How to Prepare for the
Advanced Placement Examination
Chemistry

Neil D. Jespersen, Ph.D.
Professor of Chemistry
Department of Chemistry
St. John's University
Jamaica, New York

BARRON'S

All inquiries should be addressed to:
Barron's Educational Series, Inc.
250 Wireless Boulevard
Hauppauge, New York   11788

Library of Congress Catalog Card No. 94-33294
International Standard Book No. 0-8120-1881-8

Library of Congress Cataloging-in-Publication Data

Jespersen, Neil D.
   How to prepare for the advanced placement examination. Chemistry
 / Neil D. Jespersen.
      p.   cm.
   Includes index.
   ISBN 0-8120-1881-8
   1. Chemistry—Examinations—Study guides. 2. Universities and
colleges—United States—Entrance examinations—Study guides.
3. Advanced placement programs (Education)—Study guides.
I. Title.
QD42.J47   1995
541′.076—dc20   94-33294
                                                                  CIP
                                                                  AC

PRINTED IN THE UNITED STATES OF AMERICA
5678 100 987654321

Contents

Preface

You are about to embark on one of the more intellectually challenging experiences of your life, the Advanced Placement Examination in Chemistry. Fewer than 1 percent of all high school students take this exam. Whatever the outcome, you are to be congratulated as one of a select group. As a conscientious student, you can use this review book to help you increase your score. A higher score can lead to college course credit and a head start in your selected career.

The AP Examination in Chemistry is different from other exams and tests that you have taken. *Explain, compare,* and *predict* are three important words often used on the AP Chemistry Exam. Remembered facts and calculation procedures are the basic groundwork of chemistry; however, high scores require a thorough understanding of chemical principles and relationships. Chemistry is rich in these relationships. The key to success on the exam is to think like a chemist and to apply your knowledge of one or more basic principles to provide a logical description of how chemicals behave.

This review book is designed with you, the student, in mind. It concentrates on the topics that are essential for a good score on the AP Chemistry Exam. In particular, the book is designed to provide insights into the use of basic principles to answer seemingly complex questions.

The discussion in each chapter is interspersed with exercises in which subject-matter problems are presented and solved. At the end of each chapter are questions to test your understanding of the topics discussed. These, together with the two diagnostic and three practice tests, provide hundreds of questions with a range of difficulty and complexity typical of an advanced placement exam. This review material will help you to pinpoint weak areas on which you need more preparation, and the explained answers can be used to identify sources of error or confusion.

Acknowledgments

First and foremost, a very special thank you to my wife, Marilyn Z
Jespersen, who spent countless hours reading and correcting the man
script and suggesting changes. Marilyn's contributions have made this bo
readable, understandable, and user friendly. No other person could ha
dedicated themselves to the work as she did.

I am grateful also to Professor James Brady for many fruitful discussio
and ideas in the years we have been colleagues at St. John's. We share t
idea that our job is not to teach chemistry, but to excite the student in
learning it.

Finally, I thank the editors and reviewers for their suggestions a
encouraging comments during the production of the book.

Introduction

Important Facts about the Advanced Placement Examination in Chemistry

This examination is given in May each year at selected sites throughout the country. Exact dates, locations, and application forms are available in most guidance counselor offices or from The College Board, 45 Columbus Avenue, New York, NY 10023-6992. Information is also available from the following College Board Advanced Placement Program Regional Offices

Middle States: Suite 410
3440 Market Street
Philadelphia, PA 19104-3338

Midwest: Suite 401
1800 Sherman Avenue
Evanston, IL 60201-3715

New England: 470 Totten Pond Road
Waltham, MA 02154-1982

South: Suite 250
2970 Clairmont Road
Atlanta, GA 30329-1639

Southwest: Suite 1050
98 San Jacinto Boulevard
Austin, TX 78701-4039

West: Suite 480
2099 Gateway Place
San Jose, CA 95110-1017

Denver: Suite 900
4155 East Jewell Avenue
Denver, CO 80222-4510

Canada: 212-1755 Springfield Road
Kelowna, BC
Canada V145V5

Application forms and fees for the examination are usually due 1 month before the examination date. Late registration may not be accepted and a penalty fee is charged.

Format of the Examination

The Advanced Placement Examination in Chemistry consists of a multiple-choice section and a free-response, written section. The multiple-choice section consists of 75 questions and counts for 45 percent of the total score. The time given for completion of this section is 90 minutes. Using an average of 1 minute per question assures that you will have sufficient time to answer the multiple-choice questions. A brief rest period is usually given before the free-response section.

The free-response section is also allotted 90 minutes and is divided into four parts. Fifty-five percent of the exam score is based on the free-response answers.

Part A (25%) consists of a single question that you must answer: it is usually an equilibrium problem.

Part B (25%) gives you the choice of one of two problems covering stoichiometry, the gas laws, electrochemistry, and thermodynamics.

Part C (15%) asks you to write chemical reactions from a written description. A choice of five out of eight reactions is offered.

Part D (35%) asks you to answer three of five essay-type questions covering fundamental principles and practical aspects of chemistry.

It is suggested that 50 minutes be used to answer parts A, B, and C and the remaining 40 minutes be allotted to part D. The actual division of time is up to you, however; and the proctor will not give any reminders or announcements.

Scoring of the Examination

The multiple-choice section is machine graded. Care must be taken that no stray marks are on the answer sheet, that all erasures are complete, and that each question has only one response. The total score on this section is the number correct minus 0.25 for each incorrect response. Unanswered questions do not count at all.

The free-response section is graded by trained high school and college chemistry teachers using a predefined scoring system. Each question is scored by at least two different readers, and their results must agree. Also, every question is scored by different persons, so that the grade given on one question does not influence the scores on other questions. Finally, random rescoring assures that grading standards do not drift significantly.

Scores on the multiple-choice section and free-response section are combined, using weighting factors for each part, to result in an AP grade from 0 to 160. These AP grades are then translated into the 0–5 examination grades reported to the colleges. The scoring ranges vary from year to year; the results below indicate the ranges for the 1989 examination.

AP Grade	Examination Grade	Meaning
93–160	5	Extremely well qualified
71–92	4	Well qualified
46–70	3	Qualified
25–45	2	Possibly qualified
0–24	1	No recommendation

Approximately 59 percent of all students taking the exam earn an examination grade of 3 or better.

How to Review for the AP Chemistry Examination

1. **Plan to start reviewing as soon as possible.** You don't go on a diet and lose 10 pounds in 1 day, you cannot exercise for a week and run a marathon, and you cannot read this book in one sitting and have a thorough review of chemistry. The sooner you start reviewing, the more leisurely pace you can use to digest information. Cramming does not allow time for concepts to gel and for relationships to become apparent.

2. **Set a schedule for your review**. Depending on the available time before the AP exam, divide your review into reasonable study blocks. Schedule more time than you need, plan on 2-hour study sessions, and reward yourself with time off for topics you know well.

3. **Actively review.** Don't just read this book; actively study it. Use a red pen to cancel units in problems. Write out the answers to all problems; don't solve them mentally. Make notes of topics that you find confusing.

4. **Ask questions.** AP teachers are dedicated educators who want you to succeed, but don't expect them to teach the whole course over again. Ask specific questions (write them down beforehand). If you need help with a problem, show your teacher that you've tried to solve it and indicate where you got stuck. Education is learning how to ask questions and get them answered.

5. **Assess your progress and review your weaknesses.** Use the diagnostic tests to help you concentrate on specific areas. Use the practice exams to become accustomed to test conditions.

The following schedule may be helpful in planning your review sessions. Each rectangle represents a 2-hour session. The schedule should be read horizontally, not vertically. For example, in the first week of review, you would take the first diagnostic test on Monday, review the first most needed chapter on Wednesday, and review the second most needed chapter on Friday.

The schedule requires 8 weeks to complete and leaves all weekends, as well as Tuesdays and Thursdays, free. This schedule can be compressed into as few as 3 weeks if review is done on a daily basis.

Practice Exam 3 is included for additional practice.

Monday	Tuesday	Wednesday	Thursday	Friday
Take first diagnostic test.		Review first most-needed chapter.		Review second most-needed chapter.
Take second diagnostic test.		Review first most-needed chapter.		Review second most-needed chapter.
Chapter 1		Chapter 2		Chapter 3
Chapter 4		Chapter 5		Chapter 6
Chapter 7		Chapter 8		Chapter 9
Chapter 10		Chapter 11		Chapter 12
Chapter 13		Chapter 14		Take first practice exam.
Review		Review weak areas.		Take second practice exam.

What to Expect of the AP Chemistry Examination

1. **Exam difficulty.** There is no question that the Advanced Placement Examination in Chemistry is difficult, and there are at least three reasons. First, there will be topics that you never covered in class. Because of the volume of material, even college-level courses do not include all of the topics presented on the exam. Don't waste time on questions dealing with unfamiliar material. Second, the examination is long. The multiple-choice section allows an average of slightly more than 1 minute per question. Third, many questions combine two or more concepts.

2. **Multiple-choice questions.** There are three types of questions. *Factual questions* require quick recall of important facts about chemicals and their reactions. *Conceptual questions* ask you to assess how a theory, law, or concept is applied in chemistry. *Calculation questions* require mathematical solutions, using fundamental equations of chemistry.

   Good scores are achieved by correctly answering as few as 50 percent of the 75 multiple-choice questions. On average, students who answer all the questions score 60 percent on the first 25 questions, about 50 percent on the next 25 questions, and only 30 percent on the last 25 questions. The increasing difficulty of the questions and a lack of time are the main reasons for the dramatic decrease in the scores for the last 25 questions.

3. **Free-response questions.** Parts A and B require calculated solutions to problems. Part C involves writing chemical reactions and Part D requires mostly essay answers. Part A must be answered completely,

while Parts B, C, and D allow a choice among several similar questions. This is illustrated in the practice exams at the end of the book. Concise, well-thought-out answers are important. Explain what you are doing, and state all assumptions. Before starting calculations, you should show fundamental equations, with units. A knowledge of many principles of solubility, ionization, complexation, and oxidation-reduction is required in order to write chemical equations with correct reactants and products. Identify the type of reaction: combustion, double replacement, and so on. Essay questions ask you to explain fundamental principles as applied to specific substances. Questions about common household and environmental chemicals are also asked.

Readers are looking for key terms and concepts, along with their correct usage, in explanations. Define terms clearly, and avoid using any you are not sure are correct.

How to Maximize Your Score

The Advanced Placement Examination in Chemistry is designed so that the average score will be approximately 50 percent. This is done by careful selection of the difficulty of the questions and of the length of the exam itself. There are well-known concepts and methods for assuring that you will achieve the maximum score you deserve.

The multiple choice section is designed to test your recall of fundamental chemical concepts and the use of these concepts to solve basic chemistry problems. The questions cover the entire AP course syllabus and are designed with various levels of difficulty. Each question has five choices, only one of which is the most appropriate answer. There is a penalty for incorrect answers, and the multiple-choice section is graded using the formula

$$\text{SCORE} = \left(\begin{array}{c}\text{CORRECT}\\\text{RESPONSES}\end{array}\right) - 0.25\left(\begin{array}{c}\text{INCORRECT}\\\text{RESPONSES}\end{array}\right)$$

Because of the deduction for incorrect responses, it is important to be fairly certain of your answer choices.

The free-response section involves written answers to selected questions. There are generally three problems that require numerical calculations in parts A and B and three essay questions in part D that require the use of concepts and typical chemical diagrams. There are usually several choices within each part for both the numerical and essay questions in this section. In part C the ability to deduce both molecular and ionic chemical equations from a written description is required. In the numerical and essay sections the answers are graded by well-trained teams of chemistry professionals, usually college and high school teachers. Intensive training and testing of the graders assures that the tests are graded uniformly.

The grading is reviewed by several people to confirm that grading has been done correctly.

Strategies for
Multiple-Choice
Questions

Should You Guess?

The probability of selecting the correct choice by random guessing is one in five (20%), and the deduction for an incorrect answer is one in four (25%). **Random guessing is never appropriate.** However, if it is possible to definitely eliminate any of the responses, the probability of success rises. Eliminating one choice raises the odds to 25 percent, which is the break-even point. If two or more choices can be definitely eliminated, guessing from the remaining ones is a good strategy. For this strategy to work, however, you must be certain that the eliminated choices are wrong.

If you are not totally certain that a response can be eliminated, assign it a fraction depending on your level of certainty. If you are 50 percent sure that two answers can be eliminated, that is the same as eliminating one certain response, and you may be justified in guessing between the remaining choices.

Distracters

In the design of multiple-choice questions, the writer constructs the responses so that one choice is correct and one to four are "distracters." A distracter is a response that looks good at first glance but has a serious flaw that makes it incorrect. The better the design of the test, the more distracters will be found in each question.

One popular method for constructing distracters is to use subtle changes in the wording to make a response incorrect. For example:

1. **All** chemicals become more soluble as the temperature increases.
2. **Most** chemicals become more soluble as the temperature increases.

or

1. The reaction is **exo**thermic.
2. The reaction is **endo**thermic.

Careful reading of questions and understanding of terminology are very important. The distinctions between "most" and "all" in the first set above and between "exothermic" and "endothermic" in the second are obviously significant. To ensure selecting the best answer to a nonnumerical problem, be sure to read each response before selecting one. Often a good-sounding, but incorrect, response is listed before the correct one. Another approach is to read the responses in reverse order. Pay special attention to responses that are exactly the opposite of each other as in the "exothermic"/"endothermic" example above. One response must necessarily be wrong and may also provide a clue as to whether or not both are incorrect. Also pay special attention to responses that differ by only one word, as in the first set above. Once again, they may provide a clue as to the correct way to think about the problem.

For numerical problems, some distracters provide answers in which the data are simply used in the wrong manner. For instance, for the question "What is the value of 5 divided by 2?" the answer choices may be as follows:

(A) 2.50 $\left(\dfrac{5}{2}\right)$

(B) 0.40 $\left(\dfrac{2}{5}\right)$

(C) 3.00 (5.00 − 2.00)
(D) 7.00 (5.00 + 2.00)
(E) −3.00 (2.00 − 5.00)

The parentheses show the calculation method used to obtain the answers. The question hinges on understanding the term *divided by*, and keeping in mind that 2, not 5, is the divisor, before the proper calculation can be made to obtain answer A. You must understand the proper method for using the data.

Reasonableness

There are, however, some common methods for increasing the probability of choosing the correct answer to a numerical chemistry problem. It is important to remember the principle of reasonableness. This means that answers must reflect obedience to fundamental principles, such as the conservation of matter and energy. Your personal experiences in everyday life also may provide clues as to the reasonableness of answers.

For example, if 2 grams of one reactant are mixed with 5 grams of another, it is impossible to have any more than 7 grams of product even under the best conditions (law of conservation of matter). Therefore any response that is greater than 7 grams may be eliminated very quickly. As another example, if a hot solution is added to a colder one, the final temperature must be somewhere between the low of the cold solution and the high of the hot solution. Any other responses may be eliminated as incorrect without any calculations at all.

Pointers about the reasonableness of answers will be given throughout this book.

Strategies for the Free-Response Section

Numerical Calculations

Non-programmable scientific calculators may be used on the exam. Be certain that the batteries are fresh and that you are familiar with the operation of your calculator. Write appropriate chemical reactions. Always write the fundamental equations or laws that the question requires. Identify variables. Use correct algebra in the solution, and show as many algebraic steps as possible. Clearly state any assumptions you have used, and verify that each assumption is valid before reporting the answer. Check also that you have used the correct number of significant figures in calculations.

For example, consider this problem: Calculate the pH of a 0.100 M solution of hydrofluoric acid, $K_a = 6.9 \times 10^{-4}$.

Reaction: $HF \rightleftharpoons H^+ + F^-$

Equilibrium law used: $K_a = \dfrac{[H^+][F^-]}{[HF]}$

Simplified equation: $[H^+] = \sqrt{K_a C_a}$, where C_a is the initial HF concentration and the assumption is that $[H^+] << C_a$.

Solution:
$$[H^+] = \sqrt{(6.9 \times 10^{-4})(0.100)}$$
$$= \sqrt{(6.9 \times 10^{-5})}$$
$$= 8.3 \times 10^{-3} \text{ (This agrees with the assumption.)}$$
$$pH = -\log [H^+]$$
$$= -\log (8.3 \times 10^{-3})$$
$$= 2.08$$

Chemical Equations

You will be asked to translate a written description of a chemical reaction into a chemical equation. This question draws on a storehouse of general reactions that you have encountered in your courses. All that is required are the proper reactants and products. These equations do not have to be balanced; but if a reaction can be balanced by inspection, balance it. Identify the states of the substances as (aq), (g), (s), or (ℓ) to show more knowledge.

Essay Questions

Take time to think about your answer and organize your response. The graders are often looking for key words, such as the names of physical laws (give the equation if you don't remember the name), basic concepts, or theories. They are also looking for the proper usage of these words in the context of the problem. Since incorrect statements detract from your response, avoid using terms or concepts that you are not sure apply. Write enough to fully explain your answer. Keeping in mind, however, that chemists tend to be very concise and precise, avoid complicated sentences, flowery language, and rambling, overlong responses.

Final Preparations for the Exam

Just as an athlete needs to prepare for the "big game," the student must prepare physically, mentally, and emotionally for the "big test." Here are some suggestions:

1. Eat well to have enough energy for the exam. A good dinner the night before and a relaxed breakfast on the day of the exam provide the energy essential to peak performance.
2. Get plenty of sleep. A full 8 hours of sleep is recommended for a rested body and a well-functioning mind. The night before the exam is no time to cram; in fact, such last-minute study may be detrimental.

4. The night before the exam, assemble the things you will need: plenty of #2 pencils with erasers, a scientific calculator with fresh batteries, a watch, and your admission card for the AP exam. You should also plan what you will wear to the test. Comfortable, loose-fitting clothes, including items such as sweaters that can be layered or removed to suit the room temperature, are best.

5. Be sure your transportation to the test center is reliable. Set your alarm so that you can leave early. Allow time to deal with the unexpected: a traffic jam, flat tire, or late-running bus

6. Minimize distractions and worries. Leave all valuables at home so that you do not worry about them during the test. Put all unrelated matters firmly out of your mind.

7. Be confident of your ability. A positive attitude is very important in successful test taking.

8. Relax. This one test will not make or break your career. Enjoy the exam, and show the world how well you can do.

Diagnostic Tests

1. Ⓐ Ⓑ Ⓒ Ⓓ Ⓔ	16. Ⓐ Ⓑ Ⓒ Ⓓ Ⓔ	31. Ⓐ Ⓑ Ⓒ Ⓓ Ⓔ
2. Ⓐ Ⓑ Ⓒ Ⓓ Ⓔ	17. Ⓐ Ⓑ Ⓒ Ⓓ Ⓔ	32. Ⓐ Ⓑ Ⓒ Ⓓ Ⓔ
3. Ⓐ Ⓑ Ⓒ Ⓓ Ⓔ	18. Ⓐ Ⓑ Ⓒ Ⓓ Ⓔ	33. Ⓐ Ⓑ Ⓒ Ⓓ Ⓔ
4. Ⓐ Ⓑ Ⓒ Ⓓ Ⓔ	19. Ⓐ Ⓑ Ⓒ Ⓓ Ⓔ	34. Ⓐ Ⓑ Ⓒ Ⓓ Ⓔ
5. Ⓐ Ⓑ Ⓒ Ⓓ Ⓔ	20. Ⓐ Ⓑ Ⓒ Ⓓ Ⓔ	35. Ⓐ Ⓑ Ⓒ Ⓓ Ⓔ
6. Ⓐ Ⓑ Ⓒ Ⓓ Ⓔ	21. Ⓐ Ⓑ Ⓒ Ⓓ Ⓔ	36. Ⓐ Ⓑ Ⓒ Ⓓ Ⓔ
7. Ⓐ Ⓑ Ⓒ Ⓓ Ⓔ	22. Ⓐ Ⓑ Ⓒ Ⓓ Ⓔ	37. Ⓐ Ⓑ Ⓒ Ⓓ Ⓔ
8. Ⓐ Ⓑ Ⓒ Ⓓ Ⓔ	23. Ⓐ Ⓑ Ⓒ Ⓓ Ⓔ	38. Ⓐ Ⓑ Ⓒ Ⓓ Ⓔ
9. Ⓐ Ⓑ Ⓒ Ⓓ Ⓔ	24. Ⓐ Ⓑ Ⓒ Ⓓ Ⓔ	39. Ⓐ Ⓑ Ⓒ Ⓓ Ⓔ
10. Ⓐ Ⓑ Ⓒ Ⓓ Ⓔ	25. Ⓐ Ⓑ Ⓒ Ⓓ Ⓔ	40. Ⓐ Ⓑ Ⓒ Ⓓ Ⓔ
11. Ⓐ Ⓑ Ⓒ Ⓓ Ⓔ	26. Ⓐ Ⓑ Ⓒ Ⓓ Ⓔ	41. Ⓐ Ⓑ Ⓒ Ⓓ Ⓔ
12. Ⓐ Ⓑ Ⓒ Ⓓ Ⓔ	27. Ⓐ Ⓑ Ⓒ Ⓓ Ⓔ	42. Ⓐ Ⓑ Ⓒ Ⓓ Ⓔ
13. Ⓐ Ⓑ Ⓒ Ⓓ Ⓔ	28. Ⓐ Ⓑ Ⓒ Ⓓ Ⓔ	43. Ⓐ Ⓑ Ⓒ Ⓓ Ⓔ
14. Ⓐ Ⓑ Ⓒ Ⓓ Ⓔ	29. Ⓐ Ⓑ Ⓒ Ⓓ Ⓔ	44. Ⓐ Ⓑ Ⓒ Ⓓ Ⓔ
15. Ⓐ Ⓑ Ⓒ Ⓓ Ⓔ	30. Ⓐ Ⓑ Ⓒ Ⓓ Ⓔ	45. Ⓐ Ⓑ Ⓒ Ⓓ Ⓔ

1. Ⓐ Ⓑ Ⓒ Ⓓ Ⓔ
2. Ⓐ Ⓑ Ⓒ Ⓓ Ⓔ
3. Ⓐ Ⓑ Ⓒ Ⓓ Ⓔ
4. Ⓐ Ⓑ Ⓒ Ⓓ Ⓔ
5. Ⓐ Ⓑ Ⓒ Ⓓ Ⓔ
6. Ⓐ Ⓑ Ⓒ Ⓓ Ⓔ
7. Ⓐ Ⓑ Ⓒ Ⓓ Ⓔ
8. Ⓐ Ⓑ Ⓒ Ⓓ Ⓔ
9. Ⓐ Ⓑ Ⓒ Ⓓ Ⓔ
10. Ⓐ Ⓑ Ⓒ Ⓓ Ⓔ
11. Ⓐ Ⓑ Ⓒ Ⓓ Ⓔ
12. Ⓐ Ⓑ Ⓒ Ⓓ Ⓔ
13. Ⓐ Ⓑ Ⓒ Ⓓ Ⓔ
14. Ⓐ Ⓑ Ⓒ Ⓓ Ⓔ
15. Ⓐ Ⓑ Ⓒ Ⓓ Ⓔ

16. Ⓐ Ⓑ Ⓒ Ⓓ Ⓔ
17. Ⓐ Ⓑ Ⓒ Ⓓ Ⓔ
18. Ⓐ Ⓑ Ⓒ Ⓓ Ⓔ
19. Ⓐ Ⓑ Ⓒ Ⓓ Ⓔ
20. Ⓐ Ⓑ Ⓒ Ⓓ Ⓔ
21. Ⓐ Ⓑ Ⓒ Ⓓ Ⓔ
22. Ⓐ Ⓑ Ⓒ Ⓓ Ⓔ
23. Ⓐ Ⓑ Ⓒ Ⓓ Ⓔ
24. Ⓐ Ⓑ Ⓒ Ⓓ Ⓔ
25. Ⓐ Ⓑ Ⓒ Ⓓ Ⓔ
26. Ⓐ Ⓑ Ⓒ Ⓓ Ⓔ
27. Ⓐ Ⓑ Ⓒ Ⓓ Ⓔ
28. Ⓐ Ⓑ Ⓒ Ⓓ Ⓔ
29. Ⓐ Ⓑ Ⓒ Ⓓ Ⓔ
30. Ⓐ Ⓑ Ⓒ Ⓓ Ⓔ

31. Ⓐ Ⓑ Ⓒ Ⓓ Ⓔ
32. Ⓐ Ⓑ Ⓒ Ⓓ Ⓔ
33. Ⓐ Ⓑ Ⓒ Ⓓ Ⓔ
34. Ⓐ Ⓑ Ⓒ Ⓓ Ⓔ
35. Ⓐ Ⓑ Ⓒ Ⓓ Ⓔ
36. Ⓐ Ⓑ Ⓒ Ⓓ Ⓔ
37. Ⓐ Ⓑ Ⓒ Ⓓ Ⓔ
38. Ⓐ Ⓑ Ⓒ Ⓓ Ⓔ
39. Ⓐ Ⓑ Ⓒ Ⓓ Ⓔ
40. Ⓐ Ⓑ Ⓒ Ⓓ Ⓔ
41. Ⓐ Ⓑ Ⓒ Ⓓ Ⓔ
42. Ⓐ Ⓑ Ⓒ Ⓓ Ⓔ
43. Ⓐ Ⓑ Ⓒ Ⓓ Ⓔ
44. Ⓐ Ⓑ Ⓒ Ⓓ Ⓔ
45. Ⓐ Ⓑ Ⓒ Ⓓ Ⓔ

Diagnostic Test 1

Answer the following multiple-choice problems. You may use a periodic table but no other source of information. Limit your time to 60 minutes. If you have not finished in 60 minutes, note the number of questions answered at that time and then finish the remaining questions. Score the test with the key at the end. Use the tables on pages xxvii and xxviii to determine which subjects need the most review.

1. How many completely filled orbitals are indicated by the following electronic configuration?

$$1s^2, 2s^2, 2p^6, 3s^2, 3p^6, 4s^2, 3d^6$$

    (A) 6   (B) 26   (C) 11   (D) 15   (E) 2

2. Which of the following lists the least electronegative element first and the most electronegative element last?
   (A) Fe, Mg, Cl
   (B) Na, I, Cl
   (C) S, O, C
   (D) Al, B, C
   (E) Na, Li, K

3. Millikan's oil drop experiment
   (A) demonstrated that electrons are present in all atoms
   (B) was used to calculate the electron's charge
   (C) determined the electron's charge to mass ratio
   (D) demonstrated that the atom has equal numbers of protons and electrons
   (E) demonstrated that the mass of the atom is concentrated in the nucleus

4. What is the simplest formula for a nitrogen oxide that is 69.6 percent oxygen?
   (A) NO   (B) N_2O (C) NO_2 (D) N_2O_5 (E) N_2O_4

5. When the following equation:

$$MgO + HCl \longrightarrow MgCl_2 + H_2O$$

   is balanced with the lowest possible whole-number coefficients, the sum of these coefficients is
   (A) 2   (B) 4   (C) 6   (D) 5   (E) 10

6. The compound expected when Br_2 reacts with aluminum is
   (A) AlBr   (B) $AlBr_2$ (C) Al_2Br (D) Al_2Br_3 (E) $AlBr_3$

7. The combustion of acetic acid, CH_3COOH, contains which of the following in the balanced equation?
   (A) $2CH_3COOH$ (B) $3H_2O$ (C) $3O_2$ (D) $2CO_2$ (E) O_2

8. A reaction has a rate constant of $6.3 \times 10^{-4} L^2 mol^{-2} s^{-1}$. One possible rate law for this reaction is
   (A) Rate $= k[A]^2[B]^3$
   (B) Rate $= k[A]^2$
   (C) Rate $= k[A][B][C]$
   (D) Rate $= k[A]$
   (E) Rate $= k[B]^{-1}$

9. A catalyst will NOT
   (A) increase the forward reaction rate
   (B) provide an alternative reaction pathway with a lower activation energy
   (C) increase the value of the equilibrium constant
   (D) increase the reverse reaction rate
   (E) All of the above are true.

10. The half-life of a radioactive substance is 3.0 years. How long will it take for seven-eighths of this substance to decay?
    (A) less than 1 year   (B) 9 years   (C) 27 years   (D) 3 years
    (E) 6 years

11. In which of the following pairs is the stronger acid written first?
    (A) HCl and HBr
    (B) H_2SO_4 and H_2SO_3
    (C) H_2S and HCl
    (D) HClO and $HClO_3$
    (E) H_3PO_4 and H_2SO_4

12. Which of the following is false?
    (A) Anions are negatively charged ions.
    (B) An element that loses an electron is a cation.
    (C) Cations are larger than the uncharged element.
    (D) The ionic bond is due to the attractive forces between cations and anions.
    (E) Compounds can contain both ionic and covalent bonds.

13. The oxidation number of chlorine in the ClO_4^- ion is
    (A) -1 (B) $+1$ (C) $+3$ (D) $+5$ (E) $+7$ (C) 0

14. When the following half-reaction:

$$CrO_4^{2-} \longrightarrow Cr^{3+}$$

   is balanced with the lowest possible coefficients in acid solution, there will be
    (A) three electrons on the right
    (B) six electrons on the right
    (C) no electrons needed
    (D) three electrons on the left
    (E) two electrons on the right

15. A gas has a density of 0.759 gram per liter at STP. A possible formula for this gas is
    (A) CH_4 (B) Cl_2 (C) NH_3 (D) H_2 (E) Ar

16. Given the two half-reactions below:

$$Br_2 + 2e^- \longrightarrow 2Br \qquad E^0 = 1.07 \text{ volts}$$
$$Ag^+ + e^- \longrightarrow Ag \qquad E^0 = 0.80 \text{ volt}$$

calculate the standard cell voltage for the following reaction:

$$2Ag + Br_2 \longrightarrow AgBr_2$$

(A) 1.87 volts (B) 0.27 volt (C) -0.53 volt (D) 2.67 volts
(E) -0.27 volt

17. Sulfurous acid dissociates in two steps:

$$H_2SO_3 \text{ (aq)} \longrightarrow H^+ \text{ (aq)} + HSO_3^- \text{ (aq);} \qquad K_1$$
$$HSO_3^- \text{ (aq)} \longrightarrow H^+ \text{ (aq)} + SO_3^{2-} \text{ (aq);} \qquad K_2$$

and calcium sulfite forms in the reaction

$$Ca^{2+}\text{(aq)} + SO_3^{2-}\text{(aq)} \longrightarrow CaSO_3\text{(s).}$$

The overall equilibrium constant for the reaction

$$H_2SO_3 \text{ (aq)} + Ca^{2+} \text{ (aq)} \longrightarrow CaSO_3\text{(s)} + 2H^+ \text{ (aq)}$$

is

(A) $K_1K_2K_{sp}$ (B) $K_1 + K_2 + K_{sp}$ (C) $\dfrac{K_1K_2}{K_{sp}}$ (D) $\dfrac{K_{sp}}{K_1K_2}$

(E) $\dfrac{K_w}{K_1K_2} K_{sp}$

18. Which of the following is expected to have a tetrahedral shape?
    (A) H_2O (B) NH_3 (C) CH_2Cl_2 (D) PCl_3 (E) SF_6

19. At 298 K the molecules of which of the following gases have the greatest average velocity?
    (A) CO_2 (B) NH_3 (C) Cl_2 (D) SO_2 (E) HCN

20. What ions are expected when the compound sodium acetate, $NaC_2H_3O_2$, is dissolved in water?
    (A) Na^+, $2C^{4+}$, $3H^+$, $2O^{2-}$
    (B) Na^+, $C_2H_3O_2^-$
    (C) Na^+, $2CO^-$, $3H^+$
    (D) Na, $C_2H_3O_2$
    (E) NaO_2, C_2H_3

21. Which of the following CANNOT be a Lewis or a Brönsted-Lowry acid?
    (A) NH_4^+ (B) Cu^{2+} (C) F^- (D) Na^+ (E) $H_2PO_4^-$

22. The pH of a 0.100 M solution of a weak acid is 4.44. What is the pK_a for the weak acid?
    (A) 4.44   (B) 3.22   (C) 9.56   (D) 7.88   (E) 8.88

23. If 189.6 micrograms of CuI (molar mass = 190.4) dissolves in 1 liter of distilled water, what is the K_{sp} of CuI?
    (A) 1.0×10^{-6} (B) 4.0×10^{-12} (C) 0.25×10^{-6} (D) 1.0×10^{-12}
    (E) 3.6×10^{-8}

24. A liquid is heated in a closed tube. At 453 K the liquid disappears and only one phase is present. The temperature of 453 K represents
    (A) the normal boiling point
    (B) the normal melting point
    (C) the triple point
    (D) the critical temperature
    (E) nothing; this is an optical illusion

25. A titration curve where the pH increases and the endpoint is at exactly pH 7.00 most likely represents a titration
    (A) of a strong base with a strong acid
    (B) of a polyprotic acid
    (C) of a weak acid with a strong base
    (D) of a strong acid with a strong base
    (E) of a strong base with a weak acid

26. All of the following are true of carbon EXCEPT that carbon
    (A) always forms four bonds
    (B) never has an octahedral structure
    (C) can have sp, sp^2, and sp^3 hybrids
    (D) is found only in organic compounds
    (E) conducts electricity when in the form of graphite

27. Which of the following contains two pi bonds?
    (A) N_2 (B) $CH_2\!\!=\!\!CH_2$ (C) CH_3COOH (D) Fe_2O_3
    (E) C_6H_6 (benzene)

28. N_2O_4 dissociates into two NO_2 molecules. When 0.500 mole of N_2O_4 is placed in a 2.00-liter flask and allowed to come to equilibrium, the final concentration of N_2O_4 is 0.100 mole per liter. What is the equilibrium constant for the dissociation of N_2O_4 under these conditions?
    (A) 0.200   (B) 0.900   (C) 0.225   (D) 4.44   (E) 1.11

29. At room temperature a reaction is not spontaneous. At an elevated temperature, however, the reaction is spontaneous. Which of the following describes this system?

	ΔS	ΔH
(A)	positive	positive
(B)	positive	negative
(C)	negative	positive
(D)	negative	negative
(E)	zero	positive

30. The free-energy change for a reaction at 298 K is $\Delta G^0 = -3.45$ kilojoule. What is the value of the equilibrium constant? ($R = 8.314$ J $\cdot$ mol^{-1} K^{-1}.)
    (A) 1.39×10^{-3} (B) 24.7   (C) 4.1×10^{-2} (D) 4.0   (E) 31.5

31. Which of the following functional groups do organic bases have?
    (A) —OH   (B) —COOH   (C) —C=O   (D) —NH$_2$
    (E) —C—O—C—

32. Which one of the following forms hydrogen bonds?
    (A) alcohols   (B) aldehydes   (C) ketones   (D) alkynes
    (E) ethyl groups

33. Which of the following graphs will result in a straight line for a reaction with the rate law Rate $= k$?
    (A) rate versus time
    (B) concentration versus $1/T$
    (C) concentration versus time
    (D) log concentration versus $1/t$
    (E) concentration versus log t

34. How many grams of KBr (molar mass $= 119$) are there in 125 milliliters of a 0.128 molar aqueous KBr solution?
    (A) 15.2   (B) 1.90   (C) 121.6   (D) 0.134   (E) 0.0848

35. A liquid has a vapor pressure of 345 millimeters of mercury at room temperature. A solution prepared with that liquid and a nonvolatile solute has a vapor pressure of 290 millimeters of mercury. What is the mole fraction of the solute in the solution?
    (A) 0.159   (B) 0.189   (C) 0.841   (D) 0.500   (E) Molality can be calculated, not mole fraction.

36. Which of the following CANNOT be used to determine molar masses?
    (A) osmotic pressures
    (B) freezing point depressions
    (C) vapor pressure measurements
    (D) specific heats
    (E) densities of solids

37. The equilibrium law $K = \dfrac{[A]^2[B]}{[C][D]^2}$ represents which of the following reactions?

    (A) A + B $\rightleftharpoons$ C + D
    (B) C + 2D $\rightleftharpoons$ 2A + B
    (C) 2A + B $\rightleftharpoons$ C + 2D
    (D) C + D $\rightleftharpoons$ A + B
    (E) A^2 + B $\rightleftharpoons$ C + D^2

38. A 0.300 M solution should be prepared in
    (A) a graduated cylinder
    (B) an Erlenmeyer flask
    (C) a volumetric flask
    (D) a round-bottom flask
    (E) a beaker

39. Which of the following is NOT a major group used in qualitative analysis?
    (A) the insoluble chlorides
    (B) the insoluble sulfates
    (C) the soluble sulfides and chlorides
    (D) the sulfides insoluble in acid
    (E) the sulfides insoluble in bases

40. The beta particle may also be described as
    (A) an electron   (B) a proton   (C) a helium nucleus   (D) a neutron
    (E) a hydrogen nucleus

41. A sample of a gas has a volume of 100 milliliters and a pressure of 1.25 atmospheres at 25°C. When the pressure is changed to 3.00 atmospheres and the volume changed to 50.0 milliliters, what must the temperature be if no heat is gained or lost?
    (A) 358°C   (B) 85°C   (C) 30°C   (D) 21°C   (E) −35°C

42. Which of the following represents the intermolecular attractions listed in order from the weakest to the strongest?
    (A) hydrogen bonding, London forces, dipole attractions
    (B) dipole attractions, London forces, hydrogen bonding
    (C) London forces, dipole attractions, hydrogen bonds
    (D) dipole attractions, hydrogen bonds, London forces
    (E) hydrogen bonds, dipole attractions, London forces

43. The equation for osmotic pressure is most similar to
    (A) the ideal gas law
    (B) the equilibrium law
    (C) the Nernst equation
    (D) the Henderson-Hasselbach equation
    (E) a chemical equation

44. Carbon-11 undergoes radioactive decay by emitting
    (A) a beta particle
    (B) a neutron
    (C) an alpha particle
    (D) a positron
    (E) a proton

45. When 34 grams of ethane, CH_3CH_3, is burned in excess oxygen, the theoretical yield of carbon dioxide is
    (A) 100 grams (B) 68 grams (C) 50 grams (D) 78 grams
    (E) 34 grams

Evaluation of Diagnostic Test 1

Score the test using the answer key. In the two tables below, indicate in the right-hand column the number of questions in each group that you got wrong. The first table categorizes the questions in four broad types. The second table designates specific topics and enables you to identify the ones on which you made the most errors. The two tables help you determine which types of questions caused you the most difficulty and what topics you need to emphasize in your review.

ANSWER KEY

1. C	10. B	19. B	28. B	37. B
2. B	11. B	20. B	29. A	38. C
3. B	12. C	21. C	30. D	39. B
4. C	13. E	22. D	31. D	40. A
5. D	14. D	23. D	32. A	41. B
6. E	15. C	24. D	33. C	42. C
7. D	16. B	25. D	34. B	43. A
8. C	17. C	26. D	35. C	44. D
9. C	18. C	27. A	36. E	45. A

Question Categories

Question Type	Questions	Number Wrong
Basic facts	1, 2, 3, 5, 9, 11, 12, 20, 27, 31, 32, 38, 39, 40, 44	
Basic concepts	17, 18, 19, 21, 24, 25, 29, 33, 37, 42	
Calculations	4, 10, 13, 14, 16, 22, 28, 30, 34, 35, 41, 45	
Mixed concepts	6, 7, 8, 15, 26, 36, 43	

Breakdown by Topics

Chapter	Questions	Number Wrong
1. Structure of the atom	1, 2, 3	
3. Nuclear chemistry	10, 40, 44	
4. Ionic compounds and reactions	5, 6, 12	
5. Covalent compounds	7, 18, 27	
6. Stoichiometry	4, 34, 45	
7. Gases	15, 19, 41	
8. Liquids and solids	24, 36, 42	
9. Solutions	20, 35, 43	
10. Equilibrium	17, 23, 28	
11. Kinetics	8, 9, 33	
12. Thermodynamics	29, 30, 37	
13. Redox and electrochemistry	13, 14, 16	
14. Acids and bases	11, 21, 22	
15. Organic chemistry	26, 31, 32	
16. Experiments	25, 38, 39	

This diagnostic test gives you three types of information. First, if you did not finish in 60 minutes, you know that you need to work more quickly. Second, you know the categories of questions that cause you difficulty. Third, you know the specific topics on which you are weak. Use this information to structure your review program. Read carefully the answer explanations that follow, review your major deficiencies, and then repeat the diagnostic procedure with Diagnostic Test 2.

Explanations of Answers to Diagnostic Test 1

1. **C** The 3*d* orbitals include one that is filled with a pair of electrons and four unpaired electrons. Each *s* orbital is completely filled, and three orbitals in each *p* orbital are completely filled.
2. **B** The least electronegative elements are in the lower left corner of the periodic table; the most electronegative, in the upper right corner.
3. **B** Up to the time of the experiment, only the *e/m* ratio for the electron was known.

4. **C** $? \text{ mol N} = 69.6 \text{ g O} \left(\dfrac{1 \text{ mol O}}{16 \text{ g N}} \right) = 4.35 \text{ mol O}$

   $? \text{ mol O} = (100 - 69.6) \text{ g N} \left(\dfrac{1 \text{ mol N}}{14 \text{ g N}} \right) = 2.17 \text{ mol N}$

   Divide both results by 2.17 to obtain 1 mol N and 2 mol O. The formula is NO_2.

5. **D** The balanced equation is $MgO + 2HCl \rightarrow MgCl_2 + H_2O$.
   The coefficients for MgO, $MgCl_2$, and H_2O are 1; $3 + 2 = 5$.

6. **E** Aluminum always forms a $+3$ ion.

7. **D** The balanced equation is $CH_3COOH + 2O_2 \rightarrow 2CO_2 + 2H_2O$.

8. **C** This rate constant has units for a third-order reaction.

9. **C** Only a change in temperature changes the equilibrium constant.

10. **B** One-eighth is left, and $\dfrac{1}{2} \dfrac{1}{2} \dfrac{1}{2} = \dfrac{1}{8}$. This means that three half-lives have passed.

11. **B** The extra oxygen makes H_2SO_4 stronger than H_2SO_3.

12. **C** Cations in general are smaller; most have lost an entire shell of electrons.

13. **E** Charge $= 1 \times$ (ox. # of Cl) $+ 4 \times$ (ox. # of O). The oxidation number of $O = -2$, and the charge $= -1$.
   $-1 = $ (ox. # of Cl) $- 8$, and the solution is $+7$ for Cl.

14. **D** The balanced half-reaction is $3e^- + 8H^+ + CrO_4^{2-} \rightarrow Cr^{3+} + 4H_2O$.

15. **C** At STP, 1.00 mol of gas $= 22.4$ L of gas. Calculate:

   $? \dfrac{\text{g gas}}{\text{mol gas}} = \dfrac{0.759 \text{ g gas}}{1 \text{ L gas}} \left(\dfrac{22.4 \text{ L gas}}{1 \text{ mol gas}} \right) = 17 \text{ g mol}^{-1}$.

   Ammonia has a molar mass of 17.

16. **B** $E^0_{cell} = E^0_{reduction} - E^0_{oxidation} = 1.07 \text{ V} - 0.80 \text{ V} = +0.27 \text{ V}$. Bromine is reduced in the reaction and silver is oxidized.

17. **C** When the reactions are added, the equilibrium constants are multiplied. The last reaction is the reverse of the dissolution reaction; its equilibrium constant is $\dfrac{1}{K_{sp}}$. Therefore the answer is $K_1 \cdot K_2 \cdot \dfrac{1}{K_{sp}} = \dfrac{K_1 K_2}{K_{sp}}$

18. **C** This compound has a carbon atom with four bonds and no nonbonding electron pairs.

19. **B** All have the same kinetic energy $\left(\dfrac{1}{2} mv^2 \right)$. The lower the mass, the higher the velocity; ammonia has the lowest molar mass.

20. **B** Only the sodium cation and acetate anion result.

21. **C** The fluoride ion has no ability to accept a pair of electrons and it has no protons to donate.

22. **D** $[H^+] = \sqrt{K_a C_a}$; rearrangement yields

$$K_a = \dfrac{[H^+]^2}{C_a} = \dfrac{3.63 \times 10^{-5}}{0.100} = 1.32 \times 10^{-8}$$

   The negative logarithm of the K_a value is 7.88, which is the pK_a.

23. **D** $K_{sp} = [Cu^+][I^-] = x^2$. The molar solubility, x, is 189.6×10^{-6} g CuI/ 190.4 g mol^{-1} $= 1.0 \times 10^{-6}$.
   $K_{sp} = (1.0 \times 10^{-6})^2 = 1.0 \times 10^{-12}$

24. **D** The liquid and the gas have the same density and are indistinguishable. This is called a supercritical fluid.

25. **D** An endpoint at pH = 7 indicates a reaction of a strong acid with a strong base, and the increasing pH indicates that the sample being titrated is the strong acid.

26. **D** Some inorganic compounds also contain carbon, such as calcium carbonate $CaCO_3$.

27. **A** The triple bond in N_2 consists of two pi bonds and one sigma bond. Benzene has three pi bonds.

28. **B** The equilibrium law is $K_c = \dfrac{[NO_2]^2}{[N_2O_4]}$, and the equilibrium table is as follows:

REACTION	N_2O_4	$\rightleftharpoons$	$2NO_2$
INITIAL CONCENTRATION	0.250 M		0 M
CHANGE	$-x$		$+2x$
EQUILIBRIUM	$0.250 - x$		$2x$
SOLUTION	0.100		

The value of x is calculated as $0.250 - x = 0.100$ (from the last two lines in the N_2O_4 column), and x is equal to 0.150 M. The equilibrium concentration of NO_2 is $2x = 0.300$ M. Entering these data into the equilibrium law gives the $K_c = \dfrac{(0.300)^2}{0.100} = 0.900$.

29. **A** $\Delta G^0 = \Delta H^0 - T\,\Delta S^0$, and an increasing T will result in ΔG^0 becoming negative.

30. **D** $\Delta G^0 = -RT \ln K$. Solving,

$$\ln K = \frac{-\Delta G^0}{RT} = \frac{-(-3450\ \text{J})}{(8.314\ \text{J mol}^{-1}\ \text{K}^{-1})(298\ \text{K})} = 1.39$$

Taking the antilogarithm gives $K_c = 4.0$.

31. **D** Organic bases are mostly amines, related to NH_3.

32. **A** Only alcohols have hydrogen bound to an oxygen atom.

33. **C** A straight line indicates a constant rate, independent of any concentrations. Rate $= k$ is also independent of concentration.

34. **B** ? g KBr $= 0.125$ L KBr $\left(\dfrac{0.128\ \text{mol KBr}}{1\ \text{L KBr}}\right)\left(\dfrac{119\ \text{g KBr}}{1\ \text{mol KBr}}\right) = 1.90$ g KBr

The molarity is the first conversion factor.

35. **C** $P = P^0 X_{\text{solvent}}$; therefore $\dfrac{P}{P^0} = X_{\text{solvent}} = \dfrac{290\ \text{mm Hg}}{345\ \text{mm Hg}} = 0.841$.

36. **E** Only densities of gases, not of solids, will yield molar masses.

37. **B** The exponents represent the coefficients in the reaction. Also, the reactants are in the denominator and the products in the numerator.

38. **C** A volumetric flask is the most accurately calibrated container.
39. **B** Sulfate is not used for group separations
40. **A** A beta particle and an electron are identical.
41. **B** Use the ideal gas law to obtain $\dfrac{P_1V_1}{P_2V_2} = \dfrac{T_1}{T_2}$, when R and n are canceled.

    Entering the data gives

$$\frac{(1.25 \text{ atm})(100 \text{ mL})}{(3.00 \text{ atm})(50.0 \text{ mL})} = \frac{298\text{K}}{T_2}.$$

Solving gives $T_2 = 358 \text{ K} = 85°\text{C}$.
42. **C** London forces are the weakest of all.
43. **A** $PV = nRT$ is the same as $\Pi V = nRT$, where Π is the osmotic pressure.
44. **D** Light radioactive elements with masses less than their atomic masses in the periodic table emit positrons. This process leads to a more stable electron-to-proton ratio.
45. **A** The balanced equation is $2 \text{ C}_2\text{H}_6 + 7 \text{ O}_2 \rightarrow 4 \text{ CO}_2 + 6 \text{ H}_2\text{O}$.

$$? \text{ g CO}_2 = 34 \text{ g C}_2\text{H}_6 \left(\frac{1 \text{ mol C}_2\text{H}_6}{30 \text{ g C}_2\text{H}_6}\right)\left(\frac{4 \text{ mol CO}_2}{2 \text{ mol C}_2\text{H}_6}\right)\left(\frac{44 \text{ g CO}_2}{1 \text{ mol CO}_2}\right)$$

$$= 100 \text{ g CO}_2$$

Diagnostic Test 2

Answer the following multiple-choice problems. You may use a periodic table but no other source of information. Limit your time to 60 minutes. If you have not finished in 60 minutes, note the number of questions answered at that time and then finish the remaining questions. Score the test with the key at the end. Use the tables on pages xxxviii and xxxix to determine which subjects still need the more review.

1. In qualitative analysis the Ag^+, Pb^{2+}, and Hg_2^{2+} ions are separated and confirmed with all of the following EXCEPT
   (A) HCl (B) H_2S (C) hot water (D) NH_3 (E) Na_2CrO_4

2. Which of the following is NOT related to the others?
   (A) standard Gibbs free energy
   (B) equilibrium constant
   (C) specific rate constant
   (D) standard cell voltage
   (E) standard enthalpy and entropy change

3. How many milliliters of Cl_2 at STP are needed to prepare 12.0 grams of CCl_4?
   (A) 3491 (B) 3.49 (C) 2.7 (D) 5.5 (E) 1.72

4. Under which conditions does a gas behave most like an ideal gas?
   (A) high pressure and high temperature
   (B) low pressure and low temperature
   (C) high pressure and low temperature
   (D) low pressure and high temperature
   (E) low pressure alone

5. A chemical reaction will proceed in the forward direction
   (A) if ΔG is positive and Q is greater than K
   (B) if ΔG is negative and Q is greater than K
   (C) if ΔG is positive and Q is less than K
   (D) if ΔG is negative and Q is less than K
   (E) whenever $\Delta G°$ is positive and K is greater than 1

6. A solution contains only sodium sulfate and water. When the solution is electrolyzed, the products will be
   (A) H_2 at the cathode and O_2 at the anode
   (B) H_2 at the anode and Na metal at the cathode
   (C) O_2 at the anode and Na at the cathode
   (D) Na at the cathode and SO_3 at the anode
   (E) This solution only conducts electricity.

7. A liquid has a vapor pressure of 285 millimeters of mercury at room temperature. When a nonvolatile nonelectrolyte is added so that its mole fraction is 0.150, the vapor pressure is measured as 220 millimeters of mercury. The best explanation of this result is that
    (A) the solution obeys Raoult's law
    (B) the solution obeys Henry's law
    (C) the attractive forces in the solution are greater than those in the pure compounds
    (D) the attractive forces in the solution are less than those in the pure compounds
    (E) dissociation of the solute explains the extra decrease in vapor pressure

8. Which of the following compounds has only pi bonds?
    (A) $CH_2=H_2$
    (B) $CH\equiv CH$
    (C) $N\equiv N$
    (D) $H\text{-}C\equiv N$
    (E) None of the above has only pi bonds.

9. If 25.0 milliliters of 0.0350 M sulfuric acid is titrated with 0.0500 M KOH, what volume of KOH will have been used when the endpoint is reached?
    (A) 25.0 milliliters   (B) 17.5 milliliters   (C) 35.0 milliliters
    (D) 8.75 milliliters   (E) 71.4 milliliters

10. For which reaction is K_p equal to K_c?
    (A) $CH_4(g) + 2\ O_2(g) \rightarrow CO_2(g) + 2\ H_2O(g)$
    (B) $2\ Mg(s) + O_2(g) \rightarrow 2\ MgO(s)$
    (C) $CH_4(g) + 2\ O_2(g) \rightarrow CO_2(g) + 2\ H_2O(\ell)$
    (D) $2\ HCl(aq) + Zn(s) \rightarrow ZnCl_2(aq) + H_2(g)$
    (E) $SO_2(g) + H_2O(\ell) + Ni(NO_3)_2(aq) \rightarrow NiSO_3(s) + 2\ HNO_3(aq)$

11. Two atoms whose monatomic ions have the same electronic configuration are
    (A) F and Cl   (B) Na and F   (C) Ca and Na   (D) S and Br
    (E) S and Mg

12. Which of the following is an insoluble salt?
    (A) $Fe(NO_3)_3$ (B) Na_2CO_3 (C) K_2SO_3 (D) $SrSO_4$ (E) $PbCl_2$

13. Which of the following is NOT a conjugate acid-base pair?
    (A) NH_4^+ and NH_2^-
    (B) H_2O and OH^-
    (C) HCl and Cl^-
    (D) H_2SO_4 and HSO_4^-
    (E) HCO_3^- and CO_3^{2-}

14. Which of the following can be a cis or a trans isomer?
    (A) CH_3COOH
    (B) C_6H_6 (benzene)
    (C) $HC=CH$
    (D) $(CH_3)_2C=CH_2$
    (E) $CH_3CH=CHCl$

15. The concentration of carbon-14 in an archaeological sample is 6.25 percent of the concentration found in present-day samples. If the half-life of carbon-14 is 5730 years, how old is the sample?
    (A) 5730 years (B) 11,460 years (C) 17,190 years
    (D) 22,920 years (E) 28,650 years

16. The face-centered cubic unit cell for silver atoms measures 407 picometers on each edge. The atomic radius of silver is
    (A) 204 picometers (B) 144 picometers (C) 176 picometers
    (D) 288 picometers (E) 352 picometers

17. Which of the following can react to form a peptide bond?
    (A) $CH_2{=}CH_2$ (B) CH_3NH_2 (C) $CH_3CH_2CH(NH_2)COOH$
    (D) $CH_3CH{=}CH_2$ (E) $HOOCCH_2CH_2COOH$

18. In which of the following is electromagnetic radiation listed in order from the lowest energy to the highest energy?
    (A) visible, ultraviolet, infrared
    (B) visible, ultraviolet, X rays
    (C) infrared, ultraviolet, visible
    (D) infrared, microwaves, visible
    (E) ultraviolet, visible, infrared

19. Which of the following principles is fundamental to the collision theory of reaction rates?
    (A) Reaction rates are equal to the number of collisions per second.
    (B) Only bimolecular collisions result in reactions.
    (C) Potential energy increases as reactants collide.
    (D) Effective collisions are those that involve sufficient energy and correct molecular orientation.
    (E) Reaction rate is inversely proportional to activation energy.

20. Carbonic acid, H_2CO_3, has $K_1 = 4.5 \times 10^{-7}$ and $K_2 = 4.7 \times 10^{-11}$. The pH of a 0.100 M solution of Na_2CO_3 is
    (A) 2.34 (B) 11.66 (C) 4.33 (D) 9.67 (E) 13.00

21. Which of the following measures, when applied to this endothermic reaction:

$$H_2(g) + I_2(g) \rightleftharpoons 2\ HI(g),$$

will increase the value of K_c?
    (A) Decrease the volume.
    (B) Add more H_2 to the mixture.
    (C) Remove some I_2 from the mixture.
    (D) Increase the temperature.
    (E) Add a catalyst.

22. Given this unbalanced chemical reaction:
$K_2Cr_2O_7 + H_2SO_4 + MnSO_4 \rightarrow Cr_2(SO_4)_3 + K_2SO_4 + MnO_2 + H_2O$,
the reducing agent is
(A) H_2SO_4 (B) K_2SO_4 (C) $K_2Cr_2O_7$ (D) $MnSO_4$ (E) Cr^{3+}

23. What is the volume of 1.0 gram of NH_3 at 2.30 atmospheres of pressure and 30°C? ($R = 0.0821$ L atm mol^{-1} K^{-1}.)
(A) 22.4 liters   (B) 1.32 liters   (C) 636 milliliters   (D) 10.8 liters
(E) 92.6 milliliters

24. In the nuclear reaction below, the missing substance is

$$^{121}Sb + {}^4He \rightarrow \underline{\quad} + {}^1H$$

(A) an X ray
(B) an alpha particle
(C) ^{124}Te
(D) ^{125}I
(E) $2\,^{62}Fe$

25. A liquid has a vapor pressure of 435 millimeters of mercury at room temperature and a molar mass of 122. Addition of a nonelectrolyte with a molar mass of 85 forms an ideal solution and decreases the vapor pressure to 400 millimeters of mercury. What is the molality of this solution?
(A) 0.920   (B) 0.080   (C) 0.714   (D) 0.497   (E) 2.01

26. Given the mass fraction of a solution, which of the following is needed to determine the molality of the same solution?
(A) the molar mass of the solute
(B) the molar mass of the solvent
(C) the density of the solution
(D) the density of the solvent
(E) All of the above are necessary to solve the problem.

27. Which of the following is expected to have the highest boiling point?
(A) $NaC_2H_3O_2$
(B) CH_3COOH
(C) CH_3CH_2OH
(D) CH_3OCH_3
(E) $CH_3CH=O$

28. Reaction rates double for every 10°C (approx.) temperature increase. When the temperature of a gas is increased from 100 to 110°C, what is the increase in the average velocity of a gas molecule?
(A) 2   (B) $\dfrac{110}{100}$ (C) $\dfrac{373}{383}$ (D) $\sqrt{\dfrac{100}{110}}$ (E) $\sqrt{\dfrac{383}{373}}$

29. A substance with two unshared pairs of electrons on the central atom is
(A) CO_2 (B) NH_3 (C) H_2CO (D) SO_3 (E) H_2S

30. Experimental evidence indicates that a molecule with a formula of XY_2 is a bent structure with a bond angle of 120°. The most probable hybridization is
    (A) sp (B) sp^2 (C) sp^3 (D) dsp^3 (E) d^2sp^3

31. An element, X, forms many different compounds. The mass of element X in 1 mole of five different compounds is determined to be 71, 106, 142, 213, and 177, respectively. Element X is most likely
    (A) bromine (B) germanium (C) chlorine (D) fluorine
    (E) palladium

32. Which of the following is NOT properly named?
    (A) K_2SO_3 potassium sulfite
    (B) NH_4Cl ammonium chloride
    (C) $CrSO_4$ chromium(II) sulfate
    (D) $Zn(NO_3)_2$ zinc(II) nitrate
    (E) $Fe_2(CO_3)_3$ iron(III) carbonate

33. Diamond is described as
    (A) an ionic crystal
    (B) a covalent network crystal
    (C) a molecular crystal
    (D) a metallic crystal
    (E) an sp^3 crystal

34. The following reaction is to be studied:

$$Sn^{2+} + I_2 \rightleftharpoons Sn^{4+} + 2I^-$$

The anode compartment of a galvanic cell should contain
    (A) Sn^{2+} and I_2 and a Pt electrode
    (B) Sn^{2+} and Sn^{4+} and a Pt electrode
    (C) I_2 and I^- and an iodine electrode
    (D) Sn^{2+} and a Sn metal electrode
    (E) Sn^{2+} and Sn^{4+} and a Sn metal electrode

35. In the reaction

$$Cl_2(g) + CH_2{=}CH_2(g) \rightarrow CH_2ClCH_2Cl(\ell)$$

1.00 liter of $Cl_2(g)$ at STP and 1.00 gram of $CH_2{=}CH_2$ are reacted. How many moles of product are formed?
    (A) 0.0357 (B) 0.0446 (C) 0.0803 (D) 3.54 (E) 1.00

36. In qualitative analysis H_2S is used
    (A) as a complexing agent
    (B) for confirmation tests
    (C) as a precipitating agent
    (D) as an acid to adjust the pH
    (E) as a buffer

37. Which of the following will produce the salt K_2HPO_4 in aqueous solution?
    (A) 1.00 mole Na_2HPO_4 and 2.00 moles KNO_3
    (B) 0.250 mole H_3PO_4 and 0.250 mole K_2O
    (C) 0.110 mole KH_2PO_4 and 0.220 mole KOH
    (D) 0.500 mole K_3PO_4 and 0.300 mole $Ca(OH)_2$
    (E) 1.00 mole KOH and 2.00 moles H_3PO_4

38. Which is NOT true of a rate law?
    (A) A rate law is determined from the balanced chemical reaction.
    (B) A rate law defines the elementary reaction of the rate-determining step.
    (C) A rate law relates the rate of a reaction to the reactant concentrations.
    (D) A rate law does not include the activation energy.
    (E) A rate law can be determined only from experimental evidence.

39. The equilibrium law for the following reaction:

$$CaCO_3(s) + 2HCl(aq) \rightleftharpoons CO_2(g) + H_2O(\ell) + CaCl_2(aq)$$

    is

    (A) $K_c = \dfrac{[CO_2][H_2O][CaCl_2]}{[CaCO_3][HCl]^2}$ (B) $K_p = P_{CO_2}$ (C) $K_p = \dfrac{[CO_2]}{[HCl]^2}$

    (D) $K_c = \dfrac{[CO_2][CaCl_2]}{[HCl]^2}$ (E) $K_c = \dfrac{[CO_2][H_2O][CaCl_2]}{[HCl]}$

40. The net ionic equation for the reaction between sodium sulfite and chromium(III) nitrate in aqueous solution is
    (A) $3NaSO_3(aq) + Cr(NO_3)_3(aq) \rightarrow 3\,NaNO_3(aq) + Cr(SO_3)_3(aq)$
    (B) $3SO_4^{2-}(aq) + 2\,Cr^{3+}(aq) \rightarrow Cr_2(SO_4)_3(s)$
    (C) $3SO_3^{2-}(aq) + 2\,Cr^{3+}(aq) \rightarrow Cr_2(SO_3)_3(s)$
    (D) $3Na_2SO_3(s) + 2\,Cr^{3+}(aq) \rightarrow Cr_2(SO_3)_3(s) + 6\,Na^+(aq)$
    (E) $3\,SO_3^{2-}(aq) + 2\,Cr(NO_3)_3(aq) \rightarrow Cr_2(SO_4)_3(s) + 6\,NO_3^-$

41. Which of the following is FALSE?
    (A) Radioactive decay is a first-order process.
    (B) Nuclear fusion is the combination of two nuclei.
    (C) Nuclear fission is the emission of a proton from the nucleus.
    (D) Beta particles are more penetrating than alpha particles.
    (E) Cloud chambers and Geiger counters are two detectors of nuclear events.

42. Which of the following is NOT related to the transition-state theory of reaction kinetics?
    (A) potential energy changes as reactants collide
    (B) activation energies
    (C) activated complexes
    (D) coordinate covalent bonds
    (E) reaction profiles or potential energy diagrams

43. A reaction has a $\Delta H^0 = +45.2$ kilojoules and a $\Delta S^0 = +76.3$ joules per degree K. At what temperature is the equilibrium constant equal to 1?
    (A) -592 K   (B) $-319°C$ (C) $319°C$ (D) 0.592 K   (E) $-272.4°C$

44. The number of possible isomers for the alkanes with a formula of C_4H_{10} is
   (A) 1 (B) 2 (C) 3 (D) 5 (E) 8

45. Which reactants CANNOT be used to prepare pure $MgCl_2$ under any conditions?
   (A) $MgSO_4$ and $BaCl_2$
   (B) $MgCO_3$ and HCl
   (C) Mg and HCl
   (D) $Mg(NO_3)_2$ and NaCl
   (E) $MgSO_3$ and HCl

Evaluation of Diagnostic Test 2

Score the test using the answer key. In the two tables below, indicate in the right-hand column the number of questions in each group that you got wrong. The first table categorizes the questions in four broad types. The second table designates specific topics and enables you to identify the ones on which you made the most errors. The two tables help you determine which types of questions caused you the most difficulty and what topics you need to emphasize in your review.

ANSWER KEY

1. **B**	10. **A**	19. **D**	28. **E**	37. **B**
2. **C**	11. **B**	20. **B**	29. **E**	38. **A**
3. **A**	12. **E**	21. **D**	30. **B**	39. **D**
4. **D**	13. **A**	22. **D**	31. **C**	40. **C**
5. **D**	14. **E**	23. **C**	32. **D**	41. **C**
6. **A**	15. **D**	24. **C**	33. **B**	42. **D**
7. **C**	16. **B**	25. **C**	34. **B**	43. **C**
8. **E**	17. **C**	26. **A**	35. **A**	44. **B**
9. **C**	18. **B**	27. **A**	36. **C**	45. **D**

Question Categories

Question Type	Questions	Number Wrong
Basic facts	1, 2, 6, 12, 14, 17, 18, 21, 29, 32, 33, 36, 41	
Basic concepts	4, 7, 8, 10, 11, 13, 19, 26, 27, 34, 39, 40, 42, 44	
Calculations	3, 9, 15, 16, 20, 23, 24, 25, 35, 37, 43	
Mixed concepts	5, 22, 28, 30, 31, 38, 45	

Breakdown by Topics

Chapter	Questions	Number Wrong
1. Structure of the atom	11, 18, 31	
3. Nuclear chemistry	15, 24, 41	
4. Ionic compounds and reactions	12, 33, 40	
5. Covalent compounds	8, 29, 30	
6. Stroichiometry	3, 10, 35	
7. Gases	4, 23, 28	
8. Liquids and solids	16, 27, 33	
9. Solutions	7, 25, 26	
10. Equilibrium	10, 21, 39	
11. Kinetics	19, 38, 42	
12. Thermodynamics	2, 5, 43	
13. Redox and electrochemistry	6, 21, 34	
14. Acids and bases	13, 20, 37	
15. Organic chemistry	14, 17, 44	
16. Experiments	1, 36, 45	

Compare the results of the Diagnostic Test 2 to those of Diagnostic Test 1. If your review plan has been effective, there should be overall improvement. Since the questions are different, there may be some topics that seem more difficult than before. Review all chapters before trying the practice examinations.

Explanation of Answers to Diagnostic Test 2

1. **B** H_2S is used to separate the other major groups.
2. **C** Rate constants, unlike the other choices, cannot be used to evaluate equilibrium systems.
3. **A** ? mL Cl_2 = 12.0 g CCl_4 $\left(\dfrac{1 \text{ mol } CCl_4}{154 \text{ g } CCl_4}\right)\left(\dfrac{2 \text{ mol } Cl_2}{1 \text{ mol } CCl_4}\right)$
   $\times \left(\dfrac{22{,}400 \text{ mL } Cl_2}{1 \text{ mol } Cl_2}\right)$ = 3491 mL Cl_2
4. **D** These conditions are the furthest from the condensation point.

5. **D** These characteristics define a forward reaction.

6. **A** Sulfate ions and sodium ions are not electrolyzed in aqueous solution.

7. **C** $P = P^0 X_{solvent} = (285 \text{ mm Hg})(0.850) = 242$ mm Hg. The measured vapor pressure is less than expected, indicating stronger attractions in the mixture.

8. **E** Compounds always have sigma bonds; no compound exists with only pi bonds.

9. **C** The balanced equation is $2KOH + H_2SO_4 \rightarrow K_2SO_4 + 2H_2O$.

$$? \text{ mL KOH} = 25.0 \text{ mL H}_2\text{SO}_4 \left(\frac{0.0350 \text{ mol H}_2\text{SO}_4}{1 \text{ L H}_2\text{SO}_4} \right) \left(\frac{2 \text{ mol KOH}}{1 \text{ mol H}_2\text{SO}_4} \right)$$
$$\times \left(\frac{1 \text{ L KOH}}{0.0500 \text{ mol KOH}} \right)$$

? mL KOH = 35.0 mL KOH

10. **A** The moles of gas are the same on both sides of the equation. In choice C, one product is a liquid, not a gas.

11. **B** Ions of Na and F atoms are both $1s^2, 2s^2, 2p^6$.

12. **E** $PbCl_2$ is part of the qualitative analysis scheme.

13. **A** NH_4^+ and NH_2^- differ by more than one H^+.

14. **E** $CH_3CH{=}CHCl$ has two different groups on each of the double-bonded C atoms.

15. **D** Of the original amount, 6.25% is $\frac{1}{16}$, or 4 half-lives; 4×5730 years = 22,920 years.

16. **B** The diagonal of the face represents four atomic radii, so that
$$4r = s\sqrt{2} \quad \text{and} \quad r = \frac{s\sqrt{2}}{4} = 144 \text{ pm}.$$

17. **C** $CH_3CH_2CH(NH_2)COOH$ is an amino acid, which polymerizes to form proteins.

18. **B** The ultraviolet region is just above the visible region in energy, and X rays come next.

19. **D** Not all collisions result in a reaction and b, c, and e are used in the transition-state theory.

20. **B** For a salt, $[OH^-] = \sqrt{\dfrac{K_w}{K_2} C_s}$. K_2 is used since it is the first step in the reverse of the dissociation reactions.

$[OH^-] = 4.61 \times 10^{-3}$ M. The pOH = 2.34, and the pH = 14.00 − 2.34 = 11.66.

21. **D** Only a change in temperature changes the equilibrium constant.

22. **D** In $MnSO_4$ manganese is in the $+2$ oxidation state, and in MnO_2 it is $+4$. A substance that is oxidized (oxidation number increases) in a reaction is the reducing agent.

23. **C** Solve the ideal gas equation: $PV = nRT$.

$$V = \frac{nRT}{P} = \frac{(1.0 \text{ g NH}_3/17 \text{ g mol}^{-1} \text{ NH}_3)(0.0821 \text{ L atm mol}^{-1} \text{ K}^{-1})(303\text{K})}{2.30 \text{ atm}}$$

$$= 0.636 \text{ L} = 636 \text{ mL}$$

24. **C** Tellurium-124 is the only response with a mass of 124, which makes the total masses on both sides of the equation equal:
$$^{121}\text{Sb} + {}^4\text{He} \rightarrow {}^{124}\text{Te} + {}^1\text{H}.$$

25. **C** $P = P^0 \chi_{solvent}$; $\chi_{solvent} = \dfrac{P}{P^0} = \dfrac{400}{435} = 0.920$, and $\chi_{solute} = 0.080$. A table of data is helpful. Knowledge of the mole fractions allows us to fill in the moles of the substances

	Grams	Moles
Liquid		0.920
Solute		0.080

Using the given molar masses, we convert the moles to grams to complete the table:

	Grams	Moles
Liquid	112	0.920
Solute	6.8	0.080

The molality $= \dfrac{\text{moles of solute}}{\text{kilograms of solvent}} = \dfrac{0.080 \text{ mol solute}}{0.112 \text{ kg solvent}} = 0.714 \text{ molal}$

26. **A** The molality is $= \dfrac{\text{moles of solute}}{\text{kilograms of solvent}}$, and the mass fraction is $= \dfrac{\text{grams of solute}}{\text{total mass}}$.

Only the molar mass of the solute is required to make this conversion.

27. **A** Any ionic substance will have a higher boiling point than covalent compounds of similar size.

28. **E** The kinetic energy is directly proportional to the Kelvin temperature, so $\dfrac{KE_{383K}}{KE_{373K}} = \dfrac{383}{373} = \dfrac{0.5 \, mv_{383}^2}{0.5 \, mv_{373}^2} = \left(\dfrac{v_{383}}{v_{373}}\right)^2$. The square root of the velocity term results in the square root of the temperature term, so $\sqrt{\dfrac{383}{373}} = \dfrac{v_{383}}{v_{373}}$.

29. **E** H_2S is identical in structure to water.

30. **B** Response c can result in a bent structure. However, it has approximately $109°$ angles and sp^3 hybridization, as in H_2O.

31. **C** The smallest difference between any two of these numbers is 35 or 36, and all of the numbers are multiples of 35.5. Chlorine's atomic mass is 35.5.

32. **D** Zinc has only the $+2$ oxidation state and does not use the Stock system in the names of its compounds.

33. **B** Carbon atoms are tetrahedrally bonded to each other.

34. **B** Since both Sn^{2+} and Sn^{4+} are ions, an inert platinum electrode is also required.

35. **A** The limiting reactant is calculated as follows:

$$? \text{ g C}_2\text{H}_4 = 1.00 \text{ L Cl}_2 \left(\frac{1 \text{ mol Cl}_2}{22.4 \text{ L Cl}_2}\right)\left(\frac{1 \text{ mol C}_2\text{H}_4}{1 \text{ mol Cl}_2}\right)\left(\frac{28 \text{ g C}_2\text{H}_4}{1 \text{ mol C}_2\text{H}_4}\right) =$$

1.25 g C_2H_4

Only 1.00 g C_2H_4 was given. Therefore, C_2H_4 is the limiting reactant.

$$? \text{ mol } C_2H_4Cl_2 = 1.00 \text{ g } C_2H_4 \left(\frac{1 \text{ mol C}_2\text{H}_4}{28 \text{ g C}_2\text{H}_4}\right)\left(\frac{1 \text{ mol C}_2\text{H}_4\text{Cl}_2}{1 \text{ mol C}_2\text{H}_4}\right) =$$

0.0357 mol $C_2H_4Cl_2$

36. **C** H_2S precipitates two major groups of cations.
37. **B** K_2O reacts with water: $K_2O + H_2O \rightarrow 2KOH$. This reaction has 2 mol of base for each mole of acid, as needed to produce K_2HPO_4.
38. **A** The equilibrium law can be determined from the balanced chemical reaction, but not the rate law.
39. **D** Solids and pure liquids do not appear in the equilibrium law.
40. **C** The reactants are soluble, and the sulfite ion is SO_3^{2-}. Chromium(III) sulfite is insoluble, as most sulfites are.
41. **C** Nuclear fission results in two nuclei of relatively equal size.
42. **D** Bond types are not directly related to reaction kinetics.
43. **C** $\Delta G^0 = \Delta H^0 - T\,\Delta S^0$. When $K_{eq} = 1$, $\Delta G^0 = 0.0$. The result is that $\Delta H^0 = T\,\Delta S^0$ under these conditions.

$$T = \frac{\Delta H^0}{\Delta S^0} = \frac{45,200 \text{ J}}{76.3 \text{ J K}^{-1}} = 592 \text{ K} = 319°C$$

44. **B** The two isomers are as follows:

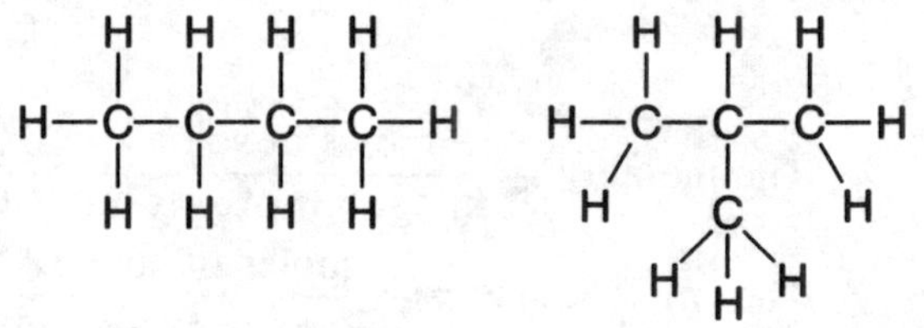

45. **D** Pure $MgCl_2$ cannot be separated from the other ions in a solution of $Mg(NO_3)_2$ and NaCl under any conditions.

PART ONE

Structure of Matter

CHAPTER ONE

Structure of the Atom

A Review of Important Discoveries About the Atom

A hypothesis by the ancient Greek philosopher Democritus (ca. 400 BC) is the first historical mention of atoms. Democritus reasoned that, if matter was discontinuous like the marbles in a box, it could be divided in half repeatedly, until eventually only one unit, such as one marble, would be left that could not be divided. He called this smallest particle of matter an **atom**. Democritus, like most ancient philosophers, had no experimental proof that atoms really exist. Roger Bacon, who is thought to have lived in the thirteenth century, established the concept that science should base its reasoning on experimental evidence. This converted science from a philosophical to an experimental study of the world.

The first chemists were the alchemists who, in the Middle Ages, tried futilely to convert base metals into gold. Despite their shortcomings (secrecy, mysticism, and at times outright fraud), the alchemists developed many experimental methods and also built an extensive body of chemical data.

Major milestones in the development of chemistry were reached in 1774, when Antoine Lavoisier performed careful experiments and measurements that led to the **law of conservation of matter**, and in 1799, when Joseph Proust made measurements on chemical reactions and compounds and developed the **law of constant composition.** The first of these important laws states that in chemical reactions matter is neither created nor destroyed. The second law states that each pure chemical compound always has the same percentage composition of each element by mass. These two laws led John Dalton to develop his **atomic theory** over the years from 1803 to 1808. Dalton's atomic theory states that:

1. All matter is composed of tiny, indivisible particles, called atoms, that cannot be destroyed or created.
2. Each element has atoms that are identical to each other in all of their properties, and these properties are different from the properties of all other atoms.
3. Chemical reactions are simple rearrangements of atoms from one combination to another in small whole-number ratios.

Every scientific theory provides new predictions that may be tested by experiments to support or disprove the theory. [It is important to remember that scientists can never prove a theory to be true. Experiments may be used to support a theory, but not to prove it.]

The atomic theory led John Dalton to propose the **law of multiple proportions**:

> When two elements can be combined to make two different compounds, and if samples of these two compounds are taken so that the masses of one of the elements in the two compounds are the same in both samples, then the ratio of the masses of the other element in these compounds will be a ratio of small whole numbers.

This law was used to help verify Dalton's atomic theory.

In 1834 Michael Faraday showed that electric current could cause chemical reactions to occur, demonstrating the electric nature of the elements. Sir William Crookes in the 1870s developed what is known today as the **cathode ray tube**. He mistakenly thought that the cathode rays were negatively charged molecules instead of electrons. (Crookes was also the first to suggest the existence of isotopes.) In 1897 J.J. Thomson determined that cathode rays were a fundamental part of matter he called electrons. He also determined their **mass to charge ratio** ($m/e = -1.76 \times 10^8$ coulombs gram^{-1}) by measuring the deflection of the cathode rays in the presence of electric and magnetic fields. Twelve years later, in 1909, Robert Millikan performed his **oil drop experiment**, which allowed him to calculate the charge of the electron (-1.60×10^{-19} coulomb). Combined with Thomson's charge to mass ratio, the mass of the electron was calculated to be 9.11×10^{-28} gram. This information led to the **"plum pudding" model** of the atom, which had electrons bathed in a sea of positive charges similar to raisins in the famous English pudding.

At this time Ernest Rutherford was interested in radioactive materials and had identified alpha and beta particles in his research. Along with Hans Geiger and Ernest Marsden, he performed the **gold foil experiment**, in which heavy alpha particles were aimed at a thin gold foil. While most of the alpha particles went through the foil with no visible effect, a few of them were deflected from their path and some actually bounced back in the direction they came from. From these results Rutherford deduced the **nuclear model of the atom**, with an extremely small, dense and positively charged nucleus surrounded by empty space sparsely occupied by electrons. Ten years later, in 1919, Rutherford discovered the basic unit of positive charge in the atom and named it the proton. The proton has a positive charge which is exactly equal in magnitude to the electron charge. It also has a mass of 1.67×10^{-24} gram, 1,836 times heavier than the electron. In 1932 James Chadwick discovered a very penetrating form of radiation. He demonstrated that it was the third major particle that makes up the atom, and it was named the neutron since it is neutral (i.e., it has no charge). The neutron has a mass almost equal to that of the proton.

While the fundamental particles of the atom (Table 1.1) were being discovered, other physicists were performing experiments that laid the foundation for a fundamental revolution in the way all matter is viewed. In the mid-1800s physicists were interested in the interaction of light and matter. One of the interesting things they found was that each element, when heated or sparked with electricity, gives off characteristic colors. A spectroscope was used to show that these colors consist of discrete wavelengths of light (line spectra), not the uniform rainbow observed when white light is separated by a prism. The line spectra of most elements and compounds are very complex. Hydrogen, however, has a seemingly simple series of lines. In 1885 Johann Balmer found an empirical mathematical relationship between the wavelengths of the lines he observed in the visible region of the spectrum. When similar series of lines were found in the infrared (Paschen series) and ultraviolet (Lyman series) regions, Johannes Rydberg extended Balmer's equation so that all of the wavelengths could be predicted.

TABLE 1.1 Fundamental Parts of the Atom

Name	Symbol	Absolute Charge (Coulomb)	Absolute Mass (Gram)	Relative Charge	Relative Mass (AMU)
Electron	e or e$^-$	-1.602×10^{-19}	9.109×10^{-28}	-1	5.486×10^{-4}
Proton	p or p$^+$	$+1.602 \times 10^{-19}$	1.673×10^{-24}	$+1$	1.0073
Neutron	n	0	1.675×10^{-24}	0	1.0087

In 1913 Niels Bohr completed his theory of how the hydrogen atom is constructed. He assumed that electrons move around the nucleus in circular orbits. Using a **solar system model**, he was able to duplicate the Rydberg equation from fundamental constants already known to physicists. Bohr's most important contribution was the concept that electrons exist in only certain "allowed orbits." This, along with Max Planck's description in 1900 of light as packets, or quanta, of energy, called photons, aided Bohr in developing the solar system model of the atom.

Louis de Broglie suggested in 1924 that, if light can be considered as particles, then the small particles such as electrons may have the characteristics of waves. In 1927 Erwin Schrödinger applied the equations for waves to the electrons in an atom and began the **wave-mechanical theory** of the atom. For hydrogen the results are very similar to Bohr's model except that the electron does not follow a precise orbit. The position of the electron in the wave-mechanical model is described by a probability of where it will be located. Also in the 1920s, Werner Heisenberg developed the uncertainty principle, which bears his name. It states that the position and the momentum of any particle cannot both be known exactly at the same time. As one is known more precisely, the other becomes less certain.

Atomic Models

Solid particle model
400 BC

Plum pudding model
1909

Nuclear model
Rutherford 1910

Solar system model
Bohr 1913

Wave-mechanical model
Schrödinger 1927

Experiments Describing the Structure of the Atom

The preceding section briefly mentioned various experiments used to determine the nature of the particles that make up the atom. In this section more detail is given to these experiments, which are considered classic examples of excellent experimentation and scientific reasoning.

Charge to Mass Ratio of the Electron

Sir William Crookes designed an evacuated tube with two electrodes, as shown in Figure 1.1. When a high voltage was applied to the electrodes, a glow was noticed between them. When an object was placed in the path of the glow, it blocked part of the beam. This experiment showed that the beam must originate at the negative electrode (cathode) and flow toward the positive electrode (anode).

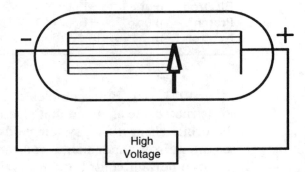

FIGURE 1.1. Cathode rays blocked by an object, showing direction of flow.

Thus the glow was called cathode rays since the rays apparently came from the cathode, or negative terminal. The path of the cathode rays could be deflected by both electric fields (Figure 1.2) and magnetic fields. The fact that these rays were attracted toward the positive electric field and repelled by the negative electric field indicated that they had a negative charge.

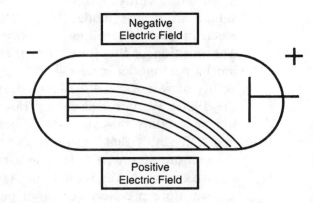

FIGURE 1.2. Deflection of cathode rays by an electric field.

In a magnetic field the magnetic force causes a negative particle to move in a circular motion with a radius of r according to the equation

$$Hev = \frac{mv^2}{r} \tag{1.1}$$

In this equation, H is the strength of the magnetic field, e is the charge of the electron, m is the mass of the electron, v is the velocity of the electron, and r is the radius of curvature caused by the magnetic field. Rearranging this equation yields

$$\frac{e}{m} = \frac{v}{rH} \tag{1.2}$$

The magnetic field H and the radius of curvature are easily measured. It is necessary to know the velocity of the electron to calculate the e/m ratio in Equation 1.2. If an electric field is applied to the beam so that it cancels the deflection of the magnetic field, the force of the electric field must be the same as the force of the magnetic field. Mathematically this is expressed as

$$Ee = Hev \tag{1.3}$$

where E is the electric field, e is the charge of the electron, and v is the velocity of the electron. Rearranging this equation gives the needed velocity of the electron.

$$v = \frac{E}{H} \tag{1.4}$$

Substituting this into Equation 1.2 gives

$$\frac{e}{m} = \frac{E}{H^2 r} \tag{1.5}$$

The experiment involves the use of a cathode ray tube with an applied magnetic field having a known strength H; the radius of deflection is measured. An electric field that may be varied is then applied to cancel the effect of the magnetic field. The value of the electric field needed to cancel the magnetic field is then used to calculate the e/m ratio. The value obtained was -1.76×10^8 coulombs per gram.

Millikan Oil Drop Experiment

Robert Millikan set up an apparatus as shown in Figure 1.3, where he could spray oil droplets (from his wife's perfume atomizer) so they would settle into a beam of X rays. The X rays caused the oil droplets to become charged with electrons. Using a small telescope, Millikan could measure the diameter of each droplet. In addition, he applied an electric voltage to the top and bottom of the chamber so that the droplet would stop falling and remain stationary. The positive plate attracted, and the negative plate repelled, the negatively charged droplet. Adjusting the voltage, Millikan was able to make the droplet stand still.

Knowing the density of the oil, Millikan could calculate the mass, m, of each oil droplet (volume × density = mass). He knew that the equation for

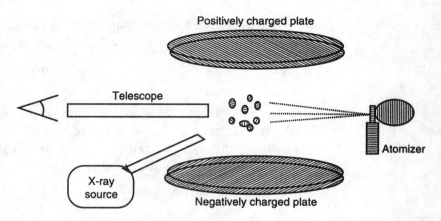

FIGURE 1.3. Diagram of apparatus used by Millikan to determine the charge of the electron.

the force of gravitational attraction was $Force = mG$, where G is the acceleration due to gravity. The equation for electrical force is $Force = Ee$, where E is the applied voltage and e is the charge of the electron. These forces are equal when the voltage is adjusted, so that the oil droplet remains stationary and

$$m_{droplet}G \quad = \quad Ee \tag{1.6}$$

From this equation the value of the charge of the electron, e, can be easily calculated.

There was one problem: the X rays did not always give an oil droplet with only one negative charge. The result was that Millikan did not get one single value for the charge of the electron. Instead he obtained a series of results that may have looked like this:

$$-3.2 \times 10^{-19} \text{ coulomb}$$
$$-6.4 \times 10^{-19} \text{ coulomb}$$
$$-8.0 \times 10^{-19} \text{ coulomb}$$
$$-4.8 \times 10^{-19} \text{ coulomb}$$

From this information, Millikan was able to deduce that the common divisor for each of these values was -1.6×10^{-19} coulomb. He reasoned that the four droplets described above must have had acquired charges of $-2, -4, -5,$ and -3, respectively, from the X rays. He had the insight to assign -1.6×10^{-19} coulomb as the charge of the electron.

Rutherford's Gold Foil Experiment

Ernest Rutherford devised an elegant experiment carried out by Johannes Geiger and Ernest Marsden. They bombarded thin foils of gold with alpha particles (helium atoms without their electrons) in order to study the structure of the atom (Figure 1.4). At that time the atom was thought to be a uniform ball of positive charge with the negative electrons embedded in it much like raisins in an English "plum pudding." If the plum pudding model was correct, the alpha particles should have gone straight through the gold foil. To the experimenters' total surprise, a small fraction of the alpha particles were deflected from their original trajectories. Even more surprising was the almost total reflection of some alpha particles.

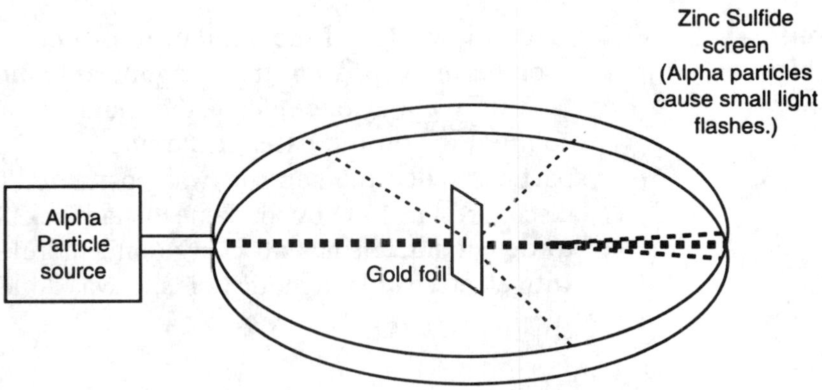

Zinc Sulfide
screen
(Alpha particles
cause small light
flashes.)

Alpha
Particle
source

Gold foil

FIGURE 1.4 Diagram of Rutherford's gold foil apparatus.

These results suggested a very massive nucleus as compared to the alpha particle. Moreover, this nucleus must be positively charged to repel the positively charged alpha particle. The nuclear model of the atom was developed by Rutherford from this information. He concluded that almost all of the mass of the atom is concentrated in a positively charged nucleus and that the rest of the atom is empty space in which the negatively charged electrons move around the nucleus.

Discovery of the Proton

Using a cathode ray tube, experimenters drilled holes into the anode (Figure 1.5) and rays moving in opposite directions to the electron were discovered. Originally called "canal rays," they were recognized as atoms with one or more electrons removed. The measurements described for the *e/m* ratio of the electron were used to determine that the lightest of the canal rays, the proton, must have a mass 1800 times greater than that of the electron. It also has a charge equal to the electron but with the opposite sign (the proton has a positive charge).

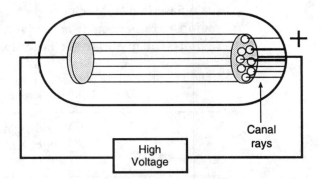

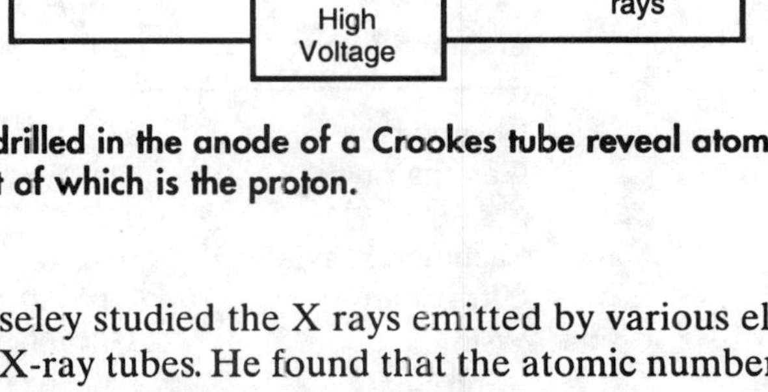

− +

High
Voltage

Canal
rays

FIGURE 1.5. Holes drilled in the anode of a Crookes tube reveal atomic ions, the lightest of which is the proton.

Determination of Atomic Numbers

In 1913 Henry Moseley studied the X rays emitted by various elements in specially designed X-ray tubes. He found that the atomic number (number of protons in the nucleus) was proportional to the square root of the frequency of the X rays emitted by the element. Moseley's brilliant scientific career was cut short when he was killed in World War I.

Discovery
of the Neutron

With knowledge of the number of protons in the nucleus of each atom, it soon became apparent that a significant amount of mass was "missing." In fact, only about one-half of the mass of each known atom could be accounted for on the basis of the number of protons it contained. Another particle, called the neutron, was postulated by Rutherford and was finally discovered in 1932 by Sir James Chadwick. The neutron was very difficult to detect since it has no charge and therefore could not be manipulated with electric and magnetic fields, as was done with the electron and proton.

Atomic Structure

Light and the
Atom

If an element is heated strongly with a flame or if it is subjected to an electrical discharge such as a high-voltage spark, the element will emit light. By studying the light emitted by the simplest of all elements, hydrogen, scientists formulated the first modern ideas of atomic structure. An understanding of visible light and other forms of electromagnetic radiation is important also in many other areas of chemistry.

The Electromagnetic Spectrum

Visible light is the most familiar form of electromagnetic radiation. All other electromagnetic radiation is invisible to the human eye but can be detected by a variety of instruments. Table 1.2 lists the various types of electromagnetic radiation, ranging from the cosmic rays with very high energy to the lowest energy radio waves. The wavelengths vary from less than a picometer (10^{-12} meter) to more than 1 kilometer. Chemists are most interested in the ultraviolet, visible, and infrared regions of the spectrum.

Figure 1.6 illustrates the electromagnetic spectrum with a logarithmic scale based on frequency and wavelength. In this representation the visible region is rather small and is surrounded by the ultraviolet and infrared regions. The names of the latter two spectral regions help to remind us that

TABLE 1.2   Regions of the Electromagnetic Spectrum

Common Name	Wavelength Range, λ (nm)	Frequency Range, ν (s^{-1})	Wavelength Range λ, (common units)
Cosmic rays	0.00005	6×10^{21}	50 fm
Gamma rays	0.0005–0.14	$6–0.02 \times 10^{20}$	0.5–140 pm
X rays	0.01–10	$300–0.3 \times 10^{17}$	10–1000 pm
Vacuum ultraviolet	10–200	$3–0.15 \times 10^{16}$	10–200 nm
Ultraviolet	200–350	$1.5–0.85 \times 10^{15}$	200–350 nm
Visible	350–700	$8.5–4 \times 10^{15}$	350–700 nm
Infrared	700–50,000	$4000–6 \times 10^{12}$	16,000–200 cm^{-1}
Microwave	$10^6–10^7$	$3–0.3 \times 10^{11}$	1–10 mm
Radio waves	$10^7–10^{12}$	$3–0.00003 \times 10^{10}$	1 cm–100 m

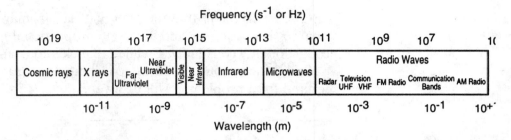

FIGURE 1.6. Pictorial representation of the electromagnetic spectrum showing approximate wavelengths and frequencies.

violet (or blue) is the high-energy end of the visible spectrum and that red is at the low-energy end. The colors of the visible spectrum are violet (highest energy), blue, green, yellow, orange, and red (lowest energy).

Wavelength, Frequency, and Energy of Light

All electromagnetic radiation may be considered as waves that are defined by the wavelength (λ) and frequency (ν). The wavelength (Figure 1.7) is the distance between two repeating points (either two minima or two maxima) on a sine wave. The frequency is defined as the number of waves that pass a point in space each second.

FIGURE 1.7. Definition of wavelength.

The wavelength and the frequency of light are inversely proportional to each other and are related by the equation

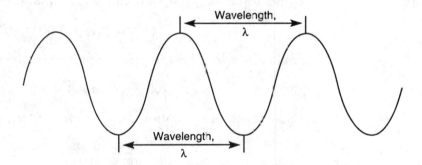

(Wavelength)(Frequency) = Speed of light

$$\lambda\nu = c$$

(1.7)

or

The speed of light is 3.00×10^8 meters per second (m s^{-1}), a number worth remembering. Wavelength has units of meters, often with the appropriate metric prefix (*cm*, *μm*, or *nm*), and frequency has units of reciprocal seconds (s^{-1}), also called hertz (Hz).

Max Planck found that the energy of electromagnetic waves is proportional to the frequency and inversely proportional to the wavelength. The proportionality constant, h, is called Planck's constant; it has a value of 6.62 $\times 10^{-34}$ joule second. [Planck's constant need not be memorized; when required for a problem, it will be given.]

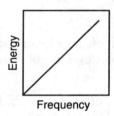

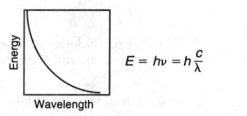

$$E = h\nu = h\frac{c}{\lambda} \tag{1.8}$$

Energy, wavelength, and frequency are all related. If the speed of light and Planck's constant are known, only one of these three variables is needed to calculate the others.

Exercise 1.1

(In this exercise and all others in this book it is recommended that you cancel the units with a red pencil or pen to verify the calculations.)

What are the frequency and the energy of blue light that has a wavelength of 400 nm? (Planck's constant = 6.62 $\times 10^{-34}$ J s.)

Solution

Substitute the given values into the equation $\lambda\nu = c$

$$(400 \text{ nm})(\nu) = 3.00 \times 10^8 \text{ m s}^{-1}$$

Substitute 10^{-9} for the prefix *nano* in the wavelength

$$(400 \times 10^{-9}\text{m})(\nu) = 3.00 \times 10^8 \text{ m s}^{-1}$$

Rearrange this equation to solve for the frequency,

$$\nu \quad = \quad \frac{3.00 \times 10^8 \text{ms}^{-1}}{400 \times 10^{-9}\text{m}} \quad = \quad 7.50 \times 10^{14} \text{ s}^{-1}$$

The energy of this light may be calculated directly from the frequency or the wavelength by using Equation 1.8.

$$E = h\nu = (6.62 \times 10^{-34} \text{ J s})(7.50 \times 10^{14} \text{ s}^{-1})$$
$$= 49.65 \times 10^{-20} \text{ J}$$
$$= 4.96 \times 10^{-19} \text{ J}$$

or

$$E = h\frac{c}{\lambda} = (6.62 \times 10^{-34} \text{ J s})\left(\frac{3.00 \times 10^8 \text{ m s}^{-1}}{400 \times 10^{-9} \text{ m}}\right)$$

$$= 4.96 \times 10^{-19} \text{ J}$$

It is very important to be sure that the units cancel properly when solving these problems. The meter units cancel each other since there is one in the numerator and another in the denominator, and the seconds units cancel because s is present in the first term and s^{-1} in the numerator of the second.

Exercise 1.2

What are the wavelength and the energy of light that has a frequency of 1.50×10^{15} s^{-1}?

Solution

The relationship between the wavelength and the frequency is $\lambda \nu = c$. Substitution of the given values yields

$$\lambda(1.5 \times 10^{15} \text{ s}^{-1}) = 3.00 \times 10^8 \text{ m s}^{-1}$$

Rearrange to solve for the wavelength, λ:

$$\lambda = \frac{3.00 \times 10^8 \text{ m s}^{-1}}{1.5 \times 10^{15} \text{ s}^{-1}}$$
$$= 2.00 \times 10^{-7} \text{ m} = 200 \times 10^{-9} \text{ m}$$

Use the metric prefix, 1 nm = 10^{-9} m, to simplify the answer:

$$\lambda = 200 \text{ nm}$$

The energy of this light is calculated from $E = h\nu$. Substituting given data yields

$$E = (6.62 \times 10^{-34} \text{ J s})(1.5 \times 10^{15} \text{ s}^{-1})$$

Canceling units and solving gives the result (remember that $s \times s^{-1}$ cancels)

$$E = 9.93 \times 10^{-19} \text{ J}$$

Atomic Spectra and Spectroscopy

Visible, ultraviolet, and infrared radiation can be separated into the various wavelengths by focusing the radiation through a triangular prism. The device used for this purpose is called a spectroscope if the light is observed by eye, and called a spectrograph if the light is detected by an electronic device and recorded on paper. A spectrometer (or spectrophotometer) is similar to a spectrograph except that the information is read from a meter. Modern instruments often have digital displays and store data in computer memories.

Using spectroscopes, experimenters found that when gaseous elements are heated they emit light. The light emitted consists of discrete wavelengths that can be measured with great accuracy. Each element emits a unique pattern of spectral wavelengths. These patterns, called atomic spectra, are used to identify elements. Figure 1.8 illustrates the spectrum of the hydrogen atom in the ultraviolet, visible, and infrared spectral regions.

Balmer discovered an empirical mathematical equation for the spectrum that bears his name. When the Lyman and Paschen series were discovered

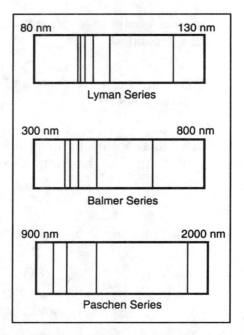

FIGURE 1.8. **Hydrogen spectra that are the basis of the Rydberg equation.**

later, Rydberg extended Balmer's equation to include them. One form of the Rydberg equation is as follows:

$$\nu = 3.2881 \times 10^{15}\ \text{s}^{-1} \left(\frac{1}{n_1^2} - \frac{1}{n_2^2} \right) \tag{1.9}$$

Balmer's and later Rydberg's equations were intriguing. Using different integers for n_1 and n_2 enabled researchers to calculate all of the spectral lines of hydrogen very accurately. It was not known why this should be true until Niels Bohr came up with a solution showing that n_1 and n_2 refer to the energy levels (orbits) of the electrons.

The Bohr Model of the Atom

Niels Bohr revolutionized concepts about the atom with his solar system model. This model of the atom required that the electron be confined to specific orbits. The energy of each orbit can be calculated by conventional physics as

$$E = \frac{-2\pi^2 m e^4}{n^2 h^2} \tag{1.10}$$

where m = mass of the electron, e = charge on the electron, h = Planck's constant, and n = orbit number.

In Bohr's theory the symbol n represents the number of each orbit, starting with the one closest to the nucleus. This theory was readily accepted because it resulted in an equation identical in form to the empirical equation of Rydberg, and the value of the Rydberg constant calculated by Bohr was almost identical to the value determined by experiment. Bohr's theory also gave meaning to Rydberg's equation. Energy in the form of light is emitted

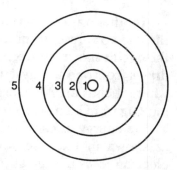

FIGURE 1.9. Diagram of Bohr orbits, showing numbering and relative sizes.

from an atom when an electron moves from its initial orbit to an orbit with a lower value of n. (Figure 1.10a). When an electron is promoted from a low orbit to a higher numbered orbit, energy must be added. (Figure 1.10b). The energy difference between any two orbits is constant, and the same amount of energy needed to raise an electron from one orbit to another will be released when the electron drops back to the original orbit.

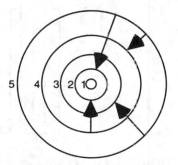

FIGURE 1.10a. Electrons dropping from outer orbits to inner orbits. They emit light energy.

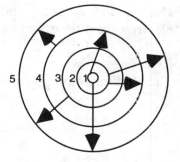

FIGURE 1.10b. Electrons excited from inner to outer orbits. They require added energy.

Line spectra all are emissions of light by atoms and therefore represent electrons in excited atoms dropping from high orbits to lower ones. To obtain a positive value for the frequency, the higher number orbit is assigned to n_2 and the lower numbered orbit to n_1 in the Rydberg equation. In the Lyman series n_2 is always equal to 1. The observed lines represent electrons dropping from the second, third, fourth, and fifth orbits down to the first orbit. In the Balmer series n_2 is always 2, and in the Paschen series $n_2 = 3$.

Another way of describing this process is the energy-level diagram, where the y-axis represents the energy of each orbit. A horizontal line, rather than the circles shown above, represents the energy level of an orbit. Arrows are drawn from one energy level to another to show where an electron starts and where it ends up. All energy-level diagrams for line spectra show electrons moving from high orbits (energy levels) to lower orbits.

The energy of each level in Figure 1.11 is calculated from Equation 1.9 as shown in Exercise 1.3. The energies have a negative sign since the electron loses energy as it drops towards the $n = 1$ level. The most stable position for the electron in the atom is the first level since the electron has lost the greatest possible amount of energy.

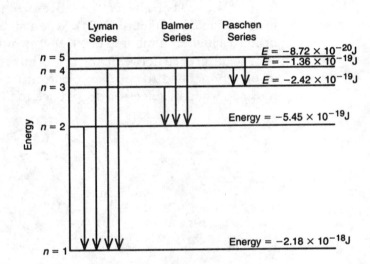

FIGURE 1.11. Energy level diagram for the Lyman, Balmer, and Paschen series of lines in the spectra of hydrogen.

Exercise 1.3

Determine the energy and the wavelength of light needed to promote an electron from the second to the fourth level in the hydrogen atom.

Solution

The Rydberg equation is solved by inserting $n_1 = 2$ and $n_2 = 4$:

$$\nu = 3.2881 \times 10^{15} \text{ s}^{-1} \left(\frac{1}{n_1^2} - \frac{1}{n_2^2} \right)$$

This becomes

$$\nu = 3.2881 \times 10^{15} \text{ s}^{-1} (0.25 - 0.00625)$$

$$= 3.2881 \times 10^{15} \text{ s}^{-1} (0.1875) = 6.165 \times 10^{14} \text{ s}^{-1}$$

$$\lambda = \frac{c}{\nu} = \frac{3.00 \times 10^8 \text{ m s}^{-1}}{6.165 \times 10^{-14} \text{ s}^{-1}}$$

$$= 4.86 \times 10^{-7} \text{ m}$$

which is converted to nanometers:

$$\lambda = (4.86 \times 10^{-7}\,m)\left(\frac{1\,nm}{10^{-9}m}\right)$$

$$= 486\,nm$$

The energy involved is calculated from

$$E = h\nu$$

$$= (6.62 \times 10^{-34}\,J\,s)\,(6.165 \times 10^{14}\,s^{-1})$$

$$= 4.08 \times 10^{-19}\,J$$

The important principle is that energy must be released (negative sign for energy) when an electron drops from an outer orbit to a lower numbered inner orbit. When an electron is promoted to a higher orbit, energy must be put into the atom and the sign of the energy term will be positive.

Ionization Energy

The Rydberg equation also makes it possible to calculate the energy needed to completely remove an electron from any level in the hydrogen atom. The process of removing an electron from an atom is called ionization, and the energy needed to do this is the ionization energy. Since moving to higher numbered orbits moves the electron away from the nucleus, moving the electron to n = infinity is the same as removing the electron from the atom. By substituting the number of the starting orbit of the electron for n_1 and infinity for n_2, we can solve the Rydberg equation for the frequency and then calculate the ionization energy using $E = h\nu$.

Exercise 1.4

What is the ionization energy of a hydrogen atom? What is the value for 1 mole of hydrogen? (1 mole of H atoms = 6.02×10^{23} H atoms.)

Solution

The normal hydrogen atom has its electron in the first orbit, or n = 1. When an atom is ionized, the electron is removed. This is equivalent to moving it to n = infinity. Solving the Rydberg equation for the energy yields

$$\nu = 3.2881 \times 10^{15}\,s^{-1}\left(\frac{1}{n_1^2} - \frac{1}{n_2^2}\right)$$

$$= 3.2881 \times 10^{15}\,s^{-1}\left(\frac{1}{1^2} - \frac{1}{\infty^2}\right)$$

$$= 3.2881 \times 10^{15}\,s^{-1}$$

$$E = h\nu = (6.626 \times 10^{-34}\,J\,s\,)(3.2881 \times 10^{15}\,s^{-1})$$

$$= 2.179 \times 10^{-18}\,J$$

To obtain the normally quoted ionization energy it is necessary to multiply by 6.02×10^{23} to find the energy needed to ionize 1.00 mol of hydrogen atoms. The result is 1312 kJ.

The Size of the Atom

Bohr arbitrarily decided that the momentum (mass × velocity) of the electron must be related to the size of the electron's orbit. The relationship he used was

$$mv = \frac{nh}{2\pi r} \qquad (1.11)$$

When Planck's constant, h, the electron mass, m, and the electron velocity, v, are entered into the equation for the first energy level, $n = 1$, a radius of $r = 53$ picometers (pm) is calculated. If $n = 2$, the orbit radius is 106 pm. The value 53 pm is often called the Bohr radius for the hydrogen atom. The radii of the other orbits are whole-number multiples of the Bohr radius. The Bohr radius gave chemists a theoretical value for the size of a hydrogen atom and confirmed that the atomic sizes determined by experiment were indeed reasonable.

The Wave-Mechanical Model of the Atom

Soon after Bohr's achievement (for which he received the Nobel Prize) Louis de Broglie suggested that the electron could behave as a wave as well as a particle. One way of looking at this duality involves the equation for the energy of a wave ($E = h\nu$) and Einstein's well-known equation for the energy of a particle ($E = mc^2$). Since the electron can have only one energy at any given moment, E in both equations must be the same, resulting in the equality

$$h\nu = mc^2 \qquad (1.12)$$

This shows the obvious relationship between the particle (mass) and wave (ν or frequency) nature of the electron.

Describing the motion of an electron as a wave required the use of complex "wave equations." Actual use of these wave equations is left for higher level college chemistry courses. However, it is important to understand the results of using these wave equations, which can be summarized as follows:

1. The wave equations require three numbers, called quantum numbers, in order to reach a solution. They are the principal quantum number, n, the azimuthal quantum number, ℓ, and the magnetic quantum number, m_ℓ. In addition, to describe an electron completely and uniquely, a fourth quantum number, called the spin quantum number, m_s, is needed. There are specific rules for assigning the four quantum numbers to electrons.

2. The wave equations changed the picture of the atom drastically (Figure 1.12). In particular, the fixed orbits of the Bohr theory are replaced with a cloud of electrons around the nucleus. The modern orbit is the region of space in which the probability of finding the electron is highest.

3. The circular orbits of the Bohr theory have been replaced with spherical electron clouds. The wave equations have shown that the shapes of most electron clouds, although more complex than Bohr's orbits, are still simple geometric shapes.

4. The arrangement of electrons deduced from wave equations agrees well with the periodic table. Many physical and chemical properties of elements and compounds are more fully understood with the knowledge gained about the electronic structure and orbit shape.

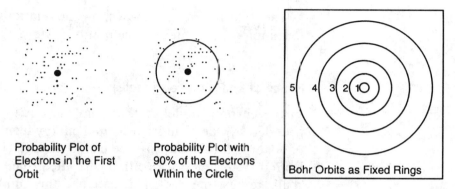

Probability Plot of
Electrons in the First
Orbit

Probability Plot with
90% of the Electrons
Within the Circle

Bohr Orbits as Fixed Rings

FIGURE 1.12. Comparison of the Bohr model and the wave model of the hydrogen atom.

5. The results of the wave equations agree completely with the Bohr model. Specifically, the energy change for an electron moving from one electron cloud to another agrees with Bohr's calculations. In addition, the identical 53 pm radius is found for the electron cloud in the wave model of the hydrogen atom.

6. The Heisenberg uncertainty principle is fundamental to the wave model of the atom. This principle states that both the position and the momentum of an electron cannot be exactly known at the same time. The more precisely that the position, x, of the electron is known, the more uncertainty exists as to its momentum, mv. Heisenberg's uncertainty equation is as follows:

$$(\Delta x)(\Delta mv) \leq \frac{h}{4\pi} \tag{1.13}$$

This equation reads, "The uncertainty in the position times the uncertainty of the momentum is equal to Planck's constant divided by four pi." The concept of this equation is important, although no questions involving a numerical solution will be asked on the AP Chemistry Exam.

Structure of the Atom

The atom is put together in a regular fashion that is not extraordinarily complex. Difficulty often arises, however, from the fact that chemists use several different models of this structure. The fact that the symbols and terminology used in these various models are not always consistent causes the subject to appear more complex than it really is. The reason behind the different models is that chemists are interested in different features of the atom, each of which is best described in a unique manner.

Some chemists desire to describe all of the electrons in an atom. Others are interested only in the outermost electrons, which are called the valence electrons. A third group are interested only in the one electron that differentiates one atom from the immediately preceding atom in the periodic table. This one electron is called the differentiating electron. Other chemists wish to see how the atom is built, adding one electron after another. Still others wish to understand how atoms lose electrons to form ions.

The following sections will show the relationships between the ideas and terminologies for all of these points of view.

Principal Energy Levels (Shells)

In the current model of the atom the positively charged nucleus is surrounded by one or more principal energy levels of electron clouds. Principal energy levels may also be called the principal shells with reference to Bohr's atomic model. In either case, the principal energy level, or principal shell, nearest the nucleus is assigned the number 1, and each succeeding energy level is numbered with consecutive integers. The largest element known needs only seven principal energy levels to hold all of its electrons. The number of the principal energy level is given the symbol n, and it is the same as the principal quantum number discussed later.

Since the principal energy levels become larger the further they are from the nucleus, they can hold correspondingly more electrons. Each can hold a maximum number of electrons equal to $2n^2$, where n is the principal energy level number. From this fact we can calculate that the first four principal energy levels can hold 2, 8, 18, and 32 electrons, respectively. The last three could hold 50, 72, and 98 electrons, but they are not completely filled.

Finally, the old style notation used upper-case letters to designate the principal energy levels. The first four were K, L, M, and N. This terminology is obsolete but may be used by scientists using and studying X rays.

Sublevels and Subshells

Each principal energy level within an atom contains one or more sublevels. These sublevels may be called subshells in the older terminology. The number of sublevels possible in each principal energy level is equal to the value of n for that energy level. For instance, the third principal energy level ($n = 3$) may contain a maximum of three sublevels. For the 109 known elements, only four sublevels are actually used. The fifth, sixth, and seventh sublevels (for $n = 5, 6$, and 7) are theoretically possible, but are not currently needed.

Sublevels are numbered with consecutive whole numbers starting with zero. These numbers are the azimuthal quantum numbers, ℓ. The value of ℓ can never be greater than $n - 1$. In addition to the numbering system, the sublevels are also given corresponding letters of s, p, d, and f. Table 1.3 shows the sublevels possible for each energy level. It is important to remember that a sublevel will not exist unless the atom has enough electrons to occupy at least part of the sublevel.

Each principal energy level has an s sublevel, all except the first and seventh have p sublevels, and the d and f sublevels also are found in more than one principal energy level. To distinguish one sublevel from another, chemists usually combine the principal energy level number with the sublevel letter in order to indicate in which principal energy level the sublevel is located. With this method, the designation $4p$ indicates a p sublevel in the fourth principal energy level.

TABLE 1.3   Sublevels in the Atom

Principal Level	Sublevel Number, ℓ	Sublevel Letter
1	0	s
2	0, 1	s, p
3	0, 1, 2	s, p, d
4	0, 1, 2, 3	s, p, d, f
5	0, 1, 2, 3	s, p, d, f
6	0, 1, 2	s, p, d
7	0	s

Orbitals

Each sublevel of the atom may contain one or more electron orbitals. An orbital is defined as a region of space that has a high electron density, and each orbital may contain a maximum of two electrons. To share an orbital, two electrons must have opposite spins. When two electrons share an orbital, they are said to be paired. Orbitals are designated as s, p, d, or f according to the sublevel they are in.

The number of orbitals that a sublevel may have depends on the azimuthal quantum number, ℓ, of the sublevel and is equal to $2\ell + 1$. From this fact we see that there is one s orbital in an s sublevel, three p orbitals in a p sublevel, five d orbitals in a d sublevel, and seven f orbitals in an f sublevel. Table 1.4 summarizes this information.

TABLE 1.4   Orbitals in the Atom

Sublevel Number, ℓ	Sublevel Letter	Number of Orbitals $2\ell + 1$	Number of Electrons per Sublevel
0	s	1	2
1	p	3	6
2	d	5	10
3	f	7	14

This table also shows why the principal energy levels contain 2, 8, 18, and 32 electrons, respectively. The first principal energy level has only one s orbital and therefore holds only 2 electrons. The second principal energy level has s and p orbitals that hold 2 and 6 electrons, respectively, or 8 for that energy level. The third principal energy level holds the sum of $2 + 6 + 10$ or 18 electrons, and the fourth principal energy level holds $2 + 6 + 10 + 14$ or 32 electrons. Orbitals take the same letter designation as the sublevel letter (s, p, d, or f). Each orbital is given a number, called the magnetic quantum number, m_ℓ. The possible values of m_ℓ range from $-\ell$ to $+\ell$, including zero, as Table 1.5 shows.

TABLE 1.5   Possible Values of m_ℓ

Orbital	m_ℓ Values
s	0
p	$-1, 0, +1$
d	$-2 -1, 0, +1, +2$
f	$-3 -2 -1, 0, +1, +2, +3$

The designation of a sublevel also tells the chemist the shape of the orbitals within that sublevel. In s sublevels the shape of the electron cloud is spherical. For the s sublevel in the first principal energy level, the highest electron density is found within a sphere 53 pm from the nucleus, as Bohr predicted. In the second and higher numbered principal energy levels, the s sublevel has a high electron density at the expected distance from the nucleus ($n \times 53$ pm). These sublevels also have an appreciable electron density at all of the lower energy level radii. Figure 1.13 illustrates this feature of the s sublevels.

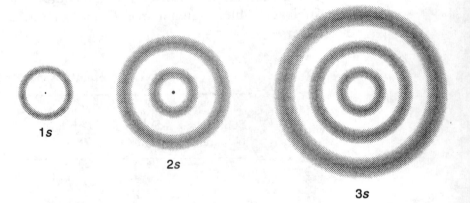

1s

2s

3s

FIGURE 1.13.   Diagrams of the 1s, 2s, and 3s orbitals, showing that electron density for the 2s and 3s orbitals occurs not only at the expected radius but also at intermediate levels.

The p orbitals have a dumbbell shape, with the electron density being greatest in two lobes on either side of the nucleus. There are three p orbitals in each p sublevel. Each is oriented along a different axis, as shown in Figure 1.14. These orbitals may be designated as p_x, p_y, and p_z.

The five d orbitals in a d sublevel have the shapes shown in Figure 1.15. They often have subscripts indicating the general locations of the orbitals on the x-, y-, and z-axes.

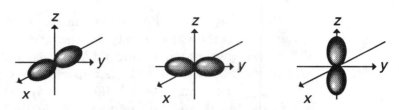

FIGURE 1.14. Diagrams of the three *p* orbitals aligned with the *x*-, *y*-, and *z*-axes.

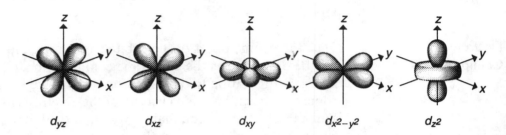

d_{yz} d_{xz} d_{xy} $d_{x^2-y^2}$ d_{z^2}

FIGURE 1.15. Shapes of the five *d* orbitals in the atom. Four of the shapes are identical; the fifth is very distinctive.

The seven *f* orbitals are slightly more complex in shape than the *d* orbitals. A knowledge of the exact shapes is not needed at this time.

Electronic Structure of the Atom

At this point we need to see how the information given above is used to develop the complete picture of an atom. The underlying principle of how the electrons are arranged is based on the energy of each orbital. Electrons will fill the orbitals that have the lowest energy first, much as water always flows downhill. While the numerical values of the energies of the orbitals are not important here, the order, from lowest to highest energy is important. That sequence

1s, 2s, 2p, 3s, 3p, 4s, 3d, 4p, 5s, 4d, 5p, 6s, 4f, 5d, 6p, 7s, 5f, 6d

is known as the aufbau, or energy order. It need not be memorized since it may be quickly obtained from the structure of the periodic table. Figure 1.16 shows the long form of the periodic table divided into shaded blocks labeled *s*, *p*, *d*, and *f* for the highest energy electron in each atom.

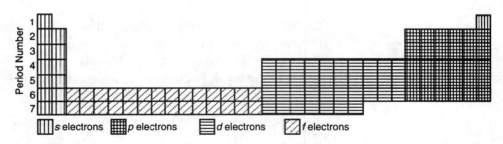

FIGURE 1.16. Periodic table divided to show the regions where *s*, *p*, *d*, and *f* electrons are the highest energy electrons in each atom.

Reading across this periodic table, we can see that the energy ordering is an integral part of this table. The first period represents the $1s$ electrons. Filling the second period adds the $2s$ and then $2p$ electrons. The third period fills with $3s$ and then $3p$ electrons, the fourth period with $4s$, $3d$, and $4p$ electrons, and the fifth with $5s$, $4d$, and $5p$ electrons. Notice that in the fourth and fifth periods a d electron has a number that is one less than the period it is in. The sixth period fills with $6s$, $4f$, $5d$, and $6p$ electrons, and the seventh with $7s$, $5f$, and $6d$ electrons. Once again, notice that the d electrons have numbers that are one less than the period number. In addition, the f orbitals have numbers that are two less than the period number.

Electronic Configurations

Once the energy order of the orbitals is known, the electrons in any atom may be described as the electronic configuration. Chemists use two forms of this configuration to display information. The first is the complete electronic configuration, which lists all of the electrons in the atom. The second is an abbreviated version that lumps all of the inner electrons together and lists only the highest energy electrons.

Complete Electronic Configurations, $n\ell^x$

In complete electronic configurations the electrons present are listed by designating the principal energy level (n) by number, the sublevel (ℓ) by letter, and the number of electrons (x) in each sublevel, x. Atoms are "built up" by adding electrons to the lowest energy sublevel possible. As shown before, the general ordering of the sublevels in the known elements is

$$1s,\ 2s,\ 2p,\ 3s,\ 3p,\ 4s,\ 3d,\ 4p,\ 5s,\ 4d,\ 5p,\ 6s,\ 4f,\ 5d,\ 6p,\ 7s,\ 5f,\ 6d$$

In addition, the maximum number of electrons in each sublevel was discussed previously and is shown in Table 1.6.

TABLE 1.6 Maximum Number of Electrons That Each Sublevel Can Hold

Sublevel	s	p	d	f
Number of electrons	2	6	10	14

To obtain an electronic configuration for an element, the number of electrons is determined from the element's atomic number. Then these electrons are placed into the sublevels, completely filling one sublevel before starting to fill the next one. Several examples are shown in Table 1.7.

Important Exceptions to Aufbau Ordering

The above examples follow the aufbau order in the filling of the sublevels. Many elements, however, do not follow the aufbau ordering, as shown in

TABLE 1.7 Electronic Comfigurations of Selected Elements

Element	Complete Electronic Configuration
Sodium, Na	$1s^2,2s^2,2p^6,3s^1$
Lead, PB	$1s^2,2s^2,2p^6,3s^2,3p^6,4s^2,3d^{10},4p^6,5s^2,4d^{10},5p^6,6s^2,4f^{14},5d^{10},6p^2$
Radom, RN	$1s^2,2s^2,2p^6,3s^2,3p^6,4s^2,3d^{10},4p^6,5^2,4d^{10},5p^6,6s^2,4f^{14},5d^{10},6p^6$
Antimony, Sb	$1s^2,2s^2,2p^6,3^2,3p^6,4s^2,3d^{10},4p^6,5s^2,4d^{10},5p^3$
Cobalt, Co	$1s^2,2s^2,2p^6,3s^2,3p^6,4s^2,3d^7$
Chlorine, Cl	$1s^2,2s^2,2p^6,3s^2,3p^5$

the table of electron configurations in Appendix 2. The only exceptions to the aufbau ordering that are important at this time occur in the electron configurations for chromium, molybdenum, copper, silver, and gold. These are listed in Table 1.8. It is apparent that the completely filled d sublevel of Cu, Ag, and Au confers stability to the atom at the expense of "unfilling" the previous s sublevel. For Cr and Mo, it appears that a half-filled d sublevel also confers stability, once again at the expense of a previously filled s sublevel.

TABLE 1.8 Common Exceptions to the Aufbau Order

Element	Electronic Configuration
Copper, Cu	$1s^2,2s^2,2p^6,3s^2,2p^6,3s^2,3p^6,3s^2,3p^6,\mathbf{4s^1,3d^{10}}$
Silver, Ag	$1s^2,2s^2,2p^6,3s^2,3p^6,4s^2,3d^{10},4p^6,\mathbf{5s^1,4d^{10}}$
Gold, Au	$1s^2,2s^2,2p^6,3s^2,3p^6,4s^2,3d^{10},4p^6,5s^2,4d^{10},5p^6,\mathbf{6s^1},4f^{14},\mathbf{5d^{10}}$
Chromium, Cr	$1s^2,2s^2,2p^6,3s^2,3p^6,\mathbf{4s^1,3d^5}$
Molybdenum, Mo	$1s^2,2s^2,2p^6,3s^2,3p^6,4s^2,3d^{10},4p^6,\mathbf{5s^1,4d^5}$

Abbreviated Electronic Configurations

When atoms react with each other, their first point of contact is the outer-most, highest energy electrons of each atom involved. In fact, the inner core of lower energy electrons and the nucleus play virtually no role in most chemical reactions. These inner electrons may be represented by the noble gas at the end of the period just before the period containing the element of interest. In a complete electronic configuration, all the electrons up to the last completely filled p^6 sublevel are the inner or core electrons. They may be replaced by the symbol, in brackets, for the appropriate noble gas. For iron, the complete and abbreviated electronic configurations are as follows:

$$Fe = 1s^2, 2s^2, 2p^6, 3s^2, 3p^6, 4s^2, 3d^6$$
$$Fe = [Ar] : 4s^2, 3d^6$$

Notice that the last completely filled p orbital is the $3p$ and that argon has the electronic configuration of all of the electrons up to and including the $3p^6$ electrons.

Valence Electrons

In many instances chemists are interested in the outermost electrons in an atom, located in the principal energy level with the highest number. In a practical sense, these include only s and p electrons of the atom. For any given atom the principal energy level of the outer d electrons will always be one less than the principal energy level of the s and p electrons. Similarly, for the f electrons the principal energy level is always two less than the outer s and p electrons.

Determining the number of valence electrons for any atom involves counting the groups (columns) from the left of the periodic table to the element of interest. The d and f electrons shown in Figure 1.16 are not counted. Valence electrons are often shown as dots surrounding the symbol of an atom, as shown in Figure 1.17.

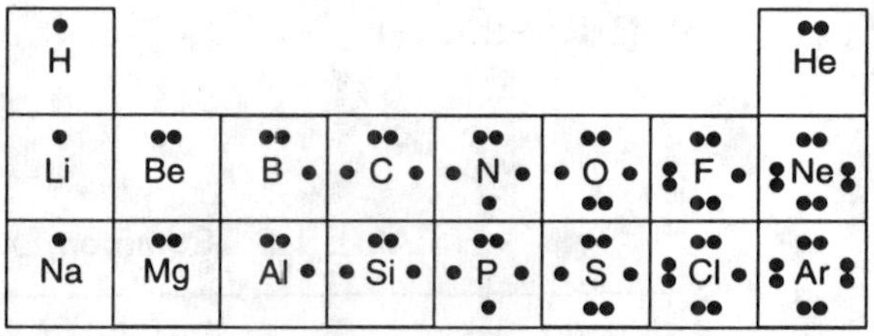

FIGURE 1.17. Representation of valence electrons as dots around the atomic symbol.

Hund's Rule

Notice that the second valence electron (second column in Figure 1.17) is represented as a pair rather than placing them on opposite sides of the symbol. This is done to indicate that the electrons are paired in the completed s orbital. The third through eighth columns fill the p orbitals. Hund's rule requires that p, d, or f orbitals in a sublevel must all be filled with one electron each before a second electron is allowed to pair in any orbital. The three separate p orbitals fill with one electron each in boron, carbon, and nitrogen, as shown by the unpaired dots in Figure 1.17. The electrons for oxygen, fluorine, and neon then form pairs until all of the p orbitals are filled. Electrons will begin to pair up only if every orbital in the sublevel is first occupied with one electron.

Hund's rule makes sense since electrons repel each other strongly because of their negative charges. This repulsion forces the electrons into separate orbitals within a sublevel until every orbital is filled with one electron. Once this occurs, additional electrons must pair up to fill each orbital with two electrons. Pairing will occur, however, only if the electrons have opposite spins. A simple view of this is that a spinning electron produces a magnetic field. If the spins are aligned with the same spin, the magnetic fields add to the repulsion of the negative charges. If the spins are opposite each other, however, the magnetic fields will attract, thus reducing the repulsion slightly.

Orbital Diagrams

Electronic configurations and valence electrons are useful for most purposes in describing the structure of the atom. However, since all of the different orbitals in a sublevel are lumped together, some detail is lost. To see that detail, orbital diagrams, which show each of the orbitals in the valence shell of the atom as a box or circle, are often used. Arrows, representing electrons, are placed in each orbital. The second electron in each orbital has the arrow facing in the opposite direction from the first, indicating that their spins are paired. Figure 1.18 shows the three possible situations for an orbital.

FIGURE 1.18. Orbital boxes that represent an empty orbital, an unpaired electron, and a pair of electrons, respectively.

Orbital diagrams are used mainly to describe the valence electrons since all of the inner electrons will be paired. At times, the *d* electrons are also shown in these diagrams. The orbital diagrams of the first ten elements are shown in Figure 1.19. The electrons are added to each sublevel, starting with the 1*s* sublevel. The arrow pointing upward traditionally represents the first electron in each orbital until each orbital in a sublevel contains one electron. Then the downward arrows, representing electrons of oppo-

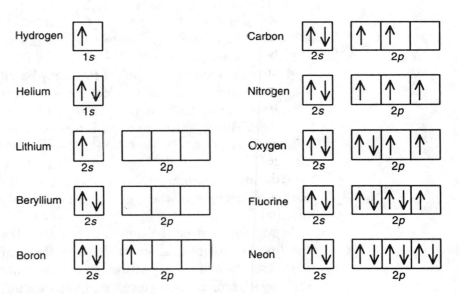

FIGURE 1.19. Orbital diagrams for the first 10 elements, showing only the valence electrons.

site spin, are added to complete the sublevel before a new sublevel starts to fill.

In later chapters we will want to show energy differences between the orbitals along with the orbital diagrams. This can be done by drawing the orbitals as shown in Figure 1.20 to indicate that the 2p orbitals are higher in energy than the 2s orbitals.

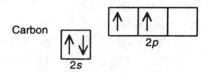

FIGURE 1.20. Orbital diagram showing that the 2s electrons in carbon have a lower energy than the 2p electrons.

Quantum Numbers

Erwin Schrödinger developed the wave equations describing the probabilities of where the electrons are located in the atom. As mentioned earlier, these equations require three integers, called quantum numbers, which describe each electron. The quantum numbers have definite rules for their possible values:

1. The **principal quantum number (n)** may have any integer value starting from 1. This represents the principal energy level of the atom in which the electron is located and is related to the average distance of the electron from the nucleus.
2. The **azimuthal quantum number (ℓ)** may have any number from 0 up to one less than the current value of n ($\ell = 0, ..., n - 1$). This designates the sublevel of the electron and also represents the shape of the orbitals in the sublevel.
3. The **magnetic quantum number (m_ℓ)** may be any integer, including 0 from $-\ell$ to $+\ell$. ($m_\ell = -\ell, ..., 0, ..., +\ell$). This quantum number designates the orientation of an orbital in space. These orientations are shown in Figures 1.13–1.15.
4. The **spin quantum number (m_s)** may be either $+\frac{1}{2}$ or $-\frac{1}{2}$ This represents the "spin" of an electron. For electrons to pair up within an orbital, one electron must have a $+\frac{1}{2}$ value and the other a value of $-\frac{1}{2}$. This quantum number is not needed for the wave equations, but it is required to satisfy the Pauli exclusion principle described below.

The final requirement, known as the Pauli exclusion principle, is that no two electrons in the same atom may have the same four quantum numbers.

When designating the quantum numbers for the electrons in an atom, the lowest possible values of the first three quantum numbers are used first. Traditionally the positive spin quantum numbers are used before the negative ones. Therefore, the hydrogen atom has the lowest possible quantum numbers, 1, 0, 0, $+\frac{1}{2}$. The quantum numbers for the first 20 elements are listed in Table 1.9. It is important to know what an appro-

TABLE 1.9 Quantum Numbers for the First 20 Elements

Element	n	ℓ	m_ℓ	ms
H	1	0	0	$+\frac{1}{2}$
He	1	0	0	$-\frac{1}{2}$
Li	2	0	0	$+\frac{1}{2}$
Be	2	0	0	$-\frac{1}{2}$
B	2	1	-1	$+\frac{1}{2}$
C	2	1	0	$+\frac{1}{2}$
N	2	1	$+1$	$+\frac{1}{2}$
O	2	1	-1	$-\frac{1}{2}$
F	2	1	0	$-\frac{1}{2}$
Ne	2	1	$+1$	$-\frac{1}{2}$
Na	3	0	0	$+\frac{1}{2}$
Mg	3	0	0	$-\frac{1}{2}$
Al	3	1	-1	$+\frac{1}{2}$
Si	3	1	0	$+\frac{1}{2}$
P	3	1	$+1$	$+\frac{1}{2}$
S	3	1	-1	$-\frac{1}{2}$
Cl	3	1	0	$-\frac{1}{2}$
Ar	3	1	$+1$	$-\frac{1}{2}$
K	4	0	0	$+\frac{1}{2}$
Ca	4	0	0	$-\frac{1}{2}$

priately formulated set of quantum numbers looks like according to the above rules.

Exercise 1.5

Designate each of the following sets of quantum numbers as possible or impossible according to the above rules.

(a) $1, 0, 0, \frac{1}{2}$ (b) $1, 3, 0, \frac{1}{2}$ (c) $3, 2, 0, \frac{1}{2}$ (d) $2, 2, 2, -\frac{1}{2}$

(e) $3, 2, 2, -\frac{1}{2}$ (f) $3, 1, -1, \frac{1}{2}$ (g) $4, 2, -2, -\frac{1}{2}$ (h) $4, 4, 0, \frac{1}{2}$

(i) $3, 2, 1, 0$ (j) $1, 1, 1, \frac{1}{2}$ (k) $6, 4, -4, -\frac{1}{2}$ (l) $5, 3, -2, \frac{1}{2}$

(m) $2, 0, 1, -\frac{1}{2}$ (n) $5, 0, 0, \frac{1}{2}$ (o) $3, 1, 2, -\frac{1}{2}$

Solution

(a), (c), (e), (f), (g), (k), (l), and (n) are valid. The others disobey one or more of the rules on page 28 as follows: (b), (d), (h) and (j) violate rule 2; (m) and (o) violate rule 3; (i) violates rule 4.

Relationship of Quantum Numbers to the Periodic Table

It must be remembered that each electron in an atom is described by a set of four quantum numbers. Calcium, for instance, will have 20 sets of quantum numbers, one set for each of its 20 electrons. In addition, the rules for the sequence in which the quantum numbers are assigned are somewhat arbitrary. Consider the electron in the hydrogen atom. There is no reason for its spin quantum number to be $+\frac{1}{2}$. In fact, since the hydrogen atoms are energetically equal, half of them will have a spin quantum number of $+\frac{1}{2}$ and half will be $-\frac{1}{2}$. In a similar fashion there is no requirement that the p orbitals fill with quantum number $m_\ell = -1$ first. In fact, all three values are equally probable. Energy levels that are the same are said to be degenerate, and all configurations are equally probable.

Referring to Figure 1.13 and the discussion about electron configurations, we can see that a knowledge of the first two quantum numbers, n and ℓ, gives us the period and sublevel (s, p, d, or f) to which the electron belongs. Because the energies of the various possibilities of m_ℓ and m_s are degenerate, they do not help in identifying the atom to which the electron belongs. For example, consider an atom that contains an electron with the quantum numbers $3, 1, 0, -\frac{1}{2}$. All that can be said about this electron is that it may exist in any element with an atomic number of 13 or greater. If this electron is specified as the last electron in a particular element, we may narrow the possibilities to the elements from aluminum to argon. Finally, strictly following the rules above, we would define this electron as the last one to fill the chlorine atom.

Any atom will have electrons that have all of the possible quantum numbers for the completely filled sublevels. If an atom has an incompletely filled sublevel, the electrons in that sublevel can have any of the quantum numbers associated with that sublevel as long as Hund's rule and the Pauli exclusion principle are followed. For instance, carbon has completely filled $1s$ and $2s$ sublevels, and each carbon atom has electrons with quantum numbers of $1, 0, 0, +\frac{1}{2}$; $1, 0, 0, -\frac{1}{2}$; $2, 0, 0, +\frac{1}{2}$; and $2, 0, 0, -\frac{1}{2}$. The two additional electrons in the incompletely filled p sublevel may be any two of the six possible sets of quantum numbers below:

$$2, 1, -1, +\tfrac{1}{2} \qquad\qquad 2, 1, -1, -\tfrac{1}{2}$$
$$2, 1, 0, +\tfrac{1}{2} \qquad\qquad 2, 1, 0, -\tfrac{1}{2}$$
$$2, 1, 1, +\tfrac{1}{2} \qquad\qquad 2, 1, 1, -\tfrac{1}{2}$$

Hund's rule requires that the third quantum number in the selected pair cannot be the same, and the Pauli exclusion principal requires that the two electrons cannot have all four quantum numbers the same.

Significance of the Quantum Numbers

The four quantum numbers are often looked upon as more data to be memorized along with the rules for obtaining valid sets. It is important to remember, however, that these numbers represent real physical properties of the atom that may be summarized in simplified form as follows:

1. The principal quantum number, n, represents the average distance of the electron from the nucleus, or the size of the principal energy level.
2. The azimuthal quantum number, l, represents the shape(s) of the orbitals within the sublevel, as shown in Figures 1.13, 1.14, and 1.15.
3. The magnetic quantum number, m_1, represents the orientation of each orbital in space.
4. The spin quantum number, m_s, represents the spin of the electron.

Important
Concepts

Bohr model of the atom
Quantum mechanical model of the atom
Electronic configurations
Atomic theory

Important
Equations

$\lambda \nu = c$
$E = h\nu$

Questions
on Chaper 1

1. Which of the following types of electromagnetic radiation has the highest energy?
   (A) visible
   (B) ultraviolet
   (C) microwave
   (D) infrared
   (E) X rays

2. What is the wavelength of light that has a frequency of $4.00 \times 10^{14} \, s^{-1}$? (The speed of light is $3.00 \times 10^8 \, m \, s^{-1}$.)
   (A) 7.5 nm
   (B) 1333 nm
   (C) 750 nm
   (D) $1.33 \, cm^{-1}$
   (E) $1.2 \times 10^{23} \, m$

3. Which of the following elements has the greatest number of p electrons?
   (A) C
   (B) Si
   (C) Fe
   (D) Cl
   (E) As

4. An electron with the four quantum numbers $3, 2, -1, -\frac{1}{2}$ may be an electron in an unfilled sublevel of
   (A) Ca
   (B) Fe
   (C) Al
   (D) Ar
   (E) Ag

5. For a d orbital:
   (A) the value of n must be 2
   (B) the value of m_s must be $+\frac{1}{2}$
   (C) the value of l must be 3
   (D) the value of m_l must be 3
   (E) the value of l must be 2

6. The numbers of electrons, protons, and neutrons, respectively, in the ^{31}P isotope are
   (A) 15, 31, 15
   (B) 15, 15, 31
   (C) 31, 15, 16
   (D) 15, 15, 16
   (E) 31, 31, 16

7. Which element has an electronic configuration that does NOT follow aufbau ordering?
   (A) Fe
   (B) Mg
   (C) Al
   (D) Ag
   (E) Ni

8. Which electronic configuration corresponds to that of a noble gas?
   (A) $1s^2, 2s^2, 2p^6, 3s^2, 3p^6, 4s^1$
   (B) $1s^2, 2s^2, 2p^6, 3s^2, 3p^4$
   (C) $1s^2, 2s^2, 2p^6, 3s^2, 3p^6$
   (D) $1s^2, 2s^2, 2p^6, 3s^1$
   (E) $1s, 2s, 2p, 3s, 3p$

9. Which electronic transition requires the addition of the most energy?
   (A) $n = 1$ to $n = 3$
   (B) $n = 5$ to $n = 2$
   (C) $n = 2$ to $n = 3$
   (D) $n = 4$ to $n = 1$
   (E) $n = 5$ to $n = 1$

10. The Heisenberg uncertainty principle states that
    (A) electrons have no momentum
    (B) the position of an electron is impossible to determine
    (C) the faster an electron moves, the more unreliable is its energy
    (D) the momentum and the position of an electron cannot be precisely defined simultaneously
    (E) Einstein's theory of relativity is still unproved

11. Which was used to determine the charge of the electron?
    (A) the gold foil experiment
    (B) deflection of cathode rays by electric and magnetic fields
    (C) the oil drop experiment
    (D) the periodic table
    (E) the mass spectrometer

12. Which of the following principles is NOT part of Dalton's atomic theory?
    (A) Atoms are the smallest, indivisible particles in nature.
    (B) Chemical reactions are simple rearrangements of atoms.
    (C) Atoms follow the law of multiple proportions.

(D) Each atom of an element is identical to every other atom of that element.
(E) All matter is composed of atoms.

13. The Rydberg equation was used
    (A) to determine energy levels in the atom
    (B) to develop the wave-mechanical model of the atom
    (C) to verify Bohr's model of the hydrogen atom
    (D) to predict atomic spectra
    (E) for nothing, but it empirically describes the spectrum of hydrogen

14. Which quantum number describes the shape of an orbital?
    (A) n
    (B) l
    (C) m_ℓ
    (D) m_s
    (E) s

15. You have just discovered a new, fundamental particle of nature. When measuring its mass, you obtain the following data for five samples:

    $4.72 \times 10^{-34}, 9.44 \times 10^{-34}, 1.180 \times 10^{-33}, 1.652 \times 10^{-33}$,
    and 7.08×10^{-34} grams

    If you make the same assumptions that Millikan did, what is the maximum mass of the new particle?
    (A) 4.72×10^{-34} g
    (B) 1.18×10^{-34} g
    (C) 9.44×10^{-34} g
    (D) 2.36×10^{-34} g
    (E) 9.91×10^{-34} g

16. Which of the following is FALSE?
    (A) The $4d$ orbitals are in the fourth period of the periodic table.
    (B) The $7s$ orbitals are in the seventh period of the periodic table.
    (C) The $4f$ orbitals are in the sixth period of the periodic table.
    (D) The $6s$ orbitals are spherical in shape.
    (E) The $5p$ orbitals are "dumb-bell" shaped.

17. The f sublevel may contain a maximum of
    (A) 2 electrons
    (B) 14 electrons
    (C) 6 electrons
    (D) 10 electrons
    (E) 8 electrons

18. The valence electrons are
    (A) all electrons in an atom beyond the preceding noble gas
    (B) all outermost electrons in a sublevel

    (C) *s* and any *p* electrons in the highest energy level or shell
    (D) electrons in the last unfilled sublevel
    (E) any electrons that can ionize

19. Which equation best expresses the energy of a photon?
    (A) $E = \frac{1}{2} mv^2$
    (B) $E = mc^2$
    (C) $E = IR$
    (D) $E = h\nu$
    (E) $E = E^0 - RT \ln K$

20. The Rydberg equation can be used
    (A) to calculate the energy released as an electron drops from a high orbit to a lower one
    (B) to calculate the ionization energy of hydrogen
    (C) to determine the energy needed to promote an electron to a higher energy level
    (D) to understand the spectra of the hydrogen atom
    (E) for all of the above purposes

Answer Key

See Appendix I for explanations of answers.

1. **E**	5. **E**	9. **A**	13. **E**	17. **B**
2. **C**	6. **D**	10. **D**	14. **B**	18. **C**
3. **E**	7. **D**	11. **C**	15. **D**	19. **D**
4. **B**	8. **C**	12. **C**	16. **A**	20. **E**

CHAPTER TWO
The Periodic Table

Chemists repeatedly refer to the **periodic table** to find specific information about the elements and to understand how the properties of the various elements are related to each other. In the table we find chemical and physical similarities between elements in the same group. We also find trends where these properties vary regularly.

This chapter reviews the periodic relationships that are necessary for a complete understanding of chemistry. The history and development of the periodic table are discussed at the end of the chapter.

The Modern Periodic Table

The periodic table summarizes a large amount of information useful to chemists and will be referred to many times throughout this book. A complete periodic table, similar to the one given with the AP Chemistry test, can be found on page 36. Basic information about its construction includes the following:

1. The **symbol** for each element is shown in a separate box, in order of increasing **atomic number**, from 1 to 109. Each box shows the atomic symbol of the element with the atomic number above the symbol and the **atomic mass** below the symbol as shown here:

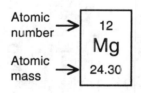

2. Each row of the periodic table is called a **period** and may contain from 2 to 32 elements. Periods with 32 elements are usually written with 14 of the elements placed below the main table
3. Each column is called a **group**, and elements within groups have similar chemical and physical properties. Within a group, the closer elements are to each other, the more similar they are.
4. The groups of the periodic table are normally numbered; however, the groups are usually not numbered on the periodic table supplied with the AP exam.

Atomic Symbols

In the periodic table each element is designated by a one- or two-letter symbol. Most symbols for the elements are simple abbreviations of their

PERIODIC TABLE OF THE ELEMENTS

1	2	3	4	5	6	7	8	9	10	11	12	13	14	15	16	17	18
1 H 1.00794																	2 He 4.002602
3 Li 6.941	4 Be 9.012182											5 B 10.811	6 C 12.011	7 N 14.00674	8 O 15.9994	9 F 18.99840	10 Ne 20.1797
11 Na 22.98976	12 Mg 24.3050											13 Al 27.98153	14 Si 28.0855	15 P 30.97376	16 S 32.066	17 Cl 35.4527	18 Ar 39.948
19 K 39.0983	20 Ca 40.078	21 Sc 44.95591	22 Ti 47.88	23 V 50.9415	24 Cr 51.9961	25 Mn 54.93805	26 Fe 55.847	27 Co 58.93320	28 Ni 58.69	29 Cu 63.546	30 Zn 65.39	31 Ga 69.723	32 Ge 72.61	33 As 74.92159	34 Se 78.96	35 Br 79.904	36 Kr 83.80
37 Rb 85.4678	38 Sr 87.62	39 Y 88.90585	40 Zr 91.224	41 Nb 92.90638	42 Mo 95.94	43 Tc (98)	44 Ru 101.07	45 Rh 102.9055	46 Pd 106.42	47 Ag 107.8682	48 Cd 112.411	49 In 114.82	50 Sn 118.710	51 Sb 121.75	52 Te 127.60	53 I 126.9044	54 Xe 131.29
55 Cs 132.9054	56 Ba 137.327	57 *La 138.9055	72 Hf 178.49	73 Ta 180.9479	74 W 183.85	75 Re 186.207	76 Os 190.2	77 Ir 192.22	78 Pt 195.08	79 Au 196.9665	80 Hg 200.59	81 Tl 204.3833	82 Pb 207.2	83 Bi 208.9803	84 Po (209)	85 At (210)	86 Rn (222)
87 Fr (223)	88 Ra 226.0254	89 #Ac 227.0278	104 Rf 261.11	105 Db 262.114	106 Jl 263.118	107 Bh 262.12	108 Hn (265)	109 Mt (266)									

*Lanthanides

58	59	60	61	62	63	64	65	66	67	68	69	70	71
Ce 140.115	Pr 140.9076	Nd 144.24	Pm (145)	Sm 150.36	Eu 151.965	Gd 157.25	Tb 158.9253	Dy 162.50	Ho 164.9303	Er 167.26	Tm 168.9342	Yb 173.04	Lu 174.967

#Actinides

90	91	92	93	94	95	96	97	98	99	100	101	102	103
Th 232.0381	Pa 231.0358	U 238.0289	Np 237.0482	Pu (244)	Am (243)	Cm (247)	Bk (247)	Cf (251)	Es (252)	Fm (257)	Md (258)	No (259)	Lr (260)

English names. The symbols for 11 elements, however, are derived from the elements' names in other languages, mainly Latin. These elements are listed in Table 2.1, and both the symbol and the name of each element should be memorized for quick recall.

TABLE 2.1 Non-English Chemical Symbols

Sodium	Na	Copper	Cu	Antimony	Sb
Mercury	Hg	Iron	Fe	Gold	Au
Potassium	K	Silver	Ag	Tungsten	W
Lead	Pb	Tin	Sn		

When chemists use atomic symbols for formulas, ions, and isotopes, chemists add subscripts and superscripts to the four corners of the symbol to represent various features of the atom. As shown below for the element calcium, the upper left-hand corner is reserved for the mass of an isotope of the

$$A \quad \text{charge}$$
$$\text{Ca}$$
$$Z \quad \text{subscript}$$

atom designated by the symbol A. The lower left-hand corner is reserved for the atomic number, Z. In the upper right-hand corner chemists place the charge of the ion that results when the element gains or loses electrons. In the lower right-hand corner are subscripts used in writing chemical formulas. These subscripts indicate how many atoms of the element are present in a formula unit. For instance, N_2 means that a molecule of nitrogen contains two atoms of nitrogen.

Electrons, Protons, and Neutrons

The periodic table may be used to quickly determine the number of **electrons** and **protons** in a particular element. The number of **neutrons** may be calculated only if a single isotope of an element is specified.

Protons

For any given element, the number of protons is always equal to the atomic number, Z, of the element:

$$\text{Number of protons} = Z \tag{2.1}$$

Electrons

For any given element, the number of electrons is equal to the atomic number:

$$\text{Number of electrons} = Z \tag{2.2}$$

For an ion of an element, the number of electrons may be calculated as:

$$\text{Number of electrons} = Z - \text{charge of the ion} \tag{2.3}$$

A positive ion (cation) has lost electrons, and a negative ion (anion) has gained electrons, compared to the element itself.

Neutrons

The number of neutrons in an element depends on the specific **isotope** of the element in question. Since the atomic masses listed in the periodic table are the **weighted averages** of all the naturally occurring isotopes, the number of neutrons in an atom cannot normally be determined from the periodic table. If the specific isotope mass number is known, however, the number of neutrons can be calculated as the difference between the isotope mass and the atomic number:

$$\text{Number of neutrons} \quad = \quad A - Z \qquad (2.4)$$

Exercise 2.1

Using a periodic table and Equations 2.1–2.4, fill in the blanks in the following table:

Symbol	Atomic Number	Isotope Mass	Number of Protons	Number of Electrons	Number of Neutrons
Fe		56			
	60	144			
		102	45	45	
		59			31
Al		27			

Solution

Symbol	Atomic Number	Isotope Mass	Number of Protons	Number of Electrons	Number of Neutrons
Fe	26	56	26	26	30
Nd	60	144	60	60	84
Rh	45	102	45	45	57
Ni	28	59	28	28	31
Al	13	27	13	13	14

Isotopes

Dalton's atomic theory states that all atoms of a given element are identical in all of their properties. However, it is now known that atoms of an element may have two or more different masses. This is due to differing numbers of neutrons in the nucleus. For instance, a carbon atom may have a mass of 12, 13, or 14 atomic mass units (^{12}C, ^{13}C, and ^{14}C). Although all carbon atoms have six electrons and six protons, the different isotopes have 6, 7, and 8 neutrons, respectively. **It is the number of electrons and protons that defines an element and its properties.**

Atomic Masses

It is important to remember that the atomic masses listed in the periodic table are all relative to the mass of the ^{12}C isotope of carbon. For this reason, masses listed in the periodic table have no units. Laboratory chemists often assign units of grams to these **relative masses** for calculation purposes, as will be shown later. Other chemists may assign units of kilograms, pounds, or even tons to the masses for large industrial uses.

A second concept to remember is that chemists may refer to the exact mass of a particular isotope of an atom, or to the weighted average of the masses of all naturally occurring isotopes. This weighted average is the relative mass listed in the periodic table, and it usually does not represent the relative mass of any particular atom of that element since most naturally occurring elements have more than one isotope. Fortunately, the percentage of each isotope is relatively constant throughout the world. As a result, the measured atomic mass is the weighted average of the masses of the individual isotopes and their relative abundances.

A weighted average is calculated as the sum of all isotope masses, each multiplied by its **natural abundance**. The natural abundance of an isotope is the fraction of all atoms of an element that have the same number of neutrons.

$$\text{Weighted average} = \sum_{i=1}^{n} (\text{mass of isotope } i)(\text{abundance of isotope } i) \qquad (2.5)$$

Exercise 2.2

Magnesium has three isotopes: ^{24}Mg, ^{25}Mg, and ^{26}Mg. They occur naturally with percentage abundances of 78.6%, 10.1%, and 11.3%, respectively. The exact masses of these isotopes are 23.9924, 24.9938, and 25.9898. What is the weighted average of the three isotopic masses?

Solution

The weighted average is calculated using Equation 2.5. In this equation the mass of each isotope is multiplied by the abundance of that isotope. These products are then added to obtain the weighted average:

$$\text{Weighted average} = (\text{mass of } ^{24}Mg)(\text{abundance of } ^{24}Mg)$$
$$+ (\text{mass of } ^{25}Mg)(\text{abundance of } ^{25}Mg)$$
$$+ (\text{mass of } ^{26}Mg)(\text{abundance of } ^{26}Mg)$$

Since the abundances are usually given as percentages, they must be converted to fractions by dividing by 100 before using them in the equation. When the appropriate numbers are substituted, the equation becomes

$$\begin{aligned}
\text{Weighted average} &= (23.9924)(0.786) + (24.9938)(0.101) + (25.9898)(0.113) \\
&= \quad 18.86 \quad + \quad 2.52 \quad + \quad 2.94 \\
&= \quad 24.32
\end{aligned}$$

You may have noticed that the atomic masses in the periodic table may have four, five, six, or seven significant figures. A greater number of significant figures suggests that an atomic mass is known with more certainty than one with fewer significant figures. Experimental difficulties are one source of uncertainty in determining atomic masses. Another source is the variation in natural isotopic abundance. If the natural isotopic abundance is fairly constant, more significant figures can be obtained for atomic masses.

Exercise 2.3

The atomic mass of bromine is listed as 79.9 in the periodic table. There is no isotope of bromine with a mass of 80. Suggest an explanation for this fact.

Solution

The masses listed in the periodic table rarely represent the masses of specific isotopes. The atomic mass of bromine (79.9) can be obtained from many possible combinations of isotope masses and their relative abundances. In this case bromine has only two natural isotopes (^{79}Br and ^{81}Br), which occur in almost equal amounts in nature.

Periodic Properties of the Elements

Two forms of the periodic table are shown in Figures 2.1 and 2.2. In Figure 2.1 the periodic table is arranged in the conventional manner with the **lanthanide** and **actinide** series placed below the body of the table. Figure 2.2 places the lanthanide and actinide elements where they normally belong. However, the form in Figure 2.2 is rarely used because the boxes become too small to read.

Chemists often speak of groups of related elements such as the **alkali metals, alkaline earth metals, transition elements, halogens,** and **noble gases**. The locations of seven of these groupings are shown in Figure 2.1. A

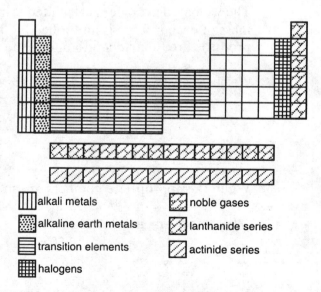

|||| alkali metals   noble gases

alkaline earth metals   lanthanide series

transition elements   actinide series

halogens

FIGURE 2.1. Common form of the periodic table, showing groups of related elements.

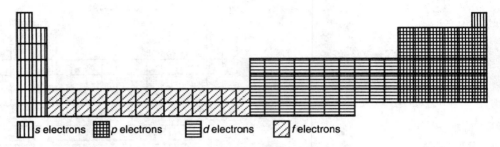

s electrons p electrons d electrons f electrons

FIGURE 2.2. Extended form of the periodic table. The shading shows the outermost electrons and their groupings.

knowledge of the names of these groupings is important, and they will be referred to frequently in the following chapters.

Chemical reactions occur when one atom collides with another. In these collisions the outermost electrons make the first contact between the atoms. For this reason, elements with similar electronic structures have similar chemical properties

After the review of the electronic structure of the atom in Chapter 1, the reasons for the chemical similarities and differences of the elements become obvious. Figure 2.2 shows the blocks of the periodic table that have s, p, d, and f electrons as the **differentiating electrons**. Each column or group has the same number and type of outermost electrons, resulting in the chemical similarities of these elements. For instance, all the noble gases have completely filled s and p sublevels, which give them extraordinary stability. The halogens are missing one p electron; otherwise, they would be electronically the same as the noble gases. The halogens tend to enter reactions that enable them to gain that one p electron. Similarly, the alkali metals and the alkaline earth metals have one and two s electrons, respectively. They readily lose these electrons to become electronically identical to (isoelectronic with) a noble gas.

Physical Properties of the Elements

Of the 109 elements in the periodic table, only two, mercury and bromine, are liquids under normal conditions. The noble gases, hydrogen, nitrogen, oxygen, fluorine, and chlorine are gases at room temperature. The remaining elements are solids.

Most of the elements in the periodic table may be considered as individual atoms. A few elements, however, exist naturally as diatomic molecules. These are H_2, O_2, N_2, and the halogens. Other elements, notably sulfur and phosphorus, exist in polyatomic units such as S_8 and P_4, but are commonly represented as single atoms in chemical reactions.

Metals and Metalloids

Metals dominate the elements in the periodic table. Most periodic tables show a heavy line dividing the metals from the nonmetals, as in Figure 2.3.

Elements bordering this line are often termed **metalloids** since they exhibit some properties of metals and some properties of nonmetals. The metallic character of the elements increases from the top of the periodic table to the bottom, as the group headed by nitrogen shows clearly. Nitro-

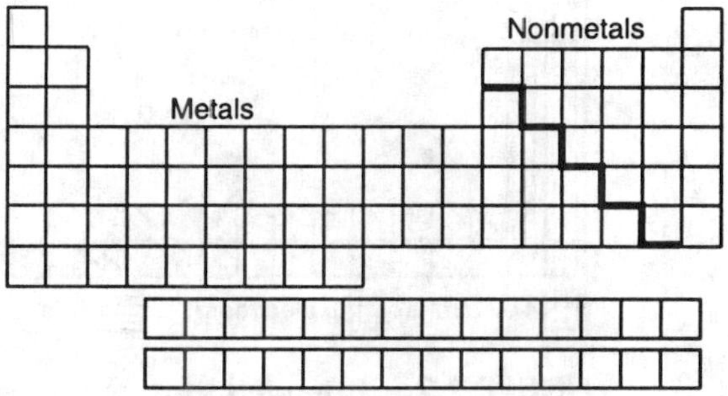

FIGURE 2.3. Location of metals and nonmetals in the periodic table. The heavy line divides the two. Elements along the line have metallic and nonmetallic properties and are called metalloids.

gen and phosphorus are nonmetals, arsenic and antimony are metalloids, and bismuth is a metal.

Allotropes

Most elements in the periodic table exist in nature in only one form. Others may have multiple forms, called **allotropes**, which are distinctly different from each other. For instance, carbon exists as graphite, diamond, and the newly discovered buckminsterfullerene. These three allotropes of carbon have distinctly different properties. Graphite conducts electricity and is slippery enough to be used as a lubricant. The diamond allotrope of carbon is the hardest of all natural materials. Large, pure diamonds are gem stones, while small diamonds are produced commercially and are used in industrial grinding machines. Buckminsterfullerene is the allotrope of carbon that exists in clusters of 60 atoms, C_{60}.

Arsenic, oxygen, phosphorus, selenium, sulfur, and tin are other elements that have more than one allotropic form. Arsenic in its gray allotrope is metallic in character, while the yellow allotrope of As_4 molecules is nonmetallic. In the same group in the periodic table, phosphorus has several allotropes, one of which is white phosphorus (P_4), which burns spontaneously when exposed to air. The red and black allotropes of phosphorus are long chains of atoms that are more stable. Sulfur has many allotropes; one is the S_8 molecule, and others are long chains of sulfur atoms. Selenium, in the same group as sulfur, has an Se_8 allotrope that is nonmetallic and another, semimetallic allotrope. Tin has three allotropes, one that has a distinctly metallic look and two that are white crystals.

Variation of Physical Properties

As mentioned earlier, the metallic character of the elements increases from the top to the bottom of a group. Many other properties also vary regularly. The melting and boiling points of metals tend to decrease from the top to the bottom of a group. Nonmetals, on the other hand, show an increase in their melting and boiling points. Similar trends in electrical properties, densities, and specific heats are also noted within each group.

Atomic Radii

Atoms range in size from hydrogen, with a radius of 37 picometers (1 pm $= 10^{-12}$ m), to francium, with a radius of 270 picometers. In each period of the periodic table the alkali metal has the largest radius and the noble gas at the end of the period has the smallest radius. In periods that have transition elements, there is a slight increase in size for the last transition elements and then a decrease in size to the smaller noble gas.

Of the atoms in a period, each succeeding atom has an additional electron and an additional proton. The electrons are added to the same shell and are located at a relatively constant distance from the nucleus, with a slight increase in atomic radius due to the electrons repelling each other. However, the increasing nuclear charge is a stronger effect and attracts the electron clouds closer to the nucleus, decreasing the overall radius. In atoms within a group, the radius increases from the top of the group to the bottom because each period has another, larger shell of electrons.

Ionization Energy

Ionization energy is defined as the energy required to remove an electron from an atom. Energy is always required to remove electrons. Francium, in the lower left corner of the periodic table, has the lowest ionization energy, while helium (the upper right corner) has the highest ionization energy. In general, a line running from the lower left to the upper right corner of the periodic table defines this diagonal relationship. We may also conclude that the ionization energy decreases from the top to the bottom of any group in the periodic table, and it increases from left to right across a period in the table.

Table 2.2 shows the ionization energies for several metals. From this table, it is clear that very little energy is required to remove one electron from sodium and potassium, but much more energy is needed to remove a second electron. This confirms the observation that sodium and potassium easily form only Na^+ and K^+ ions. For calcium and magnesium, the table shows that ionization of the first two electrons to form Ca^{2+} and Mg^{2+} ions is relatively easy but removal of a third electron requires too much energy to be feasible. Ionization energies of other metals show similar trends.

TABLE 2.2   Ionization Energies (kJ mol^{-1}) of Selected Elements

Metal	First Electron	Second Electron	Third Electron
Na	496	4563	6913
Mg	737	1450	7731
K	419	3051	4411
Ca	590	1145	4912

Electron Affinity

Electron affinity is defined as the energy needed to add an electron to an atom. Some atoms readily attract electrons, and the electron affinity has a negative value. Most atoms, however, do not accept additional electrons readily and the electron affinity is a positive value, indicating that energy must be used to add the electron.

Fluorine has the highest electron affinity, and francium the lowest. This second diagonal relationship indicates that atoms close to fluorine tend to accept electrons readily and those close to francium do not.

Electronegativity

The concept of **electronegativity** was developed by Linus Pauling to describe the attraction of electrons by individual atoms. Electronegativity is a combination of ionization energy, electron affinity, and other factors. Electronegativities show the same diagonal trend as do ionization energies and electron affinities. Fluorine has the highest electronegativity, and francium the lowest. The electronegativity concept is used in determining how electrons are distributed in molecules, as shown in later chapters. The periodic table in Figure 2.4 shows the electronegativities of the elements to illustrate the increasing trend from the lower left corner to the upper right corner of the table.

H 2.1																	
Li 1.0	Be 1.5											B 2.0	C 2.5	N 3.1	O 3.5	F 4.0
Na 1.0	Mg 1.3											Al 1.5	Si 1.8	P 2.1	S 2.4	Cl 2.9
K 0.8	Ca 1.1	Sc 1.2	Ti 1.3	V 1.5	Cr 1.6	Mn 1.6	Fe 1.7	Co 1.7	Ni 1.8	Cu 1.8	Zn 1.7	Ga 1.8	Ge 2.0	As 2.2	Se 2.5	Br 2.8
Rb 0.8	Sr 1.0	Y 1.1	Zr 1.2	Nb 1.3	Mo 1.3	Tc 1.4	Ru 1.4	Rh 1.5	Pd 1.4	Ag 1.4	Cd 1.5	In 1.5	Sn 1.7	Sb 1.8	Te 2.0	I 2.5
Cs 0.7	Ba 0.9	La 1.1	Hf 1.2	Ta 1.4	W 1.4	Re 1.5	Os 1.5	Ir 1.6	Pt 1.5	Au 1.4	Hg 1.5	Tl 1.5	Pb 1.6	Bi 1.7	Po 1.8	At 2.2
Fr 0.7	Ra 0.9	Ac 1.0														

FIGURE 2.4. Periodic table showing the electronegativities of the elements.

Ionic Radii

There are two types of ions: cations and anions. Cations are atoms that have lost one or more electrons and carry a positive charge; anions are atoms that have gained one or more electrons and carry a negative charge.

Cations are always smaller than neutral atoms of the same element. For many cations an entire shell of electrons has been lost. In those instances, the cations are only about half the size of the neutral atoms. A further decrease in size is due to the fact that cations have more protons than electrons in the nucleus.

Anions are always larger than the neutral atoms; many are almost twice the size. Since the added electron(s) go into the same shell, the gain in electrons does not fully explain the increase in size observed. Chemists reason that the outer electrons in an atom effectively shield each other from the nuclear charge. This shielding decreases the attractive forces, and the size of the electron cloud expands, resulting in the large anion radius.

Development of the Periodic Table

Atomic Masses

One of the keys to arranging the elements in the proper order was a knowledge of the correct relative masses of the atoms. By 1869 approximately 65 elements were known, as well as many of their physical and chemical properties. One of these chemical properties was that most of the known elements formed compounds with oxygen. The masses of two elements that combine with the same mass of oxygen were assumed to represent the relative masses of the atoms themselves. For example, 1.5 grams of magnesium reacts with 1 gram of oxygen, while 2.5 grams of calcium combines with 1 gram of oxygen. The ratio of 1.5/2.5 indicates that the mass of a magnesium atom is 0.6 as much as the mass of a calcium atom. Similar experiments with the other elements were thought to yield their relative masses also.

However, several complications led to disagreements over the relative atomic masses of some elements. First, scientists did not realize that hydrogen (H_2) and oxygen (O_2) are diatomic gases. Second, they assumed that one atom of each element would react with only one atom of oxygen.

Avogadro's law ("equal volumes of gases under identical conditions contain the same number of molecules") helped to solve the problem, and by 1860 there was general agreement on the formulas for most known compounds and the relative atomic masses of the elements.

Credit for Development of the Periodic Table

In the middle 1800s scientists were in the process of finding logical connections and patterns in all fields of science. For example, biologists had sorted most living matter into different groupings of species and subspecies. Chemists were trying to find order in the 65 elements known at that time. In 1864 an Englishman, J.A.R. Newlands, first proposed a periodic table. Noting that, when the elements were arranged according to mass, every eighth element seemed to have similar properties, he proposed the "law of octaves." His paper describing this theory was rejected for publication, however, and his peers were hostile to such a radical idea.

Five years later, in 1869, Dimitri Ivanovich **Mendeleev**, a Russian chemistry professor, published his periodic table. At almost the same time Julius Lothar Meyer, a German physicist, published a periodic table very similar to Mendeleev's. Although three major names are associated with the periodic table, most of the credit is given to Mendeleev. It is instructive to see why he has earned this distinction.

The primary method for assigning scientific credit is based on who publishes a discovery first. In the case of the periodic table, Mendeleev was the first to do this, since Newlands could not get his ideas published in England, and Meyer's work appeared a few months after Mendeleev's. Also, as shown below, Mendeleev showed superior insight and creativity in interpreting the meaning of his periodic table.

Details of Development of the Periodic Table

In Newlands's periodic table the elements were listed in rows of seven elements each (Table 2.3). Since the noble gases were not known at that time, and all the other elements up to calcium were known, Newlands's table worked well up to that point. After calcium, however, there was great difficulty in placing elements with similar properties in the correct groups in Newlands's table. There is also no indication that he made any revisions or improvements after 1864.

Meyer's periodic table, on the other hand, is essentially the same as Mendeleev's. Mendeleev still receives most of the credit, however, because of his insights and predictions based on his table.

TABLE 2.3   Newlands's Periodic Table

						H
Li	Be	B	C	N	O	F
Na	Mg	Al	Si	P	S	Cl
K	Ca	Cr	Ti	Mn	Fe	Co,Ni
Cu	Zn	Y	In	As	Se	Br
Rb	Sr	La,Ce	Zr	Nb,Mo	Ru,Rh	Pd
Ag	Cd	U	Sn	Sb	Te	I
Cs	Ba,V					

First, Mendeleev's periodic table (Table 2.4) left spaces for elements that were not known at that time. The first three of these were scandium, gallium, and germanium. He was able to anticipate their discovery because of his deep understanding of the chemical properties of the known elements and the periodic concept that elements with similar properties should fall in the same column. He also listed iodine and tellurium in the correct order, even though the relative atomic mass of iodine is less than that of tellurium.

TABLE 2.4   Mendeleev's Periodic Table

	I	II	III	IV	V	VI	VII	VIII
1	H							
2	Li	Be	B	C	N	O	F	
3	Na	Mg	Al	Si	P	S	Cl	
4	K	Ca		Ti	V	Cr	Mn	Fe,Co,Ni
5	Cu	Zn			As	Se	Br	
6	Rb	Sr	Yt	Zr	Nb	Mo		Ru,Rh,Pd
7	Ag	Cd	In	Sn	Sb	Te	I	
8	Cs	Ba	Di	Ce				
9								
10			Er	La	Ta	W		Os,Ir,Pt
11	Au	Hg	Tl	Pb	Bi			
12				Th		U		

Second, Mendeleev accurately predicted the chemical and physical properties of the three unknown elements that were only blank spaces in his table. The predictions fell into two general categories, chemical and physical. Mendeleev noticed that for any three adjacent elements in a column the physical properties of the middle element were close to the average of the physical properties of the elements just above and just below it. He then predicted the physical properties of each missing element by averaging the known physical data for the elements just above and below it. Mendeleev also noted that for each column of his table all the elements had the same general formulas for their oxides and chlorides. He made his chemical predictions based on the already known chemistry of the elements in the same group. Table 2.5 shows the predicted and actual values for germanium, which Mendeleev called ekasilicon.

TABLE 2.5   Mendeleev's Predicted Properties for Ekasilicon Compared to the Actual Properties of Germanium

Property	Actual Value or Formula	Predicted Value or Formula
Atomic mass	72.6 amu	72 amu
Melting point	947°C	Very high
Specific heat	$0.32 \text{ J g}^{-1}{}^{\circ}\text{C}^{-1}$	$0.31 \text{ J g}^{-1}{}^{\circ}\text{C}^{-1}$
Density	5.47 g cm^{-3}	5.5 g cm^{-3}
Oxide formula	GeO_2	MO_2
Density of oxide	4.70 g cm^{-3}	4.7 g cm^{-3}
Chloride formula	$GeCl_4$	MCl_4
Boiling point of chloride	86°C	100°C

Exercise 2.4

Predict the chloride and oxide formulas for two other elements that Mendeleev left out of his table, scandium and gallium.

Solution

The two elements were scandium and gallium. Both of these elements are in groups that tend to have +3 cations. We would expect $ScCl_3$ and Sc_2O_3. For gallium the formulas would be $GaCl_3$ and Ga_2O_3.

Important Concepts

Relationship of periodic table to electronic configuration
Chemical and physical similarities within groups
Variation of properties within groups
Diagonal relationships
Electronegativity relationships

Questions on Chapter 2

1. The differentiating electrons for transition elements are
   (A) *d* electrons
   (B) *s* electrons
   (C) *p* electrons
   (D) *f* electrons
   (E) valence electrons

2. The best way to estimate the boiling point of Pd is to
   (A) average the boiling points of Rh and Ag
   (B) average the boiling points of Ni and Pt
   (C) average the boiling points of Ir and Cu
   (D) average the boiling points of Co and Au
   (E) None of the above will work.

3. In which of the following pairs of elements is the element with the lower boiling point listed first?
   (A) Na, Cs
   (B) Te, Se
   (C) P, N
   (D) Ba, Sr
   (E) I, Br

4. In which of the following pairs is the first element expected to have a higher electronegativity than the second?
   (A) O, P
   (B) Cs, Rb
   (C) I, Br
   (D) Al, P
   (E) Sb, As

5. An element has two valence electrons. That element must be
   (A) a halogen
   (B) a noble gas
   (C) a transition element
   (D) an alkali metal
   (E) an alkaline earth metal

6. The number of electrons, protons, and neutrons in argon-40 is
   (A) 18 e, 18 p, 40 n
   (B) 40 e, 40 p, 18 n
   (C) 18 e, 22 p, 18 n
   (D) 18 e, 18 p, 22 n
   (E) 40 e, 18 p, 22 n

7. Which of the following is LEAST likely to have allotropes?
   (A) S
   (B) P
   (C) H
   (D) Se
   (E) Sn

8. Which of the following is expected to have the largest third ionization potential?
   (A) Be
   (B) B
   (C) C
   (D) N
   (E) Al

9. Which pair of elements is expected to have the most similar properties?
   (A) potassium and lithium
   (B) sulfur and phosphorus
   (C) silicon and carbon

(D) strontium and barium
(E) fluorine and iodine

10. Most elements in the periodic table are
    (A) nonmetals
    (B) liquids
    (C) gases
    (D) metals
    (E) metalloids

11. How many protons, neutrons, and electrons are in an atom of bromine?
    (A) 35 p, 45 n, 35 e
    (B) 35 p, 80 n, 35 e
    (C) 45 p, 35 n, 45 e
    (D) 80 p, 35 n, 80 e
    (E) Neutrons cannot be determined unless an isotope is specified.

12. Chemical properties of elements are defined by the
    (A) electrons
    (B) ionization energy
    (B) protons
    (C) neutrons
    (D) electronegativity

13. The chemical symbol for tin is
    (A) Sn
    (B) Ti
    (C) Au
    (D) K
    (E) Sm

14. In which pair of elements is the larger atom listed first?
    (A) K, Ca
    (B) Na, K
    (C) Cl, S
    (D) Mg, Na
    (E) O, N

15. Which of the following is LEAST likely to be a metalloid?
    (A) As
    (B) Hg
    (C) Ge
    (D) Si
    (E) Sb

Answer Key

See Appendix I for explanations of answers.

1. **A**	4. **A**	7. **C**	10. **D**	13. **A**
2. **B**	5. **E**	8. **A**	11. **E**	14. **A**
3. **D**	6. **D**	9. **D**	12. **A**	15. **B**

CHAPTER THREE

Nuclear Chemistry

The science of nuclear chemistry began with the serendipitous discovery of **radioactivity** by Antoine Becquerel in 1896. Becquerel hypothesized that a **fluorescent** compound, which glows when sunlight strikes it, also emits X rays. To test this hypothesis, he wrapped a photographic plate in black paper, placed a coin on it, and then placed fluorescent uranium ore on the coin. He exposed this apparatus to sunlight so that the uranium ore would fluoresce. When the plate was developed, a distinct image of the coin demonstrated that X rays had been produced. While Becquerel was repeating the experiment, the day became cloudy, and he stored the apparatus in a dark drawer, waiting for the weather to clear. Finally the sun reappeared; and Becquerel, thinking that the photographic plate might have been slightly exposed during the long wait, decided to develop it. To his surprise he found that, instead of being slightly exposed, the stored plate was very strongly exposed. Becquerel reasoned that the sun had nothing to do with the success of the experiment and that the uranium compound had emitted the X rays spontaneously. This was the first demonstration of natural radioactivity. In 1903 Becquerel was awarded the Nobel Prize for this discovery.

In 1919 Ernest Rutherford did what alchemists had been trying to do for centuries: he artificially converted one element into another. Rutherford did not prepare gold, however, but converted nitrogen into oxygen. This process of **transmutation** was very expensive and produced extremely small amounts of product that would not have satisfied any alchemist even if gold had been obtained. However, by bombarding nitrogen with alpha particles and producing oxygen, Rutherford demonstrated that the **nucleus** of an atom could be experimentally manipulated.

These two discoveries define the nature of nuclear chemistry. First, radioactive materials spontaneously decay into other substances by emitting energy (X rays and gamma rays) and small particles (alpha particles, beta particles, neutrons, protons and positrons). Second, by using appropriate experiments, nuclear reactions may be studied in the laboratory.

No discussion of the early years of nuclear science is complete without mention of the Curies (Marie, Pierre, and their daughter Irene). Their discoveries include radium, polonium, and the positron. They narrowly missed discovering the neutron and nuclear fission. This brilliant family accumulated a total of three Nobel Prizes. Element 96, curium, and one of the basic measures of radiation dosage, the **curie**, are named in their honor.

Radioactivity

Radioactivity is a property of matter whereby an unstable nucleus spontaneously emits small particles and/or energy in order to attain a more stable nuclear state. The process is called **radioactive decay**, and an isotope that contains an unstable nucleus is termed a **radioactive isotope** or **radioisotope**. One radioactive nucleus may decay to another radioactive nucleus, and then to another. Eventually all radioactive decay results in an isotope with a stable nucleus. Some radioactive isotopes are found to exist in nature and are called natural radioactive substances. Artificial radioactive isotopes, on the other hand, are created in the laboratory in nuclear experiments.

Radioactive isotopes, both natural and artificial, emit only a few types of **subatomic particles** as they disintegrate. These include the electron (beta particle), neutron, helium nucleus (alpha particle), and positron. When these particles are emitted in a radioactive decay process, the **nuclear mass** (nuclear mass = atomic mass = A) and/or **nuclear charge** (nuclear charge = atomic number = Z) of the nucleus changes. As a result, one isotope is converted into another with a different identity. Energy may also be released in the form of X rays or gamma rays. The energy released does not affect the identity of the isotope since these rays have neither mass nor nuclear charge. The characteristics of the particles emitted during radioactive decay are described below.

Alpha (α) particles are helium nuclei. They have a mass of 2 and a nuclear charge of +2. The symbol for the alpha particle may take many forms; the two most common are α and ^4_2He. For example, radon-222 disintegration emits an alpha particle, and the reaction may be written as

$$^{222}_{86}\text{Rn} \rightarrow \, ^{218}_{84}\text{Po} + \, ^4_2\text{He}$$

or

$$^{222}_{86}\text{Rn} \rightarrow \, ^{218}_{84}\text{Po} + \alpha$$

Beta (β) particles are electrons. They have no mass and have a nuclear charge of -1. Like the alpha particle, the beta particle is indicated by a variety of symbols, including β and $^0_{-1}\text{e}$. A decay in beta particles involves the conversion of a neutron in the nucleus into a proton and a beta particle. The beta particle is emitted and the proton remains in the nucleus. A reaction in which this occurs is the decay of carbon-14 into nitrogen-14

$$^{14}_{6}\text{C} \rightarrow \, ^{14}_{7}\text{N} + \, ^0_{-1}\text{e}$$

or

$$^{14}_{6}\text{C} \rightarrow \, ^{14}_{7}\text{N} + \beta$$

Neutrons (n) are often emitted in nuclear reactions. The symbol for a neutron is usually n or ^1_0n. A neutron has a mass of 1 and a nuclear charge of 0. When scandium-49 decays to calcium-50, a neutron and a beta particle are emitted:

$$^{49}_{21}\text{Sc} \rightarrow ^{50}_{20}\text{Ca} + ^{1}_{0}\text{n} + ^{0}_{-1}\text{e}$$

Positrons, are the positive equivalents of electrons or beta particles. The positron has essentially zero mass and a nuclear charge of +1. The symbol is either $^{0}_{+1}\beta$ or $^{0}_{+1}\text{e}$. Carbon-11 is radioactive and emits a positron when it decays to form boron-11:

$$^{11}_{6}\text{C} \rightarrow ^{11}_{5}\text{B} + ^{0}_{+1}\beta$$

The same overall reaction may occur by **electron capture**. In electron capture we visualize an electron combining with a proton to form a neutron. This reaction does not change the total mass because the electron is very light. However, converting a proton to a neutron results in decreasing the atomic number by one. The following equation represents an electron capture process:

$$^{11}_{6}\text{C} + ^{0}_{-1}\beta \rightarrow ^{11}_{5}\text{B}$$

Gamma rays (γ) are produced when some radioactive decay events occur that leave the nucleus with excess energy. When this excess energy is lost, it is sometimes in the form of gamma rays. Gamma rays have neither charge nor mass and therefore do not change the identity of the nucleus. The symbol for a gamma ray is γ.

X rays represent another form of energy that may be released in a radioactive decay event. Although X rays and gamma rays may be part of a radioactive decay event, they need not be written in the equations since they do not change the identity of the isotope.

Nuclear Reactions and Equations

Using the nuclear particles described above, we can write equations for nuclear reactions as for any other chemical reaction. In writing and balancing nuclear equations, careful attention must be paid to the total mass and the nuclear charge (atomic number) of each element. For this reason, in nuclear equations all reactants and products are usually written with *preceding* superscripts and subscripts to indicate the atomic masses, A, and atomic numbers, Z, respectively.

For example, radon-222 decays spontaneously into polonium-218 by emitting an alpha particle. This information allows us to write the nuclear equation as

$$^{222}_{86}\text{Rn} \rightarrow ^{218}_{84}\text{Po} + ^{4}_{2}\text{He}$$

If necessary, we can use the periodic table to determine the atomic number needed to write the preceding subscript (atomic number or nuclear charge) for each of the symbols. In this equation we see that the super-scripts representing the atomic masses add up to 222 on either side of the arrow $(218 + 4 = 222)$. The subscripts representing the atomic numbers add up to 86 on either side of the arrow $(84 + 2 = 86)$.

Since the atomic masses and atomic numbers must be equal on the two sides of the arrow, it is possible to deduce the identity of a missing isotope or particle in a partial equation. For example, given the partial reaction below, we can identify the particle represented by the question mark:

$$^{238}_{92}U \quad \rightarrow \quad ^{234}_{90}Th \quad + \quad ?$$

Since the total atomic mass on both sides must be 238, the question mark must represent a particle that has a mass of 4. Also, the atomic number must be 92 on both sides of the arrow, leading to the conclusion that the unknown particle has an atomic number of 2. The subatomic particle that has these characteristics is the helium nucleus, also known as the alpha particle ($^{4}_{2}He$ or $^{4}_{2}\alpha$).

Exercise 3.1

Write the equations for the following nuclear reactions:
(a) Helium-4 and sodium-23 combine to form aluminum-27.
(b) An alpha particle combines with nitrogen-14 to produce oxygen-17 and a proton.
(c) Fluorine-20 decays to neon-20 by emitting a beta particle.
(d) Uranium-238 decays to thorium-234 by emitting an alpha particle.
(e) Krypton-87 decays to krypton-86 by emitting a neutron.

Solution

(a) $^{4}_{2}He \quad + \quad ^{23}_{11}Na \quad \rightarrow \quad ^{27}_{13}Al$
(b) $^{4}_{2}He \quad + \quad ^{14}_{7}N \quad \rightarrow \quad ^{17}_{8}O \quad + \quad ^{1}_{1}H$
(c) $^{20}_{9}F \quad \rightarrow \quad ^{20}_{10}Ne \quad + \quad ^{0}_{-1}\beta$
(d) $^{238}_{92}U \quad \rightarrow \quad ^{234}_{90}Th \quad + \quad ^{4}_{2}\alpha$
(e) $^{87}_{36}Kr \quad \rightarrow \quad ^{86}_{36}Kr \quad + \quad ^{1}_{0}n$

Exercise 3.2

By balancing the masses and atomic numbers, predict the particle repre-sented by the question mark in each of the following equations:
(a) $^{14}_{7}N \quad \rightarrow \quad ? \quad + \quad ^{1}_{1}H$
(b) $^{54}_{27}Co \quad \rightarrow \quad ^{54}_{26}Fe \quad + \quad ?$
(c) $^{220}_{86}Rn \quad \rightarrow \quad ^{4}_{2}He \quad + \quad ?$
(d) $^{51}_{23}V \quad + \quad ^{2}_{1}H \quad \rightarrow \quad ?$
(e) $^{55}_{25}Mn \quad + \quad ^{1}_{1}H \quad \rightarrow \quad ^{1}_{0}n \quad + \quad ?$

Solution

(a) $^{13}_{6}C$
(b) $^{0}_{1}n$
(c) $^{216}_{84}Po$
(d) $^{53}_{24}Cr$
(e) $^{55}_{26}Fe$

Predicting Radioactivity and Radioactive Decay

It is possible to predict whether an isotope will be radioactive by using a few general principles. First, bismuth (at. no. = 83) is the last element in the periodic table that has a stable, nonradioactive isotope. All elements with atomic numbers greater than 83 are radioactive, and their isotopes decay by emitting alpha particles and beta particles and by electron capture. Alpha particles are emitted by most of these isotopes. The heavy elements often decay to other radioactive elements, which then decay to still other radioactive elements. For instance, uranium-238 decays to lead-206 in a series of 14 steps called a **radioactive disintegration series.** For uranium, this sequence is called the **uranium series** since uranium is the first element in the series. Two other radioactive disintegration series are the thorium series and the actinium series.

While the heavy isotopes ($Z > 83$) are all radioactive, the lighter radioactive elements tend to decay by emitting beta particles or positrons. We may also generalize that, if the radioactive isotope of a light element has a mass greater than the average mass of that element, it will undergo a beta emission. If the mass of the isotope is less than the average mass of the element, a positron emission may be expected. For example, the average mass of carbon is 12. Carbon-14 decays by emitting a beta particle, while carbon-10 decays by emitting a positron:

$$^{14}\text{C} \rightarrow \, _{-1}^{0}\text{e} \, + \, ^{14}\text{N}$$
$$^{10}\text{C} \rightarrow \, _{+1}^{0}\text{e} \, + \, ^{10}\text{B}$$

Why some isotopes are radioactive and some are stable is beyond the scope of this book. However, the stability of isotopes with atomic numbers less than 83 seems to depend on the ratio of neutrons to protons (n/p). Up to atomic number 20, the stable isotopes have an n/p ratio very close to 1.00. From atomic number 21 up to atomic number 83, this ratio for stable isotopes increases slowly from 1.00 to 1.5.

This stability ratio helps us to understand why carbon-14 and carbon-10 decay as they do. We predicted above that carbon-14 (n/p = 1.33) would decay to nitrogen-14 (n/p = 1.00) by beta emission. The beta particle emission reduced the n/p ratio to the value expected for a stable isotope. For the decay of carbon-10 (n/p = 0.67) to boron-10 (n/p = 1.00) by positron emission, the n/p ratio increased to a more favorable value. The examples illustrate that isotopes decay by a process that brings their n/p ratios toward the stable value.

Instead of memorizing the stable n/p ratio for each element, we can use the relative atomic mass as an average mass of the stable nuclei of a given element. This allows us to estimate the stable n/p ratio for any element. For example, the atomic mass of mercury is 200 and its atomic number is 80; therefore the number of protons is 80 and the number of neutrons is 200 − 80 = 120. The estimated stable n/p ratio for mercury is 120/80 = 1.50. The characteristic values of the stable n/p ratios for isotopes from $Z = 21$ to $Z = 83$ may be estimated in the same manner.

In another measure of stability, we find that isotopes with even numbers of **nucleons** (protons plus neutrons) tend to be more stable than those with odd numbers of nucleons. In particular, approximately 60 percent of all stable isotopes have an even number of protons *and* an even number of neutrons. Only 1.5 percent of stable isotopes have an odd number of neutrons *and* an odd number of protons.

Natural Radioactive Isotopes

Naturally radioactive elements are those from polonium ($Z = 84$) to uranium ($Z = 92$). The 17 **transuranium** elements with atomic numbers 92–109 are artificially prepared and are also radioactive. In addition to the heavy radioactive elements, a very few of the lighter elements, with atomic numbers less than 83, have naturally occurring radioactive isotopes. These lighter isotopes include potassium-40, vanadium-50, and lanthanum-138. Several interesting naturally radioactive isotopes are described below.

Radon-222 is currently an important potential environmental hazard. It forms, as part of the uranium series, from the decomposition of uranium in many rocks, particularly granite. Radon migrates from the uranium-bearing granite rocks that underlie much of the United States. Often the easiest migration route is through cracks in the basements of many dwellings. Because radon is a dense gas, it collects in the lower, unventilated areas of the house. As a gas, it is readily inhaled and exhaled with the air we breathe. However, its decomposition product, polonium, is a radioactive solid. If the radon atom happens to decay while in the lungs, it first emits an alpha particle, which may do biological damage. Second, it is transmuted into a polonium atom, which is a solid. This solid then completes the decay series within the body. This decay may result in the development of lung disease. Because radon is a noble gas, its unreactive nature makes it very difficult to eliminate from our environment. Other natural radioactive elements may also be implicated in diseases associated with smoking.

Radium-226 was one of the first radioactive elements associated with biological damage. Some radium salts are **phosphorescent** and glow in the dark. Earlier in this century, these salts were painted on watch dials by workers who licked the paint brushes to get the fine points needed for such work. Many of these workers developed cancers of the mouth. In response to this hazard, radium is no longer used for phosphorescent watch dials. It is thought that radiation was the cause of the leukemia that killed Marie Curie.

Uranium-238 is implicated in the hazards of radon gas. However, it has been used for a constructive purpose, to estimate the age of the earth. Uranium eventually decays to lead-206. The half-life of uranium, or the time required for half of the element to decay, is 4.5×10^9 years. By measuring the ratio of uranium-238 to lead-206 in rocks, we can estimate how long it has been since the rocks solidified. The best estimate is that the oldest rocks solidified approximately 4×10^9 years ago. In the following sections we will see how these calculations are made.

Potassium-40 is one of the few radioactive light elements. One way it decays is by emitting a beta particle to form argon-40. Interestingly, most of the argon in the atmosphere is argon-40, and it is thought to have been produced from the radioactive decay of potassium. This is especially likely since the amount of argon in the atmosphere is considered to be unusually high for a noble gas.

Artificial Radioactive Isotopes—Transmutation

Today, artificial radioactive isotopes are produced by bombarding a target element with nuclei of other elements that have been accelerated to high speeds. This process is carried out in a machine called a **cyclotron**, which accelerates the nuclei towards the target. Another method used to produce artificial radioactive isotopes is to bombard a target with beams of neutrons. Many new and useful radioisotopes have been generated by these methods. Some of these are listed in Table 3.1, where it will be noticed that many of the isotopes have biological applications. Isotopes, whether radioactive or not, retain their characteristic chemical and physical properties, which chemists often use to their advantage. How an isotope will act in the body and which reactions it will undergo can be predicted from its chemical properties.

For instance, the thyroid gland concentrates iodine in the body. To treat thyroid diseases, doctors use iodine-131 as a radioactive source. They know that this radioisotope, injected into the body, will concentrate exactly where they want it. This property of iodine-131 is of concern when there is an

TABLE 3.1 Some Practical Uses of Radioisotopes

Isotope Symbol	Isotope Name	Typical Application
^{3}H	Tritium	Radio-labeled organic compounds and archaeological dating
^{14}C	Carbon-14	Radio-labeled organic compounds and archaeological dating
^{24}Na	Sodium-24	Circulatory system testing for obstruction
^{32}P	Phosphorus-32	Cancer detection, agricultural tracer
^{51}Cr	Chromium-51	Determination of blood volume
^{57}Co	Cobalt-57	*In vivo* vitamin B^{12} assay
^{59}Fe	Iron-59	Measurements of red blood cell formation and lifetimes
^{60}Co	Cobalt-60	Cancer treatment
^{131}I	Iodine-131	Measurement of thyroid activity and treatment of thyroid disorders
^{153}Gd	Gadolinium-153	Measurement of bone density
^{226}Ra	Radium-226	Cancer treatment
^{235}U	Uranium-235	Nuclear reactors and weapons
^{238}U	Uranium-238	Archaeological dating
^{192}Ir	Iridium-192	Industrial tracer
^{241}Am	Americium-241	Smoke detectors
^{11}C	Carbon-11	Positron emission tomography

incident at a nuclear reactor and this radioactive substance may be released. When iodine-131 enters the food chain, increased cases of thyroid cancer are observed.

Another radioactive isotope of concern is strontium-90. We know that strontium and calcium are chemically similar since both are in the same group in the periodic table. As a result, strontium-90, which is associated with nuclear explosions, is particularly hazardous. It will become incorporated into the bone structure of all animals. From there, the beta particles it emits can do serious damage.

Radioactive isotopes may be used as tracer materials. For example, we might like to know how the phosphorus in fertilizers is used by plants. By incorporating a small amount of radioactive phosphorus in the fertilizer material, agricultural chemists can measure the time that plants take to utilize the phosphorus. In addition, they can track where in the plant the phosphorus goes.

Neutron activation analysis is the name given to a sophisticated analysis method using artificial isotopes. A sample is exposed to an intense beam of neutrons that causes many of the elements in the sample to become radioactive. These elements then decay back into the original elements at rates that are different for each element. When properly calibrated, a neutron activation analysis experiment can identify 20 or more elements in an hour or less. Often very low concentrations can be determined for trace analysis. One advantage of neutron activation analysis is that it is a nondestructive method; in other words, after the induced radiation decays occur, the sample remains unchanged.

The methods used for producing artificial isotopes were applied also to produce the transuranium elements. Many of these 17 elements were discovered during World War II, although secrecy requirements did not allow announcement until the late 1940s and 1950s. The discoverer of an element is allowed to name it. The same is true for the producers of artificial elements. Some of the newer elements have disputed names since more than one group claims credit for their discovery. The International Union of Pure and Applied Chemistry, IUPAC, now decides the names for newly discovered elements.

Rate of Radioactive Decay

Radioactive decay is a random event. We cannot predict when a single isotope will spontaneously decay. For a large group of radioactive atoms, however, we can apply the well-defined laws of kinetics (see Chapter 11). Radioactive decay is described as a first-order reaction process. The number of nuclei that disintegrate per second depends only on the number of radioactive nuclei in the sample. The equation for the number of radioactive disintegrations per second (dps) is as follows:

$$\text{Rate (dps)} = \text{(Constant)(Number of radioactive nuclei)}$$
$$= kN \tag{3.1}$$

This rate equation may be integrated by using simple calculus to obtain the expression

$$\ln\left(\frac{N_0}{N_t}\right) = kt \tag{3.2}$$

where N_0 is the original number of radioactive atoms, N_t is the number of radioactive atoms left after t seconds have elapsed, k is the **rate constant** with units of reciprocal seconds (s^{-1}), and t is the time in seconds from the start of the experiment. Since the number of atoms in a sample is directly proportional to the mass of the sample, we may interpret N_0 and N_t as the masses of radioactive atoms at the start and at time $= t$, respectively.

When half of the atoms have decayed, $N_0 = 2N_t$. Substituting $2N_t$ in place of N_0 in Equation 3.2 allows us to develop a relationship between the **half-life**, $t_{1/2}$, of an isotope and the specific rate constant, k:

$$\ln\left(\frac{2 N_t}{N_t}\right) = kt_{1/2} \tag{3.3}$$

N_t cancels on the left side of this equation to give

$$\ln(2) = kt_{1/2} \tag{3.4}$$

Since the natural logarithm of 2 is 0.693,

$$t_{1/2} = \frac{0.693}{k} \tag{3.5}$$

In Equation 3.5 $t_{1/2}$ is called the half-life of the isotope.

The half-life is an important concept. It means that one-half of the radioactive isotope present at the start of an experiment will decompose in a length of time equal to the half-life. The bar graph in Figure 3.1 shows how the amount of radioactive material declines with each half-life. After one half-life half of the isotope is left; after two half-lives half of that half, or one-quarter of the original amount, is left. With the next half-life half of what remained after the second half-life decays, and only one-eighth is left. Note that each bar in Figure 3.1 is one-half the size of the one preceding it.

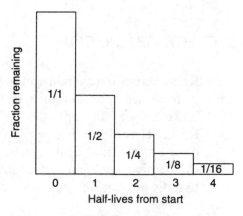

FIGURE 3.1. Bar graph illustrating how half of a radioactive material decomposes with each half-life.

We can calculate the fraction of the original sample left after a given number of half-lives by using Equation 3.6, where the fraction $\frac{1}{2}$ is raised to the power equal to the number of half-lives:

$$\text{Fraction left} \quad = \quad \left(\frac{1}{2}\right)^{\text{number of half-lives}} \tag{3.6}$$

The decimal value of these fractions multiplied by 100 gives us the percentage of the radioactive isotope remaining. The percentage that has decayed is obtained by subtracting the percentage remaining from 100.

It must be appreciated that only four half-lives are required for over 90 percent of a radioactive material to disintegrate (less than 10 percent is left). However, even a small sample of a radioactive isotope may contain upwards of 10^{18} atoms. To reduce 10^{18} atoms to just one atom will require 60 half-lives. It takes four half-lives to disintegrate the first 90 percent of an isotope, and another 56 to disintegrate the rest. This fact has important implications for policies concerning the disposal of radioactive waste materials.

Radioactive Decay Calculations

Calculations involving the disintegration of radioactive isotopes require a thorough understanding of Equations 3.1, 3.2, 3.5, and 3.6. Usually such calculations require a combination of two or more of these equations.

Exercise 3.3

The half-life of ^{210}Pb is 25 years. In a sample starting with 50 μg of ^{210}Pb, how much is left after 100 years?

Solution

Since 25 years is one half-life, 100 years is equal to four half-lives for ^{210}Pb. Therefore $\frac{1}{16}$ of the original amount will remain (see Figure 3.1). To calculate the amount remaining, the $\frac{1}{16}$ or its decimal equivalent (0.0625) is multiplied by the original amount given. Mathematically we may calculate:

$$? \text{ half-lives} \quad = \quad 100 \text{ yr}\left(\frac{1 \text{ half-life}}{25 \text{ yr}}\right) \quad = \quad 4 \text{ half-lives}$$

$$? \text{ fraction left} \quad = \quad \left(\frac{1}{2}\right)^4 \quad = \quad 0.0625$$

$$? \text{ amount left} \quad = \quad 50 \text{ }\mu\text{g }(0.0625) \quad = \quad 3.1 \text{ }\mu\text{g}$$

Whenever a problem involves a whole number of half-lives, it is usually simpler to solve it as was done here, rather than using the more complex Equation 3.2.

Exercise 3.4

How many years will 50 μg of ^{210}Pb take to decrease to 5.0 μg ($t_{1/2}$ = 25 years)?

Solution

A quick calculation shows that 5.0 μg /50 μg is 0.1 or $\frac{1}{10}$ of the original amount. From the discussion above we know that after three half-lives (75 years) $\frac{1}{8}$ remains and that after four half-lives (100 years) $\frac{1}{16}$ remains. We may estimate that the answer should be between three and four half-lives

(75 and 100 years). If a more precise answer is needed, Equation 3.2 must be used:

$$\ln\left(\frac{N_0}{N_t}\right) = kt$$

Here N_0 is the original number of atoms of the isotope, and N_t is the number remaining after time t has elapsed. We can use the mass of the isotope in place of the number of atoms since mass is directly proportional to number of atoms. Also, k is the rate constant for the radioactive disintegration, calculated from Equation 3.5. Then

$$t_{1/2} = \frac{0.693}{k}$$

Substitution yields:

$$k = \frac{0.693}{25 \text{ yr}} = 2.77 \times 10^{-2} \text{ yr}^{-1}$$

Entering our data into Equation 3.2 gives us

$$\ln\left(\frac{50 \; \mu g}{5.0 \; \mu g}\right) = (2.77 \times 10^{-2} \text{ yr}^{-1})t$$

$$\frac{2.30}{2.77 \times 10^{-2} \text{ yr}^{-1}} = t$$

As expected, the result fits the preliminary estimate of somewhere between 75 and 100 years. Effective use of good estimates cannot be overemphasized. At times an estimate allows us to select the correct answer to a multiple-choice problem. If not, the estimate serves as a check on our calculated answer.

Exercise 3.5

Ninety-nine percent of a radioactive element disintegrates in 36.0 hours. What is the half-life of this isotope?

Solution

First, it must be realized that the problem states how much of the element has disintegrated. Half-life calculations using our equations refer to the amount that is left (N_t). Subtracting 99 from 100%, we find only 1% (or $\frac{1}{100}$) left after 36.0 hours. Next we can estimate the half-life by continuing the sequence depicted in Figure 3.1. We find that $\frac{1}{32}$ is left after five half-lives, $\frac{1}{64}$ after six half-lives, and $\frac{1}{128}$ after seven half-lives. Therefore our sample has undergone at least six, but not quite seven, half-lives. Six half-lives in 36.0 hours means a half-life of 6 hours. Seven half-lives in 36.0 hours is approximately 5 hours for a half-life. Our estimate of the half-life is between 5 and 6 hours.

To calculate the exact half-life (if needed), we substitute the data into Equation 3.2:

$$\ln\left(\frac{N_0}{N_t}\right) = kt$$

$$\ln\left(\frac{100}{1}\right) = k\ (36.0\ \text{hr})$$

$$4.605 = k\ (36.0\ \text{hr})$$

$$k = \frac{4.605}{36.0} = 0.128\ \text{hr}^{-1}$$

Then we use Equation 3.5:

$$t_{1/2} = \frac{0.693}{k}$$

$$= \frac{0.693}{0.128\ \text{hr}^{-1}}$$

$$= 5.41\ \text{hr}$$

This answer agrees with our quick estimate. Often the estimate is sufficient to make an informed selection of the correct answer to a multiple-choice question. More important, it allows you to reject incorrect answers quickly.

Dating Archaeological Samples

Equation 3.2, the integrated rate equation for radioactive decay, can be used to calculate the time elapsed as long as N_0, N_t, and k are known. The rate constant can be obtained from Equation 3.3 if the half-life, $t_{1/2}$, of an isotope is known. Therefore the problem of determining the dates of very old materials involves obtaining valid data for N_0 and N_t. Two examples are presented below to illustrate the different types of logic used.

Uranium-238 decays slowly through the uranium disintegration series to lead-206. The half-life of this conversion is 4.5×10^9 years. To determine the age of a rock, we need to determine the amount of uranium present when the rock solidified, N_0, and the amount of uranium in the rock today, N_t. The amount of ^{238}U present in the rock today can be measured. It is impossible, however, to go back billions of years to obtain a sample containing the original amount of ^{238}U, which is needed to determine the value for N_0. The solution to this dilemma lies in the fact that each atom of uranium ends up as an atom of lead. Therefore, if we take a rock sample and determine the number of atoms of ^{238}U and the number of atoms of ^{206}Pb, we can say that

$$N_0 = \text{atoms } ^{238}U + \text{atoms } ^{206}Pb$$

and

$$N_t = \text{atoms } ^{238}U$$

When we set up an experiment, we must consider all possibilities for error. Two obvious ones exist in this experiment. First, if the original rock contained some ^{206}Pb, this would make our value of N_0 too high. Second, if some of the original ^{238}U did not end up as ^{206}Pb, the value for N_0 would be too low. One way this could have occurred is if radon gas, part of the uranium series, escaped from the rock before it decayed to the next solid isotope. Scientists working on this type of project evaluate these possibilities and make corrections or do additional experiments as needed.

In determining the age of carbon-containing materials, the radioactive isotope carbon-14 is measured. ^{14}C is not a natural isotope; it is constantly formed in the upper atmosphere, where ^{14}N is bombarded with neutrons. This keeps the proportion of ^{14}C relatively constant in the biosphere. While alive, animals and plants maintain that same proportion of ^{14}C in their bodies because carbon is continuously recycled. When an organism dies, however, the ^{14}C is no longer replenished by the diet and the fraction of this isotope in the dead organic matter decreases with time.

Understanding the process whereby ^{14}C enters living matter allows us to obtain reasonable measures for N_0 and N_t for our calculations. In this case we assume that the fraction of ^{14}C in the biosphere today is the same as it was in prehistoric times. With that assumption, we can write these equations:

$$N_0 = \frac{\text{living g } ^{14}C}{\text{living g total C}}$$

and

$$N_t = \frac{\text{ancient g } ^{14}C}{\text{ancient g total C}}$$

With a value for the half-life of ^{14}C we can solve Equation 3.2 to obtain the age of an ancient sample.

In using radioactive dating techniques, the equation we solve involves the ratio N_0/N_t. This ratio is difficult to determine accurately if it is very close to 1.00 or if it is very large. If the ratio is close to 1.00, very few radioactive disintegrations have occurred. If the ratio is very large, most of the sample has disintegrated (the denominator is very small in the ratio N_0/N_t). A rule of thumb for radioactive isotope dating of materials is that the age of the sample should be 0.3 to 3 half-lives of the isotope used for the dating. Uranium's half-life is close to the age of the earth and is appropriate to use for that purpose. The half-life of carbon-14 is 5730 years. As a result, we can most reliably determine the ages of biological materials that range from 1700 to 17,000 years old. Radiocarbon dating would certainly not be appropriate in verifying the age of a bottle of wine with a label date of 1865.

Nuclear Fission

Most nuclear disintegrations involve the emission of small particles, none larger than a helium nucleus. In some nuclear reactions the nucleus of a large atom breaks nearly in half. Any process that yields two nuclei of almost equivalent mass is called **nuclear fission.** Nuclear fission does not occur spontaneously, but requires that the nucleus be bombarded with energetic neutrons. Incorporation of a neutron into a **fissile** nucleus such as $^{235}_{92}U$ or $^{239}_{94}Pu$ causes the nucleus to undergo fission while releasing several more neutrons.

A fissile nucleus is one that is capable of undergoing fission. The neutrons emitted in the fission process then can react with other nuclei to cause additional fission events. Since more neutrons are released in each fission than are needed to start it, a **chain reaction** occurs.

One of the fission reactions of uranium-235 is as follows:

$$^{235}_{92}U + ^{1}_{0}n \rightarrow ^{87}_{35}Br + ^{146}_{57}La + 3^{1}_{0}n$$

If uncontrolled, the first reaction produces 3 neutrons, which will cause three more disintegrations, and 9 neutrons. These 9 neutrons then cause nine more disintegrations and the release of 27 more neutrons. Eventually the reaction is out of control.

There are two ways to keep a fission process from becoming uncontrolled. First, if the sample is small enough, the released neutrons will not hit other uranium-235 nuclei to continue the chain reaction. A **critical mass** of several pounds is needed before a chain reaction will be sustained. Second, excess neutrons can be absorbed by certain materials such as graphite and paraffin. Control rods made of graphite are used in nuclear reactors to adjust the number of available neutrons and therefore the rate of the nuclear reactions. In this use, graphite effectively absorbs some of the neutrons and keeps them from continuing the chain reaction.

Plutonium-239 is another fissile isotope. It is important because it can be produced by bombarding nonfissionable uranium-238 with neutrons. Since only 1 percent of natural uranium is ^{235}U, and most of the rest is ^{238}U, the ability to produce ^{239}Pu means that raw material is more readily available. The reactor that produces plutonium is known as a breeder reactor.

Nuclear reactors are used mainly to generate electricity. The enormous heat generated in fission reactions is used to boil water. The steam is then used to run conventional turbines that produce the electricity. In practice, the nuclear power plant is very complex in order to keep the radioactive materials contained while extracting the desired energy. Uranium reactors require expensive enriched uranium ores. Breeder reactors do not require enriched fuel; since they produce weapons-grade plutonium, their use is highly regulated and discouraged.

Nuclear Fusion

The combination of two nuclei into a larger atom is called **nuclear fusion**. The reactions within the sun are fusion reactions that combine hydrogen nuclei to form a helium atom in a three-step reaction:

$$^{1}_{1}H + ^{1}_{1}H \rightarrow ^{2}_{1}H + ^{0}_{1}e$$
$$^{1}_{1}H + ^{2}_{1}H \rightarrow ^{3}_{2}He$$
$$^{3}_{2}He + ^{3}_{2}He \rightarrow ^{4}_{2}He + ^{1}_{1}H + ^{1}_{1}H$$

Since fusion takes simple, nonradioactive materials and produces helium, it should be a clean and inexpensive source of energy.

Instead of trying to duplicate the three-step reaction in the sun, current fusion research focuses on the reaction

$$_1^3H \ + \ _1^2H \ \rightarrow \ _2^4He \ + \ _0^1n$$

Several designs for fusion reactors are being tested. Although some success has been achieved, it will be some time before this cheap, nonpolluting energy source will become a reality.

Biological Effects of Radiation

Many people are concerned about nuclear radiation. This concern is so widespread that the words *radiation* and *nuclear* are avoided in naming any consumer product. For example, one of the most useful modern medical technologies is based on a well-known technique of nuclear magnetic resonance (NMR) spectroscopy. Its name was changed to magnetic resonance imaging (MRI) to avoid the stigma of the word *nuclear*.

We must realize, however, that everyone is exposed to natural nuclear radiation. In addition, we are exposed to some manmade radiation, mostly for medical purposes. Table 3.2 lists the approximate amounts of radiation that people receive each year from various sources.

In Table 3.2 the dosage is listed in terms of millirems of radiation. This is just one unit that is used to measure radiation. In Table 3.3 we list two common units for the activity of radioisotopes and two units of dosage. The rem, or radiation equivalent for man, is not listed in Table 3.3 because it depends on the type of radiation and its energy. The rem value for any radiation source is determined by measuring the rad (radiation absorbed dose) and multiplying it by a conversion factor for the particular radiation

TABLE 3.2 Average Yearly Human Exposure to Various Radiation Sources

Source	Dose (millirems)
Natural sources:	
Cosmic rays	27
Earth and minerals	47
Building materials	3
Air (radon)	200
Body tissues	21
Subtotal	298
Manmade sources:	
Medical technologies	30
Nuclear medicine	14
TV tubes, industrial waste, jewelry	10
Other	2
Subtotal	56
Total	354

TABLE 3.3 Units for the Measurement of Radioactivity

Name of Unit	Symbol	Equivalency
Activity units:		
curie	Ci	3.7×10^{10} disintegrations per second
becquerel	Bq	1.00 disintegration per second
Dosage units:		
radiation absorbed dose	rad	10^{-5} J g^{-1}
gray	Gy	1.00 J kg^{-1}

involved. For instance, rads are multiplied by 1.0 if the radiation is beta, gamma, or X rays and by 10 if the radiation is alpha particles or neutrons. The rem unit was developed so that dosages from a variety of radiation sources could be added together. Rad values are not strictly additive.

Using rem units for radiation dosage, we may estimate the effects of different radiation dosages on the body (Table 3.4). Agreement is not complete as to the dose ranges that produce the effects listed, and constant refinements in these estimations are still being made.

TABLE 3.4 Biological Effects of Radiation

Dose (rems)	Effect on Human Body
0–25	No effect
25–100	Decrease in white blood cells
100–200	Loss of hair, nausea, vomiting
200–500	Severe radiation sickness
500 upward	Fatal dose

One major consideration in working with radiation of any sort is the type of protection needed to avoid excessive exposure. Table 3.5 lists the abilities of a variety of types of radiation to penetrate the human body. This table shows that alpha radiation has very little penetrating ability; it is dangerous mainly if an alpha-particle source is ingested. Beta particles may be stopped by a layer of clothing. Other nuclear radiation, however, requires more elaborate shielding for protection.

TABLE 3.5 Penetrating Ability of Various Types of Radiation

Radiation	Energy	Penetration of Skin
Alpha particles	5 MeV	0.05 mm
Beta particles	0.5 MeV	2 mm
Gamma rays	1 MeV	50 cm*
X rays	100 keV	20 cm*
Neutrons		VERY LARGE

*This depth represents a 10% decrease in intensity.

Measurement of Radioactivity

Radioactivity is a property of chemical substances that is noticeable only with the aid of instrumentation. The first mode of detection was the use of photographic film to detect the X rays emitted in some decay reactions. Since each particle emitted from the nucleus has its own properties, different methods and instruments have been devised to detect the various types. Some of the more common detectors are described below.

A Geiger-Müller tube is the device used to measure beta and gamma radiation. It consists of a metal tube filled with argon with a quartz window on one end. Inside the tube is a thin wire electrode. When a particle enters through the mica window, it ionizes the argon gas. These ions are accelerated by the high voltage between the anode and cathode, causing an avalanche of secondary ions. These allow a pulse of electricity to flow, and the pulses are counted to determine the number of particles entering per second. If the proper electronics are used, this device can serve also to discriminate among the energies of different types of incoming radiation.

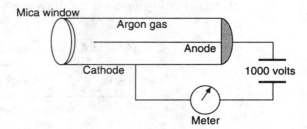

FIGURE 3.2. Diagram of a Geiger-Müller tube. Ionizing radiation that enters through the mica window ionizes some argon atoms. The ions are accelerated to the cathode and anode causing an avalanche of secondary ions. These create electrical pulses that are read on the meter.

Cloud chambers are used to measure charged particles, including alpha and beta particles. The chamber is constructed so that it is saturated with the vapor of a liquid close to its condensation point. Charged particles passing through the chamber condense the vapor into a visible trail that can be photographed and measured. The patterns of these trails can be used to identify different particles. In an electric field the paths will be curved and the charge can be determined from the curvature. When two particles collide, their relative masses can be determined from the angles at which they recoil.

Scintillation counters are used to measure many different types of radiation. The emitting material is combined with a fluorescent mixture of chemicals. Each time a particle is emitted, it strikes the fluorescent material and emits a flash of light. Phototubes are used to detect and count these flashes (scintillations) as a measure of the number of particles emitted.

Film dosimeters are used mainly as safety devices by people who work with radiation. A small plastic badge encapsulates a piece of special film, which can be made sensitive to different types of radiation. The badge is worn while working with radioactive materials. When developed, the film will reveal whether the worker was exposed to excess radiation and will also give the total dose of radiation received.

Important Concepts

Radioactivity
Nuclear fusion and fission
Balancing nuclear equations

Important Equations

Nuclear decay $= kN$

$$\ln\left(\frac{N_0}{N_t}\right) = kt$$

$$t_{1/2} = \frac{0.693}{k}$$

Questions on Chapter 3

1. In which of the following are nuclear particles listed in order of increasing penetrating power?
   (A) alpha particles < beta particles < neutrons
   (B) beta particles < alpha particles < neutrons
   (C) neutrons < alpha particles < beta particles
   (D) beta particles < neutrons < alpha particles
   (E) neutrons < beta particles < alpha particles

2. What symbol should replace the question mark in the following nuclear reaction?

$$^{238}U \rightarrow {}^{234}Th + \, ?$$

   (A) ^{4}He
   (B) $_{-1}^{0}e$
   (C) $_1^1H$
   (D) $_0^1p$
   (E) $_{+1}^{0}e$

3. Carbon-14 has a half-life of 5730 years. How old is a wooden object if 70% of the ^{14}C has decayed?
   (A) 2948 yr
   (B) 1280 yr
   (C) 9950 yr
   (D) 4321 yr
   (E) 7002 yr

4. The half-life of ^{104}Ag is 16.3 min. What is the rate constant in units of reciprocal seconds (s^{-1})?
   (A) 0.0425
   (B) 7.1×10^{-4}
   (C) 2.55
   (D) 7.25
   (E) 1411

5. Uranium-235 undergoes a fission reaction, and one of the products is ^{139}Ba. One neutron is required to induce the fission, and three neutrons are emitted. What is the other fission product?
   (A) $^{96}_{34}Se$
   (B) $^{96}_{36}Kr$
   (C) $^{84}_{35}Br$
   (D) $^{94}_{36}Kr$
   (E) $^{90}_{38}Sr$

6. Copper-67 is a radioactive form of copper with a half-life of 58.5 hours. What particle does ^{67}Cu emit when it decays?
   (A) ^4He
   (B) $^0_{-1}e$
   (C) ^1_1H
   (D) ^1_0p
   (E) $^0_{+1}e$

7. Bromine-82 has a half-life of 35.7 hours. How many milligrams of ^{82}Br will remain if 2.30-g of ^{82}Br decays for exactly 1 week?
   (A) 4.40
   (B) 238
   (C) 24.6
   (D) 88.1
   (E) 0.0669

8. Which of the following is most probably a stable isotope?
   (A) $^{68}_{29}Cu$
   (B) $^{11}_{4}Be$
   (C) $^{24}_{14}Si$
   (D) $^{66}_{30}Zn$
   (E) $^{42}_{19}K$

9. A radioactive substance decays to 75% of its original activity in 3.24 hr. What is the rate constant in units of reciprocal hours?
   (A) 0.186
   (B) 0.427
   (C) 0.339
   (D) 0.0386
   (E) 0.0888

10. A radioactive sample of ^{141}Cs has a half-life of 32.5 days. In a sample that contains 8.00×10^7 nuclei of ^{141}Cs, how many beta particles per second will be emitted?
    (A) 19.8
    (B) 1.7×10^6
    (C) 71,076
    (D) 1185
    (E) 2.47×10^{-7}

Answer Key

See Appendix I for explanations of answers.

| 1. **A** | 3. **C** | 5. **D** | 7. **D** | 9. **E** |
| 2. **A** | 4. **B** | 6. **B** | 8. **D** | 10. **A** |

PART TWO

Chemical Bonding

CHAPTER FOUR

Ionic Compounds, Formulas, and Reactions

Chemical Formulas

Chapters 1–3 show how the atom is constructed from protons, neutrons, and, most important, electrons. A good knowledge of the electronic makeup of the atom enables us to predict formulas and reactions of many chemical compounds rather than memorizing them. However, as in learning a new language, some basics must be memorized in order to use information properly and quickly.

We start with the chemical **formula**, which is a shorthand method of describing **compounds**. It uses the **atomic symbols** in the periodic table to identify the elements in a compound. If there is more than one atom of an element in the formula, a **subscript** is used to show how many atoms are present. For example, the compound potassium permanganate

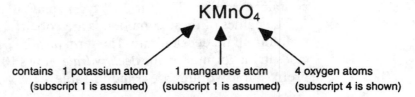

$$KMnO_4$$

contains 1 potassium atom   1 manganese atom   4 oxygen atoms
  (subscript 1 is assumed) (subscript 1 is assumed) (subscript 4 is shown)

Parentheses in chemical formulas are used to clarify and to provide additional information. A subscript placed after a closing parenthesis multiplies everything within the parentheses. For example, aluminum nitrate

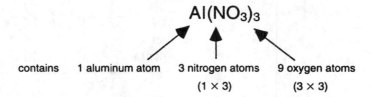

$$Al(NO_3)_3$$

contains   1 aluminum atom   3 nitrogen atoms   9 oxygen atoms
                             (1 × 3)   (3 × 3)

This formula could have been written as AlN_3O_9, which represents the same number of each atom as $Al(NO_3)_3$. However, the parentheses around the NO_3 gives the added information that the nitrogens and oxygens are in three groups of NO_3 units, called the nitrate group. (As will be seen later, the NO_3 should be properly written as the nitrate ion, NO_3^-, with a negative charge.)

The formula for ammonium phosphate is

$$(NH_4)_3PO_4$$

This compound contains 3 nitrogen, 12 hydrogen, 1 phosphorus, and 4 oxygen atoms. Here 3 ammonium groups (actually NH_4^+ ions) are shown in the formula by use of the parentheses.

Another type of formula is used for compounds called **hydrates**. These compounds have fixed numbers of water molecules, called the **water of hydration**, in their crystal lattices. To show the water of hydration clearly in the chemical formula, it is written after a dot that is placed in the middle of the line. The dot links two separate compounds into one unit. Two examples are shown below.

The hexahydrate of cobalt(II) chloride is written as

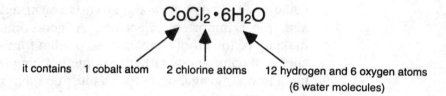

$$CoCl_2 \cdot 6H_2O$$

it contains 1 cobalt atom 2 chlorine atoms 12 hydrogen and 6 oxygen atoms (6 water molecules)

The compound

$$Na_2SO_4 \cdot 10H_2O$$

contains 2 sodium, 1 sulfur, 14 oxygen, and 20 hydrogen atoms.

The names of these compounds are cobalt(II) chloride hexahydrate and sodium sulfate decahydrate. The term *hexahydrate* indicates 6 water molecules in the formula, while *decahydrate* shows 10 water molecules. Common prefixes for hydrates are listed in Table 4.1

TABLE 4.1 Prefixes Used with Hydrates

1	mono-	6	hexa-
2	di-	7	hepta-
3	tri-	8	octa-
4	tetra-	9	nona-
5	penta-	10	deca-

The compounds discussed above are ionic, and their formulas represent the simplest ratio of the atoms in a crystal of the substance. This simplest formula is called an **empirical formula**.

For compounds that have covalent bonds **molecular formulas** are used. Benzene has a molecular formula of C_6H_6, and acetic acid has a formula of $HC_2H_3O_2$. These are not empirical formulas; they represent the actual number of each atom present in a single molecule of each of these compounds.

Another form of the molecular formula is the **structural formula**. A structural formula shows a chemist the way the atoms are connected with each other and the covalent bonds between the atoms. The structural formulas for benzene and acetic acid are shown in Figure 4.1.

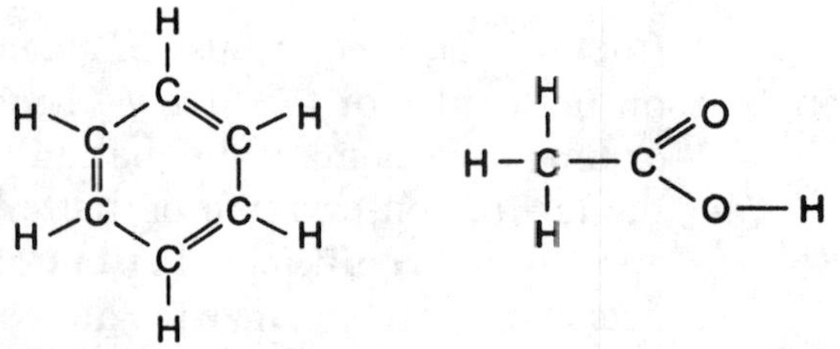

FIGURE 4.1. Structural formulas for benzene and acetic acid.

Exercise 4.1

Determine the number of each different atom represented in each of the following chemical formulas:
(a) $NaClO_4$
(b) $NH_4C_2H_3O_2$
(c) LiH_2AsO_3
(d) $Ca(C_3H_5O_3)_2 \cdot 5H_2O$
(e) $Cu(NH_3)_4SO_4 \cdot H_2O$

Solution

(a) 1 Na, 1 Cl, 4 O
(b) 1 N, 7 H, 2 C, 2 O
(c) 1 Li, 2 H, 1 As, 3 O
(d) 1 Ca, 6 C, 20 H, 11 O
(e) 1 Cu, 4 N, 14 H, 1 S, 5 O

Chemical Reactions and Equations

All chemical reactions are essentially the same, with **reactants** being converted into **products**. A chemical equation is written to describe the reaction process. The formulas of the reactants are placed on the left side, and the products on the right side, of an arrow that indicates that the reactants are converted into products:

$$\text{REACTANTS} \quad \rightarrow \quad \text{PRODUCTS}$$

On each side of the arrow, the order in which the reactants and products are written in an equation does not matter.

$$Zn \quad + \quad H_2SO_4 \quad \rightarrow \quad H_2 \quad + \quad ZnSO_4$$

has the same meaning as

$$H_2SO_4 \quad + \quad Zn \quad \rightarrow \quad ZnSO_4 \quad + \quad H_2$$

Balancing a
Chemical Equation

Chemical equations must be **balanced** with the same number of each atom on both sides of the arrow. (The arrow is similar to an equal sign in an ordinary mathematical equation.) A balanced chemical equation satisfies the law of conservation of matter. Equations are balanced by placing the appropriate **coefficients** in front of the formulas of the reactants and products in order to equalize the atoms on both sides of the arrow. A coefficient is a simple whole number, and it multiplies all of the atoms in the formula to which it is attached. Subscripts or formulas are *never altered* to balance an equation.

One common reaction is the **combustion** of propane fuel ($CH_3CH_2CH_3$) in a barbecue grill:

$$CH_3CH_2CH_3 \quad + \quad O_2 \quad \rightarrow \quad CO_2 \quad + \quad H_2O \quad \text{(unbalanced)}$$

As written, this expression simply gives the reactants ($CH_3CH_2CH_3$ + O_2) and the products (CO_2 + H_2O). It may be balanced by using the appropriate coefficients for the two reactants and two products. There are two methods for determining these coefficients. One is the **inspection method** and the other is the **ion-electron method**, which is used for complex oxidation-reduction equations. The ion-electron method will be discussed in Chapter 13.

The first step in the inspection method of balancing equations involves counting the number of each atom in the equation on the reactant side and then on the product side. This requires care and attention to detail since the smallest mistake ruins the entire effort.

The next step is to balance one atom at a time by adding a coefficient where needed and recounting the atoms. Adding coefficients and recounting continue until the same number of atoms is present on each side of the arrow.

Chemists find the process simpler if they balance the most complex molecule first, leaving the simple compounds and elements until last. Also, elements that appear in more than one compound on either the reactant or product side are left to the end. Finally, it is faster to balance groups of atoms, such as the sulfate or nitrate ions discussed later, as if they were individual atoms.

Returning to the combustion of propane, we count 3 carbon, 8 hydrogen, and 2 oxygen atoms on the reactant side. On the product side we have 1 carbon, 2 hydrogen, and 3 oxygen atoms. Since propane is the most complex molecule in the reaction, it is used as the starting point. Its 3 carbon atoms can be balanced by adding a coefficient of 3 to CO_2:

$$CH_3CH_2CH_3 \quad + \quad O_2 \quad \rightarrow \quad 3CO_2 \quad + \quad H_2O \quad \text{(still unbalanced)}$$

There are now 3 carbon atoms on both sides, but the numbers of hydrogen and oxygen atoms are still not equal.

Next, the 8 hydrogen atoms can be balanced by adding a coefficient of 4 to the water molecules:

$$CH_3CH_2CH_3 \quad + \quad O_2 \quad \rightarrow \quad 3CO_2 \quad + \quad 4H_2O \quad \text{(still unbalanced)}$$

Recounting the atoms, we find that there are now 3 carbon, 8 hydrogen, and 2 oxygen atoms on the reactant side and 3 carbon, 8 hydrogen, and 10 oxygen atoms on the product side. The carbon and hydrogen atoms are balanced, and only the oxygen atoms remain unequal. The equation can be balanced by using a coefficient of 5 for the O_2 molecule:

$$CH_3CH_2CH_3 \quad + \quad 5O_2 \quad \rightarrow \quad 3CO_2 \quad + \quad 4H_2O \quad \text{(balanced)}$$

The equation now has 3 carbon, 8 hydrogen, and 10 oxygen atoms on both the reactant and the product side. The coefficient for $CH_3CH_2CH_3$ is 1, but it is not written.

Another type of reaction is the **double-replacement** reaction. One reaction of this type is

$$Cr_2(SO_4)_3 \quad + \quad KOH \quad \rightarrow \quad Cr(OH)_3 \quad + \quad K_2SO_4 \quad \text{(unbalanced)}$$

In this unbalanced form there are 2 chromium, 3 sulfur, 13 oxygen, 1 hydrogen, and 1 potassium atom on the reactant side and 1 chromium, 1 sulfur, 7 oxygen, 3 hydrogen, and 2 potassium atoms on the product side. The chemist would see 2 chromium atoms, 3 sulfate ions (the SO_4^{2-} unit), 1 potassium atom, and 1 hydroxide ion (the OH^- unit) on the reactant side and 1 chromium atom, 1 sulfate ion, 2 potassium atoms, and 3 hydroxide ions on the product side.

Focusing on $Cr_2(SO_4)_3$, we can balance the chromium atoms with a 2 in front of $Cr(OH)_3$:

$$Cr_2(SO_4)_3 \quad + \quad KOH \quad \rightarrow \quad 2Cr(OH)3 \quad + \quad K_2SO_4 \quad \text{(unbalanced)}$$

Next, the 6 hydroxide ions in $2Cr(OH)_3$ can be balanced by placing a 6 in front of KOH:

$$Cr_2(SO_4)_3 \quad + \quad 6KOH \quad \rightarrow \quad 2Cr(OH)_3 \quad + \quad K_2SO_4 \quad \text{(unbalanced)}$$

Then the 6 potassium atoms in 6 KOH can be balanced with a 3 in front of K_2SO_4. This also balances the sulfate ions and the equation is balanced:

$$Cr_2(SO_4)_3 \quad + \quad 6KOH \quad \rightarrow \quad 2Cr(OH)_3 \quad + \quad 3K_2SO_4 \quad \text{(balanced)}$$

The reaction of hydrogen with oxygen to form water can be balanced as

$$2H_2 \quad + \quad O_2 \quad \rightarrow \quad 2H_2O$$

It will also be balanced if written as

$$4H_2 \quad + \quad 2O_2 \quad \rightarrow \quad 4H_2O$$

$$16H_2 \quad + \quad 8O_2 \quad \rightarrow \quad 16H_2O$$

$$H_2 \quad + \quad \tfrac{1}{2}O_2 \quad \rightarrow \quad H_2O$$

The last three reactions are technically balanced since they have the same numbers of hydrogen atoms and oxygen atoms on both sides of the arrow, but they are not in the best form. **Properly balanced equations have the smallest whole-number coefficients possible.** For the three reactions;

the first one should be divided by 2.
the second should be divided by 8,
the third should be multiplied by 2.

An equation may be multiplied or divided as necessary, but it should be remembered that all coefficients in the equation must be multiplied or divided by the same factor. Balancing reactions requires practice to develop skill and speed.

Exercise 4.2

Balance the following reactions by inspection:

C_6H_6 + O_2 → CO_2 + H_2O
$MgCl_2$ + $AgNO_3$ → $AgCl$ + $Mg(NO_3)_3$
Al + O_2 → Al_2O_3
CaO + H_2SO_4 → H_2O + $CaSO_4$
Al + Fe_3O_4 → Fe + Al_2O_3
NO_2 + O_2 → N_2O_5
HCl + $CaCO_3$ → $CaCl_2$ + H_2O + CO_2
O_2 + $C_4H_9NH_2$ → CO_2 + H_2O + N_2
Mg + HCl → H_2 + $MgCl_2$
Zn + $Cu(NO_3)_2$ → Cu + $Zn(NO_3)_2$
$CoCl_3$ + $Ba(OH)_2$ → $BaCl_2$ + $Co(OH)_3$
$Ba(OH)_2$ + H_3PO_4 → H_2O + Ba_3PO_4
C_6H_8 + H_2 → C_6H_{12}
SO_2 + O_2 → SO_3
C_4H_{10} + O_2 → CO_2 + H_2O
H_2S + $AuCl_3$ → Au_2S_3 + HCl

Solution

The balanced equations are given in the solution to Exercise 4.3.

Reaction Types

Many chemical reactions fall into distinct groups with definite similarities. By classifying chemical reactions, it is possible to compare the properties of the reactants and products. In addition, such classification often serves as a shorthand method in place of writing a complete chemical reaction. The combustion of propane illustrates one such classification. By calling the reaction a combustion process, it is immediately known that the other reactant is oxygen and that the products are carbon dioxide and water. Some reaction types are described below.

Combustion Reactions

In these reactions, an organic (carbon-containing) compound reacts with oxygen to form carbon dioxide and water. If the organic compound contains elements other than carbon, hydrogen, and oxygen, it is assumed that those elements end up in the elemental state as products. A typical combustion reaction is

$$C_5H_{12} + 8O_2 → 5CO_2 + 6H_2O$$

Single-Replacement Reactions

In some reactions, an element may react with a compound to produce a different element and a new compound. A typical reaction of this sort is

$$2AgNO_3 \quad + \quad Zn \quad \rightarrow \quad 2Ag \quad + \quad Zn(NO_3)_2$$

In this reaction the zinc replaces the silver in the silver nitrate. This type of reaction is also known as a single-displacement reaction.

Double-Replacement Reactions

In these reactions, two compounds react and the cation in one compound replaces the cation in the second compound and vice versa. A double replacement reaction is

$$MgSO_4 \quad + \quad BaCl_2 \quad \rightarrow \quad MgCl_2 \quad + \quad BaSO_4$$

In this type of reaction, the magnesium replaces the barium and the barium replaces the magnesium—thus the term *double replacement*.

Neutralization Reactions

These reactions are a special type of double-replacement reaction in which one reactant is an acid and the other is a base. The products are a salt and water. A typical neutralization reaction is

$$HCl \quad + \quad NaOH \quad \rightarrow \quad NaCl \quad + \quad H_2O$$

Synthesis Reactions

Reactions of two or more elements to form a compound are often called synthesis reactions. One such reaction is the formation of rust, Fe_2O_3:

$$4Fe \quad + \quad 3O_2 \quad \rightarrow \quad 2Fe_2O_3$$

Formation Reactions

A formation reaction is the same as a synthesis reaction except that the product must have a coefficient of 1. The reactants are the elements in their normal state at room temperature and atmospheric pressure. The formation reaction for $Fe(NH_4)_2(SO_4)_2$ is

$$Fe \quad + \quad N_2 \quad + \quad 4H_2 \quad + \quad 2S \quad + \quad 4O_2 \quad \rightarrow \quad Fe(NH_4)_2(SO_4)_2$$

If necessary, the use of fractional coefficients for the reactants is permitted in a formation reaction.

Addition Reactions

In these reactions a simple molecule or an element is added to another molecule, as in the addition of HCl to pentene:

$$HCl \quad + \quad C_5H_{10} \quad \rightarrow \quad C_5H_{11}Cl$$

Decomposition Reactions

These reactions result when a large molecule decomposes into its elements or into smaller molecules. When sucrose is heated strongly, this reaction occurs:

$$C_{12}H_{22}O_{11} \rightarrow 12C + 11H_2O$$

Net Ionic Reactions

When ionic compounds react in aqueous solution, usually only one ion from each compound reacts. The other ions are "spectator ions" and do not react. Writing a reaction in ionic form focuses attention on the actual reaction and allows the chemist to find substitute reactants to achieve the same result. For instance, the reaction of silver nitrate with sodium chloride produces a precipitate of silver chloride in the molecular equation

$$NaCl + AgNO_3 \rightarrow AgCl(s) + NaNO_3$$

Written as a net ionic equation, this becomes

$$Cl^- + Ag^+ \rightarrow AgCl(s)$$

The chemist now knows that any soluble chloride salt (KCl, $MgCl_2$, etc.) and any soluble silver salt ($AgClO_4$, Ag_2SO_4, etc.) will also give $AgCl$ as the product. In reactions with ions the charges must balance as well as the atoms.

Half-Reactions

These reactions are used extensively with oxidation-reduction reactions and in describing electrochemical processes in Chapter 13. The half-reaction is a reduction reaction if electrons are on the reactant side and an oxidation reaction if the electrons are products.

$$I_2 + 2e^- \rightarrow 2I^- \quad \text{(reduction half reaction)}$$
$$Fe^{2+} \rightarrow Fe^{3+} + e^- \quad \text{(oxidation half-reaction)}$$

Half-reactions may be combined to make a complete oxidation-reduction reaction as long as the electrons all cancel.

Oxidation-Reduction Reactions

These reactions involve the loss of electrons by one compound or ion and the subsequent gain of the same electrons by another compound or ion. The two half-reactions above may be added (after multiplying the second reaction by 2 and canceling the electrons) to obtain the oxidation-reduction reaction

$$I_2 + 2Fe^{2+} \rightarrow 2Fe^{3+} + 2I^-$$

The combustion and single-replacement reactions discussed above are also oxidation-reduction reactions.

Exercise 4.3

Classify each of the reactions balanced in Exercise 4.2 as one of the reaction types described in this section.

Solution

$2 C_6H_6$	$+ 15 O_2$	$\rightarrow 12 CO_2$	$- 6 H_2O$				(combustion)
$MgCl_2$	$+ 2 AgNO_3$	$\rightarrow 2 AgCl$	$+ Mg(NO_3)_2$				(double replacement)
$4 Al$	$+ 3 O_2$	$\rightarrow 2 Al_2O_3$					(synthesis)
CaO	$+ H_2SO_4$	$\rightarrow H_2O$	$+ CaSO_4$				(double replacement)
$8 Al$	$+ 3 Fe_3O_4$	$\rightarrow 9 Fe$	$+ 4 Al_2O_3$				(single replacement)
$4 NO_2$	$+ O_2$	$\rightarrow 2 N_2O_5$					(combustion or addition)
$2 HCl$	$+ CaCO_3$	$\rightarrow CaCl_2$	$+ H_2O$		$+ CO_2$	(double replacement)
$27 O_2$	$+ 4 C_4H_9NH_2$	$\rightarrow 16 CO_2$	$+ 22 H_2O$		$+ 2 N_2$	(decomposition)
Mg	$+ 2 HCl$	$\rightarrow H_2$	$+ MgCl_2$				(single replacement)
Zn	$+ Cu(NO_3)_2$	$\rightarrow Cu$	$+ Zn(NO_3)_2$				(single replacement)
$2 CoCl_3$	$+ 3 Ba(OH)_2$	$\rightarrow 3 BaCl_2$	$+ 2 Co(OH)_3$				(double replacement)
$3 Ba(OH)_2$	$+ 2 H_3PO_4$	$\rightarrow 6 H_2O$	$+ Ba_3(PO_4)_2$				(neutralization)
C_6H_8	$+ 2 H_2$	$\rightarrow C_6H_{12}$					(addition)
$2 SO_2$	$+ O_2$	$\rightarrow 2 SO_3$					(addition or combustion)
$2 C_4H_{10}$	$+ 13 O_2$	$\rightarrow 8 CO_2$	$+ 10 H_2O$				(combustion)
$3 H_2S$	$+ 2 AuCl_3$	$\rightarrow Au_2S_3$	$+ 6 HCl$				(double replacement)

Bonding

When elements combine with each other to form compounds, a chemical bond is formed. An understanding of how and why bonds are formed helps the chemist to predict many physical and chemical properties of molecules and compounds, including chemical reactivity, shape, solubility, physical state, and polarity. The key to bond formation is the behavior of the outermost, or valence, electrons. When two atoms share valence electrons to form a bond, the bond is known as a **covalent bond.** When one atom loses electrons and another gains electrons, ions are formed. The attraction between ions to form a compound is called an **ionic bond.**

The underlying principle of chemical bonding can be explained using the electronic configurations of the noble gases. Noble gases are very unreactive elements. Until 1962, when Neil Bartlett produced the first noble gas compound, they were considered inert and most periodic tables called them "inert gases." Except for helium, all noble gases have valence shells in which the outermost s and p sublevels are completely filled (ns^2, np^6), as shown in bold type in Table 4.2. This configuration gives unusual stability to the noble gases and also to atoms that can lose, gain, or share electrons to attain the same configuration.

Ionic Substances

The basis of the ionic bond is the attraction of a positively charged ion (cation) toward a negatively charged ion (anion). It is necessary to understand which elements tend to form ions and which do not. For elements that form ions we also want to develop methods to determine what kind of ion should be expected. Finally, once the ions are known, we can use that information to predict chemical formulas and chemical reactions.

TABLE 4.2 Electronic Configurations of the Noble Gases

Noble Gas	Electronic Configuration
He	$1s^2$
Ne	$1s^2, 2s^2, 2p^6$
Ar	$1s^2, 2s^2, 2p^6, 3s^2, 3p^6$
Kr	$1s^2, 2s^2, 2p^6, 3s^2, 3p^6, 4s^2, 3d^{10}, 4p^6$
Xe	$1s^2, 2s^2, 2p^6, 3s^2, 3p^6, 4s^2, 3d^{10}, 4p^6, 5s^2, 4d^{10}, 5p^6$
Rn	$1s^2, 2s^2, 2p^6, 3s^2, 3p^6, 4s^2, 3d^{10}, 4p^6, 5s^2, 4d^{10}, 5p^6, 6s^2, 4f^{14}, 5d^{10}, 6p^6$

Monatomic Ions of the Representative Elements

The representative elements are those found within the s and p blocks of the periodic table as shown in Figure 1.16. These elements have regular properties that follow basic chemical principles with very few exceptions. In the case of ion formation, the principle is that the ions of the representative elements will have electronic configurations identical to those of the noble gases.

Representative metals will lose electrons to form cations. The equation

$$M \quad \rightarrow \quad M^{n+} \quad + \quad ne^-$$

where n is the number of electrons lost by the metal, is used to represent the formation of all cations.

The electronic configuration allows the chemist to determine the number of electrons that a representative metal will lose. For instance, sodium has the electronic configuration $1s^2, 2s^2, 2p^6, 3s^1$. When the element forms the Na^+ ion, the $3s^1$ electron is lost. The electronic configuration for the Na^+ ion is then $1s^2, 2s^2, 2p^6$, which is the same as the electronic configuration of neon.

Barium has the electronic configuration

$$Ba \quad = \quad 1s^2,\ 2s^2,\ 2p^6,\ 3s^2,\ 3p^6,\ 4s^2,\ 3d^{10},\ 4p^6,\ 5s^2,\ 4d^{10},\ 5p^6,\ 6s^2$$

When the Ba^{2+} ion is formed, the two $6s$ electrons are lost, giving the barium ion the configuration

$$Ba^{2+} \quad = \quad 1s^2,\ 2s^2,\ 2p^6,\ 3s^2,\ 3p6,\ 4s^2,\ 3d^{10},\ 4p^6,\ 5s^2,\ 4d^{10},\ 5p^6$$

which is identical to the electronic configuration of xenon:

$$Xe \quad = \quad 1s^2,\ 2s^2,\ 2p^6,\ 3s^2,\ 3p6,\ 4s^2,\ 3d^{10},\ 4p^6,\ 5s^2,\ 4d^{10},\ 5p^6$$

The representative metals will lose all of their valence s and p electrons. The electronic configuration of a metal will then be identical to that of the preceding noble gas in the periodic table.

In periods 4, 5, and 6 the metals that contain outer s and p electrons may form a second ion by losing only their p electrons. We find that gallium, indium, and thallium form 1+ and 3+ ions. Tin and lead form 2+ and 4+ ions, and bismuth forms 3+ and 5+ ions.

The representative nonmetals gain electrons to form negative ions called anions. The general reaction for this process is

$$ X \quad + \quad ne^- \quad \rightarrow \quad X^{n-} $$

where n represents the number of electrons gained by the nonmetal represented by X.

As an example, bromine has the electronic configuration

$$ Br \quad = \quad 1s^2, \, 2s^2, \, 2p^6, \, 3s^2, \, 3p^6, \, 4s^2, \, 3d^{10}, \, \mathbf{4p^5} $$

When an electron is added to the $4p$ subshell, the bromide ion, Br^-, is formed. Its electronic configuration becomes

$$ Br^- \quad = \quad 1s^2, \, 2s^2, \, 2p^6, \, 3s^2, \, 3p^6, \, 4s^2, \, 3d^{10}, \, \mathbf{4p^6} $$

which is the same as that of the noble gas krypton:

$$ Kr \quad = \quad 1s^2, \, 2s^2, \, 2p^6, \, 3s^2, \, 3p^6, \, \mathbf{4s^2}, \, 3d^{10}, \, \mathbf{4p^6} $$

All halogens will gain one electron to form anions with one negative charge. Oxygen, sulfur, and selenium gain two electrons each to form 2− ions. We will see that these elements often participate in covalent bonding as well. The remaining nonmetals, nitrogen, phosphorus, and carbon, usually bond using covalent bonds, but they can form N^{3-}, P^{3-}, and C^{4-} ions.

Monatomic Ions of the Nonrepresentative Elements

The nonrepresentative elements are the remaining d block and f block metals in the periodic table. These elements are characterized by the fact that many of them may have more than one possible cation and they often form polyatomic anions. In general, it is not possible to predict with certainty the charge of the cations for these elements. However, none of these elements forms monatomic anions.

Appreciating what happens to the transition elements is not always simple, but some hints may be obtained from their electronic configurations. For these elements the electronic configurations are arranged by their principal quantum number, rather than in the aufbau order. For instance, the complete electronic configuration for lead is as follows:

$$ Pb = 1s^2, \, 2s^2, \, 2p^6, \, 3s^2, \, 3p^6, \, 4s^2, \, 3d^{10}, 4p^6, \, 5s^2, \, 4d^{10}, \, 5p^6, \, 6s^2, \, 4f^{14}, 5d^{10}, \, 6p^2 $$

Grouping the electrons by shell or principal quantum number gives

$$ Pb = 1s^2, \, 2s^2, \, 2p^6, \, 3s^2, \, 3p^6, \, 3d^{10}, \, 4s^2, \, 4p^6, \, 4d^{10}, \, 4f^{14}, \, 5s^2, \, 5p^6, \, 5d^{10}, \, \mathbf{6s^2}, \, \mathbf{6p^2} $$

and allows us to see more clearly which electrons are in the outermost shell of the atom. We can now see that the Pb^{2+} ion is formed when the two $6p$

electrons are removed and that the Pb^{4+} ion forms when all of the $6s$ and $6p$ electrons are removed.

Similarly, the 2^+ and 4^+ ions of titanium may be deduced from the electronic structure

$$Ti \quad = \quad 1s^2,\ 2s^2,\ 2p^6,\ 3s^2,\ 3p^6,\ 4s^2,\ 3d^2$$

Regrouping by shell gives

$$Ti \quad = \quad 1s^2,\ 2s^2,\ 2p^6,\ 3s^2,\ 3p^6,\ \mathbf{3d^2},\ \mathbf{4s^2}$$

Removal of just the two $4s$ electrons yields the Ti^{2+} ion, and removal of the two $3d$ and two $4s$ electrons gives the Ti^{4+} ion.

Iron is another example worth considering. It forms Fe^{2+} and Fe^{3+} ions. From the electronic configuration arranged by shells we get

$$Fe \quad = \quad 1s^2,\ 2s^2,\ 2p^6,\ 3s^2,\ 3p^6,\ 3d^6,\ \mathbf{4s^2}$$

Removal of the two $4s$ electrons gives the Fe^{2+} ion. To obtain the Fe^{3+} ion one more electron must be removed. Obviously it is one of the six $3d$ electrons that are now the outermost electrons. As we saw in Chapter 1, a d subshell that contains one electron in each orbital is a stable state. Removal of one of the $3d$ electrons results in the electronic structure

$$Fe^{3+} \quad = \quad 1s^2,\ 2s^2,\ 2p^6,\ 3s^2,\ 3p^6,\ \mathbf{3d^5}$$

which has the stable half-filled $3d$ subshell.

Not all ions in the nonrepresentative group can be rationalized without much more sophisticated reasoning. However, in the absence of additional information the logic used above provides for a reasonable first approximation of why certain ions form and others do not.

Polyatomic Ions

Many elements combine with oxygen (and sometimes hydrogen and nitrogen) to form a charged group of atoms called a **polyatomic ion**. (In older texts polyatomic ions are called radicals.) Polyatomic ions are unusually stable groups of atoms that tend to act as single units in many chemical reactions. The formulas, names, and charges of the common polyatomic ions are listed in Table 4.3 and **should be memorized.** Note that all of these are anions (negatively charged ions) except for the ammonium ion, NH_4^+.

The atoms in the polyatomic ions (Table 4.3) are bound to each other with covalent bonds, which will be described later. Polyatomic ions form ionic compounds by combining with other ions of opposite charge.

Ionic Formulas

Ionic compounds are formed when cations are attracted to anions because of their opposing charges. The formulas for ionic compounds can be deduced because no compound can have a net charge. In other words, the total positive charge of the cations must be exactly canceled by the negative

TABLE 4.3 Common Polyatomic Ions

Ion Formula	Ion Name
NH_4^+	ammonium ion
CO_3^{2-}	carbonate ion
HCO_3^-	bicarbonate ion
PO_4^{3-}	phosphate ion
ClO^-	hypochlorite ion
ClO_2^-	chlorite ion
ClO_3^-	chlorate ion
ClO_4^-	perchlorate ion
NO_2^-	nitrite ion
NO_3^-	nitrate ion
SO_3^{2-}	sulfite ion
SO_4^{2-}	sulfate ion
MnO_4^-	permanganate
$Cr_2O_7^{2-}$	dichromate ion
CrO_4^{2-}	chromate ion
$S_2O_3^{2-}$	thiosulfate ion

charge of the anions in the chemical formula. Some chemists refer to this as the **law of electroneutrality**. In addition, every ionic compound has a formula that represents the simplest ratio of the elements needed to obey the law of electroneutrality. As mentioned earlier in this chapter, this simplest ratio is called the **empirical formula.**

When the anion and cation have the same, but opposite, charges, the compound is written with only one atom of each element. This is another way of saying that the formulas for all ionic compounds are empirical formulas.

Na^+	$+$	F^-	$\rightarrow$	NaF	sodium fluoride
Mg^{2+}	$+$	O^{2-}	$\rightarrow$	MgO	magnesium oxide
Fe^{2+}	$+$	S^{2-}	$\rightarrow$	FeS	iron(II) sulfide
Al^{3+}	$+$	N^{3-}	$\rightarrow$	AlN	aluminum nitride
La^{3+}	$+$	PO_4^{3-}	$\rightarrow$	$LaPO_4$	lanthanum(III) phosphate
NH_4^+	$+$	NO_3^-	$\rightarrow$	NH_4NO_3	ammonium nitrate

When the charges of the anion and cation are not equal and opposite, it is necessary to adjust the numbers of the ions so that the total charge adds up to zero. The most convenient way to do this is to use the charge of the cation for the subscript of the anion and the charge of the anion (without the minus sign) as the subscript for the cation, as shown below. Remember that, when a subscript is 1, it is not written.

Ca^{2+}	$+$	$2Cl^-$	$\rightarrow$	$CaCl_2$	calcium chloride
$2Al^{3+}$	$+$	$3S^{2-}$	$\rightarrow$	Al_2S_3	aluminum sulfide
$3\,Na^+$	$+$	PO_4^{3-}	$\rightarrow$	Na_3PO_4	sodium phosphate
Pb^{4+}	$+$	$4Cl^-$	$\rightarrow$	$PbCl_4$	lead(IV) chloride

When a subscript must be used with a polyatomic ion, it is necessary to place parentheses around the polyatomic ion before adding the subscript, as shown in the following equations:

Ca^{2+} $+$ $2NO_3^-$ $\rightarrow$ $Ca(NO_3)_2$ calcium nitrate
$2NH_4^+$ $+$ SO_4^{2-} $\rightarrow$ $(NH_4)_2SO_4$ ammonium sulfate
$2Al^{3+}$ $+$ $3SO_4^{2-}$ $\rightarrow$ $Al_2(SO_4)_3$ aluminum sulfate

Naming Ionic Compounds

Ionic compounds contain a metal and a nonmetal. [The ammonium ion (NH_4^+) is considered a metal, and polyatomic anions are considered nonmetals for this purpose.] These compounds are also known as salts. Names are created by giving the name of the cation first and then the name of the anion.

For cations that have only one possible charge, the name is the same as that of the element. Cations that may have more than one charge, such as the lead and titanium discussed above, the element name is followed by parentheses enclosing the charge written in roman numerals. Two examples are lead(II) and lead(IV). This method, known as the Stock system, is the preferred method for naming ionic compounds.

In the old naming system, the higher charged cation was given the suffix -*ic* and the lower charged cation had the -*ous* ending. Table 4.4 lists some of these old names for reference. They are most useful for understanding the older chemical literature.

TABLE 4.4   Old Nomenclature for Some Common Ions

Ion	Stock Name	Old Name
Fe^{2+}	iron(II)	ferrous
Fe^{3+}	iron(III)	ferric
Sn^{2+}	tin(II)	stannous
Sn^{4+}	tin(IV)	stannic
Pb^{2+}	lead(II)	plumbous
Pb^{4+}	lead(IV)	plumbic
Cu^+	copper(I)	cuprous
Cu^{2+}	copper(II)	cupric
Hg^+ or Hg_2^{2+}	mercury(I)	mercurous
Hg^{2+}	mercury(II)	mercuric

Naming anions depends on whether the anion is a monatomic ion or a polyatomic anion. Monatomic anions are named by taking the root or first portion of the element name and then changing the ending to -*ide*, as shown in the accompanying table of examples. Polyatomic anions have unique names, given in Table 4.3, which must be memorized.

The entire compound is named by writing the name of the cation followed by the name

Common Anion Names	
sul**fur**	sul**fide**
oxygen	**oxide**
chlor**ine**	chlor**ide**
nitro**gen**	nitr**ide**
brom**ine**	brom**ide**
fluor**ine**	fluor**ide**

of the anion as a separate word; for example, MgF_2 is magnesium fluoride and FeI_3 is iron(III) iodide. Names of chemical compounds are not capitalized except at the beginning of a sentence. Examples of the names of representative compounds have been given in the preceding discussion of formula writing.

To name a compound which contains a metal that may have more than one possible charge, we must know the charge on the ion. Ionic is determined by "taking apart" the formula unit to find out what the charges of the ions were before the ions combined. We will know the charge of the anion, which will be either a representative monatomic anion or one of the polyatomic anions in Table 4.3. If the charge of one anion and the number of anions are known, the charge on the cation can be deduced since the formula must always have a net charge of zero. Review how formulas are determined and see how the process can be reversed.

Exercise 4.4

Name each of the following compounds:

$MgCl_2$ Na_2CrO_4 $TiBr_4$ $HgSO_4$
MnO_2 $Fe(ClO_2)_2$ Na_3PO_4 $SnCl_4$
Cr_2O_3 $Hg(NO_3)_2$ $(NH_4)_2SO_3$ BiF_3
Ca_3N_2 $Al(NO_3)_3$

Solution

$MgCl_2$	magnesium chloride	$Al(NO_3)_3$	aluminum nitrate
MnO_2	manganese(IV) oxide	$TiBr_4$	titanium(IV) bromide
Cr_2O_3	chromium(III) oxide	Na_3PO_4	sodium phosphate
Ca_3N_2	calcium nitride	$(NH_4)_2SO_3$	ammonium sulfite
Na_2CrO_4	sodium chromate	$HgSO_4$	mercury(II) sulfate
$Fe(ClO_2)_2$	iron(II) chlorite	$SnCl_4$	tin(IV) chloride
$Hg(NO_3)_2$	mercury(II) nitrate	BiF_3	bismuth(III) fluoride

Exercise 4.5

Write the formula for each of the following compounds:

aluminum sulfate   gold(III) nitrate
magnesium oxide   lithium sulfite
vanadium(III) bromide   ammonium phosphate
barium nitrite   strontium fluoride
cobalt(II) chloride   lead(IV) carbonate

Solution

Writing formulas from names is often easier than writing names from formulas since the charges of the nonrepresentative elements are given in parentheses in the names. Remember the requirement for electric neutrality or no net charge on any chemical compound.

aluminum sulfate	$Al_2(SO_4)_3$	gold(III) nitrate	$Au(NO_3)_3$
magnesium oxide	MgO	lithium sulfite	Li_2SO_3
vanadium(III) bromide	VBr_3	ammonium phosphate	$(NH_4)_3PO_4$
barium nitrite	$Ba(NO_2)_2$	strontium fluoride	SrF_2
cobalt(II) chloride	$CoCl_2$	lead(IV) carbonate	$Pb(CO_3)_2$

Ionic Reactions

Ions in Solution

Most ionic compounds dissolve in water, and in the process the compound separates into the cations and anions. This solution process may be written as

$$NaBr(s) \quad \rightarrow \quad Na^+(aq) \quad + \quad Br^-(aq)$$

The symbol in parentheses designates the state of each substance in the reaction: (s) means that the substance is a solid, and (aq) that the substance is in an aqueous solution. Other symbols used are (ℓ) for liquid and (g) for gas.

Chromium(III) nitrate dissolves according to the equation

$$Cr(NO_3)_3(s) \quad \rightarrow \quad Cr^{3+}(aq) \quad + \quad 3NO_3^-(aq)$$

One chromium(III) ion and three nitrate ions are obtained from one formula unit of chromium(III) nitrate.

The following general principles apply to the dissolution of ionic compounds.

1. Only one cation and one anion are formed. Compounds containing three or more different atoms will break apart into the appropriate polyatomic ion(s). (Exceptions are discussed in higher level chemistry courses.)
2. The charges of the ions obey the same rules as discussed above. In particular, the charges of all of the ions must add up to zero, which is the charge of any compound.
3. The subscripts of monatomic ions become coefficients for the ions. For polyatomic ions, only the subscripts after parentheses become coefficients.

Exercise 4.6

Write the ions expected when the following compounds are dissolved in water:

K_2S $\quad$ $MgBr_2$ $\quad$ $Na_2Cr_2O_7$ $\quad$ K_3PO_4
$FeCl_3$ $\quad$ $AlCl_3$ $\quad$ $(NH_4)_2S$ $\quad$ $Ti(NO_3)_4$

Solution

$$K_2S(s) \quad \rightarrow \quad 2\,K^+(aq) \quad + \quad S^{2-}(aq)$$
$$FeCl_3(s) \quad \rightarrow \quad Fe^{3+}(aq) \quad + \quad 3\,Cl^-(aq)$$
$$MgBr_2(s) \quad \rightarrow \quad Mg^{2+}(aq) \quad + \quad 2\,Br^-(aq)$$
$$AlCl_3(s) \quad \rightarrow \quad Al^{3+}(aq) \quad + \quad 3\,Cl^-(aq)$$
$$Na_2Cr_2O_7(s) \quad \rightarrow \quad 2\,Na^+(aq) \quad + \quad Cr_2O_7^{2-}(aq)$$
$$(NH_4)_2S(s) \quad \rightarrow \quad 2\,NH_4^+(aq) \quad + \quad S^{2-}(aq)$$
$$K_3PO_4(s) \quad \rightarrow \quad 3\,K^+(aq) \quad + \quad PO_4^{3-}(aq)$$
$$Ti(NO_3)_4(s) \quad \rightarrow \quad Ti^{4+}(aq) \quad + \quad 4\,NO_3^-(aq)$$

Notice that the charges on Fe^{3+} and Ti^{4+} must be calculated from the known negative charge of the anion and the fact that the total charge must add up to zero. Also observe which subscripts have become coefficients and which remained as part of a polyatomic ion. Finally, this entire process is just the reverse of the method used to determine the formulas of ionic compounds.

Any ionic compound can be broken apart into its cations and anions in this manner. Whether or not an ionic compound will dissolve to an appreciable extent in water depends on which cations and anions make up the compound. Some general guidelines for predicting solubility should be remembered.

Solubility Rules

1. All compounds containing alkali metal cations and the ammonium ion are **soluble**.
2. All compounds containing NO_3^-, ClO_4^-, ClO_3^-, and $C_2H_3O_2^-$ anions are **soluble**.
3. All chlorides, bromides, and iodides are **soluble except** those containing Ag^+, Pb^{2+}, or Hg_2^{2+}.
4. All sulfates are **soluble except** those containing Hg_2^{2+}, Pb^{2+}, Sr^{2+}, Ca^{2+}, or Ba^{2+}.
5. All hydroxides are **insoluble except** compounds of the alkali metals, Ca^{2+}, Sr^{2+}, and Ba^{2+}.
6. All compounds containing PO_4^{3-}, S^{2-}, CO_3^{2-}, and SO_3^{2-} ions are **insoluble except** those that also contain alkali metals or NH_4^+.

Double-Replacement Reactions

Predicting Products

If we know how to determine which ions make up an ionic compound, we can then take two ionic compounds, mix them together, and predict the possible products. These predictions are based on the principles involved in double-replacement reactions. As the name suggests, two replacements occur in these reactions.

> In one replacement the cation of the first salt replaces the cation of the second salt.

> In the second replacement the cation of the second salt replaces the cation of the first salt.

For example, if we mix together solutions containing $AgNO_3$ and Na_2CrO_4, what products should we predict? The first step is to determine the ions that make up the two reacting compounds. They are Ag^+, NO_3^-, $2\,Na^+$, and CrO_4^{2-}. The next step is to pair up these four ions in various ways to make two new ionic compounds that will be the predicted products. It is worthwhile to look at all of the possible pairs to see how we arrive at our conclusions.

Ag^+ + NO_3^- → $AgNO_3$ We already have this as a reactant.
Ag^+ + Na^+ → cannot form an ionic compound from two positive ions

$$2Ag^+ \quad + \quad CrO_4^{2-} \quad \rightarrow \quad Ag_2CrO_4 \text{ This is a possibility.}$$

$Ag^+ + Ag^+ \rightarrow$ cannot form an ionic compound from two identical ions

$NO_3^- + Na^+ \rightarrow$ $NaNO_3$ **This is a possibility.**

$NO_3^- + CrO_4^{2-} \rightarrow$ cannot form an ionic compound from two negative ions

$NO_3^- + NO_3^- \rightarrow$ cannot form an ionic compound from two identical ions

$2Na^+ + CrO_4^{2-} \rightarrow$ Na_2CrO_4 We already have this as a reactant.

$Na^+ + Na^+ \rightarrow$ cannot form an ionic compound from two identical ions

$CrO_4^{2-} + CrO_4^{2-} \rightarrow$ cannot form an ionic compound from two identical ions

All of the possible combinations of the four ions are given above, with the reasons why they are good or bad choices. Only two of the combinations give reasonable new compounds. Every other combination leads to either an impossible situation or back to the original compounds. Using the only reasonable results as the products, we may begin to construct a chemical equation:

$$AgNO_3 \quad + \quad Na_2CrO_4 \quad \rightarrow \quad Ag_2CrO_4 \quad + \quad NaNO_3$$

The final step is to balance the equation so it has the same number of each atom on both sides of the arrow:

$$2AgNO_3 \quad + \quad Na_2CrO_4 \quad \rightarrow \quad Ag_2CrO_4 \quad + \quad 2NaNO_3$$

Reviewing what was done to predict this equation, we see that only the positions of the silver and sodium ions have been switched on the reactant and product sides. In switching the positions of the metal atoms, we were careful to write the new formulas properly, based on the charges of the ions.

Exercise 4.7

Predict the products obtained from the following pairs of ionic compounds. Then write a balanced chemical equation for each pair.
(a) KCl and $Pb(NO_3)_2$
(b) $CaCl_2$ and $MgSO_4$
(c) $NaOH$ and $Fe_2(SO_4)_3$

Solution

(a) The ions involved are K^+, Cl^-, Pb^{2+}, and $2NO_3^-$. The possible new combinations are KNO_3 and $PbCl_2$. Placing these into a reaction and balancing it gives

$$2KCl \quad + \quad Pb(NO_3)_2 \quad \rightarrow \quad 2KNO_3 \quad + \quad PbCl_2$$

(b) The ions involved are Ca^{2+}, $2\,Cl^-$, Mg^{2+}, and SO_4^{2-}. The two new compounds are $CaSO_4$ and $MgCl_2$. The balanced chemical reaction is

$$CaCl_2 \quad + \quad MgSO_4 \quad \rightarrow \quad CaSO_4 \quad + \quad MgCl_2$$

(c) The ions are Na^+, OH^-, 2 Fe^{3+}, and 3SO_4^{2-}. Note that the charge of the iron is determined by calculation. The new compounds are Na_2SO_4 and $Fe(OH)_3$. The balanced chemical reaction is

$$6NaOH \quad + \quad Fe_2(SO_4)_3 \quad \rightarrow \quad 3Na_2SO_4 \quad + \quad 2Fe(OH)_3.$$

We can write these chemical reactions, but the major question is whether or not a chemical reaction will actually occur if the compounds are mixed together in the laboratory. In the next sections some ways in which the chemist can predict if an actual reaction will occur are presented.

Chemical Driving Forces

So far, we can predict the products of any mixture of two ionic compounds. However, not all such mixtures react. Chemists rely on three fundamental principles to make an educated guess about the possibility for a reaction to occur in a double-replacement reaction. These principles are sometimes described as **driving forces**.

1. The formation of water is perhaps the strongest driving force. In an ionic reaction where water is a product, it is almost a certainty that a double-replacement reaction is occurring.
2. Formation of a precipitate (insoluble compound) is another indicator of a strong driving force.
3. The formation of a nonionic (covalent) compound from ionic reactants is another driving force. Many of these nonionic compounds are organic acids (acetic, formic, benzoic acids) or gases such as NH_3, SO_2, and CO_2.

Some common examples of driving forces are as follows:

$HCl(aq)$	$+ NaOH(aq)$	$\rightarrow H_2O(aq)$	$+ NaCl(aq)$	(water formed)
$Na_2SO_4(aq)$	$+ Ba(NO_3)_2 (aq)$	$\rightarrow BaSO_4(s)$	$+ 2NaNO_3(aq)$	(precipitate formed)
$KC_2H_3O_2(aq)$	$+ HCl(aq)$	$\rightarrow HC_2H_3O_2(aq)$	$+ KCl(aq)$	(covalent compound formed)
$K_2SO_3(aq)$	$+ 2HNO_3(aq)$	$\rightarrow 2KNO_3(aq)$	$+ H_2O + SO_2(g)$	(gas formed)

In some reactions two of these driving forces may be present. As mentioned above, the driving force to form water is especially strong and will overcome another force that may be driving the reaction in the opposite direction. In the equation below, the formation of water overcomes the fact that CaO is a solid. Since CaO is on the reactant side of the equation, it is driving the equation toward the reactants. The production of water, however, is a stronger driving force, and the net result is that this reaction actually occurs:

$$CaO(s) \quad + \quad 2HCl(aq) \quad \rightarrow \quad CaCl_2(aq) \quad + \quad H_2O$$

Net Ionic Equations

In the process of determining the products of a reaction between ionic compounds, the ions for each substance were determined. In fact, in aqueous solution the soluble compounds appear only as ions, while insoluble compounds (precipitates), gases, and covalent compounds are written as molecules in the equation. It is possible to take a balanced double-replacement reaction and convert it into a net ionic equation that shows the actual reactants, if any, for a given reaction.

For example, a simple neutralization reaction is

$$HCl(aq) \quad + \quad NaOH(aq) \quad \rightarrow \quad NaCl(aq) \quad + \quad H_2O(\ell)$$

The ionic reaction is obtained by writing all of the soluble ionic compounds as ions

$$H^+(aq) + Cl^-(aq) + Na^+(aq) + OH^-(aq) \rightarrow Na^+(aq) + Cl^-(aq) + H_2O(\ell)$$

Since the Na^+ and the Cl^- are identical on both sides of the equation, they can be canceled to give the net ionic equation:

$$H^+(aq) \quad + \quad OH^-(aq) \quad \rightarrow \quad H_2O(\ell)$$

This allows the chemist to show that it is the H^+ and OH^- ions that are the active components of the reaction.

A reaction does not occur if potassium chloride and sodium nitrate solutions are mixed. We can demonstrate that no reaction occurs by deducing the reaction products as sodium chloride and potassium nitrate and then writing the net ionic equation. First we write the molecular equation

$$KCl(aq) + NaNO_3(aq) \rightarrow NaCl(aq) + KNO_3(aq) \quad \text{(molecular equation)}$$

Next, the ionic equation is written by separating each of the compounds into its ions:

$$K^+(aq) \quad + \quad Cl^-(aq) \quad + \quad Na^+(aq) \quad + \quad NO_3^-(aq)$$
$$\rightarrow Na^+(aq) \quad + \quad Cl^-(aq) \quad + \quad K^+(aq) \quad + \quad NO_3^-(aq) \quad \text{(ionic equation)}$$

Finally, after identical ions are canceled from both sides of this equation, nothing remains. This means that there is no net ionic equation and no reaction occurs:

NO NET IONIC EQUATION POSSIBLE

Taking a close look at the molecular equation, we see also that no driving force is present. No water, no precipitate, no covalent molecule, and no gas is formed.

A common laboratory experiment is the determination of sulfate ions by precipitation with barium ions. The precipitate is carefully collected, dried, and weighed in this experiment. The reaction between potassium sulfate and barium nitrate may be predicted to produce barium sulfate and sodium nitrate. The balanced equation is

$$K_2SO_4(aq) \quad + \quad Ba(NO_3)_3(aq) \quad \rightarrow \quad BaSO_4(aq) \quad + \quad 2KNO_3(aq)$$

The ionic equation is

$$2K^+(aq) \quad + \quad SO_4^{2-}(aq) \quad + \quad Ba^{2+}(aq) \quad + \quad 2NO_3^-(aq)$$
$$\rightarrow BaSO_4(s) \quad + \quad 2K^+(aq) \quad + \quad 2NO_3^-(aq)$$

In the ionic equation the two potassium and two nitrate ions may be canceled, resulting in

$$SO_4^{2-}(aq) \quad + \quad Ba^{2+}(aq) \quad \rightarrow \quad BaSO_4(s)$$

This balanced net ionic equation represents the reaction implied above by the words "determination of sulfate ions by precipitation with barium ions." In chemical analysis, the chemist is usually interested in a specific ion, such as the sulfate ion in this example. The net ionic equation shows us how to isolate the sulfate ion from all other ions by precipitation with barium ions.

Reactions that evolve gases are a bit more complex. Archaeologists typically carry a small bottle of hydrochloric acid on field trips. Carbonate rocks can be quickly identified since they will give off carbon dioxide (evidenced by bubbling and fizzing) when a few drops of HCl are placed on them. Most of these rocks are made of calcium carbonate. Using the techniques for a double-replacement reaction, we may predict the products to be calcium chloride and carbonic acid:

$$2HCl(aq) \quad + \quad CaCO_3(s) \quad \rightarrow \quad CaCl_2(aq) \quad + \quad H_2CO_3(aq)$$

The ionic equation is

$$2H^+(aq) + 2Cl^-(aq) + CaCO_3(s) \rightarrow Ca^{2+}(aq) + 2Cl^-(aq) + H_2CO_3(aq)$$

In this reaction only the Cl^- ions will cancel:

$$2H^+(aq) \quad + \quad CaCO_3(s) \quad \rightarrow \quad Ca^{2+}(aq) \quad + \quad H_2CO_3(aq)$$

This equation does not show any carbon dioxide gas. The key is that H_2CO_3 may also be written as $CO_2 + H_2O$. When this is substituted, the final reaction is

$$2H^+(aq) \quad + \quad CaCO_3(s) \quad \rightarrow \quad Ca^{2+}(aq) \quad + \quad H_2O(\ell) \quad + \quad CO_2(g)$$

Table 4.5 lists the common gases and their equivalents when dissolved in water. The gas and aqueous forms are interchangeable in reactions as needed.

TABLE 4.5 Common Gases and Their Equivalents in Aqueous Solution

Gas Name	Aqueous Form	Gas Form
carbon dioxide	$H_2CO_3(aq)$	$CO_2(g) + H_2O(\ell)$
sulfur dioxide	$H_2SO_3(aq)$	$SO_2(g) + H_2O(\ell)$
hydrogen sulfide	$H_2S(aq)$	$H_2S(g)$
ammonia	$NH_4OH^*(aq)$	$NH_3(g) + H_2O(\ell)$

*NH_4OH does not actually exist, and should always be written as $NH_3 + H_2O$.

Exercise 4.8

Write the balanced equation for each of the following pairs of ionic substances. Then write the ionic and net ionic equations for these reactions. Use (aq) to show soluble substances, (s) for insoluble compounds, (ℓ) for liquids, and (g) for gases.
(a) $AgNO_3$ and $CaCl_2$
(b) Na_2CO_3 and $Fe(NO_3)_3$
(c) CaF_2 and HCl
(d) NH_4Cl and KOH

Solutions

(a) $2\,AgNO_3(aq) + CaCl_2(aq)$ $\rightarrow 2\,AgCl(s) + Ca(NO_3)_3(aq)$
$2\,Ag^+(aq) + 2\,NO_3^-(aq) + Ca^{2+}(aq) + 2\,Cl^-(aq)$ $\rightarrow 2\,AgCl(s) + Ca^{2+}(aq) + 2\,NO_3^-(aq)$
$Ag^+(aq) + Cl^-(aq)$ $\rightarrow AgCl(s)$

(b) $3\,Na_2CO_3(aq) + 2\,Fe(NO_3)_3(aq)$ $\rightarrow Fe_2(CO_3)_3(s) + 6\,NaNO_3(aq)$
$6\,Na^+(aq) + 3\,CO_3^{2-}(aq) + 2\,Fe^{3+}(aq) + 6\,NO_3^-(aq) \rightarrow Fe_2(CO_3)_3(s) + 6\,Na^+(aq) + 6\,NO_3^-(aq)$
$3\,CO_3^{2-}(aq) + 2\,Fe^{3+}(aq)$ $\rightarrow Fe_2(CO_3)_3(s)$

(c) $CaF_2(aq) + 2\,HCl(aq)$ $\rightarrow 2\,HF(aq) + CaCl_2(aq)$
$Ca^{2+}(aq) + 2\,F^-(aq) + 2\,H^+(aq) + 2\,Cl^-(aq)$ $\rightarrow 2\,HF(aq) + Ca^{2+}(aq) + 2\,Cl^-(aq)$
$F^-(aq) + H^+(aq)$ $\rightarrow HF(aq)$

(d) $NH_4Cl(aq) + KOH(aq)$ $\rightarrow NH_4OH(aq) + KCl(aq)$
$NH_4^+(aq) + Cl^-(aq) + K^+(aq) + OH^-(aq)$ $\rightarrow NH_3(g) + H_2O(\ell) + K^+(aq) + Cl^-(aq)$
$NH_4^+(aq) + OH^-(aq)$ $\rightarrow NH_3(g) + H_2O(\ell)$

Note that the NH_4OH obtained from the double-replacement technique was replaced by $NH_3(g)$ and $H_2O(\ell)$ in the ionic equations since NH_4OH does not exist. It should not appear in the first equation either.

Single-Replacement Reactions

A single-replacement reaction may be described as the reaction between an element and an ionic compound (or ions in solution) to form a different element and a new ionic compound. The products of these reactions, like those of double-replacement reactions, may be predicted. In one type of single-replacement reaction the element used as a reactant may be a metal that becomes a cation as a product. The second type of single-replacement reaction involves a nonmetal as the elemental reactant that then forms an anion. Several reactions in which the reacting metal forms a cation are shown below.

One of these reactions is

$$Cu(s) + 2AgNO_3(aq) \rightarrow 2Ag(s) + Cu(NO_3)_2(aq)$$

We can write the ionic equation by breaking the $AgNO_3$ and $Cu(NO_3)_2$ into their ions:

$$Cu(s) + 2Ag^+(aq) + 2NO_3^-(aq) \rightarrow 2Ag(s) + Cu^{2+}(aq) + 2NO_3^-(aq)$$

Canceling the two nitrate ions from both sides gives the net ionic equation:

$$Cu(s) \quad + \quad 2Ag^+(aq) \quad \rightarrow \quad 2Ag(s) \quad + \quad Cu^{2+}(aq)$$

Active metals (i.e., the alkali metals) react with water. This is observed in the explosive reaction of potassium when it is placed in water.

$$2K(s) \quad + \quad H_2O(\ell) \quad \rightarrow \quad H_2(g) \quad + \quad 2KOH(aq)$$

We can write the ionic equation, which, since no ions cancel, is also the net ionic equation:

$$2K(s) \quad + \quad H_2O(\ell) \quad \rightarrow \quad H_2(g) \quad + \quad 2K^+(aq) \quad + \quad 2OH^-(aq)$$

Less active metals react with acids, as we observe with zinc and hydrochloric acid:

$$Zn(s) \quad + \quad 2HCl(aq) \quad \rightarrow \quad H_2(g) \quad + \quad ZnCl_2(aq)$$

the ionic equation is

$$Zn(s) + 2H^+(aq) + 2Cl^-(aq) \rightarrow H_2(g) + Zn^{2+}(aq) + 2Cl^-(aq)$$

and the net ionic equation is

$$Zn(s) \quad + \quad 2H^+(aq) \quad \rightarrow \quad H_2(g) \quad + \quad Zn^{2+}(aq)$$

In general, the metal reactant will form its ion, and the cation of the reactant will become the element. These reactions may be predicted when the metal reactant has only one possible cation. If, however, the metal can form several differently charged cations, as is true of lead, tin, or iron, the cation formed must be specified before the reaction can be completed.

Nonmetals that react to form anions are usually limited to the halogens. One of these reactions is

$$Cl_2(g) \quad + \quad 2KBr(aq) \quad \rightarrow \quad Br_2(\ell) \quad + \quad 2KCl(aq)$$

The net ionic reaction is

$$Cl_2(g) \quad + \quad 2Br^-(aq) \quad \rightarrow \quad Br_2(\ell) \quad + \quad 2Cl^-(aq)$$

In this reaction, the reactants Cl_2 and KBr are virtually colorless (Cl_2 is slightly yellow) and the product Br_2 produces a dark yellow or brown solution that allows us to directly observe that a reaction has occurred.

As we saw with double-replacement reactions, we can write equations for any mixture of an element and an ionic compound. To determine which reactions actually occur, we need to know whether a given element will displace an ion in a single-replacement reaction. Commonly this information is first given as the **activity series** of the elements. Later, when discussing oxidation-reduction reactions, we will find the same information in the table of standard reduction potentials. In this book we will use only an abbreviated table of standard reduction potentials (Table 4.6). We will describe the use of this table in more detail when discussing oxidation-reduction reactions. For the time being, it is important only to remember how to use this table effectively to predict whether or not single-replacement reactions will occur.

TABLE 4.6   Standard Reduction Potentials, 25°C

Half-Reaction						E° (volts)
$F_2(g)$	+	$2e^-$	→	$2F^-$		2.87
Co^{3+}	+	e^-	→	Co^{2+}		1.82
Au^{3+}	+	$3e^-$	→	Au		1.50
$Cl_2(g)$	+	$2e^-$	→	$2Cl^-$		1.36
$O_2(g)$	+	$4H^+$	+	$4e^-$	→ $2H_2O$	1.23
$Br_2(g)$	+	$2e^-$	→	$2Br^-$		1.07
$2Hg^{2+}$	+	$2e^-$	→	Hg_2^{2+}		0.92
Ag^+	+	e^-	→	Ag		0.80
Hg_2^{2+}	+	$2e^-$	→	Hg		0.79
Fe^{3+}	+	e^-	→	Fe^{2+}		0.77
I_2	+	$2e^-$	→	$2I^-$		0.53
Cu^+	+	e^-	→	Cu		0.52
Cu^{2+}	+	$2e^-$	→	Cu		0.34
Cu^{2+}	+	e^-	→	Cu^+		0.15
Sn^{4+}	+	$2e^-$	→	Sn^{2+}		0.15
S	+	$2H^+$	+	$2e^-$	→ H_2S	0.14
$2H^+$	+	$2e^-$	→	H_2		0.00
Pb^{2+}	+	$2e^-$	→	Pb		−0.13
Sn^{2+}	+	$2e^-$	→	Sn		−0.14
Ni^{2+}	+	$2e^-$	→	Ni		−0.25
Co^{2+}	+	$2e^-$	→	Co		−0.28
Tl^+	+	e^-	→	Tl		−0.34
Cd^{2+}	+	$2e^-$	→	Cd		−0.40
Cr^{3+}	+	e^-	→	Cr^{2+}		−0.41
Fe^{2+}	+	$2e^-$	→	Fe		−0.44
Cr^{3+}	+	$3e^-$	→	Cr		−0.74
Zn^{2+}	+	$2e^-$	→	Zn		−0.76
Mn^{2+}	+	$2e^-$	→	Mn		−1.18
Al^{3+}	+	$3e^-$	→	Al		−1.66
Be^{2+}	+	$2e^-$	→	Be		−1.70
Mg^{2+}	+	$2e^-$	→	Mg		−2.37
Na^+	+	e^-	→	Na		−2.71
Ca^{2+}	+	$2e^-$	→	Ca		−2.87
Sr^{2+}	+	$2e^-$	→	Sr		−2.89
Ba^{2+}	+	$2e^-$	→	Ba		−2.90
Rb^+	+	e^-	→	Rb		−2.92
K^+	+	e^-	→	K		−2.92
Cs^+	+	e^-	→	Cs		−2.92
Li^+	+	e^-	→	Li		−3.05

The table of standard reduction potentials supplied with the AP Chemistry Examination is usually arranged with the largest negative reduction potential at the top and the largest positive reduction potential at the bottom (the reverse of Table 4.6). On the exam, it is necessary only to locate the two reactants (one an element and the other an ion) in the net ionic equations listed in the table and then draw a line between the two. If the drawn line has a positive (upward) slope, the reaction will occur. If the line has a negative (downward) slope, the reaction will not occur. (In Table 4.6 a negative slope indicates a reaction will occur.) The reason why this procedure works is explained in Chapter 13 on oxidation-reduction reactions. It is instructive to take all of the single-replacement reactions above and verify, using Table 4.6, that each has a downward slope.

Exercise 4.9

A major portion of the free-response section of the AP test involves writing chemical equations from a description of the reactions. This exercise is typical of the AP questions and may be answered using the information given in this chapter.

Write the chemical formulas (ions or molecules as appropriate) for each of the following. Each reaction does occur. Where appropriate, write net ionic equations. Equations need not be balanced.

(a) A saturated solution of Br_2 in water is added to a solution containing potassium iodide.
(b) A piece of magnesium metal is placed in a solution of sulfuric acid.
(c) Sodium bromide solution is added to a silver perchlorate solution.
(d) Iron(III) nitrate solution is mixed with a potassium sulfite solution.
(e) Solid magnesium carbonate is reacted with hydrochloric acid.
(f) Ammonium chloride solution is added to a barium hydroxide solution.
(g) Chromium(III) chloride solution reacts with solid magnesium.
(h) Sodium carbonate solution is mixed with aluminum sulfate.
(i) Calcium hydroxide and sodium phosphate solutions are mixed.
(j) Carbon dioxide is bubbled into a solution of iron(III) nitrate.
(k) Solid lead(IV) oxide reacts with hydrochloric acid.
(l) Ethyl alcohol is burned in excess oxygen.
(m) Hydrogen sulfide gas is bubbled into a solution containing cobalt(II) chloride.
(n) Solid calcium oxide reacts with sulfuric acid.
(o) Chlorine gas is bubbled into a solution of potassium iodide.

Solutions

The following reactions are balanced. (Even though the question does not require balancing, it is good form to do so if possible.) Each solution gives the formulas for the reactants, the molecular equation, and the correct ionic equation if needed.

(a) Reactants: Br_2 and KI

$$Br_2 + 2KI \rightarrow I_2 + 2KBr$$
$$Br_2 + 2I^- \rightarrow I_2 + 2Br^-$$

(b) Reactants: Mg and H_2SO_4

$$Mg(s) \quad + \quad H_2SO_4 \quad \rightarrow \quad MgSO_4 \quad + \quad H_2(g)$$
$$Mg(s) \quad + \quad 2H^+ \quad \rightarrow \quad Mg^{2+} \quad + \quad H_2(g)$$

(c) Reactants: NaBr and $AgClO_4$

$$NaBr \quad + \quad AgClO_4 \quad \rightarrow \quad AgBr(s) \quad + \quad NaClO_4$$
$$Br^- \quad + \quad Ag^+ \quad \rightarrow \quad AgBr(s)$$

(d) Reactants: $Fe(NO_3)_3$ and K_2SO_3

$$2Fe(NO_3)_3 \quad + \quad 3K_2SO_3 \quad \rightarrow \quad Fe_2(SO_3)_3(s) \quad + \quad 6KNO_3$$
$$2Fe^{3+} \quad + \quad 3SO_3^{2-} \quad \rightarrow \quad Fe_2(SO_3)_3(s)$$

(e) Reactants: $MgCO_3$ and HCl

$$MgCO_3(s) \quad + \quad 2HCl \quad \rightarrow \quad MgCl_2 \quad + \quad H_2CO_3$$

(Remember that H_2CO_3 can be written as $H_2O + CO_2$.)

$$MgCO_3(s) \quad + \quad 2H^+ \quad \rightarrow \quad Mg^{2+} \quad + \quad H_2O + CO_2(g)$$

(f) Reactants: NH_4Cl and $Ba(OH)_2$

$$2NH_4Cl \quad + \quad Ba(OH)_2 \quad \rightarrow \quad BaCl_2 \quad + \quad 2NH_4OH$$

(Remember NH_4OH should always be written as $NH_3(g) + H_2O$.)

$$NH_4^+ \quad + \quad OH^- \quad \rightarrow \quad NH_3(g) \quad + \quad H_2O$$

(g) Reactants: $CrCl_3$ and Mg

$$2CrCl_3 \quad + \quad 3Mg(s) \quad \rightarrow \quad 3MgCl_2 \quad + \quad 2Cr(s)$$
$$2Cr^{3+} \quad + \quad 3Mg(s) \quad \rightarrow \quad 3Mg^{2+} \quad + \quad 2Cr(s)$$

(h) Reactants: Na_2CO_3 and $Al_2(SO_4)_3$

$$3Na_2CO_3 \quad + \quad Al_2(SO_4)_3 \quad \rightarrow \quad 3Na_2SO_4 \quad + \quad Al_2(CO_3)_3(s)$$
$$3CO_3^{2-} \quad + \quad 2Al^{3+} \quad \rightarrow \quad Al_2(CO_3)_3(s)$$

(i) Reactants: $Ca(OH)_2$ and Na_3PO_4

$$3Ca_{(OH)2} \quad + \quad 2Na_3PO_4 \quad \rightarrow \quad Ca_3(PO_4)_2(s) \quad + \quad 6NaOH$$
$$3Ca^{2+} \quad + \quad 2PO_4^{3-} \quad \rightarrow \quad Ca_3(PO_4)_2$$

(j) Reactants: CO_2, H_2O and $Fe(NO_3)_3$

$$CO_2(g) \quad + \quad 3H_2O \quad + \quad 2Fe(NO_3)_3 \quad \rightarrow \quad Fe_2(CO_3)_3(s) \quad + \quad 6HNO_3$$
$$CO_2(g) \quad + \quad 3H_2O \quad + \quad 2Fe^{3+} \quad \rightarrow \quad Fe_2(CO_3)_3(s) \quad + \quad 6H^+$$

(k) Reactants: PbO_2 and HCl

$$PbO_2(s) \quad + \quad 4HCl \quad \rightarrow \quad PbCl_4 \quad + \quad 2H_2O$$
$$PbO_2(s) \quad + \quad 4H^+ \quad \rightarrow \quad Pb^{4+} \quad + \quad 2H_2O$$

(l) Reactants: CH_3CH_2OH and O_2

$$CH_3CH_2OH \quad + \quad 3O_2(g) \quad \rightarrow \quad 2CO_2(g) \quad + \quad 3H_2O$$

No ionic reaction is possible.

(m) Reactants: H_2S and $CoCl_2$

$$H_2S(g) \quad + \quad CoCl_2 \qquad CoS(s) \quad + \quad 2HCl$$
$$H_2S(g) \quad + \quad Co^{2+} \qquad CoS(s) \quad + \quad 2H^+$$

(n) Reactants: CaO and H_2SO_4

$$CaO(s) \quad + \quad H_2SO_4 \qquad\qquad \rightarrow \quad CaSO_4(s) \quad + \quad H_2O$$
$$CaO(s) \quad + \quad 2H^+ \quad + \quad SO_4^{2-} \quad \rightarrow \quad CaSO_4(s) \quad + \quad H_2O$$

(o) Reactants: Cl_2 and KI

$$Cl_2(g) \quad + \quad 2KI \quad \rightarrow \quad I_2 \quad + \quad 2KCl$$
$$Cl_2(g) \quad + \quad 2I^- \quad \rightarrow \quad I_2 \quad + \quad 2Cl^-$$

Important Concepts

Predicting ionic charges
Balancing reactions
Writing ionic formulas and electroneutrality of compounds
Writing ionic and net ionic equations
Naming ionic compounds
Solubility rules
Polyatomic ions

Questions on Chapter 4

1. Which of the following compounds is soluble?
   (A) $MgCO_3$
   (B) $Al(OH)_3$
   (C) Cr_2S_3
   (D) K_2CrO_4
   (E) $NiSO_3$

2. Which of the following compounds is insoluble?
   (A) $Ca(OH)_2$
   (B) Fe_2S_3
   (C) Na_2CO_3
   (D) H_2SO_3
   (E) $AuCl_3$

3. Which of the following is the permanganate ion?
   (A) ClO_4^-
   (B) PO_4^{3-}
   (C) MnO_2
   (D) SO_4^{2-}
   (E) MnO_4^-

4. When ammonium oxalate, $(NH_4)_2C_2O_4$, is dissolved in water the ions formed are
   (A) $2N^{3-}(aq) + 8H^+(aq) + 2C^{4+}(aq) + 4O^{2-}(aq)$
   (B) $(NH_4)^{2+}(aq) + C_2O_4^{2-}(aq)$
   (C) $2NH_4^+(aq) + C_2O_4^{2-}(aq)$
   (D) $NH_4^{2+}(aq) + C_2O_4^{2-}(aq)$
   (E) $2NH_4^+(aq) + 2CO_2^-(aq)$

5. The correct name for $Fe(NO_3)_3$ is
   (A) iron nitrite
   (B) iron(II) nitrate
   (C) ferrous nitroxide
   (D) iron(III) sulfate
   (E) iron(III) nitrate

6. When the combustion reaction for benzene, C_6H_6, is properly balanced with the smallest whole-number coefficients possible, the sum of the coefficients is
   (A) 15
   (B) 12
   (C) 35
   (D) 17.5
   (E) 12

7. The potassium ion is isoelectronic to which noble gas?
   (A) He
   (B) Ne
   (C) Ar
   (D) Kr
   (E) Xe

8. Which two atoms will form isoelectronic ions?
   (A) Cl and Na
   (B) Cl and F
   (C) Na and F
   (D) S and Br
   (E) Fe and Ca

9. What is the formula for an ionic compound formed from aluminum and chlorine?
   (A) AlCl
   (B) Al_3Cl
   (C) Al_3Cl_3

(D) $AlCl_3$
(E) Al_2Cl_3

10. The electronic configuration $1s^2$, $2s^2$, $2p^6$, $3s^2$, $3p^6$ corresponds to the electronic configuration of
   (A) S^{2-}
   (B) Ca^{2+}
   (C) Cl^-
   (D) K^+
   (E) all of these

11. Which of the following is NOT correctly named?
   (A) Cl^- chloride ion
   (B) ClO^- hypochlorite ion
   (C) ClO_4^- perchlorate ion
   (D) ClO_2^- chlorous ion
   (E) ClO_3^- chlorate ion

12. Which of the following is NOT a correct chemical formula?
   (A) $SrBr_2$
   (B) CaO_2
   (C) Mg_3N_2
   (D) Na_2S
   (E) AlI_3

13. Which of the following is a correct formula?
   (A) NH_4SO_3
   (B) $CaC_2H_3O_2$
   (C) Na_2ClO_4
   (D) $Ba(CO_3)_2$
   (E) KH_2PO_4

14. Which of the following is a single-replacement reaction?
   (A) sodium chloride with potassium nitrate
   (B) chlorine gas with sodium metal
   (C) aluminum metal with hydrobromic acid
   (D) ethyl alcohol with oxygen
   (E) magnesium oxide with sulfur trioxide

15. Which of the following is NOT true of a net ionic equation?
   (A) All of the nonreacting ions have been canceled.
   (B) It shows the actual reactants in an equation.
   (C) It allows the chemist to substitute reactants in a logical manner.
   (D) It is used to determine which compounds are insoluble.
   (E) It must have the charges as well as the atoms balanced.

Answer Key

See Appendix I for explanations of answers.

1. **D**	4. **C**	7. **C**	10. **E**	13. **E**
2. **B**	5. **E**	8. **C**	11. **D**	14. **C**
3. **E**	6. **C**	9. **D**	12. **B**	15. **D**

CHAPTER FIVE
Covalent Compounds, Formulas, and Structure

Covalent Molecules

The **covalent bond** represents another way in which an element may form compounds and at the same time attain a noble-gas electronic configuration. In contrast to ionic bonding, where electrons are transferred from atom to atom, covalent bonding occurs when electrons are shared between two or more atoms. In addition, whereas ionic bonding is simply electrical attraction of oppositely charged ions, in covalent compounds the atoms are physically attached to each other. Compounds composed of covalently bonded groups of atoms are called **molecules**.

To conveniently show this sharing of electrons, chemists draw structures of covalent molecules using **Lewis electron-dot structures**. In the Lewis representation the outermost s and p electrons (valence electrons) are shown as dots arranged around the atomic symbol. **Lewis structures** for 18 elements are shown in Figure 5.1.

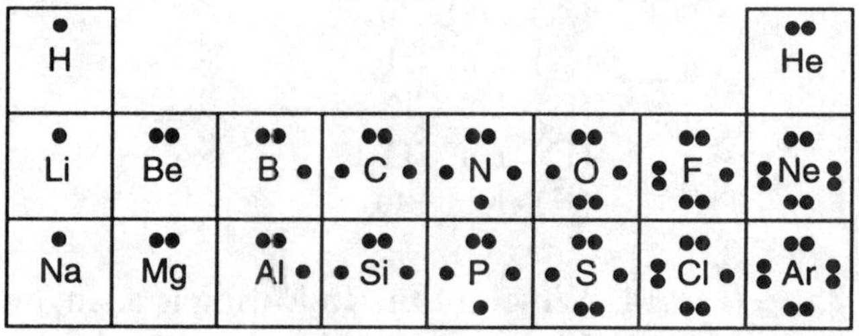

H							He
Li	Be	B	C	N	O	F	Ne
Na	Mg	Al	Si	P	S	Cl	Ar

FIGURE 5.1. Elements normally represented with Lewis electron-dot symbols.

When electrons are shared between two atoms, one atom donates one electron and the other atom donates the second electron. The shared pair of electrons represents a covalent bond. If two pairs of electrons are shared between two atoms, a **double bond** exists. When two atoms share three pairs of electrons, a **triple bond** exists.

The sharing of electrons follows the same basic principle as prevails in the formation of ions. This fact means that the atoms are trying to attain noble-gas electronic configurations. Referring to the noble-gas configurations, we see that there are two s electrons and six p electrons in complete sublevels of each noble gas. These eight electrons represent the octet of the octet rule, which governs covalent compounds. The **octet rule** states that the noble-gas configuration will be achieved if the Lewis structure shows eight electrons around each atom. Hydrogen is an exception; its "octet" is two electrons, corresponding to the two outermost electrons in the noble gas helium.

Figure 5.2 shows the Lewis electron dot structures for the **diatomic** gases. In these structures the electrons of one atom are represented as dots and those of the other atom as circles in order to illustrate that each atom contributes the same number of electrons to the bond.

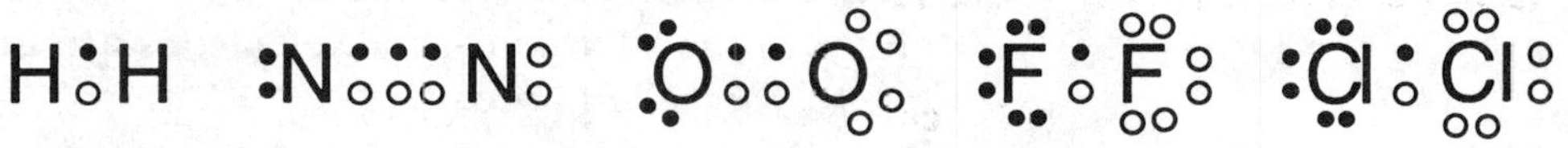

$$H \overset{\circ}{\circ} H \qquad :N \overset{\circ\circ}{\circ\circ} N \overset{\circ}{\circ} \qquad \overset{\bullet\bullet}{\underset{\bullet\bullet}{O}} \overset{\circ\circ}{\underset{\circ\circ}{O}} \qquad \overset{\bullet\bullet}{\underset{\bullet\bullet}{:F}} \overset{\circ\circ}{\underset{\circ\circ}{F}} \qquad \overset{\bullet\bullet}{\underset{\bullet\bullet}{:Cl}} \overset{\circ\circ}{\underset{\circ\circ}{Cl}}$$

FIGURE 5.2. Lewis structures of the diatomic elements

In these molecules, each atom considers the shared electrons (those electrons between the two atoms) as its own. Each hydrogen in H_2 thinks it has two electrons and an electronic configuration the same as that of helium. Nitrogen molecules have triple bonds with three pairs of shared electrons. Oxygen molecules may be represented with a double bond. Fluorine and chlorine look very similar, as expected, since both are halogens.

Oxygen has a simple Lewis structure, shown in Figure 5.2, which turns out to be incorrect. Experimental evidence shows that oxygen is paramagnetic and must contain unpaired electrons. More sophisticated molecular orbital methods must be used to obtain the correct bonding showing these unpaired electrons.

Lewis Structures of Molecules

Lewis structures of other molecules and polyatomic ions may be drawn using the basic octet rule. For larger molecules it is first necessary to determine the general arrangement of the atoms, often called the "skeleton." In most molecules this skeleton consists of a central atom with surrounding atoms bonded to it. A few general rules apply to determining the skeleton.

1. Carbon is usually a central atom in the structure. In compounds with more than one carbon atom, the carbon atoms are joined in a chain to start the skeleton.
2. Hydrogen is never a central atom because it can form only one covalent bond.
3. Halogens form only a single covalent bond when oxygen is not present, and therefore a halogen will generally not be a central atom.
4. Oxygen forms only two covalent bonds and is rarely a central atom. However, it may link two carbon atoms in a carbon chain.
5. In the simpler molecules, the atom that appears only once in the formula will be the central atom.

Once the molecular skeleton is determined, the available valence electrons must be arranged in octets around each atom. This is done in steps as follows:

1. The valence electrons of all atoms are added together.
2. If the substance is a polyatomic ion, we must take into account the electrons used to form the ion. For anions, the charge represents additional electrons that must be added to the total of the valence electrons. For cations, the charge represents missing electrons that must be subtracted from the valence electrons.
3. A pair of electrons is placed between each two atoms in the skeletal structure to represent a covalent bond. These electrons are called the **bonding pairs**.
4. The remaining electrons are used to complete the octets of all outer atoms in the skeleton. These electrons are **nonbonding pairs** of electrons (also called **lone pairs**).
5. If any electrons are left over, they are added in pairs to the central atom. These electrons are also nonbonding pairs (lone pairs).
6. When all electrons have been placed, the outer atoms will all have octets. The central atom may have an octet, or it may have more or fewer than eight electrons.
   a. If the central atom has an octet, the structure is complete (see section on formal charges, page 107).
   b. It is all right if the central atom has fewer than eight electrons, provided that the atom is boron. For other central atoms, double bonds must be constructed to obtain an octet. This is done by taking a nonbonding pair of electrons from an outer atom and placing them as a bonding pair to make a double bond. Enough double bonds are constructed to give the central atom an octet.
   c. The central atom may have more than eight electrons (as in PCl_5 shown in Figure 5.7) only if it is in period 3–7 of the periodic table. If the central atom is in period 2, it cannot have more than an octet of electrons.

For example, we may construct the Lewis diagram for methane, CH_4, in the following manner. First we draw the skeleton with carbon in the center and the hydrogen atoms arranged symmetrically around it. Next we count the valence electrons. There are four valence electrons on the carbon atom and one on each of the four hydrogen atoms, for a total of eight electrons. In the next step we add the bonding pairs of electrons to the structure. This uses up all of the electrons, and we check to see whether each atom has an octet. (Remember that for hydrogen an "octet" is simply one pair of electrons.) Finally, to simplify the structure, we can replace the bonding pairs of electrons by a line representing a bond. These steps are shown in Figure 5.3.

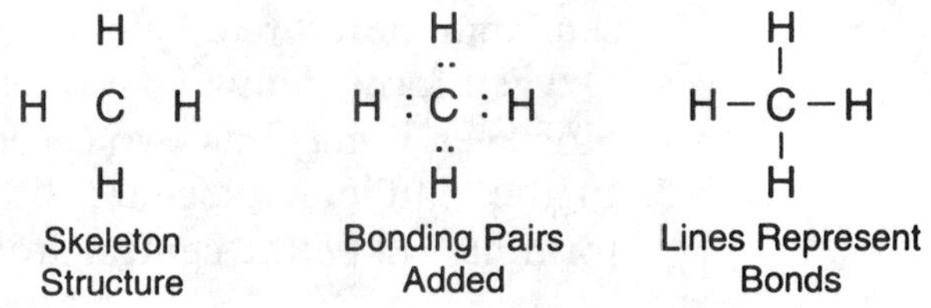

FIGURE 5.3. Construction of the Lewis structure for methane. Because of its simplicity, the structure is complete once the bonding pairs are added.

The most common **electron-deficient** molecules involve boron. The structure of boron trifluoride, BF_3, is constructed as illustrated in Figure 5.4.

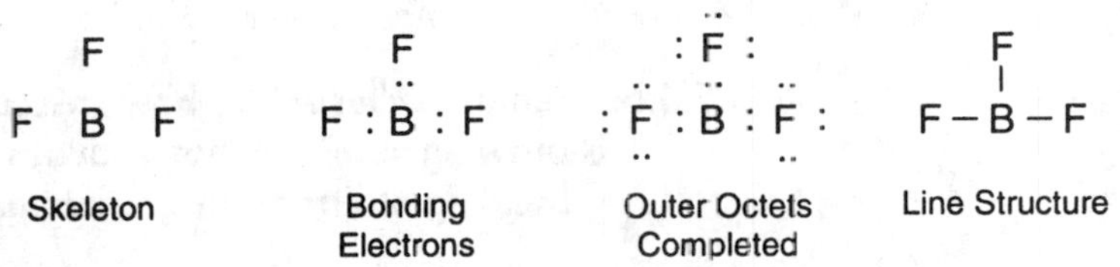

$$
\begin{array}{cccc}
\text{F} & \text{F} & : \overset{\cdot\cdot}{\text{F}} : & \text{F} \\
\text{F B F} & \text{F} \overset{\cdot\cdot}{:} \text{B} : \text{F} & : \overset{\cdot\cdot}{\text{F}} : \text{B} : \overset{\cdot\cdot}{\text{F}} : & \text{F} - \text{B} - \text{F} \\
\text{Skeleton} & \begin{array}{c}\text{Bonding}\\\text{Electrons}\end{array} & \begin{array}{c}\text{Outer Octets}\\\text{Completed}\end{array} & \text{Line Structure}
\end{array}
$$

FIGURE 5.4. **Construction of the BF_3 molecule. Compared to methane, this construction requires the additional step of constructing octets around the fluorine atoms.**

The skeleton is arranged with boron as the central atom. Adding up the valence electrons, we get $3 + 7 + 7 + 7 = 24$ electrons for the boron and three fluorine atoms. Next, bonding pairs are added between each fluorine and the boron atom, using six electrons and leaving 18 to be placed. Six more electrons are placed around each fluorine atom to complete its octet. All of the remaining electrons are now utilized. Since boron is commonly found with an electron-deficient structure (i.e., with less than an octet of electrons), the structure is complete. The line structure may be drawn for simplicity. The nonbonding pairs of the outer atoms are generally not shown in a line structure.

Phosphorus forms two compounds with chlorine, PCl_3 and PCl_5. Examining their Lewis structures, we find first that PCl_3 is constructed as shown in Figure 5.5.

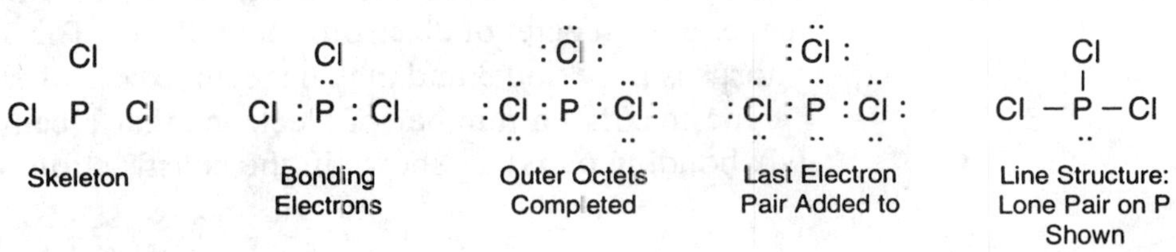

$$
\begin{array}{ccccc}
\text{Cl} & \text{Cl} & : \overset{\cdot\cdot}{\text{Cl}} : & : \overset{\cdot\cdot}{\text{Cl}} : & \text{Cl} \\
\text{Cl P Cl} & \text{Cl} \overset{\cdot\cdot}{:} \text{P} : \text{Cl} & : \overset{\cdot\cdot}{\text{Cl}} : \text{P} : \overset{\cdot\cdot}{\text{Cl}} : & : \overset{\cdot\cdot}{\text{Cl}} : \overset{\cdot\cdot}{\text{P}} : \overset{\cdot\cdot}{\text{Cl}} : & \text{Cl} - \overset{\cdot\cdot}{\text{P}} - \text{Cl} \\
\text{Skeleton} & \begin{array}{c}\text{Bonding}\\\text{Electrons}\end{array} & \begin{array}{c}\text{Outer Octets}\\\text{Completed}\end{array} & \begin{array}{c}\text{Last Electron}\\\text{Pair Added to}\end{array} & \begin{array}{c}\text{Line Structure:}\\\text{Lone Pair on P}\\\text{Shown}\end{array}
\end{array}
$$

FIGURE 5.5. **Construction of the Lewis structure for PCl_3. Compared to BCl_3, this construction requires the addition of a pair of nonbonding electrons to the central atom in step 4.**

As before, the skeleton is drawn and the valence electrons counted. There are $5 + 7 + 7 + 7 = 26$ electrons. The bonding electron pairs and the outer octets are completed in the next two steps, leaving two electrons unused. These are placed on the central phosphorus atom as shown in Figure 5.5, completing its octet. All atoms are checked to see that each has an octet of electrons. One way to do this is to draw a circle around all of the electrons adjacent to each atom, as shown in Figure 5.6.

Finally, the line structure may be used. Since nonbonding pairs on the central atom are important in determining the molecular geometry, they are shown in the line structure (see the last structure in Figure 5.5).

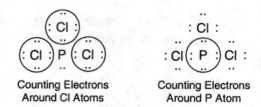

FIGURE 5.6. Diagram illustrating how to count electrons around each atom by drawing a circle that includes all nonbonding electrons and all bonding electrons for that atom.

In constructing the PCl_5 molecule, we observe some differences, as shown in Figure 5.7.

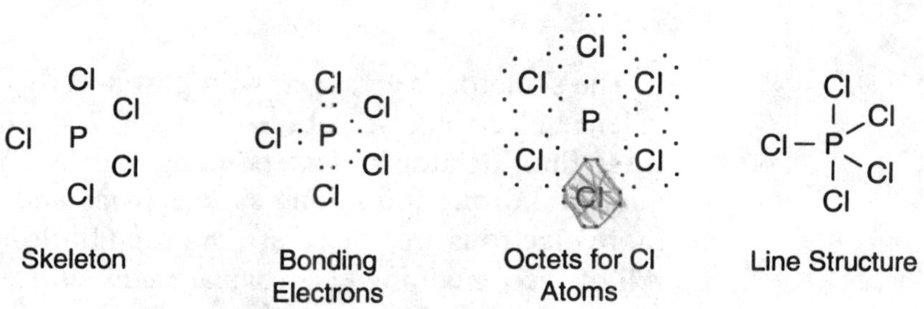

Skeleton	Bonding Electrons	Octets for Cl Atoms	Line Structure

FIGURE 5.7. Construction of the PCl_5 molecule. The phosphorus atom has 10 bonding electrons (five pairs), which are allowed since phosphorus is in period 3 of the periodic table.

There is a total of 40 valence electrons in PCl_5, which need to be placed. The skeleton is drawn, bonding pairs are added, and then the octets for clorine are completed. This step uses up all 40 electrons, and the line structure may be drawn for clarity. Notice that the phosphorus atom has more than an octet of electrons (actually 10). This is reasonable since phosphorus is in period 3 and may have an excess of electrons.

The maximum number of electrons that a central atom can have is 12 (six bonding pairs), as shown in the construction of SF_6 (Figure 5.8).

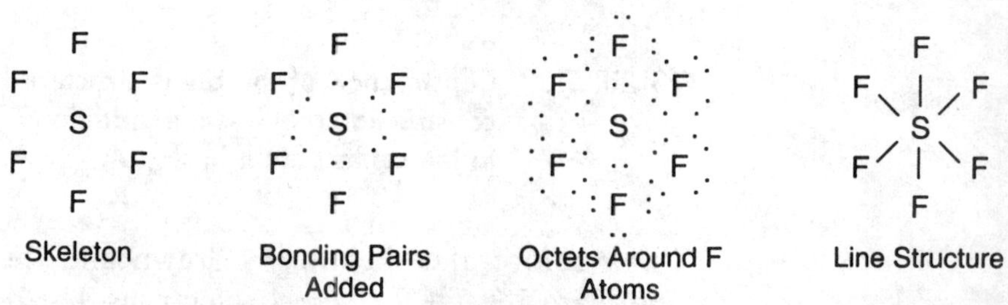

Skeleton	Bonding Pairs Added	Octets Around F Atoms	Line Structure

FIGURE 5.8. Construction of the SF_6 molecule. This structure shows 12 bonding electrons (six pairs) around the sulfur atom.

Multiple Covalent Bonds

Some compounds require the use of double bonds, which are represented by two pairs of electrons between atoms. Sulfur dioxide, SO_2, is one of those substances. There are 18 valence electrons ($6 + 6 + 6 = 18$) to distribute on the O S O skeleton so as to obtain octets on all atoms. The steps are illustrated in Figure 5.9.

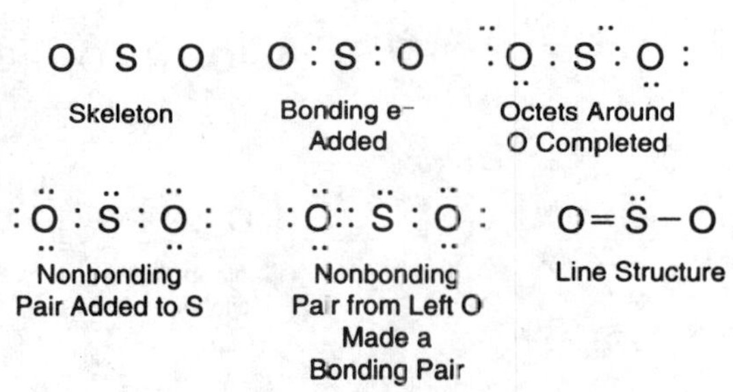

O S O   O : S : O   :Ö : S : Ö :

Skeleton   Bonding e⁻   Octets Around
            Added   O Completed

:Ö : S : Ö :   :Ö :: S : Ö :   O = S̈ − O

Nonbonding   Nonbonding   Line Structure
Pair Added to S   Pair from Left O
              Made a
              Bonding Pair

FIGURE 5.9. Construction of the Lewis structure for the SO$_2$ molecule. This involves the formation of a double bond as shown in the fifth diagram.

After the last two electrons are added to the sulfur atom as a nonbonding pair, the sulfur still has only six electrons. To obtain an octet, a nonbonding electron pair from the left oxygen atom is moved to a position between the sulfur and the oxygen. The result is an additional bonding pair, creating a double bond. Notice that the left oxygen atom still has an octet, and now the sulfur also has an octet of electrons. Finally, although the nonbonding pair was moved from the left oxygen, we could have chosen to move a pair from the oxygen atom on the right to obtain a similar structure with the double bond on the right. These two, equally probable structures (Figure 5.10) are called **resonance structures** (see page 110).

O = S̈ − O   O − S̈ = O

FIGURE 5.10. The two resonance structures of SO$_2$. These molecules differ only in the position of the double bond.

Some molecules contain triple bonds. Common examples are nitrogen, N_2, acetylene, C_2H_2, and the cyanide ion, CN^-. A triple bond is formed by first constructing a double bond as described above. If the atoms still do not have octets, a second pair of nonbonding electrons may be moved to a bonding position.

Lewis Structures of Ions

In addition to the Lewis structures for molecules, we may also draw Lewis structures for covalently bonded polyatomic ions. The methods are the same as those for molecules except that we must account for the electrons that give an ion its charge. One electron is added to the valence electrons for each negative charge on an ion and one electron is subtracted from the valence electrons for each positive charge. The structure of the nitrite ion, NO_2^-, is an example. As with molecules, we count the valence electrons, $6 + 6 + 5 = 17$. The negative charge adds one electron for a total of 18. As shown in Figure 5.11, we construct the skeleton, add the bonding electrons, complete the octets around the oxygen atoms, add one nonbonding pair to nitrogen to use the remaining electrons, and finally construct a double bond so that all atoms have octets. When writing Lewis structures for ions, it is necessary to enclose the ion in brackets and indicate the charge of the ion as shown.

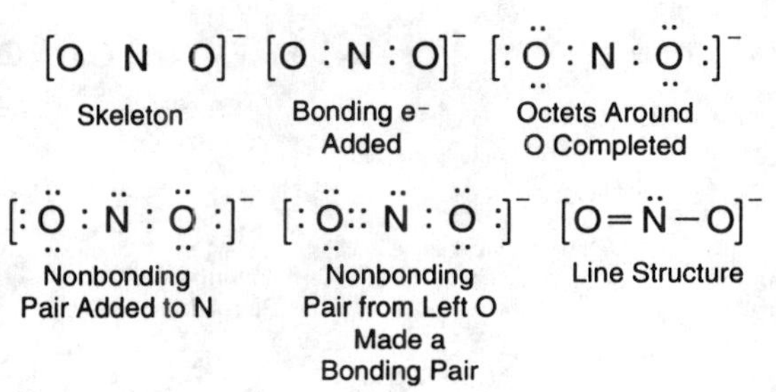

$$[\text{O} \quad \text{N} \quad \text{O}]^- \quad [\text{O} : \text{N} : \text{O}]^- \quad [:\ddot{\text{O}} : \text{N} : \ddot{\text{O}} :]^-$$

Skeleton   Bonding e⁻   Octets Around
             Added   O Completed

$$[:\ddot{\text{O}} : \ddot{\text{N}} : \ddot{\text{O}} :]^- \quad [:\ddot{\text{O}} :: \ddot{\text{N}} : \ddot{\text{O}} :]^- \quad [\text{O}=\ddot{\text{N}}-\text{O}]^-$$

Nonbonding   Nonbonding   Line Structure
Pair Added to N   Pair from Left O
               Made a
            Bonding Pair

FIGURE 5.11. Construction of the Lewis structure of the nitrite ion.

We notice a distinct similarity in the structures of the SO_2 molecule and the NO_2^- ion. The electrons are arranged in exactly the same manner. Since the nitrogen atom has one less electron than sulfur does, the nitrite ion requires an extra electron, which results in its -1 charge.

Exercise 5.1

1. Construct the Lewis structure for each of the following compounds.
   (a) CH_3Cl (b) CS_2 (c) PH_3
   (d) SiF_4 (e) H_2S

2. Construct the Lewis structure for each of the following ions.
   (a) NO_3^- (b) CO_3^{2-} (c) PO_4^{3-}
   (d) SO_3^{2-} (e) ClO_4^-

Solution

1. (a) 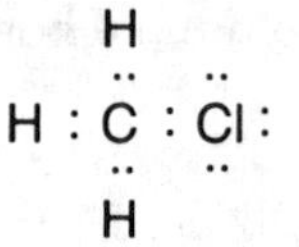
```
      H
      ..
H : C : Cl :
      ..   ..
      H
```

(c)
```
      H
      ..
H : P : H
      ..
```

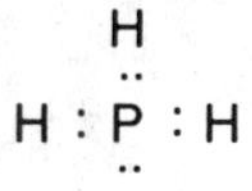

(e) 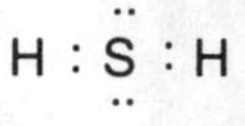
```
     ..
H : S : H
     ..
```

(b) 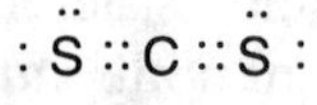 $\quad :\ddot{\text{S}} :: \text{C} :: \ddot{\text{S}} :$

(d) 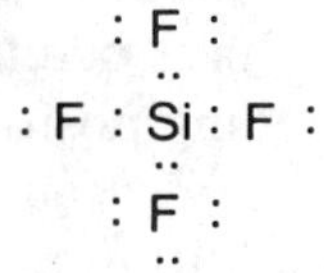
```
      : F :
        ..
: F : Si : F :
        ..
      : F :
        ..
```

2. (a) 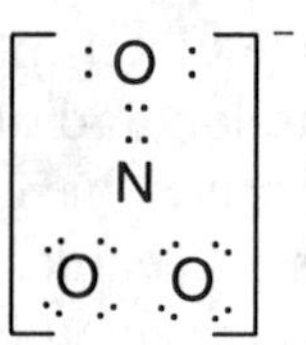
$$\begin{bmatrix} :\text{O}: \\ \text{N} \\ .\ddot{\text{O}} \quad \ddot{\text{O}}. \end{bmatrix}^-$$

(c) 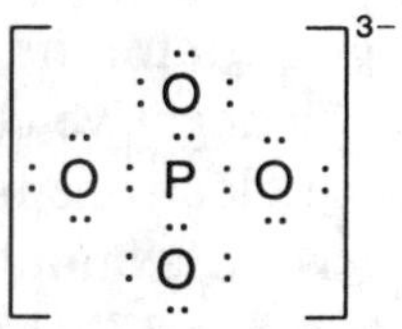
$$\begin{bmatrix} :\ddot{\text{O}}: \\ :\text{O}:\text{P}:\text{O}: \\ :\ddot{\text{O}}: \end{bmatrix}^{3-}$$

(e) 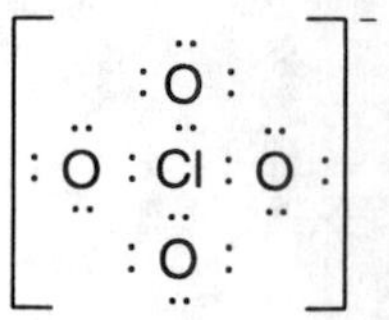
$$\begin{bmatrix} :\ddot{\text{O}}: \\ :\text{O}:\text{Cl}:\text{O}: \\ :\ddot{\text{O}}: \end{bmatrix}^-$$

(b) 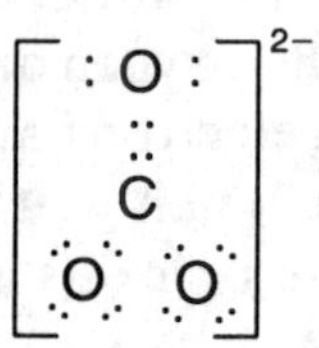
$$\begin{bmatrix} :\text{O}: \\ .. \\ \text{C} \\ .\ddot{\text{O}} \quad \ddot{\text{O}}. \end{bmatrix}^{2-}$$

(d) 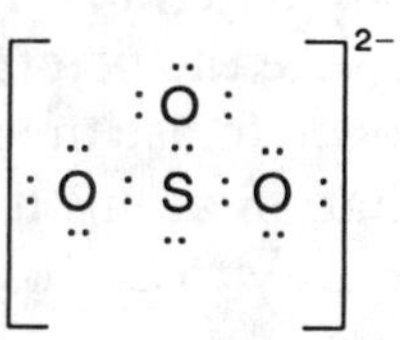
$$\begin{bmatrix} :\ddot{\text{O}}: \\ :\ddot{\text{O}}:\text{S}:\ddot{\text{O}}: \end{bmatrix}^{2-}$$

Lewis Structures of Odd Electron Compounds

Some compounds have formulas in which the total number of valence electrons is an odd number. In such cases it is impossible to construct a Lewis structure with an octet around each atom. Nitrogen dioxide, NO_2, is one such compound. One possible Lewis structure is shown in Figure 5.12.

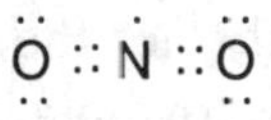

$$\ddot{O} :: \overset{\displaystyle \cdot}{N} :: \ddot{O}$$

FIGURE 5.12 Lewis structure of the NO_2 molecule, showing the unpaired electron on the nitrogen atom.

Molecules that have Lewis structures with an unpaired electron are often called **free radicals**. The unpaired electron makes the molecule unusually reactive. Free radicals have been implicated in such biological processes as aging and cancer. In an effort to pair up the single electron, free radicals may also form **dimers** or pairs of molecules. For example, the molecule NO_2 dimerizes to produce the N_2O_4 molecule in the reaction

$$2NO_2 \rightarrow N_2O_4$$

Formal Charges

How do we know whether or not a Lewis structure is reasonable? Calculation of the **formal charge** on each atom is one technique that may be used to make this judgment. The formal charge is the difference between the number of electrons an atom has in a Lewis structure and its number of valence electrons. This calculation is described in detail below.

First it is important to understand the concept of formal charges. In a covalent compound an atom shares some of its valence electrons to form bonds, while the rest of the valence electrons remain as nonbonding electron pairs. If we count these nonbonding electrons and the electrons that an atom shares to form bonds, we should end up with a number equal to the valence of the atom. A different number means that the atom has lost or gained one or more electrons, an unlikely event since the loss or gain of electrons implies ionic behavior. Technically the formal charge is a separation of charge. In fact, some Lewis structures do require charge separation, but it is the minimum possible. In addition, we know, based on the electronegativities of the atoms, that the element with the greater electronegativity will be the atom with a negative charge. If the formal charges show elements with large electronegativities as positive compared to other atoms in the structure, we must question the validity of the structure.

In calculating the formal charge, each electron in a proposed Lewis structure is assigned to a specific atom. The number of electrons assigned to an atom is then compared to the number of that atom's valence electrons. If the assigned electrons and the number of valence electrons are equal, the formal charge is zero. If more electrons are assigned to an atom than there are valence electrons, the formal charge will be a negative value equal to the number of extra electrons. Similarly, if fewer electrons are assigned to an atom than there are valence electrons, the atom has a positive formal charge equal to the number of missing electrons. To calculate the formal charge on each atom in a Lewis structure the following steps are taken:

1. For each atom count all electrons not used for bonding by the atom.
2. Count half of the atom's bonding electrons.
3. Add steps 1 and 2 to obtain the electrons assigned to that atom.
4. Subtract the assigned electrons from the valence electrons to obtain the formal charge.

In equation form the formal charge is calculated as follows:

Formal charge = Valence e⁻ − [Number of nonbonding e⁻
+ ½ (Number of bonding e⁻)]   (5.1)

The formal charge calculations may be quickly checked since the formal charges on the atoms in a molecule must add up to zero, obeying the law of electroneutrality. For a polyatomic ion the formal charges must add up to the charge on the ion.

A molecule or polyatomic ion with the lowest possible formal charge on each atom is usually judged to be a more probable structure than one where the formal charge is larger. Consider the sulfate ion, SO_4^{2-}. Its Lewis structure may be drawn as shown in Figure 5.13.

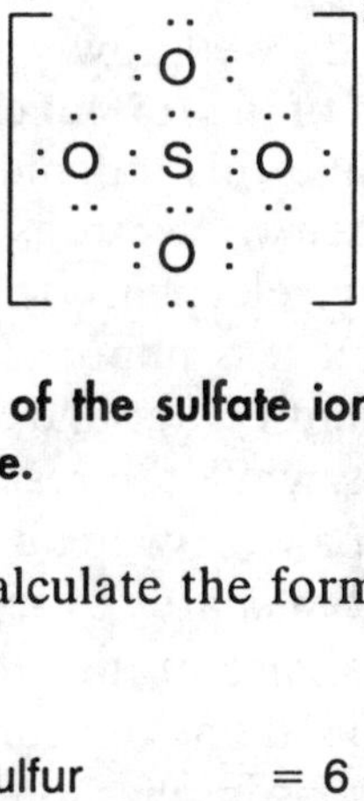

FIGURE 5.13. Lewis structure of the sulfate ion, constructed by the procedures described above.

From this structure we calculate the formal charges on sulfur and oxygen:

Formal charge on sulfur   = 6 − 0 − ½(8) = +2
Formal charge on **each** oxygen = 6 − 6 − ½(2) = −1

We find that the formal charge on each oxygen is −1 and the formal charge on sulfur is +2. These charges add up to the charge of the ion, as they should (+2 −1 −1 −1 −1 = −2). These formal charges are large, and an alternative structure should be sought. The structure shown in Figure 5.14 is one possible variation.

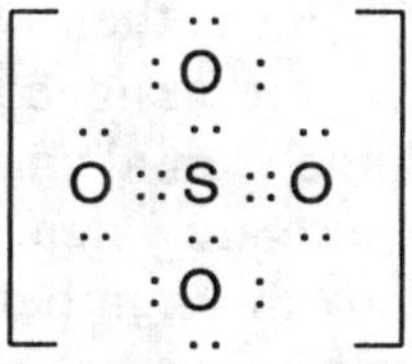

FIGURE 5.14. Alternative Lewis structures for the sulfate ion.

There are now two types of oxygen-sulfur bonds (two with a single bond and two with a double bond). When the formal charges are calculated, we have these results:

Formal charge on sulfur $= 6 - 0 - \frac{1}{2}(12) = 0$
Formal charge on each
   oxygen with double bond $= 6 - 4 - \frac{1}{2}(4) = 0$
Formal charge on each
   oxygen with single bond $= 6 - 6 - \frac{1}{2}(2) = -1$

This is the preferred structure since it has the minimum formal charges. The formal charges add up to the charge of the ion $(-1 - 1 = -2)$ and cannot be any lower.

Formal charges may also be used to deduce the appropriate structure for a compound that has many possible Lewis structures. For instance, the NOCl molecule can be drawn with the four structures shown in Figure 5.15.

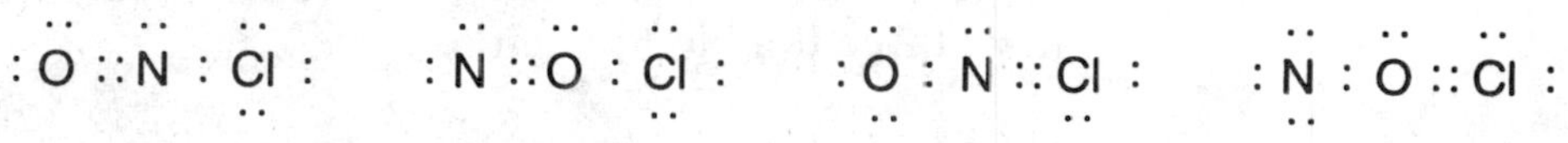

$$: \overset{..}{O} :: N : \overset{..}{\underset{..}{Cl}} : \qquad : N :: \overset{..}{\underset{..}{O}} : \overset{..}{\underset{..}{Cl}} : \qquad : \overset{..}{\underset{..}{O}} : N :: \overset{..}{\underset{..}{Cl}} : \qquad : N : \overset{..}{\underset{..}{O}} :: \overset{..}{\underset{..}{Cl}} :$$

Structure 1   Structure 2   Structure 3   Structure 4

FIGURE 5.15. Possible Lewis structures for the NOCl molecule.

To determine which of these structures is the most reasonable, we calculate the formal charges. Using the rules for determining these charges, we obtain the values in Table 5.1.

TABLE 5.1 Formal Charges on NOCl Structures

Element	Structure 1	Structure 2	Structure 3	Structure 4
Oxygen	0	+1	−1	+1
Nitrogen	0	−1	0	−2
Chlorine	0	0	+1	+1

From Table 5.1 we see that the first structure has the lowest formal charges on all atoms, and it is preferred. Structure 2 has larger formal charges, but also has a negative charge on nitrogen even though nitrogen is less electronegative than oxygen. This is not a reasonable situation since the more electronegative atom is expected to have the more negative formal charge. Structures 3 and 4 also have negative charges on the less electronegative elements as well as formal charges greater than zero. We therefore conclude that structure 1 is the most reasonable structure.

Exercise 5.2

In Exercise 5.1 the Lewis structures of the molecules and ions listed below were constructed. Now calculate the formal charges for each of those structures. Also, suggest which ones may have better structures, and draw them.

(a) CH_3Cl (c) PH_3 (e) H_2S (g) CO_3^{2-} (i) SO_3^{2-}
(b) CS_2 (d) SiF_4 (f) NO_3^- (h) PO_4^{2-} (j) ClO_4^-

Solution

(a) all zero
(b) all zero
(c) all zero
(d) all zero
(e) all zero
(f) $N = +1$ O(single bonded) $= -1$ O(double bonded) $= 0$
(g) $C = 0$ O(single bonded) $= -1$ O(double bonded) $= 0$
(h) $P = +1$ $O = -1$
(i) $S = +1$ $O = -1$
(j) $Cl = +3$ $O = -1$

It is possible to find better structures for (f), (h), (i), and (j). Structures (f), (h), and (i) should each have another double-bonded oxygen; (j) should have three double-bonded oxygens.

Resonance Structures

In the discussion above we found that, when there are several possible structures, the most reasonable one can be selected by using the concept of formal charges. At times we can construct several Lewis structures for a substance that are totally equivalent, even down to the formal charges on the atoms. Chemists call these structures **resonance structures**.

Most resonance structures are very similar for a given substance, usually differing only in the geometry of the molecule or ion. It is found experimentally that none of the resonance Lewis structures properly describes the molecule. The true properties of the substance are found by blending all of the resonance structures together. For example, the resonance of the SO_3 molecule is shown in Figure 5.16 with the three possible Lewis structures.

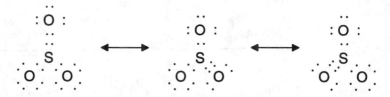

FIGURE 5.16. Three resonance structures of SO_3. They differ only in the position of the double bond.

It is important to understand the nature of resonance. In Figure 5.16, each SO_3 has two single bonds and one double bond. In a variety of experiments it is found that all of the sulfur-oxygen bonds are identical. The measured properties of these bonds indicate that they are not purely single bonds or purely double bonds. Sulfur-oxygen bonds have characteristics in between those of the single and those of the double bond. To properly visualize the SO_3 molecule we must think of three identical sulfur-oxygen bonds as a blend of bonds that is approximately two-thirds single bond and one-third double bond in character.

When discussing resonance, the benzene ring must be mentioned. The formula for benzene is C_6H_6. The molecule is a ring of six carbon atoms with one hydrogen atom attached to each. Assigning electrons to this skeleton results in the resonance structures shown in Figure 5.17.

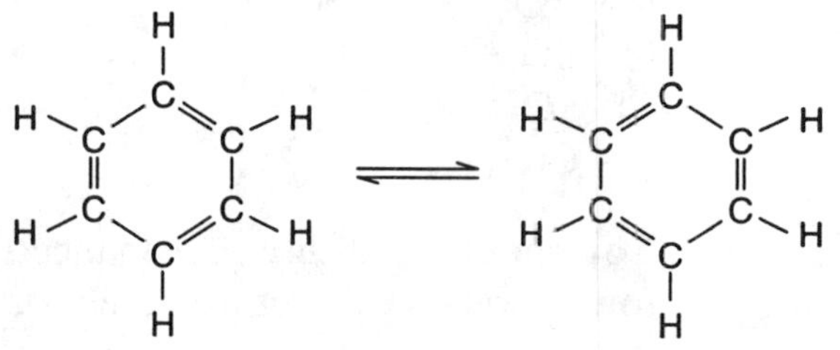

FIGURE 5.17. Structural formulas for the two resonance forms of benzene.

These structures are often summarized as shown in Figure 5.18. Each corner of the hexagon is assumed to represent a carbon atom, and a hydrogen atom is assumed to be attached to each carbon.

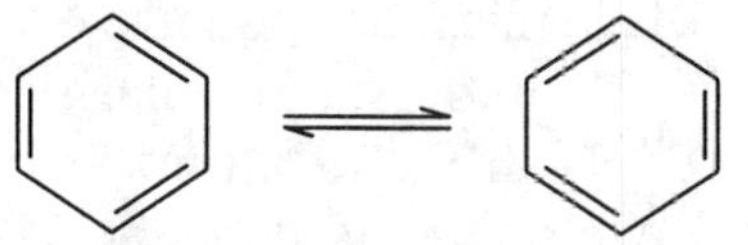

FIGURE 5.18. Abbreviated resonance structures of benzene.

Finally, since we know that the actual structure of the benzene molecule is not properly represented by either resonance structure, but rather involves a blending of the two, organic chemists often represent the benzene ring as shown in Figure 5.19.

FIGURE 5.19. Structure of benzene with a central circle representing the resonant nature of the molecule.

The circle within the ring reminds us that the double bonds are distributed (delocalized) over the entire molecule.

Benzene is one of many organic compounds classified as **aromatic molecules**. They definitely have a smell, but current chemical terminology recognizes the term *aromatic* as meaning that the structure contains one or more benzene rings. The benzene ring is found in such diverse compounds as aspirin, morphine, nicotine, proteins, saccharin, and many plastics. Benzene and many other aromatic compounds are considered carcinogens; however, a large number of beneficial compounds with aromatic character are not carcinogenic. Prudence dictates, however, that all aromatic compounds be treated with care in the laboratory.

Exercise 5.3

In exercises 5.1 and 5.2 simple Lewis structures were constructed and then modified, based on the formal charges. Use those structures to draw the resonance structures of the following ions:

(a) NO_3^-

(b) CO_3^{2-}

(c) PO_4^{3-}

(d) SO_3^{2-}

(e) ClO_4^-

Solution

You should find three resonance structures each for (a), (b), and (d) and four resonance structures each for (c) and (e).

Covalent Bond Polarity and Electronegativity

Electrons are shared equally only in a covalent bond between two identical atoms (e.g., H_2, F_2, and N_2). If the electrons are not shared equally by two atoms, they will spend more time localized near one atom or the other. The result is that the atom that attracts the electrons will be relatively more negative than the other atom. When this occurs, we say that the bond between the atoms is **polar** with a positive end and a negative end. Understanding bond polarities allows the chemist to explain many physical properties of chemical compounds. We will use this concept frequently in later chapters.

To understand polarities, we need a method to determine how effectively different atoms attract electrons toward themselves. Linus Pauling developed the concept of **electronegativity** to numerically represent the ability of an atom to attract electrons. Figure 5.20 shows the periodic table with the electronegativity value for each element. We see that electronegativity increases from left to right in each period of the periodic table. In addition, the electronegativity within any group increases from the bottom of the group to the top. In general, the electronegativity increases from the lower left corner of the periodic table up to the upper right corner. This is one of the important **diagonal relationships** in the periodic table.

H 2.1																	
Li 1.0	Be 1.5											B 2.0	C 2.5	N 3.1	O 3.5	F 4.0
Na 1.0	Mg 1.3											Al 1.5	Si 1.8	P 2.1	S 2.4	Cl 2.9
K 0.8	Ca 1.1	Sc 1.2	Ti 1.3	V 1.5	Cr 1.6	Mn 1.6	Fe 1.7	Co 1.7	Ni 1.8	Cu 1.8	Zn 1.7	Ga 1.8	Ge 2.0	As 2.2	Se 2.5	Br 2.8
Rb 0.8	Sr 1.0	Y 1.1	Zr 1.2	Nb 1.3	Mo 1.3	Tc 1.4	Ru 1.4	Rh 1.5	Pd 1.4	Ag 1.4	Cd 1.5	In 1.5	Sn 1.7	Sb 1.8	Te 2.0	I 2.5
Cs 0.7	Ba 0.9	La 1.1	Hf 1.2	Ta 1.4	W 1.4	Re 1.5	Os 1.5	Ir 1.6	Pt 1.5	Au 1.4	Hg 1.5	Tl 1.5	Pb 1.6	Bi 1.7	Po 1.8	At 2.2
Fr 0.7	Ra 0.9	Ac 1.0														

FIGURE 5.20 Periodic table showing the electronegativities of the elements.

The diagonal relationship of the electronegativities allows chemists to determine quickly which end of a bond is negative and which end is positive. In a bond, the element closest to fluorine will be relatively negative and the element furthest from fluorine will be relatively positive. Polarities are indicated by the symbols $\delta+$ and $\delta-$ for partially positive and partially negative atoms respectively. Full positive and negative charges are used only for ions. For example, the baron-oxygen bond would be written as $^{\delta+}B\!-\!O^{\delta-}$ to show that the boron atom is more positive than the oxygen atom.

Exercise 5.4

Without using Figure 5.20, indicate the positive and negative ends of each of the following bonds by the symbols $\delta+$ and $\delta-$:
(a) S—O
(b) C—N
(c) S—P
(d) C—F
(e) Si—0
(f) H—Br
(g) H—O

Solution

Using the diagonal relationships in the periodic table, we identify the positive and negative ends as follows:
(a) $^{\delta+}S\!-\!O^{\delta-}$
(b) $^{\delta+}C\!-\!N^{\delta-}$
(c) $^{\delta-}S\!-\!P^{\delta+}$
(d) $^{\delta+}C\!-\!F^{\delta-}$
(e) $^{\delta+}Si\!-\!O^{\delta-}$
(f) $^{\delta+}H\!-\!Br^{\delta-}$
(g) $^{\delta+}H\!-\!O^{\delta-}$

The electronegativity table in Figure 5.20 gives numerical data that may be used to evaluate the magnitude of bond polarity. This is done by taking the absolute value of the difference in the electronegativities of the two atoms participating in a bond. We may call this value delta EN or, in written form, ΔEN:

$$\Delta EN = \text{Atom with largest electronegativity} - \text{Atom with smallest electronegativity} \qquad (5.2)$$

The larger the value of ΔEN, the greater the polarity of the bond. If ΔEN is zero, the bond is considered to be nonpolar.

Exercise 5.5

For the bonds in Exercise 5.4, determine the ΔEN values, and predict which bond is the least polar and which is the most polar.

Solution

(a) 1.7
(b) 0.6
(c) 0.3
(d) 1.5
(e) 1.7
(f) 0.7
(g) 1.4

The S—O and Si—O bonds are the most polar, and the S—P bond is the least polar.

Without an electronegativity table, it is possible to determine which of two bonds is the more polar if the bonds have one atom in common. The more polar bond will be the one where the second atom is furthest in the periodic table from the common atom. For instance, the nitrogen-fluorine bond is more polar than the oxygen-fluorine bond since nitrogen is further from fluorine than is oxygen.

Exercise 5.6

Using a periodic table, but not a table of electronegativities, estimate, for each of the following pairs, which bond is more polar:
(a) C—N or C—O
(b) H—Cl or H—Br
(c) S—O or S—Br
(d) H—S or H—O
(e) P—Br or S—Br

Solution

The more polar bond in each pair belongs to (a) C—O, (b) H—Cl, (c) S—O, (d) H—O, and (e) P—Br.

Electronegativity and Ionic Character

At one end of the polarity scale are the completely **nonpolar** bonds between diatomic elements. We may visualize ionic compounds as being at the other end of the polarity scale since the electrons are actually transferred from one atom to another. From the table of electronegativities in Figure 5.2, we see that the largest ΔEN is 3.3 for the ionic compound FrF. The well-known ionic compounds NaCl and $CaBr_2$ have ΔEN values of 3.0 and 1.7, respectively. The ΔEN of a bond has been used to estimate the percentage ionic character of a bond. Chemists say that a ΔEN of 1.7 represents a bond that is 50 percent ionic and 50 percent covalent in character. A bond with a ΔEN of 1.7 or greater is considered ionic. Bonds with ΔEN's of less than 1.7 are polar covalent, and those for which ΔEN is zero are nonpolar bonds.

Bond Order

Bond order is a term that refers to the average number of bonds that an atom makes in all of its bonds to other atoms. From the Lewis structures of the diatomic elements in Figure 5.2, we see that fluorine (F_2) and chlorine (Cl_2) have one bond each and a bond order of 1. Oxygen (O_2) has a double bond and a bond order of 2, and nitrogen (N_2) has a triple bond and thus a bond order of 3. In the SO_3 resonance structures there is a total of four bonds: two single bonds and one double bond. Since the sulfur is bonded to three oxygen atoms, the average number of bonds that sulfur has with its oxygen atoms is $\frac{\text{four bonds}}{\text{three O atoms}}$, and the bond order of sulfur is $\frac{4}{3}$. In benzene, the bond order for each carbon atom is $\frac{3}{2}$.

Exercise 5.7

Determine the bond order of the central atom of each of the following compounds. You may use the structures determined in Exercises 5.1 and 5.2.
(a) CH_3Cl (c) PH_3 (e) H_2S (g) CO_3^{2-} (i) SO_3^{2-}
(b) CS_2 (d) SiF_4 (f) NO_3^- (h) PO_4^{3-} (j) ClO_4^-

Solution

If we use the simple Lewis structures, we obtain:

(a) 1   (c) 1   (e) 1   (g) $\frac{4}{3}$ (i) 1
(b) 2   (d) 1   (f) $\frac{4}{3}$ (h) 1

If we use the best formal charge structures, we obtain:

(a) 1   (c) 1   (e) 1   (g) $\frac{4}{3}$ (i) $\frac{4}{3}$
(b) 2   (d) 1   (f) $\frac{5}{3}$ (h) $\frac{5}{4}$ (j) $\frac{7}{4}$

Bond Strength, Bond Energy, and Bond Length

Just as two ropes are twice as strong as one rope, a double bond is almost twice as strong as a single bond. The strength of a covalent bond is expressed as its bond energy. When two atoms are covalently bonded together, they vibrate in the same way that a spring vibrates. The frequency of this vibration is related to the two masses attached to the ends of the spring and to the strength of the spring itself. Since we know the masses of the two atoms, the frequency of vibration will be related to the strength of the bond. Frequency is related to bond energy (bond strength) by Equation 5.3, where the energy is equal to Planck's constant times the frequency of vibration.

$$E = h\nu \qquad (5.3)$$

Bond vibrations may be observed in the infrared spectral region by using an infrared spectrometer. Infrared spectra confirm that single bonds have the lowest energy, double bonds have a higher energy, and triple bonds have the highest energy.

Another method used to measure bond energies involves measurement of the energy released when organic compounds are burned. Ethane, C_2H_6, contains only single bonds; ethylene, C_2H_4, contains a double bond; and acetylene, C_2H_2, contains a triple bond. When burned, ethane yields 1540 kilojoules, ethylene 1387 kilojoules, and acetylene 1305 kilojoules of energy. The fact that the lowest energy is released by acetylene is taken to indicate that this compound's bonds are already in the highest energy configuration. The high energy of combustion for ethane, on the other hand, indicates that its bonds have lower energy to start with and can release more energy upon combustion.

The length of a covalent bond may be measured in several ways. One way is by X-ray crystallography, as described in Chapter 8. The positions of the atoms in a crystal can be determined based on the diffraction of X rays by a crystal. Another method involves the fact that the frequency of vibration and the length of the vibrating medium are related. As described above, these vibrations are measured using infrared spectroscopy. Whatever method is used to measure bond lengths, consistent results are obtained. In particular, a single bond has the longest length and a triple bond has the shortest.

We have discussed resonance structures and the fact that the actual structure of a molecule is a blend of all equivalent resonance structures. In these molecules we do not have pure single, double, or triple bonds. We can, however, calculate bond order, which represents the average number of bonds per atom. Bond order is related to bond strength and length also. The general rule is that the greater the bond order, the shorter the bond length. Table 5.2 lists some typical bond lengths and energies.

TABLE 5.2 Typical Bond Lengths and Energies

Bond	Bond Order	Bond Length (pm)	Bond Energy (kJ mol^{-1})
C—C	1	154	347
C=C	2	134	612
C≡C	3	120	820
N—N	1	145	159
N=N	2	123	418
N≡N	3	110	914
C—O	1	143	351
C=O	2	120	715

Nomenclature

The naming of covalently bonded binary molecules (these are predominately molecules with two nonmetals) is quite different from the naming of ionic compounds, and the two methods should not be confused. In addition, many of these covalent substances were discovered long before the modern method of naming compounds was developed. Common covalent compounds often have trivial (older) and systematic (modern) names. Some important trivial names are shown in Table 5.3, along with their modern equivalents.

TABLE 5.3 Trivial and Systematic Names of Some Common Covalent Molecules

Molecule	Trivial Name	Systematic Name
H_2O	water	dihydrogen oxide*
CH_4	methane	carbon tetrahydride*
N_2O	nitrous oxide	dinitrogen oxide
NO	nitric oxide	nitrogen oxide
N_2O_3	nitrous anhydride	dinitrogen trioxide
N_2O_5	nitric anhydride	dinitrogen pentoxide
NH_3	ammonia	nitrogen trihydride*
AsH_3	arsine	arsenic trihydride
H_2O_2	hydrogen peroxide	dihydrogen dioxide*
N_2H_4	hydrazine	dinitrogen tetrahydride

*These names are almost never used.

In the systematic naming of covalent compounds, the prefixes in the names in column 3 of Table 4.1 indicate the number of each atom present in a molecular formula. Some of these prefixes are indicated in the systematic names in Table 5.3. Other examples of the use of these prefixes can also be given. The formula for carbon dioxide is CO_2, and the name indicates one carbon atom and, because of the prefix *di*−, two oxygen atoms. Sulfur forms two compounds, SO_2 and SO_3, named sulfur dioxide and sulfur trioxide, respectively. Again the prefixes, *di*− and *tri*−, indicate the number of oxygen atoms bound to the sulfur in the two compounds. The compound N_2O_4 has two nitrogen and four oxygen atoms and is named dinitrogen tetroxide.

Exercise 5.8

Name each of the following covalent molecules:
(a) SiO_2 (c) N_2O_3 (e) PBr_5 (g) $BrCl_3$
(b) P_4O_{10} (d) SF_4 (f) XeF_4 (h) S_4N_4

Solution

(a) sulfur dioxide   (e) phosphorus pentabromide
(b) tetraphosphorus decaoxide   (f) xenon tetrafluoride
(c) dinitrogen trioxide   (g) bromine trichloride
(d) sulfur tetrafluoride   (h) tetrasulfur tetranitride

Exercise 5.9

Give the formula for each of the following compounds:
(a) diboron tetrabromide   (e) diphosphorus pentoxide
(b) boron trifluoride   (f) carbon disulfide
(c) carbon tetrafluoride   (g) sulfur trioxide
(d) carbon monoxide   (h) nitrogen triiodide

Solution

(a) B_2Br_4 (c) CF_4 (e) P_2O_5 (g) SO_3
(b) BF_3 (d) CO (f) CS_2 (h) NI_3

Additional rules and names for compounds are given in Chapter 14 on acids and bases and in Chapter 15 on common organic compounds.

Molecular Geometry

Once a valid Lewis structure has been determined, the overall geometry of a simple molecule with one central atom can be established. The process can be extended to very large macromolecules, such as proteins and DNA, by determining the geometries around individual atoms and then combining them to obtain the entire structure. This overall geometry is extremely important in understanding the properties of chemical compounds. The key to the discovery of DNA's double helix was the geometric structures of the four bases, which must hydrogen-bond to each other in order to hold the total structure together.

The **valence-shell electron-pair repulsion theory** (VSEPR theory) allows us to determine the three-dimensional shapes of covalently bonded molecules with a minimum of information. This theory states that the geometry around each atom will depend on the repulsion of the valence-shell electrons (bonding electrons and nonbonding pairs) away from each other. This repulsion, due to the negative charges, results in electron pairs being aligned as far away from each other as possible.

Basic Structures

To determine the three-dimensional geometry around a central atom, A, all we need to know is how many atoms, X, are covalently bonded to it. The one restriction is that central atom A must have no nonbonding pairs of electrons. Table 5.4 lists the **basic structures** for the six possible geometries.

TABLE 5.4 Basic Structures for Six Geometries

Notation	Shape	Example	Angle(s)
AX	Linear	HBr	180°
AX$_2$	Linear	CS$_2$	180°
AX$_3$	Planar triangle	BCl$_3$	120°
AX$_4$	Tetrahedron	CCl$_4$	109.5°
AX$_5$	Trigonal bipyramid	PCl$_5$	120°,90°
AX$_6$	Octahedron	XeF$_6$	90°

In this table we use the AX$_n$ notation to represent the number of atoms, X, attached to the central atom, A.

The angles listed in this table are the angles between the bonds, assuming that the central atom is the vertex of the angle. For structures AX to AX$_4$ every bond is equidistant from every other one. For the AX$_5$ and AX$_6$ structures bond angles are measured between the nearest neighbors. For the AX$_5$ structure, the 120° angle is for the three equatorial atoms and the 90° angle is the angle between the axial atoms and the equatorial atoms. Figure 5.21 illustrates these shapes in diagram format. The AX structure is omitted from many texts as being trivial since any molecule that contains only two atoms must be linear.

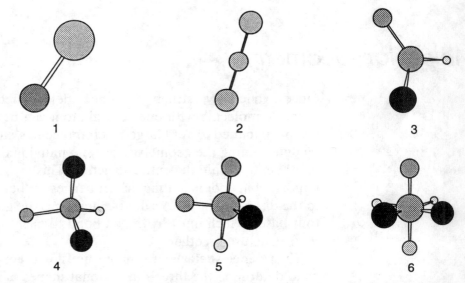

FIGURE 5.21. Perspective diagrams of the six basic geometric structures. Darkest atoms are closest to the viewer, structures are tilted to show all atoms. 1—linear diatomic; 2—linear triatomic; 3—planar triangle; 4—tetrahedron; 5—trigonal bipyramid; 6—octahedron. For diagrams 5 and 6 the axial atoms are at the top and bottom of the figures, while the equatorial atoms are in the center.

The geometry around a central atom that does not have any nonbonding electron pairs is determined by counting the atoms bonded to it. For instance, three atoms bound to a central atom with no nonbonding pairs must be a planar triangle. Five atoms bound to a central atom must have the shape of a trigonal bipyramid.

Derived Structures

Nonbonding electron pairs on the central atom take up space, just as an atom does. In fact, a nonbonding electron pair takes up slightly more space than an atom. As a result, we count the number of nonbonding pairs, as well as the atoms attached to the central atom, to determine the *basic structure* as we did above. Since the nonbonding pairs of electrons are not "seen" when a structure is drawn, the actual geometries of the atoms we do see will be only part of this basic structure. The part that we see is called the **derived structure.** The possible derived structures are listed in Table 5.5. The symbol E in the notation represents a nonbonding pair of electrons on the central atom.

TABLE 5.5 Derived Structures with Nonbonding Electron Pairs on the Central Atom

Basic Structure Notation	Derived Structure Notation	Shape	Example	Angle(s)
AX	AE	Single atom	None	None
AX_2	AXE	Linear diatomic	CN^-	180°
AX_3	AX_2E	Bent	$SnCl_2$	120°
AX_4	AX_3E	Triangular pyramid	NH_3	109.5°
AX_4	AX_2E_2	Bent	H_2O	109.5°
AX_5	AX_4E	Distorted tetrahedron	SF_4	120°, 90°
AX_5	AX_3E_2	T-shape	ICl_3	90°
AX_5	AX_2E_3	Linear	I_3^-	180°
AX_6	AX_5E	Square pyramid	IF_5	90°
AX_6	AX_4E_2	Square planar	XeF_4	90°

Since the first two entries in Table 5.5 represent single atoms and diatomic substances, their structures need not be drawn. The geometries that correspond to the other derived structures are shown in Figures 5.22–5.25.

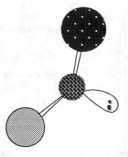

FIGURE 5.22. Bent AX_2E derived structure, showing an electron pair occupying the space formerly occupied by an atom in the basic AX_3 (trigonal planar) structure.

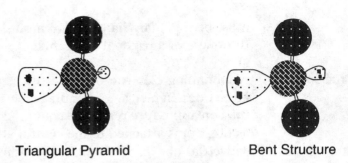

Triangular Pyramid   Bent Structure

FIGURE 5.23. Pictorial representation of the AX$_3$E (triangular pyramid) and AX$_2$E$_2$ (bent) derived structures that are derived from the AX$_4$ (tetrahedral) basic structure.

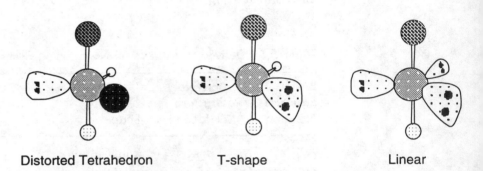

Distorted Tetrahedron   T-shape   Linear

FGURE 5.24. The three possible derived structures obtained from the AX$_5$ (trigonal bipyramid) basic structure. Notice that the equatorial atoms are replaced by electron pairs.

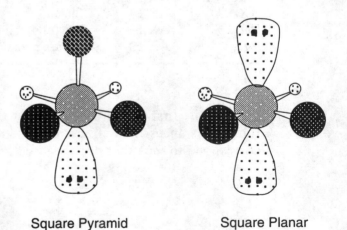

Square Pyramid   Square Planar

FIGURE 5.25. The two derived structures obtained from the AX$_6$ (octahedral) basic structure. Note that the second atom replaced by an electron pair is on the opposite side of the molecule, so that the electron clouds have the extra space they need.

In Table 5.5 and Figures 5.22 and 5.23 we find two bent structures, AX$_2$E and AX$_2$E$_2$. The bond angles for these two structures will be very different, and we can distinguish the structures on the basis of their angles. Since the AX$_2$E bent structure is derived from the trigonal planar AX$_3$ structure, we expect its angle to be approximately 120°. The AX_2E_2 structure is derived from the tetrahedral AX_4 basic structure; and, bond angles of approximately 109.5° are expected for structures related to the tetrahedron.

In forming the derived structures from the basic structures, we are, in effect, replacing one or more atoms with pairs of nonbonding electrons. Up to the AX_4 structure, it does not matter which atom is replaced by an electron pair; we get the same derived structure. However, AX_5 and AX_6 will have different shapes, when we make the derived structures, depending on which atom is replaced by a nonbonding electron pair. The actual shapes of the molecules can be explained by the fact that a nonbonding pair of electrons takes up relatively more space than a bonded atom. In the AX_5 structure, the nonbonding electron pairs will replace the equatorial atoms since more room is available (120° between the atoms compared to 90° for the axial atoms) for the electron cloud. In the AX_6 structure, it does not matter which atom is replaced by the first nonbonding electron pair; the result is always a square pyramid. The second nonbonding electron pair always replaces the atom opposite the first nonbonding electron pair. This positioning allows the nonbonding electron pairs the most room possible on the molecule.

When determining the geometry around a central atom, it is necessary to count the number of atoms bound to the central atom and the number of nonbonding pairs of electrons, if any. We now understand why it is so important to show nonbonding pairs of electrons in Lewis structures. Of particular importance are the nonbonding pairs on the central atom.

Exercise 5.10

Construct the Lewis structure and predict the shape of each of the following molecules and ions:
(a) CH_3Cl (c) PH_3 (e) H_2S (g) CO_3^{2-} (i) SO_3^{2-}
(b) CS_2 (d) SiF_4 (f) NO_3^- (h) PO_4^{3-} (j) ClO_4^-

Solution

The shapes are as follows:
(a) tetrahedron   (e) bent   (i) tetrahedron
(b) linear   (f) triangular planar   (j) tetrahedron
(c) triangular pyramid   (g) triangular planar
(d) tetrahedron   (h) tetrahedron

These shapes are the same whether we use the simple Lewis structure or the structures optimized for the best formal charges.

Complex Structures

Geometries of more complex molecules are constructed by determining the geometry around each atom in sequence and then stringing the geometries together. Organic (carbon-based) compounds often have complex structures where these geometries are very important. The three-dimensional structures of these compounds often help define chemical, physical, and biological properties.

Carbon, with its four valence electrons, can form a maximum of four covalent bonds with four other atoms. It can also bond to three atoms as long as one of the bonds is a double bond. In bonding to two atoms, carbon will form either two double bonds, as in carbon dioxide, CO_2, or one single bond and one triple bond, as in hydrogen cyanide, HCN. In all instances, carbon never has a nonbonding pair of electrons. As a result, a carbon bonded to four atoms is tetrahedral; if bonded to three atoms, trigonal planar; and if bonded to two atoms, linear.

For instance, the molecule of ethylene, CH_2CH_2 has the structure shown in Figure 5.26.

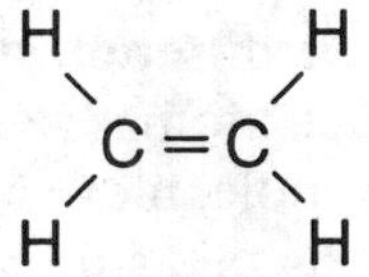

$$\begin{array}{ccc} H & & H \\ \diagdown & & \diagup \\ & C = C & \\ \diagup & & \diagdown \\ H & & H \end{array}$$

FIGURE 5.26.   Ethylene molecule.

Since each carbon atom is bonded to only three atoms (two hydrogen and one carbon), the carbon atoms must each have a trigonal planar geometry. We will see the reason later, but both planes are lined up so that this molecule is perfectly flat. We can also predict that the benzene ring shown in Figure 5.19 must be flat also since each of its six carbon atoms is trigonal planar.

When we have a molecule such as butane, $CH_3CH_2CH_2CH_3$, we may draw the structure shown in Figure 5.27.

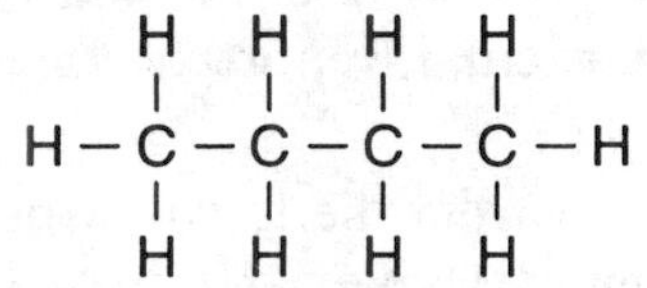

$$\begin{array}{ccccccc} & H & H & H & H & \\ & | & | & | & | & \\ H - & C - & C - & C - & C & - H \\ & | & | & | & | & \\ & H & H & H & H & \end{array}$$

FIGURE 5.27.   Line structure of butane, C_4H_{10}.

Each carbon atom is bonded to four other atoms; therefore, the geometries of the carbon atoms are all tetrahedral. Placing the four tetrahedral structures together, we obtain the three-dimensional structure illustrated in Figure 5.28.

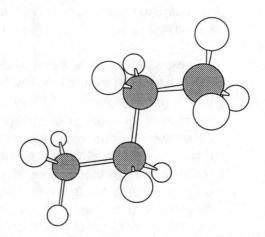

FIGURE 5.28.   Three-dimensional computer-generated structure for butane, showing the tetrahedral arrangement of atoms around each carbon (shaded circles).

Since three-dimensional structures are difficult to draw on paper, organic chemists often find it convenient to build models of these structures so that they can inspect their features more easily.

Oxygen atoms in organic compounds always have two nonbonding pairs of electrons. An oxygen bonded to two atoms will have an AX_2E_2 derived structure (bent), and a double-bonded oxygen with an AXE_2 derived structure (linear) will be bonded to only a single atom. Nitrogen atoms in organic compounds will have one nonbonding pair of electrons. The nitrogen atom will have an AX_3E structure (triangular pyramid) if bonded to three other atoms. When bonded to only two atoms, one with a double bond, it will have an AX_2E structure (bent).

Exercise 5.11

Predict the geometry around each of the carbon atoms in this molecule:

$$\underset{}{CH_3CH_2CH} = \overset{\overset{\displaystyle CH_3}{\displaystyle |}}{C}\underset{\underset{\displaystyle OH}{\displaystyle |}}{CH_2C} = O$$

Solution

From left to right along the main chain, the geometries are tetrahedral, tetrahedral, triangular planar, triangular planar, tetrahedral, triangular planar, respectively. The CH_3 above the molecule is tetrahedral. Using this information, it is possible to make a more realistic drawing, or molecular model, of the compound.

Molecular Polarity

Bond polarities depend on the electronegativities of the two elements bonded together. Very few molecules are diatomic, meaning that for most molecules more than one bond must be considered in determining the polarity of the molecule as a whole. These bonds are arranged geometrically in space as described in the preceding section. The result is that, even if a bond is polar, the molecule as a whole may or may not be polar. There are four general rules for determining whether a molecule is polar.

1. A molecule that is symmetrical is nonpolar. It does not matter how polar the individual bonds are.
2. A nonsymmetrical molecule is polar if the bonds are polar.
3. A molecule with more than one type of atom attached to the central atom is often nonsymmetrical and therefore polar.
4. A central atom with nonbonding electron pairs is often nonsymmetrical and polar.

When determining the polarity of a molecule, we must remember that there is only one positive end and one negative end, directly opposite each other. We recognize the CH_3Cl and CBr_4 molecules as tetrahedral structures. As Figure 5.29 indicates, CH_3Cl is polar because it is not symmetrical, and CBr_4 is symmetrical and nonpolar.

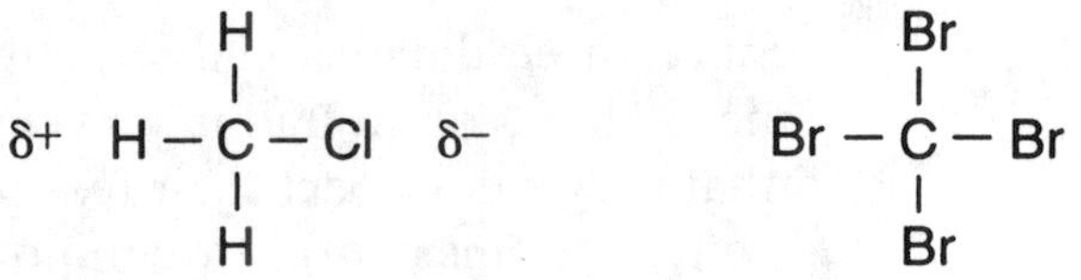

$$\begin{matrix} & & H & & & & & Br \\ & & | & & & & & | \\ \delta+ & H- & C- & Cl & \delta- & & Br- & C- & Br \\ & & | & & & & & | \\ & & H & & & & & Br \end{matrix}$$

FIGURE 5.29. Line structures of CH_3Cl, showing the polarity of the molecule, and of CBr_4, showing its symmetry and nonpolarity.

From our knowledge of electronegativities we may predict that the negative end of the CH_3Cl molecule is located near the chlorine atom and that the positive end is opposite the chlorine atom in a region of space between the three hydrogen atoms.

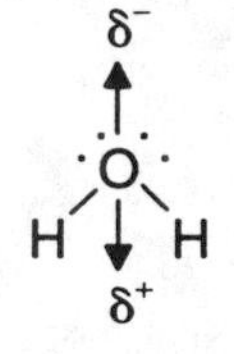

FIGURE 5.30. Structure of water and its polarity.

For the water molecule we may draw the structure shown in Figure 5.30. The electronegativity of the oxygen indicates that it is the negative end of the molecule and that the region of space opposite the oxygen, between the two hydrogen atoms, is the positive end.

Exercise 5.12

Construct the Lewis structure and predict the polarity of each of the following:
(a) CH_3Cl (c) PH_3 (e) H_2S (g) CO_3^{2-} (i) SO_3^{2-}
(b) CS_2 (d) SiF_4 (f) NO_3^- (h) PO_4^{3-} (j) ClO_4^-

Solution

(a) polar with Cl the negative end.   (e) polar with S the negative end
(b) nonpolar   (f–j) nonpolar because of resonance;
(c) polar with P the negative end   charge on ion is distributed
(d) nonpolar   evenly over the ion. These
       ions are charged but not polar.

Covalent Bond Formation

Orbital Overlap Model (Sigma Bonds)

Up to now we have constructed molecules only according to the octet rule. We now turn to the actual nature of the covalent bond and the ways the electrons are shared in these bonds. When an electron is present in an atom, its orbital is called an **atomic orbital**. When a bond is formed, the shared electrons merge into a new orbital called a **molecular orbital**, in which the electrons are paired and localized around two nuclei. In the formation of hydrogen, H_2, from two hydrogen atoms we visualize the process as shown in Figure 5.31. Here H represents the nucleus of the hydrogen atom, and

FIGURE 5.31. Combination of two hydrogen atoms to form the hydrogen molecule. The electrons in the hydrogen atoms have opposing spins so that they can pair in the molecular orbital.

the shading indicates that the spin of each electron in one hydrogen atom is the opposite of the spin in the other atom. When the electrons are paired with opposite spins, the molecular orbital is formed. The dashed line between the two hydrogen nuclei in this orbital is an imaginary line called the **internuclear axis**. A bond of this type has a high electron density along the internuclear axis. A bond with a high electron density along the internuclear axis is called a **sigma bond** (σ bond). We may view this molecular orbital as the overlap of two s orbitals (Figure 5.32).

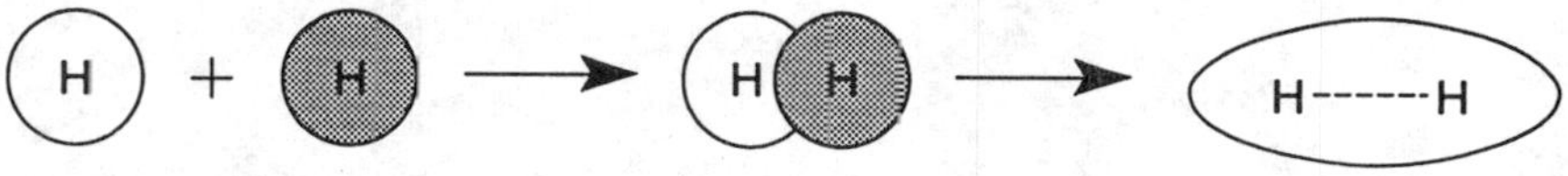

FIGURE 5.32. Overlap of two s atomic orbitals to form a molecular orbital in hydrogen.

Sigma bonds may also be formed by the overlap of an s orbital and a p orbital (Figure 5.33), as in the formation of hydrogen fluoride, HF, or by the overlap of two p orbitals (Figure 5.34).

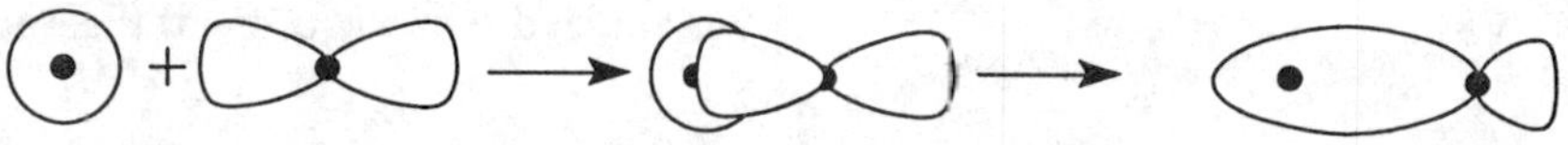

FIGURE 5.33. Overlap of an s orbital and a p orbital to form a sigma bond in a substance such as HF.

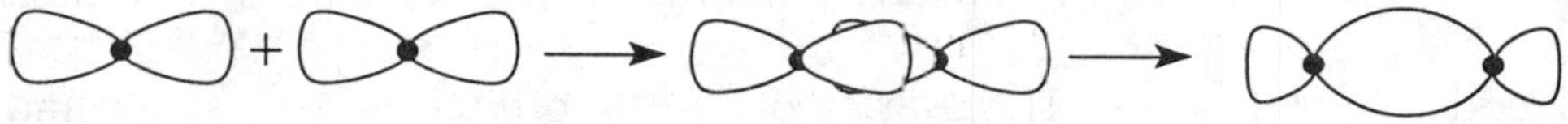

FIGURE 5.34. Overlap of two p orbitals to form a sigma bond in a molecule such as F_2.

Orbital Overlap Model (Pi Bonds)

We have described the three important ways in which sigma bonds are formed. Every covalent bond has one and only one sigma bond. If a compound has a double or triple covalent bond, additional overlap of orbitals is needed. Such a bond, called a **pi bond** (π bond), is formed by the sideways overlap of two p orbitals as shown in Figure 5.35.

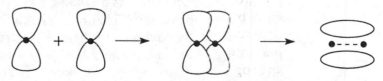

FIGURE 5.35. Sideways overlap of p orbitals to form a pi bond.

The **pi bond** has its electron density arranged in two electron clouds, one above and one below the internuclear axis (dashed line). When arranged in this manner, the electrons in the pi bond do not interfere with the electrons in the sigma bond.

A double bond involves one sigma bond and one pi bond. A triple bond between two atoms may be formed by adding a second pi bond, which has its two electron clouds centered behind and in front of the two nuclei.

If we place one atom in front of the other and look down the internuclear axis, the positions of the sigma and pi bonds are as shown in Figure 5.36.

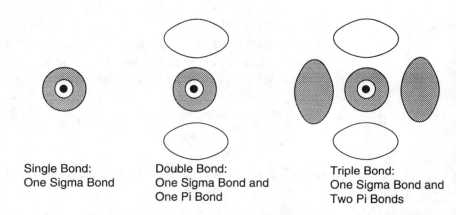

Single Bond:
One Sigma Bond

Double Bond:
One Sigma Bond and
One Pi Bond

Triple Bond:
One Sigma Bond and
Two Pi Bonds

FIGURE 5.36. End view of the single, double, and triple bonds, looking down the internuclear axis. The dot and white circle represent the two nuclei. The shaded circle represents the sigma bond present in all three bonds. The two white ovals represent one of the pi bonds, and the two shaded ovals represent the second pi bond.

From this discussion we see that a single covalent bond is always a sigma bond. A double covalent bond has one sigma and one pi bond, while a triple covalent bond has one sigma and two pi bonds. All of these bonds are arranged so that their electron clouds do not interfere with each other.

Hybrid
Orbital Model

The overlap of s and p orbitals to form sigma and pi bonds works well to describe some features of the covalent bond and for molecules with two and sometimes three atoms. Larger molecules require another model of bond formation.

To understand why a new model is needed, we need to review the implications of the overlap model. First, p orbitals are oriented at 90° from each other and s orbitals are spherical, having no directionality. If all covalent compounds were formed from the overlap of these orbitals, we would expect all covalent molecules to have 90° bond angles. As we have seen, however, few molecular geometries have angles of 90°. Second, even a simple molecule such as methane, CH_4, cannot be adequately explained by the overlap model. We know that methane is a tetrahedral molecule with four totally equivalent C-H bonds. Using the overlap method, we see that the carbon in methane has only two unpaired p electrons (the s electrons are paired), and we would expect the formation of the CH_2 molecule. The bonds would be oriented at a 90° angle since p orbitals are

90° apart. If we allowed the two *s* electrons to unpair so that they could also form bonds, we could obtain the CH_4 molecule. However, the bond angles would still not be correct, and we would expect two distinctly different C-H bond types in methane, one from the overlap of *s* orbitals and the other from the overlap of *p* orbitals. Our new model must be able to explain correctly the molecular geometries and bonding in larger molecules.

sp³ Hybrid Orbitals

The problem posed by the CH_4 molecule requires that we develop a better model of sigma bond formation. To construct this model, we postulate the formation of hybrid orbitals. A **hybrid orbital** may be defined as a set of orbitals with identical properties formed from the combination of two or more different orbitals with different energies. The orbital diagram of carbon is presented in Figure 5.37, along with the conversion of the *s* and *p* electrons into hybrid orbitals called *sp³* orbitals.

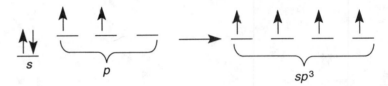

FIGURE 5.37.   **The *s* and *p* electrons of the carbon atom and their conversion into the *sp³* hybrid orbitals used in bonding.**

The designation *sp³* indicates that one *s* and three *p* orbitals have been combined to form the hybrid orbital. In this orbital diagram for carbon, the *p* electrons are shown as having a higher energy than the *s* electrons by placing the orbitals at different levels. When carbon forms methane, its electrons reorganize into the four identical *sp³* hybrid orbitals shown on the right. The energy of the electrons in the hybrid orbitals lies between the original *s* and *p* energies, as shown. When the *sp³* hybrid orbitals form, their orientation is tetrahedral. Overlap of the four identical *sp³* electrons with electrons from hydrogen atoms forms the tetrahedral methane molecule as we know it. Any molecule whose basic structure is the tetrahedron will have *sp³* hybrid orbitals. This includes the CH_4, NH_3, and H_2O molecules described previously.

sp² Hybrid Orbitals

Formaldehyde, CH_2O, is a carbon compound having single bonds to the hydrogen atoms and a double bond with the oxygen atom. Carbon has three sigma bonds and one pi bond in this compound. The structure is triangular planar because there are no nonbonding electron pairs on carbon. The orbitals in this compound are designated as *sp²* hybrids. The formation of these orbitals can be diagrammed as shown in Figure 5.38. Here we see that three electrons are in three identical orbitals, called *sp²* hybrids. The remaining electron stays in an unhybridized *p* orbital and overlaps with a *p* orbital on the oxygen atom to form the pi bond in the C=O double bond.

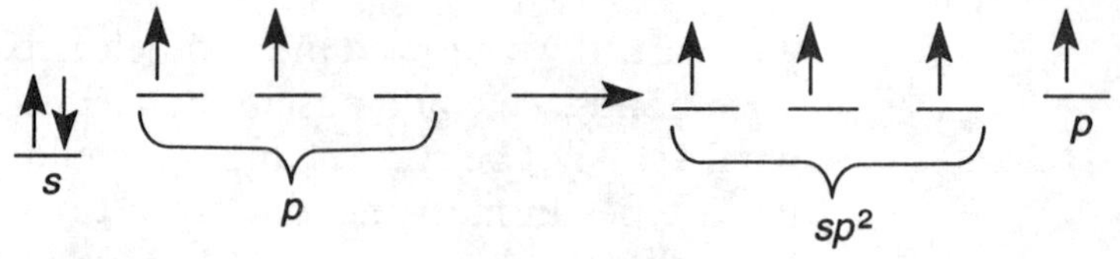

FIGURE 5.38.   Formation of the *sp²* hybrid orbitals for carbon.

In the earlier discussion of the ethylene and benzene molecules, it was stated that these molecules are totally flat. Figure 5.39 shows why. In order for the *p* orbitals to overlap, they must be aligned as shown. This requirement fixes the remaining *sp²* bonds in one plane, resulting in the planar ethylene molecule. Proper alignment of the *p* orbitals in benzene forces this molecule also to be planar.

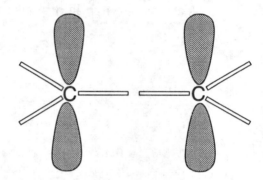

FIGURE 5.39.   Two carbon atoms with *sp²* hybridization. The thin lines are the triangular planar *sp²* bonding orbitals. The large orbitals are the unhybridized *p* orbitals that overlap to form a pi bond.

sp Hybrid Orbitals

Carbon dioxide, O=C=O, has two sigma bonds and two pi bonds. The hybridization for this molecule is shown in Figure 5.40.

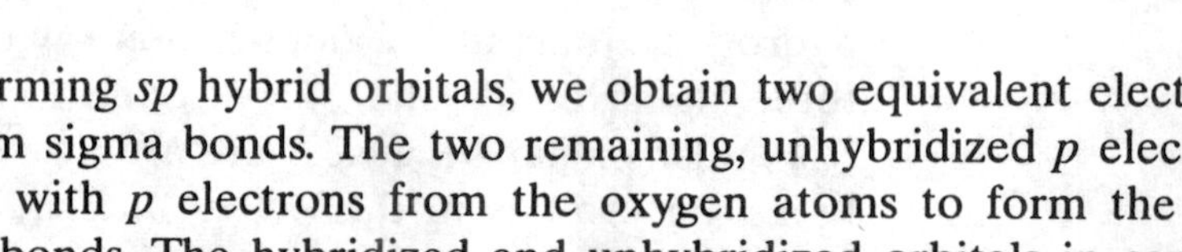

FIGURE 5.40.   Hybridization of carbon to produce the *sp* hybrid orbitals. The two unhybridized *p* electrons are available to form pi bonds.

In forming *sp* hybrid orbitals, we obtain two equivalent electrons that can form sigma bonds. The two remaining, unhybridized *p* electrons can overlap with *p* electrons from the oxygen atoms to form the required double bonds. The hybridized and unhybridized orbitals in carbon's *sp²* hybrid may be pictured as shown in Figure 5.41. This diagram shows the *p* orbitals available for pi bonding. Since there are two *p* orbitals, two additional pi bonds can form. These two pi bonds can be directed toward different atoms to form compounds, such as O=C=O, with two double

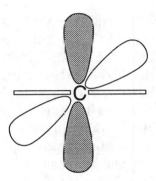

FIGURE 5.41. The *sp* hybrid orbitals, shown as thin lines. The remaining two *p* orbitals (one is shaded, and the other is not) are shown as larger lobes. These *p* orbitals overlap with other *p* orbitals to form two pi bonds to the carbon.

bonds. They can also be directed toward the same atom to form a triple bond, as in the cyanide ion, $C\equiv N^-$.

*dsp*³ Hybrid Orbitals

The *dsp*³ notation indicates a hybrid that has five equivalent orbitals with at least one electron in each orbital. Since carbon has only four valence electrons, it cannot form a *dsp*³ hybrid. In addition, only atoms that have available *d* orbitals can form these hybrids. This requirement means that an element must be in period 3 or higher. Phosphorus, which has five valence electrons and is in period 3, is a typical element that can form the *dsp*³ hybrid. The orbital diagram for phosphorus in Figure 5.42 shows the *3d* orbitals, even though they are empty before hybridization.

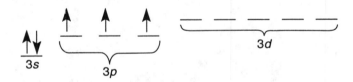

FIGURE 5.42. Orbital diagram for a phosphorus atom. Energy levels are shown by the positions of the orbitals.

When the hybrid orbitals are formed, they may be represented as shown in Figure 5.43. The five electrons in the *dsp*³ hybrid will form five sigma bonds in a covalent compound. The basic structure for the *dsp*³ hybrid is the trigonal bipyramid.

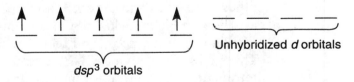

FIGURE 5.43. Five identical *dsp*³ hybrid orbitals for phosphorus. Four unoccupied d orbitals are not used and remain unhybridized.

Not all compounds of phosphorus will be dsp^3 hybrids. When phosphorus forms PCl_3, for example, the three chlorine atoms can readily combine with the three unpaired electrons in phosphorus without hybridization involving the d orbitals. However, since the structure of PCl_3 is tetrahedral, there must be some hybridization. Here the s and p orbitals hybridize into the sp^3 form, as shown in Figure 5.44. Since one of the hybrid orbitals is filled with a pair of electrons, this hybrid of phosphorus will form compounds with only three sigma bonds, such as phosphorus trichloride. PCl_3 has an AX_3E configuration and a triangular pyramid shape (a derived structure).

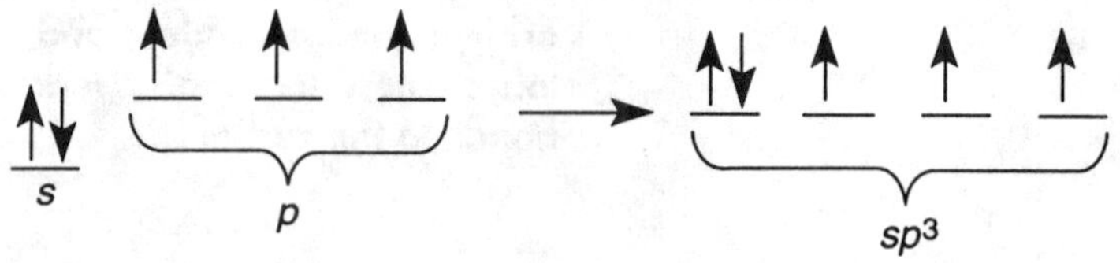

FIGURE 5.44.   The sp^3 hybridization for phosphorus.

d^2sp^3 Hybrid Orbitals

As is true for dsp^3 hybrids, an element must be in period 3 or higher to be able to participate in d^2sp^3 hybrids. At least six valence electrons are required. Sulfur is one element that forms d^2sp^3 hybrids. Sulfur's orbital configuration and the d^2sp^3 hybrid are shown in Figure 5.45.

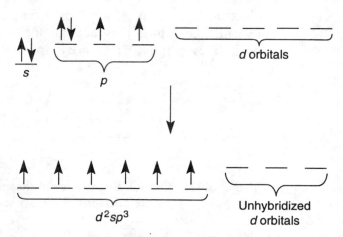

FIGURE 5.45.   Orbital diagram of the valence electrons in sulfur and the conversion to the d^2sp^3 hybrid orbitals.

The d^2sp^3 hybrid allows sulfur to form six covalent bonds with an octahedral structure. One of those compounds is sulfur hexafluoride. In addition, we have seen a variety of other sulfur compounds that result from other types of hybridization. Sulfur dichloride, SCl_2, uses sp^3 hybridization, as shown in Figure 5.46. In SCl_2, two unpaired electrons form sigma bonds with the chlorine atoms, and there are two pairs of nonbonding electrons. This sp^3 hybrid gives an AX_2E_2 structure, which also corresponds to a basic tetrahedral configuration. Since the two nonbonding pairs of electrons are not seen, SCl_2 has a bent shape with an angle close to 109.5°. Whereas sulfur can form both d^2sp^3 and sp^3 hybrids, oxygen in period 2 does not have

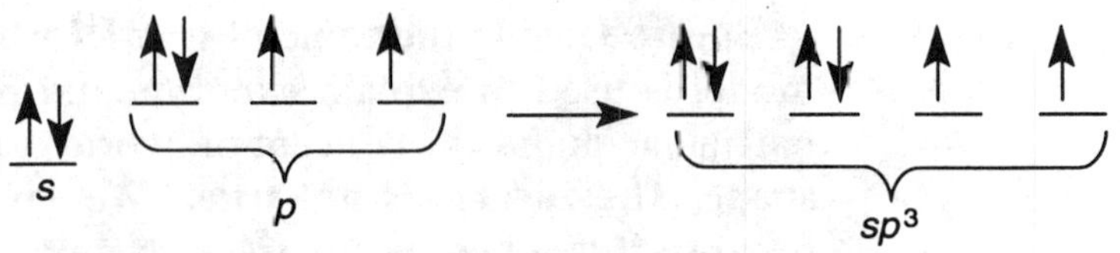

FIGURE. 5.46. **Hybridization used to explain the structure of molecules such as SCl_2.**

available d orbitals to form the d^2sp^3 hybrid and can form only single bonded compounds with an sp^3 hybrid.

There is a direct correspondence between hybridization and structure, which is shown in Table 5.6. If the basic structure is known, the hybridization can be determined; similarly, if the hybridization is known, the structure is likewise known.

TABLE 5.6   **Correspondence Between Hybridization and Structure**

Basic Structure*	Derived Structure*	Hybrid	Bonding e⁻ Pairs	Nonbonding e⁻ Pairs
Linear		sp	2	0
Planar triangle		sp^2	3	0
Planar triangle	Bent	sp^2	2	1
Tetrahedron		sp^3	4	0
Tetrahedron	Triangular pyramid	sp^3	3	1
Tetrahedron	Bent	sp^3	2	2
Trigonal bipyramid		dsp^3	5	0
Trigonal bipyramid	Distorted tetrahedron	dsp^3	4	1
Trigonal bipyramid	T-shape	dsp^3	3	2
Trigonal bipyramid	Linear	dsp^3	2	3
Octahedron		d^2sp^3	6	0
Octahedron	Square pyramid	d^2sp^3	5	1
Octahedron	Square planar	d^2sp^3	4	2

*Basic structures are listed for substances that have no nonbonding electron pairs. Derived structures are listed only for substances that have nonbonding electron pairs.

Exercise 5.13

Determine the total number of sigma and pi bonds in each of the following. Using the simple Lewis structure, also determine the hybridization for each.

(a) CH_3Cl (c) PH_3 (e) H_2S (g) CO_3^{2-} (i) SO_3^{2-}
(b) CS_2 (d) SiF_4 (f) NO_3^- (h) PO_4^{3-} (j) ClO_4^-

Solution

(a) $4\,\sigma, 0\,\pi, sp^3$ (e) $2\,\sigma, 0\,\pi, sp^3$ (i) $3\,\sigma, 0\,\pi, sp^2$
(b) $2\,\sigma, 2\,\pi, sp$ (f) $3\,\sigma, 1\,\pi, sp^2$ (j) $4\,\sigma, 0\,\pi, sp^3$
(c) $3\,\sigma, 0\,\pi, sp^3$ (g) $3\,\sigma, 1\,\pi, sp^2$
(d) $4\,\sigma, 0\,\pi, sp^3$ (h) $4\,\sigma, 0\,\pi, sp^3$

Before leaving the topic of hybrid orbitals, we must recognize that this model is used to explain experimental results. For a molecule that has a particular shape, the concept of hybrid orbitals may be used to explain that shape. **The reverse is not true.** We say that H_2O has sp^3 hybridization because it is a bent structure with a bond angle of 104°, which is close to the 109.5° bond angle expected for a tetrahedral structure. Experiments show, however, that the similar molecule H_2S has a bond angle of 90°. In this case the simple overlap of the p orbitals of sulfur with the s orbitals of hydrogen is sufficient to explain the structure. Hybridization is not needed, and is apparently unwarranted, in this example.

Important
Concepts

Octed rule and when it can be disobeyed
Lewis structures and formal charges
Molecular geometry and molecular polarity
Hybrid orbitals

Questions
on Chapter 5

1. In which of the following are the elements listed in order of increasing electronegativity?
   (A) Ba, Zn, C, Cl
   (B) N, O, S, Cl
   (C) N, P, As, Sb
   (D) K, Ba, Si, Ga
   (E) Li, K, Na, Ca

2. Which of the following bonds is expected to be the most polar?
   (A) C—Si
   (B) C—N
   (C) O—C
   (D) S—C
   (E) H—C

3. For which of the following may we draw both polar and nonpolar Lewis structures?
   (A) $CHCl_3$
   (B) NH_3
   (C) BF_3
   (D) SF_2Cl_4
   (E) PCl_5

4. Which of the following has the fewest pi bonds and is nonpolar?
   (A) HCCH
   (B) CO_2
   (C) CO_3^{2-}
   (D) N_2
   (E) SO_2

5. The SF_5^- ion has a square pyramid structure. The hybridization of the *s* orbitals in sulfur is
   (A) dsp^3
   (B) sp
   (C) d^2sp^3
   (D) sp^3
   (E) sp^2

6. Which of the following is NOT a linear structure?
   (A) I_2
   (B) I_3^-
   (C) CO_2
   (D) H_2S
   (E) $H-C\equiv C-H$

7. The cyanide ion most resembles
   (A) N_2
   (B) O_2
   (C) CO_2
   (D) NO
   (E) C_2H_2

8. In which of the following pairs are the two items NOT properly related?
   (A) sp^3 and $109.5°$
   (B) trigonal planar and $120°$
   (C) octahedral and dsp^3
   (D) sp and $180°$
   (E) square planar and d^2sp^3

9. How many resonance structures are possible for the SO_3 molecule?
   (A) none
   (B) 2
   (C) 3
   (D) 4
   (E) $\frac{4}{3}$

10. Which of the following has a nonbonding pair of electrons on the central atom?
    (A) BCl_3
    (B) NH_3
    (C) CCl_2Br_2
    (D) PF_5
    (E) SO_4^{2-}

11. Which of the following is true when the $C=C$ and $C\equiv C$ bonds are compared?
    (A) The triple bond is shorter than the double bond.
    (B) The double bond vibrates at a lower frequency than the triple bond.
    (C) The double-bond energy is lower than the triple-bond energy.
    (D) Both are composed of sigma and pi bonds.
    (E) All of the above are true.

12. How many valence electrons are available to construct the Lewis structure of the sulfite ion?
    (A) 24
    (B) 18
    (C) 26
    (D) 22
    (E) 20

13. The correct name for N_2O_3 is
    (A) dinitrogen tetroxide
    (B) dinitrogen trioxide
    (C) dinitrogen oxide
    (D) trinitrogen dioxide
    (E) nitric anhydride

14. Which angle is NOT expected in any simple molecule?
    (A) 60°
    (B) 90°
    (C) 109.5°
    (D) 120°
    (E) All of these are reasonable angles.

15. Sulfur forms the following compounds: SO_2, SF_6, SCl_4, SCl_2. Which form of hybridization is NOT represented by these molecules?
    (A) sp
    (B) sp^2
    (C) sp^3
    (D) dsp^3
    (E) d^2sp^3

Answer Key

See Appendix I for explanations of answers.

1. **A**	4. **C**	7. **A**	10. **B**	13. **B**
2. **C**	5. **C**	8. **C**	11. **E**	14. **A**
3. **D**	6. **D**	9. **C**	12. **C**	15. **A**

CHAPTER SIX

Stoichiometry

Stoichiometry (measurement of the elements) is the name given to the quantitative relationships between the compounds in a chemical reaction. These quantitative relationships allow chemists to calculate the amounts of reactants needed for a reaction and to predict the quantity of product. Using stoichiometric methods, chemists can determine the formulas of compounds and can simplify procedures in chemical analysis. This chapter discusses and illustrates stoichiometric calculations and the fundamental concepts that make stoichiometry the most important topic in chemistry.

Quantitative calculations in chemistry fall into two groups. The first group involves taking a memorized equation, entering data for all but one variable, and then solving for the remaining variable. The second group involves converting information with one set of units into an answer with another set of units. All stoichiometric calculations are the conversion type.

The **factor-label method** has become the predominant method taught for solving stoichiometry problems. Over the years many methods have been used to perform stoichiometric conversions. Many of these methods were limited in their utility, were complex, and involved a large amount of memorization. Today, the factor-label method is used in most courses. It has the advantage of minimizing memorization while applying basic chemical concepts to define the conversion process.

Factor-Label Method

Defining Factor Labels

A conversion problem changes the units of a measurement but not its magnitude. For instance, a distance of 2.0 yards may be converted into 72 inches by multiplying 2.0 by the factor 36. This does not indicate, however, how the units of yards became units of inches. If, instead of using just the factor 36, we multiply by the factor with its units, it is clear how the yards became inches:

$$2.0 \text{ yards}\left(\frac{36 \text{ inches}}{1 \text{ yard}}\right) = 72 \text{ inches}$$

In this equation the yard units cancel, and it is clear that the remaining units are inches. The ratio $\left(\dfrac{36 \text{ inches}}{1 \text{ yard}}\right)$ is known as the **factor label.** Using labels along with the numerical factors enables us to keep track of the units and to produce an answer with the correct units. Proper use of factor labels also tells us when to multiply and when to divide.

A factor label is derived from a defined relationship between two sets of units. The factor label above was obtained from the definition of 1 yard:

$$1 \text{ yard} = 36 \text{ inches}$$

Two factor labels can be obtained from every defined equality. For example, dividing both sides of the above equivalence by 1 yard gives

$$\frac{1 \text{ yard}}{1 \text{ yard}} = \frac{36 \text{ inches}}{1 \text{ yard}} = 1$$

Factor Label

Dividing both sides by 36 inches gives

$$\frac{1 \text{ yard}}{36 \text{ inches}} = \frac{36 \text{ inches}}{36 \text{ inches}} = 1$$

Factor Label

The two possible factor labels are inverses of each other. In addition, they are both equal to 1. When a measurement is multiplied by a factor label, it is multiplied, in effect, by 1, and its true value does not change, although the units do change.

Using Factor Labels

Every conversion problem must start with two pieces of information: (1) the number and the units that need to be converted and (2) the units of the answer. This is set up as

$$? \text{ answer units} = xxx \text{ given units}$$

On the right side is *xxx*, which represents the number given in the problem, and its units, which will be converted. The left side of the equal sign reminds us of the units needed for the solution to the problem.

After this step, it is necessary to find the equalities that can be used to produce the factor labels needed to solve the problem. For example, we might be required to convert 35 yards into feet and to convert 624 feet into yards. The solution starts with the initial setup of the question with the desired units as the unknown in an equation and the given data as the starting point:

$$? \text{ feet} = 35 \text{ yards} \quad \text{(initial setup)}$$

Being familiar with the English system of measurement, we know that 1 yard is defined as being 3 feet in length:

$$1 \text{ yard} = 3 \text{ feet}$$

From this equality two conversion factors, $\left(\dfrac{3 \text{ feet}}{1 \text{ yard}}\right)$ and $\left(\dfrac{1 \text{ yard}}{3 \text{ feet}}\right)$, can be written. The correct conversion factor is the one that allows us to cancel the yard units, leaving units of feet. This factor label is used to multiply the given 35 yards:

$$? \text{ feet} \quad = \quad 35 \text{ yards} \left(\frac{3 \text{ feet}}{1 \text{ yard}} \right)$$

After being sure that the units properly cancel, we calculate the answer as 105 feet. The following equation illustrates what happens if the wrong form of the factor label is chosen:

$$? \text{ feet} = 35 \text{ yards} \left(\frac{1 \text{ yard}}{3 \text{ feet}} \right) = 11.7 \text{ yards}^2\text{feet}^{-1} \quad \text{(wrong factor label chosen)}$$

This conversion will not work since the units do not cancel; in fact the final unit is the meaningless yard² per foot. The correct answer is

$$? \text{ feet} \quad = \quad 35 \text{ yards} \left(\frac{3 \text{ feet}}{1 \text{ yard}} \right) \quad = \quad 105 \text{ feet}$$

> IN ALL OF THE FOLLOWING EXAMPLES, THE CANCELLATION OF THE UNITS IS NOT SHOWN. IT IS SUGGESTED THAT YOU TAKE A COLORED PENCIL AND PERFORM ALL OF THE CANCELLATIONS TO ASSURE YOURSELF THAT EACH FACTOR LABEL DOES INDEED CANCEL PROPERLY.

In the second part of the question, the reverse calculation, from feet to yards, is requested. Starting as before with the question and the data supplied, we write

$$? \text{ yards} \quad = \quad 624 \text{ feet} \quad \text{(initial setup)}$$

Selecting the correct conversion factor gives

$$? \text{ yards} \quad = \quad 624 \text{ feet} \left(\frac{1 \text{ yard}}{3 \text{ feet}} \right) \quad = \quad 208 \text{ yards}$$

For this conversion the same equality, but a different factor label, was used. One of these factor labels converts from yards to feet, and the other converts feet to yards.

Many conversions require more than one step to reach the desired units. These problems may be solved stepwise, one factor label at a time, or the factor labels may be combined in one large equation. Both methods are illustrated in Exercise 6.1.

Exercise 6.1

A typical school year includes 180 days of classes. How many minutes are there in those days?

Solution

We start with the question and the given information to obtain

$$? \text{ minutes} = 180 \text{ days}$$

Next, we find the conversion equalities that may be useful. These are as follows:

$$1 \text{ day} = 24 \text{ hours}$$
$$1 \text{ hour} = 60 \text{ minutes}$$

The given data have units of days, and the only equality that also has units of days is the first one. The ratio needed for the conversion must have the day units in the denominator so that these units will cancel. Multiplying by this ratio yields

$$? \text{ minutes} = 180 \text{ days}\left(\frac{24 \text{ hr}}{1 \text{ day}}\right) = 4320 \text{ hr}$$

This result still does not have the desired units, so another step is needed. Starting with the result obtained above, we write

$$? \text{ minutes} = 4320 \text{ hr}$$

In our second conversion equality there is a relationship between hours and minutes, 1 hour = 60 minutes. When the next factor label is inserted, the hour units cancel:

$$? \text{ minutes} = 4320 \text{ hr}\left(\frac{60 \text{ min}}{1 \text{ hr}}\right) = 2.59 \times 10^5 \text{ min}$$

Since the units of this answer match the units that the question requires, the problem is solved. This answer is rounded off to 2.59×10^5 min.

Solving this same problem with one large equation involves writing all of the factor labels needed until the units match:

$$? \text{ minutes} = 180 \text{ days}\left(\frac{24 \text{ hr}}{1 \text{ day}}\right)\left(\frac{60 \text{ min}}{1 \text{ hr}}\right) = 2.59 \times 10^5 \text{ min}$$

The step-by-step and the combined methods result in exactly the same answer, and either method is correct.

Conversion of Metric Units

Chemistry students in the United States are hampered by the fact that the metric system is used in chemistry, whereas the English system of measurement governs everyday life. The examples above were done in **English units** because these units are often more familiar. From this point onward, however, only **metric units** will be used. The original metric system was developed in 1790 in France. Our modern version of the metric system is called the Systeme Internationale, or S.I. The seven base units of the S.I. are defined in Table 6.1.

These seven base units may be combined in a variety of ways to obtain other common units. For example, area can be expressed as square meters

TABLE 6.1 Seven Metric Base Units

Property Defined	Unit Name	Abbreviation
Mass	kilogram	kg
Length	meter	m
Time	second	s
Temperature	kelvin	K
Quantity	mole	mol
Electric current	ampere	A
Light intensity	candela	cd

(m^2), and volume as cubic meters (m^3). These base units are often too large or too small, however, for practical use in a laboratory. The base units may be modified by the use of a metric prefix. Each **metric prefix** represents a number that multiplies the base unit. The most commonly used prefixes for metric units are listed in Table 6.2.

TABLE 6.2 Metric Prefixes

Prefix Name	Prefix Symbol	Exponential Value
mega-	M	10^6
kilo-	k	10^3
deci-	d	10^{-1}
centi-	c	10^{-2}
milli-	m	10^{-3}
micro-	μ	10^{-6}
nano-	n	10^{-9}
pico-	p	10^{-12}

It is essential to remember the first five of the metric base units in Table 6.1 and all of the metric prefixes in Table 6.2. Factor labels between a unit with a prefix and the corresponding metric base unit may be quickly obtained by first writing an equality:

$$1 \text{ cm} = 1 \text{ cm}$$

and then replacing one of the prefixes with the corresponding exponent:

$$1 \text{ centimeter} = 1 \times 10^{-2} \text{ meter}$$

This equality can be used to write the two possible factor labels as $\left(\frac{\text{cm}}{10^{-2}\text{ m}}\right)$ and $\left(\frac{10^{-2}\text{ m}}{\text{cm}}\right)$. Conversion between a prefix and a base unit is a one-step calculation, but conversion between two different prefixes requires two steps.

Exercise 6.2

Convert 2.38 cm to meters and millimeters.

Solution

For the first conversion one of the factor labels above may be used:

$$? \; m = 2.38 \; cm \; \text{(setup)}$$

$$= 2.38 \; cm \left(\frac{10^{-2} \; m}{cm} \right)$$

$$= 0.0238 \; m = 2.38 \times 10^{-2} \; m$$

For the second conversion, centimeters to millimeters, two conversion factors are needed. The first converts the prefix to the base unit, and the second converts the base unit to the new prefix.

$$? \; mm = 2.38 \; cm \; \text{(setup)}$$

$$= 2.38 \; cm \left(\frac{10^{-2} \; m}{cm} \right) \left(\frac{mm}{10^{-3} \; m} \right)$$

$$= 23.8 \; m = 2.38 \times 10^{-1} \; mm$$

The answers to both parts of this exercise were written in exponential notation in order to show that the number 2.38 does not change in these conversions, but the exponent does.

Conversion of
Complex Units

Many times the data used in chemistry involve complex units. There are area measurements that have squared units such as square kilometers (km^2), square meters (m^2), or square centimeters (cm^2). There are volume measurements with cubic units such as cubic centimeters (cm^3), cubic millimeters (mm^3), and cubic meters (m^3). For velocity the units may be meters per second, which is abbreviated as m/s or $m \; s^{-1}$. Acceleration has units of meters per second squared ($m \; s^{-2}$), and energy has units of kilogram meters squared per second squared ($kg \; m^2 \; s^{-2}$).

The following exercises illustrate the conversion method used when the units have squared or cubed terms and when they involve a ratio.

Exercise 6.3

How many square centimeters are there in 180 m^2?

Solution

Setting up the problem as before, we have

$$? \; cm^2 = 180 \; m^2$$

The units are square centimeters and square meters. For clarity it is best to write the setup of this problem as

$$? \; cm \times cm = 180 \; m \times m$$

We can use the equality that says that 10^{-2} m is equal to 1 cm to write the needed factor label. Using the ratio that will cancel out the meter units, we obtain

$$? \; cm \times cm = 180 \; m \times m \left(\frac{1 \; cm}{10^{-2} \; m} \right)$$

By using the conversion ratio only once, we have canceled only one of the meter units, leaving the mixed units of centimeter meter. Applying the conversion ratio a second time cancels all of the meter units and leaves us with the desired square centimeters:

$$? \text{ m} \quad \times \quad \text{cm} \quad = \quad 180 \text{ m} \quad \times \quad \text{m} \left(\frac{1 \text{ cm}}{10^{-2} \text{ m}} \right) \left(\frac{1 \text{ cm}}{10^{-2} \text{ m}} \right)$$

Once the units cancel properly, the answer can be calculated as $1.80 \times 10^6 \text{ cm}^2$. For volumes, which have cubic units, each factor label is used three times.

When the units involve ratios that need to be converted, the units in the numerator are converted into the units required by the problem. Then the units in the denominator are converted.

Exercise 6.4

A train is moving at a speed of 25 km hr^{-1}. How fast is it moving in units of meters per minute?

Solution

Set up the problem as before, with the desired units as the question and the given speed as the starting point in the conversion.

$$? \frac{\text{m}}{\text{min}} \quad = \quad \frac{25 \text{ km}}{\text{h}} \quad \text{(setup)}$$

The two equalities that must be used to construct factor labels for this problem are

$$
\begin{aligned}
1 \text{ kilometer} &= 10^3 \text{ meters} \\
1 \text{ hour} &= 60 \text{ minutes}
\end{aligned}
$$

Applying the factor obtained from the first equality converts the kilometers to meters:

$$? \frac{\text{m}}{\text{min}} \quad = \quad \frac{25 \text{ km}}{\text{h}} \left(\frac{10^3 \text{ m}}{1 \text{ km}} \right)$$

Next, the second equality is used to convert the hour units in the denominator to the minutes required:

$$? \frac{\text{m}}{\text{min}} \quad = \quad \frac{25 \text{ km}}{\text{h}} \left(\frac{10^3 \text{ m}}{1 \text{ km}} \right) \left(\frac{1 \text{ h}}{60 \text{ min}} \right)$$

The units cancel properly, leaving the desired meters per minute units. The answer is then calculated to be 417 m min^{-1}.

Exercises 6.1–6.4 illustrate three important principles about the factor-label method. First, it is necessary to know the equalities required to obtain the proper conversion factors. Second, there is often a proper sequence in which to use these conversion factors. Third, if the units for the given value are in the form of a ratio, they must be converted into units that also represent a ratio. Similarly, if the problem requests an answer where the units must be a ratio, the starting data must have units in the form of a ratio.

Exercise 6.5

Convert each of the following:
(a) 8.89 nm to mm
(b) 3.89×10^5 cm^2 to μm^2
(c) 2.43×10^2 kg m^2 s^{-2} to g cm^2 s^{-2}

Solution

(a) 8.89×10^{-6} mm
(b) 3.89×10^{13} μm^2
(c) 2.43×10^9 g cm^2 s^{-2}

Chemical Equalities and Relationships

The Mole and Avogadro's Number

The **mole** (mol) is the central unit of measurement in chemistry. Numerically 1 mole represents 6.02×10^{23} units of a chemical substance. For the elements 1 mole represents 6.02×10^{23} atoms of the element. In compounds such as CH_4 or CO_2, 1 mole represents 6.02×10^{23} molecules. For ionic compounds it represents 6.02×10^{23} empirical formula units of a substance such as NaCl, or MgBr$_2$. The value 6.02×10^{23} is called **Avogadro's number** in honor of that chemist-physicist's pioneering work in stoichiometry.

In mathematical equations the number of moles is given the symbol n. This symbol is also used for many other purposes, however, and only a thorough understanding of any equation will tell whether n represents moles or some other quantity.

In general,

$$1 \text{ mole of X} = 6.02 \times 10^{23} \text{ units of X} \tag{6.1}$$

Some specific chemistry examples are as follows:

1 mole of argon atoms	=	6.02×10^{23} Ar atoms
1 mole of CH$_4$ molecules	=	6.02×10^{23} CH$_4$ molecules
1 mole of Mg^{2+} ions	=	6.02×10^{23} Mg^{2+} ions
1 mole of NaCl formula units	=	6.02×10^{23} NaCl formula units

Molar Mass

The periodic table used for the AP Chemistry Exam lists the **relative atomic mass** of each element directly underneath the chemical symbol. Relative atomic mass has no units and simply indicates the mass of one element as compared to that of another. In chemistry it is customary to add grams units to the atomic masses listed in the periodic table, calling them **gram-atomic masses**. One mole of an element is equal to the gram-atomic mass of that element:

$$1 \text{ mole of an element} = \text{gram-atomic mass of that element} \tag{6.2}$$

For a chemical compound the gram-molar mass is equal to the sum of the gram-atomic masses of all atoms in the chemical formula:

$$\text{gram-molar mass of a compound} = \Sigma \text{ (gram-atomic masses in formula)} \tag{6.3}$$

Similar to the cases for elements, the **gram-molar mass** of a compound is equal to 1 mole of that compound. Gram-molar masses of ions are determined by the atom(s) present in the ion since the gain or loss of electrons has virtually no effect on the total mass.

1 mole of a compound = gram-molar mass of that compound (6.4)

Some specific examples of the molar-mass relationships are as follows:

1 mole of argon   =   39.948 grams of argon
1 mole of uranium =   238.029 grams of uranium
1 mole of CH_4 =   16.043 grams of CH_4
1 mole of NaCl   =   58.4424 grams of NaCl
1 mole of Mg^{2+} = 24.3050 grams of Mg^{2+}

For most calculations, masses may be rounded off to whole numbers. In addition, standard abbreviations are used for the equalities. The five examples above are more commonly written as

1 mol Ar   =   40 g Ar
1 mol U   =   238 g U
1 mol CH_4 =   16 g CH_4
1 mol NaCl   =   58 g NaCl
1 mol Mg^{2+} = 24 g Mg^{2+}

Although it is correct to refer to the gram-atomic mass of an element and the gram-molar mass of a compound, it is common usage to refer to these as simply the atomic mass, A, and molar mass, MM, respectively.

The equalities defined in this section can be used to produce the appropriate factor labels for conversion calculations. Currently more than ten million compounds are known, and these definitions will give twice as many factor labels.

Exercise 6.6

Using the periodic table, determine the molar mass of each of the following compounds and round to two decimal places:
(a) $Cd(NO_3)_2$
(b) $CH_3(CH_2)_4Br$
(c) $(NH_4)_2SO_4$
(d) $(CH_3CH_2CH_2)_2O$
(e) $CuSO_4 \cdot 5H_2O$

Solution

(a) 236.42
(b) 151.04
(c) 132.14
(d) 102.18
(e) 249.69

Factor Labels from Chemical Formulas

Because of its structure, the formula for an ionic compound is an empirical formula representing the simplest ratio of atoms. Formulas for molecular compounds give the numbers and types of all the atoms that make up one molecule. All chemical formulas represent the ratio of atoms within the formula. This fact allows the chemist to write relationships between a formula as a whole and the individual atoms in that formula. For example, common table sugar is sucrose with the formula $C_{12}H_{22}O_{11}$. On the atomic scale this gives the following relationships, where the equal sign is read as "is chemically equivalent to":

1 molecule of $C_{12}H_{22}O_{11}$	=	12 atoms of carbon
1 molecule of $C_{12}H_{22}O_{11}$	=	22 atoms of hydrogen
1 molecule of $C_{12}H_{22}O_{11}$	=	11 atoms of oxygen
12 atoms of carbon	=	22 atoms of hydrogen
12 atoms of carbon	=	11 atoms of oxygen
22 atoms of hydrogen	=	11 atoms of oxygen

In short, one sucrose molecule gives the chemist six different relationships with which to construct factor labels. (It should be emphasized that these are not true equalities. The equal signs in these equations should be read as "is chemically equivalent to"; then the first relationship actually says that 1 molecule of $C_{12}H_{22}O_{11}$ "is chemically equivalent to" 12 atoms of carbon.)

It is rare that the chemist thinks of these relationships in terms of molecules and atoms. Rather they are viewed as moles of molecules or moles of atoms. In essence, each side of the relationships given above is multiplied by Avogadro's number to obtain the chemical equivalences:

1 mol $C_{12}H_{22}O_{11}$	=	12 mol C
1 mol $C_{12}H_{22}O_{11}$	=	22 mol H
1 mol $C_{12}H_{22}O_{11}$	=	11 mol O
12 mol C	=	22 mol H
12 mol C	=	11 mol O
22 mol H	=	11 mol O

Finally, it is important to remember that these relationships are true only for the specified compound. They may be different for other compounds.

Exercise 6.7

How many different chemical equivalences may be written for the following formulas?
(a) NaCl
(b) $FeCl_3$
(c) $NiSO_4$
(d) $(NH_4)_3PO_4$
(e) O_3

Solution

(a) 3
(b) 3
(c) 6
(d) 10
(e) 1

Factor Labels from Balanced Chemical Equations

While the chemical formula of a compound provides many relationships for factor labels, these relationships are limited to that single compound. A balanced chemical equation, however, gives a group of relationships that can be used to generate additional factor labels. Consider the balanced equation for the combustion of benzene, C_6H_6:

$$2C_6H_6 \quad + \quad 15O_2 \quad \rightarrow \quad 12CO_2 \quad + \quad 6H_2O$$

On a mole basis the following relationships can be obtained:

$$2 \text{ mol } C_6H_6 \ = \ 15 \text{ mol } O_2$$
$$2 \text{ Mol } C_6H_6 \ = \ 12 \text{ mol } CO_2$$
$$2 \text{ Mol } C_6H_6 \ = \ 6 \text{ mol } H_2O$$
$$15 \text{ mol } O_2 \ = \ 12 \text{ mol } CO_2$$
$$15 \text{ mol } O_2 \ = \ 6 \text{ mol } H_2O$$
$$12 \text{ mol } CO_2 \ = \ 6 \text{ mol } H_2O$$

Once again, the equal sign does not represent mathematical equality and should be read as "is equivalent to." These equalities apply only to the balanced equation from which they are derived.

Concentration and Density as Factor Labels

The concentration of a solution can also be used as a factor label for conversion calculations. The most common concentration unit used in chemistry is molarity. **Molarity** (M) is the number of moles of a solute that are dissolved in 1 liter of solution. When a problem gives the concentration of a solution, such as 0.250 molar NaOH (also written as 0.250 M NaOH), this value can be made into a factor label by specifying its units:

$$0.250 \text{ M NaOH} \ = \ \frac{0.250 \text{ mol NaOH}}{1 \text{ L NaOH}}$$

This ratio is a factor label for conversions between moles of NaOH and liters of NaOH solution. As with all conversion factors, its inverse is also a conversion factor:

$$\frac{1 \text{ L NaOH}}{0.250 \text{ mol NaOH}}$$

In many instances the volume is expressed in milliliters (mL). Then the two factor labels can be written as

$$\frac{0.250 \text{ mol NaOH}}{1000 \text{ mL NaOH}} \quad \text{and} \quad \frac{1000 \text{ mL NaOH}}{0.250 \text{ mol NaOH}}$$

since there are 1000 mL in each liter.

The density of a substance may be used as a factor label for conversions between volume and mass. Most densities in chemistry are given in units of grams per cubic centimeter (g cm^{-3}). If an organic liquid has a density of 0.741 g cm^{-3}, this fact may be written as the factor label:

$$\text{Density} \ = \ \frac{0.741 \text{ g}}{cm^3}$$

As with molarity, the inverse of this ratio is the other factor label obtained from the density:

$$\frac{cm^3}{0.741\ g}$$

Since 1 cm³ is the same as 1 mL, we can interchange the two terms as needed to obtain

$$\frac{mL}{0.741\ g} \quad \text{and} \quad \frac{0.741\ g}{mL}$$

Other Conversion Factors

Another useful equality for constructing a factor label is the relationship between the moles of a gas and the volume of a gas at standard temperature and pressure (see Chapter 4). Standard temperature is 0°C, and standard pressure is 1 atmosphere of pressure. Under these conditions 1 mole of a gas occupies 22.4 liters. The equality and its two conversion factors are as follows:

$$1\ mol\ gas \quad = \quad 22.4\ L\ gas$$

$$1 \quad = \quad \frac{22.4\ L}{1\ mol\ gas}$$

and

$$1 \quad = \quad \frac{1\ mol\ gas}{22.4\ L}$$

While this expression specifically refers to an ideal gas, this factor label can be used for calculations involving most real gases with little error.

Finally, there are several equalities that are very useful to remember:

$$
\begin{aligned}
1\ cm^3 \quad &= \quad 1\ mL \\
1\ L \quad &= \quad 1000\ mL \quad = \quad 1000\ cm^3 \\
1\ cm^3\ (H_2O) \quad &= \quad 1\ g\ H_2O
\end{aligned}
$$

The Conversion Sequence

Once the various equalities and relationships are known, they must be used in the correct way to perform stoichiometric calculations. It is important to understand the sequence of operations required to perform any conversion successfully and efficiently.

Figure 6.1 illustrates how conversions in chemistry are related to each other. This diagram shows the sequence of conversions from any given item of chemical information to any other that may be desired. The notations along the arrows indicate the type of factor label needed to perform each conversion. At most, a conversion will require three steps, not including any conversions of metric prefixes.

SUBSTANCE A

SUBSTANCE B

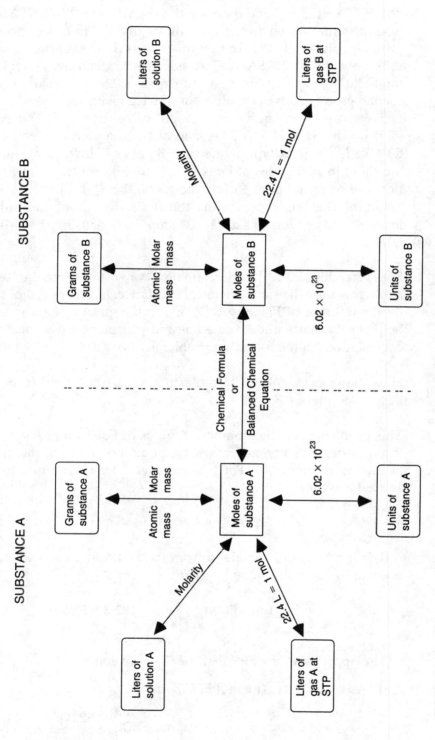

FIGURE 6.1. Diagram of the sequence of steps used in stoichiometry calculations. The box corresponding to the given data is found on the **SUBSTANCE A** side of the diagram. The box corresponding to the desired data is then located. Arrows between boxes indicate from what data factor labels are derived.

To start analyzing this diagram, note that the left-side boxes all refer to "SUBSTANCE A," and those on the right side to "SUBSTANCE B." The examples that follow in the text will be divided into two groups. The first group involves only the conversion of units of one substance and therefore uses only the SUBSTANCE A side of the diagram. A typical question might be "How many atoms of iron are in a 2.00-gram sample of Fe?". The second group involves problems in which a given amount of substance A is converted into an equivalent amount of substance B. These conversions start on the SUBSTANCE A side of the diagram and end on the SUBSTANCE B side. A typical question might be "How many grams of carbon are there in 10.0 grams of $Fe_2(CO_3)_3$?". In all problems the given information will be found as one of the boxes on the SUBSTANCE A side of the diagram. The box representing the desired units of the answer is then located, and conversions are made step by step, using the indicated factor labels.

Calculations Involving One Substance

Some stoichiometric questions involve converting from one set of units to another set for the same chemical substance. In this case we focus entirely on the left side of Figure 6.1. Some sample questions are given below. To help clarify the method, use a colored pen or pencil to perform the unit cancellations in the following problems.

Exercise 6.8

How many grams of $FeCl_3$ (molar mass = 162.3) need to be weighed to have 0.456 mol of $FeCl_3$?

Solution

This problem gives the number of moles of $FeCl_3$ and asks for grams. This is a one-step conversion that uses the equality between the molar mass of $FeCl_3$ and the moles of $FeCl_3$ as the factor label. The question to be answered is set up as

$$? \text{ g FeCl}_3 \quad = \quad 0.456 \text{ mol FeCl}_3$$

The factor label is obtained from the fact that 1 mole of any substance is equal to the molar mass in grams:

$$1 \text{ mol FeCl}_3 \quad = \quad 162.3 \text{ g FeCl}_3$$

The appropriate factor label for the conversion is $\left(\dfrac{162.3 \text{ g FeCl}_3}{1 \text{ mol FeCl}_3}\right)$ since it allows us to cancel the mol FeCl3 units:

$$? \text{ g FeCl}_3 \quad = \quad 0.456 \text{ mol FeCl}_3 \left(\frac{162.3 \text{ g FeCl}_3}{1 \text{ mol FeCl}_3}\right)$$

The mol $FeCl_3$ units cancel, and the g $FeCl_3$ units remaining are the ones requested in the question. No other factor labels are needed, and the answer is calculated as

$$? \text{ g FeCl}_3 \quad = \quad 0.456 \text{ mol FeCl}_3 \left(\frac{162.3 \text{ g FeCl}_3}{1 \text{ mol FeCl}_3}\right) \quad = \quad 74.0 \text{ g FeCl}_3$$

Exercise 6.9

A sample contains 24.6 g of CaO. How many moles of CaO (molar mass = 56.0) are in this sample?

Solution

This problem gives the grams of sample and asks for the number of moles. In effect, it is the reverse process of the preceding calculation. The question is set up as

$$? \text{ mol CaO} = 24.6 \text{ g CaO}$$

The conversion equality is 1 mol CaO = 56.0 g CaO, which can be made into a factor label with g CaO in the denominator. Multiplying by the conversion factor gives

$$? \text{ mol CaO} = 24.6 \text{ g CaO}\left(\frac{1 \text{ mol CaO}}{56.0 \text{ g CaO}}\right)$$

When the g CaO units are canceled, the mol CaO units remain. These are the desired units, and the result is then calculated as

$$? \text{ mol CaO} = 24.6 \text{ g CaO}\left(\frac{1 \text{ mol CaO}}{56.0 \text{ g CaO}}\right) = 0.439 \text{ mol CaO}$$

Exercise 6.10

A solution has a molarity of 0.658 mol $MgBr_2$ L^{-1}. How many moles of $MgBr_2$ are in 0.400 L of this solution?

Solution

This problem requires that the moles of $MgBr_2$ be determined, but two numerical items of information are given. From Figure 6.1 it is seen that the molarity is used as a factor label, and therefore the starting point is the liters of solution given. The question is set up as

$$? \text{ mol MgBr}_2 = 0.400 \text{ L MgBr}_2$$

The molarity is already a ratio:

$$0.658 \text{ M MgBr}_2 = \frac{0.658 \text{ mol MgBr}_2}{1 \text{ L MgBr}_2}$$

and may be used as the conversion factor:

$$? \text{ mol MgBr}_2 = 0.400 \text{ L MgBr}_2\left(\frac{0.658 \text{ mol MgBr}_2}{1 \text{ L MgBr}_2}\right)$$

Canceling the units and solving give the answer:

$$? \text{ mol MgBr}_2 = 0.263 \text{ mol MgBr}_2$$

Exercise 6.11

The same $MgBr_2$ solution as in the Exercise 6.10 must be used to obtain 0.500 mol of $MgBr_2$. How many milliliters of this solution are needed?

Solution

Now we must calculate the volume from the number of moles given, and the setup starts with

$$? \text{ mL MgBr}_2 \quad = \quad 0.500 \text{ mol MgBr}_2$$

Once again, the molarity is the conversion factor. However, it cannot be used directly since the units will not cancel. The molarity ratio is inverted and then used in the equation as

$$? \text{ mL MgBr}_2 \quad = \quad 0.500 \text{ L MgBr}_2 \left(\frac{1 \text{ L MgBr}_2}{0.658 \text{ mol MgBr}_2} \right)$$

Although the mol units cancel properly, the answer will be calculated in liters, not the milliliters requested. We must use an additional factor label to change the prefix of the liter units. The appropriate factor label is $\left(\frac{1 \text{ mL}}{10^{-3} \text{ L}} \right)$. Multiplying by this factor label and canceling the L units, we obtain the desired mL units:

$$? \text{ mL MgBr}_2 \quad = \quad 0.500 \text{ mol MgBr}_2 \left(\frac{1 \text{ L MgBr}_2}{0.658 \text{ mol MgBr}_2} \right) \left(\frac{1 \text{ mL}}{10^{-3} \text{ L}} \right)$$

The answer is 760 mL of MgBr$_2$ solution.

Exercises 6.8–6.11 demonstrated the one-step conversion of data to and from mole units. Many common calculations, however, involve two steps, as shown below.

Exercise 6.12

How many grams of KCl (molar mass = 74.6) are there in 0.250 L of a 0.300 molar solution of KCl?

Solution

From Figure 6.1 we see that to get from the given volume of the solution to the grams required for the answer involves two steps. The first step uses the molarity as a factor label to convert to moles, and then the second step uses the molar mass factor label to convert to grams. The problem starts with the volume of the solution:

$$? \text{ g KCl} \quad = \quad 0.250 \text{ L KCl}$$

Next the molarity is used to convert to moles:

$$? \text{ g KCl} \quad = \quad 0.250 \text{ L KCl} \left(\frac{0.300 \text{ mol KCl}}{1 \text{ L KCl}} \right)$$

Then the conversion factor for the molar mass is used:

$$? \text{ g KCl} \quad = \quad 0.250 \text{ L KCl} \left(\frac{0.300 \text{ mol KCl}}{1 \text{ L KCl}} \right) \left(\frac{74.6 \text{ g KCl}}{1 \text{ mol KCl}} \right)$$

After canceling the L KCl and mol KCl units, we have the desired g KCl units, and the calculation, can be made:

$$? \text{ g KCl} \quad = \quad 0.250 \text{ L KCl} \left(\frac{0.300 \text{ mol KCl}}{1 \text{ L KCl}} \right) \left(\frac{74.6 \text{ g KCl}}{1 \text{ mol KCl}} \right)$$

$$= \quad 5.60 \text{ g KCl}$$

Exercise 6.13

What is the mass of one molecule of CH_4 (molar mass = 16)?

Solution

This problem involves another two-step calculation, starting with one molecule of CH_4 and ending with the number of grams of CH_4. The conversion involves the use of Avogadro's number and the molar mass of CH_4 as the factor labels. The question is set up as

$$? \text{ g CH}_4 \quad = \quad 1 \text{ molecule CH}_4$$

Figure 6.1 shows that the first conversion uses Avogadro's number, 6.02×10^{23}, as a factor label. The units for Avogadro's number in this problem are molecules of CH_4, and the equality used is:

$$1 \text{ mol CH}_4 \quad = \quad 6.02 \times 10^{23} \text{ molecules CH}_4$$

Setting up the factor label properly, so that the units of molecules CH_4 cancel, gives

$$? \text{ g CH}_4 \quad = \quad 1 \text{ molecule CH}_4 \left(\frac{1 \text{ mol CH}_4}{6.02 \times 10^{23} \text{ molecules CH}_4} \right)$$

The next step is to use the molar mass to convert from moles to grams:

$$? \text{ g CH}_4 \quad = \quad 1 \text{ molecule CH}_4 \left(\frac{1 \text{ mol CH}_4}{6.02 \times 10^{23} \text{ molecules CH}_4} \right) \left(\frac{16 \text{ g CH}_4}{1 \text{ mol CH}_4} \right)$$

Since all units cancel properly, the calculation can now be performed to obtain

$$? \text{ g CH}_4 \quad = \quad 2.66 \times 10^{-23} \text{ g CH}_4$$

as the mass of one molecule of CH_4.

Exercise 6.14

How many molecules of CO_2 are contained in a 3.00-L flask at standard temperature and pressure? (Assume that CO_2 behaves as an ideal gas.)

Solution

This problem starts with the volume of a gas and ends with the number of molecules of CO_2. In the first step the volume of gas is converted to moles, using the fact that 1 mol of a gas occupies 22.4 L; then the moles are converted to molecules using Avogadro's number. The setup of the question is

$$? \text{ molecules CO}_2 \quad = \quad 3.00 \text{ L CO}_2$$

This is multiplied by the ratio $\left(\dfrac{1 \text{ mol } CO_2}{22.4 \text{ L } CO_2}\right)$:

$$? \text{ molecules } CO_2 \quad = \quad 3.00 \text{ L } CO\left(\dfrac{1 \text{ mol } CO_2}{22.4 \text{ L } CO_2}\right)$$

The next step is to convert to molecules, being sure that the units of the ratio cancel properly:

$$? \text{ molecules } CO_2 \quad = \quad 3.00 \text{ L } CO_2\left(\dfrac{1 \text{ mol } CO_2}{22.4 \text{ L } CO_2}\right)\left(\dfrac{6.02 \times 10^{23} \text{ molecules } CO_2}{1 \text{ mol } CO_2}\right)$$

The units cancel properly, and the answer is calculated as

$$? \text{ molecules } CO_2 \quad = \quad 8.06 \times 10^{22} \text{ molecules } CO_2$$

Exercise 6.15

Perform each of the following conversions:
(a)   26.5 g of $MgCl_2$ to moles of $MgCl_2$
(b)   3.456 mol of CH_4 to grams of CH_4
(c) 6.57×10^{18} atoms of Fe to moles of Fe
(d)   2.22 mol of O_2 to molecules of O_2
(e)   1.45 mol of KCl to liters of KCl with a molarity of 0.135
(f)   23.5 mL of 0.766 M HF to moles of HF
(g)   1.46 L of CO_2 at STP to moles of CO_2
(h)   0.025 mol of N_2 to liters of N_2
(i)   26.5 g of $MgCl_2$ to liters of 0.200 M $MgCl_2$ solution
(j)   3.456 g of CH_4 to liters of CH_4 at STP
(k) 6.57×10^{18} atoms of Fe to grams of Fe
(l)   2.22 g of O_2 to molecules of O_2
(m)   1.45 L of HCl at STP to liters of HCl with a molarity of 0.135
(n)   23.5 mL of 0.766 M HF to liters of HF gas at STP
(o)   0.025 g of N_2 to liters of N_2
(p)   1.46 L of CO_2 at STP to molecules of CO_2

Solution

(a)   0.278 mol $MgCl_2$
(b)   55.44 g CH_4
(c) 1.09×10^{-5} mol Fe
(d) 1.34×10^{24} molecules O_2
(e)   10.7 L KCl
(f)   0.0180 mol HF
(g)   0.0652 mol CO_2
(h)   0.56 L N_2
(i)   1.39 L $MgCl_2$
(j)   4.83 L CH_4
(k) 6.10×10^{-4} g Fe
(l) 4.18×10^{22} molecules O_2
(m)   0.479 L HCl(aq)
(n)   0.403 L HF(g)
(o)   0.0200 L N_2
(p) 3.92×10^{22} molecules CO_2

Calculations
Involving Two
Substances

To this point all the sample calculations have involved the same substance. In Figure 6.1, all of the conversions took place between the boxes labeled "SUBSTANCE A." When we start with one substance and end up with a different one, however, the conversion **must always** include the central conversion from moles of substance A to moles of substance B. There is simply no other possible way to perform the conversions. These conversions must use information obtained from a given chemical formula or from a balanced chemical reaction.

The simplest two-substance conversions are mole-to-mole conversions, as shown in Exercises 6.16 and 6.17.

Exercise 6.16

How many moles of nitrogen are there in 6.50 mol of ammonium phosphate, $(NH_4)_3PO_4$?

Solution

The chemical formula gives the information for the factor label; this compound has three nitrogen atoms for each unit of ammonium phosphate. The setup states the question as

$$? \text{ mol N} \quad = \quad 6.50 \text{ mol } (NH_4)_3PO_4$$

This is then multiplied by the factor-label $\left(\dfrac{3 \text{ mol N}}{1 \text{ mol } (NH_4)_3PO_4} \right)$:

$$? \text{ mol N} \quad = \quad 6.50 \text{ mol } (NH_4)_3 PO_4 \left(\dfrac{3 \text{ mol N}}{1 \text{ mol } (NH_4)_3 PO_4} \right)$$

The mol $(NH_4)_3PO_4$ units cancel, leaving the mol N units that the problem requests. The answer is calculated as

$$? \text{ mol N} \quad = \quad 19.5 \text{ mol N}$$

Exercise 6.17

How many moles of water will be formed in the complete combustion of 2.50 mol of methane, CH_4?

Solution

This problem starts with one substance, methane, and asks a question about a second very different substance, water. A chemical reaction will be needed to solve the problem. Every combustion reaction has oxygen as a reactant and carbon dioxide and water as the products:

$$CH_4 \quad + \quad 2O_2 \quad \rightarrow \quad CO_2 \quad + \quad 2H_2O$$

This equation tells us that 1 mol of methane will form 2 mol of water, and this information is used to construct the factor label, $\left(\dfrac{2 \text{ mol } H_2O}{1 \text{ mol } CH_4} \right)$. The question is written as

$$? \text{ mol } H_2O \quad = \quad 2.50 \text{ mol } CH_4$$

Multiplying this by the factor label yields

$$? \text{ mol H}_2\text{O} \quad = \quad 2.50 \text{ mol CH}_4 \left(\frac{2 \text{ mol H}_2\text{O}}{1 \text{ mol CH}_4} \right)$$

After canceling the mol CH_4 units and verifying that the proper units, mol H_2O, have been obtained to satisfy the question, the answer is calculated:

$$? \text{ mol H}_2\text{O} \quad = \quad 2.50 \text{ mol CH}_4 \left(\frac{2 \text{ mol H}_2\text{O}}{1 \text{ mol CH}_4} \right) \quad = \quad 5.00 \text{ mol H}_2\text{O}$$

More complex calculations involve adding a step before the mole-to-mole conversion and a step afterwards. In all of these calculations the units for the given information in the problem are found in one of the five boxes on the left or SUBSTANCE A side of Figure 6.1. Then the units requested by the problem are found on the SUBSTANCE B side of the diagram. Proceeding from the given units to the requested units defines the sequence of conversions, and the factor labels, that are needed to obtain the correct answer.

One of the more common calculations involves calculating the mass of a compound given the mass of another compound and the balanced chemical reaction. Figure 6.1 shows that this procedure involves three steps:

1. Convert the starting mass to moles, using the molar mass of the given compound.
2. Convert the moles of compound A to moles of compound B, using the equivalencies derived from the balanced chemical reaction.
3. Convert from moles back to grams, using the molar mass of the requested compound.

Exercise 6.18

Propane, C_3H_8, is a common heating and cooking fuel in rural areas of the country. Propane is also the fuel used in outdoor grills and in small hand-held torches. If 100 g of propane is burned in excess oxygen, how many grams of oxygen will be needed? In addition, how many grams of carbon dioxide and water will be formed in the reaction?

Solution

This problem asks for the calculation of three quantities, O_2, CO_2, and H_2O. These will be calculated as three separate problems. First, a balanced chemical equation is needed to determine the relationships between the reactants and products. The reactants and products are listed in Equation (a):

$$C_3H_8 \quad + \quad O_2 \quad \rightarrow \quad CO_2 \quad + \quad H_2O \qquad \text{(a)}$$

This is then balanced to obtain

$$C_3H_8 \quad + \quad 5O_2 \quad \rightarrow \quad 3CO_2 \quad + \quad 4H_2O \qquad \text{(b)}$$

To calculate the oxygen needed, the question is set up as

$$? \text{ g O}_2 \quad = \quad 100 \text{ g C}_3\text{H}_8$$

The first conversion uses the molar mass of the C_3H_8 molecule, which is $3(12) + 8(1) = 44$:

$$? \text{ g } O_2 \quad = \quad 100 \text{ g } C_3H_8 \left(\frac{1 \text{ mol } C_3H_8}{44 \text{ g } C_3H_8} \right)$$

The next conversion factor is obtained from Equation (b), which says that 1 mol of C_3H_8 is equivalent to 5 mol of O_2.

$$? \text{ g } O_2 \quad = \quad 100 \text{ g } C_3H_8 \left(\frac{1 \text{ mol } C_3H_8}{44 \text{ g } C_3H_8} \right)\left(\frac{5 \text{ mol } O_2}{1 \text{ mol } C_3H_8} \right)$$

The final factor label uses the molar mass of the O_2 molecule, $16 + 16 = 32$:

$$? \text{ g } O_2 \quad = \quad 100 \text{ g } C_3H_8 \left(\frac{1 \text{ mol } C_3H_8}{44 \text{ g } C_3H_8} \right)\left(\frac{5 \text{ mol } O_2}{1 \text{ mol } C_3H_8} \right)\left(\frac{32 \text{ g } O_2}{1 \text{ mol } O_2} \right)$$

The units cancel to leave only units of g O_2. The answer is calculated as

$$? \text{ g } O_2 \quad = \quad 364 \text{ g } O_2$$

The remaining question in the statement of the problem is answered by using the following setups:

$$? \text{ g } CO_2 = 100 \text{ g } C_3H_8 \left(\frac{1 \text{ mol } C_3H_8}{44 \text{ g } C_3H_8} \right)\left(\frac{3 \text{ mol } CO_2}{1 \text{ mol } C_3H_8} \right)\left(\frac{44 \text{ g } CO_2}{1 \text{ mol } CO_2} \right)$$

$$= 300 \text{ g } CO_2$$

$$? \text{ g } H_2O = 100 \text{ g } C_3H_8 \left(\frac{1 \text{ mol } C_3H_8}{44 \text{ g } C_3H_8} \right)\left(\frac{4 \text{ mol } HO_2}{1 \text{ mol } C_3H_8} \right)\left(\frac{18 \text{ g } H_2O}{1 \text{ mol } H_2O} \right)$$

$$= 164 \text{ g } H_2O$$

Reviewing this problem, we see that it started with 100 grams of C_3H_8, which was found to require 364 grams of O_2 for complete combustion. The masses of the products were calculated as 300 grams of CO_2 and 164 grams of H_2O.

The total mass of the reactants, 100 g C_3H_8 and 364 g O_2, is 464 grams. At the end of the reaction, the total mass of the products, 300 g CO_2 and 164 g H_2O, is also 464 grams. The law of conservation of mass states that matter cannot be created or destroyed in a chemical reaction. Since this law cannot be violated, we expect that the results of our calculations will obey it. Obtaining the same total mass for the reactants and the products indicates that the law of conservation of mass was not violated.

It is always an advantage to be able to estimate an answer to a problem to assure that no errors were made in calculations. In stoichiometry problems, only mass to mass conversions allow us to do this. In 95 percent of these problems, the calculated mass is between one-fifth and five times the given mass. For the problem above, this means that the answers should be between 20 and 500 grams. All of our results fell in that range, giving added confidence that the conversions were correctly done. If the results did not fit the estimates, we would be well advised to carefully recheck our calculations. The 5 percent of reactions that do not follow this general rule are those in which the molar masses of the compounds are very different, as, for example, those of H_2 and Zn.

In some instances the information given is in the form of the volume and molarity of a reactant that produces a precipitate. These calculations also involve a three-step conversion:

1. Start with the given volume and convert to moles, using the molarity of the given solution.
2. Use the balanced chemical reaction to calculate the moles of product.
3. Convert the moles of product to grams, using the molar mass.

Exercise 6.19

A 45.0 mL sample of 0.300 molar $FeCl_3$ is reacted with enough NaOH solution to precipitate all the iron as $Fe(OH)_3$. How many grams of $Fe(OH)_3$ will be precipitated?

Solution

First a balanced chemical reaction must be written:

$$FeCl_3 \quad + \quad 3\,NaOH \quad \rightarrow \quad Fe(OH)_3 \quad + \quad 3\,NaCl \qquad (c)$$

The question is set up as

$$?\ g\ Fe(OH)_3 \quad = \quad 45.0\ mL\ FeCl_3$$

The first factor label is the molarity, written as

$$0.300\ M\ FeCl_3 \quad = \quad \frac{0.300\ mol\ FeCl_3}{1000\ mL\ FeCl_3}$$

The denominator of this factor label includes the conversion from liters to milliliters without using another factor label:

$$?\ g\ Fe(OH)_3 \quad = \quad 45.0\ mL\ FeCl_3 \left(\frac{0.300\ mol\ FeCl_3}{1000\ mL\ FeCl_3} \right)$$

The next factor label is obtained from the relationships in the chemical reaction shown in Equation (c), where 1 mol of $FeCl_3$ is equivalent to 1 mol of $Fe(OH)_3$:

$$?\ g\ Fe(OH)_3 \quad = \quad 45.0\ mL\ FeCl_3 \left(\frac{0.300\ mol\ FeCl_3}{1000\ mL\ FeCl_3} \right) \left(\frac{1\ mol\ Fe(OH)_3}{1\ mol\ FeCl_3} \right)$$

Finally, the moles of $Fe(OH)_3$ are converted to grams by using the molar mass, 107, for $Fe(OH)_3$:

$$?\ g\ Fe(OH)_3 \quad = \quad 45.0\ mL\ FeCl_3 \left(\frac{0.300\ mol\ FeCl_3}{1000\ mL\ FeCl_3} \right) \cdot$$

$$\left(\frac{1\ mol\ Fe(OH)_3}{1\ mol\ FeCl_3} \right) \left(\frac{107\ g\ Fe(OH)_3}{1\ mol\ Fe(OH)_3} \right)$$

Since the units cancel, the answer is calculated as

$$? \text{ g Fe(OH)}_3 \quad = \quad 1.44 \text{ g Fe(OH)}_3$$

In many reactions it is important to know the volume of one reactant that will react with a given volume of a second reactant. The molarities of both reactants must be given for this type of problem to be solved.

Exercise 6.20

How many milliliters of a 0.250 M NaOH solution are needed to completely neutralize 65.0 mL of a 0.400 M solution of sulfuric acid?

Solution

A balanced equation is required. Since the problem states that the sulfuric acid, H_2SO_4, is completely neutralized, both protons on the sulfuric acid react with the NaOH:

$$H_2SO_4 \quad + \quad 2NaOH \quad \rightarrow \quad Na_2SO_4 \quad + \quad 2H_2O \qquad \text{(d)}$$

Figure 6.1 indicates another three-step calculation:

1. Convert milliliters of H_2SO_4 to moles of H_2SO_4, using the molarity of H_2SO_4.
2. Convert moles of H_2SO_4 to moles of NaOH.
3. Convert moles of NaOH to milliliters, using the molarity of NaOH.

The initial setup of the question is

$$? \text{ mL NaOH} \quad = \quad 65.0 \text{ mL } H_2SO_4$$

Using the molarity of the H_2SO_4 as a conversion factor gives

$$? \text{ ml NaOH} \quad = \quad 65.0 \text{ mL } H_2SO_4 \left(\frac{0.400 \text{ mol } H_2SO_4}{1000 \text{ mL } H_2SO_4} \right)$$

Then Equation (d) is used to convert to moles NaOH:

$$? \text{ ml NaOH} \quad = \quad 65.0 \text{ mL } H_2SO_4 \left(\frac{0.400 \text{ mol } H_2SO_4}{1000 \text{ mL } H_2SO_4} \right) \left(\frac{2 \text{ mol NaOH}}{1 \text{ mol } H_2SO_4} \right)$$

Finally, the molarity of the NaOH is used to convert moles NaOH to milliliters NaOH:

$$? \text{ ml NaOH} \quad = \quad 65.0 \text{ mL } H_2SO_4 \left(\frac{0.400 \text{ mol } H_2SO_4}{1000 \text{ mL } H_2SO_4} \right) \cdot$$

$$\left(\frac{2 \text{ mol NaOH}}{1 \text{ mol } H_2SO_4} \right) \left(\frac{1000 \text{ mL NaOH}}{0.250 \text{ mol NaOH}} \right)$$

Since the units cancel properly, the answer may be calculated as 208 mL.

In some chemical reactions a gas is evolved as one of the products. The most common cases are the reactions of active metals with mineral acids and the reactions of carbonates with acids. It is possible to calculate the volume of gas from a chemical reaction at standard temperature and pressure (STP = 0°C and 1 atm). (If the final conditions are not at STP, see Chapter 4 on gases for further calculations using the ideal gas law.) The volume of gas evolved from a given mass or volume of reactant is calculated in Exercises 6.21–6.23.

Exercise 6.21

Metallic copper reacts with concentrated nitric acid to produce nitrogen dioxide. Calculate the volume of NO_2 that will form at STP when 1.25 g of copper is completely reacted according to the equation

$$Cu(s) + 4HNO_3(aq) \rightarrow Cu(NO_3)_2(aq) + 2NO_2(g) + 2H_2O(\ell) \quad (e)$$

Solution

We have the chemical reaction, and need to follow three steps to convert the grams of copper to the volume of $NO_2(g)$ formed:

1. Convert grams Cu to moles Cu, using the atomic mass.
2. Convert moles Cu to moles NO_2, using the balanced equation
3. Convert moles NO_2 to volume, using the molar volume of an ideal gas.

We start with the setup of the question:

$$? \text{ L } NO_2 \quad = \quad 1.25 \text{ g Cu}$$

Using the atomic mass of copper as a factor label, we get

$$? \text{ L } NO_2 \quad = \quad 1.25 \text{ g Cu}\left(\frac{1 \text{ mol Cu}}{63.55 \text{ g Cu}}\right)$$

The next factor label involves the balanced chemical equation given in Equation (e), which states that 1 mol Cu will form 2 mol NO_2. The equation becomes

$$? \text{ L } NO_2 \quad = \quad 1.25 \text{ g Cu}\left(\frac{1 \text{ mol Cu}}{63.55 \text{ g Cu}}\right)\left(\frac{2 \text{ mol } NO_2}{1 \text{ mol Cu}}\right)$$

Finally, the fact that 1 mol of an ideal gas at STP occupies 22.4 L is used as a conversion factor to obtain

$$? \text{ L } NO_2 \quad = \quad 1.25 \text{ g Cu}\left(\frac{1 \text{ mol Cu}}{63.55 \text{ g Cu}}\right)\left(\frac{2 \text{ mol } NO_2}{1 \text{ mol Cu}}\right)\left(\frac{22.4 \text{ L } NO_2}{1 \text{ mol } NO_2}\right)$$

Since all of the units cancel properly, the answer may be calculated as

$$? \text{ L } NO_2 \quad = \quad 0.881 \text{ L } NO_2 \text{ at STP}$$

Exercise 6.22

Blackboard chalk is almost 100% calcium carbonate, $CaCO_3$. What volume of carbon dioxide, CO_2, will be evolved at STP if an excess of chalk is reacted with 35.0 mL of 0.888 molar hydrochloric acid?

Solution

The chemical reaction may be obtained from the facts given in the problem. Knowing that the reactants are HCl and $CaCO_3$ and that one of the products is CO_2, we can readily deduce the other products, H_2O and $CaCl_2$:

$$2HCl(aq) + CaCO_3(s) \rightarrow CO_2(g) + H_2O(\ell) + 2CaCl_2(aq) \quad (f)$$

The starting point for the calculation is

$$? \, L \, CO_2 \quad = \quad 35.0 \; mL \; HCl$$

The molarity of the HCl is used to convert to moles HCl:

$$? \, L \, CO_2 \quad = \quad 35.0 \; mL \; HCl \left(\frac{0.888 \; mol \; HCl}{1000 \; mL \; HCl} \right)$$

Next the chemical reaction shown in Equation (f) is used to obtain a factor label for the conversion from moles HCl to moles CO_2:

$$? \, L \, CO_2 \quad = \quad 35.0 \; mL \; HCl \left(\frac{0.888 \; mol \; HCl}{1000 \; mL \; HCl} \right) \left(\frac{1 \; mol \; CO_2}{2 \; mol \; HCl} \right)$$

Finally, the molar volume of a gas is used to convert to the volume of CO_2 formed:

$$? \, L \, CO_2 \quad = \quad 35.0 \; mL \; HCl \left(\frac{0.888 \; mol \; HCl}{1000 \; mL \; HCl} \right) \left(\frac{1 \; mol \; CO_2}{2 \; mol \; HCl} \right) \left(\frac{22.4 \; L \; CO_2}{1 \; mol \; CO_2} \right)$$

The units cancel properly, and the answer is calculated as

$$? \, L \, CO_2 \quad = \quad 0.348 \; L \; CO_2 \; at \; STP$$

Exercise 6.23
(a) How many grams of water are obtained when 35.6 g of benzene, C_6H_6, are burned in excess oxygen? How many liters of CO_2 at STP will be produced in the same reaction?
(b) How many milliliters of 0.248 M HCl are needed to react with 1.36 g of zinc to produce hydrogen gas? How many milliliters of hydrogen gas are expected at STP?

Solution
(a) The balanced reaction is

$$2C_6H_6 \quad + \quad 15O_2 \quad \rightarrow \quad 12CO_2 \quad + \quad 6H_2O$$

$$? \, g \, H_2O \quad = \quad 35.6 \; g \; C_6H_6 \left(\frac{1 \; mol \; C_6H_6}{78.0 \; g \; C_6H_6} \right) \left(\frac{6 \; mol \; H_2O}{2 \; mol \; C_6H_6} \right) \left(\frac{18.0 \; g \; H_2O}{1 \; mol \; H_2O} \right)$$

$$= \quad 16.4 \; g \; H_2O$$

$$? \, L \, CO_2 \quad = \quad 35.6 \; g \; C_6H_6 \left(\frac{1 \; mol \; C_6H_6}{78.0 \; g \; C_6H_6} \right) \left(\frac{12 \; mol \; CO_2}{2 \; mol \; C_6 H_6} \right) \left(\frac{22.4 \; L \; CO_2}{1 \; mol \; CO_2} \right)$$

$$= \quad 61.3 \; L \; CO_2$$

(b) The balanced reaction is

$$2HCl \quad + \quad Zn \quad \rightarrow \quad ZnCl_2 \quad + \quad H_2$$

$$? \, mL \, HCl \quad = \quad 1.36 \; g \; Zn \left(\frac{1 \; mol \; Zn}{65.38 \; g \; Zn} \right) \left(\frac{2 \; mol \; HCl}{1 \; mol \; Zn} \right) \left(\frac{1000 \; mL \; HCl}{0.248 \; mol \; HCl} \right)$$

$$= \quad 168 \; mL \; HCl$$

$$? \text{ mL } H_2 \quad = \quad 1.36 \text{ g Zn} \left(\frac{1 \text{ mol Zn}}{65.38 \text{ g Zn}} \right) \left(\frac{1 \text{ mol } H_2}{1 \text{ mol Zn}} \right) \left(\frac{22400 \text{ mL } H_2}{1 \text{ mol } H_2} \right)$$

$$= \quad 466 \text{ mL } H_2$$

Limiting Reactant Calculations

When chemicals are mixed together under the appropriate conditions, a chemical reaction is started. The reaction will stop when one of the reactants is completely used up. The reactant that is totally consumed, stopping the reaction, is called the **limiting reactant** or **limiting reagent**. The other reactant or reactant(s) are called the excess reactant(s). The amount of the limiting reactant determines how much of the other reactant(s) react and how much of each product is formed. Up to this point, only the amount of one reactant has been given in a problem, and this reactant was assumed to be the limiting reactant. When the amounts of two or more reactants are given, special procedures for limiting reactant calculations must be used.

To understand the concept of a limiting reactant more fully, consider a vending machine that accepts quarters and dimes only and does not give any change. If an item in that machine costs 45 cents, the only way it can be purchased is with two dimes and one quarter. If you have ten dimes and ten quarters, only five 45-cent items can be obtained from this machine since the dimes will run out before the quarters do. Figure 6.2 illustrates this example.

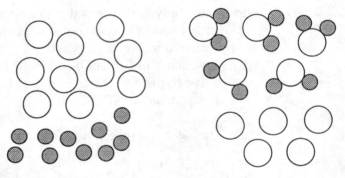

FIGURE 6.2. The vending machine example of a limiting reactant. On the left are the ten quarters (large circles) and ten dimes (small circles). On the right are five groups of one quarter and two dimes each used for 45-cent purchases. Also on the right are five left-over quarters. The dimes are the limiting reactant.

A variety of problems can be solved in the context of the limiting reactant concept. These include the determination of which reactant is the limiting reactant, the amount of product formed, and the amount of excess reactant that does not react. Examples of these calculations are shown in Exercises 6.24–6.29.

PROCEDURES FOR SOLVING LIMITING REACTANT PROBLEMS MUST ALWAYS BE USED WHEN THE AMOUNTS OF TWO OR MORE REACTANTS ARE GIVEN IN THE STATEMENT OF THE PROBLEM.

Finding the Limiting Reactant:

Exercise 6.24

For the reaction below, determine the limiting reactant if 100 g of $FeCl_3$ is reacted with 50.0 g of H_2S:

$$2FeCl_3(aq)\ +\ 3H_2S(g)\quad\rightarrow\quad Fe_2S_3(s)\ +\ 6HCl(aq)$$

Solution

The first thing to remember is that the compound present in the smallest amount is not necessarily the limiting reactant. To determine the limiting reactant, the amount given for one reactant is converted into the amount of the other reactant that is needed to react with it. Using the procedures above, we can convert the 50 g of H_2S into the number of grams of $FeCl_3$ needed to react with it as follows:

$$?\ g\ FeCl_3\quad=\quad 50.0\ g\ HS\left(\frac{1\ mol\ H_2S}{34\ g\ H_2S}\right)\left(\frac{2\ mol\ FeCl_3}{3\ mol\ H_2S}\right)\left(\frac{162\ g\ FeCl_3}{1\ mol\ FeCl_3}\right)$$

$$=\quad 159\ g\ FeCl_3$$

From this result we see that 159 g of $FeCl_3$ is needed to react with all 50.0 g of H_2S. However, the amount of $FeCl_3$ given in the problem is only 100 g. The conclusion must be that we will run out of $FeCl_3$ before all of the H_2S can be reacted. Since the $FeCl_3$ is used up first, it is the limiting reactant.

(If the problem had stated that 200 g of $FeCl_3$, instead of 100 g, was available, it would be apparent that we had more than enough $FeCl_3$ to react all of the H_2S. Then we would have concluded that H_2S was the limiting reactant.)

Determining the Theoretical Yield

The term **theoretical yield** refers to the maximum amount of product formed in a reaction based on the amounts of reactants used. This amount is a theoretical yield since no laboratory work is done. Many events can occur in the laboratory that result in less than the theoretical amount of product. One is that the reactants do not combine completely. Another is the possibility of side reactions that produce different products. Products can also be lost by poor lab techniques or in the purification process. In most cases, the theoretical yield refers to the maximum mass of product that can be produced.

> ONCE A LIMITING REACTANT IS IDENTIFIED, ALL FURTHER CALCULATIONS ARE BASED ON THE AMOUNT OF THE LIMITING REACTANT GIVEN IN THE ORIGINAL STATEMENT OF THE PROBLEM.

Exercise 6.25

What is the theoretical yield of Fe_2S_3 that can be obtained from 100 g of $FeCl_3$ and 50.0 g of H_2S?

Solution

These are the same data as in Exercise 6.24, but the question has changed. To solve the problem, we need to know the limiting reactant. In this case it has already been determined as the $FeCl_3$. We now use the 100 g of $FeCl_3$ given in the problem to calculate the mass of the Fe_2S_3.

$$? \text{ g } Fe_2S_3 \quad = \quad 100 \text{ g } FeCl_3 \left(\frac{1 \text{ mol } FeCl_3}{162.5 \text{ g } FeCl_3} \right) \left(\frac{1 \text{ mol } Fe_2S_3}{2 \text{ mol } FeCl_3} \right) \left(\frac{208 \text{ g } Fe_2S_3}{1 \text{ mol } Fe_2S_3} \right)$$

$$= \quad 64.0 \text{ g } Fe_2S_3$$

(It is essential that the 100 g of $FeCl_3$ given in the problem be used for this calculation. If we had used the 159 grams calculated in Exercise 6.24, a totally incorrect answer would have been obtained.)

Another question that can be asked in a limiting reactant problem is how much of the excess reactant is left over when the reaction stops. In the vending machine example in Figure 6.2 this can be done by counting the five quarters that combine with two dimes and then subtracting them from the ten quarters we started with. In the chemical calculation the amount of the excess reactant that reacts with the limiting reactant is calculated. This is then subtracted from the starting amount of the excess reactant as given in the problem. Exercise 6.26 illustrates the procedure.

Exercise 6.26

When 100 g of $FeCl_3$ is reacted with 50.0 g of H_2S, how many grams of which reactant will be left over when the reaction is complete?

Solution

To determine which reactant is left over, the limiting reactant is identified and then all other reactants become the excess reactants. Since the data are the same for this problem as for Exercises 6.24 and 6.25, we know that $FeCl_3$ is the limiting reactant and, therefore, H_2S is the excess reactant. To determine how much H_2S is left over, we first calculate the number of the grams of H_2S that react:

$$? \text{ g } H_2S \quad = \quad 100 \text{ g } FeCl_3 \left(\frac{1 \text{ mol } FeCl_3}{162.5 \text{ g } FeCl_3} \right) \left(\frac{3 \text{ mol } H_2S}{2 \text{ mol } FeCl_3} \right) \left(\frac{34 \text{ g } H_2S}{1 \text{ mol } H_2S} \right)$$

$$= \quad 31.4 \text{ g } H_2S$$

Since the problem started with 50.0 g of H_2S and 31.5 g reacted, the remaining amount of H_2S must be

$$? \text{ g } H_2S \text{ (left)} \quad = \quad 50.0 \text{ g } H_2S \text{ (start)} \quad - \quad 31.4 \text{ g } H_2S \text{ (reacted)}$$

$$= \quad 18.6 \text{ g } H_2S$$

To complete all of the information about this reaction, we can calculate the theoretical yield of HCl in the same way that the theoretical yield of Fe_2S_3 was calculated.

Exercise 6.27

When 100 g of $FeCl_3$ is reacted with 50.0 g of H_2S, how many grams of HCl are formed?

Solution

As before, the limiting reactant must be determined; we already know that it is $FeCl_3$. The 100 grams of $FeCl_3$ given in the problem is used as the starting point for the calculation:

$$? \text{ g HCl} = 100 \text{ g } FeCl_3$$

$$= 100 \text{ g FeCl}\left(\frac{1 \text{ mol } FeCl_3}{162.5 \text{ g } FeCl_3}\right)\left(\frac{6 \text{ mol HCl}}{2 \text{ mol } FeCl_3}\right)\left(\frac{36.5 \text{ g HCl}}{1 \text{ mol HCl}}\right)$$

$$= 67.4 \text{ g HCl}$$

This calculation follows the same principles as the calculation of the amount of Fe_2S_3 in Exercise 6.25.

With this calculation we have determined the masses of all reactants and products in the chemical equation. Listing the masses of the substances before and after reaction demonstrates once again that the law of conservation of matter is obeyed.

REACTION:	$2\,FeCl_3$	+	$3\,H_2S$	→	Fe_2S_3	+	$6\,HCl$
Start	100 g		50.0 g		0 g		0 g
End	0 g		18.6 g		64.0 g		67.4 g

In this table we can add up the masses of all of the substances at the start of the reaction to get a total of 150 grams. At the end of the reaction the masses again add up to 150 grams. These results show that the law of conservation of mass has been obeyed since total mass at the start and at the end of the reaction is the same.

Exercise 6.28

Silver tarnishes in air because of a complex reaction with oxygen and hydrogen sulfide, H_2S, in the air, which may be written as

$$2Ag + O_2 + H_2S \rightarrow Ag_2S + 2H_2O$$

What is the theoretical yield of silver sulfide, Ag_2S, that can be produced from a mixture of 0.200 g of silver, 1.50 L of oxygen at STP, and 65.0 mL of 0.350 molar H_2S solution?

Solution

This is a limiting reactant problem since the amounts of three different reactants are given. An added complexity is that each of these amounts has a different type of unit. To begin with, the identity of the limiting reactant must be determined. Because there are three reactants, Ag, O_2, and H_2S, a process of elimination is used. First, one pair of reactants is selected to determine which *might be* the limiting reactant, while eliminating the excess reactant. Next, the third reactant and the possible limiting reactant from the first step are used to determine the actual limiting reactant. Choosing silver and oxygen as the first pair, we have

$$? \text{ L } O_2 \;=\; 0.200 \text{ g Ag}\left(\frac{1 \text{ mol Ag}}{108 \text{ g Ag}}\right)\left(\frac{1 \text{ mol } O_2}{2 \text{ mol Ag}}\right)\left(\frac{22.4 \text{ L } O_2}{1 \text{ mol } O_2}\right)$$

$$=\; 0.0207 \text{ L } O_2$$

Since the problem gives the amount of oxygen as 1.5 L, there is plenty of this reactant and it cannot be the limiting reactant, but silver may be. The next step determines the amount of hydrogen sulfide:

$$? \text{ mL } H_2S \;=\; 0.200 \text{ g Ag}\left(\frac{1 \text{ mol Ag}}{108 \text{ g Ag}}\right)\left(\frac{1 \text{ mol } H_2S}{2 \text{ mol Ag}}\right)\left(\frac{1000 \text{ mL } H_2S}{0.350 \text{ mol } H_2S}\right)$$

$$=\; 2.65 \text{ mL } H_2S$$

Since the question states that there is 65.0 mL of H_2S solution and all that is needed is 2.65 mL, H_2S cannot be the limiting reactant. Because neither H_2S nor O_2 can be the limiting reactant, it must be the silver. Now the theoretical yield of Ag_2S can be calculated, based on the 0.200 g of silver given in the original problem:

$$? \text{ g } Ag_2S \;=\; 0.200 \text{ g Ag}\left(\frac{1 \text{ mol Ag}}{108 \text{ g Ag}}\right)\left(\frac{1 \text{ mol } Ag_2S}{2 \text{ mol Ag}}\right)\left(\frac{248 \text{ g } Ag_2S}{1 \text{ mol } Ag_2S}\right)$$

$$=\; 0.230 \text{ g AgS}$$

Exercise 6.29

Silver nitrate, $AgNO_3$ (molar mass = 170), reacts with sodium chromate, Na_2CrO_4 (molar mass = 162), to form silver chromate (molar mass = 332) and sodium nitrate. If 45.5 mL of 0.200 M $AgNO_3$ is mixed with 35.8 mL of 0.436 M Na_2CrO_4, what is the theoretical yield of the precipitate silver chromate? How many grams of which reactant are left over?

Solution

The reaction is

$$2AgNO_3(aq) \;+\; Na_2CrO_4(aq) \;\rightarrow\; Ag_2CrO_4(s) \;+\; 2NaNO_3(aq)$$

To determine the limiting reactant, the calculation is

$$? \text{ mL } Na_2CrO_4 \;=\; 45.5 \text{ mL } AgNO_3\left(\frac{0.200 \text{ mol } AgNO_3}{1000 \text{ mL } AgNO_3}\right)\cdot$$

$$\left(\frac{1 \text{ mol } Na_2CrO_4}{2 \text{ mol } AgNO_3}\right)\left(\frac{1000 \text{ mL } Na_2CrO_4}{0.436 \text{ mol } Na_2CrO_4}\right)$$

$$=\; 10.4 \text{ mL } Na_2CrO_4$$

Since we were given 35.8 mL of Na_2CrO_4, the conclusion is that $AgNO_3$ is the limiting reactant, and all further calculations are based on the given amount of $AgNO_3$:

$$? \text{ g Ag}_2\text{CrO}_4 \quad = \quad 45.5 \text{ mL AgNO}_3 \left(\frac{0.200 \text{ mol AgNO}_3}{1000 \text{ mL AgNO}_3} \right) \cdot$$

$$\left(\frac{1 \text{ mol Ag}_2\text{CrO}_4}{2 \text{ mol AgNO}_3} \right)\left(\frac{332 \text{ g Ag}_2\text{CrO}_4}{1 \text{ mol Ag}_2\text{CrO}_4} \right)$$

$$= \quad 1.51 \text{ g Ag}_2\text{CrO}_4$$

Since $AgNO_3$ is the limiting reactant, Na_2CrO_4 is the excess reactant. The amount of Na_2CrO_4 that reacts is calculated and subtracted from the given amount:

$$? \text{ g Na}_2\text{CrO}_4 \quad = \quad 45.5 \text{ mL AgNO}_3 \left(\frac{0.200 \text{ mol AgNO}_3}{1000 \text{ mL AgNO}_3} \right) \cdot$$

$$\left(\frac{1 \text{ mol Na}_2\text{CrO}_4}{2 \text{ mol AgNO}_3} \right)\left(\frac{162 \text{ g Na}_2\text{CrO}_4}{1 \text{ mol Na}_2\text{CrO}_4} \right)$$

$$= \quad 0.737 \text{ g Na}_2\text{CrO}_4 \text{ reacts}$$

The original number of grams of Na_2CrO_4 is calculated as

$$? \text{ g Na}_2\text{CrO}_4 \quad = \quad 35.8 \text{ mL Na}_2\text{CrO}_4 \left(\frac{0.436 \text{ mol Na}_2\text{CrO}_4}{1000 \text{ mL Na}_2\text{CrO}_4} \right)\left(\frac{162 \text{ g Na}_2\text{CrO}_4}{1 \text{ mol Na}_2\text{CrO}_4} \right)$$

$$= \quad 2.529 \text{ g Na}_2\text{CrO}_4 \text{ initially present}$$

The amount of sodium chromate left over is calculated by subtraction:

$$? \text{ g Na}_2\text{CrO}_4 \text{ left over} \quad = \quad 2.529 \text{ g Na}_2\text{CrO}_4 \quad - \quad 0.737 \text{ g Na}_2\text{CrO}_4$$

$$= \quad 1.792 \text{ g Na}_2\text{CrO}_4$$

Titrations

The titration technique used for chemical analysis utilizes the reactions of two solutions. One reactant solution is placed in a beaker, and the other in a buret, which is a long, graduated tube with a stopcock. The stopcock is a valve that allows the chemist to add controlled amounts of solution from the buret to the beaker. An indicator, that is, a compound that changes color when the reaction is complete, is added to the solution in the beaker. The chemist reads the volume of solution in the buret at the start of the experiment and again at the point where the indicator changes color. The difference in these volumes represents the volume of reactant delivered from the buret. Figure 6.3 illustrates the experimental setup.

The crucial point about the titration experiment is that the indicator is designed to change color when the amount of reactant delivered from the buret is exactly the amount needed to react with the solution in the beaker. From this experiment, a variety of calculations may be made as shown below.

A classic chemical reaction is the one between Fe^{2+} and the permanganate ion MnO_4^-:

$$5Fe^{2+} + MnO_4^- + 8H^+ \rightarrow Mn^{2+} + 5Fe^{3+} + 4H_2O \quad (6.5)$$

In titrations, the purple permanganate ion is the indicator of the point where the correct amount has been added to completely react all of the

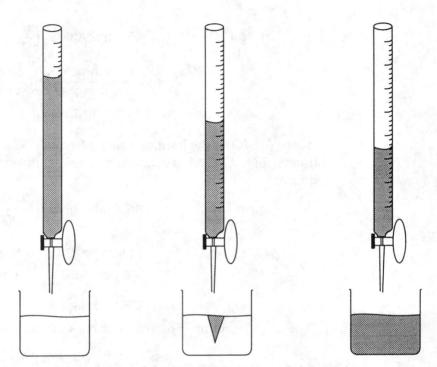

FIGURE 6.3. Titration experiment showing the initial setup, the slight color change of the indicator before the endpoint is reached, and the colored solution at the endpoint.

Fe^{2+} ions in the sample. All of the calculations in Exercises 6.30–6.32 refer to Equation 6.5.

Exercise 6.30

It takes 34.35 mL of a 0.240 M solution of $KMnO_4$ (0.240 M MnO_4^-) to titrate an unknown sample of Fe^{2+} to its endpoint. How many grams of Fe^{2+} are in the sample?

Solution

This problem gives the amount of MnO_4^-, and the grams of Fe^{2+} are to be calculated. Figure 6.1 shows the sequence of steps, and the required factor labels can be determined. The question is set up as

$$? \text{ g } Fe^{2+} \quad = \quad 34.35 \text{ mL } MnO_4^-$$

Then the necessary factor labels are entered:

$$? \text{ g } Fe^{2+} \quad = \quad 34.35 \text{ mL } MnO_4^- \left(\frac{0.240 \text{ mol } MnO_4^-}{1000 \text{ mL } MnO_4^-} \right) \cdot$$

$$\left(\frac{5 \text{ mol } Fe^{2+}}{1 \text{ mol } MnO_4^-} \right) \left(\frac{55.85 \text{ g } Fe^{2+}}{1 \text{ mol } Fe^{2+}} \right)$$

$$= \quad 2.30 \text{ g } Fe^{2+}$$

Exercise 6.31

How many milliliters of 0.240 M MnO_4^- solution will be needed to titrate a 1.56 g sample of pure $Fe(NO_3)_2$?

Solution

The question is set up as

$$? \text{ mL MnO}_4^- \quad = \quad 1.56 \text{ g Fe(NO}_3)_2$$

The grams are converted to moles by using the molar mass of $Fe(NO_3)_2$:

$$? \text{ mL MnO}_4^- \quad = \quad 1.56 \text{ g Fe (NO}_3)_2 \left(\frac{1 \text{ mol Fe (NO}_3)_2}{180 \text{ g Fe (NO}_3)_2} \right)$$

Using the ionization reaction

$$Fe(NO_3)_2 \quad \rightarrow \quad Fe^{2+} \quad + \quad 2NO_3^-$$

we can apply the factor label $\left(\dfrac{1 \text{ mol Fe}^{2+}}{1 \text{ mol Fe(NO}_3)_2} \right)$ to convert to the Fe^{2+} ion:

$$? \text{ mL MnO}_4^- \quad = \quad 1.56 \text{ g Fe (NO}_3)_2 \left(\frac{1 \text{ mol Fe (NO}_3)_2}{180 \text{ g Fe (NO}_3)_2} \right) \left(\frac{1 \text{ mol Fe}^{2+}}{1 \text{ mol Fe (NO}_3)_2} \right)$$

Equation 6.5 is used to convert to moles of MnO_4^-, and then the molarity is used to convert to milliliters of MnO_4^-.

$$? \text{ mL MnO}_4^- \quad = \quad 1.56 \text{ g Fe (NO}_3)_2 \left(\frac{1 \text{ mol Fe (NO}_3)_2}{180 \text{ g Fe (NO}_3)_2} \right) \left(\frac{1 \text{ mol Fe}^{2+}}{1 \text{ mol Fe (NO}_3)_2} \right) \cdot$$

$$\left(\frac{1 \text{ mol MnO}_4^-}{5 \text{ mol Fe}^{2-}} \right) \left(\frac{1000 \text{ mL MnO}_4^2}{0.240 \text{ mol MnO}_4^-} \right)$$

$$= \quad 7.22 \text{ mL MnO}_4^-$$

This exercise demonstrates that the stoichiometry calculations described above can be used also for calculations in titration experiments. There is one calculation, however, that the stoichiometry calculations do not address—conversion of the molarity of one solution to the molarity of another. Since the answer desired is molarity, and molarity is not one of the possible starting points in Figure 6.1, a new method for using factor labels must be developed.

Exercise 6.32

What is the molarity of an Fe^{2+} solution if 4.53 mL of a 0.687 M MnO_4^- solution is required to titrate 30.00 mL of the Fe^{2+}-containing solution to the endpoint?

Solution

The desired information is the molarity of the Fe^{2+} solution. The units of molarity are a ratio, and we look for a ratio of units with which to start the problem. The appropriate term is the molarity of the MnO_4^- solution. The setup of the question is as follows:

$$? \frac{\text{mol Fe}^{2+}}{\text{L Fe}^{2+}} \quad = \quad \frac{0.687 \text{ mol MnO}_4^-}{1 \text{ L MnO}_4^-}$$

We need factor labels to convert the numerator from mol MnO_4^- to mol Fe^{2+} and the denominator from L MnO_4^- to L Fe^{2+}. The factor label for the numerator comes from Equation 6.31. We obtain the factor label for the denominator from the ratio of the volumes of the two solutions at the endpoint of the titration:

$$? \frac{\text{mol Fe}^{2+}}{\text{L Fe}^{2+}} = \left(\frac{0.687 \text{ mol MnO}_4^-}{1000 \text{ mL MnO}_4^-}\right)\left(\frac{5 \text{ mol Fe}^{2+}}{1 \text{ mol MnO}_4^-}\right)\left(\frac{4.53 \text{ mL MnO}_4^-}{30.00 \text{ mL Fe}^{2+}}\right)$$

$$= \frac{0.519 \text{ mol Fe}^{2+}}{1000 \text{ mL Fe}^{2+}} = 0.519 \text{ M Fe}^{2+}$$

Exercise 6.33

A 0.235 M solution of HCl is titrated to the endpoint with 23.4 mL of 0.216 M NaOH. (a) How many grams of HCl were in the titrated sample? (b) If the volume of the HCl sample is 50.0 mL, what is the molarity of the HCl solution?

Solution

The reaction is

$$\text{HCl} + \text{NaOH} \rightarrow \text{NaCl} + \text{H}_2\text{O}$$

(a) To calculate the grams of HCl, we use the equation

$$? \text{ g HCl} = 23.4 \text{ mL NaOH}\left(\frac{0.216 \text{ mol NaOH}}{1000 \text{ mL NaOH}}\right) \cdot$$

$$\left(\frac{1 \text{ mol HCl}}{1 \text{ mol NaOH}}\right)\left(\frac{36.461 \text{ g HCl}}{1 \text{ mol HCl}}\right)$$

$$= 0.184 \text{ g HCl}$$

(b) Calculating the molarity of the HCl solution involves units that are a ratio. The starting point is the molarity of the NaOH, which is also a ratio of units:

$$? \frac{\text{mol HCl}}{\text{L HCl}} = \left(\frac{0.216 \text{ mol NaOH}}{1 \text{ L NaOH}}\right)\left(\frac{1 \text{ mol HCl}}{1 \text{ mol NaOH}}\right)\left(\frac{23.4 \text{ mL NaOH}}{50.0 \text{ mL HCl}}\right)$$

$$= \frac{0.101 \text{ mol HCl}}{\text{L HCl}} = 0.101 \text{ M HCl}$$

Percent Composition

The percent composition of a chemical substance tells the chemist how much of each element, or polyatomic ion, is present in a compound on a percent basis. In other words, the percent composition is the mass of an element or polyatomic ion that is present in 100 grams of a chemical compound.

Exercise 6.34

What is the percentage of Fe, O, H, and the OH^- polyatomic ion in $Fe(OH)_3$?

Solution

Each of these calculations will start with 100 g of $Fe(OH)_3$, and we calculate the grams of each element in turn to obtain their percentages:

$$? \text{ g Fe} = 100 \text{ g Fe(OH)}_3 \left(\frac{1 \text{ mol Fe(OH)}_3}{106.8 \text{ g Fe(OH)}_3} \right) \cdot$$

$$\left(\frac{1 \text{ mol Fe}}{1 \text{ mol Fe(OH)}_3} \right)\left(\frac{55.8 \text{ g Fe}}{1 \text{ mol Fe}} \right)$$

$$= 52.2 \text{ g Fe}$$

$$\% \text{ Fe} = \frac{52.2 \text{ g Fe}}{100 \text{ g Fe(OH)}_3} \times 100 = 52.2\% \text{ Fe}$$

$$? \text{ g O} = 100 \text{ g Fe(OH)}_3 \left(\frac{1 \text{ mol Fe(OH)}_3}{106.8 \text{ g Fe(OH)}_3} \right) \cdot$$

$$\left(\frac{3 \text{ mol O}}{1 \text{ mol Fe(OH)}_3} \right)\left(\frac{16.0 \text{ g O}}{1 \text{ mol O}} \right)$$

$$= 44.9 \text{ g O}$$

$$\% \text{ O} = \frac{44.9 \text{ g O}}{100 \text{ g Fe(OH)}_3} \times 100 = 44.9\% \text{ O}$$

$$? \text{ g H} = 100 \text{ g Fe(OH)}_3 \left(\frac{1 \text{ mol Fe(OH)}_3}{106.8 \text{ g Fe(OH)}_3} \right) \cdot$$

$$\left(\frac{3 \text{ mol H}}{1 \text{ mol Fe(OH)}_3} \right)\left(\frac{1.0 \text{ g H}}{1 \text{ mol H}} \right)$$

$$= 2.8 \text{ g H}$$

$$\% \text{ H} = \frac{2.8 \text{ g H}}{100 \text{ g Fe(OH)}_3} \times 100 = 2.8\% \text{ H}$$

$$? \text{ g OH}^- = 100 \text{ g Fe(OH)}_3 \left(\frac{1 \text{ mol Fe(OH)}_3}{106.8 \text{ g Fe(OH)}_3} \right) \cdot$$

$$\left(\frac{3 \text{ mol OH}^-}{1 \text{ mol Fe(OH)}_3} \right)\left(\frac{17.0 \text{ g OH}^-}{1 \text{ mol OH}^-} \right)$$

$$= 47.8 \text{ g OH}^-$$

$$\% \text{ OH}^- = \frac{47.8 \text{ g OH}^-}{100 \text{ g Fe(OH)}_3} \times 100 = 47.8\% \text{ OH}^-$$

The percentages of the elements add up to 99.9%. The sum should equal 100%, but does not because the numbers were rounded to one decimal place.

Another method for calculating the percentage composition is to use the formula

$$\text{percent of element} = \frac{\left(\begin{array}{c}\text{atomic mass} \\ \text{of element}\end{array}\right)\left(\begin{array}{c}\text{number of atoms} \\ \text{in formula}\end{array}\right)}{\text{molar mass of compound}} \times 100 \quad (6.6)$$

A close look at the stoichiometry equations in Exercise 6.34 shows that Equation 6.6 is just a summary of these stoichiometric calculations.

Exercise 6.35

What is the percentage of each element in (a) $Ca(NO_3)_2$ and (b) $CH_3CH_2NH_2$?

Solution

(a) Ca = 34.52%, N = 24.13%, O = 41.35%
(b) C = 53.28%, H = 15.65%, N = 31.07%

Empirical Formulas

Given a chemical formula and the atomic masses of the elements, it is possible to calculate the percent composition of a compound. More important is the fact that, with a knowledge of the percent composition and atomic masses, we can deduce the empirical formula of a compound, that is, the simplest ratio of atoms in the compound. Butyric acid has the molecular formula $HC_4H_7O_2$. Its empirical formula is C_2H_4O. Benzene, C_6H_6, has the empirical formula CH. The empirical formula of the sugar glucose, $C_6H_{12}O_6$, is CH_2O. All sugars have the same empirical formula, which is why they are also called carbohydrates (carbo- for the carbon and -hydrate for the water molecule).

To determine the empirical formula of a compound, the simplest ratio of the moles of the atoms in the compound is found by using the following steps:

1. From the given data, calculate the number of moles of each element in the compound.
2. Divide the number of moles of each element obtained in step 1 by the smallest value found to obtain whole-number subscripts for the empirical formula.
3. Note that, if step 2 does not give whole numbers (within ±0.1), the decimal portion of each number will be close to a rational fraction; for example, 0.5 = ½, 0.33 = ⅓, 0.67 = ⅔. In this situation, multiply each item of the data by the denominator of the rational fraction to remove the fraction and end up with a whole-number subscript for the empirical formula.

Exercise 6.36

What is the empirical formula of a compound that contains 4.0 g of calcium and 7.1 g of chlorine?

Solution

The first step involves converting the grams of Ca and Cl to moles:

$$? \text{ mol Ca} = 4.0 \text{ g Ca}\left(\frac{1 \text{ mol Ca}}{40.0 \text{ g Ca}}\right) = 0.10 \text{ mol Ca}$$

$$? \text{ mol Cl} = 7.1 \text{ g Cl}\left(\frac{1 \text{ mol Cl}}{35.5 \text{ g Cl}}\right) = 0.20 \text{ mol Cl}$$

The second step is to divide both of these answers by the smaller value, 0.10:

$$\frac{0.10 \text{ mol Ca}}{0.10} = 1 \text{ mol Ca}$$

$$\frac{0.20 \text{ mol Cl}}{0.10} = 2 \text{ mol Cl}$$

This tells us that the empirical formula contains 1 mol Ca and 2 mol Cl and is written as $CaCl_2$.

Exercise 6.37

A compound containing carbon, hydrogen, and oxygen is found to contain 9.1% H and 54.5% C. What is its empirical formula?

Solution

Since the percentage of an element is the number of grams per 100 g of compound, we may assume a 100 g sample of compound and convert the percent sign directly to gram units. Also, since the percent hydrogen and percent carbon do not add up to 100%, we may conclude that the missing 36.4 % is oxygen. Step 1 of the procedure on page 170 is used to calculate the number of moles of each element:

$$? \text{ mol C} = 54.5 \text{ g C}\left(\frac{1 \text{ mol C}}{12 \text{ g C}}\right) = 4.54 \text{ mol C}$$

$$? \text{ mol H} = 9.1 \text{ g H}\left(\frac{1 \text{ mol H}}{1 \text{ g H}}\right) = 9.1 \text{ mol H}$$

$$? \text{ mol O} = 36.4 \text{ g O}\left(\frac{1 \text{ mol O}}{16 \text{ g O}}\right) = 2.28 \text{ mol O}$$

Using step 2 and dividing by the smallest number, 2.28, we obtain

$$\frac{4.54 \text{ mol C}}{2.28} = 1.99 \text{ mol C}$$

$$\frac{9.1 \text{ mol H}}{2.28} = 3.99 \text{ mol H}$$

$$\frac{2.28 \text{ mol O}}{2.28} = 1.00 \text{ mol O}$$

Since these numbers are within ±0.1 of a whole number, they are rounded to 2 mol C, 4 mol H, and 1 mol O, and the empirical formula is written as C_2H_4O.

Exercise 6.38

A compound is analyzed and found to contain 74.1% oxygen and 25.9% nitrogen. What is its empirical formula?

Solution

Assuming a 100 g sample, we convert the percentages directly to gram units, and the moles of N and O are calculated as

$$? \text{ mol N} = 25.9 \text{ g N}\left(\frac{1 \text{ mol N}}{14 \text{ g N}}\right) = 1.85 \text{ mol N}$$

$$? \text{ mol O} = 74.1 \text{ g N}\left(\frac{1 \text{ mol O}}{16 \text{ g O}}\right) = 4.63 \text{ mol O}$$

Dividing both answers by 1.85 (step 2) gives

$$\frac{1.85 \text{ mol N}}{1.85} = 1.00 \text{ mol N}$$

$$\frac{4.63 \text{ mol O}}{1.85} = 2.50 \text{ mol O}$$

The 2.50 mol O cannot be rounded to a whole number, but the decimal 0.50 represents the rational fraction ½. We must use step 3, in which all of the data are multiplied by the denominator of the rational fraction—in this case, 2 is used.

$$1.00 \text{ mol N} \times 2 = 2.00 \text{ mol N}$$
$$2.50 \text{ mol O} \times 2 = 5.00 \text{ mol O}$$

These whole numbers are used to write the empirical formula N_2O_5.

Exercise 6.39

Determine the empirical formula for each of the following compounds, given its composition:
(a) A compound composed of 17.72 g Cl and 3.10 g P.
(b) A compound that is 24.74% K, 40.50% O, and 34.76% Mn.
(c) A compound containing carbon, hydrogen, and oxygen that is 40.0% C and 6.66% H.

Solution

(a) PCl_5
(b) $KMnO_4$
(c) CH_2O

Molecular Formulas

An empirical formula, which gives the simplest ratio of atoms in a molecule, is used to represent an ionic compound. For a molecular, covalent compound, however, the actual molecular formula may be the empirical formula or some whole-number multiple of the empirical formula. Once the empirical formula has been determined as shown in the preceding section, the molar mass of the compound can be used to determine the molecular formula.

The number of empirical formula units in the molecular formula of a compound is determined by dividing the molar mass of the compound by the empirical formula mass. This will result in a small whole number:

$$\frac{\text{molar mass}}{\text{empirical formula mass}} = \text{small whole number} \qquad (6.7)$$

Each and every subscript in the empirical formula is then multiplied by this small whole number to obtain the molecular formula.

Exercise 6.40

A compound has an empirical formula of CH_2O, and its molar mass is determined in a separate experiment to be 180 g mol^{-1}. What is the molecular formula of this compound?

Solution

The number of CH_2O units in the molecule is determined from Equation 6.7:

$$\frac{180 \text{ g mol}^{-1}}{30 \text{ g emp. form.}^{-1}} = 6 \text{ empirical formula units per mole}$$

Each subscript in the empirical formula is multiplied by 6 to obtain $C_6H_{12}O_6$.

Exercise 6.41

The following empirical formulas were determined, and their molar masses are given in parentheses after the formulas. Determine the molecular formulas.
(a) C_3H_7 (86)
(b) CH_2 (70)
(c) $C_4H_3O_2$ (165)
(d) BH_3 (27.7)
(e) CH_2ON (176)

Solution

(a) C_6H_{14}
(b) C_5H_{10}
(c) $C_8H_6O_4$
(d) B_2H_6
(e) $C_4H_8O_4N_4$

Other Stoichiometric Equations

Chemists become very familiar with the factor-label method and see shortcuts in the calculation of the moles of a substance from a variety of units, as shown below:

$$\text{moles} = \frac{\text{grams}}{\text{molar mass}} \tag{6.8}$$

$$\text{moles} = \text{molarity} \times \text{liters of solution} \tag{6.9}$$

$$\text{moles} = \frac{\text{liters of gas}}{22.4} \tag{6.10}$$

$$\text{moles} = \frac{\text{molecules or atoms}}{6.02 \times 10^{23}} \tag{6.11}$$

These relationships can speed the calculations, but must be used with care to ensure that the proper units are chosen in all instances.

Important
Concepts

Factor-label method
Equalities from: Avogador's number, molar masses, chemical formulas and
   chemical equations
Stoichiometric conversion sequence
Limiting reactant calculations
Percent composition and empirical formulas
Titrations

Important
Equations

moles = grams/molar mass
molarity = moles/liter
moles = molecules or atoms/6.02×10^{23}
moles = liters of gas at STP/22.4

Questions on
Chapter 6

1. What weight of $KClO_3$ (molar mass = 122.6) is needed to make 200 mL
   of a 0.150 M solution of this salt?
   (A) 2.73 g
   (B) 3.68 g
   (C) 27.3 g
   (D) 164 g
   (E) 3.69 kg

2. In an experiment 35.0 mL of 0.345 M HNO_3 is titrated with 0.130 M
   NaOH. What volume of NaOH will have been used when the indicator
   changes color?
   (A) 35.0 mL
   (B) 13.2 mL
   (C) 26.4 mL
   (D) 50.0 mL
   (E) 92.9 mL

3. In the reaction

$$CaCO_3 \quad + \quad 2HCl \quad \rightarrow \quad H_2O \quad + \quad CO_2 \quad + \quad CaCl_2$$

   how many grams of $CaCO_3$ (molar mass = 100) are needed to produce
   3.00 L of CO_2 at STP?
   (A) 13.4
   (B) 9.11
   (C) 5.89
   (D) 300
   (E) 7.47

4. What is the simplest formula for a compound composed of only carbon
   and hydrogen and containing 14.3% H?
   (A) CH
   (B) CH_4
   (C) C_4H
   (D) CH_2
   (E) CH_3

5. What is the molar mass of $Al(NO_3)_3$?
   (A) 165.00
   (B) 56.99
   (C) 213.00
   (D) 88.99
   (E) 184.99

6. How many milligrams of Na_2SO_4 (molar mass = 142) are needed to prepare 100 mL of a solution that is 0.00100 M in Na^+ ions?
   (A) 28.4
   (B) 14,200
   (C) 1.00
   (D) 7.1
   (E) 14.2

7. The wavelength of blue light is 400 nm. What is the wavelength in centimeters?
   (A) 4.00×10^{-5} cm
   (B) 400×10^{-9} cm
   (C) 400×10^{-2} cm
   (D) 2.5×10^6 cm
   (E) 2.5×10^8 cm

8. In the reaction below, how many moles of aluminum will produce 1 mol of iron?

$$8Al \quad + \quad 3Fe_3O_4 \quad \rightarrow \quad 9Fe \quad + \quad 4Al_2O_3$$

   (A) 1
   (B) $\frac{3}{4}$
   (C) $\frac{9}{8}$
   (D) $\frac{8}{9}$
   (E) $\frac{4}{3}$

9. In the following reaction:

$$2KOH \quad + \quad H_2SO_4 \quad \rightarrow \quad K_2SO_4 \quad + \quad 2H_2O$$

   35.4 mL of 0.125 M KOH is required to titrate 50.0 mL of H_2SO_4. What is the molarity of the H_2SO_4 solution?
   (A) 0.0883 M
   (B) 0.100 M
   (C) 0.0443 M
   (D) 0.125 M
   (E) 0.177 M

10. A substance has an empirical formula of CH_2. Its molar mass is determined in a separate experiment as 83.5. What is the most probable molecular formula for this compound?
   (A) C_2H_4
   (B) C_6H_2
   (C) C_4H_2
   (D) CH_{12}
   (E) C_6H_{12}

11. The mass of one atom of iron is
    (A) 1.66×10^{-24} g
    (B) 2.11×10^{-22} g
    (C) 3.15×10^{-22} g
    (D) 9.28×10^{-23} g
    (E) 3.36×10^{25} g

12. How many grams of SO_2 are there in a 4.00-L sample of this compound at STP?
    (A) 256.2
    (B) 11.4
    (C) 358.7
    (D) 2.78×10^{-3}
    (E) 2.86

13. What is the percentage of potassium in K_3PO_4?
    (A) 14.6%
    (B) 29.2%
    (C) 18.4%
    (D) 55.2%
    (E) 39.1%

14. A 0.200-g sample of a compound containing only carbon, hydrogen, and oxygen is burned, and 0.357 g of CO_2 and 0.146 g of H_2O are collected. What is the percentage of carbon in this compound?
    (A) 56.0%
    (B) 73.0%
    (C) 48.7%
    (D) 24.3%
    (E) 43.2%

15. Which of the following is NOT a base metric unit?
    (A) meter
    (B) liter
    (C) mole
    (D) second
    (E) kilogram

16. In the reaction

    $$2AgNO_3 \quad + \quad CaCl_2 \quad \rightarrow \quad 2AgCl \quad + \quad Ca(NO_3)_2$$

    how many grams of AgCl (molar mass = 143.5) will precipitate when 20.0 g $AgNO_3$ (molar mass = 170) is reacted with 15.0 g $CaCl_2$ (molar mass = 111)?
    (A) 16.9
    (B) 38.8
    (C) 33.8
    (D) 8.45
    (E) 67.6

17. In the reaction

$$2AgNO_3 \quad + \quad CaCl_2 \quad \rightarrow \quad 2AgCl \quad + \quad Ca(NO_3)_2$$

how many grams of which reactant will remain when 20.0 g $AgNO_3$ (molar mass = 170) is reacted with 15.0 g $CaCl_2$ (molar mass = 111)?
(A) 6.53 g $CaCl_2$
(B) 6.53 g $AgNO_3$
(C) 45.9 g $CaCl_2$
(D) 8.47 g $CaCl_2$
(E) 25.9 g $AgNO_3$

18. A 50.0-g sample of impure $CaCl_2$ is reacted with excess $AgNO_3$ according to the reaction

$$2AgNO_3 \quad + \quad CaCl_2 \quad \rightarrow \quad 2AgCl \quad + \quad Ca(NO_3)_2$$

If 5.86 g of AgCl (molar mass = 143.5) precipitates, what is the percentage of chlorine (molar mass = 35.5) in the sample?
(A) 1.45%
(B) 2.90%
(C) 3.80%
(D) 11.7%
(E) 8.53%

19. How many liters of air are needed to completely burn 1 mol of methane in air (20% oxygen) at STP according to the reaction

$$CH_4 \quad + \quad 2O_2 \quad \rightarrow \quad CO_2 \quad + \quad 2H_2O?$$

(A) 22.4
(B) 44.8
(C) 11.2
(D) 224
(E) 64.0

20. Determine the empirical formula for a compound that is 25% hydrogen and 75% carbon.
(A) CH
(B) CH_2
(C) CH_4
(D) C_2H_8
(E) C_4H

Answer Key

See Appendix I for explanations of answers.

1. **B**	5. **C**	9. **C**	13. **D**	17. **D**
2. **E**	6. **D**	10. **E**	14. **C**	18. **B**
3. **A**	7. **A**	11. **D**	15. **B**	19. **D**
4. **D**	8. **D**	12. **B**	16. **A**	20. **C**

PART THREE

States of Matter

CHAPTER SEVEN

Gases

The gaseous state is characterized as a form of matter that will expand to completely fill any container in which it is placed. Gases are noted for having low densities, usually in the range of 10^{-4} to 10^{-2} gram per cubic centimeter. This means that gases are 100 to 10,000 times less dense than water. Gases have a wide range of other physical properties, as do the other two states of matter. Many gases are colorless or only lightly colored and are difficult to see. However, some gases, such as NO_2, $Br_2(g)$, and $I_2(g)$, are highly colored and quite visible. Gases can be felt in the same manner as the wind is felt on a breezy day. Gases may also stimulate the sense of smell. Ammonia and hydrogen chloride have pungent, irritating odors. Other gases, such as N_2, O_2, CO, and the noble gases, have no noticeable smell.

While the physical properties of gases vary widely, the physical behavior of all gases is extraordinarily similar, to the extent that one equation, the **ideal gas law**, defines the relationships among the volume, pressure, temperature, and moles of gas in any sample. Similarly, only one theory, the **kinetic molecular theory**, is commonly used to describe the behavior of all gases. A thorough understanding of the ideal gas law is necessary for numerical calculations based on gases, and a similar understanding of the kinetic molecular theory provides the basis for explaining why gases behave as they do.

Development of the Ideal Gas Law (PV = nRT)

Historically, the ideal gas law was formulated from a combination of Boyle's law, Charles's law, Gay-Lussac's law, and Avogadro's principle.

In 1660 Robert Boyle discovered the **inverse relationship** between the pressure and volume of a gas, which is given below in equation and in graphical form:

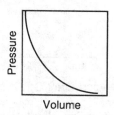

$$P \propto \frac{1}{V} \quad \text{or} \quad PV = \text{constant} \tag{7.1}$$

If a sample of gas starts with initial conditions of pressure and volume, and an experiment is done to change those conditions (without changing T or the amount of gas), then the relationship

$$P_iV_i \quad = \quad P_fV_f \qquad (7.2)$$

is obtained. The subscripts i and f represent the initial and the final conditions, respectively. This form of **Boyle's law** shows that, if the pressure on a gas is increased, the volume must correspondingly decrease. If the pressure decreases, the volume will increase.

In 1787, over 100 years later, Jacques Charles discovered the **direct relationship** between the volume of a gas and its temperature, as illustrated in the following equations and graph:

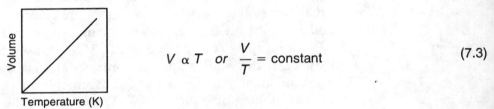

$$V \propto T \quad or \quad \frac{V}{T} = constant \qquad (7.3)$$

If a gas sample starts with initial conditions of volume and temperature that are changed to some final conditions (while the pressure and the amount of gas do not change), **Charles's law** may be reformulated as

$$\frac{V_i}{T_i} \quad = \quad \frac{V_f}{T_f} \qquad (7.4)$$

Another way of stating this law is to say that, as the temperature of a gas decreases, its volume will decrease.

Absolute zero is the lowest possible temperature. It is zero on the Kelvin and −273 degrees on the Celsius temperature scales. One method of determining absolute zero is to construct a graph of the volume of a gas as its temperature is changed and to extrapolate the data to the temperature that corresponds to zero volume of the gas, as shown in Figure 7.1.

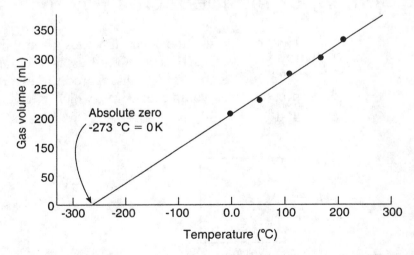

FIGURE 7.1. Using Charles's law to determine absolute zero. Each dot represents an experimental measurement. The line is the best straight line through the data, and the intercept is at −273°C.

At about the same time, Gay-Lussac, along with Charles, discovered the direct relationship between pressure and temperature:

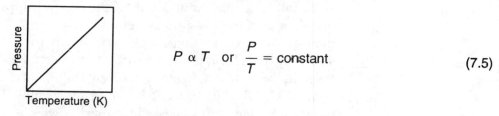

$$P \propto T \quad \text{or} \quad \frac{P}{T} = \text{constant} \qquad (7.5)$$

If initial conditions of P and T are changed to some final conditions, **Gay-Lussac's law** requires that

$$\frac{P_i}{T_i} = \frac{P_f}{T_f} \qquad (7.6)$$

Finally, in 1811, Avogadro suggested the principle that equal volumes of gases contain equal numbers of molecules or atoms (i.e., moles of a gas) under identical conditions of temperature and pressure. This direct relationship between the number of moles and volume is written in equation form and shown graphically as:

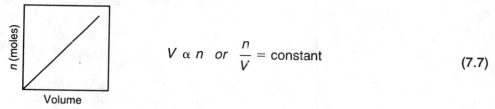

$$V \propto n \quad \text{or} \quad \frac{n}{V} = \text{constant} \qquad (7.7)$$

If initial conditions of n or V are changed to some final conditions, **Avogadro's principle** requires that

$$\frac{n_i}{V_i} = \frac{n_f}{V_f} \qquad (7.8)$$

Avogadro's principle can be interpreted as meaning that, at constant temperature and pressure, the volume of the container must increase as the moles of gas increase.

Each of these laws considers the relationship between only two of the four variables, P, V, T, and n, that affect gases. This fact means that the other two variables must remain constant, or the law will not be applicable.

deal Gas Law

The four laws of Boyle, Charles, Gay-Lussac, and Avogadro are combined into the ideal gas law:

$$PV = nRT \qquad (7.9)$$

where P is the pressure, V the volume, n the number of moles of gas, and T the temperature in Kelvin units. The constant, R, called the **universal gas constant**, is needed to make all of the relationships fit together. Table 7.1 gives some of the possible values and units for R. This constant appears in many different equations, and selection of the proper value and corresponding units for it is often critical. The selection of R is based on the units given in the problem. In many problems not all of the data are given in units compatible with the units of R. For instance, most problems give the temperature in degrees Celsius, which must *always* be converted to kelvins. In other instances the pressure or volume may need to be converted to the appropriate units. Units must be watched very carefully in gas law calculations.

TABLE 7.1 Different Formulations of the Universal Gas Constant, R (These are given with problems and need not be memorized.)

Value	Units
0.0821	L atm mol^{-1} K^{-1}
8.314	J mol^{-1} K^{-1}
6.24×10^4	L mm Hg mol^{-1} K^{-1}
1.99	cal mol^{-1} K^{-1}
8.314	V C mol^{-1} K^{-1}

Instead of memorizing the four laws developed by Boyle, Charles, Gay-Lussac, and Avogadro, it is more convenient to use only the ideal gas law equation for all problems. There are two ways to use the ideal gas law. First, a problem may give three of the four variables and ask that the fourth be calculated. This involves direct substitution of data into the ideal gas law equation. The second way to use the law involves taking a gas under certain initial conditions of P, V, T, and n and changing to some different, final conditions of these four variables. To solve this type of problem the ratio of the ideal gas law equations for the initial and final conditions is written as:

$$\frac{P_i V_i}{P_f V_f} = \frac{n_i R T_i}{n_f R T_f} \tag{7.10}$$

Variables that the problem states (or implies) as constants are canceled, along with R, and then the appropriate substitutions are made from the given data to perform the calculation. Using this approach, it can be seen that the ideal gas law becomes Boyle's law if n and T are constant (i.e., they cancel), and becomes Charles's law if n and P are held constant. If V and n are held constant, Equation 7.10 cancels to become Gay-Lussac's law, and it becomes Avogadro's principle if P and T are held constant. Only one equation need be remembered for all ideal gas law calculations!

DERIVATION OF THE IDEAL GAS LAW

One method for deriving the ideal gas law uses Avogadro's principle, $\frac{n}{V} = C$, and Guy-Lussac's law, $\frac{P}{T} = C'$. Since C and C' are not the same constants, we multiply Avogadro's principle by a constant, R, so that $CR = C'$. Then

$$CR = C'$$

$$\frac{nR}{V} = \frac{P}{T}$$

Rearranging the last two terms in this expression yields

$$PV = nRT$$

the ideal gas law, and R is the universal gas constant.

Exercise 7.1

A gas occupies 250 mL, and its pressure is 550 mm Hg at 25°C.
(a) If the gas is expanded to 450 mL, what is the pressure of the gas now?
(b) What temperature is needed to increase the pressure of the gas to exactly 1 at 250 mL?
(c) How many moles of gas are in this sample?
(d) The sample is an element and has a mass of 0.525 g. What is it?

Solution

(a) Use the ratio of two ideal gas law equations as shown in Equation 7.10:

$$\frac{P_i V_i}{P_f V_f} = \frac{n_i R T_i}{n_f R T_f}$$

Cancel all but the P and V terms since no change is specified for the other terms and they are assumed to be constant:

$$\frac{P_i V_i}{P_f V_f} = 1$$

Assign the data to the variables: P_i = 550 mm Hg, V_i = 250 mL, and V_f = 450 mL, enter the data in the equation, and solve:

$$\frac{(550 \text{ mm Hg})(250 \text{ mL})}{P_f (450 \text{ mL})} = 1$$

$$\frac{(550 \text{ mm Hg})(250 \text{ mL})}{450 \text{ mL}} = P_f$$

$$306 \text{ mm Hg} = P_f$$

(b) Use the same procedure as in part (a) but cancel n, R, and V since they remain constant:

$$\frac{P_i V_i}{P_f V_f} = \frac{n_i R T_i}{n_f R T_f}$$

$$\frac{P_i}{P_f} = \frac{T_i}{T_f}$$

Assign the data: $P_i = 550$ mm Hg, $T_i = 25 + 273 = 298$ K, and $P_f = 1$ atm $= 760$ mm Hg.

$$\frac{550 \text{ mm Hg}}{760 \text{ mm Hg}} = \frac{298 \text{ K}}{T_f}$$

$$T_f = 298 \text{ K} \left(\frac{760 \text{ mm Hg}}{550 \text{ mm Hg}} \right)$$

$$= 412 \text{ K} = 139°C$$

(c) To solve this question we use the ideal gas law equation and substitute the given values:

$$P V = n R T$$

To use the constant $R = 0.0821$ L atm mol^{-1} K^{-1}, the data must be converted to the proper units so that $P = 550$ mm Hg $\left(\dfrac{1 \text{ atm}}{760 \text{ mm Hg}} \right) =$ 0.724 atm, $V = 250$ mL $\left(\dfrac{1L}{1000 \text{ mL}} \right) = 0.250$ L and, $T = 25°C = 298$ K. Enter these data and solve:

$$(0.724 \text{ atm})(0.250 \text{ L}) = n \,(0.0821 \text{ L atm mol}^{-1} \text{ K}^{-1})(298 \text{ K})$$

$$n = \frac{(0.724 \text{ atm})(0.250 \text{ L})}{(0.0821 \text{ L atm mol}^{-1} \text{ K}^{-1})(298 \text{ K})}$$

$$= 7.40 \times 10^{-3} \text{ mol}$$

(d) We can identify a gas by its molar mass. The molar mass is

$$\text{molar mass} = \frac{\text{mass of sample}}{\text{moles of sample}}$$

$$= \frac{0.525 \text{ g}}{7.40 \times 10^{-3} \text{ mol}}$$

$$= 70.9 \text{ g mol}^{-1}$$

The element with a molar mass closest to 70.9 is chlorine, Cl_2.

Standard Temperature and Pressure (STP)

The ideal gas law has four variables, P, V, n, and T, along with the constant R. By defining the standard pressure as exactly 1 atmosphere and the standard temperature as exactly 0 degrees Celsius, two of the variables can be stated quickly and easily. Therefore any gas at **STP** is understood to have $P = 1.00$ atm and $T = 273$ K, and only n and V need be stated in a problem.

Besides making the statement of problems simpler, gases at STP can be compared to each other. The next section shows how the molar mass and density of a gas and the molar volume of a gas at STP are calculated. Differences between the densities and molar volumes calculated from the ideal gas law and the densities and molar volumes determined by experimental measurements indicate to scientists the difference between ideal gases and real gases.

Molar Mass, Density, and Molar Volume

In the ideal gas law n represents the number of moles of gas. The number of moles is calculated as $n = \dfrac{\text{grams of gas}}{\text{molar mass}}$. Substituting this equivalency into the ideal gas law yields

$$P V = \frac{g}{\text{molar mass}} R T \tag{7.11}$$

This equation can be used to determine the **molar mass** of a gas if P, V, g, and T are known for a given sample.

Rearranging Equation 7.11 algebraically yields another useful relationship:

$$P \,(\text{molar mass}) = \frac{g}{V} R T \tag{7.12}$$

In this equation $\dfrac{g}{V}$ is the density of the gas in grams per liter. The **density** of a gas can be determined if P, T, and the molar mass are known.

Finally, at standard temperature, 0 degree Celsius, and pressure, 1.0 atmosphere, the ideal gas law can be solved to calculate the **molar volume**, $\dfrac{V}{n}$, as

$$\frac{V}{n} = \frac{RT}{P} = \frac{(0.0821 \text{ L atm mol}^{-1} \text{ K}^{-1})(273 \text{ K})}{1.00 \text{ atm}}$$

$$= \quad 22.4 \text{ L mol}^{-1} \tag{7.13}$$

This indicates that 1 mole of an **ideal gas** at STP has a volume of 22.4 liters, a fact that is useful in stoichiometry calculations. Table 7.2 lists the molar volumes of some real gases at STP. They are all close to 22.4 liters indicating that they behave as ideal gases under these conditions.

TABLE 7.2 Molar Volumes of Some Gases at STP

Gas	Symbol	Molar (L) Volume
Argon	Ar	22.401
Carbon dioxide	CO_2	22.414
Helium	He	22.398
Hydrogen	H_2	22.410
Nitrogen	N_2	22.413
Oxygen	O_2	22.414

Exercise 7.2

What are the expected densities of argon, neon, and air at STP?

Solution

Each density is calculated, using Equation 7.12, as

$$\text{density} = \frac{g}{V} = \frac{(\text{molar mass})\,P}{RT}$$

At STP, $P = 1.00$ atm and $T = 273$ K. Substituting these data gives

$$\text{density Ar} = \frac{(39.95 \text{ g mol}^{-1})(1.00 \text{ atm})}{(0.0821 \text{ L atm mol}^{-1} \text{ K}^{-1})(273 \text{ K})} = 1.78 \text{ g L}^{-1}$$

$$\text{density Ne} = \frac{(20.18 \text{ g mol}^{-1})(1.00 \text{ atm})}{(0.0821 \text{ L atm mol}^{-1} \text{ K}^{-1})(273 \text{ K})} = 0.900 \text{ g L}^{-1}$$

$$\text{density air} = \frac{(28.8 \text{ g mol}^{-1})(1.00 \text{ atm})}{(0.0821 \text{ L atm mol}^{-1} \text{ K}^{-1})(273 \text{ K})} = 1.28 \text{ g L}^{-1}$$

The molar mass of air is approximated from the fact that air is 80 percent nitrogen and 20 percent oxygen.

$$\text{molar mass} = (0.80)\left(\frac{28 \text{ g N}_2}{\text{mol}}\right) + (0.20)\left(\frac{32 \text{ g O}_2}{\text{mol}}\right)$$
$$= 28.8 \text{ g mol}$$

We may also conclude that a balloon full of neon will rise in air whereas an argon-filled balloon will sink to the floor.

Kinetic Molecular Theory

The ideal gas law describes the relationships among P, V, T, and n for ideal gases. The **kinetic molecular theory** describes gases at the level of individual particles. This theory, developed largely by Boltzmann, Clausius, and Maxwell between 1850 and 1880, is often stated as five postulates:

1. Gases consist of molecules or atoms in continuous random motion.
2. Collisions between these molecules and/or atoms in a gas are elastic.

3. The volume occupied by the atoms and/or molecules in a gas is negligibly small.
4. The attractive forces between the atoms and/or molecules in a gas are negligible.
5. The average kinetic energy of a molecule or atom in a gas is directly proportional to the Kelvin temperature of the gas.

The concept of gas **pressure** is important to understand since it is central to the kinetic molecular theory. Pressure is defined in physics as the force exerted per unit area. The English units for pressure, pounds per square inch, are familiar. For gases, the force is generated by collisions of the gas particles with the container walls. Each collision has a certain force, which is related to the velocity of the gas particle. The total force is the sum of the forces of all the collisions occurring each second per unit area. Thus the pressure is dependent on the velocity of the gas particles and the collision frequency. In turn, the collision frequency depends on the velocity of the gas particle and the distance to the container walls. Changing the temperature changes the force of the collisions, as well as the frequency of collision. The frequency of collision can be changed also by altering the size of the container; the force of the collisions is not affected.

Based on this understanding of pressure, the molecular meanings of the gas laws can be appreciated as follows.

Boyle's law states the inverse relationship between pressure and volume $\left(P \propto \dfrac{1}{V} \right)$. The kinetic molecular theory agrees with this observation. If the volume of a gas is decreased, the gas particles will strike the walls of the container more frequently. Increasing the frequency of these collisions increases the observed pressure of the gas.

Gay-Lussac's law finds a direct relationship between temperature and pressure $(P \propto T)$. In this case, an increase in temperature increases the kinetic energy of the gas particles. This increase has two effects. First, the force of each collision is greater; second, since the average velocity of the gas particles increases with temperature, the frequency of collisions with the container walls also increases. Thus the kinetic molecular theory predicts an increase in gas pressure as temperature rises.

Charles's law predicts a direct relationship between temperature and volume $(V \propto T)$. An increase in temperature increases both the force of each collision and the frequency of collisions. Both of these effects increase the pressure. If the pressure of the gas is to remain constant, the volume must increase to correspondingly decrease the frequency of collisions with the walls of the container.

Finally, the kinetic molecular theory also explains **Graham's law of effusion**. The last of the five postulates given above may be stated as the following equation:

$$\overline{\text{KE}} = cT = \frac{1}{2} m \bar{v}^2 \tag{7.14}$$

where $\overline{\text{KE}}$ is the average **kinetic energy**, c is a constant that is the same for all gases, T is the temperature in Kelvin, m is the mass of the gas, and $\bar{v}$ is the average velocity of the gas. Since cT will be the same for all gases at the same temperature, the average kinetic energy of any two gases at the same temperature will also be the same:

$$\overline{KE}_1 = \overline{KE}_2$$

and

$$\frac{1}{2}m_1\overline{v}_1^2 = \frac{1}{2}m_2\overline{v}_2^2$$

Then

$$\sqrt{\frac{m_1}{m_2}} = \frac{\overline{v}_2}{\overline{v}_1} \tag{7.15}$$

Equation 7.15 is Graham's law of effusion. When the rates at which two gases will effuse through a pinhole in a container are compared, they are found to be inversely related to the square roots of the molecular masses of the gas particles. **Effusion** through a pinhole requires that a gas particle hit the pinhole just right to pass through it. The more collisions a gas has with the walls of a container, the higher the probability is that it will hit the pinhole and go through it. This demonstrates that an increase in the average velocity of a gas particle results in more frequent collisions with the container walls.

Equation 7.15 is also the mathematical statement of the relative rates of **diffusion** of gases. All gases will expand to fill a container, but filling it may take some time, depending on the conditions present. This equation illustrates that the velocity of the gas will be inversely proportional to the square root of the masses of the individual gas particles. Since this is a ratio and the units cancel, m_1 and m_2 may be either the actual mass or the molar mass of the gas particles. Heavier gases would be expected to diffuse more slowly than lighter gases, and they do.

Exercise 7.3

Helium leaks through a very small hole at a rate of 3.22×10^{-5} mol s^{-1}. How fast will oxygen effuse through the same hole under the same conditions?

Solution

Graham's law of effusion is

$$\sqrt{\frac{m_1}{m_2}} = \frac{\overline{v}_2}{\overline{v}_1}$$

and we assign the molar masses as $m_1 = 4$ and $m_2 = 32$. Correspondingly, $\overline{v}_1 = 3.22 \times 10^{-5}$ mol s^{-1} while $\overline{v}_2$ is the unknown:

$$\sqrt{\frac{4}{32}} = \frac{\overline{v}_2}{3.22 \times 10^{-5} \text{ mol s}^{-1}}$$

$$\overline{v}_2 = 1.14 \times 10^{-5} \text{ mol s}^{-1}$$

Average Kinetic Energies and Velocities

Much experimentation has shown that the average kinetic energy is directly proportional to the temperature of a gas, some gas molecules will have kinetic energies above the average, and some will have kinetic energies below the average. Figure 7.2 shows the distribution of the kinetic energies of gas particles at two different temperatures. It should also be noted from Figure 7.2 that the average kinetic energy is not the same as the most probable kinetic energy. The reason is that the curves in Figure 7.2 are not symmetrical and the point at which half of the molecules have higher and half have lower kinetic energies lies to the right of the peak.

Since

$$KE = \frac{1}{2} m \, v^2$$

Figure 7.2 can also be drawn with the x-axis representing the square of the molecular velocity. Some molecules would have velocities above the average, and others would have lower than average velocities.

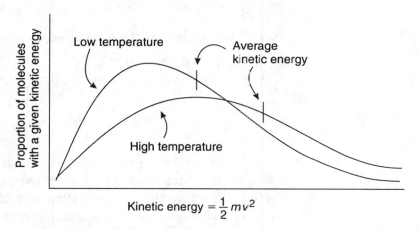

FIGURE 7.2.   Kinetic energy distribution diagrams for gas particles at two different temperatures. Note that average kinetic energy is not at the curve maximum.

Real Gases

The ideal gas law works very well for most gases; however, the law does not work well for gases under high pressures or gases at very low temperatures. These conditions are the same conditions used to condense gases, and therefore it may be generalized that any gas close to its boiling point (condensation point) will deviate significantly from the ideal gas law. The kinetic molecular theory makes two fundamental assumptions about the properties of gas particles themselves: (1) gases have no volume, and (2) they exhibit no attractive or repulsive forces. These two assumptions define an **ideal gas**. They work quite well, since gas particles are often widely separated and what little volume they have is relatively unimportant. Similarly, because of the large average distance between gas particles the attractive forces and repulsive forces are very weak. As a **real gas** is cooled and/or compressed, the distance between the particles decreases dramatically, and these real volumes and forces can no longer be ignored.

Johannes van der Waals developed a modification of the ideal gas law to deal with the nonideal behavior of real gases. He reasoned that, if the gas particles each occupied some volume, there would be a net decrease in the useful volume of the container. (Imagine a fishbowl filled with marbles. Little useful room would be left for the fish.) This decrease in volume must be proportional to the moles of gas particles present. By using the letter b for the proportionality constant, the volume term in the ideal gas law could be replaced by $(V - nb)$.

In evaluating the effect of intermolecular attractions, it was reasoned that, if gas particles attracted each other, they would have curved paths and therefore would take longer to collide with the container walls. The result would be a decreased collision frequency and a lower pressure for the real gas than the pressure of an ideal gas under the same conditions. The frequency of attractions between gas particles would be expected to rise with greater concentrations of the gas. The best correction factor was found to be based on the square of the concentration of the gas, $(n/V)^2$. The proportionality constant was given the symbol a, and the entire correction factor was added to the measured pressure $\left(P + a\left(\dfrac{n}{v}\right)^2\right)$ to obtain the equivalent ideal pressure.

The van der Waals equation for real gases takes the form

$$\left(P + \frac{an^2}{V^2}\right)(V - bn) \quad = \quad nRT \tag{7.16}$$

The value of the proportionality constant a represents the relative strength of attractive forces acting between the gas molecules, with larger values of a indicating stronger attractive forces such as dipole-dipole attractions. The value of the constant b represents the relative size of the gas molecule. The larger the value of b, the larger is the size of the molecule.

The size of gas molecules does not vary greatly from one molecule to another, and this contribution to deviations from the ideal gas law is similar for many molecules. Attractive forces, however, vary greatly, depending on molecular polarity, and contribute the most to deviations from the ideal gas law.

Dalton's Law of Partial Pressures

Dalton's law of partial pressures is based on the fact that, when two gases are mixed together, the gas particles tend to act independently of each other. The result is that, for a mixture of gases, the total pressure is equal to the sum of the pressures of all of the components of the mixture:

$$P_{total} \quad = \quad p_1 \quad + \quad p_2 \quad + \quad \cdots \tag{7.17}$$

In this equation, the lower-case p stands for the **partial pressure** of each individual gas. The ellipsis (three dots) at the end of the equation indicates that, if more than two gases are mixed, the equation should be expanded to include the additional components.

Exercise 7.4

A mixture of gases contains 2.00 mol of O_2, 3.00 mol of N_2, and 5.00 mol of He. The total pressure of the mixture is 850 mm Hg. What is the partial pressure of each gas?

Solution

The ideal gas law can be interpreted to mean that the pressure is proportional to the number of moles of gas present when T and V are constant. In this problem we have a total of 10.00 mol of gases. Since there are 2.00 mol of O_2, 2.00/10.00 of all moles of gas are O_2; therefore, the same ratio applies to the partial pressure of O_2:

$$p_{O_2} = 850 \text{ mm Hg} \left(\frac{2.00 \text{ mol } O_2}{10.00 \text{ mol total}} \right) = 170 \text{ mm Hg}$$

Using similar calculations for N_2 and He gives

$$p_{N_2} = 850 \text{ mm Hg} \left(\frac{3.00 \text{ mol } N_2}{10.00 \text{ mol total}} \right) = 255 \text{ mm Hg}$$

$$p_{He} = 850 \text{ mm Hg} \left(\frac{5.00 \text{ mol He}}{10.00 \text{ mol total}} \right) = 425 \text{ mm Hg}$$

To check the calculations, we determine the total pressure from the three partial pressures:

$$P_{total} = 170 \text{ mm Hg} + 255 \text{ mm Hg} + 425 \text{ mm Hg}$$

$$= 850 \text{ mm Hg}$$

This result agrees with the total pressure given in the problem.

Gas Measurements

The physical properties of gases depend on the four variables of volume, temperature, pressure, and number of moles. Each of these quantities may be measured independently. Often, however, it is easier to measure three of these four variables and to calculate the last one from the ideal gas law equation. The measurement methods for the variables are reviewed briefly below.

Volume is expressed in liters (sometimes milliliters) and may be determined in several ways, including:

1. Careful measurement of the dimensions of the container followed by the appropriate geometric calculations.
2. Measurement of the mass of a liquid of known density that fills the container to capacity.

Temperature is measured with standard thermometers. Special instruments may be used if high accuracy and precision are needed or if the temperature of the gas is extremely high or low. Since gases have very low densities, sufficient time must be allowed for a thermometer to reach the correct temperature. Often, the temperature of the gas is determined by measuring the temperature of its surroundings after sufficient time has elapsed for the container and the surroundings to reach the same temperature (thermal equilibrium). The container may be submersed in a liquid such as water to thermostat the system (i.e., keep its temperature constant) and also to speed the attainment of thermal equilibrium.

Pressure is the force exerted per unit area. Pressures may be recorded in SI units of kilopascals (kPa) or in experimental units, such as millimeters of mercury (also known as torr) or atmospheres (1 atm = 760 mm Hg). Pressure may be determined either by direct reading of an instrument called a pressure gauge or by using a **manometer**. Two types of manometer, the closed-end and open-end, are available. Both are U-shaped pieces of glass with one end open so that it can be attached to a vessel containing a gas. The other end may be open or closed, as the names suggest, and as shown in Figure 7.3.

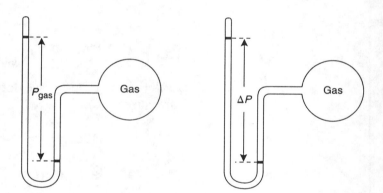

FIGURE 7.3. On the left, a closed-end manometer measures the gas pressure directly. On the right, an open-end manometer measures the difference between the atmospheric pressure and the gas pressure.

The closed-end manometer (also called a **eudiometer**) is completely filled with mercury. When the instrument is set up, the difference in the mercury levels indicates the pressure of whatever system is attached to the apparatus. If this device is not attached to an experimental setup, but is left open to the atmosphere, it measures atmospheric pressure and is then called a **barometer**.

The open-end manometer is usually filled with mercury, and the two ends are connected to gases at different pressures. The difference in pressure will be equal to the difference in the level of the mercury in the two sides of the manometer. This method gives only the difference in pressure between the two sides of the manometer. If one side is left open to the atmosphere, as shown in Figure 7.3, the difference represents the difference between the gas pressure and the atmospheric pressure.

If a fluid other than mercury is used in a manometer, the difference in the heights of this fluid represents the pressure. However, for comparison with a normal mercury manometer, the readings must be corrected for the relative densities of the fluid used and of mercury by using the equation

$$\text{mm Hg} = \text{mm fluid}\left(\frac{\text{density fluid}}{\text{density Hg}}\right) \tag{7.18}$$

Exercise 7.5

Medical devices for anesthesiology must not restrict the air flow to the patient by more than 2.50 mm Hg. Suggest a method for making these measurements accurately.

Solution

It is difficult to measure 2.50 mm Hg with accuracy in a mercury-filled manometer. If a water manometer is used, the difference in liquid levels will be much greater and will be easier to measure. For example, the difference in water levels equal to 2.50 mm Hg is calculated from Equation 7.18 as

$$2.50 \text{ mm Hg} = \text{mm H}_2\text{O}\left(\frac{1.00 \text{ g H}_2\text{O/mL H}_2\text{O}}{13.6 \text{ g Hg/mL Hg}}\right)$$

$$\text{mm H}_2\text{O} = 34 \text{ mm H}_2\text{O}$$

It is much easier to measure 34 mm than 2.5 mm.

The *number of moles of gas* is given the symbol "n". This is determined by measuring the mass of the gas and using the molecular mass to convert it to moles ($n = \text{mol} = \text{g/MM}$). Measuring the mass of any gas involves evacuating a vessel to a very low pressure using a vacuum pump. The evacuated vessel is weighed and then the gas sample is introduced to the vessel and it is weighed again to determine the increase in mass due to the gas.

Experiments Involving Gases

As a candidate for advanced placement in chemistry, you should be familiar with a variety of experiments for producing, collecting, and manipulating gases in the laboratory. A few of the more familiar reactions for producing gases are these:

$$2\text{KClO}_3(s) \rightarrow 2\text{KCl}(s) + 3\text{O}_2(g) \quad \text{(with heat and MnO}_2 \text{ as a catalyst)}$$

$$\text{NH}_4^+(aq) + \text{OH}^-(aq) \rightarrow \text{NH}_3(g) + \text{H}_2\text{O}(\ell)$$

$$\text{CaCO}_3(s) + \text{HCl}(aq) \rightarrow \text{CO}_2(g) + \text{CaCl}_2(aq) + \text{H}_2\text{O}(\ell)$$

$$2\text{HCl}(aq) + \text{Zn}(s) \rightarrow \text{ZnCl}_2(aq) + \text{H}_2(g)$$

In addition to knowledge of the chemical reactions, the use of a **pneumatic trough** for collecting gas samples over water should be familiar. Figure 7.4 illustrates a pneumatic trough with a bottle full of water sub-

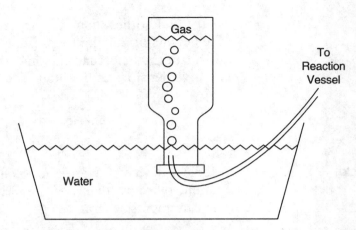

FIGURE 7.4. Collection of gases in a pneumatic trough. When the reaction is complete, the position of the bottle is adjusted so that the water level in the bottle is equal to the water level in the trough. At that point $P_{gas} = P_{atm}$.

mersed. The gas from the chemical reaction bubbles into the bottle, displacing the water as it is collected.

The pressure of the gas inside the collecting bottle must be determined in order to solve the ideal gas equation. When the reaction is complete, the gas pressure is determined by moving the bottle in the water until the two liquid levels coincide. At this point the pressure inside the bottle is the same as the barometric pressure outside the bottle.

When gases are collected over water, there will always be some water vapor in the collecting bottle. The pressure of the water vapor depends on the temperature only and is obtained from the appropriate reference table. (The AP chemistry test does not include this table; the information will be given in the problem if needed.) The pressure of the gas that was generated is calculated from Dalton's law of partial pressures as

$$p_{gas} = P_{atm} - p_{water} \tag{7.19}$$

The volume of gas may be determined by marking the jar when the liquid levels are equal and then measuring the jar's volume to the mark at a later time. This is done by filling the jar to the mark with water and then carefully pouring the water into a graduated cylinder to determine the volume.

Temperature is measured with a laboratory thermometer, and atmospheric pressure is determined from a barometer for use in Equation 7.19. These measurements give P, V, and T for the ideal gas law equation, and the amount of gas produced, n, can be calculated.

Exercise 7.6

A 0.060-g piece of magnesium is placed in hydrochloric acid to generate hydrogen according to the equation

$$Mg(s) \quad + \quad 2HCl(aq) \quad \rightarrow \quad MgCl_2(aq) \quad + \quad H_2(g)$$

The gas is collected in a pneumatic trough at 25°C. A barometer reading of 755 mm Hg is made during the experiment. When bubbles of hydrogen cease forming, the bottle is adjusted to the water level in the trough and the water level is marked on the bottle. Afterwards, 65 mL of water is needed to fill the bottle to the same mark. The vapor pressure of water at 25°C is 23.8 mm Hg. How many moles of hydrogen were produced?

Solution

The volume of the gas is 0.065 L, its temperature is 298 K, and its pressure is calculated from Equation 7.19 as

$$P_{H_2} \quad = \quad 755 \text{ mm Hg} \quad - \quad 23.8 \text{ mm Hg} \quad = \quad 731 \text{ mm Hg}$$

This is converted to 0.962 atm. The ideal gas law is then used to calculate n, the number of moles of hydrogen:

$$(0.962 \text{ atm})(0.065 \text{ L}) \quad = \quad n(0.0821 \text{ L atm mol}^{-1} \text{ K}^{-1}) \, (298 \text{ K})$$

$$n \quad = \quad 2.6 \quad \times \quad 10^{-3} \text{ mol } H_2(g)$$

Important
Concepts

Ideal gas law and ideal gas
Standard temperature and pressure, STP
Universal gas law constant, R
Dalton's law of partial pressures
Kinetic molecular theory
Average kinetic energy
Graham's law of effusion

Important
Equations

$$PV = nRT$$

$$\sqrt{\frac{m_1}{m_2}} = \frac{\bar{v}_2}{\bar{v}_1}$$

$$P_{total} = p_1 + p_2 + \ldots$$

Questions on
Chapter 7

1. What volume will 2.50 mol of N_2 occupy at 45°C and 1.50 atm of pressure?
   (A) 43.5 L
   (B) 6.08 L
   (C) 0.0233 L
   (D) 56.00 L
   (E) 14.9 L

2. How many moles of helium are needed to fill a balloon that has a volume of 6.45 L and a pressure of 800 mm Hg at a room temperature of 24°C? Assume ideal gas behavior.
   (A) 0.288
   (B) 214
   (C) 0.278
   (D) 2.65×10^3
   (E) 0.255

3. If ideal gas behavior is assumed, what is the density of neon at STP?
   (A) 1.11 g L^{-1}
   (B) 448 g L^{-1}
   (C) 0.009 g L^{-1}
   (D) 0.901 g L^{-1}
   (E) 1.25 g L^{-1}

4. A sample of CO has a pressure of 58 mm Hg and a volume of 155 mL. When the CO is quantitatively transferred to a 1.00-L flask, the pressure of the gas will be
   (A) 374 mm Hg
   (B) 8990 mm Hg
   (C) 111 mm Hg
   (D) 8.99 mm Hg
   (E) 2.67 mm Hg

5. At 30°C a sample of hydrogen is collected over water $[p_{30°C} = 31.82$ mm Hg] in a 500-mL flask. The total pressure in the collection flask is 745 mm Hg. What will be the percent of error in the amount of hydrogen reported if the correction for the vapor pressure of water is not made?
   (A) 0.0%
   (B) +4.5%
   (C) −4.5%
   (D) +4.3%
   (E) −4.3%

6. What will the total pressure be in a 2.50-L flask at 25°C if it contains 0.016 mol of CO_2 and 0.035 mol of CH_4?
   (A) 31.4 mm Hg
   (B) 380 mm Hg
   (C) 0.041 mm Hg
   (D) 935 mm Hg
   (E) 1.23 atm

7. The carbon dioxide from the combustion of 1.50 g of C_2H_6 is collected over water at 25°C. The pressure of CO_2 in the collection flask is 746 mm Hg, and the volume is 2.00 L. How much of the CO_2 formed apparently dissolved in the water of the pneumatic trough?
   (A) 0.0814 mol
   (B) 0.87 g
   (C) 1.79 g
   (D) 0.100 mol
   (E) 2.55 g

8. In which of the following is it impossible to predict the direction in which the pressure of a gas will change?
   (A) A gas sample is heated.
   (B) A gas sample is heated, and the volume is increased.
   (C) A gas sample is cooled, and some gas is withdrawn.
   (D) Additional gas is added to a sample of gas.
   (E) A gas sample is cooled, and the volume is increased.

9. The kinetic molecular theory predicts that at a given temperature
   (A) all gas molecules have the same kinetic energy
   (B) all gas molecules have the same average velocity
   (C) only real gas molecules collide with each other
   (D) on the average, heavier molecules move more slowly
   (E) elastic collisions result in the loss of energy

10. The effect of increasing the temperature on the pressure may be explained by the kinetic molecular theory as due to
    (A) the increase in force with which the gas molecules collide with the container walls
    (B) the increase in rotational energy of the gas molecules
    (C) the increase in average velocity of the gas molecules, which causes a corresponding increase in the rate of collision with the container walls
    (D) a decrease in the attractive forces between gas molecules
    (E) a combination of A and C.

11. Ideal gases
    (A) have no volume
    (B) have no mass
    (C) have no attractive forces between them
    (D) have a combination of A and C
    (E) have a combination of A and B

12. Under which conditions will a real gas behave most like an ideal gas?
    (A) high pressure and high temperature
    (B) low pressure and low temperature
    (C) low volume and high temperature
    (D) low pressure and high temperature
    (E) high pressure and low temperature

13. Real gases tend to have
    (A) larger volumes than ideal gases
    (B) greater kinetic energies than ideal gases
    (C) lower average kinetic energies than ideal gases
    (D) lower pressures than ideal gases
    (E) both A and D

14. Under identical conditions gaseous CO_2 and CCl_4 are allowed to effuse through a pinhole. If the rate of effusion of the CO_2 is 6.3×10^{-2} mol s^{-1}, what is the rate of effusion of the CCl_4?
    (A) 6.3×10^{-2} mol s^{-1}
    (B) 2.2×10^{-1} mol s^{-1}
    (C) 1.8×10^{-2} mol s^{-1}
    (D) 3.4×10^{-2} mol s^{-1}
    (E) 1.2×10^{-1} mol s^{-1}

15. A gas has a density, at STP, of 3.48 g L^{-1}. The most reasonable formula for this compound is
    (A) C_2H_6
    (B) HF
    (C) CCl_4
    (D) C_6H_6
    (E) CaF_2

16. The number of moles of an ideal gas in a 2.50-L container at 300 K and a pressure of 0.450 atm is ($R = 0.0821$ L atm mol^{-1} K^{-1})
    (A) 0.0457
    (B) 21.9
    (C) 4.93×10^{-5}
    (D) 2.03×10^{4}
    (E) 6.02

17. A gas mixture contains twice as many moles of O_2 as N_2. Addition of 0.200 mol of argon to this mixture increases the pressure from 0.800 atm to 1.10 atm. How many moles of O_2 are in the mixture?
    (A) 0.355
    (B) 0.178
    (C) 0.533
    (D) 0.200
    (E) 0.0750

18. A gas in a 1.50-L container has a pressure of 245 mm Hg. When the gas is transferred completely to a 350-mL container at the same temperature, the pressure will be
    (A) 1.05 mm Hg
    (B) 1.05 atm
    (C) 2.14 mm Hg
    (D) 1050 mm Hg
    (E) 9.5×10^{-4} atm

19. At STP a 5.00-L flask filled with air has a mass of 543.251 g. The air in the flask is replaced with another gas, and the mass of the flask is then determined to be 566.107 g. The density of air is 1.290 g L^{-1}. What is the gas that replaced the air?
    (A) Ne
    (B) O_2
    (C) Ar
    (D) Xe
    (E) He

20. What volume of hydrogen gas, at STP, will a 0.100-g sample of magnesium (molar mass = 24.31) produce when reacted with an excess of HCl? (Mg + 2HCl → $MgCl_2$ + H_2)
    (A) 92.1 mL
    (B) 46.1 mL
    (C) 184 mL
    (D) 9.2 mL
    (E) 4.6 L

Answer Key   See Appendix I for explanations of answers.

1. **A**	5. **B**	9. **D**	13. **E**	17. **A**
2. **C**	6. **B**	10. **E**	14. **D**	18. **D**
3. **D**	7. **B**	11. **D**	15. **D**	19. **D**
4. **D**	8. **B**	12. **D**	16. **A**	20. **A**

CHAPTER EIGHT

Liquids and Solids

Comparison of Liquids and Solids to Gases

Liquids and solids are distinctly different from the gases discussed in Chapter 7. First, liquids and solids are much more dense than gases. Inorganic liquids and solids have densities that range from 1 to 8 g cm^{-3}; a few have densities up to 20 g cm^{-3}. Most organic liquids and solids have densities from 0.7 to 2.0 g cm^{-3}. In contrast, gas densities at STP are generally between 10^{-2} and 10^{-4} g cm^{-3}. Second, gases expand to fill all available space and must be kept in an enclosed container, while a liquid fills any container from the bottom up to a level dictated only by the mass of liquid present. Liquids also conform to the shape of the container. Solids maintain their shape without any container. Third, and most important, is the lack of significant attractive forces in gases and the presence of significant attractive forces in liquids and solids. The obvious physical differences between the three states of matter are explained on the basis of these forces.

Intermolecular Forces

In discussing gases, we found that the ideal gas law can be used to describe gases for two reasons. First, the volume of a gas molecule is so small that 99.9 percent of a gas is empty space. Second, the gas molecules are so far apart that there is no significant intermolecular attraction. If gases were truly ideal (zero volume and zero attractive forces), it would be impossible to condense them to liquids.

For condensation to occur, intermolecular attractive forces must overcome the kinetic energy of the gas molecules. A real gas can be condensed to a liquid by increasing the pressure and/or decreasing the temperature. Pressure is increased to force the gas molecules closer together, thereby increasing the attractive forces. Temperature is decreased to lower the average kinetic energy.

By understanding the attractive forces between molecules, it is possible to appreciate many of the physical properties of both liquids and solids, including the condensation process. We can identify several of these **intermolecular forces** of attraction as dipole-dipole attractive forces, London forces, and hydrogen bonding. These forces are described below.

**Dipole-Dipole
Attractive Forces**

Molecular compounds share electrons in a covalent bond. This electron sharing is rarely equal, particularly between dissimilar elements. Consequently, the electrons may congregate at one end of the molecule, giving it polarity. Polar molecules are also called **dipoles** to remind us that there is only one positive and only one negative end to each molecule. The positive end has a partial positive charge, indicated as $\delta+$. Similarly, the negative end of a molecule is only partially negative and is designated as $\delta-$. Polar molecules are attracted toward each other, with the negative end of one molecule attracted to the positive end of another molecule.

One of the simplest dipoles is hydrogen chloride. In Figure 8.1 the electron clouds around the nonpolar H_2 and the polar HCl molecules are compared.

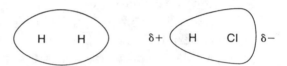

FIGURE 8.1. Representations of the electron clouds around the nonpolar H_2 and the polar HCl molecules.

In the gaseous state, polar molecules show little attraction for each other because they are so far apart (about 3000 pm). The molecules in solids and liquids, however, are approximately ten times closer (about 300 pm). Attractive forces between dipoles may be represented by Equation 8.1:

$$\text{Force} = \frac{(\delta+)(\delta-)}{r^2} \qquad (8.1)$$

This equation shows that the attractive force is inversely proportional to the square of the distance, r, between two polar molecules. In gases r is so large that the attractive force is negligibly small. In liquids, where the distance between molecules is much smaller, these forces are significant.

For a gas to become a liquid, the attractive forces must overcome the kinetic energy of the moving gas molecule. Equation 8.1 indicates that decreasing the distance between molecules will increase the attractive force. Increasing the pressure on a gas forces the molecules closer together, and cooling a gas reduces its average kinetic energy. Therefore, decreasing the temperature of a gas and/or increasing the pressure on it will help condense the gas to the liquid phase. The boiling point, which is also the same as the condensation point, is an indication of the attractive forces between molecules since it is a measure of how much the kinetic energy must be increased so that it can overcome the attractive forces in a liquid. Low boiling points indicate low attractive forces, and high boiling points indicate higher attractive forces.

In the condensed state of a liquid the dipole-dipole forces define many of the observed properties. For instance, highly polar molecules have higher boiling points than molecules with lower polarities. The vapor pressure, surface tension, viscosity, and solubilities of liquids are also based on considerations involving attractive forces, as described in the following sections.

London Forces of Attraction

Dipole-dipole interactions are used to explain how and why polar molecules may be condensed to the liquid state. It remained for Fritz London, in 1928, to give a logical explanation of how nonpolar gases develop the forces necessary for condensation. He postulated that nonpolar atoms and molecules may become momentarily polar when an unsymmetrical distribution of their electrons results in the formation of instantaneous dipoles. These instantaneous dipoles provide weak attractive forces in nonpolar substances. **London forces** may also be called **dispersion forces**, **instantaneous dipole forces**, or **induced dipole forces**.

To describe how London forces develop, consider a noble gas such as argon. Previously, argon was described as an atom with 14 electrons arranged in symmetrical orbitals around the 14 protons in its nucleus. The electrons around the argon nucleus are in constant motion. This motion results in a high probability that, at any moment in time, the electrons will not be arranged symmetrically. To illustrate this, several "instantaneous snapshots" of the argon atom are shown in Figure 8.2.

FIGURE 8.2. Random distribution of electrons around an argon nucleus. The first two obviously have more electrons on one side (the upper left quadrant). The third looks symmetrical but a close examination shows more electrons in the lower left quadrant.

When the electrons are not evenly distributed, argon will be a dipole for an instant before the electrons move to new positions. This instantaneous dipole may be attracted to another nearby instantaneous dipole, or it may induce another dipole in a neighboring atom by distorting the neighboring atom's electron cloud. The result is a very weak, attractive force, allowing argon to condense. Since such forces are very weak, argon and the other noble gases have very low boiling points.

The halogens are like the noble gases in having no permanent dipoles. Yet iodine is a solid, and bromine is a liquid, at room temperature and all of the halogens have much higher boiling points than the neighboring noble gases. The explanation for this seeming paradox lies in the **polarizability** of the electron clouds of the halogen molecules. Polarizability refers to the ease with which the electron cloud around an atom or molecule can be deformed into a dipole. Small atoms and molecules, with their electrons tightly held near the nucleus, have a low polarizability. Large atoms or molecules, with many loosely held electrons, have electron clouds with high polarizability. The difference may be visualized by comparing a small, hard golf ball and a large, soft sponge basketball. Since the large electron clouds of bromine and iodine are easily polarized, they have much higher boiling points than the neighboring noble gases.

We can explain the behavior of many molecules on the basis of London forces. For instance, methane, CH_4, is a nonpolar tetrahedral molecule.

Instantaneous dipoles are used to explain why methane condenses to a liquid. Ethane, C_2H_6, has a higher boiling point than methane because the six hydrogen atoms may become instantaneous dipoles, resulting in a stronger attractive force. The related propane, C_3H_8, and butane, C_4H_{10}, have increasingly more hydrogens to form more instantaneous dipoles; therefore, they have higher boiling points. These four compounds are the first four in a series of compounds called the **normal alkanes**. All n-alkanes have the general formula C_nH_{2n+2}. Figure 8.3, with the number of carbon atoms on one axis and the boiling point on the other axis, shows that boiling points rise because of increased instantaneous dipole forces.

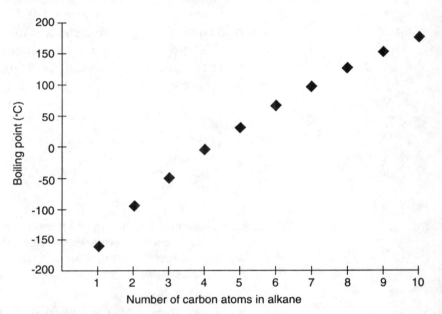

FIGURE 8.3. Plot of boiling points of the normal alkanes versus the number of carbon atoms in each n-alkane. The number of hydrogen atoms is proportional to the number of carbon atoms.

In general, we may conclude that the more atoms in a molecule, the more opportunity there is to form instantaneous dipoles. The result is to increase the attractive forces and raise the boiling point.

Hydrogen Bonding

Figure 8.3 shows a plot of the boiling points of the n-alkanes. These compounds are called a **homologous series** because their formulas vary in a regular fashion. For the n-alkanes in the graph, we added one extra carbon atom for each compound. Chemists make similar plots of other homologous series of compounds to help visualize trends in physical properties.

Figure 8.4 illustrates such a plot for the hydrogen compounds of the elements in the four groups of the periodic table headed by fluorine, oxygen, nitrogen, and carbon. We see that the compounds headed by carbon all fall on a reasonably straight line, and we conclude that they all act in a similar manner. We see also that the first compound, H_2O, NH_3, and HF, in each of the other three groups in the periodic table has a much greater boiling point than expected based on the boiling points of the other compounds in these groups.

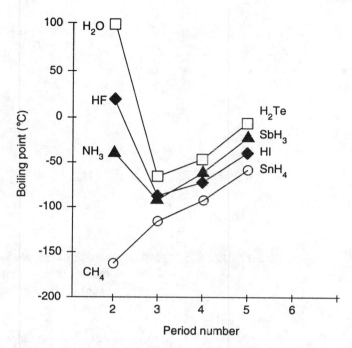

FIGURE 8.4. Plot of the boiling points of the hydrogen compounds in the groups headed by fluorine (HF, HCl, HBr, and HI), oxygen (H_2O, H_2S, H_2Se, H_2Te), nitrogen (NH_3, PH_3, AsH_3, SbH_3), and carbon (CH_4, SiH_4, GeH_4, SnH_4). Only the first and last compounds of each group are shown on the graph.

This behavior may be attributed to the large electronegativity difference (ΔEN) between hydrogen and fluorine, oxygen, and nitrogen. This large ΔEN means that H_2O, NH_3, and HF are very polar molecules with very strong dipole-dipole forces. These extraordinarily large dipole forces are given a special name, **hydrogen bonds.**

The hydrogen-bonded liquid states of HF, NH_3, and H_2O are somewhat structured. In hydrogen fluoride, the hydrogen of one HF molecule is attracted to the fluorine on another HF molecule. This attraction can extend for many HF units, creating a chainlike structure (Figure 8.5).

··· H — F ··· H — F ··· H — F ··· H — F ··· H — F ··· H — F ··· H — F ···

FIGURE 8.5. A structure illustrating the chain structure of the HF hydrogen bonding. The dotted lines indicate hydrogen bonds.

For ammonia also, a chainlike structure can form. Although NH_3 has three hydrogen atoms, it has only one nonbonding pair of electrons on its nitrogen, limiting it to a chainlike structure similar to that of HF. The increase in boiling point over the expected boiling point for both HF and NH_3 is similar, although it is slightly greater for HF since HF has a larger electronegativity difference.

Water is different. It has two hydrogen atoms, which can participate in two hydrogen bonds with neighboring oxygen atoms. In addition, the oxygen atoms have two lone pairs of electrons, which can hydrogen-bond with two hydrogen atoms. Water can form a large network structure, as diagrammed in Figure 8.6.

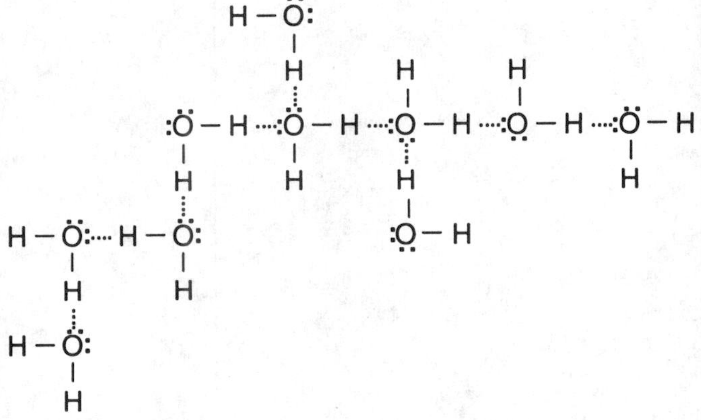

FIGURE 8.6. Network structure of water with hydrogen bonding. Tetrahedral water molecules are shown as planar structures for clarity. Dotted lines represent hydrogen bonds.

As a result of this network structure, water has the greatest increase in boiling point compared to its expected boiling point. The boiling point increase is higher in water than in HF, even though HF has a larger electronegativity difference.

Exercise 8.1

Determine the boiling points that would be expected for HF, H_2O, and NH_3 if hydrogen bonding did not exist.

Solution

Using Figure 8.4, we extrapolate each group to period 2 and read the temperature at that point. The approximate answers are HF $= -105°C$, $H_2O = -95°C$, $NH_3 = -120°C$.

Hydrogen bonding is not limited to HF, H_2O, and NH_3. This effect is observed whenever hydrogen is covalently bonded to fluorine, oxygen, or nitrogen. In the case of fluorine, there is only one compound that hydrogen-bonds: HF itself. Many compounds, however, contain the O-H bond. These include alcohols, sugars, organic acids, and phenol-type compounds. In addition to ammonia, primary and secondary amines are nitrogen containing compounds that form hydrogen bonds. These compounds are described in more detail in Chapter 15.

Hydrogen bonding is a phenomenon that has wide-reaching effects. It causes water to be a liquid at the temperatures normally encountered on Earth. It causes solid water, ice, to be less dense than liquid water, so that ice floats. If ice did not float on water, the entire planet would be ice covered all year, winter, spring, summer, and fall. In addition, it is hydrogen bonding that holds the two strands of the double helix together in DNA, and gives structure to proteins such as hemoglobin and antibodies. Life as we know it is dependent on hydrogen bonding.

Exercise 8.2

Predict the type of intermolecular forces expected for each of the following compounds:

C_6H_6 (benzene), CH_3OH, CH_3NH_2, CF_4, SO_3, XeF_6, $C_{12}H_{26}$, CH_3OCH_3.

Solution

The key to this problem lies in determining the polarities of the compounds. Polarities were discussed in Chapter 5. For these compounds the intermolecular forces are, in order, London forces, hydrogen bonding, hydrogen bonding, London forces, London forces, London forces, London forces, dipole-dipole forces.

Physical Properties of Liquids

We may use the forces discussed above to describe the liquid state. Some of the physical properties of liquids are surface tension, viscosity, evaporation, vapor pressure, boiling point, and heat of vaporization.

Surface Tension

Surface tension is due to an increase in the attractive forces between molecules at the surface of a liquid compared to the forces between molecules in the center, or bulk, of the liquid. This property causes fluids to minimize their surface areas. As a result, small droplets of liquids tend to form spheres. Surface tension produces a "skin" on a liquid surface that allows small insects to literally stand on water. Also, carefully placed small iron objects such as needles and pins can float on the surface of water even though iron is almost eight times as dense as water.

To visualize surface tension, consider the attractive forces that hold a molecule in the liquid state (Figure 8.7). In the interior of the liquid each molecule is attracted to other molecules from every direction (top, bottom, front, rear, left, and right). When a molecule is at the surface of a liquid, it has the same ability to attract neighboring molecules; however, at the surface there are no molecules to attract on its top side. Since the same total attractive force is now divided between fewer adjacent molecules, the result is a stronger attraction of a surface molecule toward the bulk of the liquid. This increased attractive force per molecule is responsible for the surface tension.

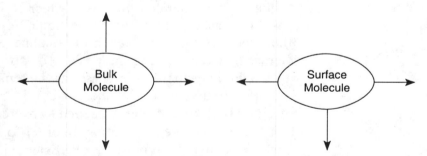

FIGURE 8.7.   Diagram illustrating attractive forces for molecules in the bulk of a liquid compared to those at the surface. Arrows indicate attractive forces; front and rear arrows are not shown.

Surface tension determines whether or not droplets of a liquid will bead up, as on a freshly waxed car, or spread out when placed on a flat surface. To describe this phenomenon, we define **cohesive forces** as attractions between identical molecules in the liquid, and **adhesive forces** as attractions between different molecules, such as those in the liquid and a flat surface. If the cohesive forces of the liquid are strong compared to the adhesive forces between that liquid and the flat surface, the liquid will retain its shape and form beads. If, however, the adhesive forces between the flat surface and the liquid are strong enough, the liquid will spread uniformly.

Very clean glass has low adhesive forces, and water beads readily on it. In dishwashers these beads of water evaporate, leaving undesired spots on glasses and dishes. For this reason dishwasher detergents contain chemicals called **surfactants**. A surfactant decreases the cohesive forces, and therefore the surface tension, of liquids. The surfactant in dishwasher detergent lowers the cohesive forces of water so that the adhesive forces between water and glass are small. Then water does not bead up on glassware, and the spotting problem is reduced.

Viscosity

Viscosity refers to a liquid's resistance to flow. A liquid such as water has a fairly low viscosity and flows easily. Pancake syrup, on the other hand, has a high viscosity, particularly when cold, and flows slowly. The attractive forces within the liquid are responsible for viscosity. In order for a liquid to flow, the molecules must move past each other. Molecules are able to move more freely in solutions that have relatively low attractive forces. The liquid alkanes have lower viscosities than water because alkanes are attracted to each other only by London forces. Water is more viscous because of hydrogen bonding. Syrup is very viscous since its bulky sugar molecules contain many —OH groups, which hydrogen-bond to the water in the mixture.

Viscosity usually decreases as the temperature of a liquid is increased. Pancake syrup flows much more easily at room temperature than it does when first taken from the refrigerator. The reason is that at the higher temperature the molecules have a higher kinetic energy since $KE = kT$. This increase in kinetic energy weakens the intermolecular forces, thus decreasing the viscosity.

Evaporation

Evaporation is a familiar process in which a liquid in an open container is slowly converted into a gas. Some liquids evaporate more rapidly than others. For example, a beaker of gasoline evaporates in a few hours, whereas a beaker of water may take a day or two. In addition, the rate at which a liquid evaporates increases as the temperature increases.

Evaporation may be explained by considering the attractive forces involved and the kinetic energy needed to overcome these forces. This process is the reverse of condensation. In order for a molecule to be converted from a liquid to a gas, it must have sufficient kinetic energy to overcome its attractive forces. In any group of molecules the average kinetic energy is proportional to the Kelvin temperature. The actual kinetic energies are distributed as shown in Figure 8.8. Some molecules have low, and others have high, kinetic energies. The escape energy is defined as the minimum kinetic energy needed for a molecule to escape from the liquid into the gas phase. All molecules with kinetic energies greater than the escape energy are capable of evaporating.

The area under the curve in Figure 8.8 represents the total number of molecules. The shaded area represents the number of molecules that have

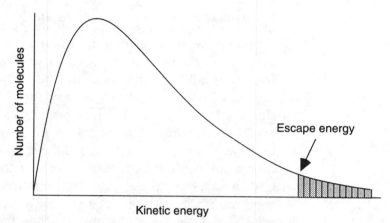

FIGURE 8.8. Distribution of kinetic energies of a group of molecules at a given temperature. Total area under the curve represents all molecules, and shaded area represents molecules with kinetic energies greater than the escape energy.

kinetic energies equal to or exceeding the escape energy. The ratio of these two areas is a constant as long as the temperature is constant. Molecules that are close enough to the surface and traveling in the correct direction will escape as gas molecules. At constant temperature, the proportion of molecules with enough kinetic energy to escape will remain constant and the liquid will evaporate at a uniform rate until all molecules have entered the gas phase.

Since only molecules near the surface may escape into the gas phase, the surface area of the liquid is a factor in evaporation (Figure 8.9). Fifty milliliters of a liquid in a narrow test tube will evaporate more slowly than the same 50 milliliters in a beaker. If the liquid is poured into an evaporating dish, it will evaporate even more quickly. The reason is found in the increased proportion of molecules that are close enough to the surface to escape readily.

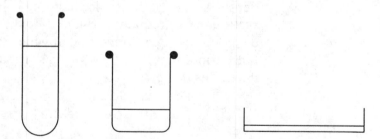

FIGURE 8.9. Surface areas of a test tube, beaker, and evaporating dish, each holding 10 mL of liquid. The increasing surface area indicates that evaporation will be slowest from the test tube and fastest from the evaporating dish.

Temperature is another important factor in the evaporation process. An increase in temperature increases the proportion of the molecules that have kinetic energies above the escape energy. Lowering the temperature decreases the proportion with enough kinetic energy to escape.

The temperature of a beaker of liquid evaporating on a lab bench is usually constant because it can absorb heat from its surroundings easily and quickly. If the beaker is insulated from the surroundings, however, the liquid cools and the rate of evaporation decreases. These phenomena are explained using curves similar to the one in Figure 8.8. First, when a molecule escapes from the liquid into the gas phase, the average kinetic energy of the remaining molecules decreases. A decrease in the average kinetic energy means that the temperature also decreases, explaining the cooling observed. Second, as the average kinetic energy decreases, the proportion of molecules that have kinetic energies above the escape energy decreases. Since fewer molecules have enough energy to escape, the rate of evaporation decreases.

Conversely, increasing the temperature of a liquid increases the rate of evaporation. This rise occurs because a greater proportion of all molecules now have a kinetic energy greater than the escape energy. When the temperature is increased sufficiently, boiling occurs. Boiling is recognized as the formation, throughout the solution, of gas bubbles which then rise to the surface. At the boiling point, the molecules do not have to reach the surface to enter the gas phase. Enough molecules, with the appropriate escape energy, can come together within the solution to form the bubbles we observe.

Vapor Pressure

Vapor pressure is the pressure that develops in the gas phase above a liquid when the liquid is placed in a closed container. Evaporation of molecules from the liquid still occurs in the closed container, but the gas molecules cannot escape to the surroundings. As more molecules enter the gas phase, the pressure increases, finally stopping at a level that is dependent only on the temperature. This final pressure is called the vapor pressure.

When a liquid is placed in a closed container, it starts evaporating just as it would in an open beaker. In the closed container, however, gas molecules cannot escape. As the gas molecules move, they collide with the walls of the container, the liquid in the lower part of the container being one of these "walls." When the gas molecules collide with the liquid, very few bounce off; almost all condense to the liquid state again. Initially the rate at which the molecules evaporate is much greater than the rate at which they condense. As the gas molecules increase in number, they collide with the liquid surface more frequently. Eventually the rate at which the liquid molecules evaporate is equal to the rate at which the gas molecules condense. Under these conditions the liquid and gas are said to be in **equilibrium**. Figure 8.10 illustrates this process.

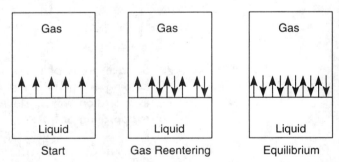

FIGURE 8.10. Diagrams illustrating the establishment of the equilibrium vapor pressure. At the start molecules leave the liquid into empty space. The middle frame shows some gas reentering the liquid but not as rapidly as molecules leave. At equilibrium molecules leave and enter the liquid at the same rate.

At equilibrium, the rate at which molecules leave the liquid must equal the rate at which they reenter the liquid. The rate at which molecules escape the liquid (evaporate) depends on the temperature. The rate at which they enter the liquid (condense) depends on the frequency at which the gas molecules collide with the liquid "wall" of the container. In Chapter 7 on gases it was shown that the frequency of collision is part of the definition of gas pressure. As a result, the vapor pressure depends only on the nature of the liquid (attractive forces) and the temperature (kinetic energy). As the temperature increases, the vapor pressure increases as shown in Figure 8.11.

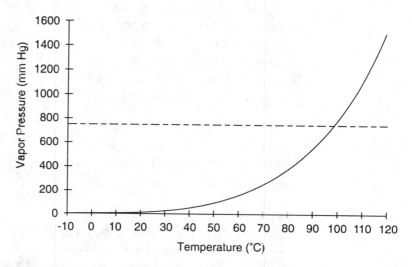

FIGURE 8.11   *Vapor pressure curve for water. Dashed line at 760 mm Hg intersects the curve at 100°C, the normal boiling point of water.*

A vapor pressure curve such as the one shown in Figure 8.11, or the tabular form of the data, may be used to determine the vapor pressure of a liquid at any temperature. Therefore chemists do not have to repeatedly determine the vapor pressure; it may be looked up in a convenient source.

Vapor pressure data point to some interesting facts about the boiling process.

Boiling occurs when the vapor pressure of a liquid is equal to the prevailing atmospheric pressure around that liquid. The vapor pressure curve shows that the temperature at which a liquid boils can vary greatly with changes in the atmospheric pressure. Therefore the boiling point of a compound is not a constant unless the pressure is also specified. The term *normal boiling point* refers to a boiling point measured when the atmospheric pressure is 760 mm Hg (1.00 atm.).

The change in boiling point with pressure has many practical aspects. Suppose a liquid decomposes instead of boiling. Decomposition may be avoided if the pressure is reduced so that boiling occurs at a much lower temperature. This technique is used in **vacuum distillation** to purify heat- sensitive materials.

The normal atmospheric pressure in Denver, Colorado, is much lower than 760 millimeters of mercury beause of the mile-high altitude of the city. The result is that water boils at a lower temperature. At high elevations longer heating times are needed to cook food properly. For this reason many people in Denver (and elsewhere) use pressure cookers. These covered pots increase the pressure and therefore the boiling point of water. At the increased temperature foods cook faster.

Heat of Vaporization

The **heat of vaporization** is the energy needed to convert 1 gram of liquid into 1 gram of gas at a temperature equal to the normal boiling point of the liquid. The units for the heat of vaporization are joules per gram (J g^{-1}). If 1 mole of liquid is vaporized, we call the energy the molar heat of vaporization and use the units joules per mole (J mol^{-1}). In either case the symbol is ΔH_{vap}. Since energy must always be added to a liquid to cause it to vaporize, ΔH_{vap} is always positive. In Chapter 12 on thermodynamics, a positive ΔH_{vap} is defined as indicating an endothermic process. The reverse process, condensation, requires the gas to give off heat in an exothermic process. Since vaporization and condensation describe the same process from different directions, their heats are related by the equation.

$$\Delta H_{vap} = -\Delta H_{cond} \tag{8.2}$$

Table 8.1 lists some heats of vaporization for compounds with different types of intermolecular forces.

TABLE 8.1 Heats of Vaporization of Representative Compounds

Compound	Formula	Heat of Vaporization (kJ mol^{-1})	Attractive Force
Water	H_2O	+43.9	Hydrogen bonding
Ammonia	NH_3	+21.7	Hydrogen bonding
Hydrogen fluoride	HF	+30.2	Hydrogen bonding
Hydrogen chloride	HCl	+15.6	Dipole-dipole
Hydrogen sulfide	H_2S	+18.8	Dipole-dipole
Fluorine	F_2	+ 5.9	London
Chlorine	Cl_2	+10.0	London
Bromine	Br_2	+15.0	London
Methane	CH_4	+ 8.2	London
Ethane	C_2H_6	+15.1	London
Propane	C_3H_8	+16.9	London

There are differences in the heats of vaporization that can be related to the intermolecular attractive forces. For similar-size molecules, hydrogen-bonded substances have the largest ΔH_{vap} values. Polar substances have higher heats of vaporization than similar-size nonpolar substances. Molecules that have the same intermolecular attractive forces also show trends in their heats of vaporization. Water has the highest ΔH_{vap}, and ammonia the lowest, among hydrogen-bonded molecules. Fluorine, chlorine, and bromine show a regular increase in ΔH_{vap}, and methane, ethane, and propane also have increasing ΔH_{vap} values because of increasing London forces.

The amount of heat required to vaporize a liquid is very large. For example, the heat energy needed to vaporize 1 gram of water could be used to raise the temperature of six times as much water from zero to 100°C. This fact explains why water can be quickly raised to its boiling point, but a long time is needed to boil away all of the water.

Exercise 8.3

For each of the following pairs, predict which compound will have (1) the lower boiling point, (2) the higher heat of vaporization, (3) the higher evaporation rate, and (4) the lower vapor pressure.

(a) C_6H_{14} or C_8H_{18} (c) HF or HCl   (e) $C_6H_{13}OH$ or $C_3H_7OC_3H_7$
(b) C_6H_{14} or $C_6H_{13}OH$ (d) HBr or HCl   (f) PBr_3 or PBr_5

Solution

For these pairs we have to assess the relative attractive forces. The one with the greater attractive forces will have the higher boiling point, higher heat of vaporization, lower evaporation rate, and lower vapor pressure. For the six pairs, the substances with the greater attractive forces are as follows: (a) C_8H_{18} since it has more hydrogen atoms for greater London forces; (b) $C_6H_{13}OH$ since it has the —OH group, which forms hydrogen bonds; (c) HF since it forms hydrogen bonds; (d) HBr since its electron cloud is more polarizable; (e) $C_6H_{13}OH$ since it forms hydrogen bonds; (f) PBr_5 since it has more polarizable bromine atoms (the polarity of PBr_3 is a minor factor). Once the attractive forces are determined, the answers can be obtained:

(a) 1. C_6H_{14} (c) 1. HCl   (e) 1. $C_3H_7OC_3H_7$
   2. C_8H_{18} 2. HF   2. $C_6H_{13}OH$
   3. C_6H_{14} 3. HCl   3. $C_3H_7OC_3H_7$
   4. C_8H_{18} 4. HF   4. $C_6H_{13}OH$
(b) 1. C_6H_{14} (d) 1. HCl   (f) 1. PBr_3
   2. $C_6H_{13}OH$ 2. HBr   2. PBr_5
   3. C_6H_{14} 3. HCl   3. PBr_3
   4. $C_6H_{13}OH$ 4. HBr   4. PBr_5

Clausius-Clapeyron equation

The heat of vaporization and the vapor pressure are both measures of the intermolecular forces that attract molecules together in the liquid state. Because they describe the same forces, there is a mathematical relationship, called the **Clausius-Clapeyron equation**, between the two:

$$\ln P = \frac{\Delta H_{vap}}{RT} + C \tag{8.3}$$

In this equation P represents the vapor pressure, ΔH_{vap} is the heat of vaporization, R is the universal gas law constant, T is the Kelvin temperature, and C is a constant. A plot of the natural logarithm of the vapor pressure versus $1/T$ will produce a straight-line graph in which the slope of the line will be $-\Delta H_{vap}/R$.

Another form of the Clausius-Clapeyron equation relates the vapor pressures at two temperatures to ΔH_{vap} as shown in Equation 8.4.

$$\ln\left(\frac{P_1}{P_2}\right) = \frac{\Delta H_{vap}}{R}\left(\frac{1}{T_2} - \frac{1}{T_1}\right) \tag{8.4}$$

In this form the constant C has been eliminated. Equation 8.4 has five variables: two temperatures, two pressures, and ΔH_{vap}. It can be solved for any one of these if the other four variables are known. For instance, ΔH_{vap} can be determined by measuring the vapor pressures at two different temperatures. Or, if the heat of vaporization is known, the vapor pressure at any temperature can be determined if the vapor pressure is known for any other temperature. Finally, the normal boiling point of a liquid can be determined from the ΔH_{vap} value and a known vapor pressure at any temperature. This calculation is possible since the normal boiling point is always at 760 millimeters of mercury, or 1.00 atmospheres, of pressure.

Exercise 8.4

What are the heat of vaporization (in kJ mol^{-1}) and the normal boiling point of a liquid that has a vapor pressure of 254 mm Hg at 25°C and a vapor pressure of 648 mm Hg at 45°C? ($R = 8.314$ J mol^{-1} K^{-1})

Solution

The Clausius-Clapeyron equation, Equation 8.3, is used first to determine ΔH_{vap}, and then to determine the normal boiling point at 760 mm Hg. At this point, the necessary units are considered. The temperature must be converted to the Kelvin temperature units. The pressures may have any units as long as they are identical since the units for pressure will cancel in the ratio P_1/P_2.

$$\ln\left(\frac{P_1}{P_2}\right) = \frac{\Delta H_{vap}}{R}\left(\frac{1}{T_2} - \frac{1}{T_1}\right)$$

In solving this equation, we assign 298 K and 254 mm Hg to T_1 and P_1 respectively. T_2 and P_2 are 318 K and 648 mm Hg. Substituting these values into the equation, we have

$$\ln\left(\frac{254 \text{ mm Hg}}{648 \text{ mm Hg}}\right) = \frac{\Delta H_{vap}}{8.314 \text{ } J \text{ mol}^{-1} \text{ K}^{-1}}\left(\frac{1}{318} - \frac{1}{298}\right)$$

Solving yields

$$-0.937 = \Delta H_{vap}\left(-2.53 \times 10^{-5} \text{ J}^{-1} \text{ mol}\right)$$

Then

$$\Delta H_{vap} = \frac{-0.937}{-2.53 \times 10^{-5} \text{ J}^{-1} \text{ mol}}$$

$$= +36,911 \text{ J mol}^{-1}$$

$$= +36.9 \text{ kJ mol}^{-1}$$

Once the heat of vaporization has been determined, one of the two vapor pressure measurements can be combined with it to calculate the normal boiling point. Assigning $P_1 = 648$ mm Hg, $P_2 = 760$ mm Hg, and $T_1 = 318$ K, we enter the data into the equation and calculate T_2, the normal boiling point.

Before actually solving the equation, we can estimate the answer. First, it must be above 318 K since 648 torr is less than 760 torr. Second, the normal boiling point cannot be very much greater than 318 K since 648 torr is not far from 760 torr.

Entering the data into the Clausius-Clapeyron equation we have

$$\ln\left(\frac{648 \text{ mm Hg}}{760 \text{ mm Hg}}\right) = \frac{36{,}900 \text{ J mol}^{-1}}{8.314 \text{ J mol}^{-1} \text{ K}^{-1}} \left(\frac{1}{T_2} - \frac{1}{318}\right)$$

We can solve this for T_2, which will be the boiling temperature:

$$-0.159 = 4438 \text{ K}\left(\frac{1}{T_2} - 3.14 \times 10^{-3} \text{ K}^{-1}\right)$$

$$= \frac{4438 \text{ K}}{T_2} - 13.94$$

$$13.78 = \frac{4438 \text{ K}}{T_2}$$

$$T_2 = \frac{4438 \text{ K}}{13.78}$$

$$= 322 \text{ K } (49 \text{ }^\circ\text{C})$$

The value of 322 K for this part of the problem fits well with the estimate (slightly above 318 K) made beforehand.

Solids

At room temperature and atmospheric pressure many substances exist as solids. In the periodic table there are two liquids and 11 gases; the remaining 96 elements are solids. Solids have the property of retaining their shapes with or without a container. This occurs because solids have rigid crystal structures. These solid structures may be defined based on the attractive forces that hold them together or on the arrangement of the atoms in the crystals themselves.

Crystal Types Based on Attractive Forces

Metallic Crystals

All metals in the periodic table are solids at 25°C, except mercury. The **metallic crystal** is visualized as a rigid structure of metal nuclei and inner electrons. The valence electrons are thought to be very mobile in the structure, moving freely from atom to atom. These mobile electrons act to bond metal atoms together with widely varying degrees of force. Metals such as iron, chromium, cobalt, gold, platinum, and copper have melting points above 1000°C. Others, for example, mercury and gallium, have melting points near or below room temperature. Melting points are one measure of the attractive forces since melting disrupts the crystal bonding, producing a liquid. The energy needed to disrupt a crystal is often called the lattice energy.

The mobile valence electrons provide an explanation for the ability of metals to conduct electricity and heat. In both cases the electrons can quickly carry charge (electricity) and thermal energy (heat) throughout the metal. Also, the interaction of light with these electrons is responsible for the characteristic metallic luster. Most metals have a color similar to that of silver or aluminum. A few, notably copper and gold, are yellow.

Metals such as lead, gold, sodium, and potassium are soft and can be cut with a knife. Other metals, for example, tin and zinc, are somewhat brittle. Most metals are malleable and can be formed into various shapes with a hammer or extruded into thin wires. These properties are due to the metallic crystal structure, which allows the atoms to move from one position to another without a major disruption of the crystal. The softness, hardness, and brittleness of metals can be altered by preparing solutions of one metal dissolved in another. These solutions are known as alloys.

The atoms in metallic crystals are arranged in the most compact form possible. As a result, the atoms usually crystallize in either the face-centered cubic structure or the body-centered cubic structure. Both of these are described below.

Ionic Crystals

The attraction of a cation (positive ion) toward an anion (negative ion) is the strongest attractive force known in chemistry. The result is that almost all ionic compounds are solids with rigid crystalline structures (lattices). Because of these strong attractions, a large amount of energy, called the lattice energy, is required to separate the ions. The high lattice energy of ionic compounds gives them very high melting and boiling points compared to molecular compounds of similar size and molar mass. For example, sodium chloride melts at 801°C and boils at 1,413°C, while butane (C_4H_{10}, molar mass = 58) melts at −135°C and boils at approximately 0°C. The melting points of ionic crystals are consistently high in contrast to the variability evident in the metals.

An **ionic crystal** has a regular structure, or lattice, of alternating positive and negative ions. Many of these crystals are cubic structures, which will be described later. Other structures may provide shapes seen in many natural minerals. It is relatively simple to describe the crystal structures of the metals since all of the atoms are the same size. Ionic crystals, however, usually have ions of different sizes, which affect the manner in which they pack. These sizes also may limit the closeness with which the ions approach each other.

Ionic bonding causes these crystals to be rigid and brittle. To understand this property, we visualize a simple ionic substance such as NaCl with alternating sodium cations and chloride anions in a crystal lattice. The strong attraction of the positive and negative charges holds the crystal rigidly together. Hitting an ionic crystal with a hammer has a very different result compared to hitting a metallic crystal with the same force. In both, the atoms can be forced to move. In a metallic crystal, the atoms shift their positions but the metallic bond is not disrupted. In an ionic crystal, however, movement of the atoms by as little as one ionic diameter will cause positive ions to be aligned with positive ions and negative ions to be aligned with negative ions. The repulsion between like-charged ions is so great that the crystal shatters, as diagrammed in Figure 8.12.

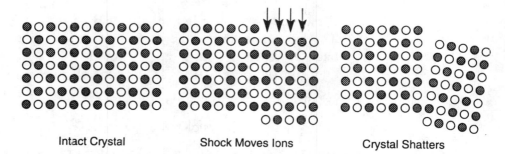

Intact Crystal   Shock Moves Ions   Crystal Shatters

FIGURE 8.12. Illustration of why ionic crystals shatter. Light circles are cations, and dark circles are anions.

Molecular Crystals

Molecular crystals may be composed of either atoms of the nonmetals or of covalent molecules. These crystals are held together by London forces, dipole-dipole attractions, hydrogen bonding, or a mixture of these. All of these forces are much weaker than the attractive forces between ions in ionic crystals. As a result, molecular crystals tend to be soft, with low melting points. Some substances that form molecular crystals with London forces holding the crystal together are neon, xenon, sulfur, fluorine, methane (CH_4), and decane ($C_{10}H_{22}$). Dipole-dipole attractive forces hold crystals of SO_2, CO_2 $CHCl_3$, and other polar molecules together. Hydrogen bonding is responsible for the attractive forces in crystals of H_2O and NH_3. In many molecules there may be a combination of attractive forces. For example, n-decanol has the structure

$$CH_3CH_2CH_2CH_2CH_2CH_2CH_2CH_2CH_2CH_2OH$$

The long carbon chain is responsible for London forces, while the —OH at the end of the molecule provides hydrogen bonding.

Network (Covalent) Crystals

A **network crystal** has a lattice structure in which the atoms are covalently bonded to each other. The result is that the crystal is one large molecule with a continuous network of covalent bonds. A diamond is pure carbon with each carbon atom covalently bonded to four other carbon atoms in a tetrahedral (sp^3) geometry. The totality of this network of covalent bonds makes the diamond the hardest natural substance known. SiO_2 is the empirical formula for sand and quartz. Silicon dioxide forms a covalent crystal with each silicon forming bonds to four oxygen atoms and each oxygen bonding to two silicon atoms with a tetrahedral geometry. Silicon carbide is another network crystal similar to diamond with alternating tetrahedral silicon and carbon atoms. It is very hard and is used as an industrial substitute for diamonds. Network crystals, like ionic substances, are represented by their empirical formulas.

Graphite is another form (allotrope) of carbon in a covalent crystal. In graphite each carbon atom is covalently bonded to three other carbon atoms in a trigonal planar (sp^2) geometry that gives graphite its structure of flat sheets. The extra p electron that is not used in the sp^2 bonding holds these sheets together in a manner similar to that seen in a metallic crystal. The weak bonding of the p electrons allows the flat sheets to slide over each other easily and is responsible for the slippery feel of graphite. In addition, these p electrons are responsible for ability of graphite to conduct electricity.

Amorphous (Noncrystalline) Substances

Some materials are **amorphous** and do not form crystals. One characteristic of a noncrystalline substance is that it does not have a distinct, sharp melting point. Rather, these materials soften gradually over a large temperature range. Ordinary glass is an example. Although glass is composed mainly of SiO_2, the atoms are not arranged in a network crystal as discussed above. Glass has often been described as a supercooled liquid. Many plastics (polymers) have combined characteristics; they are partially crystalline and partially amorphous.

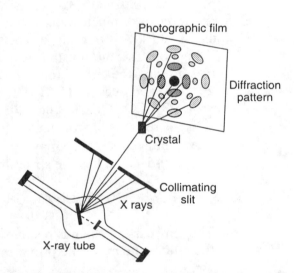

FIGURE 8.13   An X-ray diffraction apparatus for the determination of crystal structures.

Crystal Lattices

We can determine the positions of atoms in a crystal by using an experimental method called **X-ray diffraction** (Figure 8.13). In an X-ray diffraction experiment a narrow beam of **monochromatic** (single-wavelength) X rays is aimed at a crystal. On the other side of the crystal is a photographic plate to detect the X rays as they emerge from the crystal. When developed, the photographic plate shows a regular pattern of spots, which can be deciphered to determine arrangement of the atoms and the distances between them.

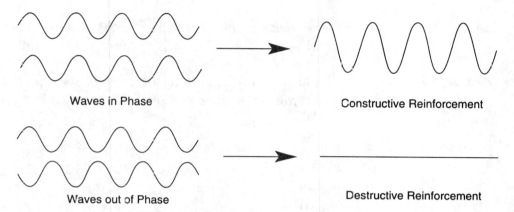

FIGURE 8.14. How waves in phase constructively reinforce and waves out of phase destructively reinforce.

In this technique X rays are diffracted by the layers of atoms within the crystal itself. In diffraction separate light waves may **constructively reinforce** or **destructively reinforce** each other when they combine. Figure 8.14 diagrams the two types of reinforcement by representing light as waves, and the combination of two waves as the addition of their amplitudes. If the waves are in phase, with their maxima (peaks) aligned, addition results in a wave with an increased amplitude. If the two waves are out of phase, with maxima aligned with minima, the addition results in zero amplitude or no wave at all.

X rays generated by an X-ray tube must be in phase. When the waves enter the crystal, they are reflected by the layers of atoms within the crystal as shown in Figure 8.15. When the waves emerge from the crystal, they may or may not be in phase because the lower wave has traveled a longer distance than the upper wave.

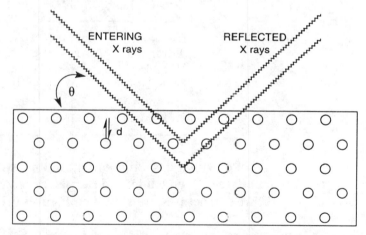

FIGURE 8.15. Reflection of X rays by the layers of atoms within a crystal.

The **Bragg equation** defines the relationship between the angles and the spacing between the layers in the crystal that results in constructive reinforcement:

$$n\lambda = 2d \sin \theta \qquad (8.5)$$

where λ is the wavelength of the X rays, d is the distance between the layers in the crystal, and θ is the angle at which the X ray enters the crystal. Also in this equation, n is the order of diffraction and may be any integer value; in most cases n is equal to 1.

Exercise 8.5

What is the minimum spacing between atoms if X rays with a wavelength of 216 pm are constructively reinforced when reflected at an angle of 31.2°?

Solution

We have all of the data to solve the Bragg equation, Equation 8.5, except *n*. We will solve the equation as far as possible by substituting the data:

$$n\lambda = 2d \sin \theta$$

$$n(216\ pm) = 2d \sin 31.2$$

$$d = \frac{n(216\ pm)}{2 \sin(31.2)} = n(208\ pm)$$

Since *n* may be any integer, starting with 1, we see that the minimum spacing will be 1(208 pm), or 208 pm.

The arrangement of the atoms in a solid is called the **crystal lattice**. Since crystal is made up of repeating **unit cells** stacked together, the crystal observable to the naked eye is an enlarged version of the unit cell itself. Sodium chloride is an example. If we closely examine ordinary table salt, we see many tiny cubes. X-ray diffraction experiments confirm that the atoms are actually arranged in a cubic structure. Basalt, a common rock, forms long crystals with a hexagonal cross section that also describes the shape of the unit cell. Since unit cells must pack together without any spaces, there are only six fundamental crystal shapes, as listed in Table 8.2.

TABLE 8.2   Basic Crystal Shapes

Crystal Name	Sides	Angles
Cubic	$A = B = C$	$a = b = c = 90°$
Tetragonal	$A = B <> C$	$a = b = c = 90°$
Rhombic	$A <> B <> C$	$a = b = c = 90°$
Monoclinic	$A <> B <> C$	$a <> b = c = 90°$
Triclinic	$A <> B <> C$	$a <> b <> c <> 90°$
Hexagonal	$A <> B$	$a = b = 90°, c = 120°$

We will focus only on the cubic structures, called the **simple cubic**, **body-centered cubic**, and **face-centered cubic**. Two different views of these three structures are shown in Figures 8.16 and 8.17.

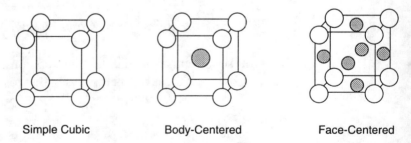

Simple Cubic   Body-Centered   Face-Centered

FIGURE 8.16.   The three cubic structures of crystals: simple cubic, body-centered cubic, and face-centered cubic. Diagrams are drawn as "ball and stick" models to show placements of all atoms.

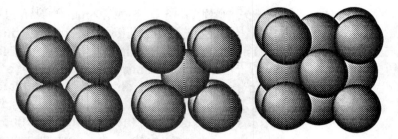

FIGURE 8.17. The three cubic structures of crystals: simple cubic, body-centered cubic, and face-centered cubic. Diagrams are drawn as "space filling" models to show which atoms actually contact each other.

In the simple cubic structure, the corner atoms are all in contact with each other. In the body-centered cubic, the corner atoms are not in contact, but all of the corner atoms touch the center atom. In the face-centered cubic, the corner atoms do not touch each other, but they all do touch the face atoms.

Another view of the unit cell is obtained by determining the number of atoms that are actually contained within that cell. In Figures 8.16 and 8.17 atoms are placed at the corners and faces of the unit cell. Only parts of these atoms, however, are within the unit cell itself. Figure 8.18 shows the simple cubic structure and the parts of the atoms that are actually within the cell. In this example, only one-eighth of each corner atom is within the unit cell. The other parts of these corner atoms are parts of neighboring unit cells.

FIGURE 8.18. The simple cubic unit cell, showing that only one-eighth of each corner atom is actually part of the cell.

Table 8.3 lists the positions of other atoms and the fractions that are completely inside the unit cell.

TABLE 8.3 Fractional Parts of Atoms Within a Unit Cell

Atom Position	Fraction Inside Cell
Body	$\frac{1}{1}$
Face	$\frac{1}{2}$
Edge	$\frac{1}{4}$
Corner	$\frac{1}{8}$

Using the information in Table 8.3, we may calculate that there is only one atom inside the simple cubic, unit cell (one-eighth each of eight corner atoms). For the face-centered cell we have four atoms in the unit cell (eight corner atoms and six face atoms). For the body-centered structure we have two atoms inside the unit cell (eight corner atoms and one body atom).

The length of a side of the cubic cell can be obtained from X-ray diffraction experiments. This measurement, along with the geometry of the atoms in the unit cell, allows us to calculate the radius of an atom. For the simple cubic structures there is a nucleus at each corner of the cube. If the atoms are in contact, the edge of the cube represents two atomic radii. In the face-centered cubic, the corner atoms are in contact with the face atoms. The diagonal of one side of the cube is equal to four radii (one radius for each corner atom and two radii for the face atom). In the body-centered cubic structure the atoms are in contact along the diagonal running through the cube from one corner to the opposite corner. Again, there are four radii, as in the face-centered cubic. The three equations for determining the radius, r, of the atom from the length of the side, s, of the unit cell are as follows:

$$2r = s \qquad \text{(simple cubic)} \qquad (8.6)$$

$$4r = \sqrt{s^2 + s^2} \qquad \text{(face-centered cubic)} \qquad (8.7)$$

$$4r = \sqrt{s^2 + s^2 + s^2} \qquad \text{(body-centered cubic)} \qquad (8.8)$$

This approach is often used to determine the atomic radii of the elements. The structure of an element is relatively easy to analyze since all of the atoms are identical in size.

The unit cell of a cubic ionic compound may be constructed with one cation at each corner of the cube or, alternatively, with an anion at each corner of the cube. Geometrically the structures are the same. In some ionic compounds there is sufficient space for the smaller cation to fit between the larger anions. The result is that the anions will be as close as possible to each other. Lithium bromide is an example. In other compounds the ions are of almost equal size, and the cation will force the anions apart so that they are not in contact with each other. Sodium fluoride is an example. The size of an ion is more difficult to determine than the size of a metallic atom for two reasons. First, the size of an ion depends upon the cation in the compound. Second, because cations and anions are not the same size, it is sometimes difficult to choose the correct geometry for the calculation. Ionic radii are usually average values determined from many compounds.

Exercise 8.6

Calcium metal has a density of 1.55 g cm^{-3}. Assuming that it crystallizes into one of the three cubic structures, determine the dimensions of each of these cubes.

Solution

We can use Avogadro's number, 6.02×10^{23}, along with the gram-atomic mass of calcium, 40.078 g mol^{-1}, to calculate the volume occupied by one atom. We start by deciding on the units for the answer, which are $\dfrac{\text{cm}^3}{\text{Ca atom}}$, and then we look at the given data to find a starting point. Since our answer requires a ratio of units, we choose density as the starting point since it also has a ratio of units. Setting up the problem, we see that this calculation involves a conversion from grams to atoms, which we have seen before:

$$? \frac{cm^3}{Ca \; atom} = \frac{cm^3}{1.55 \; g \; Ca}$$

Now we convert the denominator from grams Ca to atoms Ca:

$$? \frac{cm^3}{atom \; Ca} = \frac{cm^3}{1.55 \; g \; Ca} \left(\frac{40.078 \; g \; Ca}{1 \; mol \; Ca} \right) \left(\frac{1 \; mol \; Ca}{6.02 \times 10^{23} \; atoms \; Ca} \right)$$

We solve this to obtain

$$? \frac{cm^3}{atom \; Ca} = 4.30 \times 10^{-23} \; cm^3 \; per \; Ca \; atom$$

$$= 4.30 \times 10^{-29} \; m^3 \; per \; Ca \; atom$$

Since a simple cubic structure has one atom in its unit cell, the unit cell must have a volume of $4.30 \times 10^{-29} \; m^3$. Taking the cube root of this gives us the length of one side of the cube, or 3.50×10^{-10} m. This can be converted into the more convenient 350 pm.

In a body-centered cubic structure there are two atoms in a unit cell, for a volume of $8.60 \times 10^{-29} \; m^3$. Taking the cube root gives us 441 pm.

The face-centered structure has four atoms per unit cell, for a total volume of $1.72 \times 10^{-28} \; m^3$. Taking the cube root gives the length of a side as 556 pm.

Exercise 8.7

Using the data from Exercise 8.6, estimate the atomic radius of the calcium atom for all three possible structures. If the accepted radius is 197 pm, what crystal structure does calcium have?

Solution

For the simple cubic structure, $2r = s$, and our value of 350 pm for s gives us a radius of 175 pm.

For the face-centered cubic, $4r = \sqrt{s^2 + s^2}$. Solving this for r, we obtain 197 pm.

For the body-centered cubic, $4r = \sqrt{s^2 + s^2 + s^2}$. Solving this, we obtain $r = 191$ pm.

These data indicate that calcium crystallizes in the face-centered cubic structure.

Phase Changes

Solids, liquids, and gases can be converted from one phase to another by temperature and pressure changes, and we can make qualitative and quantitative observations about these conversions. There are two ways to represent these changes: the heating or cooling curve and the phase diagram. If the pressure is held constant, the effect of heat may be explained by a heating or cooling curve. If we are interested in the effects of both temperature and pressure, a phase diagram is used.

Heating and Cooling Curves

Starting with a solid material well below its melting point and adding heat at a constant rate will produce the following effects:

1. The temperature of the solid will increase at a constant rate until the solid starts to melt.
2. When melting begins, the temperature stops rising and remains constant until all of the solid is converted into a liquid.
3. The temperature of the liquid starts increasing at a constant rate until boiling starts.
4. When boiling begins, the temperature stops rising and remains constant until all of the liquid has been converted into gas.
5. The temperature of the gas increases at a constant rate.

This process is often summarized in a **heating curve** as shown in Figure 8.19.

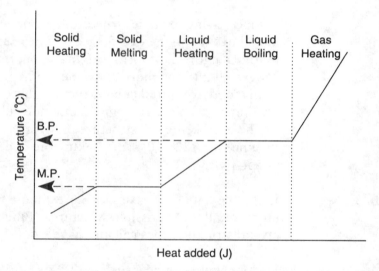

FIGURE 8.19. Typical heating curve, bringing a sample from the solid state on the left to the gaseous state on the right.

In a heating curve there are several points of interest. Adding heat to a pure solid, liquid, or gas phase increases its temperature. The **heat capacity** ($J°C^{-1}$) of a solid, liquid, or gas is the reciprocal of the slope of the curve (change in joules divided by the change in temperature) in those regions where the temperature increases as heat is added. The **specific heat** ($J g^{-1}°C^{-1}$) is the heat capacity divided by the number of grams of sample used. The plateaus represent the melting and boiling processes. The temperature does not change during melting and boiling, and two phases are present. During melting both the solid and the liquid are in equilibrium; during boiling both the liquid and the gas phase are in equilibrium. The **heat of fusion** (melting) may be determined as the length of the first (solid-melting) plateau, which represents the heat added, divided by the number of moles of sample. The **heat of vaporization** is the length of the second (liquid-boiling) plateau divided by the number of moles of sample.

Both the heat of fusion and the heat of vaporization have units of joules per mole ($J\ mol^{-1}$). These are also called the enthalpy of fusion and enthalpy of vaporization, respectively.

The **cooling curve** is the reverse of the heating curve, as shown in Figure 8.20. All of the features are the same except that we start with a gas and end with a solid as the heat is removed from the sample. The gas condenses to a liquid at the same temperature at which the liquid boils, and the liquid crystallizes at the same temperature at which the solid melts. The terms **condensation point** and **crystallization point** are sometimes used in place of boiling point and melting point.

Some liquids exhibit an ability to be supercooled. **Supercooling** is observed when a liquid that is cooled to a temperature below its melting point remains a liquid. A supercooled liquid is described as being in a metastable state. A metastable liquid will crystallize rapidly if sufficiently disturbed by shaking or by adding a seed crystal to initiate crystallization. In Figure 8.20 the dashed line on the curve shows the alternative path taken by a substance that supercools. Gases do not supercool as some liquids can.

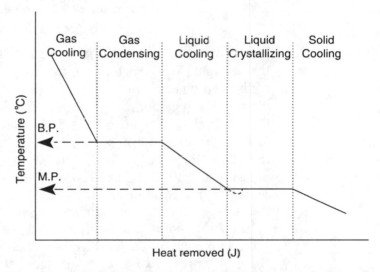

FIGURE 8.20.   A cooling curve, showing the effect of removing heat from a gas to form first a liquid and then a solid. The dashed line shows an alternative path for a liquid that supercools.

Exercise 8.8

List all of the information that can be obtained from a heating curve.

Solution

We can obtain the following data from a heating curve: (1) melting point; (2) boiling point; (3) specific heats and heat capacities of the solid, liquid, and gas; (4) heat of fusion of the solid; (5) heat of vaporization of the liquid.

Phase Diagrams

We can draw a diagram, called a **phase diagram,** that shows the relationship between pressure and temperature and the three states of matter. A phase diagram of a substance allows us to make many predictions about the physical behaviors of a wide variety of materials. Most phase diagrams are similar to the one shown in Figure 8.21. Pressure is plotted on the y-axis, and temperature on the x-axis. The diagram is divided into the three physical states by three lines that meet at the **triple point.** Solids exist at pressures and temperatures in the upper left of the diagram. Liquids exist at

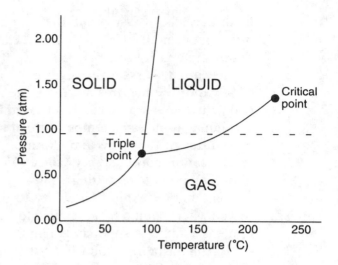

Figure 8.21. A typical phase diagram of the pressure-temperature regions where gas, liquid, and solid phases exist. Each line represents an equilibrium between two phases, and the triple point indicates the pressure and temperature at which all three phases are in equilibrium.

pressures and temperatures in the upper right, and gases in the lower part, of the diagram. Along each line in the diagram there is an **equilibrium** mixture of the two phases on the two sides of that line. At the triple point all three phases exist together in equilibrium. The liquid-solid line is usually a straight line, while the gas-solid and liquid-gas lines are curved upward, as shown.

Temperature and pressure are the two variables that define a point in the phase diagram. We may draw a horizontal line representing a selected pressure and a vertical line representing a selected temperature. The intersection of the two lines on the phase diagram will indicate the phase(s) of the substance at that particular combination of temperature and pressure.

The **triple point** is the only point where all three phases are in equilibrium with each other. At this point each phase has the same temperature and vapor pressure. For each substance there is only one temperature and one pressure at which the triple point occurs. (Helium is the only substance that does not have a triple point since it has no solid phase.) The triple point of water is at 0.01°C and 4.58 mm Hg.

Three equilibrium lines radiate from the triple point in the phase diagram. The pressures and temperatures along these lines indicate the pressures and temperatures where two adjoining phases will be in equilibrium.

The solid-liquid equilibrium line:

$$SOLID \rightleftharpoons LIQUID$$

points upward from the triple point. This line is nearly vertical because changes in pressure have very little effect on solids and liquids (these two phases are only slightly compressible in comparison to gases). For almost all compounds the line slopes slightly toward higher temperatures. For water, however, it slopes in the opposite direction. The slight tilt of this equilibrium line may be explained based on the relative densities of the solid and liquid phases. When the pressure is increased, the equilibrium will be shifted toward the denser phase. To counter this shift, the temperature must change to reestablish the equilibrium. Most solids are denser than their liquids. Increasing the pressure forces the reaction toward the formation of solid. To maintain equilibrium, the temperature must be increased; therefore, the line slopes slightly toward the right. Liquid water, however, is denser than solid ice. As a result, an increase in pressure favors the formation of liquid water. To maintain equilibrium, the temperature must decrease, and therefore the solid-liquid equilibrium line tilts slightly toward the left. The normal melting point is the point on this line at 760 millimeters of mercury (1 atmosphere) of pressure. We can change the melting point only slightly by changing the pressure.

The liquid-gas equilibrium line:

$$\text{LIQUID} \rightleftharpoons \text{GAS}$$

extends in a curved manner upward and to the higher temperature side from the triple point. This line shows a pronounced curvature because of the compressibility of gases. We find that this line ends abruptly at the **critical point**, that is, the maximum temperature at which any liquid can exist. Above the critical point the differences between gases and liquids disappear and the substance is often called a **supercritical fluid**. The normal boiling point of a liquid is the point where the liquid-gas equilibrium line crosses the dashed line, indicating a pressure of 760 millimeters of mercury. Unlike the melting point, the boiling point may vary greatly with pressure.

The solid-gas equilibrium line:

$$\text{SOLID} \rightleftharpoons \text{GAS}$$

extends downward and to lower temperatures. This line is also highly curved because of the compressibility of gases. The process of converting a solid directly into a gas is called **sublimation**. In this portion of the diagram, pressures are usually at very low levels not normally encountered in the laboratory. Some substances, such as iodine, have solid-gas equilibrium lines at atmospheric pressure. Solid iodine readily sublimes from the solid to a vapor without any liquid phase.

Exercise 8.9

Determine the temperatures and pressures for the critical point, triple point, normal boiling point, and normal melting point for the substance described in Figure 8.21.

Solution

We may estimate the critical point at 220°C and 1.4 of atmospheres pressure. The triple point is at 95°C and 0.75 of atmospheres pressure. The normal boiling and melting points must be at 1.00 atm of pressure, and they are 180°C and 100°C, respectively.

Important Concepts

Intermolecular forces, dipole-dipole, London and hydrogen bonds
Physical properties and intermolecular forces
Solid crystals and crystal structures
Heating and cooling curves
Phase diagrams

1. In which of the following are the intermolecular forces listed from the weakest to the strongest?
   (A) dipole-dipole > London > hydrogen bonds
   (B) London < dipole-dipole < hydrogen bonds
   (C) hydrogen bonds < dipole-dipole < London
   (D) London > hydrogen bonds > dipole-dipole
   (E) London < hydrogen-bonds < dipole-dipole

2. Which of the following consistently have the highest melting points?
   (A) metals
   (B) salts
   (C) molecular crystals
   (D) alkanes
   (E) dipoles

3. Carbon dioxide sublimes. Which physical transformation occurs in sublimation?
   (A) gas to liquid
   (B) gas to solid
   (C) solid to liquid to gas
   (D) solid to gas
   (E) solid to liquid

4. Which element is expected to have the greatest polarizability?
   (A) Fe
   (B) Ca
   (C) Ne
   (D) S
   (E) Al

5. Which of the following compounds will NOT hydrogen-bond?
   (A) CF_4
   (b) CH_3OH
   (C) $H_2NCH_2CH_2CH_3$
   (C) $CH_3CH_2CH_2CH_2COOH$
   (D) $HOCH_2CH_2OH$
   (E) $HClO$

6. When the following compounds are kept at the same temperature, the compound expected to evaporate most quickly is
   (A) C_8H_{18}
   (B) $C_8H_{17}OH$
   (C) $C_8H_{17}NH_2$
   (D) C_6H_{14}
   (E) $C_7H_{15}COOH$

7. Which of the following will have the greatest *change* in its boiling point if the pressure at which it is boiled is changed from 1.00 atm to 0.900 atm? (The numbers in parentheses are the heats of vaporization in kilojoules per mole.)
   (A) water (43.9)
   (B) ammonia (21.7)
   (C) methane (8.2)
   (D) bromine (15.0)
   (E) fluorine (5.9)

8. Which of the following statements is NOT consistent with the crystal properties of the substance?
   (A) SiC is used to grind metal parts to shape.
   (B) Tungsten is drawn into thin wires.
   (C) Aluminum is used to cut glass.
   (D) Graphite is used to lubricate locks.
   (E) MgF_2 shatters when dropped.

9. Which structure has the most atoms in its unit cell?
   (A) face-centered cubic
   (B) simple cubic
   (C) body-centered cubic
   (D) tetrahedron
   (E) octahedron

10. Which physical property can be determined if the unit cell and its dimensions are determined by X-ray diffraction?
    (A) heat capacity
    (B) heat of fusion
    (C) boiling and melting points
    (D) vapor pressure
    (E) density

Questions 11 and 12 refer to the heating curve below.

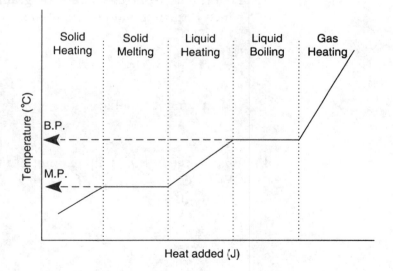

11. On the basis of this heating curve, which of the following statements is true?
    (A) The heat of fusion and heat of vaporization are about equal.
    (B) The heat capacities of the solid, liquid, and gas are approximately equal.
    (C) The heat capacity of the gas is greater than that of the liquid.
    (D) The heat capacity of the gas is greater than the heat of fusion.
    (E) The heat of vaporization is less than the heat of fusion.

12. On the basis of this heating curve, which of the following statements is correct about the substance?
    (A) The substance supercools easily.
    (B) The gas is a metastable state.
    (C) The substance must be a salt that dissociates on heating.
    (D) The density of the liquid is greater than that of the solid.
    (E) The specific heat can be determined if the mass is known.

Questions 13–15 refer to the phase diagram below.

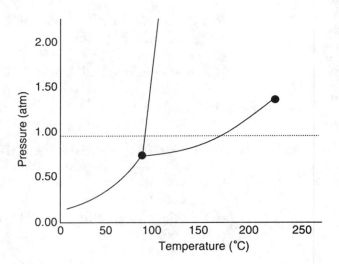

13. Determine, from this phase diagram, the maximum temperature at which this compound will sublime.
    (A) 100°C
    (B) 230°C
    (C) 115°C
    (D) 95°C
    (E) It cannot sublime.

14. What is the normal boiling point of this compound?
    (A) 95°C
    (B) 100°C
    (C) 50°C
    (D) 180°C
    (E) 150°C

15. At 125°C and 1.50 atm of pressure this substance will be
    (A) a liquid
    (B) a solid
    (C) a gas
    (D) a solid and liquid in equilibrium
    (E) a gas and liquid in equilibrium

16. Which pair of temperatures and pressures will produce a supercritical fluid?
    (A) 150°C and 2.00 atm
    (B) 95°C and 1.00 atm
    (C) 145°C and 230 atm
    (D) 10°C and 0.15 atm
    (E) 250°C and 2.00 atm

17. The crystal structure in which all sides and angles are different is given the name
    (A) cubic
    (B) rhombic
    (C) hexagonal
    (D) triclinic
    (E) tetragonal

18. The Bragg equation is used to determine
    (A) the spacing between atoms in a crystal
    (B) ionization energies
    (C) the wavelength of X rays
    (D) empirical formulas
    (E) intermolecular forces

19. Diamond is classified as
    (A) a covalent crystal
    (B) an ionic crystal
    (C) an amorphous solid
    (D) a metallic crystal
    (E) a molecular crystal

20. A liquid substance that exhibits low intermolecular attractions is expected to have
    (A) low viscosity, low boiling point, and low heat of vaporization
    (B) high viscosity, low boiling point, and low heat of vaporization
    (C) low viscosity, high boiling point, and low heat of vaporization
    (D) low viscosity, low boiling point, and high heat of vaporization
    (E) high viscosity, high boiling point, and high heat of vaporization

Answer Key

See Appendix I for explanation of answers.

1. B	5. A	9. A	13. D	17. D
2. B	6. D	10. E	14. D	18. A
3. D	7. A	11. A	15. A	19. A
4. A	8. C	12. E	16. E	20. A

CHAPTER NINE

Solutions

Introduction and Definitions

Chemical reactions occur only when atoms, molecules, or ions directly interact, or collide, with each other. Reactants separated by as much as a few molecular diameters may as well be separated by miles. Consequently, most reactions are carried out either in liquid solutions or in the gas phase where freely moving molecules or ions may effectively collide millions of times per second.

Every **solution** is a uniform mixture of one or more **solutes** dissolved in a **solvent**. Of all the possible mixtures of substances, only a few form solutions. These include all gas mixtures, gases, liquids, or solids dissolved in a liquid, and many **alloys**, which are solid solutions of two or more metals.

In a gas the attractive forces are very small; and, as stated above, gaseous molecules or atoms interact only when they collide. The absence of major attractive forces means that gases can be mixed in all proportions, and there are no gases that are "insoluble" in other gases. Liquid solutions are more complex and more common. The presence of attractive forces is the basis of our understanding of liquid-phase solutions, which are described in detail in this chapter. Alloys are generally described in higher level chemistry courses.

To describe a solution in **quantitative**, or numerical, terms, chemists specify the amount of solute dissolved in a specified amount of solvent. This is generally called the **concentration** of a solution. The various concentration units used by chemists are defined later in this chapter. **Solubility** is the quantitative term for the maximum amount, in units of grams per liter, of solute that can dissolve in a solvent. **Molar solubility** is the maximum amount, in moles per liter, of solute that can dissolve. Solubility depends on the temperature of the solution, as described later.

Chemists also use several **qualitative,** or nonnumerical, terms to describe solutions. In a **concentrated** solution a large amount of solute is dissolved in the solvent. A **dilute** solution has a small amount of solute dissolved in the solvent. Solutions that have the maximum amount of solute dissolved in the solvent are called **saturated solutions**. A saturated solution may be identified as one in which the solution is in equilibrium with undissolved solute. An **unsaturated solution** has less than the maximum amount of solute dissolved in the solvent. An unsaturated solution never has any undissolved solute present. In a **supersaturated solution** more than the maximum amount of solute is dissolved. With many solutes a supersaturated solution can be obtained by preparing a saturated solution at a high temperature and then carefully cooling the liquid to avoid crystallizing the excess solute. Supersaturated solutions are **metastable**, meaning that the excess solute will crystallize if the solution is shaken or if a seed crystal is added to start the crystallization process.

The terms *concentrated* and *dilute* have no relationship to the terms *saturated, supersaturated,* and *unsaturated*. Some saturated solutions may be very dilute. An example is silver chloride, which is saturated at a concentration of 1.0×10^{-5} mol AgCl per liter. On the other hand, 10 moles of sucrose dissolved in a liter of solution is a concentrated solution, but it is not saturated at 100°C.

Solubility and the Solution Process

Whether or not a substance will dissolve in a solvent is of major importance in chemistry. Separating and purifying compounds often depends on the difference in solubility between two compounds. The effectiveness of drugs depends on their solubilities in water and body fats. The ability of plants to use nutrients in the soil depends on the solubilities of the nutrients in water.

Since all gases are soluble in each other in all proportions and the consideration of alloys is outside the scope of this book, we shall focus on liquid-phase solutions. With liquids, the general rule for solubility is often stated as "**like dissolves like.**" This means that solutions can be made from solutes and solvents with similar polarities, but not from solutes and solvents that have very different polarities.

Focusing on the solution process more closely, we note that the dissolution of one substance in another involves three distinct steps, as shown in Figure 9.1. First, the solute molecules are separated so that the solvent can fit in between them (step A energy is used to break attractions between solute molecules). Second, the solvent molecules are separated so that the solute can fit between them (step B energy is used to break attractions between solvent molecules). Third, the separated solute and solvent molecules are combined to form the solution (step C energy is released when new attractions are formed between solute and solvent molecules). When more energy is released in step C than is used in steps A and B, the solvent will dissolve the solute. This excess energy is released as heat when the solute and solvent are mixed, and an increase in temperature is observed.

In addition to the breaking and making of attractions between molecules, Figure 9.1 illustrates that the randomness of molecules is another factor in the solution process. In diagram form, the solute is shown as an ordered crystal and in the solution the solute is shown randomly arranged. This increase in randomness, more precisely called **entropy**, helps the solution process. In some solutions the energy released in step C is slightly less than the energy used in steps A and B. When this occurs, the solution cools as the solvent and solute are mixed. For the solute to dissolve, however, the shortfall in energy must be compensated by the increased randomness of the solution. Solutes that are solids have the greatest increase in randomness when dissolved. Liquids have a moderate increase, and gases have virtually no increase, in randomness when dissolved.

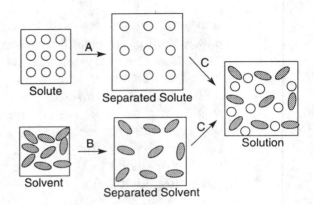

FIGURE 9.1. The three steps involved in forming a solution. Step A separates the solute, step B separates the solvent, and step C combines the separated solvent and solute into a solution.

Examples of the Solution Process

Ionic Solutions

This example describes why ionic compounds dissolve to form aqueous solutions. Ionic compounds have the strongest attractive forces holding the ions in the crystal lattice. The energy needed to disrupt the crystal (step A in the solution process) is known as the lattice energy. Lattice energies are so high that dissolution of an ionic compound seems impossible. However, water, with its high polarity, is strongly attracted to the charged ions in the solution. As a result, many water molecules are attracted to each ion and enough energy is released (step C of the solution process) so that the dissolution is favored. The increase in entropy due to the breakup of the crystal structure also aids the solution process. Still, many ionic compounds are insoluble in water because the hydration of the ions cannot offset the lattice energy. Chapter 4 lists the solubility rules for ionic compounds.

Gas Mixtures

In a second example we see that gases mix freely with other gases solely on the basis of the entropy increase since there are virtually no attractive forces between gas molecules. When a gas is allowed to expand into a vacuum, it does so because the increased volume means more disorder for the molecules, as shown in Figure 9.2.

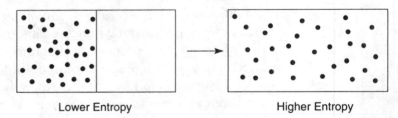

Lower Entropy   Higher Entropy

FIGURE 9.2. Increase in the entropy of a gas when the volume is increased.

When two gases are allowed to expand (Figure 9.3), each into the volume occupied by the other, the entropy of each gas increases. Since there are no attractive forces, each gas "thinks" it is expanding into a vacuum.

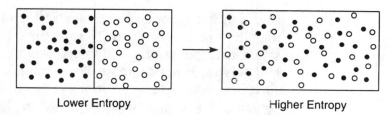

Lower Entropy   Higher Entropy

FIGURE 9.3. Mixing of two gases, illustrating the increase in entropy for each.

Detergents

As a final example, the solubility effects of compounds called detergents are described. Detergents are compounds that have two types of attractive forces. As shown in Figure 9.4, one end of a long-chain carbon molecule contains an ionic group and the other end is a long-chain hydrocarbon. The ionic end causes a detergent molecule to be soluble in water. The hydrocarbon end can dissolve in nonpolar substances. An aqueous solution of a detergent can remove nonpolar stains from clothes because fats and greases dissolve in the hydrocarbon end of the detergent molecule.

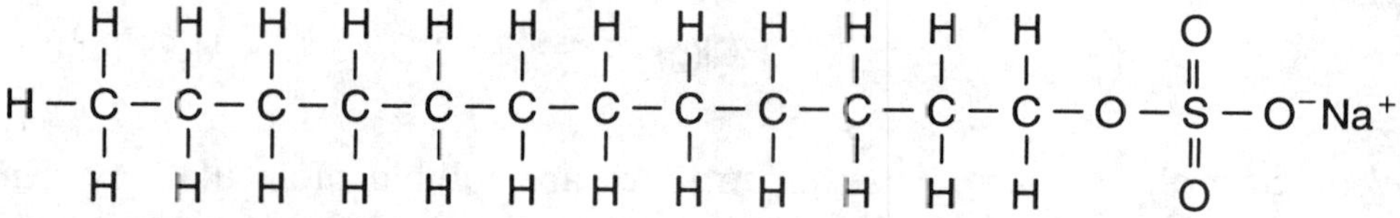

$$H-\overset{\overset{\displaystyle H}{|}}{\underset{\underset{\displaystyle H}{|}}{C}}-\overset{\overset{\displaystyle H}{|}}{\underset{\underset{\displaystyle H}{|}}{C}}-\overset{\overset{\displaystyle H}{|}}{\underset{\underset{\displaystyle H}{|}}{C}}-\overset{\overset{\displaystyle H}{|}}{\underset{\underset{\displaystyle H}{|}}{C}}-\overset{\overset{\displaystyle H}{|}}{\underset{\underset{\displaystyle H}{|}}{C}}-\overset{\overset{\displaystyle H}{|}}{\underset{\underset{\displaystyle H}{|}}{C}}-\overset{\overset{\displaystyle H}{|}}{\underset{\underset{\displaystyle H}{|}}{C}}-\overset{\overset{\displaystyle H}{|}}{\underset{\underset{\displaystyle H}{|}}{C}}-\overset{\overset{\displaystyle H}{|}}{\underset{\underset{\displaystyle H}{|}}{C}}-\overset{\overset{\displaystyle H}{|}}{\underset{\underset{\displaystyle H}{|}}{C}}-\overset{\overset{\displaystyle H}{|}}{\underset{\underset{\displaystyle H}{|}}{C}}-\overset{\overset{\displaystyle H}{|}}{\underset{\underset{\displaystyle H}{|}}{C}}-O-\overset{\overset{\displaystyle O}{\|}}{\underset{\underset{\displaystyle O}{\|}}{S}}-O^-Na^+$$

FIGURE 9.4. Structure of the detergent sodium dodecyl sulfate. The ionic end dissolves in water, and the hydrocarbon end dissolves in nonpolar substances such as fats and grease.

Rates of Dissolution

In addition to the attractive forces that determine whether or not solutes will dissolve, we are interested in the rate at which solutes dissolve. Almost intuitively, we heat solutions to increase the speed of dissolution. We also grind chemicals into small particles and stir solutions vigorously to accelerate the solution process. All three of these operations speed the rate at which solvent molecules can reach the surface of a solid and start the dissolution process. Heating accelerates the motion of the solvent molecules so that they collide with the solid more rapidly. Grinding a solute into fine particles allows more of the solute to be exposed to the solvent. Stirring a solution moves dissolved solute away from the surface of the solute and brings less concentrated solvent in contact with the solute. While heating, grinding, and stirring increase the rate of dissolution, it must be remembered that the maximum concentration achieved depends only on the temperature of the solution and the chemical identity of the solute.

Aqueous Solutions

Classification of Solutes

Solutions in which water is the solvent are known as **aqueous** solutions. Ionic substances **dissociate** (break apart) completely into ions when dissolved in water. Some molecular compounds, notably HCl, also break apart into ions when dissolved in water in a process called **ionization**. Their solutions conduct electricity very well, and these compounds are called **electrolytes**. Other compounds dissociate or ionize only slightly when dissolved in water; their solutions conduct electricity, but not well. These compounds are called **weak electrolytes**. The rest of the soluble compounds form absolutely no ions when dissolved in water. Their solutions do not conduct electricity, and these compounds are called **nonelectrolytes**.

Dissociation is a term usually reserved for the sparation of ions in an ionic compound when it is dissolved. *Ionization* is a term that should be reserved for molecular (nonionic) compounds that form ions upon dissolution. Often the terms dissociation and ionization are used interchangeably.

Electrolytes

Electrolytes are ionic compounds, such as NaCl, KBr, and $Mg(NO_3)_2$, that are soluble in water. In addition, there are three electrolytes that are molecular (covalent) compounds in the gas phase but ionize completely when dissolved in water. These compounds are HCl, HBr, and HI. A typical reaction is

$$HCl(g) \quad + \quad H_2O(\ell) \quad \rightarrow \quad H_3O^+(aq) \quad + \quad Cl^-(aq)$$

Weak Electrolytes

Weak electrolytes are soluble molecular compounds that only partially ionize into ions when dissolved in water. Most weak electrolytes ionize less than 10 percent, meaning that more than 90 percent of the molecules remain intact. Weak electrolytes are the weak acids and weak bases. Some weak acids are listed in Table 9.1.

TABLE 9.1 Some Common Weak Acids

Name	Formula	Alternative Formula
Acetic acid	$HC_2H_3O_2$	CH_3COOH
Formic Acid	$HCHO_2$	$HCOOH$
Propionic acid	$HC_3H_5O_2$	CH_3CH_2COOH
Benzoic acid	$HC_7H_5O_2$	C_6H_5COOH
Hypochlorous acid	$HClO$	$HOCl$
Chlorous acid	$HClO_2$	None
Chloric acid	$HClO_3$	None
Hydrosulfuric acid	H_2S	None
Hydrofluoric acid	HF	None
Phosphoric acid	H_3PO_4	None
Water	H_2O	HOH

All weak bases are related to the weak base ammonia. Three weak bases are methylamine, CH_3NH_2; diethylamine, $(CH_3CH_2)_2NH$; and ethylenediamine, $H_2NCH_2CH_2NH_2$. The reaction of a weak electrolyte with water results in an **equilibrium**, which is shown by a double arrow in a reaction:

$$NH_3(g) \quad + \quad H_2O(\ell) \quad \rightleftharpoons \quad NH_4^+(aq) \quad + \quad OH^-(aq)$$

Nonelectrolytes

Non-electrolytes are molecular compounds that dissolve but show absolutely no tendency to form ions. Sugars such as glucose, $C_6H_{12}O_6$, and sucrose, $C_{12}H_{22}O_{11}$, and alcohols such as methanol, CH_3OH; ethanol, CH_3CH_2OH; and propanol, $CH_3CH_2CH_2OH$ are some examples of soluble nonelectrolytes.

Concentrations of Solutions

Definitions and Units

Molarity (M)

The most common unit of concentration used by chemists is **molarity.** It is defined as the number of moles of solute dissolved in 1 liter of solution and is abbreviated as the upper-case letter M:

$$\text{molarity (M)} \quad = \quad \frac{\text{number of moles of solute}}{\text{1 L of solution}} \tag{9.1}$$

A molar solution is prepared by measuring the solute in an appropriate manner and quantitatively transferring it to a volumetric flask of the desired size. Enough solvent is then added to fill the flask about half full, and the mixture is shaken to dissolve all of the solute. Once the solute is dissolved, solvent is added exactly to the mark on the volumetric flask and mixing is repeated.

Molality (m)

Molality is defined as the number of moles of solute dissolved in 1 kilogram of solvent and is abbreviated as the lower-case letter m:

$$\text{molality} \quad = \quad \frac{\text{number of moles of solute}}{\text{1 kg of solvent}} \tag{9.2}$$

Preparation of solutions with molality units involves measuring the moles of solute and mixing the solute with the required mass of solvent.

Care must be used in distinguishing the terms *molarity* and *molality*, which have very similar spellings and abbreviations. Chemists use the upper-case M only for molarity and the lower-case m only for molality. In addition, the denominator for molarity is the total volume of the solvent and solute after mixing, while the denominator for molality is the mass of the solvent only, as shown in Equation 9.2.

Mole Fraction (X)

The **mole fraction**, X, of one component, A, of a mixture is defined as the number of moles of that component divided by the sum of all of the moles in the solution:

$$X_A = \frac{mol_A}{mol_A + mol_B} + \cdots \tag{9.3}$$

The three dots (an ellipsis) in the denominator means that we must add in also the moles for any additional components of the solution. The mole fraction does not distinguish the solute from the solvent. For any solution, we can calculate the mole fraction of each compound in the mixture. The mole fraction always has a value from 0.00 to 1.00, and the sum of the mole fractions of all the compounds in a solution must add up to 1.00. At times, chemists may use a variation of this and report the **mole percent**, which is the mole fraction multiplied by 100.

A solution with mole fraction units is prepared by carefully measuring the desired number of moles of each of the components and then mixing.

Mass (Weight) Fraction (wt/wt)

The **mass fraction** is also known as the weight fraction. It may be used in situations in which it is inconvenient or impossible to use mole units. One such situation occurs when the molar mass of a compound has not been accurately determined.

The mass fraction, usually symbolized as wt/wt, is the ratio of the mass of the solute, A, to the mass of the entire solution:

$$\frac{wt}{wt} = \frac{mass_A}{mass_A + mass_B} + \cdots \tag{9.4}$$

Like the mole fraction, the mass fraction must be a value between 0.00 and 1.00, and the sum of all mass fractions must add up to 1.00. The mass percent is obtained by multiplying the mass fraction by 100.

Mass-fraction solutions are prepared by weighing each component and then mixing the components together.

Mass-Volume Fraction (wt/vol)

The mass dissolved per liter of solution is another common concentration unit. It may be used to specify the concentration as

$$\frac{wt}{vol} = \frac{\text{number of grams of solute}}{\text{number of milliliters of solution}} \tag{9.5}$$

Since the weight of 1 milliliter of water is very close to 1 gram, the weight-volume (wt/vol) unit is considered to be identical to the wt/wt unit in dilute aqueous solutions. The wt/vol unit is often expressed as a percentage by multiplying Equation 9.5 by 100. Dilute weight/volume solutions are prepared in the same manner as solutions with molarity units.

Volume Fraction (vol/vol)

When working with solutions of one liquid dissolved in another liquid, it is often more convenient to measure the volumes of the liquids rather than their masses:

$$\frac{vol}{vol} = \frac{\text{volume of liquid}_A}{\text{volume of liquid}_A + \text{volume of liquid}_B} + \cdots \tag{9.6}$$

Preparation of volume-volume solutions involves measuring the appropriate volume of each liquid separately and then mixing the liquids thoroughly. It should be noted that for many liquids the total volume of a mixture is not equal to the sum of the the combined volumes. For example, 50 milliliters of water and 50 milliliters of ethyl alcohol yield a mixture with a volume of about 93 milliliters. As a result, it is incorrect to prepare a 0.50 vol/vol mixture of water and alcohol by measuring 50 mL of alcohol and diluting it with water to 100 mL.

Parts per Million and Parts per Billion

A value expressed in any of the units above that has the word *fraction* in its name (mole fraction, mass fraction, mass-volume fraction, and volume fraction) may be converted to a percent (literally parts per hundred) by multiplying it by 100. In addition, the mass fraction and the volume fraction are often multiplied by 1 million (10^6) to obtain parts per million units or by 1 billion (10^9) to obtain parts per billion units. This is particularly true for solutions that contain only trace quantities of solutes.

To perform any calculations, however, the percent, parts per million, and parts per billion units must be converted back to their fractional forms first. This is done by dividing these units by 100, 10^6, and 10^9, respectively. The fractional form must always have a value between 0.00 and 1.00.

Exercise 9.1

Determine the concentration of each of the following solutions:
(a) A solution prepared by dissolving 25.0 g of $MgCl_2$ in enough water to make 450 mL of solution. Calculate the molarity and the mass-volume fraction of the solute.
(b) A solution is prepared by mixing 85.0 g of hexane, C_6H_{14}, and 45.0 g of decane, $C_{10}H_{22}$. Calculate the molality, the mole fraction of decane, and the mass fraction of hexane.

Solution

(a) The number of moles of $MgCl_2$ is calculated:

$$? \text{ mol } MgCl_2 \quad = \quad 25.0 \text{ g } MgCl_2 \left(\frac{1 \text{ mol } MgCl_2}{95.21 \text{ g } MgCl_2} \right) \quad = \quad 0.263 \text{ mol } MgCl_2$$

From the definitions

$$\text{molarity (M)} \quad = \quad \frac{0.263 \text{ mol } MgCl_2}{0.450 \text{ L solution}} \quad = \quad 0.0584 \text{ M } MgCl_2$$

$$\frac{\text{wt}}{\text{vol}} \quad = \quad \frac{25.0 \text{ g MgCl}}{450 \text{ ml}} \quad = \quad 0.0556 \text{ g per ml } MgCl_2$$

(b) The number of moles of each compound is calculated:

$$? \text{ mol } C_6H_{14} \quad = \quad 85.0 \text{ g } C_6H_{14} \left(\frac{1 \text{ mol } C_6H_{14}}{86.0 \text{ g } C_6H_{14}} \right) \quad = \quad 0.988 \text{ mol } C_6H_{14}$$

$$? \text{ mol } C_{10}H_{22} \quad = \quad 45 \text{ g } C_{10}H_{22} \left(\frac{1 \text{ mol } C_{10}H_{22}}{142 \text{ g } C_{10}H_{22}} \right) \quad = \quad 0.317 \text{ mol } C_{10}H_{22}$$

The molality is calculated by assuming that the hexane is the solvent since it is the major component in the mixture.

$$\text{molality (m)} = \frac{0.317 \text{ mol } C_{10}H_{22}}{0.085 \text{ kg } C_6H_{14}} = 3.73 \text{ molal } C_{10}H_{22}$$

$$X_{decane} = \frac{0.317 \text{ mol } C_{10}H_{22}}{0.317 \text{ mol } C_{10}H_{22} + 0.988 \text{ mol } C_6H_{14}} = 0.243$$

$$\text{mass fraction}_{hexane} = \frac{45.0 \text{ g } C_6H_{14}}{45.0 \text{ g } C_6H_{14} + 85.0 \text{ g } C_{10}H_{22}} = 0.346$$

Concentration-Conversion Calculations

Concentration units may be classified as temperature dependent or temperature independent. The temperature-dependent units are molarity, volume fraction, and mass-volume fraction. Since the volume of liquid changes slightly with temperature, temperature-dependent concentrations are identified as those that have volume units in their definitions. Molality, mole fraction, and mass fraction units are not affected by temperature changes. These units are defined on the basis of mass or moles, which do not change with temperature.

The three types of conversions between units may be summarized as follows.

1. Conversions from one temperature-independent unit to another temperature-independent unit.
2. Conversions from one temperature-dependent unit to another temperature-dependent unit.
3. Conversions between temperature-dependent units and temperature-independent units.

Each of these has its own techniques and logic, which are described below.

Conversions Between Temperature-Independent Concentration Units

When converting one temperature-independent concentration into another, the given concentration is used to construct a table showing the masses and moles of each component of the solution. This table of information is then used to calculate the desired concentration from its definition.

Exercise 9.2

Given an aqueous solution that is 0.500 molal in NaCl, what are the corresponding mass and mole fractions of NaCl?

Solution

To solve the problem we construct a table as shown:

	Grams	Moles
NaCl		
H_2O		

A 0.500 molal solution is defined as 0.500 mol of solute dissolved in 1.00 kg of solvent, which is water. These values may be entered directly in the table.

	Grams	Moles
NaCl		0.500
H$_2$O	1000	

To complete the table, the 1000 g of water may be converted into moles (55.5 mol) and the molar mass of NaCl can be used to convert the 0.500 mol of NaCl to 29.22 g. (Review stoichiometry calculations like these in Chapter 6 if necessary.)

	Grams	Moles
NaCl	28.22	0.500
H$_2$O	1000	55.5

From the information now available in the table, the mass fraction and mole fraction definitions can be used to calculate these values:

$$\text{mass fraction} = \frac{\text{g NaCl}}{\text{g NaCl} + \text{g H}_2\text{O}} = \frac{28.22 \text{ g}}{28.22 \text{ g} + 1000 \text{ g}} = 0.0274$$

$$X = \frac{\text{mol NaCl}}{\text{mol NaCl} + \text{mol H}_2\text{O}} = \frac{0.500 \text{ mol}}{0.500 \text{ mol} + 55.5 \text{ mol}}$$

$$= 0.00893$$

Exercise 9.3

In another example, an aqueous solution of glucose, C$_6$H$_{12}$O$_6$ (molar mass = 180), has a mole fraction of 0.400 for glucose. What are the molality and the mass fraction of this solution?

Solution

A table is constructed for the solution components:

	Grams	Moles
Glucose		
Water		

The definition of the mole fraction

$$X = \frac{\text{mol glucose}}{\text{mol glucose} + \text{mol H}_2\text{O}} = 0.400$$

shows that, if the denominator is assumed to equal 1.00, then the numerator, which is the number of moles of glucose, must equal 0.400. At the same time, since the denominator is assumed to equal 1.00, 1.00 = mol glucose + mol H_2O. Therefore, there must be 0.600 mol of water. Entering these values in the table gives

	Grams	Moles
Glucose		0.400
Water		0.600

From the molar masses of water and glucose, the grams of each can be calculated and entered in the table.

	Grams	Moles
Glucose	72.0	0.400
Water	10.8	0.600

The mass fraction and molality are calculated from the tabulated data as

$$\text{mass fraction} = \frac{\text{g glucose}}{\text{g glucose} + \text{g } H_2O} = \frac{72.0 \text{ g}}{72.0 \text{ g} + 10.8 \text{ g}}$$

$$= 0.870$$

$$\text{molality (m)} = \frac{\text{mol glucose}}{\text{kg water}} = \frac{0.400 \text{ mol}}{0.0108 \text{ kg}} = 37.0 \text{ molal}$$

Conversions Between Temperature-Dependent Concentration Units

Temperature-dependent conversions involve the molarity (M) and the mass-volume concentration units. These conversions require a direct conversion of units and may be done in a manner similar to the stoichiometry calculations in Chapter 6. Exercise 9.4 illustrates the technique.

Exercise 9.4

Suppose that you are given a solution that is 3.50×10^{-4} M in $Pb(NO_3)_2$. What is the concentration in weight-volume units?

Solution

Conversions of this type are treated as ordinary stoichiometric conversions. We start by stating the requested units and the given data:

$$? \text{ mass/vol} = 3.50 \times 10^{-4} \text{ M } Pb(NO_3)_2$$

Although M stands for molarity, when solving problems it is better to write the actual ratio of units that molarity represents (mol/L). The setup is rewritten as

$$\frac{g}{ml} = \frac{3.50 \times 10^{-4} \text{ mol Pb (NO}_3)_2}{1 \text{ L Pb (NO}_3)_2}$$

This setup indicates that a conversion from mol $Pb(NO_3)_2$ to g $Pb(NO_3)_2$ in the numerator and a conversion from L $Pb(NO_3)_2$ to mL $Pb(NO_3)_2$ in the denominator are needed. These conversions may be done as follows:

$$\frac{g}{ml} = \left(\frac{3.50 \times 10^{-4} \text{ mol Pb (NO}_3)_2}{1 \text{ L Pb (NO}_3)_2}\right)\left(\frac{331 \text{ g Pb (NO}_3)_2}{1 \text{ mol Pb (NO}_3)_2}\right)\left(\frac{1 \text{ L}}{1000 \text{ mL}}\right)$$

$$\frac{g}{ml} = \frac{0.116 \text{ g Pb (NO}_3)_2}{1000 \text{ mL Pb (NO}_3)_2} = \frac{0.000116 \text{ g Pb (NO}_3)_2}{\text{mL Pb (NO}_3)_2}$$

Conversions Between Temperature-Dependent and Temperature-Independent Concentration Units

Temperature-dependent units have volume units in their definitions, and temperature-independent concentrations have masses or moles. At some time during the conversion of units there will be a conversion between mass and volume. *Density is the factor that must be used for such a conversion.* Aside from the need for density to convert between mass and volume, the calculations for this type of problem are a combination of those for the two types discussed above.

Exercise 9.5

The molarities of concentrated reagents such as ammonia, hydrochloric acid, sulfuric acid, and nitric acid are not specified when these substances are purchased from a supplier. Instead, these reagents have labels that list the weight percent (% wt/wt) and density. For instance, commercial hydrochloric acid is 36% (wt/wt) hydrogen chloride and has a density of 1.18 g mL^{-1}. Determine the molarity of commercial HCl.

Solution

The 36% (wt/wt) indicates that every 100 g of commercial acid contains 36 g of HCl. Setting up a stoichiometry-type conversion for this problem yields

$$? \text{ M HCl} = \frac{36 \text{ g HCl}}{100 \text{ g solution}}$$

Converting the symbol M to its actual units gives

$$? \frac{\text{mol HCl}}{\text{L sol'n}} = \frac{36 \text{ g HCl}}{100 \text{ g sol'n}}$$

The molar mass of HCl is used to convert g HCl to mol HCl, and the density is the conversion factor needed to convert grams of solution into liters:

$$? \frac{\text{mol HCl}}{\text{L sol'n}} = \left(\frac{36 \text{ g HCl}}{100 \text{ g sol'n}}\right)\left(\frac{1 \text{ mol HCl}}{36.46 \text{ g HCl}}\right)\left(\frac{1.18 \text{ g sol'n}}{1 \text{ mL sol'n}}\right)\left(\frac{1000 \text{ mL sol'n}}{1 \text{ L sol'n}}\right)$$

$$= 11.7 \text{ M HCl}$$

Exercise 9.6

The molarity of a solution of potassium fluoride, KF, is 0.748.
(a) What is the molality of this solution if the density is 1.035 g mL^{-1}?
(b) What is the mole fraction of KF?

43.4 g

Solution

(a) The given solution contains 0.748 mol in 1.00 L of solution. From this fact the number of grams of KF is calculated to be 31.4 g. The mass of the 1.00 L of solution is obtained by multiplying by the density to get 1035 g. Of this 1035 g, 31.4 g is KF and the remaining 1003.6 g is water. If needed, a table may be constructed to summarize this information:

	Grams	Moles
KF	31.4	0.748
H$_2$O	1003.6	

This table contains enough information to calculate the molality from the definition:

$$\text{molality KF} = \frac{\text{mol KF}}{\text{kg H}_2\text{O}} = \frac{0.748 \text{ mol KF}}{1.0036 \text{ kg H}_2\text{O}}$$

$$= 0.745 \text{ m}$$

(b) To calculate the mole fraction, the 1003.6 g of water is converted into 55.8 mol of water. The data are then substituted into the definition of the mole fraction:

$$X = \frac{\text{mol KF}}{\text{mol KF} + \text{mol H}_2\text{O}}$$

$$= \frac{0.748 \text{ mol KF}}{0.748 \text{ mol glucose} + 55.8 \text{ mol H}_2\text{O}}$$

$$= 0.0132$$

In Exercise 9.6 an aqueous solution that had a molarity of 0.748 was calculated to have a molality of 0.745. This is less than 0.5 percent difference. We may generalize that dilute aqueous solutions (less than 0.5 M or 0.5 m) have the same molality and molarity.

IN DILUTE AQUEOUS SOLUTIONS
MOLARITY = MOLALITY.

The same concepts that yielded the molarity-molality simplification are used to conclude that in dilute solutions the mass fraction is equal to the mass-volume fraction. This is particularly true for solutions in which the solute is present in trace quantities and the concentrations are expressed as parts per million or parts per billion.

Effect of Temperature on Solubility

This topic is rather complex, and the details are usually left for more advanced courses. The basic principle of the temperature effect on solubility lies in the randomness (entropy) of the molecules. To begin, we recall that gas molecules are always more random than the molecules in liquids and that the molecules in liquids are more randomly arranged than the molecules in highly structured crystals:

Randomness of Molecules

SOLIDS << LIQUIDS << GASES

As a general rule, increasing temperatures drive molecules toward the more random phase. Thus an increase in temperature usually increases the solubility of solids in a liquid and always decreases the solubility of gases in a liquid. Decreasing temperatures have the opposite effect.

Most solids are more soluble in hot solvents than in cold solvents. Figure 9.5 illustrates the changes in solubility of a few solid compounds as temperature is increased. A simple explanation is that increasing the temperature increases the disorder of all molecules. If two states are present, molecules will tend to move from an ordered state to a more disordered state. A more precise explanation is left for more advanced chemistry courses.

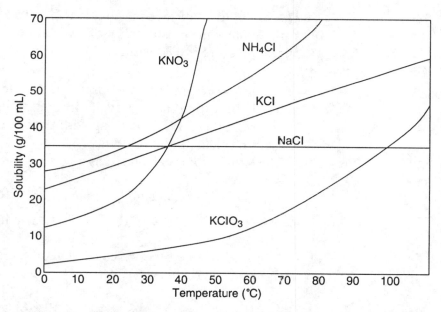

FIGURE 9.5. Temperature dependence of solubility for several representative ionic compounds.

In agreement with the general principle above, the solubility of gases in liquids always decreases as the temperature is increased. You may have noticed that a warm bottle of soda fizzes more than a cold bottle. In this case the increased disorder caused by an increase in temperature favors molecules leaving the liquid phase and entering the gas phase. This occurs because molecules are always more random in the gas phase than in the liquid phase.

Effect of Pressure on Solubility

External pressure has no significant effect on the solubility of solids or liquids because solids and liquids are not appreciably compressed when pressure is increased. Gases, on the other hand, are easily compressed. Compression increases the frequency with which gas molecules hit the liquid phase and enter it, thereby increasing the solubility.

The effect of pressure on the solubility of gases is expressed in Henry's law:

$$\text{solubility}_{gas} = kP_{gas} \qquad (9.7)$$

Solubility$_{gas}$ is usually expressed as molarity or as wt/vol concentration units, k is the Henry's law proportionality constant, and p_{gas} is the partial pressure of the gas.

If the solubility of a gas is known at one pressure, Henry's law can be used to determine the solubility at another pressure as long as the temperature is the same in both cases.

Exercise 9.7

The solubility of oxygen in water is 1.25×10^{-3} M at 25°C at sea level (1.00 atm). What will the solubility of oxygen be in Denver, where the atmospheric pressure is 0.800 atm?

Solution

The solution requires two steps. First, the Henry's law constant is determined by inserting the sea level information into the equation and solving for k. Next, the value of k along with the atmospheric pressure in Denver is used to calculate the solubility.

The value of k is calculated as

$$k\,(1.00\ \text{atm}) = 1.25 \times 10^{-3}\ \text{M O}_2$$
$$k = 1.25 \times 10^{-3}\ \text{M O}_2\ \text{atm}^{-1}$$

Using this value of k, we can calculate the solubility of oxygen at Denver's atmospheric pressure:

$$\text{solubility}_{O_2} = (1.25 \times 10^{-3}\ \text{M O}_2\ \text{atm}^{-1})\,(0.800\ \text{atm})$$
$$= 1.00 \times 10^{-3}\ \text{M O}_2$$

Alternative Solution

Another method for solving this type of problem is to write the Henry's law equation for two states, indicated by the subscripts 1 and 2:

$$\text{solubility}_1 = kP_1 \quad \text{and} \quad \text{solubility}_2 = kP_2$$

The k does not need a subscript since it is constant under all conditions. Next, the ratio of these two equations is taken:

$$\frac{\text{solubility}_1}{\text{solubility}_2} = \frac{kP_1}{kP_2}$$

The constants k cancel, leaving

$$\frac{\text{solubility}_1}{\text{solubility}_2} = \frac{P_1}{P_2}$$

For ease of calculation we define solubility$_1$ as the solubility in Denver and P_1 = 0.800 atm. Then solubility$_2$ = 1.25 x 10^{-3} M and P_2 = 1.00 atm. Entering these data gives

$$\frac{\text{solubility}_1}{1.25 \times 10^{-3} \text{ M}} = \frac{0.800 \text{ atm}}{1.00 \text{ atm}}$$

$$\text{solubility}_1 = \frac{(0.800 \text{ atm})(1.25 \times 10^{-3} \text{ M})}{1.00 \text{ atm}} = 1.00 \times 10^{-3} \text{ M O}_2$$

In this method the algebra was done with the symbolic variables before any data were entered or any calculations performed.

Colligative Properties of Solutions

The physical properties of pure liquids are altered when solutes are dissolved in these liquids. The word *colligative*, meaning collective, is used to describe physical properties that are changed by the presence of any solute particles. The chemical identity of the solute is not important. Only the concentration of the solute particles is significant in altering physical properties. The physical properties that change when a solute is present include vapor pressure, boiling point, melting point, and osmotic pressure.

Vapor-Pressure Lowering by Nonelectrolytes

If a nonvolatile nonelectrolyte is dissolved in a liquid, it causes the vapor pressure to decrease in proportion to its concentration. This effect is explained on the basis that some of the nonvolatile solute molecules take up space at the surface of the liquid and decrease the effective surface area of the solute available for evaporation. The result is to decrease the evaporation rate and the vapor pressure.

In the 1880s F.M. Raoult was the first to observe this effect and to show that the vapor pressure is proportional to the mole fraction of the solvent in a solution. This is entirely reasonable since the mole fraction of the solvent represents the proportion of solvent molecules at the surface of the liquid. **Raoult's law** states that the actual vapor pressure, P_{actual}, is equal to the vapor pressure of the pure solvent, P^0, multiplied by the mole fraction of the solvent:

$$P_{actual} = P^0 X_{solvent} \tag{9.8}$$

Exercise 9.8

Many people use 2 teaspoons (18 g each) of sugar in each cup (250 mL) of coffee. The vapor pressure of water at 80°C is 355 mm Hg. What is the vapor pressure of sugared coffee at the same temperature?

Solution

Sucrose, $C_{12}H_{22}O_{11}$, has a molar mass of 342 g mol^{-1}, and 2 teaspoons represents 0.105 mol. The cup of coffee has a volume of 250 mL; and since the density of water is 1.00 g mL^{-1}, the mass of the solvent is 250 g, or 13.89 mol. The mole fraction of solvent is

$$X = \frac{\text{mol } H_2O}{\text{mol sucrose} + \text{mol } H_2O}$$

$$= \frac{13.89 \text{ mol } H_2O}{0.108 \text{ mol sucrose} + 13.89 \text{ mol } H_2O}$$

$$= 0.992$$

The vapor pressure of the sugared coffee is then

$$P = (355 \text{ mm Hg}) (0.992)$$

$$= 352 \text{ mm Hg}$$

We see from this result that the small mole fraction of sucrose, $X = 0.008$, has only a small effect on the vapor pressure. Larger amounts will of course have a larger effect.

Vapor Pressures of Volatile Liquid Mixtures

When one liquid is dissolved in another, the vapor pressure of the entire mixture depends on the vapor pressures of the individual liquids and the proportions in which these liquids are mixed. We may use the same logic as for the nonvolatile solute to understand what is happening. In this case the solute liquid occupies space at the surface of the solution, inhibiting the vaporization of the solvent and decreasing its vapor pressure. Now, however, the solute itself is volatile, and the space it occupies at the surface allows it to vaporize. By using Raoult's law for both volatile components of the solution, we obtain

$$P_{total} = X_1 \, p_1^0 + X_2 \, p_2^0 + \cdots \tag{9.9}$$

The subscripts 1 and 2 represent the two different volatile liquids in the mixture, and the ellipsis indicates that for mixtures of more than two volatile liquids similar terms are added. At this point we notice that, if one solute is not volatile ($p_2^0 = 0$), Equation 9.9 becomes the same as Equation 9.8.

Exercise 9.9

Calculate the vapor pressure of a mixture of equal weights of water and ethyl alcohol, C_2H_5OH, at 35°C, when the vapor pressures of the two substances are 42.0 and 100 mm Hg, respectively.

Solution

If there are equal masses of the two liquids, let us assume that 100 g of one liquid is mixed with 100 g of the other. This gives us 5.56 mol of water and 2.17 mol of ethyl alcohol.

The mole fraction of water is

$$X_1 = \frac{5.56 \text{ mol } H_2O}{5.56 \text{ mol } H_2O + 2.17 \text{ mol } C_2H_5OH} = 0.719$$

The mole fraction of ethyl alcohol is

$$X_2 = \frac{2.17 \text{ mol } C_2H_5OH}{5.56 \text{ mol } HO + 2.17 \text{ mol } C_2H_5OH} = 0.281$$

Entering this information, along with the corresponding vapor pressures of the pure liquids, into the Raoult's law equation yields

$$P_{total} = (42 \text{ mm Hg}) (0.719) + (100 \text{ mm Hg}) (0.281)$$

$$= 58.3 \text{ mm Hg}$$

From Raoult's law for mixtures of liquids, we can make the generalization that the total vapor pressure of a liquid-liquid solution will always lie somewhere between the lowest and highest vapor pressures of the two liquids.

Figure 9.6 is a pictoral representation of Raoult's law for a binary mixture of water and ethyl alcohol.

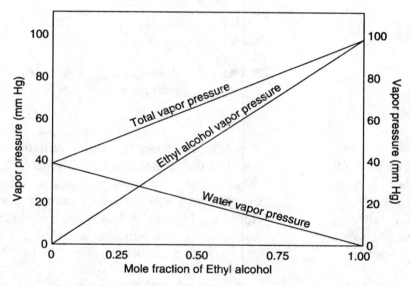

FIGURE 9.6. Graphical representation of Raoult's law for a binary liquid mixture of water and ethyl alcohol at 35°C.

Ideal Solutions and Raoult's Law

The preceding discussion of Raoult's law assumes that the solutions are ideal solutions. An ideal solution is one in which the energy used to disrupt the attractive forces in the solvent and solute is exactly balanced by the energy released when the solution forms. In other words, the attractive forces in the pure solute and solvent are the same as the attractive forces in the solution. If the solution is not ideal, deviations from Raoult's law are found. These deviations may be summarized as follows:

1. *Positive deviation*: The vapor pressure of the solution is greater than expected from Raoult's law because the solution has weaker attrac-

tive forces than those in the pure solute and solvent. A solution with positive deviation cools as the mixture is prepared since the extra energy needed to break the attractions is absorbed from the surroundings.

2. *Negative deviation*: The vapor pressure is lower than expected from Raoult's law because the attractive forces in the solution are greater than those in the pure solute and solvent. These solutions produce extra energy that is given off as heat. A mixture of this type becomes warmer when the solution is prepared.

Figure 9.7 illustrates the effects of positive and negative deviations from Raoult's law.

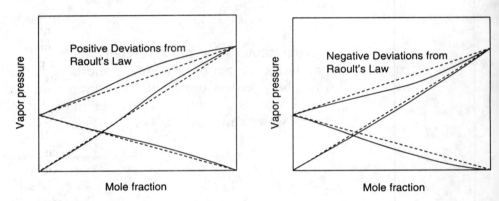

FIGURE 9.7. **Positive and negative deviations from Raoult's law. Dashed lines indicate Raoult's law for ideal solutions.**

Boiling-Point Elevation and Freezing-Point Depression of Nonvolatile Nonelectrolyte Solutions

A solute decreases the vapor pressure of a solvent according to Raoult's law. The phase diagram (see Chapter 8 for a complete description of phase diagrams) of a solution is similar to the phase diagram for the pure solvent except that the decrease in vapor pressure lowers the liquid-gas equilibrium line. Figure 9.8 illustrates the change in the position of the liquid-gas equilibrium line, which establishes a new triple point and also shifts the solid-liquid equilibrium line for the solution as compared to the pure solvent.

From Figure 9.8 it is apparent that a decrease in the vapor pressure must also cause the boiling point to increase and the melting point to decrease. The increase in the boiling point is directly related to the decrease in vapor pressure caused by the presence of a solute. As a result, higher temperatures are needed to make the vapor pressure of the solution equal to atmospheric pressure. The decrease in the melting point arises because the attractive forces between the solute and solvent interfere with the crystallization process.

The changes in the boiling and melting points of a solution depend on the solvent and on the molal concentration of the solute. For the increase in the boiling point, ΔT,

$$\Delta T = k_b m \qquad (9.10)$$

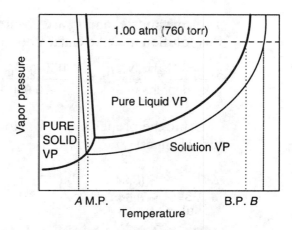

FIGURE 9.8. Change in the phase diagram of a solvent when a nonvolatile solute is dissolved in it. Heavy lines represent the phase diagram for the pure solvent. Lighter lines represent changes to the solid-liquid and liquid-gas equilibrium lines. M.P. and B.P. indicate the melting and boiling points, respectively, of the pure solvent, while A and B are the new melting and boiling points.

where m is the molality of the solution and k_b is the boiling-point-elevation constant for the solvent. For the decrease in the melting point the equation is similar to Equation 9.10 except that it has a negative sign to indicate a decrease in temperature and a different constant, k_f, called the freezing-point-depression constant:

$$\Delta T = -k_f m \qquad (9.11)$$

Note that freezing point and melting point are the same. In either boiling or freezing, the calculated ΔT must be added to the boiling point or freezing point of the pure solvent to determine the actual boiling and freezing points. Table 9.2 lists some common solvents with their boiling-point-elevation and freezing-point-depression constants.

TABLE 9.2 Freezing-Point-Depression and Boiling-Point-Elevation Constants for Some Common Solvents

Solvent	Freezing Point (°C)	k_F (°C m^{-1})	Boiling Point (°C)	k_B (°C m^{-1})
Acetic acid	16.66	3.90	117.90	2.53
Benzene	5.50	5.10	80.10	2.53
Cyclohexane	6.50	20.2	80.72	2.75
Camphor	178.40	40.0	207.42	5.61
p-Dichlorobenzene	53.10	7.1	174.1	6.2
Naphthalene	80.29	6.94	217.96	6.2
Water	0.00	1.86	100.0	0.52

Exercise 9.10

What are the freezing and boiling points of naphthalene when 10.0 g of nicotine, $C_{10}H_{14}N_2$, is dissolved in 50.0 g of naphthalene?

Solution

The constants k_f and k_b are given in Table 9.2. The molality of nicotine in this solution must be calculated to obtain ΔT:

$$? \frac{\text{mol } C_{10}H_{14}N_2}{\text{kg naphthalene}} = \frac{10.0 \text{ g } C_{10}H_{14}N_2 / 162 \text{ g mol}^{-1}}{0.050 \text{ kg naphthalene}} = 1.23 \text{ m } C_{10}H_{14}N_2$$

Using the proper k_f and k_b, along with this molality, gives the temperature changes:

$$\Delta T_f = -(6.94°\text{C m}^{-1})(1.23 \text{ m}) \qquad \text{and} \qquad \Delta T_b = (6.2°\text{C m}^{-1})(1.23 \text{ m})$$
$$= -8.54°\text{C} \qquad\qquad \text{and} \qquad\qquad = 7.63°\text{C}$$

These changes are then added to the freezing and boiling temperatures of the pure solvent to obtain the freezing point and boiling point of the solution:

$$\text{Freezing point} = 80.29°\text{C} - 8.54°\text{C} = 71.75°\text{C}$$

$$\text{Boiling point} = 217.96°\text{C} + 7.63°\text{C} = 225.59°\text{C}.$$

Uses of Boiling-Point Elevation and Freezing-Point Depression

Chemists take advantage of the freezing-point depression to make cooling baths below 0°C. This is done by dissolving large quantities of salt in water and then adding ice. Daniel Fahrenheit used this method to make the coldest solution he could and defined it as zero on his temperature scale. Everyone takes advantage of antifreeze in his or her car engine. Antifreeze lowers the freezing point of water by adding a high concentration of ethylene glycol. Antifreeze solutions must also increase the boiling point of water to allow engines to run above 100°C without boiling over.

The most important use of the freezing-point-depression and boiling-point-elevation phenomenon is in the determination of molar masses. The molality used to calculate ΔT_f and ΔT_b is defined as number of moles of solute per kilogram of solvent. The number of moles of solute is equal to the mass of the solute divided by its molar mass (g solute/molar mass solute). The equations for ΔT_f and ΔT_b may be expanded to read as

$$\Delta T_f = -k_f \left(\frac{\text{g solute/molar mass solute}}{\text{kg solvent}} \right) \qquad (9.12)$$

$$\Delta T_b = k_b \left(\frac{\text{g solute/molar mass solute}}{\text{kg solvent}} \right) \qquad (9.13)$$

To obtain the molar mass of a substance, we need to know the number of grams of solute dissolved in each kilogram of solvent, the change in either the boiling point or the freezing point, and the appropriate constant, k_f or k_b, for the solvent.

Exercise 9.11

When 10.0 g of elemental sulfur is dissolved in 100.0 g of cyclohexane, the freezing point of this solution is found to be $-1.40°\text{C}$. What is the molar mass of sulfur?

Solution

Expanded Equation 9.12 will be used:

$$\Delta T_f \quad = \quad -k_f \left(\frac{\text{g solute/molar mass solute}}{\text{kg solvent}} \right)$$

Since the freezing point of the solution is $-1.40°C$ and the normal freezing point of cyclohexane is $6.50°C$, $\Delta T_f = -7.90°C$. From Table 9.2, the freezing-point-depression constant is $20.2°C\,m^{-1}$. Entering the data in the equation yields

$$-7.90°C \quad = \quad -20.2°C\,m^- \left(\frac{10.0 \text{ g S/ molar mass S}}{0.100 \text{ kg cyclohexane}} \right)$$

$$= \quad \frac{-2020°C \text{ g S/mol S}}{\text{molar mass S}}$$

$$\text{molar mass of sulfur} \quad = \quad \frac{-2020°C \text{ g S/mol S}}{-7.90°C}$$

$$= \quad 256 \text{ g S/mol S}$$

This result tells us that one molecule of sulfur has a mass of 256 g. Since the atomic mass of sulfur is 32 in the periodic table, there must be eight sulfur atoms in one molecule of sulfur (256/32 = 8). This means that elemental sulfur exists as S_8 molecules.

Osmotic Pressure

Freezing-point-depression and boiling-point-elevation measurements have constants in the range of a few degrees Celsius per molal. Therefore, to attain any reasonable measurements, solutions must be fairly concentrated, since small temperature changes are often difficult to measure.

Modern chemistry is often interested in extremely large molecules such as polymers, proteins, peptides, and DNA. These molecules, which have molar masses exceeding 100,000 g mol^{-1}, are impossible to dissolve in sufficient quantities to obtain temperature changes that can be accurately measured. However, dilute solutions produce an osmotic pressure that is easily measured even in very dilute solutions.

The principle of **osmosis** explains the flow of solvent through semipermeable membranes. It is the basic mechanism that transports water from the roots to the upper branches of trees that may be over 100 feet tall.

In explaining osmosis, we start by observing that two solutions of different concentrations will diffuse into each other until the concentrations are uniform. There is a natural tendency for solutes and solvents to diffuse from regions of high concentration to regions of lower concentration until the concentration is uniform throughout the solution.

A semipermeable membrane placed between two solutions with different concentrations will allow only the solvent to diffuse. Solute molecules, which are often larger than solvent molecules, cannot pass through the semipermeable membrane. Diffusion of the solvent through the semipermeable membrane will stop when the concentrations have been equalized or when an opposing force is applied to stop the diffusion. This opposing force is known as **osmotic pressure**.

The osmotic pressure experiment is diagrammed in Figure 9.9. At the start of the experiment two compartments are separated by a semipermeable membrane; one compartment holds a solution containing the solute,

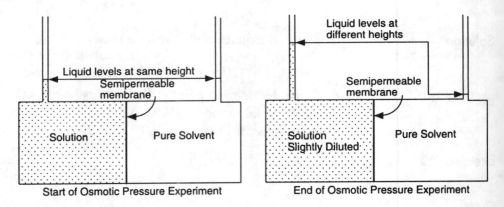

FIGURE 9.9. **Start of an osmotic pressure experiment with equal pressures acting on both compartments. At the end of the experiment the pressure developed is the osmotic pressure.**

and the other holds a pure solvent. The heights of the two liquids in the measuring tubes are equal at the start, indicating that the same atmospheric pressure is acting on both compartments.

Since the solution is more concentrated than the solvent, solvent immediately starts diffusing from the solvent side to the solution side in an attempt to equalize the concentrations. This dilutes the solution by increasing its volume, and the liquid level in the measuring tube for the solution increases. Conversely, the loss of solvent from the solvent compartment makes the liquid level in its measuring tube decrease. The difference in liquid levels between the two compartments represents the opposing force, called the osmotic pressure, that will stop the diffusion at some point. When the liquid levels stop changing, the osmotic pressure is the difference between the heights of the two liquid levels.

The equation that governs this process is the ideal gas law equation from Chapter 7:

$$PV = nRT \tag{9.14}$$

The symbol Π replaces P for an osmotic pressure experiment:

$$\Pi V = nRT \tag{9.15}$$

Exercise 9.12

Calculate the osmotic pressure that would result from dissolving 2 teaspoons of sucrose in a cup of coffee at 80°C. ($R = 0.0821$ L atm mol^{-1} K^{-1}).

Solution

In Exercise 9.8 we determined that one cup of coffee is 0.250 L and 2 teaspoons of sucrose is equivalent to 0.105 mol of sucrose. Since the temperature is given in degrees Celsius, it must be converted to kelvin units: 353 K. Substituting these data into the osmotic pressure equation yields

$$\Pi(0.250 \text{ L}) \quad = \quad (0.105 \text{ mol})(0.0821 \text{ L atm mol}^{-1} \text{ K}^{-1})(353 \text{ K})$$

Solving, we obtain an osmotic pressure of 12.17 atm or 9251 mm Hg (9.2 m of mercury or 125 m of water!).

This exercise shows that the osmotic pressure is very large for a 0.1

This exercise shows that the osmotic pressure is very large for a 0.1 molar solution. A 10 micromolar solution will result in more than a centimeter difference in pressure for aqueous solutions. This fact makes osmotic pressure measurements ideal for very dilute solutions. Of particular interest is the use of osmotic pressure to determine molar mass, as shown in the next exercise.

Exercise 9.13

A large polymer is synthesized, and 100 mL of a solution containing 1.00 g of this polymer is tested in an osmotic pressure experiment. The resulting pressure is measured as 55 mm of water at 25°C. From this information calculate the molar mass of the polymer.

Solution

First, the pressure must be converted to millimeters of mercury and then to atmospheres since we intend to use a value of R that is 0.0821 L atm mol^{-1}K^{-1}. This is done by using the ratio of the densities of water and mercury:

$$? \text{ atm} = 55 \text{ mm H}_2\text{O} \left(\frac{1.00 \text{ g H}_2\text{O mL}^{-1}}{13.5 \text{g Hg mL}^{-1}} \right) = 4.07 \text{ mm Hg}$$

$$= 4.07 \text{ mm Hg} \left(\frac{1 \text{ atm}}{760 \text{ mm Hg}} \right) = 5.36 \times 10^{-3} \text{ atm}$$

Entering the data into the osmotic pressure equation yields the number of moles of polymer:

298 K

$$(5.36 \times 10^{-3} \text{ atm})(0.100 \text{ L}) = n(0.0821 \text{ L atm mol}^{-1} \text{ K}^{-1})(\cancel{353 \text{ K}})$$

$$n = 1.85 \times 10^{-5} \text{ mol}$$

Since the number of moles of any substance is the mass divided by the molar mass, M, we can write

$$n = \frac{\text{g compound}}{\text{molar mass}}$$

or

$$\text{molar mass compound} = \frac{\text{g compound}}{n}$$

Entering the data, we obtain

$$\text{molar mass compound} = \frac{1.00 \text{ g compound}}{1.85 \times 10^{-5} \text{ mol compound}}$$

$$= 54,054 \text{ g mol}^{-1} \text{ or } 54.1 \text{ kg mol}^{-1}$$

Since this solution is very dilute, the molarity and molality can be considered to be the same. In aqueous solution the freezing-point depression would have been 4×10^{-4} °C. This is a temperature change that is difficult to measure precisely, and it indicates the utility of the osmotic pressure measurement.

Colligative Properties of Electrolytes

As defined earlier, electrolytes are compounds that dissociate completely into two or more ions when dissolved in water. Each ion acts as a discrete particle as far as the colligative properties are concerned. The result is that NaCl solutions will have twice the effect on vapor pressure, boiling and freezing points, and osmotic pressure as the same concentration of a non-dissociating solute such as sucrose. Compounds such as $MgCl_2$ and $(NH_4)_2SO_4$ will have three times the effect since they dissociate into three ions each. $AlCl_3$ and Na_3PO_4 will each dissociate into four ions.

Exercise 9.14

(a) Calculate the expected osmotic pressure of a 3.5×10^{-3} M aqueous solution of the electrolyte $Al(NO_3)_3$ at 30°C.

(b) What are the expected normal boiling and melting points of this solution?

Solution

(a) The dissociation equation for $Al(NO_3)_3$ is

$$Al(NO_3)_3 \rightleftharpoons Al^{3+} + 3\,NO_3^-$$

Four ions are produced for each $Al(NO_3)_3$ dissolved. The concentration of all ions is $4 \times 3.5 \times 10^{-3}$ M = 1.4×10^{-2} M ions. Converting 30°C to 303 K and substituting into the osmotic pressure equation gives

$$\Pi V = nRT$$

Rearranging and noting that $\frac{n}{V}$ = M yields

$$\Pi = \left(\frac{n}{V}\right)RT = MRT$$

$$= (14 \times 10^{-3})\,(0.082 \text{ L atm mol}^{-1}\text{K}^{-1})\,(303 \text{ K})$$

$$= 0.348 \text{ atm} = 264 \text{ mm Hg}$$

(b) To calculate the freezing-point depression and the boiling-point elevation, we first assume that M = m since the concentration is so small. From this assumption we obtain

$$\Delta T_f = -(1.86°C \text{ m}^{-1})(1.4 \times 10^{-2}) = -0.026°C$$

$$\Delta T_b = (0.52°C \text{ m}^{-1})(1.4 \times 10^{-2}) = 0.0073°C$$

This gives us a melting point of $0.00 - 0.026 = -0.026$°C and a boiling point of $100 + 0.0073 = 100.0073$°C. The osmotic pressure is obviously easier to measure.

Ion Pairing

Solutions with high concentrations of an electrolyte exhibit a behavior called ion-pairing. At high concentrations the positive and negative ions are relatively close to each other, and some ions form pairs. These pairs act as single particles, not separate ions. A result of ion pairing is that electrolyte solutions often have smaller than expected effects on colligative properties of solutions. For example, a 0.1 molal aqueous solution of NaCl is expected to have a freezing point depression of $-0.372°C$, while experiments give a lesser value of $-0.348°C$.

Important Concepts

Molecular view of the solution process
Attractive forces and randomness in the solution process
Solubility related to attractive forces
Concentration units, particularly molarity and molality
Colligative properties
Osmotic pressure

Important Equations

M = moles/liter solution
m = moles/kg solvent
$\Delta T = -k_f m$
$\Delta T = k_b m$
$\Pi V = nRT$
$d = grams/cm^3$

Questions on Chapter 9

1. The solubility of cadmium chloride, $CdCl_2$, is 140 g per 100 mL of solution. What is the molar solubility (molarity) of a saturated solution of $CdCl_2$?
   (A) 0.765 M
   (B) 1.31 M
   (C) 7.65 M
   (D) 12.61 M
   (E) 0.131 M

2. The vapor pressure of an ideal solution is 456 mm Hg. If the vapor pressure of the pure solvent is 832 mm Hg, what is the mole fraction of the nonvolatile solute?
   (A) 0.548
   (B) 0.354
   (C) 0.645
   (D) 1.82
   (E) 0.452

3. All of the following physical properties change as solute is added to the solution. Which is NOT a colligative property?
   (A) boiling point
   (B) surface tension
   (C) vapor pressure
   (D) melting point
   (E) osmotic pressure

4. Which of the following is expected to be the most soluble in hexane, C_6H_{14}?
   (A) KCl
   (B) C_2H_5OH
   (C) C_6H_6
   (D) H_2O
   (E) $HC_2H_3O_2$

5. Molarity units are most appropriate in calculating which of the following?
   (A) freezing-point depression
   (B) vapor pressure
   (C) boiling-point elevation
   (D) surface tension
   (E) osmotic pressure

6. All of the following may be used to determine molar masses. Which one requires an ideal solution for accurate results?
   (A) freezing-point depression
   (B) boiling-point elevation
   (C) osmotic pressure
   (D) vapor pressure
   (E) gas density

7. To make a solution, 3.45 mol of $C_6H_{13}Cl$ and 1.26 mol of C_5H_{12} are mixed. Which of the following is needed, but not readily available, to calculate the molarity of this solution?
   (A) the density of the solution
   (B) the densities of $C_6H_{13}Cl$ and C_5H_{12}
   (C) the temperature
   (D) the molar masses of $C_6H_{13}Cl$ and C_5H_{12}
   (E) the volumes of $C_6H_{13}Cl$ and C_5H_{12}

8. Which of the following when added to 1.00 kg H_2O is expected to give the greatest increase in the boiling point of water? ($k_b = 0.052°C\ m^{-1}$)
   (A) 1.25 mol sucrose
   (B) 0.25 mol iron(III) nitrate
   (C) 0.50 mol ammonium chloride
   (D) 0.66 mol calcium sulfate
   (E) 1.00 mol acetic acid

9. Ethyl alcohol, C_2H_5OH, and water become noticeably warmer when mixed. This is due to
   (A) the decrease in volume when they are mixed
   (B) smaller attractive forces in the mixture than in the pure liquids
   (C) the hydrogen bonding of the two liquids
   (D) the change in vapor pressure observed
   (E) stronger attractive forces in the mixture than in the pure liquids

10. Which is the most appropriate method for determining the molar mass of a newly discovered enzyme?
    (A) freezing-point depression
    (B) osmotic pressure
    (C) boiling-point depression
    (D) gas density
    (E) vapor pressure

11. A polluted pond contains 25 ppb of lead ions. What is the concentration of lead ions in molarity units?
    (A) 1.2×10^8 M
    (B) 1.2×10^{-7} M
    (C) 2.5×10^{-8} M
    (D) 0.121 M
    (E) 1.2×10^{-10} M

12. When algae decay in a pond, the process uses up the available oxygen. Which of the following factors will also contribute to a decrease in oxygen in a pond?
    (A) decreasing salinity (salt concentration)
    (B) increasing acidity due to acid rain
    (C) increasing temperature
    (D) increasing surface tension of the water
    (E) increasing atmospheric pressure

13. Liquid A has a vapor pressure of 437 mm Hg, and liquid B has a vapor pressure of 0.880 atm at 85°C. Which of the following represents a possible solution of the two liquids?
    (A) a mixture with a vapor pressure of 345 mm Hg
    (B) a mixture with a vapor pressure of 0.750 atm
    (C) a mixture with a boiling point of 65.2°C
    (D) a mixture with a vapor pressure of 1106 mm Hg
    (E) a mixture with a boiling point of 85°C

14. The freezing-point-depression constant for water is 1.86°C m^{-1}. When 100 g of a compound is dissolved in 500 g H_2O, the freezing point is -10.0°C. Of the five possibilities below, which is the identity of the compound?
    (A) $Mg(NO_3)_2$
    (B) KCl
    (C) Na_2SO_4
    (D) HCOOH
    (E) HF

15. Which of the following compounds is incorrectly classified?
    (A) NaF   electrolyte
    (B) CH_3OH weak electrolyte
    (C) $Mg(C_2H_3O_2)_2$ electrolyte
    (D) CH_3CH_2COOH weak electrolyte
    (E) glucose   nonelectrolyte

16. The k_f and k_b values for water are 1.86 and 0.52°C m^{-1}, respectively. A solution boils at 107.5°C. At what temperature does this solution freeze?
    (A) 7.5°C
    (B) -7.5°C
    (C) 0.0°C
    (D) -26.8°C
    (E) -284.5°C

17. If equal numbers of moles of each of the following are dissolved in 1 kg of distilled water, the one with the lowest boiling point will be
    (A) NaF
    (B) AlCl$_3$
    (C) Mg(C$_2$H$_3$O$_2$)$_2$
    (D) CH$_3$CH$_2$COOH
    (E) glucose

18. When ethyl alcohol and water are mixed, the solution becomes noticeably warm to the touch. It may be concluded that
    (A) the mixture will show a negative deviation from Raoult's law
    (B) ethyl alcohol and water are more strongly attracted to each other than are two water molecules.
    (C) ethyl alcohol and water are more strongly attracted to each other than are two ethyl alcohol molecules.
    (D) only B and C are true
    (E) A, B, and C are all true.

19. When KCl dissolves in water, the solution cools noticeably to the touch. It may be concluded that
    (A) the solvation energy is greater than the lattice energy
    (B) KCl is relatively insoluble in water
    (C) the entropy decreases when KCl dissolves
    (D) the boiling point of the solution will be less than 100°C
    (E) the entropy increase overcomes the unfavorable heat of dissolution

20. If 20.0 g of ethanol (molar mass = 46) and 30.0 g of water (molar mass = 18) are mixed together, the mole fraction of ethanol in this mixture is
    (A) 0.207
    (B) 0.261
    (C) 0.739
    (D) 0.793
    (E) 4.83

Answers

See Appendix I for explanation of answers.

1. **C**	5. **E**	9. **E**	13. **B**	17. **E**
2. **E**	6. **D**	10. **B**	14. **B**	18. **A**
3. **B**	7. **A**	11. **B**	15. **B**	19. **E**
4. **C**	8. **A**	12. **C**	16. **D**	20. **A**

PART FOUR

Physical Chemistry

CHAPTER TEN

Chemical Equilibrium

The concept of a **dynamic equilibrium** is central to many aspects of chemistry. In a dynamic equilibrium chemicals are reacting rapidly at the molecular scale, while their concentrations remain constant on the macroscopic scale. Many physical and chemical processes participate in dynamic equilibria. For example, (1) in a closed container gas molecules condense just as fast as liquid molecules evaporate; (2) a saturated solution involves a solid dissolving at the same rate as solute crystallizes; and (3) in a weak electrolyte solution the ions recombine into molecules just as fast as other molecules dissociate into ions. In all of these chemical and physical processes the rate in one direction is exactly equal to the rate in the other direction. It is important that, although reactions never stop in a dynamic equilibrium, the overall concentrations remain constant.

Figure 10.1 shows that a chemical reaction has two well-defined regions in time, and these regions are studied and measured in very different ways. When compounds are first mixed in a chemical reaction, they interact to form other compounds. During the reaction process the concentrations of the reactants decrease and the concentrations of the products increase. While the concentrations are changing, the reaction is studied using the principles of **chemical kinetics**, which are reviewed in Chapter 11. At some point in time the concentrations of the reactants and products stop changing. Although reactions do not stop at the molecular level, at the macroscopic level the concentrations of compounds in a dynamic equilibrium remain constant. At this point the compounds are in a dynamic chemical equilibrium with each other, and they are studied and described using the concepts of **chemical equilibrium**.

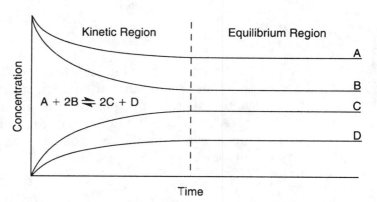

FIGURE 10.1. The two regions of chemical reactions. On the left, in the kinetic region, concentrations are changing with time. On the right, in the equilibrium region, the concentrations, on a macroscopic or laboratory scale, no longer appear to change.

The Equilibrium Law

In a chemical reaction the actual concentrations of the reactants and products, at equilibrium, are dependent on the initial concentrations of the reacting mixture. When several experiments with different initial concentrations of reactants are performed, they result in equilibrium mixtures with different concentrations. Although these mixtures may be different, they all obey the **equilibrium law**. This law states that the concentrations of all of the products multiplied together, divided by the concentrations of all the reactants multiplied together, will be equal to a number called the **equilibrium constant**, K. The value of the equilibrium constant depends only on the specific reaction and the temperature of the reaction mixture when equilibrium is reached.

The upper-case letter K is reserved as the symbol for the equilibrium constant. To describe the type of equilibrium constant a subscript is often used after the K. The symbol K_c represents the equilibrium constant when concentration is expressed in molarity units (mol L^{-1}). The symbol K_p is used when the partial pressures of gases represent the amounts of reactants and products. Special symbols for the equilibrium constant are K_{sp} for the solubility product, K_a for the acid dissociation constant, K_b for the base dissociation constant, K_f for the formation constant of complexes, and K_d for the dissociation constant in complexation reactions. These special forms of K are described in later sections of this chapter.

The equilibrium law depends on the chemical equation for the reaction under study. A general equilibrium reaction may be written as

$$aA \quad + \quad bB \quad \rightleftharpoons \quad pP \quad + \quad nN \tag{10.1}$$

and its equilibrium law will be written as

$$K_c \quad = \quad \frac{[P]^p[N]^n}{[A]^a[B]^b} \tag{10.2}$$

Whenever possible, the chemical reaction is balanced with the smallest possible whole-number coefficients. All tabulated values for equilibrium constants refer to equations with the simplest coefficients.

A more specific example of the formulation of the equilibrium law can be shown using the reaction between hydrogen and chlorine to form hydrogen chloride:

$$H_2(g) \quad + \quad Cl_2(g) \quad \rightleftharpoons \quad HCl(g) + HCl(g) \tag{10.3}$$

or

$$H_2(g) \quad + \quad Cl_2(g) \quad \rightleftharpoons \quad 2HCl(g) \tag{10.4}$$

The equilibrium law for this reaction is written as

$$K_c = \frac{[HCl] \times [HCl]}{[H_2] \times [Cl_2]} = \frac{[HCl]^2}{[H_2] \times [Cl_2]} \qquad (10.5)$$

Writing the chemical reaction with two separate HCl molecules as in Equation 10.3 illustrates that the concentration of HCl, written with square brackets as [HCl], should be multiplied by itself in the equilibrium law. Writing the chemical equation in the form of Equation 10.4 illustrates that the coefficient in a chemical equation will be used as an exponent in the equilibrium law.

For the combustion of propane, C_3H_8, the reaction is

$$C_3H_8(g) \quad + \quad 5O_2(g) \quad \rightleftharpoons \quad 3CO_2(g) \quad + \quad 4H_2O(g) \quad (10.6)$$

and the equilibrium law for this equation is written as

$$K_c = \frac{[CO_2]^3 \times [H_2O]^4}{[C_3H_8] \times [O_2]^5} \qquad (10.7)$$

The coefficients of the reactants and products are written as exponents of the concentrations in the equilibrium law.

Any substance that has a constant concentration during a reaction, including solids and all pure liquids, is not written as part of the equilibrium law. In dilute solutions, the solvent concentration is also constant and is not written in the equilibrium law.

Three examples are a reaction where water is a pure liquid:

$$CH_4(g) \quad + \quad 2O_2(g) \quad \rightleftharpoons \quad CO_2(g) \quad + \quad 2H_2O(\ell) \quad (10.8)$$

$$K_c = \frac{[CO_2]}{[CH_4] \times [O_2]^2} \qquad (10.9)$$

a reaction where AgCl is a solid:

$$AgCl(s) \quad \rightleftharpoons \quad Ag^+(aq) \quad + \quad Cl^-(aq) \qquad (10.10)$$

$$K_c = [Ag^+] \times [Cl^-] \qquad (10.11)$$

and a reaction where water is the solvent for dulute solutions:

$$NH_3(g) \quad + \quad H_2O(\ell) \quad \rightleftharpoons \quad NH_4^+(aq) \quad + \quad OH^-(aq) \quad (10.12)$$

$$K_c = \frac{[NH_4^+] \times [OH^-]}{[NH_3]} \qquad (10.13)$$

In most cases a solution is considered to be dilute when the concentration of the solute is less than 1 mole per liter.

Exercise 10.1

Write the equilibrium law for each of the following chemical equations:
- (a) $HF(aq)$ + $H_2O(\ell)$ ⇌ $F^-(aq)$ + $H_3O^+(aq)$
- (b) $2NH_3(aq)$ + $3I_2(s)$ ⇌ $2NI_3(s)$ + $3H_2(g)$
- (c) $CO(g)$ + $H_2O(g)$ ⇌ $CO_2(g)$ + $H_2(g)$
- (d) $Ba^{2+}(aq)$ + $SO_4^{2-}(aq)$ ⇌ $BaSO_4(s)$
- (e) $C_2H_4(g)$ + $3O_2(g)$ ⇌ $2CO_2(g)$ + $2H_2O(g)$

Solution

(a) $K_c = \dfrac{[F^-][H_3O^+]}{[HF]}$

(b) $K_c = \dfrac{[H_2]^3}{[NH_3]^2}$

(c) $K_c = \dfrac{[CO_2][H_2]}{[CO][H_2O]}$

(d) $K_c = \dfrac{1}{[Ba^{2+}][SO_4^{2-}]}$

(e) $K_c = \dfrac{[CO_2]^2[H_2O]^2}{[C_2H_4][O_2]^3}$

Manipulating the Equilibrium Law

The equilibrium law is written directly from the balanced chemical equation. On paper, chemical equations are easily manipulated. We can reverse the direction of the reaction by writing the reactants as products and the products as reactants. The coefficients of an equation can all be multiplied or divided by a constant factor. Equations can be added and subtracted. Each of these operations results in a different equilibrium law and a different value for the equilibrium constant.

Reversing a
Chemical Equation

The chemical equation with the corresponding K_c

$$O_2(g) + 2SO_2(g) \rightleftharpoons 2SO_3(g) \qquad K_c = \frac{[SO_3]^2}{[O_2] \times [SO_2]^2} \qquad (10.14)$$

can be written in the reverse direction as

$$2SO_3(g) \rightleftharpoons O_2(g) + 2SO_2(g) \qquad K_c' = \frac{[O_2] \times [SO_2]^2}{[SO_3]^2} \qquad (10.15)$$

The two equilibrium constants, K_c and K_c', are inversely related to each other:

$$K_c = \frac{1}{K_c'} \qquad (10.16)$$

If a chemical reaction is reversed, the value of the new equilibrium constant will be the inverse of the original equilibrium constant.

Multiplying or Dividing Coefficients by a Constant

Taking the same reaction, Equation 10.14, of sulfur dioxide with oxygen:

$$O2(g) + 2SO_2(g) \rightleftharpoons 2SO_3(g) \quad K_c = \frac{[SO_3]^2}{[O_2] \times [SO_2]^2}$$

we can multiply each of the coefficients by 3 to obtain another balanced equation:

$$3O_2(g) + 6SO_2(g) \rightleftharpoons 6SO_3(g) \quad K_c' = \frac{[SO_3]^6}{[O_2]^3 \times [SO_2]^6} \quad (10.17)$$

The relationship between K_c and K_c' can be shown since

$$\frac{[SO_3]^6}{[O_2]^3 [SO_2]^6} = \left(\frac{[SO_3]^2}{[O_2][SO_2]^2}\right)\left(\frac{[SO_3]^2}{[O_2][SO_2]^2}\right)\left(\frac{[SO_3]^2}{[O_2][SO_2]^2}\right) \quad (10.18)$$

$$= \left(\frac{[SO_3]^2}{[O_2][SO_2]^2}\right)^3$$

$$K_c' = K_c K_c K_c = K^3 \quad (10.19)$$

We see that the original equilibrium constant is raised to the power equal to the factor used in the multiplication.

Dividing an equation by 2 is the same as multiplying the equation by ½. Therefore, when an equation is divided by 2, the new equilibrium constant, K_c', is the square root of the original K_c:

$$K_c' = K_c^{1/2} = \sqrt{K_c} \quad (10.20)$$

Finally, reversing a reaction may also be considered mathematically the same as multiplying it by −1. The result is that

$$K_c' = K_c^{-1} = \frac{1}{K_c} \quad (10.21)$$

which agrees with Equation 10.16.

Adding Chemical Reactions

Chemical reactions are added by adding all reactants and all products in two equations and writing them as one equation. For example:

$$2S(g) + 2O_2(g) \rightleftharpoons 2SO_2(g) \quad K_1 = \frac{[SO_2]^2}{[S]^2 \times [O_2]^2} \quad (10.22)$$

$$O_2(g) + 2SO_2(g) \rightleftharpoons 2SO_3(g) \quad K_2 = \frac{[SO_3]^2}{[O_2] \times [SO_2]^2} \quad (10.23)$$

Adding these two equations and canceling the $2SO_2(g)$, which are identical on both sides, yields

$$2S(g) + 3O_2(g) \rightleftharpoons 2SO_3(g) \quad K_{overall} = \frac{[SO_3]^2}{[S]^2 \times [O_2]^3} \quad (10.24)$$

Mathematically we find that

$$K_{overall} = K_1 \times K_2 \qquad (10.25)$$

When equations are added, the overall equilibrium constant will be the product of the equilibrium constants of the reactions that were added.

Exercise 10.2

Given the following two reactions and their equilibrium constants:

$$Ag^+(aq) + Cl^-(aq) \rightleftharpoons AgCl(s) \qquad K_c = 1.0 \times 10^{10} \quad (a)$$

$$Ag^+(aq) + 2NH_3(aq) \rightleftharpoons Ag(NH_3)_2^+(aq) \qquad K_c = 1.6 \times 10^7 \quad (b)$$

what is the equilibrium constant of the reaction

$$AgCl(s) + 2NH_3(aq) \rightleftharpoons Ag(NH_3)_2^+(aq) + Cl^-(aq) \qquad K_{overall} = ? \quad (c)$$

Show how reactions (a) and (b) are added to obtain reaction (c).

Solution

To add the given equations, it is necessary to reverse equation (a) to make $AgCl(s)$ a reactant and Cl^- a product as required in the overall reaction:

$$AgCl(s) \rightleftharpoons Ag^+(aq) + Cl^-(aq) \qquad K_c = 1/1.0 \times 10^{10} = 1.0 \times 10^{-10} \quad (d)$$

The equilibrium constant is inverted, as shown, when a reaction is reversed. Equation (d) is added to equation (b), and the $Ag^+(aq)$ ions cancel. When reactions are added, the equilibrium constants are multiplied:

$$K_{overall} = (1.0 \times 10^{-10})(1.6 \times 10^7) = 1.6 \times 10^{-3}$$

Determining the Value of the Equilibrium Constant

The equilibrium constant, K, has a numerical value that may be determined by a variety of methods. The most direct method is to measure the concentration of each reactant and product in the mixture. For example, when sulfur dioxide reacts with oxygen to produce sulfur trioxide, the reaction and equilibrium law may be written as in Equation 10.14:

$$O_2(g) + 2SO_2(g) \rightleftharpoons 2SO_3(g) \qquad K_c = \frac{[SO_3]^2}{[O_2] \times [SO_2]^2}$$

If the concentrations at equilibrium are determined as $[O_2] = 2.0 \times 10^{-8}$ M, $[SO_2] = 3.4 \times 10^{-9}$ M, and $[SO_3] = 0.971$ M, they can be substituted into the equilibrium law to calculate the value of the equilibrium constant:

$$K_c = \frac{(0.971)^2}{(2.0 \times 10^{-8}) \times (3.4 \times 10^{-9})^2}$$

$$= 4.2 \times 10^{24}$$

This method of determining the value of an equilibrium constant requires three measurements, and, if K_c is very large or very small, it can lead to considerable experimental error. In addition, it may be impossible to analyze the mixture for all possible components. Other ways to determine the equilibrium constant, based on chemical stoichiometry, are described later in this chapter.

Using the Equilibrium Law

Extent of Reaction and Spontaneous Reactions

The value of the equilibrium constant indicates the extent to which reactants are converted into products in a chemical reaction. If the equilibrium constant is large, it indicates that the amount of products present at equilibrium is much greater than the amount of reactants. A very large equilibrium constant, greater than 10^{10}, for example, means that for all intents and purposes the reaction goes to completion. Conversely, when K is very small, less than 10^{-10}, very little product is formed and virtually no visible reaction occurs. If $K = 1$, the equilibrium mixture contains approximately equal amounts of reactants and products. These general ideas allow us to quickly estimate the composition of an equilibrium mixture.

In a **spontaneous reaction** products are formed when reactants are mixed, without any additional assistance. Chemists generally define a spontaneous reaction as one with an equilibrium constant greater than 1.00. A reaction with an equilibrium constant less than 1.00 is called a **nonspontaneous reaction**. The fact that $K' = 1/K_c$ when a reaction is reversed tells the chemist that a reaction that is nonspontaneous in one direction is spontaneous if written in the opposite direction.

Exercise 10.3

Which of the following reactions is spontaneous? List the reactions in order from the greatest extent of reaction to the lowest.

(a) $H_2(g) + I_2(g) \rightleftharpoons 2HI$ $K_c = 49$
(b) $Br_2 + Cl_2 \rightleftharpoons 2BrCl$ $K_c = 6.9$
(c) $HF(aq) + H_2O(l) \rightleftharpoons F^-(aq) + H_3O^+(aq)$ $K_c = 6.8 \times 10^{-4}$
(d) $2H_2(g) + O_2(g) \rightleftharpoons 2H_2O(g)$ $K_c = 9.1 \times 10^{80}$
(e) $2N_2O(g) \rightleftharpoons 2N_2(g) + O_2(g)$ $K_c = 7.0 \times 10^{34}$

Solution

All the reactions except (c) have equilibrium constants greater than 1 and are spontaneous.

The extent of reaction follows the order (d) > (e) > (a) > (b) > (c), based on the magnitude of the equilibrium constants.

The Reaction Quotient and Predicting the Direction of a Reaction

The **reaction quotient**, Q, is defined as the number obtained by entering all of the required concentrations into the equilibrium law and calculating the result. For the sulfur dioxide reaction discussed previously (Equation 10.14):

$$O_2(g) + 2SO_2(g) \rightleftharpoons 2SO_3(g)$$

$$K_c = \frac{[SO_3]^2}{[O_2] \times [SO_2]^2} \quad \text{(equilibrium law)} \tag{10.26}$$

$$Q = \frac{[SO_3]^2}{[O_2] \times [SO_2]^2} \quad \text{(reaction quotient)} \tag{10.27}$$

The equilibrium constant is the numerical value of K_c when the reaction is at equilibrium. If the chemicals in the reaction are not in equilibrium, the numerical value of the equilibrium law is called the reaction quotient, Q. Q has exactly the same form as the equilibrium law except that K_c has been replaced by Q.

Four principles may be ascribed to the value of Q:

1. If Q does not change with time, the reaction is in a state of equilibrium and $Q = K_c$.
2. If $Q = K_c$, the reaction is in a state of equilibrium.
3. If $Q < K_c$, the reaction will move in the forward direction (to the right) in order reach equilibrium.
4. If $Q > K_c$, the reaction will move in the reverse direction (to the left) in order reach equilibrium.

The first principle tells us how to determine whether a chemical reaction has reached equilibrium. It is necessary to measure the concentrations at different times (e.g., 1 hour, 2 hours, and 5 hours after the reaction has started). If the value of Q does not change, the system is in equilibrium and $Q = K_c$.

The second principle tells us that, if K_c is known from a prior experiment, the determination of Q will tell us whether the reactants and products have reached equilibrium. In particular, if $Q = K_c$, the system is in equilibrium.

The third and fourth principles tell us what will happen if Q is not equal to K_c. A value of Q that is less than the value of K_c means that the numerator of the equilibrium law must increase, while the denominator decreases, to raise the value of Q up to that of K_c. The fact that the numerator represents the concentrations of the products indicates that the reaction must proceed toward the product side of the reaction, or in the forward direction.

A value of Q that is larger than the value of K_c indicates that the numerator must decrease, while the denominator increases, to reach equilibrium. Again, the numerator represents the concentrations of products, and a decrease in products indicates that the reaction must proceed in the reverse direction.

If the value of K_c is known, we can tell whether or not a reaction is at equilibrium by determining Q and comparing it to K_c. If the reaction is not at equilibrium, we can also predict in which direction it will go in order to reach equilibrium.

Exercise 10.4

Using the equilibrium constants and reactions below, determine whether or not each of the following systems is in equilibrium. If the system is not in equilibrium, predict whether it will proceed in the forward or reverse direction.

(a) $H_2(g) + I_2(g) \rightarrow 2HI(g)$ $K_c = 49$
$[H_2] = 0.10$ M; $[I_2] = 0.10$ M; $[HI] = 0.70$ M

(b) $Br_2 + Cl_2 \rightarrow BrCl$ $K_c = 6.9$
$[Br_2] = 0.10$ M; $[Cl_2] = 0.20$ M; $[BrCl] = 0.45$ M

(c) $HF(aq) + H_2O(\ell) \rightarrow F^-(aq) + H_3O^+(aq)$ $\quad K_c = 6.8 \times 10^{-4}$
$[HF] = 0.20$ M; $[F^-] = 2.0 \times 10^{-4}$ M; $[H_3O^+] = 2.0 \times 10^{-4}$ M
(d) $2H_2(g) + O_2(g) \rightarrow 2H_2O(g)$ $\quad K_c = 9.1 \times 10^{80}$
$[H_2] = 3.0 \times 10^{-30}$ M; $[O_2] = 2.2 \times 10^{-24}$ M; $[H_2O] = 0.0180$ M
(e) $2N_2O(g) \rightarrow 2N_2(g) + O_2(g)$ $\quad K_c = 7.0 \times 10^{34}$
$[N_2O] = 2.4 \times 10^{-18}$ M; $[N_2] = 0.0360$ M; $[O_2] = 0.0090$ M

Solution

The values of Q are calculated as follows: (a) 49; (b) 10.1; (c) 2×10^{-7}; (d) 9.1×10^{80}; (e) 2.0×10^{30}.

Reactions (a) and (d) are in equilibrium since $Q = K_c$. Reaction (b) has $Q > K_c$, indicating that the reaction must go in the reverse direction to reach equilibrium. Reactions (c) and (e) have $Q < K_c$, so the reaction must go forward to attain equilibrium.

Equilibrium Calculations

Previously it was shown how the equilibrium constant may be calculated by measuring the concentrations of all of the molecules in a chemical reaction. Chemists take advantage of stoichiometric relationships to make experiments easier and more reliable. With experience, these relationships become more obvious. A tabular system of analysis allows us to summarize our knowledge and perform calculations of considerable sophistication without many years of experience.

The Equilibrium Table

In solving equilibrium problems, it is convenient to organize the data in a logical format so that the proper conclusions may be drawn. To do this we construct a table of information called an **equilibrium table**. The basic table has five lines: the first line is used for the balanced chemical reaction; the next line is for the initial conditions stated in the problem; the third line represents the stoichiometric relationships, showing how the conditions on line 2 will change; the fourth line is the sum of the second and third lines and represents the concentrations at equilibrium; and the fifth will show the actual equilibrium amounts, calculated by solving the expression on line 4.

To illustrate such a table, we start with a chemical reaction, for example:

$$NO_2(g) + SO_2(g) \rightleftharpoons NO(g) + SO_3(g) \quad (10.28)$$

The table to be constructed will look like this:

REACTION	NO_2(g)	+	SO_2(g)	$\rightleftharpoons$	NO(g)	+	SO_3(g)
INITIAL CONDITIONS							
CHANGE							
EQUILIBRIUM							
ANSWER							

In this table, the first line is always the balanced chemical REACTION, as shown. The second and last lines will contain numerical data with units of molarity or partial pressure. All entries on these lines must have identical units. The CHANGE line represents the stoichiometric relationships inherent in the reaction. In this line the change is represented as the unknown, x. The coefficient for the x in each column is the same as the coefficient of the substance in the chemical reaction at the top of the same column. The algebraic signs of all reactants are the opposite of the signs of the products of the reaction on the third line. (Mathematically it does not matter which x's are positive and which are negative as long as all reactants have the same sign and all products have the opposite sign.) The EQUILIBRIUM line is the sum of the INITIAL CONDITIONS and CHANGE lines. Finally, the ANSWER and EQUILIBRIUM lines are mathematically equal to each other.

To illustrate a table filled out with the data given in a problem, let us assume that a 4.00-liter flask is filled with 1 mole of each of the four compounds in the given reaction. The molarity of each compound is 1.00 mole/4.00 liters = 0.250 M. The table will look like this:

REACTION	$NO_2(g)$	+	$SO_2(g)$	$\rightleftharpoons$	$NO(g)$	+	$SO_3(g)$
INITIAL CONDITIONS	0.250 M		0.250 M		0.250 M		0.250 M
CHANGE	$+x$		$+x$		$-x$		$-x$
EQUILIBRIUM	$0.250 + x$		$0.250 + x$		$0.250 - x$		$0.250 - x$
ANSWER							

Using this table, we can then perform the appropriate algebraic calculations.

Calculation of Equilibrium Constants

In the example on page 268, the equilibrium constant was determined by measuring all of the concentrations of a mixture when equilibrium was established. Using stoichiometric relationships provides an easier way to do the same thing. To determine the equilibrium constant for the reaction in Equation 10.28:

$$NO_2(g) \quad + \quad SO_2(g) \quad \rightleftharpoons \quad NO(g) \quad + \quad SO_3(g)$$

an experiment can be set up where the initial amount of every compound is 0.250 M. The equilibrium table is the same as before:

REACTION	$NO_2(g)$	+	$SO_2(g)$	$\rightleftharpoons$	$NO(g)$	+	$SO_3(g)$
INITIAL CONDITIONS	0.250 M		0.250 M		0.250 M		0.250 M
CHANGE	$+x$		$+x$		$-x$		$-x$
EQUILIBRIUM	$0.250 + x$		$0.250 + x$		$0.250 - x$		$0.250 - x$
ANSWER							

When equilibrium is reached, the concentration of NO_2 is measured as 0.261 M. This value may be entered in the ANSWER row of the table under the NO_2 column as shown below:

REACTION	$NO_2(g)$	+	$SO_2(g)$	⇌	$NO(g)$	+	$SO_3(g)$
INITIAL CONDITIONS	0.250 M		0.250 M		0.250 M		0.250 M
CHANGE	+x		+x		−x		−x
EQUILIBRIUM	0.250 + x		0.250 + x		0.250 − x		0.250 − x
ANSWER	**0.261 M**						

Since the values in the last two lines of the $NO_2(g)$ column are mathematically equal, we write

$$0.261 \text{ M} = 0.250 \text{ M} + x$$

and

$$x = 0.011$$

Since the value of x is now known, the ANSWER line can be completed for all of the other compounds in the reaction by evaluating the expression on the EQUILIBRIUM line:

REACTION	$NO_2(g)$	+	$SO_2(g)$	⇌	$NO(g)$	+	$SO_3(g)$
INITIAL CONDITIONS	0.250 M		0.250 M		0.250 M		0.250 M
CHANGE	+x		+x		−x		−x
EQUILIBRIUM	0.250 + x		0.250 + x		0.250 − x		0.250 − x
ANSWER	**0.261 M**		**0.261 M**		**0.239 M**		**0.239 M**

These values are then entered into the equilibrium law to determine the value of K_c:

$$K_c = \frac{[NO][SO_3]}{[NO_2][SO_2]}$$

$$= \frac{(0.239)(0.239)}{(0.261)(0.261)} \qquad (10.29)$$

$$= 0.839$$

Only one measurement, the concentration of NO_2, was needed to determine the value of K_c, instead of four measurements.

Exercise 10.5

In the example above, rewrite the table so that all reactants are $-x$ and all products $+x$ on the CHANGE line. Verify that the same answer is obtained.

Solution

The signs of x on the EQUILIBRIUM line must also be changed. In this form $x = -0.011$, and the calculated value of K_c is the same as before.

Determination of Equilibrium Concentrations by Direct Analysis

When a reaction is at equilibrium, it obeys the equilibrium law. The concentration of any compound in a reaction can be determined by measuring the concentrations of all the other compounds involved in the reaction. For instance, the reaction between H_2 and I_2 to form HI has an equilibrium constant equal to 49. At equilibrium, if $[I_2] = 0.200$ M and $[HI] = 0.050$ M, we can calculate the concentration of H_2:

$$H_2 \quad + \quad I_2 \quad \rightleftharpoons \quad 2HI \tag{10.30}$$

$$K \quad = \quad \frac{[HI]^2}{[H_2] \times [I_2]}$$

$$49 \quad = \quad \frac{(0.050)^2}{[H] \times (0.200)} \tag{10.31}$$

$$[H_2] \quad = \quad \frac{(0.050)^2}{(49) \times (0.200)}$$

$$= \quad 2.6 \times 10^{-4}$$

Determination of Equilibrium Concentrations from Initial Concentrations and Stoichiometric Relationships

Given initial concentrations and a known value for the equilibrium constant, we can determine the equilibrium concentrations of all compounds in a reaction. For example, the reaction

$$Br_2 \quad + \quad Cl_2 \quad \rightleftharpoons \quad 2BrCl \tag{10.32}$$

has an equilibrium constant of 6.90. If 0.100 mole of BrCl is introduced into a 500-milliliter flask, the equilibrium concentrations of Br_2, Cl_2, and BrCl can be calculated.

The solution starts with setting up the equilibrium table. The initial concentration of BrCl is 0.100 mole/0.500 liter = 0.200 M; and since no Br_2 or Cl_2 is added to the flask, their concentrations are entered as zero. On the CHANGE line a positive x for Br_2 and Cl_2 is chosen because their concentrations cannot be less than zero. The change in BrCl must then be entered as $-2x$. If the signs of all the x's were reversed, the same answer would be obtained. Writing the table as suggested, however, indicates a better understanding of the equilibrium process.

REACTION	Br$_2$(g)	+	Cl$_2$(g)	⇌	2BrCl(g)
INITIAL CONDITIONS	0 M		0 M		0.200 M
CHANGE	+x		+x		−2x
EQUILIBRIUM	+x		+x		0.200 − 2x
ANSWER					

The algebraic expressions on the EQUILIBRIUM line are entered into the equilibrium law:

$$K_c = \frac{[BrCl]^2}{[Br_2] \times [Cl_2]}$$

(10.33)

$$6.90 = \frac{(0.200 - 2x)^2}{(x)(x)}$$

Taking the square root of both sides of this equation yields

$$2.63 = \frac{0.200 - 2x}{x}$$

$$2.63\,x = 0.200 - 2x$$

$$4.63\,x = 0.200$$

$$x = 0.0432$$

Once a value for x is determined, we return to the table and calculate the values for the ANSWER line:

REACTION	Br$_2$(g)	+	Cl$_2$(g)	⇌	2BrCl(g)
INITIAL CONDITIONS	0 M		0 M		0.200 M
CHANGE	+x		+x		−2x
EQUILIBRIUM	+x		+x		0.200 − 2x
ANSWER	0.0432 M		0.0432 M		0.114 M

In another example using the same reaction, let us mix together 0.200 M Br$_2$ and 0.300 M Cl$_2$ and determine the concentrations at equilibrium. We set up the equilibrium table and enter the initial concentrations:

REACTION	$Br_2(g)$	+	$Cl_2(g)$	⇌	$2BrCl(g)$
INITIAL CONDITIONS	0.200 M		0.300 M		0 M
CHANGE	$-x$		$-x$		$+2x$
EQUILIBRIUM	$0.200 - x$		$0.300 - x$		$+2x$
ANSWER					

Since BrCl cannot have a concentration less than zero, the change for it must be $+2x$ and Br_2 and Cl_2 must have $-x$ for their changes since the reactants must decrease if the product increases. We make the appropriate entries in the CHANGE line. Adding the INITIAL CONDITIONS to the CHANGE, we obtain the expressions for the EQUILIBRIUM line, using Equation 10.33, and enter them into the equilibrium law:

$$K_c = \frac{[BrCl]^2}{[Br_2]\,[Cl_2]}$$

$$6.90 = \frac{(2x)^2}{(0.200 - x)\,(0.300 - x)}$$

The square root cannot be taken to simplify this equation since the denominator is not an exact square. Multiplying out the denominator of the ratio yields

$$6.90 = \frac{(2x)^2}{x^2 - 0.5x + 0.06}$$

$$6.90\,x^2 - 3.45\,x + 0.414 = 4\,x^2$$

$$2.90\,x^2 - 3.45\,x + 0.414 = 0$$

This is a quadratic equation of the form $ax^2 + bx + c = 0$, which is solved for x by using the quadratic formula:

$$x = \frac{-b \pm \sqrt{b^2 - 4ac}}{2a} \qquad (10.34)$$

Making the substitutions into the quadratic equation yields

$$x = \frac{-(-3.45) \pm \sqrt{(-3.45)^2 - 4(2.90)(0.414)}}{2(2.90)}$$

$$= \frac{3.45 \pm 2.66}{5.8}$$

There are two roots to this equation:

$$x = 1.05 \text{ or } 0.136$$

If the root 1.05 is chosen, we calculate a negative value for the Br_2 and Cl_2 concentrations, which is clearly impossible. The root 0.136 gives the reasonable results shown in the complete table:

REACTION	$Br_2(g)$	+	$Cl_2(g)$	⇌	$2BrCl(g)$
INITIAL CONDITIONS	0.200 M		0.300 M		0 M
CHANGE	$-x$		$-x$		$+2x$
EQUILIBRIUM	$0.200 - x$		$0.300 - x$		$+2x$
ANSWER	**0.064 M**		**0.164 M**		**0.272 M**

In the two examples above, the answers were obtained by standard mathematical methods. Such solutions are called **analytical solutions**. In other problems the mathematics becomes very time consuming, if not impossible, to solve analytically. Sometimes, however, as shown below, the chemist can make simplifying assumptions that result in answers that are accurate to better than ±10 percent. Other problems, which will not be described further, can be solved by making logical estimates of the answer. One way of making logical estimates is called the **method of successive approximations**. Other methods use sophisticated computer programs to make repeated estimates.

When the equilibrium constant is very small and the initial concentrations of the reactants are given, quadratic equations, or even higher order equations, may be avoided by making some assumptions based on our knowledge of the meaning of K_c. For example, the reaction in Equation 10.15:

$$2SO_3(g) \rightleftharpoons 2SO_2(g) + O_2(g)$$

has an equilibrium constant, $K_c = 2.4 \times 10^{-25}$. An equilibrium constant this small indicates that very little SO_3 will react to form the products. If 2.00 moles of SO_3 is placed in a 1.00-liter flask, we can calculate the concentrations of all three molecules when the system comes to equilibrium. First the equilibrium table is constructed:

REACTION	$2SO_3$	⇌	$2SO_2$	+	O_2
INITIAL CONDITIONS	2.00 M ~~0.200 M~~		0 M		0 M
CHANGE	$-2x$		$+2x$		$+x$
EQUILIBRIUM	2.00 ~~0.200~~ $- 2x$		$+2x$		$+x$
ANSWER					

Entering the expressions from the EQUILIBRIUM line into the equilibrium law gives

$$K_c = \frac{[SO_2]^2\,[O_2]}{[SO_3]^2}$$

(10.35)

$$2.4 \times 10^{-25} = \frac{(2x)^2(x)}{(2.00 - 2x)^2}$$

Equation 10.35 is a quadratic equation and may be solved using the quadratic formula as before. However, because K_c is very small, it is possible to simplify this equation with an assumption based on our knowledge that this reaction produces very little product. The assumption is that $2x$ will be very small and that, when $2x$ is subtracted from 2.00 M, we will still have 2.00 M SO_3 left.

ASSUME: $2x << 2.00$ M so that 2.00 M $- 2x = 2.00$ M

The assumption allows us to simplify the denominator in the equation to

$$2.4 \times 10^{-25} = \frac{(2x)^2(x)}{(2.00)^2}$$

A solution can now be obtained with much simpler mathematical operations. Multiplying both sides by $(2.00)^2$ and placing the unknown x on the left, we obtain

$$4x^3 = 9.6 \times 10^{-25}$$

$$x^3 = 2.4 \times 10^{-25}$$

$$x = 6.2 \times 10^{-9} \text{ M}$$

Before using the calculated x to fill in the ANSWER line in the table, we check the assumption to be sure it was valid. The assumption is true since $2.00 - 6.2 \times 10^{-9}$ is equal to 2.00. (The actual value is 1.9999999938, which rounds off to 2.00.) Once x is shown to be reasonable, we can complete the table:

REACTION	2SO$_3$	⇌	2SO$_2$	+	O$_2$
INITIAL CONDITIONS	0.200 M		0 M		0 M
CHANGE	$-2x$		$+2x$		$+x$
EQUILIBRIUM	$0.200 - 2x$		$+2x$		$+x$
ANSWER	**2.00 M**		**1.24×10^{-9} M**		**6.2×10^{-9} M**

Simplifying assumptions are used only for items on the EQUILIBRIUM line of the table. In addition, these assumptions can only be used with terms that are themselves sums or differences. In the table on page 278 it is impossible to make any simplifying assumptions regarding the $+2x$ for SO_2 or the $+x$ for O_2.

In another example, the reverse of the reaction in Equation 10.15 is

$$O_2 \quad + \quad 2SO_2 \quad \rightleftharpoons \quad 2SO_3 \qquad (10.36)$$

and its equilibrium constant will be

$$\frac{1}{2.4 \times 10^{-25}} = 4.2 \times 10^{24}$$

If the initial concentration of SO_3 is 2.00 M, the concentrations of O_2 and SO_2 can be determined by the same method as in the preceding example, which gives exactly the same results.

A general principle about equilibrium calculations and the assumptions used can be deduced from the two preceding examples. If the initial concentrations of reactants are given for a reaction with a very small equilibrium constant, we may assume that these concentrations will not change significantly when equilibrium is reached. Similarly, if the initial concentrations are given for the products of a reaction with a large equilibrium constant, we may assume that the concentrations of the products will not change significantly when equilibrium is reached.

The above principle indicates also, that, if the equilibrium constant is large and the initial concentrations of the reactants are given, there will be a significant change in concentration that cannot be ignored. For example, we will use the reaction in Equation 10.36 with its equilibrium constant $K_c = 4.2 \times 10^{24}$, and determine the equilibrium concentrations if 2.00 moles of O_2 and 2.00 moles of SO_2 are placed in a 1.00-liter flask.

The equilibrium table can be set up as follows:

REACTION	$O_2(g)$	+	$2SO_2(g)$	$\rightleftharpoons$	$2SO_3(g)$
INITIAL CONDITIONS	2.00 M ~~0.200 M~~		2.00 M		0 M
CHANGE	$-x$		$-2x$		$+2x$
EQUILIBRIUM	$2.00 - x$		$2.00 - 2x$		$+2x$
ANSWER					

The equilibrium law for this case is written as

$$4.2 \times 10^{24} = \frac{(2x)^2}{(2.00 - x)(2.00 - 2x)^2}$$

Because the equilibrium constant is so large, we cannot ignore the x in the $2.00 - x$ and $2.00 - 2x$ terms on the EQUILIBRIUM line. This equation is too complex to solve analytically, and estimation methods are too time consuming. The method used to solve this problem requires us to assume that the reaction goes to completion. Calculating the concentrations that would be found if the reaction went to completion provides a new set of initial concentrations that allow us to solve the problem easily.

This reaction is a limiting reactant problem since the concentrations of two reactants are given. Using the equilibrium table, we can simplify the calculation by remembering that the limiting reactant is completely consumed in the reaction. If a reactant is completely used up, its concentration will be zero on the ANSWER line of the table. We can test whether O_2 is the limiting reactant by entering 0 for it on the ANSWER line of the table:

REACTION	$O_2(g)$	+	$2SO_2(g)$	⇌	$2SO_3(g)$
INITIAL CONDITIONS	0.200 M		2.00 M		0 M
CHANGE	$-x$		$-2x$		$+2x$
EQUILIBRIUM	$2.00 - x$		$2.00 - 2x$		$+2x$
ANSWER	**0 M**				

With 0 on the ANSWER line for O_2 the other concentrations can be calculated since $0 M = 2.00 - x$ and therefore $x = 2.00$.

REACTION	$O_2(g)$	+	$2SO_2(g)$	⇌	$2SO_3(g)$
INITIAL CONDITIONS	0.200 M		2.00 M		0 M
CHANGE	$-x$		$-2x$		$+2x$
EQUILIBRIUM	$2.00 - x$		$2.00 - 2x$		$+2x$
ANSWER	**0 M**		**−2.00 M**		**4.00 M**

It is impossible for O_2 to be the limiting reactant since the concentration of SO_2 would then have to be negative as shown in the table above. Next we try SO_2 as the limiting reactant:

REACTION	$O_2(g)$	+	$2SO_2(g)$	⇌	$2SO_3(g)$
INITIAL CONDITIONS	0.200 M		2.00 M		0 M
CHANGE	$-x$		$-2x$		$+2x$
EQUILIBRIUM	$2.00 - x$		$2.00 - 2x$		$+2x$
ANSWER			**0 M**		

Since $0 M = 2.00 - 2x$, then $x = 1.00$ and the remaining items on the ANSWER line can be calculated:

REACTION	$O_2(g)$	+	$2SO_2(g)$	$\rightleftharpoons$	$2SO_3(g)$
INITIAL CONDITIONS	0.200 M		2.00 M		0 M
CHANGE	$-x$		$-2x$		$+2x$
EQUILIBRIUM	$2.00 - x$		$2.00 - 2x$		$+2x$
ANSWER	**1.00 M**		**0 M**		**2.00 M**

These results are reasonable. To continue with the solution of the problem, the concentrations on the ANSWER line of the table above are entered in a new table as the initial concentrations, and new CHANGE and EQUILIBRIUM lines are written:

REACTION	$O_2(g)$	+	$2SO_2(g)$	$\rightleftharpoons$	$2SO_3(g)$
INITIAL CONDITIONS	**1.00 M**		**0 M**		**2.00 M**
CHANGE	$+x$		$+2x$		$-2x$
EQUILIBRIUM	$1.00 + x$		$+2x$		$2.00 - 2x$
ANSWER					

The terms on the EQUILIBRIUM line are then entered into the equilibrium law:

$$4.2 \times 10^{24} = \frac{(2.00 - 2x)^2}{(1.00 + x)(2x)^2}$$

This equation is simplified by using two assumptions based on the fact that SO_3 is not expected to react to a large extent:

ASSUME $1.00 \gg x$ so that $1.00 + x = 1.00$
ASSUME $2.00 \gg 2x$ so that $2.00 - 2x = 2.00$

Then the equilibrium law becomes

$$4.2 \times 10^{24} = \frac{(2.00)^2}{(1.00)(2x)^2}$$

Solving this equation yields

$$4x^2 = \frac{(2.00)^2}{(1.00)\,(4.2 \times 10^{24})}$$

$$= 9.5 \times 10^{-25}$$

$$x^2 = 2.4 \times 10^{-25}$$

$$x = 4.9 \times 10^{-13}$$

The assumption is valid, and the table with answers entered becomes as follows:

REACTION	$O_2(g)$	+	$2SO_2(g)$	$\rightleftharpoons$	$2SO_3(g)$
INITIAL CONDITIONS	1.00 M		0 M		2.00 M
CHANGE	$+x$		$+2x$		$-2x$
EQUILIBRIUM	$1.00 + x$		$+2x$		$2.00 - 2x$
ANSWER	**1.00 M**		**4.9×10^{-13} M**		**2.00 M**

This problem illustrates another principle of chemical equilibrium. As long as the same number of moles of each *element* is present initially in different reacting mixtures, and these mixtures have identical volumes, the final composition of these equilibrium mixtures will always be the same.

There are a variety of methods for solving problems involving initial concentrations. If the equilibrium constant is very large or very small, approximations and stoichiometric calculations can be used to simplify the mathematics. In general, a very large equilibrium constant is one where the value of K_c is at least 100 times greater than the initial concentrations. The value of K_c is considered to be very small when the equilibrium constant is less than one one-hundredth (< 0.01) of the initial concentrations. If K_c is neither very large nor very small, assumptions cannot be used and analytical solutions are then sought.

K_p, an Equilibrium Constant for Gas-Phase Reactions

The ideal gas law

$$PV = nRT \tag{10.37}$$

can be rearranged to read

$$\frac{n}{V} = \frac{P}{RT} \tag{10.38}$$

Since the n/V term is the concentration in moles per liter, the pressure of a gas, at a constant temperature, is directly proportional to its concentration. Therefore, the equilibrium law may be written using the partial pressures of the gaseous reactants and products. Under these conditions the equilibrium constant is given the symbol K_p. Usually only reactions that are entirely in the gas phase are written in this manner.

One gas-phase reaction is

$$H_2(g) \quad + \quad I_2(g) \quad \rightleftharpoons \quad 2HI(g)$$

and its equilibrium law is written as

$$K_p \quad = \quad \frac{p_{HI}^2}{p_{H_2} p_{Br_2}} \tag{10.39}$$

where p represents the partial pressure of each gas. All calculations and procedures illustrated with the examples using K_c are done in exactly the same manner when the equilibrium constant is K_p.

Exercise 10.6

For the reaction of gaseous sulfur with oxygen at high temperatures:

$$2S(g) \quad + \quad 3O_2(g) \quad \rightleftharpoons \quad 2SO_3(g)$$

when the system reaches equilibrium the partial pressures are measured as $p_S = 0.0035$ atm, $p_{SO_3} = 0.0050$ atm, and $p_{O_2} = 0.0021$ atm. What is the value of K_p under these conditions?

Solution

This problem is solved by writing the correct equilibrium law. Since all of the chemicals in the reaction are gases and are measured in partial pressures, the equilibrium law should be written with the constant K_p:

$$K_p \quad = \quad \frac{p_{SO_2}^2}{p_S^2 p_{O_2}^3}$$

With this equilibrium law, the values for the partial pressures are entered and the solution is calculated:

$$K_p \quad = \quad \frac{(0.0050)^2}{(0.0021)^3 \, (0.0035)^2}$$

$$= \quad 2.2 \times 10^8$$

Exercise 10.7

With the known value of $K_p = 2.2 \times 10^8$ from Exercise 10.6, determine whether each of the following systems is in equilibrium. If a system is not, determine in which direction the reaction will proceed.

System 1: $p_{SO_3} = 1.25$ atm $\qquad p_{O_2} = 0.256$ atm $\qquad p_S = 0.0112$ atm
System 2: $p_{SO_3} = 0.00677$ atm $\qquad p_{O_2} = 0.122$ atm $\qquad p_S = 0.212$ atm
System 3: $p_{SO_3} = 0.123$ atm $\qquad p_{O_2} = 0.00145$ atm $\qquad p_S = 0.0332$ atm

Solution

The values for the pressures are entered into the equilibrium-law equation to calculate the reaction quotient, Q, which is then compared to the known value of K_p:

System 1:

$$Q = \frac{p_{SO_3}^2}{p_S^2 p_{O_2}^3} = \frac{(1.25)^2}{(0.256)^3 (0.0112)^2} = 7.4 \times 10^5$$

System 2:

$$Q = \frac{p_{SO_3}^2}{p_S^2 p_{O_2}^3} = \frac{(0.00677)^2}{(0.122)^3 (0.212)^2} = 5.6 \times 10^{-1}$$

System 3:

$$Q = \frac{p_{SO_3}^2}{p_S^2 p_{O_2}^3} = \frac{(0.123)^2}{(0.00145)^3 (0.0332)^2} = 4.5 \times 10^9$$

For none of the three systems is the value of Q equal to the known K_p of 2.2×10^8, indicating that none of the systems is in equilibrium.

In System 1 and System 2 Q is smaller than the known K_p. Q must increase as these systems approach equilibrium, and the numerator of the ratio will increase while the denominator decreases. Since the numerator contains the products and the denominator contains the reactants, the products must increase and the reactants decrease. Therefore the reaction in these systems must proceed in the forward direction.

System 3 has a value of Q that is greater than the known K_p. The ratio must decrease for the reaction to reach equilibrium. Products must be used to form more reactants, and the reaction in this system must proceed in the reverse direction.

Relationship Between K_p and K_c

The equilibrium constant for a gas-phase reaction can be written as K_p or K_c, and the two can be converted from one to another. Equation 10.38 shows that $\left(\dfrac{P}{RT}\right)$ can be substituted for the molar concentrations in the equilibrium law, resulting in the relationship

$$K_p = K_c (RT)^{\Delta n_g} \tag{10.40}$$

In this equation R is the universal gas law constant (0.0821 L atm mol^{-1} K^{-1}), T is the Kelvin temperature, and Δn_g is the change in the number of moles of gas in the balanced reaction:

$$\Delta n_g = \text{moles of gas products} - \text{moles of gas reactants} \tag{10.41}$$

In a preceding example (page 269) the reaction

$$I_2(g) + H_2(g) \rightleftharpoons 2HI(g)$$

had a $K_c = 49$. The equivalent K_p at 100°C is calculated by determining Δn_g:

$$\Delta n_g = 2 \text{ mol HI} - (1\text{mol } I_2 + 1 \text{ mol } H_2)$$

$$= 0$$

If $\Delta n_g = 0$, then $K_p = K_c$ for this reaction.

In the reaction of sulfur with oxygen the value of Δn_g is not zero:

$$\Delta n_g = (2 \text{ mol } SO_3) - (2 \text{ mol S} - 3 \text{ mol } O_2)$$

$$= -3$$

With $K_p = 2.2 \times 10^8$ at 573 K, we can calculate K_c as

$$2.2 \times 10^8 = K_c [(0.0821)(573)]^{-3}$$

$$K_c = (2.2 \times 10^8)[(0.0821)(573)]^3$$

$$= 2.3 \times 10^{13}$$

Exercise 10.8

The value of K_c for the following reaction:

$$2NO(g) + O_2(g) \rightleftharpoons 2NO_2(g)$$

is 5.6×10^{12} at 290 K. What is the value of K_p?

Solution

In this problem we are required to solve Equation 10.40. Since K_p is the unknown, we need values for K_c, R, T, and Δn_g. All of these are given in the problem except Δn_g. To determine the value for Δn_g, we note that this reaction has 3 mol of gases as reactants and 2 mol of gases as products. This is a decrease of 1 mol of gas in going from reactants to products, and therefore Δn_g is -1. Entering the numbers into the equation, we get

$$K_p = 5.6 \times 10^{12}[(0.081)(290)]^{-1}$$

Rearranging the equation, we calculate the value of K_p as

$$K_p = \frac{5.6 \times 10^{12}}{(0.081)(290)} = 2.4 \times 10^{11}$$

Units of Equilibrium Constants

In the exact derivation of equilibrium constants there are no units, and we say that the equilibrium constants are dimensionless quantities. At times, however, it is convenient to assign dimensions to an equilibrium constant. To assign units to K_p or K_c, we determine the value of Δn as

$$\Delta n = \text{moles of products} - \text{moles of reactants} \qquad (10.42)$$

which represents the sum of the coefficients of the reactants subtracted from the sum of the coefficients of the products in a balanced chemical reaction.

With Δn determined, the units are assigned as follows:

$$\text{units for } K_p \quad = \quad (\text{atm})^{\Delta n}$$

and

$$\text{units for } K_c \quad = \quad (M)^{\Delta n} \quad = \quad \left(\frac{\text{mol}}{L}\right)^{\Delta n}$$

Special Equilibrium Constants

Solubility Product

In Chapter 4 rules for determining solubility were given. These rules are used to determine whether an ionic compound will dissolve to an appreciable extent in water. In quantitative terms, it is loosely agreed that a salt is soluble if at least 0.1 mol of it will dissolve in 1 liter of water (0.1 M solution). Saturated solutions of insoluble salts have concentrations that are less than 0.1 molar. However, most insoluble salts do dissolve to a small extent.

The solution process may be written in a form similar to a chemical reaction. For solid $Fe_2(OH)_3$ we have

$$Fe(OH)_3(s) \quad \rightleftharpoons \quad Fe^{3+}(aq) \quad + \quad 3OH^-(aq) \tag{10.43}$$

The equilibrium law for this is written as

$$K_c \quad = \quad [Fe^{3+}][OH^-]^3 \tag{10.44}$$

$Fe(OH)_3(s)$ does not appear in the equilibrium law because it is a solid. In the special case of the solubility of slightly soluble compounds the equilibrium law always represents the product of the ions produced when the compound dissolves. The equilibrium constant is called the **solubility product** constant and is given the symbol K_{sp}.

$$K_{sp} \quad = \quad [Fe^{3+}][OH^-]^3 \tag{10.45}$$

Questions involving K_{sp} are solved in the same way as other equilibrium problems. For example, K_{sp} has a value of 1.6×10^{-39} for $Fe(OH)_3$. The molar solubility is calculated by setting up an equilibrium table:

REACTION	Fe(OH)$_3$	$\rightleftharpoons$	Fe^{3+}	+	3OH$^-$
INITIAL CONDITIONS	Solid		0 M		0 M
CHANGE	$-x$		$+x$		$+3x$
EQUILIBRIUM	Not used		$+x$		$+3x$
ANSWER					

Entering the information from the EQUILIBRIUM line into the K_{sp} equilibrium law gives

$$1.6 \times 10^{-39} = (x)(3x)^3$$
$$= (x)(27x^3)$$
$$= 27x^4$$
$$x^4 = 5.9 \times 10^{-41}$$
$$x = 8.8 \times 10^{-11}$$

The value of x is used to calculate the molar concentrations of Fe^{3+} and OH^- in the solution. We enter these data in the table:

REACTION	$Fe(OH)_3$	$\rightleftharpoons$	Fe^{3+}	+	$3OH^-$
INITIAL CONDITIONS	Solid		0 M		0 M
CHANGE	$-x$		$+x$		$+3x$
EQUILIBRIUM	Not used		$+x$		$+3x$
ANSWER			8.8×10^{-11} M		1.2×10^{-10} M

The solubility of $Fe(OH)_3$ may be deduced from this table also. The CHANGE line indicates that $-x$ of the compound dissolves, and therefore x represents the solubility of $Fe(OH)_3$, or 8.8×10^{-11} mol L^{-1}.

If $Fe(OH)_3$ is dissolved in a solution that already contains the Fe^{3+} ion, the **common ion effect** is observed. The common ion effect is a decrease in the solubility of a compound when it is dissolved in a solution that already contains an ion in common with the salt being dissolved. As an example, we can calculate the solubility of $Fe(OH)_3$ in a solution that already has a 6.5×10^{-5} M concentration of Fe^{3+}. The equilibrium table is constructed as follows:

REACTION	$Fe(OH)_3$	$\rightleftharpoons$	Fe^{3+}	+	$3OH^-$
INITIAL CONDITIONS	**Solid**		6.5×10^{-5} M		0 M
CHANGE	$-x$		$+x$		$+3x$
EQUILIBRIUM	Not used		$6.5 \times 10^{-5} + x$		$+3x$
ANSWER					

Entering the information into the K_{sp} equation yields

$$1.6 \times 10^{-39} = (6.5 \times 10^{-5} + x)(3x)^3$$

To avoid a very complex fifth-order equation, we can use the results of the preceding problem to assume that x will be very small compared to 6.5×10^{-5}:

ASSUME: $x \ll 6.5 \times 10^{-5}$ so that $6.5 \times 10^{-5} + x = 6.5 \times 10^{-5}$

Entering this assumption into the equation gives

$$1.6 \times 10^{-39} = (6.5 \times 10^{-5})(3x)^3$$

$$27x^3 = \frac{1.6 \times 10^{-39}}{6.5 \times 10^{-5}}$$

$$x^3 = 9.1 \times 10^{-37}$$

$$= 9.7 \times 10^{-13}$$

This result satisfies the simplifying assumption and may be entered in the table:

REACTION	Fe(OH)$_3$	$\rightleftharpoons$	Fe^{3+}	+	3OH$^-$
INITIAL CONDITIONS	Solid		6.5×10^{-5} M		0 M
CHANGE	$-x$		$+x$		$+3x$
EQUILIBRIUM	Not used		$6.5 \times 10^{-5} + x$		$+3x$
ANSWER			6.5×10^{-5} M		2.9×10^{-12} M

In addition we may conclude that the solubility of Fe(OH)$_3$ is 9.7×10^{-13} M.

To determine the value of the solubility product, a variety of experiments may be performed. In one of the simplest, the molar solubility of a compound is determined by measuring the amount that dissolves in 1 liter of water. For example, if the molar solubility of MgF$_2$ is determined to be 0.00118 mol per liter, what is its K_{sp}? When solid MgF$_2$ dissolves, the reaction is

$$MgF_2(s) \rightleftharpoons Mg^{2+}(aq) + 2F^-(aq) \qquad (10.46)$$

and the K_{sp} expression is

$$K_{sp} = [Mg^{2+}][F^-]^2 \qquad (10.47)$$

The equilibrium table is set up as follows:

REACTION	MgF$_2$	⇌	Mg^{2+}	+	2F$^-$
INITIAL CONDITIONS	Solid		0 M		0 M
CHANGE	$-x$		$+x$		$+2x$
EQUILIBRIUM	Not used		$+x$		$+2x$
ANSWER					

The solubility given in the problem is the amount dissolved, which is also x. Knowing x, we can immediately complete the ANSWER line:

REACTION	MgF$_2$	⇌	Mg^{2+}	+	2F$^-$
INITIAL CONDITIONS	Solid		0 M		0 M
CHANGE	$-x$		$+x$		$+2x$
EQUILIBRIUM	Not used		$+x$		$+2x$
ANSWER			0.00118 M		0.00236 M

Substituting the values from the ANSWER line into the K_{sp} expression yields

$$K_{sp} = (0.00118)(0.00236)^2$$
$$= 6.6 \times 10^{-9}$$

Weak-Acid and Weak-Base Equilibria

Weak acids and weak bases are compounds that dissociate only slightly when dissolved in water, as shown for acetic acid and ammonia in the following equations:

$$CH_3COOH(aq) + H_2O(\ell) \rightleftharpoons CH_3COO^-(aq) + H_3O^+(aq) \quad (10.48)$$

$$NH_3(aq) + H_2O(\ell) \rightleftharpoons NH_4^+(aq) + OH^-(aq) \quad (10.49)$$

The equilibrium laws for these two reactions are as follows:

$$K_c = K_a = \frac{[CH_3COO^-][H_3O^+]}{[CH_3COOH]} \quad (10.50)$$

and

$$K_c = K_b = \frac{[NH_4^+][OH^-]}{[NH_3]} \quad (10.51)$$

For weak acids the equilibrium constant is called the **acid dissociation constant** and is given the symbol K_a. Weak bases have a corresponding **base dissociation constant**, K_b. Since all weak acids dissociate to form an anion and the hydronium ion, H_3O^+, all of their dissociation reactions have the same form as the one for acetic acid and their K_a expressions are similar. Weak bases all dissociate the same way as ammonia, and their base dissociation expressions are similar to that for ammonia. Acid and base equilibrium problems are approached in exactly the same manner as other equilibrium problems.

For example, when 0.100 mole of NH_3 is dissolved in 1 liter of solution, what are the equilibrium concentrations of all solutes? First, the equation for the dissociation of ammonia is written, along with its equilibrium law, as shown in Equations 10.49 and 10.51. Next, K_b will be needed and can be found in a table of dissociation constants of the bases; for ammonia $K_b = 1.8 \times 10^{-5}$. Then an equilibrium table is constructed to summarize the given information and the stoichiometric relationships:

REACTION	NH_3	+	H_2O	$\rightleftharpoons$	NH_4^+	+	OH^-
INITIAL CONDITIONS	0.100 M		Pure solvent		0 M		0 M
CHANGE	$-x$		$-x$		$+x$		$+x$
EQUILIBRIUM	$0.100 - x$		Not used		$+x$		$+x$
ANSWER							

For acetic acid K_a is 1.8×10^{-5}, and this value can be used in the equilibrium law, along with the expressions on the EQUILIBRIUM line of the equilibrium table, to obtain

$$1.8 \times 10^{-5} = \frac{(x)(x)}{0.100 - x}$$

Since the equilibrium constant is small, it is expected that x will be much smaller than 0.100:

ASSUME: $x << 0.100$ so that $0.100 - x = 0.100$

Using this simplifying assumption, we have

$$1.8 \times 10^{-5} = \frac{(x)(x)}{0.100}$$

$$x^2 = 1.8 \times 10^{-6}$$

$$x = 1.3 \times 10^{-3}$$

Since x is much smaller than 0.100, the equilibrium table can be completed as follows:

REACTION	NH_3	+	H_2O	$\rightleftharpoons$	NH_4^+	+	OH^-
INITIAL CONDITIONS	0.100 M		Pure solvent		0 M		0 M
CHANGE	$-x$		$-x$		$+x$		$+x$
EQUILIBRIUM	$0.100 - x$		Not used		$+x$		$+x$
ANSWER	**0.099**				**0.0013 M**		**0.0013 M**

There are many different calculations involving acids and bases that interest chemists. Chapter 14 provides the details for weak-acid and weak-base calculations, buffer calculations, and hydrolysis calculations. All of these calculations are based on the equilibrium concept developed here.

Formation Constants

Metal ions can react with anions and molecules to form chemical species called **complexes**. Ammonia complexes with copper ions in solution, turning the solution from light blue to a much darker blue. The reaction is

$$Cu^{2+}(aq) \quad + \quad 4NH_3(aq) \quad \rightleftharpoons \quad Cu(NH_3)_4^{2+} \qquad (10.52)$$

$Cu(NH_3)_4^{2+}$ is a complex ion of copper and ammonia. Since this reaction is written as an equilibrium, its equilibrium law is written as

$$K_c \quad = \quad K_f \quad \frac{[Cu(NH_3)_4^{2+}]}{[Cu^{2+}][NH_3]^4} \qquad (10.53)$$

The reaction represents the formation of the complex, and the equilibrium constant is known as the **formation constant**, K_f.

When the complexation reaction is reversed, it represents the dissociation of the complex into its parts. The equilibrium constant for the dissociation is often called the **dissociation constant**, K_d. K_f and K_d are inversely proportional to each other:

$$K_f \quad = \quad \frac{1}{K_d} \qquad (10.54)$$

Problems involving complexation equilibria are solved in exactly the same fashion as other equilibrium problems.

Le Châtelier's Principle

In 1888 Henry Le Châtelier proposed his fundamental principle of chemical equilibrium. He observed that chemical systems react until they reach a state of equilibrium. He also observed that, if chemicals in a state of equilibrium are disturbed in some manner, they will react again until equilibrium is reestablished.

Le Châtelier's Principle

Whenever a system in dynamic equilibrium is disrupted by changes in chemical concentrations or physical conditions, the system will respond with internal physical and chemical changes to reestablish the equilibrium state.

Chemical changes to a system involve the addition or removal of one or more of the products or reactants. Physical changes to a system include changes in temperature, pressure, and volume. An understanding of how these factors affect chemical equilibria allows chemists to adjust experimental conditions to maximize the desired products and minimize waste.

Effect of Concentration

Changing the concentration of any reactant or product in a chemical reaction will alter the concentrations of the other chemicals present as the system reacts to reestablish equilibrium. Figure 10.2 illustrates how this process works. A two-compartment container is set up. Dividing the compartments is a very porous barrier such as a window screen. When a liquid is added to the container, the fluid flows easily to equal heights in both compartments to establish Equilibrium 1. If some more liquid is then added to the reactant (R) compartment, the equilibrium is momentarily disturbed, as shown in the middle diagram. However, the liquid flows through the barrier and reestablishes a new equilibrium condition, Equilibrium 2, in the last diagram.

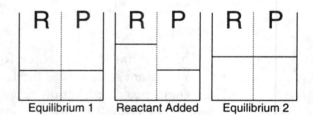

| Equilibrium 1 | Reactant Added | Equilibrium 2 |

FIGURE 10.2. Diagrams illustrating an initial equilibrium of two liquids with a porous barrier, a disturbance to the equilibrium by adding liquid to one side, and finally the reestablishment of equilibrium.

Figure 10.2 clearly illustrates the action of a chemical system. Adding a reactant to an equilibrium system disturbs it by raising the reactant concentration. This disturbance causes the reaction to produce a greater amount of product and to reduce the amount of reactant in order to reestablish equilibrium. Also important is the fact that the final equilibrium has different amounts of reactants and products than were present in the initial equilibrium state.

Illustrations similar to Figure 10.2 can be used to visualize other possible concentration changes and their effects. Increasing the concentration of a product will cause an increase in reactant formation (reverse reaction). Decreasing the concentration of a reactant will cause more reactant to form (reverse reaction), and decreasing the concentration of a product will cause more product to form (forward reaction).

Increasing the concentration of a reactant or product is a simple experimental process of adding more chemicals to the reaction mixture. Decreasing the concentration of a product or reactant, however, is experimentally more difficult. Some techniques that are used to remove products or reactants from a reaction mixture are described below.

In the reaction to form ammonia:

$$N_2(g) \quad + \quad 3H_2(g) \quad \rightleftharpoons \quad 2NH_3(g)$$

the ammonia gas produced is very soluble in water:

$$NH_3(g) \quad \xrightarrow{H_2O} \quad NH_3(aq)$$

so that a little water in the reaction system effectively removes the product NH_3. Another method used to remove a gas from a reaction is to condense it into a pure liquid.

Substances in solution can be removed by causing them to precipitate as solids. Additional chemicals may be added to a reaction mixture in order to cause precipitation.

Formation of a complex is an effective method for removing metal ions from solution. Complexing a metal ion changes it into a distinctly different substance, the complex. For example, the dissolution of AgCl with ammonia is a complexation reaction. The $Ag(NH_3)_2^+$ complex is very soluble, and it removes Ag^+ from the solution so that more AgCl may dissolve. The two separate steps of the reaction are as follows:

$$AgCl(s) \quad \rightleftharpoons \quad Ag^+(aq) \quad + \quad Cl^-(aq)$$

and

$$Ag^+(aq) \quad + \quad NH_3(aq) \quad \rightleftharpoons \quad Ag(NH_3)_2^+(aq)$$

which add up to

$$AgCl(s) \quad + \quad 2NH_3(aq) \quad \rightleftharpoons \quad Ag(NH_3)_2^+(aq) \quad + \quad Cl^-(aq)$$

The effects of changing reactant and product concentrations are summarized in Table 10.1.

TABLE 10.1 Effect of Changing Concentrations

Concentration Change	Observed Effect
Increase reactant	Favors products
Decrease reactant	Favors reactants
Increase product	Favors reactants
Decrease product	Favors products

Effect of Pressure

An increase in pressure easily compresses gases but has little effect on solids and liquids. Increasing the pressure of a gas increases its molar concentration. Changing the pressures of individual gaseous reactants by adding or removing a gas follows the same principles as changing the concentrations discussed in the preceding section. Changing the pressure of a system by adding an inert gas does nothing, however, since the gases originally present still have the same partial pressures and concentrations.

Increasing the pressure of a gaseous reaction system by decreasing its volume will have an effect on the equilibrium only if Δn_g is not zero (Δn_g is the difference between the moles of gaseous products and of gaseous reactants, used previously to make conversions between K_c and K_p). If $\Delta n_g = 0$, there will be no shift in the equilibrium since there is the same number of moles of gaseous products and of gaseous reactants. When $\Delta n_g > 0$, however, the reaction will be forced toward the reactant side because the larger number of moles of product will be compressed to a higher concentration than the reactants. Similarly, if $\Delta n_g < 0$, there will be more moles of gaseous reactant and the reaction will be forced toward producing more product. Decreasing the pressure will have the opposite effects.

These effects are summarized in Table 10.2.

TABLE 10.2   Effect of Pressure on Gaseous Reactions

Value of Δn_g	Increasing Pressure	Decreasing Pressure
Positive	Favors reactants	Favors products
Zero	No effect	No effect
Negative	Favors products	Favors reactants

Effect of Temperature

The only experimental variable that has any effect on the value of the equilibrium constant is temperature. For some reactions the equilibrium constant increases as the temperature increases; for others the equilibrium constant decreases. Which direction the equilibrium constant changes depends on whether the reaction is exothermic (ΔH is negative) or endothermic (ΔH is positive). An exothermic reaction gives off heat to the surroundings, and an endothermic reaction absorbs heat from the surroundings.

An exothermic reaction may be represented as a reaction in which one of the products is heat:

$$\text{Reactants} \quad \rightleftharpoons \quad \text{Products} \quad + \quad \text{Heat} \qquad (10.55)$$

Raising the temperature for an exothermic reaction is similar to increasing the concentrations of the products. As occurs with a chemical change, increasing the amounts of product will move the reaction toward the left, or reactant, side.

For an endothermic reaction, increasing the temperature is equivalent to increasing the concentrations of the reactants. The result is to move the equilibrium toward the product side:

$$\text{Heat} \quad + \quad \text{Reactants} \quad \rightleftharpoons \quad \text{Products} \qquad (10.56)$$

and represents an increase in the equilibrium constant.

TABLE 10.3 Effect of Temperature Changes

Temperature Change	Reaction Type	Effect On Reaction	Effect On K
Increase	Exothermic	Favors reactants	Decrease
Increase	Endothermic	Favors products	Increase
Decrease	Exothermic	Favors products	Increase
Decrease	Endothermic	Favors reactants	Decrease

The effects of temperature changes are summarized in Table 10.3. The last column of the table indicates that the actual effect of a change in temperature is a change in the value of the equilibrium constant. In addition to the direction of change, we will see in Chapter 12 on thermodynamics that the amount of increase or decrease in the equilibrium constant is related to the magnitude of the heat of reaction.

Important Concepts

Dynamic equilibrium
Equilibrium law
Equilibrium constant and the reaction quotient
Solving equilibrium problems
Le Châtelier principle

Important Equations

$K = [A]^a[B]^b/[C]^c[D]^d$ for reaction $cC \, 1 \, dD \rightleftharpoons aA \, 1 \, bB$

Questions on Chapter 10

1. A chemical system in equilibrium will
   (A) have the same concentrations of all products and reactants
   (B) form more products if the temperature is increased
   (C) have a specific ratio of product to reactant concentrations
   (D) not have any precipitates
   (E) represent a spontaneous chemical process

2. Chemical equilibrium may be used to describe
   (A) chemical reactions
   (B) acidity
   (C) solubility
   (D) A and C
   (E) A, B, and C

3. For the following reaction:

$$\text{heat} \quad + \quad 2NO_2(g) \quad \rightleftharpoons \quad N_2O_4(g)$$

   which change will not be effective in increasing the amount of $N_2O_4(g)$?
   (A) decreasing the volume of the reaction vessel
   (B) increasing the temperature
   (C) adding N_2 to increase the pressure
   (D) adsorbing the $N_2O_4(g)$ with a solid adsorbant
   (E) adding more $NO_2(g)$ to the reaction vessel

4. The reaction

$$2NO_2(g) \quad \rightleftharpoons \quad N_2O_4(g)$$

has an equilibrium constant of 4.5×10^3 at a certain temperature. What is the equilibrium constant of

$$2N_2O_4(g) \quad \rightleftharpoons \quad 4NO_2(g)?$$

(A) 4.5×10^3
(B) 9.0×10^6
(C) 2.2×10^{-4}
(D) 2.0×10^7
(E) 4.9×10^{-8}

5. The correct form of the solubility product for silver chromate, Ag_2CrO_4, is
(A) $[Ag^+]^2[CrO_4^{2-}]$
(B) $[Ag^+][CrO_4^{2-}]$
(C) $[Ag^+][CrO_4^{2-}]^2$
(D) $[Ag^+]^2[CrO^{2-}]^4$
(E) $[Ag]^2[CrO_4]$

6. For which of the following will $K_p = K_c$?
(A) $MgCO_3(s) + 2HCl(g) \rightleftharpoons MgCl_2(s) + CO_2(g) + H_2O(\ell)$
(B) $C(s) + O_2(g) \rightleftharpoons CO_2(g)$
(C) $CH_4(g) + 3O_2(g) \rightleftharpoons CO_2(g) + 2H_2O(g)$
(D) $Zn(s) + 2HCl(aq) \rightleftharpoons H_2(g) + ZnCl_2(aq)$
(E) $2NO_2(g) + O_2(g) \rightleftharpoons N_2O_5(g)$

7. Which is an appropriate formulation of the equilibrium law for the reaction

$$MgCO_3(s) + 2HCl(g) \rightleftharpoons MgCl_2(s) + CO_2(g) + H_2O(\ell)?$$

(A) $\dfrac{[CO_2]}{[HCl]}$

(B) $\dfrac{[MgCl_2][CO_2][H_2O]}{[HCl]^2[MgCO_3]}$

(C) $\dfrac{[HCl]^2[MgCO_3]}{[MgCl_2][CO_2][H_2O]}$

(D) $\dfrac{[CO_2]}{[HCl]^2}$

(E) $\dfrac{[CO_2][H_2O]}{[HCl]^2}$

8. In the reaction

$$2HI(g) \quad \rightleftharpoons \quad H_2(g) \quad + \quad I_2(g)$$

the equilibrium constant is 0.020. If 0.200 mol of HI is placed in a 10.0-L flask, how many moles of $I_2(g)$ will be in the flask when equilibrium is reached?
(A) 0.022
(B) 0.025
(C) 0.0022
(D) 2.2
(E) 0.0025

9. For the reaction

$$2NO_2(g) \quad \rightleftharpoons \quad N_2O_4(g)$$

K_p = 8.8 when pressures are measured in atmospheres. Under which of the following conditions will the reaction proceed in the reverse direction?

$NO_2(g)$	$N_2O_4(g)$
(A) 0.200 atm	0.352 atm
(B) 250 mm Hg	400 mm Hg
(C) 0.00255 atm	0.000134 atm
(D) 46.5 mm Hg	82.3 mm Hg
(E) 0.138 atm	0.764 atm

10. The solubility product of PbI_2 is 7.9×10^{-9}. What is the molar solubility of PbI_2 in distilled water?
(A) 2.0×10^{-3}
(B) 1.25×10^{-3}
(C) 5.0×10^{-4}
(D) 8.9×10^{-5}
(E) 7.9×10^{-3}

11. The solubility of gold(III) chloride is 1.00×10^{-4} g L^{-1}. What is the solubility product of $AuCl_3$ (molar mass = 303)?
(A) 1.00×10^{-16}
(B) 2.7×10^{-15}
(C) 1.2×10^{-26}
(D) 3.2×10^{-25}
(E) 9.6×10^{-25}

12. If units were used with the equilibrium constant, K_c, for the following reaction:

$$CH_4(g) \quad + \quad 3O_2(g) \quad \rightleftharpoons \quad CO_2(g) \quad + \quad 2H_2O(g)$$

they would be
(A) M^{-2}
(B) M^2

(C) M

(D) M^{-1}

(E) M^3

13. Which of the following CANNOT affect the extent of reaction?
    (A) changing the temperature
    (B) adding a catalyst
    (C) increasing the amounts of reactants
    (D) removing some product
    (E) changing the volume

14. In which of the following cases is the reaction expected to be exothermic?
    (A) Increasing the pressure increases the amount of product formed.
    (B) Increasing the amount of reactants increases the amount of product formed.
    (C) Increasing the temperature increases the amount of product formed.
    (D) Increasing the volume decreases the amount of product formed.
    (E) Increasing the temperature decreases the amount of product formed.

15. A reaction has a very large equilibrium constant of 3.3×10^{13}. Which statement is NOT true about this reaction?
    (A) The reaction is very fast.
    (B) The reaction is essentially complete.
    (C) The reaction is spontaneous.
    (D) The equilibrium constant will change if the temperature is changed.
    (E) The products will react to yield very little reactant.

16. The K_{sp} of AgCl is 1.0×10^{-10}, and the K_{sp} of AgI is 8.3×10^{-17}. A solution is 0.100 M in I^- and Cl^-. What is the molarity of iodide ions when AgCl just starts to precipitate?
    (A) 1.0×10^{-5}
    (B) 9.1×10^{-9}
    (C) 8.3×10^{-7}
    (D) 8.3×10^{-8}
    (E) 1.2×10^4

17. One liter of solution contains 2.4×10^{-3} mol of sulfate ions. What is the molar solubility of $BaSO_4$ in this solution? ($K_{sp} = 1.1 \times 10^{-10}$ for $BaSO_4$)
    (A) 1.05×10^{-5}
    (B) 1.1×10^{-9}
    (C) 2.6×10^{-13}
    (D) 2.2×10^7
    (E) 4.6×10^{-8}

18. The equilibrium constant for the reaction

$$H_2(g) \quad + \quad I_2(g) \quad \rightleftharpoons \quad 2HI(g)$$

must be determined. If 1.00 g of HI is placed in a 2.00-L flask, which of the following is LEAST important in determining the equilibrium constant?
(A) The temperature must remain constant at the desired value.
(B) Several measurements must be made to assure that the reaction is at equilibrium.
(C) Only one of the three concentrations needs to be accurately determined.
(D) All three concentrations must be accurately measured.
(E) The original mass and volume of the flask must be accurately measured.

19. In an experiment 0.0300 mol each of $SO_3(g)$, $SO_2(g)$, and $O_2(g)$ were placed in a 10.0-L flask at a certain temperature. When the reaction came to equilibrium, the concentration of $SO_2(g)$ in the flask was 3.50×10^{-5} M. What is K_c for the reaction

$$2SO_2(g) \quad + \quad O_2(g) \quad \rightleftharpoons \quad 2SO_3(g)$$

(A) 3.5×10^{-5}
(B) 1.9×10^7
(C) 5.2×10^{-8}
(D) 1.2×10^{-9}
(E) 8.2×10^8

20. The weak acid H_2A ionizes in two steps with these equilibrium constants:

$$H_2A \quad \rightleftharpoons \quad H^+ \quad + \quad HA^- \quad K_{a1} \quad = \quad 2.3 \times 10^{-4}$$

$$HA^- \quad \rightleftharpoons \quad H^+ \quad + \quad A^{2-} \quad K_{a2} \quad = \quad 4.5 \times 10^{-7}$$

What is the equilibrium constant for the reaction:

$$H_2A \quad \rightleftharpoons \quad 2H^+ \quad + \quad A^{2-}$$

(A) 6.8×10^{-11}
(B) 1.0×10^{-10}
(C) 2.3045×10^{-4}
(D) 2.0×10^{-3}
(E) 5.1×10^2

Answer Key

See Appendix I for explanations of answers.

1. C	5. A	9. B	13. B	17. E
2. E	6. B	10. B	14. E	18. D
3. C	7. D	11. D	15. A	19. B
4. E	8. A	12. D	16. D	20. B

CHAPTER ELEVEN
Kinetics

Kinetics is the field of chemistry that deals with the rate at which chemical reactions occur. It covers the period of time between the mixing of reactants and the point at which the chemical reaction stops or reaches equilibrium. A knowledge of how fast chemicals react, and the factors that influence this rate, allows chemists to exercise precise control over chemical reactions. For example, using chemical kinetics, chemists can predict what conditions are necessary to retard the spoilage of foods and medicines. Expiration dates on consumer products are all based on rates of chemical reactions. Efficient, rapid production of desirable products for industry and consumers can be optimized if the kinetics of the chemical reactions involved are understood. Also, environmental hazards can be avoided or minimized if the basic reaction rates of pollutants in air, water, and soil are known. Catalysts speed up chemical reactions, and many chemists are employed to find new catalysts to increase the yield of useful products and, at the same time, reduce byproducts that may end up as pollutants. Finally, chemists study chemical kinetics to deduce the fundamental sequences, called chemical mechanisms, in which chemicals react to form products.

Reaction Rates

The rate of a chemical reaction is the rate of change in the concentration per unit time. It is expressed as the number of moles per liter that react each second, and the units, in abbreviated form, are always mol L^{-1} s^{-1}. **Reaction rates** are determined by measuring the concentration of one or more of the chemicals involved in the reaction at different times during the course of the reaction. Figure 11.1 illustrates the results of such measurements as a **kinetic curve**, also called a **concentration versus time curve**. The kinetic curve on the left is obtained from five individual measurements of the concentration of a reaction product. These points are connected with a smooth line. The second kinetic curve is one that may be obtained using instrumentation that continuously monitors the concentration of the same product. Figure 11.1 illustrates the increase in product as a reaction occurs. If the concentration of a reactant is measured, a decrease in concentration with time will be recorded as shown in Figure 11.2.

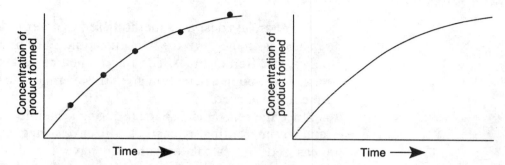

FIGURE 11.1. Kinetic curves obtained by measuring the formation of a product of a chemical reaction. The first curve is obtained from five individual measurements connected with a smooth line. The second curve is recorded automatically by an instrument designed to monitor the concentration continuously.

The rate of a chemical reaction is obtained from a kinetic curve by determining the slope of the curve at the desired point in time. The slope of a curve is determined in a three-step process:

1. Select the desired point on the curve, and draw a tangent to it.
2. Select two points on the tangent, and determine the concentrations, c, and times, t, corresponding to these points.
3. Use Equation 11.1 to calculate the slope:

$$\text{Rate} = -\left(\frac{C_2 - C_1}{t_2 - t_1}\right) = -\frac{\Delta C}{\Delta t} \tag{11.1}$$

Figure 11.2 illustrates the construction of the tangents for the determination of the initial rate, $t = 0$, and the rate at 180 seconds, $t = 180$. The small triangles on the tangents connect point 1 and point 2 with a right triangle. The necessary values for ΔC ($C_2 - C_1$) and Δt ($t_2 - t_1$) are the lengths of the sides of these triangles.

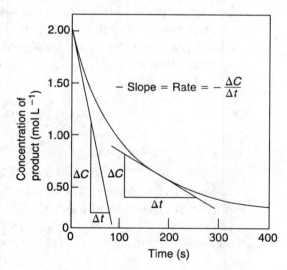

FIGURE 11.2. Tangents drawn to a kinetic curve, showing how the slope at $t = 0$ and $t = 180$ s are determined. This curve decreases with time since it was obtained by measuring the concentration of a reactant.

Another, less desirable method used to determine the rate of a chemical reaction is to measure the concentration, C, of one reactant or product at only two different times. The rate is then calculated using Equation 11.1. Such a two-point calculation gives the average rate of the reaction over the time interval used.

Since the reactants disappear during a chemical reaction, the rate calculated by measuring a reactant will have a negative sign. If a product is measured, the calculated rate will have a positive sign. By convention, however, chemists always use a positive value for the rate of a reaction, whether it is the positive rate of the appearance of products or the negative rate of disappearance of reactants:

$$\text{Rate} = \frac{\Delta C_{products}}{\Delta t} \qquad (11.2)$$

$$\text{Rate} = \frac{-\Delta C_{reactants}}{\Delta t} \qquad (11.3)$$

The sign for the rate is implied by calling the rate either the rate for the appearance (implied positive sign) of products or the rate of disappearance (implied negative sign) of reactants.

The value of a reaction rate depends on which reactant or product is measured. After the rate has been measured based on one component of the reaction, the rates of change of the other components may be calculated by a stoichiometric conversion.

Consider the following reaction:

$$2C_2H_6 \quad + \quad 7O_2 \quad \rightarrow \quad 4CO_2 \quad + \quad 6H_2O \qquad (11.4)$$

and assume that the rate of reaction was determined by measuring the CO_2 produced and was found to be 2.50 mol CO_2 L^{-1} s^{-1}. This can be converted to the rates of appearance or disappearance of all other chemical species by using the stoichiometric relationships in Equation 11.4.

First the problem is set up in the form of a stoichiometry question. The equation below can be interpreted to read "What will the rate of consumption of C_2H_6 be if the rate of production of CO_2 is 2.50 mol CO_2 L^{-1} s^{-1}?"

$$? \frac{\text{mol } C_2H_6}{\text{L s}} = \frac{2.50 \text{ mol } CO_2}{\text{L s}}$$

Since the denominators of both ratios are the same, the problem involves only the conversion of mol CO_2 into mol C_2H_6. The chemical reaction gives us a conversion factor of $\left(\dfrac{2 \text{ mol } C_2H_6}{4 \text{ mol } CO_2}\right)$, which is used to obtain

$$? \frac{\text{mol } C_2H_6}{\text{L s}} = \frac{2.50 \text{ mol } CO_2}{\text{L s}} \left(\frac{2 \text{ mol } C_2H_6}{4 \text{ mol } CO_2}\right)$$

Since the units of mol CO_2 cancel, leaving the units desired, the problem is finished, and the answer can be calculated as

$$? \frac{\text{mol } C_2H_6}{L \; s} = \frac{1.25 \; \text{mol } C_2H_6}{L \; s}$$

In a similar fashion we can calculate the corresponding rates based on O_2 and H_2O:

$$? \frac{\text{mol } O_2}{L \; s} = \frac{2.50 \; \text{mol } CO_2}{L \; s} \left(\frac{7 \; \text{mol } O_2}{4 \; \text{mol } CO_2} \right)$$

$$= \frac{4.38 \; \text{mol } O_2}{L \; s}$$

and

$$? \frac{\text{mol } H_2O}{L \; s} = \frac{2.50 \; \text{mol } CO_2}{L \; s} \left(\frac{6 \; \text{mol } H_2O}{4 \; \text{mol } CO_2} \right)$$

$$= \frac{3.75 \; \text{mol } H_2O}{L \; s}$$

$$= 3.75 \; \text{mol } H_2O \; L^{-1} \; s^{-1}$$

It is apparent that any reaction rate must specify to which reactant or product that rate actually applies.

Exercise 11.1

Using Figure 11.2, determine the rate, for the reaction illustrated, at 100 s and 200 s after the reaction starts.

Solution

When the tangents are drawn, the slopes are determined to be -6.5×10^{-3} and -2.8×10^{-3} mol $L^{-1}s^{-1}$. Since this curve represents the disappearance of a reactant, the rate is the negative of the slope, or 6.5×10^{-1} mol $L^{-1}s^{-1}$ at 100 s and 2.8×10^{-3} mol $L^{-1}s^{-1}$ at 200 s.

Exercise 11.2

In the reaction

$$N_2(g) \quad + \quad 3H_2(g) \quad \rightarrow \quad 2NH_3(g)$$

the rate of disappearance of $H_2(g)$ is found to be 4.8×10^{-2} mol $L^{-1} \; s^{-1}$. What is the rate at which $N_2(g)$ is reacting, and what is the rate at which $NH_3(g)$ is being produced under the same conditions?

Solution

This problem requires the conversion of one rate into another. The initial setup is

$$? \frac{\text{mol } N_2}{L \; s} = \frac{4.8 \times 10^{-2} \; \text{mol } H_2}{L \; s}$$

The next step uses the factor label for the conversion between $N_2(g)$ and $H_2(g)$ as

$$? \frac{\text{mol } N_2}{L \; s} = \frac{4.8 \times 10^{-2} \; \text{mol } H_2}{L \; s} \left(\frac{1 \; \text{mol } N_2}{3 \; \text{mol } H_2} \right)$$

$$= 1.6 \times 10^{-2} \; \text{mol } N_2 \; L^{-1} s^{-1}$$

The same steps are used to determine the rate for the production of $NH_3(g)$:

$$? \frac{mol\ NH_3}{L\ s} = \frac{4.8 \times 10^{-2}\ mol\ H_2}{L\ s}$$

$$? \frac{mol\ NH_3}{L\ s} = \frac{4.8 \times 10^{-2}\ mol\ H_2}{L\ s} \left(\frac{2\ mol\ NH_3}{3\ mol\ H_2} \right)$$

$$= 3.2 \times 10^{-2}\ mol\ NH_3\ L^{-1}\ s^{-1}$$

Factors That Affect Reaction Rates

Concentration, Temperature, and Catalysts

Most people are aware of the factors that increase reaction rates, perhaps without even realizing it. To make a fire burn more fiercely, we add wood to it. A car travels faster if we press on the accelerator pedal to give the engine more gas. In any chemical reaction the **concentration of reactants** is an important factor in the observed rate.

In addition, to get food to cook faster, we turn up the heat on the stove. To decrease the spoilage of foods, we refrigerate or, even better, freeze them. Obviously, **temperature** is another important factor in chemical reaction rates. As a consequence, in all rate experiments temperatures must be carefully controlled. It is important to remember that increasing temperature *always* increases reaction rates and decreasing temperature *always* decreases reaction rates.

Finally, a **catalyst** will increase the rate of reaction. A catalyst is a substance that participates in a chemical reaction but does not appear in the balanced equation. Perhaps the most familiar catalysts are those in the catalytic converters in automobiles. The platinum in a catalytic converter provides a surface on which reactants meet and react more efficiently. Although the platinum promotes the effective reaction of two other chemicals, it is not included in the balanced equation.

Other experimental factors, as long as they do not affect the concentration, temperature, or catalysts, will have no effect on the rate of a chemical reaction.

Effect of Concentration on Reaction Rates

The effect of concentration on a chemical reaction is expressed in the **rate law**. All rate laws start with the same form

$$Rate = k[A]^x[B]^y[C]^z \tag{11.5}$$

In this equation k stands for the **rate constant**, and the square brackets indicate the concentrations of the reactants A, B, and C, which have exponents $x, y,$ and z. These exponents are usually small whole numbers. In more complex rate laws they may be negative numbers or rational fractions. Exponents must be determined from laboratory experiments and have no relationship to the stoichiometric coefficients of the balanced chemical equation.

Determination of Rate Laws

All rate laws must be determined by using the data from a group of well-planned experiments. By changing the concentration of one reactant while holding all other concentrations constant, we can determine whether the change we made has an effect on the rate; and, if it does, we can calculate the exponent for the changed reactant in the rate law. **There is no theoretical way to predict the exponents of a rate law.**

An example of the method used to determine rate laws can be shown using the reaction of peroxydisulfate with iodide ions according to the equation

$$S_2O_8^{2-} \quad + \quad 3I^- \quad \rightarrow \quad 2SO_4^{2-} \quad + \quad I_3^- \tag{11.6}$$

Table 11.1 shows three experiments using this reaction. In experiments 1 and 2 the concentration of iodide ion is the same and the concentrations of peroxydisulfate ions are different. In experiments 2 and 3 the iodide ion concentration is changed while the peroxydisulfate concentration is held constant. The measured initial rate for each experiment is given in the last column.

TABLE 11.1 Kinetic Data for the Peroxydisulfate Reaction at 20.0°C

Experiment Number	$[S_2O_8^{2-}]$ (mol L^{-1})	$[I^-]$ (mol L^{-1})	Initial Rate of Reaction (mol L^{-1}s^{-1})
1	0.200	0.200	2.2×10^{-3}
2	0.400	0.200	4.4×10^{-3}
3	0.400	0.400	8.8×10^{-3}

The rate law will have the form

$$\text{Rate} \quad = \quad k[S_2O_8^{2-}]^x[I^-]^y \tag{11.7}$$

where the exponents x and y need to be determined.

To determine the exponent for the peroxydisulfate ion, we focus attention on the change in reaction rate as the concentration of $S_2O_8^{2-}$ is changed in experiments 1 and 2. A rate law can be written for experiment 1 and another for experiment 2 by entering the data from the table into Equation 11.7:

$$\text{Rate}_1 \quad = \quad 2.2 \times 10^{-3} \quad = \quad k(0.200)^x(0.200)^y$$

$$\text{Rate}_2 \quad = \quad 4.4 \times 10^{-3} \quad = \quad k(0.400)^x(0.200)^y$$

The ratio of these two equations is then written (the calculations are usually easier if the larger numbers are used for the numerator) as

$$\frac{\text{Rate}_2}{\text{Rate}_1} \quad = \quad \frac{4.4 \times 10^{-3}}{2.2 \times 10^{-3}} \quad = \quad \frac{k(0.400)^x(0.200)^y}{k(0.200)^x(0.200)^y}$$

The two k's and the two $(0.200)^y$ factors cancel to yield

$$\frac{\text{Rate}_2}{\text{Rate}_1} = \frac{4.4 \times 10^{-3}}{2.2 \times 10^{-3}} = \frac{(0.400)^x}{(0.200)^x}$$

Since both exponents are x, the right-hand term can be rewritten as

$$\frac{\text{Rate}_2}{\text{Rate}_1} = \frac{4.4 \times 10^{-3}}{2.2 \times 10^{-3}} = \left(\frac{0.400}{0.200}\right)^x$$

Solving this gives

$$2.0 = 2.00^x$$
$$= 2.00^1$$

From this result we conclude that exponent $x = 1$. In a similar manner the value of exponent y is determined using experiments 2 and 3, where the concentration of $S_2O_8^{2-}$ is held constant and I^- is varied. The ratio of rate laws for experiments 2 and 3 is

$$\frac{\text{Rate}_3}{\text{Rate}_2} = \frac{8.8 \times 10^{-3}}{4.4 \times 10^{-3}} = \frac{k(0.400)^x(0.400)^y}{k(0.400)^x(0.200)^y}$$
$$2.0 = 2.00^y$$
$$= 2.00^1$$

The value of exponent y is 1. Using the exponents determined in this manner, we write the rate law:

$$\text{Rate} = k[S_2O_8^{2-}]^1[I^-]^1 \quad \text{or} \quad k[S_2O_8^{2-}][I^-] \tag{11.8}$$

The exponents in the rate law are definitely not the same as the exponents in balanced Equation 11.6.

Once the rate law is known, the rate constant can be calculated. This is done by taking *any* one of the three experiments in Table 11.1, substituting the values into the rate equation, and solving for the rate constant k. The rate constant should be the same whether experiment 1, 2, or 3 is chosen for this calculation. To verify this, we will calculate the rate constant for each experiment and express it in the proper units:

> Observe how the units cancel in these calculations.

$$\text{Experiment 1: } k = \frac{2.2 \times 10^{-3} \text{ mol L}^{-1} \text{ s}^{-1}}{(0.200 \text{ mol L}^{-1})(0.200 \text{ mol L}^{-1})}$$
$$= 0.055 \text{ L mol}^{-1} \text{ s}^{-1}$$

Experiment 2: k = $\dfrac{4.4 \times 10^{-3} \text{ mol L}^{-1} \text{ s}^{-1}}{(0.400 \text{ mol L}^{-1})(0.200 \text{ mol L}^{-1})}$

= $0.055 \text{ L mol}^{-1} \text{ s}^{-1}$

Experiment 3: k = $\dfrac{8.8 \times 10^{-3} \text{ mol L}^{-1} \text{ s}^{-1}}{(0.400 \text{ mol L}^{-1})(0.400 \text{ mol L}^{-1})}$

= $0.055 \text{ L mol}^{-1} \text{ s}^{-1}$

We have demonstrated that an easy way to verify the rate law is to calculate the rate constant for each experiment. The rate constants should all agree within experimental error; if they do not, something is wrong with the rate law.

Chemists use the term **order of reaction** to indicate the exponents in the rate law. The reaction we have been considering is said to be **first order** with respect to peroxydisulfate and first order with respect to iodide ions. It is also said to be **second order** overall. Individual reactants have the same orders as their exponents. The order of the overall reaction is the sum of all of the exponents.

REMEMBER THE DIFFERENCE

REACTION RATE
(or simply rate). This varies with the concentration of reactants and time. Rate always has units of mol L^{-1} s^{-1}.

RATE CONSTANT
This is a constant value at a fixed temperature for a given reaction. The units of a rate constant depend on the order of the reaction.

To summarize, we can say that in this reaction:

(a) the order with respect to peroxydisulfate is 1 (first order with respect to peroxydisulfate);

(b) the order with respect to iodide ion is one (first order with respect to iodide);

(c) the overall order is $1 + 1 = 2$ (second order overall);

(d) the units for the reaction rate are always mol L^{-1} s^{-1};

(e) the units for the rate constant are (mol L^{-1} s^{-1})/(mol L^{-1})^2 = L mol^{-1} s^{-1}.

Exercise 11.3

Determine the rate law and value of the rate constant, with its units, for the data in the table below.

Experiment Number	[A] (mol L^{-1})	[B] (mol L^{-1})	Initial Rate of Reaction (mol L^{-1}s^{-1})
1	0.100	0.200	1.1×10^{-6}
2	0.100	0.600	9.9×10^{-6}
3	0.400	0.600	9.9×10^{-6}

Solution

The general form of the rate law will be

$$\text{Rate} = k[A]^x[B]^y$$

Taking the ratio of the rate laws for experiments 1 and 2 yields

$$\frac{\text{Rate}_2}{\text{Rate}_1} = \frac{k(0.100)^x(0.600)^y}{k(0.100)^x(0.200)^y}$$

Canceling the identical terms, k and $(0.100)^x$, on the right and entering the rates on the left yields

$$\frac{9.9 \times 10^{-6}}{1.1 \times 10^{-6}} = \frac{(0.600)^y}{(0.200)^y}$$

$$9 = 3^y$$

Three squared is equal to 9, and therefore $y = 2$.

To determine exponent x, the ratio of the rate laws for experiments 2 and 3 are used:

$$\frac{\text{Rate}_3}{\text{Rate}_2} = \frac{k(0.400)^x(0.600)^y}{k(0.100)^x(0.600)^y}$$

Entering the rates and canceling as before gives

$$\frac{9.9 \times 10^{-6}}{9.9 \times 10^{-6}} = \frac{(0.400)^x}{(0.100)^x}$$

$$1.0 = 4^x$$

Any number raised to the zero power is equal to 1, and therefore $x = 0$. The rate law is

$$\text{Rate} = k[A]^0[B]^2 = k[B]^2$$

Since the concentration of A has no effect on the reaction rate, it is not part of the rate law.

The rate constant is determined by taking any of the three experiments, substituting the rate and concentrations into the rate law, and calculating k. Using the data from experiment 1 yields

$$1.1 \times 10^{-6}\ \text{mol B L}^{-1}\ \text{s}^{-1} = k(0.200\ \text{mol B L}^{-1})^2$$

$$k = \frac{1.1 \times 10^{-6}\ \text{mol B L}^{-1}\ \text{s}^{-1}}{(0.200\ \text{mol B L}^{-1})^2}$$

$$= 2.75 \times 10^{-5}\ \text{L mol}^{-1}\ \text{s}^{-1}$$

Exercise 11.4

What is the overall order of each of the following rate laws, and what are the units of the rate constant, k, in each of these rate laws?
(a) Rate = $k[A][B][C]$
(b) Rate = $k[X]^2[Y]^3$
(c) Rate = $k[M]^2[N]$
(d) Rate = k
(e) Rate = $k[R]$

Solution

(a) Order = 3. Units are $L^2\,mol^{-2}\,s^{-1}$.
(b) Order = 5. Units are $L^4\,mol^{-4}\,s^{-1}$.
(c) Order = 3. Units are $L^2\,mol^{-2}\,s^{-1}$.
(d) Order = 0. Units are $mol\,L^{-1}\,s^{-1}$.
(e) Order = 1. Units are s^{-1}.

Effect of Temperature on Reaction Rates

Almost instinctively we add heat when we wish to increase the speed of a reaction. Higher temperatures increase the rates at which foods cook and solids dissolve in water. Cold-blooded animals such as snakes and lizards are almost immobile in cold temperatures, and they sun themselves to warm up in order to hunt for food.

In 1889 Svante Arrhenius developed the equation for the relationship between the rate constant and temperature. It is called the **Arrhenius equation** in his honor.

$$k = Ae^{-E_a/RT} \tag{11.9}$$

This equation includes the rate constant, k; the activation energy, E_a; the universal gas law constant, R, which equals 8.314 J mol^{-1} K^{-1}; the Kelvin temperature, T; a proportionality constant, A; and the base of natural logarithms, e. When the natural logarithm of Equation 11.9 is taken, the result is

$$\ln k = \frac{-E_a}{RT} + \ln A \tag{11.10}$$

This equation can be utilized in two ways to eliminate the need to know the value of the constant A. First, a graph of $\ln k$ versus $1/T$ can be constructed after determining the rate constant at a variety of temperatures. This graph, shown in Figure 11.3, is often called an Arrhenius plot. The slope of the line is equal to $-E_a/R$. Arrhenius plots are used to determine the activation energy, E_a, and also the rate constant at any desired temperature.

The second way to apply Equation 11.10 is a two-point approach using only the rate constants determined at two different temperatures. With this

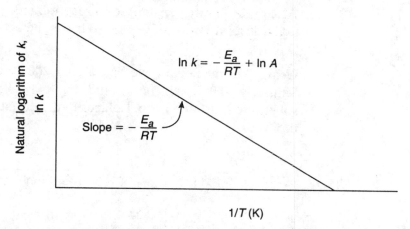

FIGURE 11.3. An Arrhenius plot of $\ln k$ versus $1/T$. The activation energy, E_a, is determined from the slope of the straight line.

method, an Arrhenius equation is written for the rate constant determined at each temperature, shown by subscripts 1 and 2 in the equations below:

$$\ln k_1 = \frac{-E_a}{RT_2} + \ln A$$

$$\ln k_2 = \frac{-E_a}{RT_2} + \ln A$$

When the second equation is subtracted from the first, the result is

$$\ln k_1 - \ln k_2 = \frac{-E_a}{RT_1} - \frac{-E_a}{RT_2} \qquad (11.11)$$

which is commonly rewritten with the ln terms combined on the left and the $-E_a/R$ factored from the right side.

$$\ln\left(\frac{k_1}{k_2}\right) = \frac{-E_a}{R}\left(\frac{1}{T_1} - \frac{1}{T_2}\right) \qquad (11.12)$$

This equation has five variables, E_a, k_1, k_2, T_1, and T_2. Given four of these, we can determine the fifth by substitution into the equation. Equation 11.12 may also be written using the ratio of the rates rather than the rate constants:

$$\ln\left(\frac{\text{rate}_1}{\text{rate}_2}\right) = \frac{-E_a}{R}\left(\frac{1}{T_1} - \frac{1}{T_2}\right) \qquad (11.13)$$

The rate and the rate constant are directly proportional to each other as long as the concentrations are held constant.

Often the signs in this equation become confused since the calculation is somewhat involved. It is always possible, however, to test the answer for reasonableness. Two principles must be remembered:

1. The larger rate constant (or rate) will *always* be associated with the higher temperature.
2. The activation energy *always* has a positive sign.

Exercise 11.5

At 200 K the rate constant for a reaction is 3.5×10^{-3} s^{-1}, and at 250 K the rate constant is 4.0×10^{-3} s^{-1}. What is the activation energy?

Solution

Using the given data, we can assign 200 K as T_1 and 3.5×10^{-3} as k_1. Similarly, 250 K will be T_2 and 4.0×10^{-3} must be k_2. These are then substituted into the proper places in the equation, along with $R = 8.3145$ mol^{-1} K^{-1}

$$\ln\left(\frac{3.5 \times 10^{-3}}{4.0 \times 10^{-3}}\right) = \frac{-E_a}{8.3145 \text{ J mol}^{-1} \text{ K}^{-1}}\left(\frac{1}{200 \text{ K}} - \frac{1}{250 \text{ K}}\right)$$

$$-0.1335 = (-1.20 \ 10^{-4} \text{ mol J}^{-1})\, E_a$$

$$E_a = 1.11 \times 10^3 \text{ J mol}^{-1} = 1.11 \text{ kJ mol}^{-1}$$

Exercise 11.6

A common rule of thumb is that, near room temperature, the rate of a reaction will double with each 10°C rise in temperature. Estimate the activation energy needed for this rule to hold true.

Solution

Choose two temperatures 10°C apart, such as 290 K and 300 K, which are close to room temperature of 298 K. The rates double, meaning that the rate constants must double. We can assign rate constants of 1.00 to the 290 K temperature and 2.00 to the 300 K temperature. Now the problem is solved as above:

$$\ln\left(\frac{1}{2}\right) = \frac{-E_a}{8.3145 \text{ J mol}^{-1} \text{ K}^{-1}}\left(\frac{1}{200 \text{ K}} - \frac{1}{300 \text{ K}}\right)$$

$$-0.693 = (-1.382 \times 10^{-5} \text{ mol J}^{-1})E_a$$

$$E_a = 5.01 \times 10^4 \text{ J mol}^{-1} = 50.1 \text{ kJ mol}^{-1}$$

Choosing other temperatures near 298 K will result in slightly different answers, but all will be close to 50 kJ mol^{-1}. Many common reactions have activation energies near this value.

Exercise 11.7

What is the rate of reaction at 450°C if the reaction rate is 6.75×10^{-6} mol L^{-1} s^{-1} at 25°C? The activation energy was previously determined to be 35.5 kJ mol^{-1}.

Solution

Using the equation with rates, we can enter the variables given, after converting kilojoules to joules, to obtain

$$\ln\left(\frac{\text{rate}_1}{6.75 \times 10^{-6}}\right) = \frac{-35500 \text{ J mol}^{-1}}{8.3145 \text{ J mol}^{-1} \text{ K}^{-1}}\left(\frac{1}{723} - \frac{1}{298}\right)$$

Remembering that the logarithm of a ratio can be written as the logarithm of the numerator minus the logarithm of the denominator, we obtain

$$\ln \text{rate}_1 - \ln (6.75 \times 10^{-6}) = 8.42$$

$$\ln \text{rate}_1 - (-11.91) = 8.42$$

$$\ln (\text{rate}_1) = -3.49$$

$$\text{rate}_1 = 3.05 \times 10^{-2} \text{ mol L}^{-1} \text{ s}^{-1}$$

As expected, the reaction rate is greater at a higher temperature.

Applications of Selected Rate Laws

Zero-Order Reactions

A reaction that is **zero order** has a rate law in which the exponents of all of the reactants are zero. Since any number raised to the zero power is equal to 1 ($x^0 = 1$), the rate law is

$$\text{Rate} = k \tag{11.14}$$

This type of reaction does not depend on the concentration of any reactant. Its rate is equal to the rate constant, and the rate constant has the same units (mol L^{-1} s^{-1}) as a rate.

Catalytic reactions are often zero-order reactions. One catalyzed reaction is the decomposition of hydrogen peroxide in the presence of platinum metal:

$$2H_2O_2 \quad \rightarrow \quad 2H_2O \quad + \quad O_2 \tag{11.15}$$

The concentration versus time plot for any zero-order reaction is a straight line, as shown in Figure 11.4.

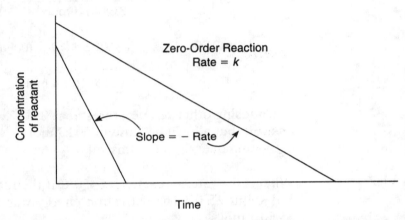

FIGURE 11.4. Kinetic curves of two different zero-order reactions, illustrating the straight-line relationship between concentration and time.

First-Order Reactions

Any rate law in which the sum of the exponents is 1 is a **first-order reaction.** There are a variety of ways in which a reaction can be first order, including the case where the exponents of two reactants are 0.5 each. In the most common case the concentration of one reactant, A, has an exponent of 1 as in the following rate law:

$$\text{Rate} \quad = \quad k[A] \tag{11.16}$$

As a first-order reaction progresses, the concentration of reactant A decreases and the rate decreases. When the concentration of A has decreased to half its original amount, the rate will be half the initial rate. The time required for this to occur is called the **half-life,** $t_{1/2}$. In another half-life the concentration will decrease by half again, to one-fourth of the initial concentration. Figure 11.5 illustrates the shape of the kinetic curve for all first-order reactions.

The Integrated Equation

Using elementary calculus, we can integrate the first-order rate equation to give an equation that allows us to calculate concentrations at any time after the reaction has started:

$$\ln \left(\frac{[A]_0}{[A]_t} \right) \quad = \quad kt \tag{11.17}$$

or

$$\ln [A]_0 \quad - \quad \ln [A]_t \quad = \quad kt \tag{11.18}$$

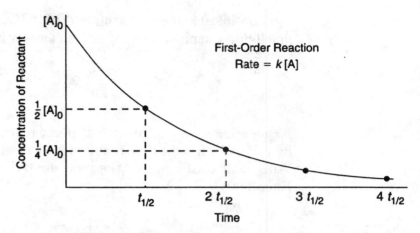

FIGURE 11.5. Kinetic curve for all first-order reactions. The time at which the concentration is one-half the original concentration is the half-life, $t_{1/2}$.

Each form of the integrated equation contains four variables: the time, t; the rate constant, k; an initial concentration of A, $[A]_0$; and the concentration at some time after the reaction is started, $[A]_t$. Using Equation 11.18, chemists often plot the natural logarithm of the reactant concentration versus time in a graph as shown in Figure 11.6. In this type of graph, only a first-order reaction will result in a straight line, and the slope will be equal to $-k$.

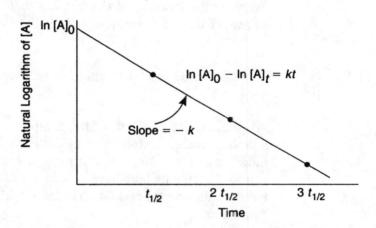

FIGURE 11.6. Logarithmic plot of a first-order reaction.

Exercise 11.8

A certain first-order reaction has a rate constant of $4.5 \times 10^{-3} \text{s}^{-1}$. How much of a 50.0 millimolar (mM) sample will have reacted after 75.0 s?

Solution

Substitution of the data into integrated rate Equation 11.18 yields

$$
\begin{aligned}
\ln (0.0500) \quad - \quad \ln [A]_t \quad &= \quad (4.5 \times 10^{-3} \text{ s}^{-1})(75.0 \text{ s}) \\
-2.995 \quad - \quad \ln [A]_t \quad &= \quad 0.3375 \\
\ln [A]_t \quad &= \quad -3.333 \\
[A]_t \quad &= \quad 0.0356 \text{ M}
\end{aligned}
$$

This indicates that the sample is now 35.6 mM. The question asks how much of the sample has reacted; the answer is

$$50.0 \text{ mM} \quad - \quad 35.6 \text{ mM} \quad = \quad 14.4 \text{ mM}$$

Half-Lives

As mentioned previously, a first-order reaction has a property called the half-life, which is the time required for half of the reactant to be consumed. When half of the reactant is used up, $[A]_t = 0.5 [A]_0$. Substituting into Equation 11.17 yields

$$\ln \left(\frac{0.5[A]_0}{[A]_0} \right) \quad = \quad -kt_{1/2}$$

$$\ln (0.5) \quad = \quad -kt_{1/2}$$

$$-0.693 \quad = \quad -kt_{1/2}$$

$$t_{1/2} \quad = \quad \frac{0.693}{k} \tag{11.19}$$

where $t_{1/2}$ is the half-life of the reaction. Half-lives may be used to quickly estimate the fraction of the starting material left after it has been allowed to react for a given number of half-lives.

Exercise 11.9

What percentage of a sample has reacted after six half-lives?

Solution

After each half-life, half of the sample present at the start of that half-life will be reacted. After one half-life, ½ of the sample is left; after two half-lives, ½ × ½ or ¼ will remain; after three half-lives, ½ × ½ × ½ or ⅛ remains. After six half-lives ½ × ½ × ½ × ½ × ½ × ½ = ¹⁄₆₄ of the original is left, meaning that 63/64 has reacted. The percentage that has reacted is calculated as

$$\frac{63}{64} \times 100 = 98.4\% \text{ reacted}$$

The most prominent first-order processes in chemistry are those associated with radioactive decay of the elements. The decay of radioactive elements follows first-order kinetics, as shown in Chapter 3.

Second-Order Reactions

Two second-order rate laws are

$$\text{Rate} \quad = \quad k[A]^2 \tag{11.20}$$

$$\text{Rate} \quad = \quad k[A][B] \tag{11.21}$$

In the special case where [A] = [B] the two rate laws can be integrated to obtain the same equation.

$$\frac{1}{[A]_t} - \frac{1}{[A]_0} = kt \tag{11.22}$$

The half-life of the second-order reactions specified above may be determined by substituting 0.5 $[A]_0$ for $[A]_t$ in Equation 11.21.

$$\frac{1}{0.5[A]_0} - \frac{1}{[A]_0} = kt_{1/2}$$

$$\frac{2}{[A]_0} - \frac{1}{[A]_0} = kt_{1/2}$$

$$\frac{1}{[A]_0} = kt_{1/2} \tag{11.23}$$

$$t_{1/2} = \frac{1}{k\,[A]_0} \tag{11.24}$$

The important information derived from these equations is that the half-life of a second-order reaction depends on the starting concentrations of the reactants. In addition, a straight-line graph will be obtained by plotting 1/[A] versus time. The slope of the line will be equal to k, as shown in Figure 11.7.

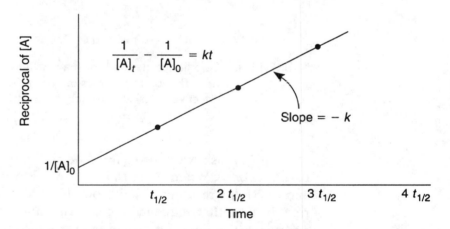

FIGURE 11.7. Plot of 1/[A] versus time, illustrating the straight-line relationship for a second-order reaction.

Theory of Reaction Rates

Collision Theory

The **collision theory** states that the reaction rate is equal to the frequency of effective collisions between reactants. For a collision to be effective, the molecules must collide with sufficient energy and in the proper orientation so that products can form.

The minimum energy needed for a reaction is the activation energy, E_a. If two molecules collide head on, they will stop at some point and all of the kinetic energy will be converted into potential energy. If the molecules strike each other with a glancing blow, however, only part of the kinetic energy will be converted into potential energy. As long as the increase in potential energy is greater than E_a, a reaction is possible. The fraction of all collisions that have the minimum energy needed for reaction can be calculated using the **kinetic molecular theory** of gases discussed in Chapter 7. The fraction of collisions with this minimum energy increases with rising temperature since the average kinetic energy of molecules increases as temperature increases.

In addition to the energy requirement, for an effective collision the molecules must collide in the proper orientation. An example is the reaction of hydrogen iodide molecules with chlorine atoms. In this reaction the chlorine replaces the iodine in the molecule:

$$HI \quad + \quad Cl \quad \rightarrow \quad HCl \quad + \quad I$$

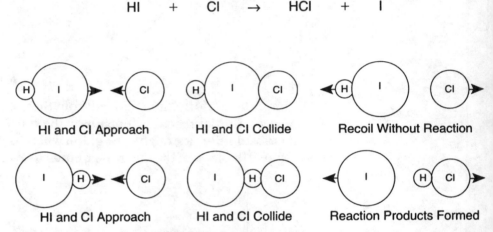

| HI and Cl Approach | HI and Cl Collide | Recoil Without Reaction |
| HI and Cl Approach | HI and Cl Collide | Reaction Products Formed |

FIGURE 11.8. Orientation needed for the reaction of hydrogen iodide with chlorine. The top row shows an ineffective collision; the bottom row, an effective collision, forming products.

Figure 11.8 shows hydrogen iodide colliding with a chlorine atom from two directions. When, as in the top row, chlorine collides with the iodide end of HI, the reactants recoil from the collision without a reaction occurring. In the other sequence the chlorine atom collides with the hydrogen end of HI. This collision can cause the iodine atom to be released while the chlorine bonds with the hydrogen. After collision the products HCl and I are present.

The overall reaction rate predicted by the collision theory may be summarized by the equation

$$\text{Reaction rate} \quad = \quad N f_e f_o \tag{11.25}$$

where N represents the number of collisions per second, which depends on the temperature and concentration of the reactants; f_e is the fraction of the collisions with the minimum energy; and f_o is the fraction of collisions with the correct orientation. The fraction f_e will increase as temperature increases, while f_o remains constant for a given reaction.

Transition-State Theory

The **transition-state theory** attempts to describe in detail the molecular configurations and energies as a collision of reactants occurs. This theory recognizes that, as molecules approach on a collision course, they do not act like billiard balls simply bouncing off each other. Instead, as the molecules get closer, their orbitals interact and distort each other. This distortion weakens bonds within the molecules so that at the moment of collision some bonds are so weak that they break and new bonds may form.

Using the diagram in Figure 11.8, we can visualize the effective collision in this sequence. First the chlorine approaches the hydrogen end of the HI molecule. As the Cl and HI get closer, the very electronegative Cl starts attracting the electrons that the hydrogen shares with the iodine atom. As a result the H-I bond is weakened and a H-Cl bond starts to form. At the moment of collision, the H-I bond is approximately half broken and the H-Cl bond is approximately half formed. This state is called the **activated complex.** When the atoms recoil, the activated complex breaks apart. The result may be a successful reaction giving new products, or an unsuccessful collision with the original reactants remaining intact.

The Reaction Profile

In the transition-state theory the energies of the reactants during the collision are described by a reaction profile. As the molecules approach, interact, and become distorted, their potential energy must increase. This potential energy increase comes from an equal decrease in the kinetic energy of the molecules. In other words, as the molecules approach a collision they slow down because their kinetic energy is converted to potential energy.

The **reaction profile** plots the increase in potential energy of the reactants as they approach, reaching a maximum at the moment of collision, and then the decrease in potential energy as the products recoil. A reaction profile is shown in Figure 11.9. In a reaction profile the minimum amount of kinetic energy that must be converted into potential energy in order to form products is called the activation energy, E_a. It is often referred to as an energy barrier between the reactants and the products.

The transition-state theory is based on the same considerations as the collision theory. First, if reactants collide with enough energy to surmount

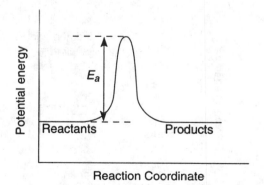

FIGURE 11.9. Reaction profile illustrating the energy barrier between reactants and products.

the energy barrier, a reaction may occur. Second, if the activated complex formed at the moment of collision (top of the energy barrier) has the proper structure, it can proceed to fall apart into products. If it has the wrong structure, however, products cannot form and the molecules recoil as the original reactants. These energy and orientation factors are the same ones that are important to the collision theory.

The major difference in the two theories is that the collision theory views reactions as collisions between hard spheres, similar to the collisions between billiard balls. The transition-state theory, on the other hand, views the collisions as interactions between sponge balls that are deformed in the collision process. The transition-state theory involves more details about the energy and shapes of the molecules as they collide than the collision theory.

Interpretation of Reaction Profiles

Reaction profiles provide a rich source of information about the rates of chemical reactions and are also a graphical view of the conversion of reactants into products. These graphs are often more informative than words alone in describing features of the reaction process.

In a reaction profile, the rate constant, and therefore the rate of a chemical reaction, are inversely related to the height of the energy barrier, E_a. When the activation energy is low, a large proportion of the collisions will have sufficient energy for a reaction to occur. Conversely, a high activation energy indicates that few collisions will have enough energy to convert reactants into products.

Reaction profiles can be used to determine whether a reaction is endothermic or exothermic. This is possible because the potential energy difference between the products and the reactants is equal to the heat of reaction, ΔH:

$$\Delta H = PE_{products} - PE_{reactants} \tag{11.26}$$

When heat is absorbed from the surroundings, the reaction is endothermic and ΔH has a positive sign. For **endothermic reactions** the potential energy of the products is greater than the potential energy of the reactants. The reverse is true for **exothermic reactions**. The reaction profiles for these two cases are shown in Figure 11.10.

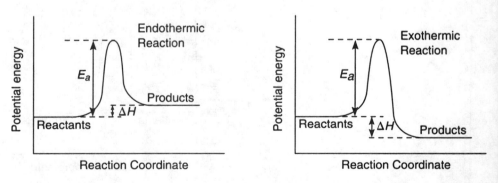

FIGURE 11.10. Reaction profiles illustrating the difference between an endothermic reaction and an exothermic reaction.

Another aspect of the reaction profile is that it allows the chemist to explain the reverse as well as the forward chemical reaction. To visualize what occurs in the reverse process, we look at the reaction profile, starting on the product side and proceeding toward the reactant side. When the products are reacting to form reactants, there is a different energy of activation and a different heat of reaction. The activation energy for the reverse reaction is the difference between the potential energy of the products and the maximum energy of the curve. For the heat of reaction the sign of ΔH will be opposite to that for the forward reaction. Figure 11.11 is the same as Figure 11.10 except that it shows the activation energies and heats of reaction for the reverse reactions.

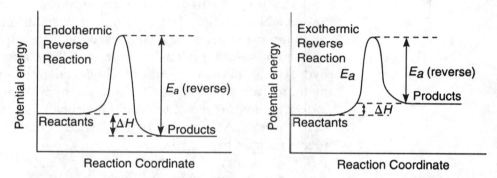

FIGURE 11.11. Reaction profiles illustrating the activation energy of reverse re-actions and the fact that ΔH of the reverse reaction is opposite in sign to ΔH of the forward reaction.

Reaction profiles also allow us to explain the action of **catalysts** (Figure 11.12). As mentioned previously, a catalyst is a substance that increases the rate of a chemical reaction without itself being reacted. It speeds up a reaction by providing an alternative reaction pathway that has a lower energy barrier in the reaction profile. As a result the energies of activation of both the forward and reverse reactions are simultaneously decreased by the same amount, so that the reaction comes to chemical equilibrium more

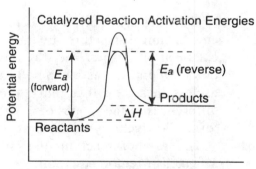

FIGURE 11.12. Reaction profile of a catalyzed reaction, illustrating that the for-ward and reverse activation energies are both reversed. The heat of reaction is not affected, nor is the position of equilibrium because the potential energies of the reactants and products are not affected.

quickly. It must be kept in mind that a catalyst will not increase the amount of product formed, nor will it alter the composition of the equilibrium mixture, as indicated by the unchanged potential energy plateaus for the reactants and products.

An example of a catalyst is the platinum metal used in the hydrogenation of ethylene. Ethylene has a double bond to which two hydrogen atoms may be added to form ethane:

$$
\begin{array}{ccc}
\text{H} \quad \text{H} & & \text{H} \quad \text{H} \\
\text{C} = \text{C} \ + \ \text{H}_2 \ \leftrightarrow \ & \text{H} - \text{C} - \text{C} - \text{H} \\
\text{H} \quad \text{H} & & \text{H} \quad \text{H}
\end{array}
$$

A mixture of hydrogen and ethylene at room temperature does not show appreciable reaction, but addition of a small amount of finely divided platinum catalyzes a very rapid reaction. The apparent reason is that the hydrogen molecule is fairly stable, and the energy required to break the hydrogen atoms apart results in a high activation energy. Platinum adsorbs hydrogen readily on its surface and the hydrogen molecule separates into individual hydrogen atoms. These hydrogen atoms then readily react with the ethylene. At the end of the process, the original platinum can be recovered and used again.

The discovery of new, more effective, and more specific catalysts is a major objective of many industrial chemists. Many catalysts are naturally occurring minerals whose properties are often discovered by trial and error. Others are synthetic compounds designed by studying natural catalysts and using chemical methods to improve upon them.

Enzymes, another class of natural catalysts found in living organisms, catalyze very specific reactions. Most enzyme reactions have an optimum temperature around 36°C. Generally the enzyme, E, and the reactant(s), called the substrate, S, react to form an enzyme-substrate, ES, complex. The **enzyme-substrate complex** then decomposes into the product(s), P, and the original enzyme. This process is written as:

$$
\text{E} \ + \ \text{S} \ \rightleftharpoons \ \text{ES} \ \rightleftharpoons \ \text{P} \ + \ \text{E} \tag{11.27}
$$

Enzymes are specific for certain reactions because they recognize specific chemical structures by their three-dimensional shape as well as their chemical properties. The way this occurs is often called the **lock and key** model of enzyme action. Small changes in the shape of a key will make it useless in a lock that the key once was able to open. Similarly, small differences in the shapes of molecules will determine whether or not they form effective enzyme-substrate complexes.

The rate of reaction of a simple enzyme reaction is given by the **Michaelis-Menton equation**:

$$
\text{Rate} \ = \ \frac{k[\text{E}][\text{S}]}{C \ + \ [\text{S}]} \tag{11.28}
$$

In this equation k is the rate constant for the formation of the ES complex. The constant C is a combination of the other rate constants in the process. When the substrate concentration is very large, this equation becomes

$$\text{Rate} = k [E] \qquad (11.29)$$

When the substrate concentration is very low, the equation becomes

$$\text{Rate} = \left(\frac{k}{C}\right) [E] [S] \qquad (11.30)$$

To understand these equations, we may visualize the rate at which cars pass through a toll booth on an expressway. When there is a large volume of traffic, [S], the rate at which cars go through the toll depends on the number of booths, [E]. When there is little traffic, the rate depends on the frequency, [S], with which cars reach the toll booths. Similarly, at low substrate concentrations the rate depends on [S], while at high substrate concentrations the rate depends on [E], as shown in Figure 11.13.

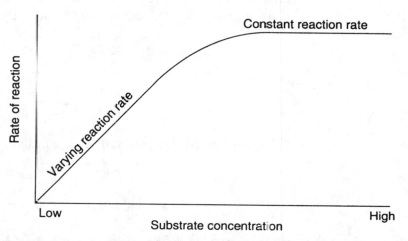

FIGURE 11.13. Dependence of the reaction rate of enzyme-catalyzed reactions on substrate concentrations, [S]. At low substrate concentration the rate is proportional to [S]. At high substrate concentrations the rate is independent of [S]. The enzyme concentration, [E], is assumed to be constant.

Reaction Mechanisms

One of the most important uses of chemical kinetics is to decipher the sequence of steps that lead to an observed chemical reaction. Chemists write chemical equations for reactions as a single step. However, most chemical reactions occur in a series of steps called elementary reactions. All of the elementary reactions in a mechanism must add up to the overall balanced equation. The complete sequence of steps is called a **reaction mechanism**.

Elementary reactions

In a mechanism, the **elementary reactions** usually involve the collision of only two reactant molecules. It is extremely rare that three molecules will collide simultaneously, and the simultaneous collision of more than three molecules is so infrequent that such collisions are hardly ever considered. Collisions between just two molecules, however, occur millions of times each second. Therefore, the most probable elementary reaction is one in which only two molecules collide. Another feature of the elementary reaction is that its **coefficients are the exponents** used in the rate law.

A sequence of elementary reactions will always have one step that is slower than all the rest. This slowest step determines the overall rate of reaction and is called the **rate-determining step** or the **rate-limiting step**. Since chemists can measure only the overall reaction rate in the laboratory, they are in fact measuring the rate of the slowest, rate-determining elementary reaction in the mechanism. Thus the rate law determined for a reaction is directly related to the rate-determining step.

Using these principles, chemists determine the rate law for a chemical reaction. They then postulate a series of elementary reactions based on the fact that one of the steps in the mechanism must obey the experimental rate law. When two or more mechanisms satisfy the rate law requirement, additional experiments must be done to decide which mechanism is correct.

To illustrate the procedure, we consider the reaction

$$H_2 \quad + \quad 2ICl \quad \rightarrow \quad I_2 \quad + \quad 2HCl \tag{11.31}$$

which has rate law

$$Rate \quad = \quad k\,[H_2]\,[ICl] \tag{11.32}$$

A two-step mechanism that satisfies this rate law is

$$H_2 \quad + \quad ICl \quad \rightarrow \quad HI \quad + \quad HCl \tag{11.33}$$

$$HI \quad + \quad ICl \quad \rightarrow \quad I_2 \quad + \quad HCl \tag{11.34}$$

The two steps in this mechanism, Equations 11.33 and 11.34, add up to the overall reaction. They also involve only two molecules as reactants in each elementary reaction. The rate law describes the first step of the mechanism, which is presumably the slow step. Chemists can easily demonstrate that the second step is a much faster reaction by reacting HI and ICl.

The HI in the above mechanism does not appear in the balanced equation, Equation 11.31. Any chemical species that is part of a mechanism but not of the balanced equation is called an **intermediate**. In this example, the intermediate HI is also a known compound that made possible the experimental verification of the mechanism. In other cases intermediates are very unstable and often exotic chemical species. Demonstrating the presence of an intermediate provides evidence to support one mechanism over another.

Considering the above example, we see that there is another mechanism that might also be considered. This is a three-step process:

$$H_2 \quad + \quad ICl \quad \rightarrow \quad HI \quad + \quad HCl \tag{11.35}$$

$$H_2 \quad + \quad ICl \quad \rightarrow \quad HI \quad + \quad HCl \tag{11.36}$$

$$2HI \quad \rightarrow \quad H_2 \quad + \quad I_2 \tag{11.37}$$

When added, these three reactions give the same overall reaction. To decide whether this mechanism is possible, scientists determined the rate of decomposition of the intermediate HI to H_2 and I_2 (the last step, Equation 11.37, in the mechanism). This reaction was found to be much slower than the reaction between H_2 and ICl. It was concluded that this is not the correct mechanism since the rate-determining step would give a completely different rate law.

From this description we can see that a kinetic study of a reaction will determine the rate law for the slowest step in the mechanism. Possible mechanisms are proposed, and the correct mechanism must have one step that obeys the observed rate law. If there are still several possible mechanisms, appropriate experiments must be devised to decide which mechanism is correct.

Determining Rate Laws for Elementary Reactions

The coefficients of the reactants in an elementary reaction are the exponents of the reactant concentrations in the rate law. Therefore the rate law for each step of a mechanism can be predicted directly. One complication is that, after the first step, most of the elementary reactions in a mechanism will have an intermediate as a reactant. To compare an experimental rate law with the rate laws of the elementary reactions, it will be necessary to convert the rate law that has an intermediate into one that has only reactants.

For example, the reaction

$$2NO \quad + \quad O_2 \quad \rightarrow \quad 2NO_2 \tag{11.38}$$

has a possible mechanism consisting of the two elementary reactions

$$NO \quad + \quad O_2 \quad \rightarrow \quad NO_3 \tag{11.39}$$

$$NO_3 \quad + \quad NO \quad \rightarrow \quad 2NO_2 \tag{11.40}$$

The rate law for the first step is

$$\text{Rate} \quad = \quad k[NO][O_2] \tag{11.41}$$

The rate law for the second step includes the intermediate NO_3:

$$\text{Rate} \quad = \quad k[NO_3][NO] \tag{11.42}$$

To eliminate the NO_3 and convert it into one of the reactants, we use the **steady-state assumption**, which says that, if the second step is the rate-determining step, the first reaction, Equation 11.39, must be relatively fast and reversible. This means that the rate at which NO_3 is formed is equal to the rate at which it disappears:

$$\text{NO}_3 \text{ rate formation} \quad = \quad \text{NO}_3 \text{ rate disappearance} \tag{11.43}$$

The rate laws governing the forward and reverse reactions in the first step are

$$\text{Rate}_{\text{forward}} = k_f\,[NO]\,[O_2] \qquad (11.44)$$

$$\text{Rate}_{\text{reverse}} = k_r\,[NO_3] \qquad (11.45)$$

Since the forward and reverse rates are equal, we can write

$$k_f\,[NO]\,[O_2] = k_r\,[NO_3] \qquad (11.46)$$

Solving for $[NO_3]$ gives

$$[NO]_3 = \frac{k_f}{k_r}\,[NO]\,[O_2] \qquad (11.47)$$

Substituting this result for the intermediate, NO_3, in the rate law gives

$$\text{Rate} = k\!\left(\frac{k_f}{k_r}\right)[NO]\,[O_2]\,[NO] \qquad (11.48)$$

Combining all of the k, k_f, and k_r rate constants, we can write the rate law for the second step of the mechanism:

$$\text{Rate} = k[NO]^2[O_2] \qquad (11.49)$$

Exercise 11.10

The kinetics of the following reaction is studied:

$$2NO + O_2 \rightarrow 2NO_2$$

Two possible mechanisms are

$$2NO \rightarrow N_2O_2$$
$$N_2O_2 + O_2 \rightarrow 2NO_2$$

and

$$NO + O_2 \rightarrow NO_3$$
$$NO_3 + NO \rightarrow 2NO_2$$

Describe the method you would use to determine which mechanism is correct.

Solution

The rate laws for each of these elementary reactions can be determined. For the first mechanism they are

$$\text{Rate}_1 = k\,[NO]^2$$

$$\text{Rate}_2 = k[N_2O_2]\,[O_2]$$

Using the steady-state assumption to obtain the rate law of the second elementary reaction in terms of measurable reactants, we obtain

$$k_f[NO]^2 \quad = \quad k_r\,[N_2O_2]$$

and the rate law will be

$$Rate_2 \quad = \quad k[NO]^2[O_2]$$

For the second mechanism the rate laws are

$$Rate_1 \quad = \quad k[NO]\,[O_2]$$
$$Rate_2 \quad = \quad k[NO]^2[O_2]$$

The second rate law was derived above.

We can see that, if the first step is the slow step, the two mechanisms give two distinctly different rate laws and the decision is clear cut. If the second step is the slow step, however, both mechanisms yield the same rate law. To determine which mechanism is correct, additional experiments must be designed to identify the intermediate, NO_3 or N_2O_2, that is formed during the reaction.

Rate Laws and Reverse Reactions

The rate law determined from initial concentrations describes the kinetic curves shown in Figures 11.1 and 11.2 as long as no other significant reactions are occurring. Since the concentrations of the reactants decrease as the reaction progresses, we expect the rate of reaction to decrease as the rates do in Figures 11.1 and 11.2.

At the same time as there is a decrease in the concentration of reactants, the increasing concentration of products may result in products reacting with each other to make more reactants. This reverse reaction also slows the reaction rate. The rate law for the forward reaction

$$A \quad + \quad B \quad \rightarrow \quad C \quad + \quad D \tag{11.50}$$

is

$$Rate_f \quad = \quad k_f[A]^x[B]^y \tag{11.51}$$

where the subscript f indicates the forward reaction.

When products C and D react to form the original reactants, the reverse reaction

$$C \quad + \quad D \quad \rightarrow \quad A \quad + \quad B \tag{11.52}$$

occurs. Its rate law is written as

$$Rate_r \quad = \quad k_r[C]^z[D]^w \tag{11.53}$$

The overall rate of this reaction is

$$Rate_{overall} \quad = \quad Rate_f \quad - \quad Rate_r \tag{11.54}$$

$$Rate_{overall} \quad = \quad k_f[A]^x[B]^y \quad - \quad k_r[C]^z[D]^w \tag{11.55}$$

Equation 11.55 indicates that, as products C and D increase in concentration, the reaction rate will decrease. Chemists use initial reaction rates to determine rate laws in order to avoid the errors that a reverse reaction may introduce into the results.

Chemical Equilibrium

When a chemical reaction stops, there are two possibilities. One is that the reaction goes all the way to completion, and the reaction stops because the limiting reactant is used up. The other is that the reaction comes to chemical equilibrium. Chemical equilibrium may be viewed as a situation where the overall rate is zero and therefore the forward and reverse rates are equal:

$$Rate_{overall} \quad = \quad 0 \tag{11.56}$$

and

$$Rate_f \quad = \quad Rate_r \tag{11.57}$$

If the two rates are equal, then, using the individual rate laws, we can write the relationship as

$$k_f[A]^x[B]^y \quad = \quad k_r[C]^z[D]^w \tag{11.58}$$

Rearranging this equation so the constants are all on the same side gives

$$\frac{k_f}{k_r} \quad = \quad \frac{[C]^z[D]^w}{[A]^x[B]^y} \tag{11.59}$$

Equation 11.59 is known as the equilibrium law. The left side is the ratio of two constants, which are combined into the equilibrium constant, K_{eq}. The right-hand side is the ratio of the concentrations of the products divided by the concentrations of the reactants.

This derivation of the equilibrium constant clearly shows the nature of chemical equilibrium as a dynamic equilibrium. Reaction is constantly occurring in both the forward and the reverse direction at a tremendous rate. Since the rates are equal, no change is observed in the concentrations of the reactants and products at equilibrium.

It was emphasized previously that the exponents in the rate law are not necessarily equal to the coefficients in the chemical reaction except for elementary reactions. In Chapter 10, it was shown that in the equilibrium law the exponents are the coefficients present in the balanced chemical equation. Equation 11.59 seems to indicate that the exponents of the rate law should be equal to the reaction coefficients. The answer to this seeming inconsistency lies in a detailed understanding of reaction mechanisms, which is beyond the scope of this book. Here we simply state that both principles are true; the reaction coefficients are the exponents in the equilibrium law but are not necessarily the exponents in the rate laws.

It is important to realize that, although Equation 11.59 shows a relationship between rate constants and the equilibrium constant, a single rate constant indicates nothing about the equilibrium constant. Similarly, since the equilibrium constant is a ratio of rate constants, it indicates only the relative sizes of the forward and reverse rate constants. The equilibrium constant tells us nothing about the actual reaction rate.

Important Concepts

Reaction rates
Rate laws
Order of reaction
Half-lives
Collision theory
Transition-state theory and reaction profiles
Arrhenius equation

Important Equations

$Rate = k[A]^x[B]^y \dots$

$t_{1/2} = 0.693/k$

$\ln\left(\dfrac{[A_0]}{[A_t]}\right) = kt$ for a first-order reaction

$\ln\left(\dfrac{k_1}{k_2}\right) = \dfrac{-E_a}{R}\left(\dfrac{1}{T_1} - \dfrac{1}{T_2}\right)$

Questions on Chapter 11

1. The activated complex may be described as
   (A) an elementary reaction in a mechanism
   (B) the shape of the molecules at the moment of collision
   (C) the shape of the reaction product
   (D) the phase—liquid, solid, or gas—in which a reaction takes place
   (E) the transition state

2. A reaction in which the rate and the rate constant have the same units is
   (A) a radioactive decay
   (B) a second-order reaction
   (C) a reaction with a one-step mechanism
   (D) a first-order reaction
   (E) a zero-order reaction

Questions 3–5 refer to the following diagram:

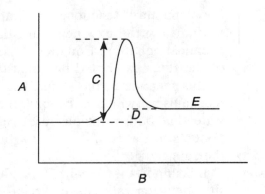

3. In the reaction profile, A, B, and C should be labeled as shown in

	A	B	C
(A)	potential energy	reaction coordinate	activation energy
(B)	heat of reaction	reaction coordinate	potential energy
(C)	potential energy	reaction coordinate	heat of reaction
(D)	heat of reaction	potential energy	activation energy
(E)	activation energy	extent of reaction	heat of reaction

4. In the reaction described by the reaction profile,
   (A) forward E_a > reverse E_a and ΔH is exothermic
   (B) reverse E_a > forward E_a and ΔH is endothermic
   (C) forward E_a < reverse E_a and ΔH is exothermic
   (D) reverse E_a < forward E_a and ΔH is endothermic
   (E) reverse E_a = forward E_a and ΔH is zero

5. Addition of a catalyst to the reaction mixture will affect only
   (A) A
   (B) B
   (C) C
   (D) D
   (E) E

6. A fast reaction should have
   (A) a high activation energy
   (B) a catalyst present
   (C) a large equilibrium constant
   (D) a low activation energy
   (E) an exothermic heat of reaction

7. Which of the following rate laws has a rate constant with units of L^2 mol^{-2} s^{-1}?
   (A) Rate = k [A]
   (B) Rate = k [A]^2
   (C) Rate = k [A] [B]
   (D) Rate = k [A][B]^2
   (E) Rate = k [A]^0

8. Which of the following is LEAST effective in increasing the rate of a reaction?
   (A) increasing the pressure by adding an inert gas
   (B) grinding a solid reactant into small particles
   (C) increasing the temperature
   (D) eliminating reverse reactions
   (E) adding a catalyst

9. A first-order reaction has a half-life of 36 min. What is the value of the rate constant?
   (A) 3.2×10^{-4} s^{-1}
   (B) 1.9×10^{-3} L mol^{-1} s^{-1}
   (C) 1.2 s^{-1}
   (D) 0.028 s^{-1}
   (E) 9.3×10^{-4} L mol^{-1}s^{-1}

10. If a reactant's concentration is doubled and the reaction rate increases by a factor of 8, the exponent for that reactant in the rate law should be.
    (A) 0
    (B) 1
    (C) 2
    (D) 3
    (E) ½

11. If the temperature of a reaction is raised from 300 K to 320 K, the reaction rate will increase by a factor of approximately
    (A) $\dfrac{320 \text{ K}}{300 \text{ K}}$
    (B) $\dfrac{22°\text{C}}{2°\text{C}}$
    (C) 4
    (D) 2
    (E) 20

12. A graph of the reciprocal of reactant concentration versus time will give a straight line for
    (A) a zero-order reaction
    (B) a first-order reaction
    (C) a second-order reaction
    (D) both A and C
    (E) A, B, and C

13. The rate at which CO_2 is produced in the following reaction:

    $$2C_6H_6(g) \quad + \quad 15O_2(g) \quad \rightarrow \quad 12CO_2(g) \quad + \quad 6H_2O(\ell)$$

    is 2.2×10^{-2} mol L^{-1}s^{-1}. What is the rate at which O_2 is consumed?
    (A) 2.2×10^{-2} mol L^{-1}s^{-1}
    (B) 1.3×10^{-1} mol L^{-1}s^{-1}

(C) 2.8×10^{-2} mol L^{-1}s^{-1}
(D) 1.8×10^{-3} mol L^{-1}s^{-1}
(E) -2.2×10^{-2} mol L^{-1}s^{-1}

14. Which of the following will be most helpful in determining the shelf life of an new drug?
(A) the reaction mechanism for its decomposition
(B) the rate law for its decomposition
(C) the Arrhenius plot of the decomposition reaction
(D) the integrated rate law plot
(E) the overall chemical reaction

15. An Arrhenius plot is a graph of
(A) the rate constant versus concentration
(B) the natural logarithm (ln) of the rate constant versus concentration
(C) the reciprocal of the rate constant versus ln T
(D) the rate constant versus ln $\dfrac{1}{T}$

(E) the natural logarithm (ln) of the rate constant versus $\dfrac{1}{T}$

16. A first-order reaction has a half-life of 85 s. What fraction of the reactant is left after 255 s?
(A) ½
(B) ¼
(C) ⅛
(D) ⅓
(E) ⅞

17. A rate law is found to be

$$\text{Rate} = k[A]^2[B]$$

The order of the reaction is
(A) first order
(B) second order
(C) third order
(D) fourth order
(E) The rate order cannot be determined.

18. A rate law is found to be

$$\text{Rate} = k[A]^2[B]$$

Which of the following actions will NOT change the initial reaction rate?
(A) doubling the concentrations of both A and B
(B) doubling the concentration of A and halving the concentration of B

(C) halving the concentration of A and doubling the concentration of B
(D) halving the concentration of A and quadrupling the concentration of B
(E) doubling the concentration of A and quadrupling the concentration of B

19. Using the rule of thumb that the reaction rate doubles for each 10°C increase in temperature, estimate the shelf life of a new product at 25°C if it takes 2 days to decompose at 125 °C.
   (A) 2048 days
   (B) 20 days
   (C) 200 days
   (D) 11585 days
   (E) 365 days

20. Modern automobiles use a catalytic converter to
   (A) increase horsepower by burning more gasoline
   (B) absorb pollutants from the exhaust
   (C) complete the combustion of unburned gases
   (D) cool the exhaust gases
   (E) convert pollutants into water

Answer Key

See Appendix I for explanations of answers.

1. **B**	5. **C**	9. **A**	13. **C**	17. **C**
2. **E**	6. **D**	10. **D**	14. **C**	18. **D**
3. **A**	7. **D**	11. **C**	15. **E**	19. **A**
4. **D**	8. **A**	12. **C**	16. **C**	20. **C**

CHAPTER TWELVE
Thermodynamics

Thermodynamics is a field of study aimed at understanding energy and the energy changes that occur during chemical reactions or physical changes. The unifying principle in this chapter is that energy changes govern whether or not chemical changes occur. Energy changes also define the extent to which reactants are converted into products. To reach these conclusions it is necessary to have a very thorough understanding of the properties of energy in all forms.

Essential Definitions

In the discussion of thermodynamics precise terminology is used to avoid confusion and to ensure that experimental results may be compared from one laboratory to another. Some of the important terms defined in this chapter are *system*, *state function*, *standard state*, and the *exo-* and *endo-* prefixes.

System

A **system** is that part of the universe that is under study. Everything else in the universe is called the **surroundings**. When hydrogen and oxygen are placed in a bomb calorimeter to study the formation of water, all of the hydrogen and oxygen atoms and the calorimeter are the system. The surrounding laboratory, the building, the city, and so on are parts of the surroundings.

There are several types of systems. An **open system** can transfer both energy and matter to and from the surroundings. An open bottle of perfume is an example of an open system. A **closed system** is one where energy can be transferred to the surroundings but matter cannot. A well-stoppered bottle of perfume is a closed system. In an **isolated system** there is no transfer of energy or matter to or from the surroundings. A thermos bottle is almost a closed system since it minimizes heat transfer to the surroundings. Calorimeters are designed to be as close as possible to a closed system.

State Function

In this chapter we will encounter enthalpy change, ΔH; entropy change, ΔS; free-energy change, ΔG; and energy change, ΔE. The numerical values and mathematical signs of these **state functions** depend only on the difference between the final state and the initial state of the system.

The state of a system is defined by the mass and phase (solid, liquid, or gas) of the matter in the system, as well as the temperature and pressure of the system. For the melting of 1 mole of ice, the initial state is described as 18 g $H_2O(s)$ at 1.00 atm pressure and 273 K, and the final state as 18 g

$H_2O(\ell)$ at 1.00 atm pressure and 273 K. With this precise description all scientists should, within experimental error, obtain identical values of ΔH, ΔS, ΔG, and ΔE for the melting of ice.

Two quantities that are *not* state functions are heat (q) and work (w). The values for these quantities depend on the sequence of steps used to transform matter from the initial state to the final state.

Standard State

The thermodynamic quantities ΔH, ΔS, ΔG, and ΔE are **extensive properties** of matter, meaning that they change as the amount of sample changes. To make these quantities **intensive properties** of matter, we must define precisely the temperature, pressure, mass, and physical state of the substance. A system is in the **standard state** when the pressure is 1 atmosphere, the temperature is 25°C, and 1 mole of compound is present. When the thermodynamic quantities are determined at standard state, they are intensive properties and a superscript 0 is added to their symbols: as ΔH^0, ΔS^0, ΔG^0 and ΔE^0. For a chemical reaction, the standard state involves the number of moles designated by the stoichiometric coefficients in the simplest balanced chemical equation.

Exo- and Endo- Prefixes and Sign Conventions

The prefix *exo-*, as in *exothermic*, indicates that energy is being lost from the system to the surroundings. Mathematically, the prefix *exo-* corresponds to a negative sign for numerical thermodynamic quantities. For an exothermic reaction the heat of reaction, ΔH, is a negative number.

The prefix *endo-* indicates that energy is gained from the surroundings. An *endothermic* reaction absorbs heat energy and appears to cool as it progresses. For an endothermic reaction the heat of reaction, ΔH, is a positive number.

Types of Energy

Energy takes many forms. Heat and light, along with chemical, nuclear, electrical, and mechanical energy, are some of the common types. Any one of these forms of energy can be converted into any of the other forms. In addition, the **law of conservation of energy** states that energy is never created or destroyed. As a result of these properties, all forms of energy can be converted into heat energy, which we can measure in a calorimeter as described below.

Energy can also be categorized as either kinetic energy, KE, or potential energy, PE. **Kinetic energy** is the energy that matter possesses because of its motion. There is one equation to describe kinetic energy:

$$\text{KE} \quad = \quad \tfrac{1}{2}m\,v^2 \tag{12.1}$$

When the mass, m, is expressed in kilograms and the velocity, v, in meters per second, the energy units are joules.

Potential energy is stored energy, which may be released under the appropriate conditions, as in a nuclear reaction. There are several forms of potential energy, such as **gravitational energy** and the energy of **electro-**

static attraction between oppositely charged ions. Each form of potential energy is described by its own equation, but these equations are similar to each other. They all have the forms

$$\text{PE}_{\text{grav}} = K_{\text{grav}}\left(\frac{m_1 m_2}{r}\right) \quad \text{and} \quad \text{PE}_{\text{elect}} = K_{\text{elect}}\left(\frac{q_1 q_2}{r}\right) \quad (12.2)$$

The two masses, m, in gravitational attraction and the two charges, q, in electrostatic attraction are separated by a distance, r. K is a proportionality constant that is different for each type of potential energy.

The total energy of a substance is the sum of its kinetic and potential energies.

$$\text{Energy } (E) = \text{Potential energy (PE)} + \text{Kinetic energy (KE)} \quad (12.3)$$

In chemical substances, the kinetic energy is the motion of the molecules. The potential energy of a chemical is the sum of all attractions, including all the covalent bonds, ionic bonds, or electrostatic attractions in the substance.

Measurement of Energy

Heat is often called the "lowest form" of energy. In this form it is easily measurable by determining temperature changes caused by the release or absorbtion of heat in a chemical process.

Specific Heat

Heat energy was originally defined in terms of the calorie, which is the amount of heat needed to raise the temperature of 1 gram of pure water from 14.5 to 15.5°C. The joule is the metric unit for energy; 1 calorie is equal to exactly 4.184 joules. By virtue of these definitions, 4.184 joules of energy is needed to raise the temperature of 1 gram of water by 1 degree Celsius. This quantity is known as the **specific heat** of water:

$$\text{Specific heat of water} = 4.184 \text{ J g}^{-1}{}^{\circ}\text{C}^{-1} \quad (12.4)$$

Once the specific heat of water is defined, the specific heat of any other substance can be determined. One method is to immerse a hot object in a known quantity of water and then measure the temperature change that occurs. This method is illustrated in Exercise 12.1.

As an interesting sidelight, in 1818 Pierre Dulong and A.T. Petit discovered that for most metals the specific heat multiplied by the atomic mass of the metal was equal to a constant. The **law of Dulong and Petit** is as follows:

$$\text{Specific heat} \times \text{Molar mass} = 25 \text{ J mol}^{-1}{}^{\circ}\text{C}^{-1} \quad (12.5)$$

This law helped confirm the molar masses of the elements when disagreements occurred. In addition, specific heat is an intensive physical property of all elements and compounds and can be used to identify substances. 12.6

Equation ~~12.4~~ enables chemists to determine the heat energy of any process by measuring the change in temperature of a known mass of water. The equation is as follows:

Heat energy $\quad = \quad$ (Specific heat) (Mass) (Temperature change)

$$q \quad = \quad \text{sp. ht.} \quad \times \quad g \quad \times \quad \Delta T \qquad (12.6)$$

In this equation q, the heat energy, is expressed in joules. The temperature change is always determined as the final temperature minus the initial temperature ($°C_{final} - °C_{initial}$). Equation 12.6 is applicable to any substance, not just water.

There is a distinct difference between heat energy and temperature, as Equation 12.6 indicates. Temperature is a measure of the average kinetic energy of a group of atoms, and a temperature change is a change in the average kinetic energy. Heat energy is produced when both the kinetic energy and the energy of attractions between the atoms in the group change in a chemical process.

Exercise 12.1

An insulated cup contains 75.0 g of water at 24.00°C. A 26.00-g sample of a metal at 85.25°C is added. The final temperature of the water and metal is 28.34°C.
(a) What is the specific heat of the metal?
(b) According to the law of Dulong and Petit, what is the approximate molar mass, M, of the metal?
(c) What is the apparent identity of the metal?

Solution

(a) The law of conservation of energy requires that the heat energy gained by the water be exactly equal to the heat energy lost by the metal as it cools in the water. Mathematically this is written as

$$+q_{water} \quad = \quad -q_{metal}$$

Using Equation 12.6, we expand this equation:

$$(\text{sp. heat}_{H_2O})(\text{g } H_2O)(\Delta T_{water}) \quad = \quad -(\text{sp. heat}_{metal})(\text{g metal})(\Delta T_{metal})$$

Entering the data yields

$$4.184 \text{ J g}^{-1} °C^{-1}(75.0 \text{ g})(4.34°C) \quad = \quad -(\text{sp. heat}_{metal})(26.00 \text{ g})(-56.91°C)$$

$$1362 \text{ J} \quad = \quad 1480 \text{ g } °C(\text{sp. heat}_{metal})$$

$$\text{sp. heat}_{metal} \quad = \quad 0.920 \text{ J g}^{-1} °C^{-1}$$

(b) Using Equation 12.5 for the law of Dulong and Petit we obtain

$$0.920 \text{ J g}^{-1}°C^{-1}(\text{molar mass}) \quad = \quad 25 \text{ J mol}^{-1} °C^{-1}$$

$$\text{molar mass} \quad = \quad 27 \text{ g mol}^{-1}$$

(c) Aluminum is the only metal with a molar mass of 27 g mol^{-1}.

Calorimeters and
Heat
Measurements

A **calorimeter** is the device used for measuring the heat energy produced by chemical reactions and physical changes. Figure 12.1 illustrates the design features of a calorimeter. The reaction vessel, usually made of metal, efficiently transfers heat to the rest of the apparatus, which includes a large mass of water in an insulated container that prevents heat from being lost to the surroundings. Also included are a stirrer and a very accurate thermometer. All parts of the calorimeter heat up or cool down as heat is released or absorbed in the chemical process. Water is the major part of the system; however, for the most accurate measurements the specific heats and masses of the reaction vessel, the thermometer, the stirrer, and the container itself must be included in the calculation.

The total **heat capacity**, C, of the calorimeter, sometimes called the calorimeter constant, is defined as the sum of the products of the specific heat and the mass of all components of the calorimeter:

$$C \, (\text{J} \, {}^\circ\text{C}^{-1}) \quad = \quad (\text{sp. ht.})_1 (\text{mass})_1 \quad + \quad (\text{sp. ht.})_2 (\text{mass})_2$$
$$+ \quad (\text{sp. ht.})_3 (\text{mass})_3 \quad + \ldots \quad (12.7)$$

The heat energy produced in the calorimeter is then calculated as

$$q \quad = \quad C \, ({}^\circ\text{C}_{\text{final}} - {}^\circ\text{C}_{\text{initial}}) \tag{12.8}$$

where C replaces the (sp. ht $\times$ g) terms in Equation 12.6.

The most convenient method for determining the heat capacity, C, of a calorimeter is to calibrate the device, using a reaction that will produce a known amount of heat, and then calculate C from the observed temperature change using Equation 12.8.

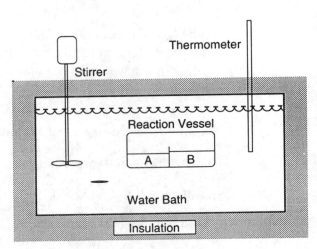

FIGURE 12.1. Diagram of a calorimeter and its essential components. Reactant A and B may be mixed by rotating the reaction vessel. In a bomb calorimeter the reaction vessel is filled with reactant and O_2, which are then ignited with an electric spark.

Exercise 12.2

A calorimeter has a heat capacity of 1265 J $°C^{-1}$. A reaction causes the temperature of the calorimeter to change from 22.34°C to 25.12°C. How many joules of heat were released in this process?

Solution

The heat released in a calorimeter is given in Equation 12.8. We calculate ΔT as $25.12 - 22.34 = +2.78°C$. Entering these data into the equation gives

$$q = 1265 \text{ J } °C^{-1} (2.78°C)$$

$$= 3517 \text{ J of heat energy is released}$$

First Law of Thermodynamics

The **first law of thermodynamics** states that energy is always conserved. In chemistry this law means that the measurable quantities heat (q) and work (w) must add up to the total energy change in a system:

$$\Delta E = q + w \tag{12.9}$$

The value of q has a positive sign if heat is added to the system. The value of w is positive if work is done on the system. Similarly, q is a negative value if heat is released from the system, and w is a negative value if work is done by the system.

If the system cools, q has a positive sign and the process is said to be endothermic. If the system heats up, it is exothermic and q has a negative sign. As we will see later, work is equal to the pressure times the change in volume, $P \Delta V$. If the volume increases, work is done by the system and w has a negative sign. When work is done on the system, the volume decreases and w has a positive sign.

The change in energy of a system, at constant temperature, is also the difference in potential energy between the final and initial states of the system:

$$\Delta E = PE_{final} - PE_{initial} \tag{12.10}$$

As we will see later, ΔE is mainly heat energy. Therefore a system that increases its potential energy is often said to be endothermic, while a decrease in potential energy indicates an exothermic process.

Work

In Equation 12.9 the energy change is the sum of the heat and the work. Heat is measured using a calorimeter, and work is also easily measured. **Work** is defined as the force applied to an object as it moves a certain distance:

$$\text{Work} = \text{Force} \times \text{Distance moved} \tag{12.11}$$

Force can be defined as the pressure exerted over a given area, so

$$\text{Work} = \text{Pressure} \times \text{Area} \times \text{Distance moved}$$

Multiplying the area by the distance results in volume units or an overall volume change:

$$\text{Work} = \text{Pressure} \times \text{Volume change}$$

$$w = P \Delta V \tag{12.12}$$

Work is the product of the pressure and the change in volume that occurs during a chemical reaction.

Exercise 12.3

Demonstrate that work is not a state function by calculating the work involved in expanding a gas from an initial state of 1.00 L and 10.0 atm of pressure to (a) 10.0 L and 1.0 atm pressure, (b) 5.00 L and 2.00 atm and then to 10.0 L and 1.00 atm pressure.

Solution

(a) $w = -P \Delta V = -(1.00 \text{ atm})(10.0 \text{ L} - 1.00 \text{ L}) = -9.00 \text{ L atm}$
(b) $w = -P \Delta V = -(2.00 \text{ atm})(5.0 \text{ L} - 1.00 \text{ L})$
$\quad - (1.00 \text{ atm})(0.0 \text{ L} - 5.00 \text{ L}) = -13.0 \text{ L atm}$

In both parts of this exercise the sample starts at the same state (1.00 L and 10.0 atm) and ends in the same state (10.0 L and 1.00 atm). However, the work in units of liter atmospheres is different. This can occur only if w is not a state function.

Definition of q_p, q_v, ΔE, and ΔH

The first law of thermodynamics may be rewritten as

$$\Delta E = q_p - P \Delta V \qquad (12.13)$$

The minus sign enters this equation because an increase in volume means that the system does work on the surroundings, and such work has been defined as a negative quantity. The heat term, q, is given the subscript p indicate that the pressure must be constant.

When the heat energy is measured in a calorimeter that does not allow the volume to change, $P \Delta V$ must be zero. As a result $\Delta E = q_v$, where the subscript v indicates that the volume is held constant. Calorimeters that do not allow the volume to change are called **bomb calorimeters**, a name derived from the heavy stainless steel reaction vessel, which was known to explode if not used correctly.

For most real reactions chemists are interested in the heat generated at constant pressure, q_p. This variable is called the enthalpy change and is given the symbol ΔH. **Enthalpy**, H, is the heat content of a chemical, and ΔH is the difference in heat content of the products and reactants:

$$\Delta H = H_{\text{products}} - H_{\text{reactants}} \qquad (12.14)$$

Using Equations 12.9 and 12.12, we can write the relationship between ΔE and ΔH is

$$\Delta E = \Delta H - P \Delta V \qquad (12.15)$$

For many reactions, the value of ΔH is very large and the value of $P \Delta V$ is relatively small, so that ΔE and ΔH are approximately equal.

Standard Enthalpy Changes and the Standard Heat of Reaction, ΔH^0

The heat energy or enthalpy change, ΔH, produced by a chemical reaction is an **extensive property**, since reacting a larger amount of chemicals produces a larger amount of heat. For example, when propane is burned according to the equation

$$CH_3CH_2CH_3(g) + 5O_2(g) \rightarrow 3CO_2(g) + 4H_2O(g) \qquad (12.16)$$

more heat is generated as more propane is burned. To make the heat produced by a reaction an **intensive property**, the amount of chemical that reacts must be specified. The standard heat of a reaction, ΔH^0, is generally defined as the heat produced when the number of moles specified in the balanced chemical equation reacts. For the reaction of propane the heat of reaction, ΔH^0_{react}, equals $-2{,}044$ kJ when 1 mole of propane reacts with 5 moles of oxygen as shown in Equation 12.16. The negative sign indicates that a large amount of heat is released in this reaction, making propane an excellent fuel for cooking.

Hess's Law

Hess's law states that, whatever mathematical operations are performed on a chemical reaction, the same mathematical operations are applied also to the heat of reaction. Hess's law is summarized as follows:

1. If the coefficients of a chemical reaction are all multiplied by a constant, the ΔH^0_{react} is multiplied by that same constant.
2. If two or more reactions are added together to obtain an overall reaction, the heats of these reactions are also added to give the heat of the overall reaction.

Hess's law allows the chemist to measure ΔH^0_{react} for several reactions and then to combine the reactions and their heats to obtain ΔH^0_{react} for a completely different reaction.

For example, we saw above that the burning of propane produces a large amount of heat. The reaction in Equation 12.16 is easy to perform by igniting propane in the presence of oxygen. The reverse reaction for the synthesis of 1 mole of propane from carbon dioxide and water is impossible to perform, but it may be written as

$$3CO_2(g) + 4H_2O(g) \rightarrow CH_3CH_2CH_3(g) + 5O_2(g) \qquad (12.17)$$

Since reversing a reaction is the same as multiplying it by -1, the heat needed for this reaction is $+2{,}044$ kJ. The change from a negative to positive value is explained on the basis that ΔH^0, which is a state function, depends only on the final and initial states of the system. Synthesis of 1 mole of propane has the same final and initial states as the combustion of 1 mole of propane. The only difference is the direction of the process. We must reach the conclusion that ΔH^0 has the same magnitude for these two reactions, but they have different signs because they go in opposite directions. Figure 12.2 illustrates this process.

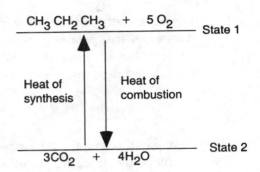

FIGURE 12.2 Diagram illustrating that the heat of a reaction has the same magnitude whether the reaction is run in the forward or reverse direction. The sign of the heat of reaction, however, is positive in one direction and negative in the other.

The general principle that $\Delta H^0_{\text{forward react}} = -\Delta H^0_{\text{reverse react}}$ is an essential part of Hess's law.

For the combustion of propane, Hess's first rule (page 339) tells us that multiplying the reaction by 2 will result in ΔH^0 also being multiplied by 2:

$$2CH_3CH_2CH_3(g) + 10O_2(g) \rightarrow 6CO_2(g) + 8H_2O(g) \quad \Delta H = 4,088 \text{ kJ}$$

If the reaction is multiplied by ½, the ΔH^0 will also be multiplied by ½.

$$\tfrac{1}{2}CH_3CH_2CH_3(g) + 2.5O_2(g) \rightarrow 1.5CO_2(g) + 2H_2O(g) \quad \Delta H = -1,011 \text{ kJ}$$

If the reaction is multiplied by 6, the ΔH^0 will also be multiplied by 6

$$6CH_3CH_2CH_3(g) + 30O_2(g) \rightarrow 18CO_2(g) + 24H_2O(g) \quad \Delta H = -12,264 \text{ kJ}$$

Once ΔH^0 is multiplied by any coefficient, the system is no longer standard state and the superscript zero is dropped as shown.

The second of Hess's rules concerns the addition of chemical reactions. To repeat, when chemical reactions are added, all of the reactants are written as reactants of the overall reaction. All of the products are combined as products of the overall reaction. The last step in adding reactions is the cancellation of any identical reactants and products in the overall reaction.

To add the two reactions below, the reactants and products in Equations 12.18 and 12.19 are combined in an overall reaction, 12.20:

$$N_2(g) + O_2(g) \rightarrow 2NO(g) \quad (12.18)$$

$$2NO(g) + O_2(g) \rightarrow 2NO_2(g) \quad (12.19)$$

$$N_2(g) + 2NO(g) + 2O_2(g) \rightarrow 2NO(g) + 2NO_2(g) \quad (12.20)$$

Two molecules of NO(g) are canceled from both the reactant and product sides of Equation 12.20 to obtain the overall reaction:

$$N_2(g) \quad + \quad 2O_2(g) \quad \rightarrow \quad 2NO_2(g) \tag{12.21}$$

Since the two reactions were added, their heats of reaction are also added:

$N_2(g)$	+	$O_2(g)$	$\rightarrow$	$2NO(g)$	ΔH_1^0	= +180.5 kJ
$2NO(g)$	+	$O2(g)$	$\rightarrow$	$2NO_2(g)$	ΔH_2^0	= −114.1 kJ

$$N_2(g) \quad + \quad 2O_2(g) \quad \rightarrow \quad 2NO_2(g) \qquad \Delta H_{overall}^0 = +66.4 \text{ kJ}$$

In this example $\Delta H_1^0 + \Delta H_2^0 = \Delta H_{overall}^0$.

The heats of many reactions can be determined if the heats of combustion are known for each of the reactants and products. To illustrate this more complex combination of reactions, we can determine the heat of reaction for the synthesis of propane from carbon and hydrogen:

$$3C(s) \quad + \quad 4H_2(g) \quad \rightarrow \quad CH_3CH_2CH_3(g) \tag{12.22}$$

from the combustion reactions of propane, hydrogen, and carbon. These reactions, along with their ΔH^0 values, are as follows:

(1) $CH_3CH_2CH_3(g) + 5O_2(g) \rightarrow 3CO_2(g) + 4H_2O(g)$ $\qquad \Delta H_1^0 = -2{,}044 \text{ kJ}$

(2) $2H_2(g) \qquad\qquad + O_2(g) \rightarrow 2H_2O(g)$ $\qquad\qquad\qquad \Delta H_2^0 = -483.6 \text{ kJ}$

(3) $C(s) \qquad\qquad\quad + O_2(g) \rightarrow CO_2(g)$ $\qquad\qquad\qquad\quad \Delta H_3^0 = -393.5 \text{ kJ}$

If it is not immediately obvious how these three equations should be combined, some general principles on how to approach the problem logically are helpful. In the list below, the first three principles tell us how to find which equation to start with. Once Equation 1 is established, the same principles are used to select and manipulate the remaining reactions. If needed, the fourth principle may be used.

1. Focus on the most complex molecules first.
2. Focus only on atoms and molecules that occur in just one reaction.
3. Focus on atoms and molecules that are in the overall equation.
4. Focus on finding atoms and molecules to cancel unneeded ones from already selected equations.

Using principles 1-3, we see that the combustion of propane in Equation 1 should be considered first. This equation contains 1 mole of propane and so does the overall equation, Equation 12.22. However, in the combustion reaction Equation 1, propane is a reactant and in Equation 12.22 it is a product. Consequently, Equation 1 must be reversed by multiplying it by −1. This reverses the equation and at the same time changes the sign of ΔH^0:

$$3CO_2(g) + 4H_2O(g) \rightarrow CH_3CH_2CH_3(g) + 5O_2(g) \qquad \Delta H^0 = -2{,}044 \text{ kJ} \times (-1)$$

Using principle 3, we now focus on the reaction in Equation 2 and note that it includes 2 $H_2(g)$ and that we need 4 $H_2(g)$ in our overall equation. The hydrogens are reactants in both Equation 2 and Equation 12.22, but Equation 2 must be multiplied by 2 so that we have the correct number of H_2 in the final reaction. We will also have to multiply ΔH^0 by 2:

$$4H_2(g) \quad + \quad 2O_2(g) \quad \rightarrow \quad 4H_2O(g) \quad \Delta H \quad = \quad -483.6 \text{ kJ} \times 2$$

To demonstrate the use of principle 4, we see that the remaining reaction, Equation 3, contains one $CO_2(g)$ as a product. We need to cancel three $CO_2(g)$ molecules from the already selected equations. Since $CO_2(g)$ is a product in Equation 3 and a reactant in the rearranged Equation 3, the CO_2's will cancel when the reactions are added. However, Equation 3 must be multiplied by 3 so that all three $CO_2(g)$ molecules will cancel:

$$3C(s) \quad + \quad 3O_2(g) \quad \rightarrow \quad 3CO_2(g) \quad \Delta H \quad = \quad 2393.5 \text{ kJ} \times 3$$

Adding the three equations gives us

$$3C(s) + 3O_2(g) + \; +4H_2(g) + 3O_2(g) + 3CO_2(g) \; + 4H_2O(g)$$
$$\rightarrow 3CO_2(g) + 4H_2O(g) + 5O_2(g) + CH_3CH_2CH_3(g)$$

After canceling the three $CO_2(g)$, four $H_2O(g)$ and five $O_2(g)$ molecules the equation becomes

$$3C(s) \quad + \quad 4H_2(g) \quad \rightarrow \quad CH_3CH_2CH_3(g) \qquad (12.23)$$

The heat of reaction is the sum of the three ΔH^0 values multiplied by the operations performed:

$$
\begin{aligned}
\Delta H^0_{overall} &= \Delta H^0_1 \times (-1) &+ \quad \Delta H^0_2 \times 2 &+ \quad \Delta H^0_3 \times 3 \\
&= -2044 \text{ kJ} \times (-1) &+ \quad -483.6 \text{ kJ} \times 2 &+ \quad -393.5 \text{ kJ} \times 3 \\
&= +2044 \text{ kJ} &- \quad 967.2 \text{ kJ} &- \quad 1180.5 \text{ kJ} \\
&= -103.7 \text{ kJ}
\end{aligned}
$$

The advantage of being able to perform some simple experiments to obtain data for complex, even impossible reactions was recognized very quickly. During the energy crisis of the 1970's, the feasibility of producing alternative fuels was determined from thermochemical calculations.

Exercise 12.4

We may wish to synthesize methane from carbon and hydrogen:

$$C(s) \quad + \quad 2H_2(g) \quad \rightarrow \quad CH_4(g)$$

In terms of the heat energy needed for this reaction and the heat of combustion for methane, is this effort worthwhile? The heats of combustion are as follows: $CH_4 = -890.3$ kJ; $H_2 = -571.8$ kJ, and $C = -393.5$ k

Solution

The three combustion reactions are written as

$$CH_4(g) + 2O_2(g) \rightarrow CO_2(g) + 2H_2O(l) \quad \Delta H = -890.3 \text{ kJ}$$

$$2H_2(g) + O_2(g) \rightarrow 2H_2O(l) \quad \Delta H = -571.8 \text{ kJ}$$

$$C(s) + O_2(g) \rightarrow CO_2(g) \quad \Delta H = -393.5 \text{ kJ}$$

To obtain the desired reaction we need to reverse the combustion of methane and add it to the remaining reactions. The heat of this reaction is

$$\Delta H^0_{react} = -890.3 \text{ kJ}(-1) + -571.8 \text{ kJ} + -393.5 \text{ kJ}$$
$$= -75.0 \text{ kJ}$$

Ignoring all other factors, we see that the formation of CH_4 produces heat and its combustion produces a much greater amount of heat. On this basis, the synthesis of CH_4 is a feasible process. If, however, the energy required to make $H_2(g)$ from water is included in the calculation, the energy gain is very small and the investment in such a project may be suspect.

In this reaction, methane is formed from the elements carbon and hydrogen. This is known as a formation reaction, and we have determined the heat of formation.

Formation
Reactions and
Heats of
Formation

In the preceding section we saw that the heats of many chemical reactions can be determined if the heats of combustion of all reactants and products are known. For other types of reactions the heat of combustion can also be tabulated. Such a table would be very long and complex, however, and finding the appropriate reactions to combine would be a monumental task. **Heats of formation** allow chemists to tabulate thermochemical data in a short, easy-to-use format.

A **formation reaction** is defined as one in which the reactants are elements in their standard state at 25°C and 1 atmosphere of pressure, and there is only 1 mole of product. Here are some examples of formation reactions:

$$Fe(s) + O_2(g) \rightarrow FeO(s) \tag{12.24}$$

$$2Fe(s) + \tfrac{3}{2}O_2(g) \rightarrow Fe_2O_3(s) \tag{12.25}$$

$$2K(s) + \tfrac{1}{2}H_2(g) + 2O_2(g) + P(s) \rightarrow K_2HPO_4(s) \tag{12.26}$$

Fractional coefficients may be used in formation reactions. Since there is always 1 mole of product, the standard heats of formation, ΔH^0_f, are tabulated as the heat produced per mole of product.

Since the reaction can easily be deduced if the product is known, a table of data need contain only the name or formula of the product and its corresponding ΔH^0_f. A tabulation of some heats of formation is given in Appendix 3.

Heats of formation of the elements are always zero, whether they are molecules or atoms. The reason is that the formation reaction for an element such as oxygen is defined as

$$O_2(g) \quad \rightarrow \quad O_2(g) \qquad (12.27)$$

Since the oxygen is at 25°C and 1.00 atmosphere pressure as both the product and the reactant, the initial and final states of the oxygen in Equation 12.27 are the same, and their difference must be zero:

$$\Delta H_f^0 \text{ (any element)} \quad = \quad 0 \qquad (12.28)$$

Heats of formation can be calculated from heats of combustion, as was shown in Exercise 12.4.

For the combustion of propane (Equation 12.16):

$$CH_3CH_2CH_3(g) \quad + \quad 5O_2(g) \quad \rightarrow \quad 3CO_2(g) \quad + \quad 4H_2O(g)$$

ΔH^0 can be calculated using the formation reactions and the tabulated heats of formation. Again, we will need a formation reaction for each of the reactants and products. Elements are excluded, however, since their heats of formation are always zero. In this example, the formation reactions for propane, carbon dioxide, and water are needed:

$$3C(s) \quad + \quad 4H_2(g) \quad \rightarrow \quad CH_3CH_2CH_3(g) \qquad \Delta H_f^0 \quad = \quad -103.8 \text{ kJ mol}^{-1}$$

$$C(s) \quad + \quad O_2(g) \quad \rightarrow \quad CO_2(g) \qquad \Delta H_f^0 \quad = \quad -393.5 \text{ kJ mol}^{-1}$$

$$H_2(g) \quad + \quad \tfrac{1}{2}O_2(g) \quad \rightarrow \quad H_2O(g) \qquad \Delta H_f^0 \quad = \quad -241.8 \text{ kJ mol}^{-1}$$

The following operations are performed on these reactions so that they can be combined to yield the combustion reaction:

The propane formation reaction is reversed.

$$CH_3CH_2CH_3(g) \quad \rightarrow \quad 3C(s) \quad + \quad 4H_2(g)$$
$$\Delta H \quad = \quad -103.8 \text{ kJ mol}^{-1} \times (-1 \text{ mol})$$

The carbon dioxide formation reaction is multiplied by 3.

$$3C(s) \quad + \quad 3O_2(g) \quad \rightarrow \quad 3CO_2(g)$$
$$\Delta H \quad = \quad -393.5 \text{ kJ mol}^{-1} \times 3 \text{ mol}$$

The $H_2O(g)$ formation reaction is multiplied by 4.

$$4H_2(g) \quad + \quad 2O_2(g) \quad \rightarrow \quad 4H_2O(g)$$
$$\Delta H \quad = \quad -241.8 \text{ kJ mol}^{-1} \times 4 \text{ mol}$$

After these three operations, adding the three reactions yields the combustion reaction:

$$CH_3CH_2CH_3(g) \quad + \quad 5O2(g) \quad \rightarrow \quad 3CO_2(g) \quad + \quad 4H_2O(g)$$

The corresponding sum of the heats is the heat of reaction:

$$\Delta H^0 = (-103.8 \text{ kJ mol}^{-1})(-1 \text{ mol}) + (-393.5 \text{ kJ mol}^{-1})(3 \text{ mol})$$
$$+ (-241.8 \text{ kJ mol}^{-1})(4 \text{ mol})$$

$$= -2,044 \text{ kJ}$$

After several calculations using heats of formation have been made, a pattern appears. The heat of any reaction will be the sum of ($\Delta H_f^0 \times$ mol$_{\text{product}}$) for all the products minus the sum of ($\Delta H_f^0 \times$ mol$_{\text{reactant}}$) for all the reactants. The mol$_{\text{product}}$ and mol$_{\text{reactant}}$ terms refer to the stoichiometric coefficients in the balanced equation for the reaction:

$$\Delta H^0 = \sum(\Delta H_f^0 \times \text{coeff})_{\text{products}} - \sum(\Delta H_f^0 \times \text{coeff})_{\text{reactants}} \qquad (12.29)$$

Exercise 12.5

Calculate the heat of combustion of CH_4. The heats of formation are as follows: ΔH_f^0 ($CH_4(g)$) = -74.8 kJ mol^{-1}, ΔH_f^0 ($CO_2(g)$) = -110.5 kJ mol^{-1}, and ΔH_f^0 ($H_2O(g)$) = -241.8 kJ mol^{-1}.

Solution

For the combustion of CH_4 the equation is

$$CH_4(g) + 2O_2(g) \rightarrow CO_2(g) + 2H_2O(g)$$

The heat of this reaction is calculated as

$$\Delta H_{react}^0 = [(-110.5 \text{ kJ mol}^{-1})(1 \text{ mol}) + (-241.8 \text{ kJ mol}^{-1})(2 \text{ mol})]$$
$$- [(-74.8 \text{ kJ mol}^{-1})(1) + (0.00 \text{ kJ mol}^{-1})(2 \text{ mol})]$$

$$= -519.3 \text{ kJ}$$

The value of 0.00 kJ mol^{-1} in this calculation represents the heat of formation of $O_2(g)$, which, by definition, is zero.

Entropy and the Second Law of Thermodynamics

The degree of randomness in a sample of matter is called its **entropy**, S. The change in entropy is a state function just as ΔH and ΔE are state functions. The more randomly the atoms and molecules move or are arranged, the greater is the entropy of a given substance. We can immediately visualize, for example, that ice has a very ordered structure compared to liquid water; therefore, water has greater entropy. Similarly, since the H_2O molecules are much more randomly arranged in steam than they are in liquid water, the gas has a higher entropy. The units for entropy are joules per degrees Celsius ($J°C^{-1}$); thus entropy is an extensive property of matter. Chemists transform it into an intensive property by calculating the entropy of 1 mole of matter, in which case the units become joules per mole per degree Celsius [$J \cdot (\text{mol}°C)^{-1}$], and the symbol is S^0. A table of standard entropy values for selected elements and compounds is given in Appendix 3. It should be noted that the entropy values of the elements are not zero.

Unlike other thermodynamic quantities, such as energy, E, and enthalpy, H, the actual value for the entropy, S, of a substance can be determined. From fundamental principles, a perfect crystal at absolute zero (0 K or $-273.16°C$) has zero entropy since all motion ceases and there is perfect order. As the temperature of 1 mole of a chemical is increased from absolute zero, the entropy increases and the standard entropy is defined as

$$S^0 = \frac{q_{rev}}{T} \tag{12.30}$$

In this equation T represents the temperature in kelvins, and q_{rev} is the heat added to raise the temperature very slowly from absolute zero up to T. Heat, q, is not a state function, and it seems that S should not be a state function either. However, if heat is always added in a carefully defined manner, the results will always be the same. This carefully defined path is called a **reversible process**, and the heat added is symbolized as q_{rev}. A reversible process is defined as one that occurs in infinitesimally small steps from the initial to the final state.

Entropy changes due to a chemical process are calculated in the same fashion as the heats of reaction. Just as is done for ΔH_f^0 values, the tables list entropies for 1 mole of substance, making entropy an intensive physical property. This can be written as

$$\Delta S^0 = \Sigma (S_f^0 \times coeff)_{products} - \Sigma (S_f^0 \times coeff)_{reactants} \tag{12.31}$$

For example, we can calculate the entropy change for the combustion of propane from the data in Appendix 3:

$$CH_3CH_2CH_3(g) \quad + \quad 5O_2(g) \quad \rightarrow \quad 3CO_2(g) \quad + \quad 4H_2O(g)$$

$$\Delta S^0 \quad = \quad ? \text{ J}°C^{-1}$$

$$\Delta S^0 \quad = \quad \left[\left(\frac{213.6 \text{ J}}{\text{mol K}}\right)(3 \text{ mol}) + \left(\frac{188.7 \text{ J}}{\text{mol K}}\right)(4 \text{ mol})\right] -$$

$$\left[\left(\frac{205.0 \text{ J}}{\text{mol K}}\right)(5 \text{ mol}) + \left(\frac{270.2 \text{ J}}{\text{mol K}}\right)(1 \text{ mol})\right]$$

$$= \quad 1395.6 \text{ J K}^{-1} - 1295.2 \text{ J K}^{-1}$$

$$= \quad + 100.4 \text{ J K}^{-1}$$

This result represents an increase in entropy. We might have predicted an increase for this reaction since there are 7 moles of gaseous products and only 6 moles of gaseous reactants. The increase in the number of moles of gas in this reaction is 1 ($\Delta n_g = 1$), indicating that the entropy change is expected to be positive.

In addition to calculating the entropy change from tabulated data, we can estimate the sign and, to some degree, the magnitude of an entropy change for a chemical process. In making such an estimate, the following principles are important:

1. Formation of a gas increases entropy greatly. The greater the value of Δn_g, the greater the entropy increase. The reverse is true for a decrease in entropy.
2. If $\Delta n_g = 0$, changes from the solid to the liquid phase are the next leading contributors to an increase in entropy. A solid that melts or a solute that dissolves in a solvent both exhibit an increase in entropy. Conversely, the formation of solids always results in a decrease in entropy.
3. An increase in temperature increases the entropy of a system, and a temperature decrease decreases the entropy.

Gibbs Free-Energy, ΔG

This thermodynamic quantity was named in honor of J. Willard Gibbs, a preeminent physical chemist who developed the concept. The **free-energy change**, represented by the symbol ΔG^0, is the maximum amount of energy available from any chemical reaction. Two forces drive chemical reactions. The first is the enthalpy, ΔH^0, which represents the change in the internal potential energy of the atoms. The second is the drive toward increased randomness, or an increase in the entropy of the system. If the enthalpy is negative, it means that the internal potential energy of the system is decreased, and this favors a spontaneous reaction. If the entropy increases, a spontaneous reaction is also favored. The combination of these two driving forces is represented as

$$\Delta G^0 = \Delta H^0 - T\Delta S^0 \tag{12.32}$$

The Gibbs free-energy equation is derived directly from the **second law of thermodynamics**, which states that any physical or chemical change must result in an increase in the entropy of the universe.

Since ΔG^0 is a combination of ΔH^0 and ΔS^0 we can make some generalizations, shown in Table 12.1, based only on the signs of these quantities.

TABLE 12.1 Relationships of the Signs of ΔH^0 and ΔS^0 to the Sign of ΔG^0

ΔH^0	ΔS^0	ΔG^0	Comment
Negative	Positive	Negative	Always spontaneous
Positive	Negative	Positive	Never spontaneous
Negative	Negative	Positive or negative	Decrease temperature to make spontaneous
Positive	Positive	Positive or negative	Increase temperature to make spontaneous

When ΔH^0 is negative and ΔS^0 is positive, the only value possible for ΔG^0 is a negative one. In this case the reaction will be spontaneous at all temperatures. Similarly, when ΔH^0 is positive and ΔS^0 is negative, ΔG^0 must be positive, indicating a nonspontaneous reaction at all temperatures.

When ΔH^0 is negative and ΔS^0 is negative, ΔG^0 may be either negative or positive, depending on the relative magnitudes of ΔH^0 and ΔS^0. However, the $-T \Delta S^0$ term will always be positive. It will have a larger magnitude at high temperatures and a smaller magnitude at low temperatures. This fact suggests that lowering the temperature may make the positive magnitude of $T \Delta S^0$ small enough so that, when it is combined with the negative ΔH^0, the resulting ΔG^0 will be negative and the reaction will be spontaneous.

The reverse is true when ΔH^0 is positive and ΔS^0 is positive. Again, ΔG^0 may be either positive or negative. The same reasoning leads to the conclusion that increasing the temperature will eventually cause the reaction to be spontaneous with a negative ΔG^0.

SPONTANEITY OF REACTIONS

When ΔG^0 is negative, a reaction is spontaneous. When ΔG^0 is positive, a reaction is nonspontaneous.

When the signs of ΔS^0 and ΔH^0 are different, the reaction will **always** be either spontaneous or nonspontaneous.

When the signs of ΔS^0 and ΔH^0 are the same, the reaction may be either spontaneous or nonspontaneous, depending on the Kelvin temperature.

As is true of ΔH^0 and ΔS^0 calculations, we can calculate the value of ΔG^0 for a reaction from tabulated values of free energies of formation. These values are listed in a table in Appendix 3. Since temperature is an important variable that affects the value of the free energy, the temperature must be specified. It is most common to list ΔG^0 values for room temperature of 25°C or 298 K. The symbol for free energy incorporates the temperature, as in ΔG^0_{298}. In using the free-energy table, we subtract the ΔG^0_{298} of the reactants from the ΔG^0_{298} values of the products in the equation:

$$\Delta G^0_{298} = \sum(\Delta G^0_{298} \times \text{coeff})_{\text{products}} - \sum(\Delta G^0_{298} \times \text{coeff})_{\text{reactants}} \quad (12.33)$$

For the combustion of propane (Equation 12.16) we obtain

$$\Delta G^0_{298} = \left[\left(\frac{-394.4 \text{ kJ}}{\text{mol}}\right)(3\,\text{mol}) + \left(\frac{-228.6 \text{ kJ}}{\text{mol}}\right)(4\,\text{mol})\right] - \left[\left(\frac{-23.5 \text{ kJ}}{\text{mol}}\right)(1\,\text{mol})\right]$$

$$= (-1183.2 \text{ kJ} - 914.4 \text{ kJ}) - (-23.5 \text{ kJ})$$

$$= -2074.1 \text{ kJ}$$

The negative value indicates that the reaction is spontaneous, as anyone who has used a barbecue grill or propane torch already knows.

We have calculated ΔH^0 and ΔS^0 for this reaction in preceding sections of this chapter. Using those values, along with a temperature of 298 K, we have a second way to determine the value of ΔG^0_{298}:

$$
\begin{aligned}
\Delta G^0_{298} &= \Delta H^0 & - & \quad T\Delta S^0 \\
&= -2044 \text{ kJ} & - & \quad (298 \text{ K})(100.4 \text{ J K}^{-1}) \\
&= -2044 \text{ kJ} & - & \quad 29.9 \text{ kJ} \\
&= -2074 \text{ kJ}
\end{aligned}
$$

Free Energy at Temperatures Other Than 298 K

Using the table of standard free energies of formation in Appendix 3, we can calculate the free-energy change at 298 K. Standard free-energy changes at other temperatures can also be calculated. For this purpose we need to know the standard heat of reaction, ΔH^0_{react}, and the standard entropy change, ΔS^0_{react}, for the reaction. These values are correct for 298 K, but we may assume that they do not change significantly with temperature. Using these values in the free-energy equation with a temperature other than 298 K gives the free-energy change at that different temperature.

Exercise 12.6

For a certain reaction, $\Delta H^0 = +2.98$ kJ and $\Delta S^0 = +12.3$ J K^{-1}. What is G^0 at 298 K, 200 K, and 400 K?

Solution

The equation to be solved is

$$
\Delta G^0 = \Delta H^0 - T\Delta S^0
$$

Substituting the values given in the problem yields

$$
\begin{aligned}
\Delta G^0_{298} &= 2.98 \text{ kJ} & - & \quad 298\,(12.3 \text{ J K}^{-1}) \\
&= 2.98 \text{ kJ} & - & \quad 3665 \text{ J}
\end{aligned}
$$

To complete the solution, -3665 J must be converted to -3.67 kJ. Then

$$
\Delta G^0 = -0.69 \text{ kJ} \quad \text{(a spontaneous reaction)}
$$

At 200 K and 400 K the answers are

$$
\Delta G^0_{200} = 2.98 \text{ kJ} - 200 \text{ K}\,(12.3 \text{ J K}^{-1}) = +0.52 \text{ kJ}
$$

and

$$
\Delta G^0_{400} = 2.98 \text{ kJ} - 400 \text{ K}\,(12.3 \text{ J K}^{-1}) = -1.94 \text{ kJ}
$$

In this exercise we see that the reaction is not spontaneous at 200 K but is spontaneous at 298 and 400 K.

Exercise 12.7

For a certain reaction, $\Delta H^0 = -13.65$ kJ and a $\Delta S^0 = -75.8$ J K^{-1}. (a) What is ΔG^0_{298} at 298 K? (b) Will increasing or decreasing the temperature make the reaction spontaneous? If so, at what temperature will the reaction become spontaneous?

Solution

(a) At 298 K the free energy is

$$\Delta G^0_{298} \quad = \quad -13.65 \text{ kJ} \quad - \quad 298 \text{ K } (-75.8 \text{ J K}^{-1}) \quad = \quad +8.94 \text{ kJ}$$

(b) The reaction is not spontaneous at 298 K. Since ΔH^0 and ΔS^0 both have the same sign, the free energy will change from positive to negative at some temperature. Since the number zero divides the positive numbers from the negative numbers, we may conclude that $\Delta G^0 = 0.00$ kJ is the dividing line between spontaneous and nonspontaneous reactions. Consequently, the free-energy equation is set up as

$$\Delta G^0_{react} \quad = \quad \Delta H^0_{react} \quad - \quad T \Delta S^0_{react}$$

$$0.00 \text{ kJ} \quad = \quad -13.65 \text{ kJ} \quad - \quad T(-75.8 \text{ JK}^{-1})$$

$$T \quad = \quad \frac{13.65 \text{ kJ}}{0.0758 \text{ kJ K}^{-1}} \quad = \quad 180 \text{ K}$$

From this result we predict that the reaction will be spontaneous below 180 K and nonspontaneous above 180 K.

The condensation of a gas and the crystallization of a liquid are two physical processes that are spontaneous at low temperatures and nonspontaneous at higher temperatures.

Free Energy and Equilibrium

When a system is not at standard state, the free-energy change is represented by ΔG, not ΔG^0. Equation 12.34 shows the relationship between ΔG and ΔG^0:

$$\Delta G \quad = \quad \Delta G^0 \quad + \quad RT \ln Q \tag{12.34}$$

From Chapter 10 we recall that Q is the reaction quotient. If the value of Q is not equal to the equilibrium constant, further reaction occurs until the system reaches equilibrium.

Using Equation 12.34, we find that when a system is at standard state all concentrations are equal to 1 and $Q = 1$. The natural logarithm of 1 is zero ($\ln 1 = 0$), and consequently $\Delta G = \Delta G^0$.

The value of ΔG (without the superscript) tells us whether the reaction will continue and, if so, in which direction it will go. When ΔG is negative, the reaction will proceed in the forward direction. When ΔG is positive, the reaction proceeds in the reverse direction. If ΔG is zero, the reaction is at equilibrium and no further reaction occurs. For the equilibrium condition we find that

$$\Delta G^0 \quad = \quad -RT \ln K \tag{12.35}$$

by setting $\Delta G = 0$, substituting the equilibrium constant, K, for the reaction quotient, Q, in Equation 12.34, and rearranging.

The relationships between ΔG and ΔG^0 are diagrammed in Figure 12.3. The standard free energies, ΔG^0, are shown for the reactants on the left side and for the products on the right side of each graph. The difference between the two is ΔG^0 for the reaction. In each diagram the curved line connecting the two G^0 values represents the value of G for the reaction mixture. The slope of the curved line is ΔG, and at the minimum, where the slope $= 0$, the reaction is in equilibrium.

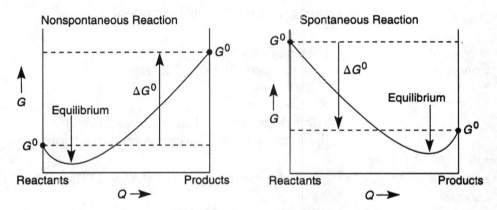

Figure 12.3.   Free-energy diagrams for a nonspontaneous reaction and a spontaneous reaction. The difference between the G^0 points is ΔG^0. The slope of the curved line is ΔG, and the equilibrium point is at the minimum of the curve.

The curves in Figure 12.3 illustrate that in a nonspontaneous reaction a small amount of reactants is converted into products at equilibrium (minimum of curved line). A spontaneous reaction, on the other hand, has most of the reactants converted into products because the minimum is closer toward the product side. The slope of the curved line is negative to the left of the equilibrium point, so that ΔG is negative and the reaction moves toward the products and also toward the minimum. On the right-hand side of the equilibrium point, the slope and ΔG are positive. The reaction proceeds toward the reactants and also toward the minimum.

Exercise 12.8

The value of the equilibrium constant is 45 at 298 K. At the same temperature $Q = 35$. Determine the value of ΔG^0 for the reaction at 298 K, and show that the value of G indicates the same direction for the reaction as Q predicts.

Solution

The value of ΔG^0 is calculated as

$$\Delta G^0 = -RT \ln K$$
$$= -(8.314 \text{ J mol}^{-1} \text{ K}^{-1})(298 \text{ K})[\ln (45)]$$
$$= -9.43 \text{ kJ mol}^{-1}$$

The value of ΔG is calculated as

$$\Delta G = \Delta G^0 + RT \ln Q$$
$$= -9.43 \text{ kJ mol}^{-1} + (8.314 \text{ J mol}^{-1} \text{ K}^{-1})(298 \text{ K})[\ln (35)]$$
$$= -9.43 \text{ kJ mol}^{-1} + 8.81 \text{ kJ mol}^{-1}$$
$$= -0.62 \text{ kJ mol}^{-1}$$

The value of ΔG predicts that the reaction will proceed in the forward direction. The fact that Q is less than K also indicates that the reaction will proceed in the forward direction.

Important Concepts

Forms of energy
Law of Conservation of Energy
Hess's Law
Standard State
Gibbs Free Energy, Entropy and Enthalpy
Spontaneous and Nonspontaneous reactions

Important Equations

$q = (\text{SPECIFIC HEAT})(\text{MASS})(\text{TEMPERATURE CHANGE})$
$\Delta E = q + w$
$\Delta G^0 = \Delta H^0 - T\Delta S^0$
$\Delta G^0 = -RT \ln K$

Questions on Chapter 12

1. When 0.400 g of CH_4 is burned in excess oxygen in a bomb calorimeter that has a heat capacity of 3245 J °C^{-1}, a temperature increase of 6.795°C is observed. What is the value of q_v?
   (A) 220 kJ mol^{-1}
   (B) −882 kJ
   (C) 477 kJ
   (D) −22.05 kJ
   (E) 8.820 kJ g^{-1}

2. Using the data in question 1, determine ΔH^0 for the combustion of methane.
   (A) −22.05 kJ mol^{-1}
   (B) −882 kJ
   (C) +22.05 kJ
   (D) −8.820 kJ g^{-1}
   (E) This value cannot be determined because w is not known.

3. Which of the following describes a system that CANNOT be spontaneous?
   (A) ΔH^0 is positive, and ΔS^0 is negative.
   (B) ΔH^0 is positive, and ΔS^0 is positive.
   (C) ΔH^0 is negative, and ΔS^0 is negative.
   (D) ΔH^0 is negative, and ΔS^0 is positive.
   (E) ΔH^0 is 0.00, and ΔS^0 is positive.

4. Which of the following explains the fact that, when KCl is dissolved, water condenses on the outside of the beaker?
   (A) ΔH^0 is positive, and ΔS^0 is negative.
   (B) ΔH^0 is positive, and ΔS^0 is positive.
   (C) ΔH^0 is negative, and ΔS^0 is negative.
   (D) ΔH^0 is negative, and ΔS^0 is positive.
   (E) ΔH^0 is 0.00, and ΔS^0 is negative.

5. The reaction with the greatest expected entropy decrease is
   (A) $CH_4(g)$ + $2O_2(g)$ → $CO_2(g)$ + $2H_2O(g)$
   (B) $CH_4(\ell)$ + $2O_2(g)$ → $CO_2(g)$ + $2H_2O(g)$
   (C) $CH_4(g)$ + $2O_2(g)$ → $CO_2(g)$ + $2H_2O(\ell)$
   (D) $CH_4(g)$ + $2O_2(g)$ → $CO_2(s)$ + $2H_2O(g)$
   (E) $CH_4(\ell)$ + $2O_2(g)$ → $CO_2(g)$ + $2H_2O(\ell)$

6. Water boils at 100°C with a molar heat of vaporization of +43.9 kJ. What is the entropy change when

$$H_2O(g) \quad → \quad H_2O(\ell)$$

   at 100°C?
   (A) Problem cannot be solved; ΔG^0 must also be known.
   (B) Problem cannot be solved; this is not a chemical reaction.
   (C) -439 J K^{-1}
   (D) $+0.439 \text{ J K}^{-1}$
   (E) -118 J K^{-1}

7. The law of Dulong and Petit says that the molar specific heat of metals is approximately 25 J mol^{-1} K^{-1}. This suggests that
   (A) the heat absorbed depends only on the number of atoms
   (B) the heat absorbed depends on the volume change with temperature
   (C) the first law of thermodynamics is true
   (D) potential energy and kinetic energy are inversely related
   (E) this law is an oddity since it does not apply to nonmetals

8. A gas is allowed to expand from an initial volume of 5.00 L and pressure of 3.00 atm to a volume of 15.0 L and pressure of 1.00 atm. What is the value of w?
   (A) 30.0 L atm
   (B) 10.0 L atm
   (C) 45.0 L atm
   (D) 15.0 L atm
   (E) -10.0 L atm

9. In question 8 the units of work are given as L atm. To convert L atm to the metric unit of joules, we need to know
   (A) Avogadro's constant and Planck's constant
   (B) the universal gas law constant in units of L atm mol^{-1} K^{-1}
   (C) the universal gas law constant in units of J mol^{-1} K^{-1}

(D) both B and C
(E) A, B, and C

10. Which of the following is the LEAST probable for a combustion reaction?
(A) ΔG^0 is a large negative number.
(B) ΔS^0 is a large negative number.
(C) ΔH^0 is a large negative number·
(D) K_{eq} is a large positive number.
(E) Q, the reaction quotient, is a small number.

11. Of the following, which can be precisely determined for a chemical substance?
(A) entropy, S
(B) enthalpy, H
(C) free energy, G
(D) internal energy, E
(E) all of these

12. The heat of formation of $CH_3OH(\ell)$ = -238.6 kJ mol^{-1}, of $CO_2(g)$ = -393.5 kJ mol^{-1}, and of $H_2O(g)$ = -241.8 kJ mol^{-1}. What is ΔH^0 for the heat of combustion of methanol?
(A) -396.7 kJ
(B) -1277 kJ
(C) -638.5 kJ
(D) $+ 396.7$ kJ
(E) This value cannot be calculated without the heat of formation for $O_2(g)$.

13. The rate of reaction will be large if
(A) ΔG^0 is a large negative number
(B) ΔS^0 is a large negative number
(C) ΔH^0 is a large negative number
(D) K_{eq} is a large positive number
(E) None of the above can be used to estimate reaction rates.

14. Given the following thermochemical data:

$N_2O_4(g) \rightarrow 2NO_2(g)$ $\qquad \Delta H^0 = +57.93$ kJ

$2NO(g) + O_2(g) \rightarrow 2NO_2(g)$ $\qquad \Delta H^0 = -113.14$ kJ

determine the heat of the reaction

$2NO(g) + O_2(g) \rightarrow N_2O_4(g)$.

(A) 171.07 kJ
(B) -55.21 kJ
(C) -171.07 kJ
(D) $+ 55.21$ kJ
(E) -85.54 kJ

15. Which of the following can change the value of ΔG^0 for a chemical reaction?
    (A) changes in the total pressure
    (B) changes in the pressures of the reactants
    (C) changes in the concentrations of the reactants
    (D) changes in the temperature in °C
    (E) the presence of a catalyst

16. At what temperature is $K_{eq} = 1.00$ if $\Delta S^0 = 22.6$ J K^{-1} and $\Delta H^0 = 15.3$ kJ for a chemical reaction?
    (A) 404°C
    (B) 677°C
    (C) 0.67°C
    (D) 1477°C
    (E) 1204°C

17. The standard heat of formation of $SO_3(g)$ is -396 kJ mol^{-1}. The standard entropies of $S(s)$, $O_2(g)$, and $SO_3(g)$ are 31.8, 205.0, and 256 J mol^{-1} K^{-1}, respectively. Calculate the free energy for the decomposition of SO_3 in the reaction

$$2SO_3(g) \quad \rightarrow \quad 2S(s) \quad + \quad 3O_2(g)$$

    at 25°C.
    (A) 396 kJ
    (B) 446 kJ
    (C) 346 kJ
    (D) -346 kJ
    (E) 742 kJ

18. The reaction

$$2C_6H_6(l) \quad + \quad 15O_2(g) \quad \rightarrow \quad 12CO_2(g) \quad + \quad 6H_2O(\ell)$$

    is expected to have.
    (A) a positive ΔH and a negative ΔS
    (B) a negative ΔH and a negative ΔS
    (C) a positive ΔH and a positive ΔS
    (D) a negative ΔH and a negative ΔS
    (E) These predictions cannot be made.

19. The evaporation of any liquid is expected to have
    (A) a positive ΔH and a negative ΔS
    (B) a negative ΔH and a negative ΔS
    (C) a positive ΔH and a positive ΔS
    (D) a positive ΔH and a negative ΔS
    (E) These predictions cannot be made.

20. Which of the following is most likely to be true?
    (A) No products are formed in a nonspontaneous reaction.
    (B) A positive ΔG° indicates a spontaneous reaction.

(C) A positive ΔS° always means that the reaction is spontaneous.

(D) A spontaneous reaction always goes to completion.

(E) Combustion of organic compounds has a negative ΔH^0.

Answer Key

See Appendix I for explanations of answers.

1. **D**	5. **C**	9. **B**	13. **E**	17. **E**
2. **B**	6. **E**	10. **B**	14. **C**	18. **B**
3. **A**	7. **A**	11. **A**	15. **D**	19. **C**
4. **B**	8. **E**	12. **B**	16. **A**	20. **E**

PART FIVE

Chemical Reactions

CHAPTER THIRTEEN

Oxidation-Reduction Reactions and Electrochemistry

Chemical reactions in which electrons are transferred from one atom to another are called **oxidation-reduction** reactions. As a group, more reactions may be classified as oxidation-reduction reactions than as acid-base, double-replacement, or complexation reactions combined.

Oxidation is the loss of electrons, and **reduction is the gain of electrons**. When an atom of barium reacts with an atom of sulfur, the barium loses its two valence electrons and is oxidized, while the sulfur gains these two electrons and is reduced.

$$Ba \; + \; \cdot \overset{..}{\underset{..}{S}} \cdot \; \longrightarrow \; Ba : \overset{..}{\underset{..}{S}} : \qquad (13.1)$$

This reaction may be written as two **half-reactions** that show the individual oxidation and reduction steps:

$$Ba \; \rightarrow \; Ba^{2-} \; + \; 2e^{-} \qquad \text{(oxidation)} \qquad (13.2)$$

$$S \; + \; 2e^{-} \; \rightarrow \; S^{2-} \qquad \text{(reduction)} \qquad (13.3)$$

Although we may write separate half-reactions, they cannot exist without each other. Perhaps the word *redox* was coined to emphasize this point.

In the oxidation-reduction reaction of Equation 13.1, the barium atom loses its electrons to the sulfur atom, causing the sulfur atom to be reduced. Consequently, barium is called the **reducing agent**. The opposite view is that sulfur gains electrons from the barium atom, causing the barium atom to be oxidized. Consequently, sulfur is called the **oxidizing agent**. In any redox reaction, the substance oxidized is the reducing agent and the substance reduced is the oxidizing agent.

Oxidation Numbers

Determining Oxidation Numbers

In more complex reactions it is not always obvious that electrons are transferred. To determine whether a substance has lost or gained electrons, chemists calculate the **oxidation number**, also called the **oxidation state**, of each element. If the oxidation number changes during a reaction, electrons have been transferred.

To determine the oxidation numbers of the elements in a compound or polyatomic ion, we follow a short set of rules:

Oxidation Number Rules

1. The oxidation numbers of all atoms add up to the charge on the molecule or ion.
2. The oxidation number of an alkali metal is +1, for an alkaline earth element it is +2, and for the metals in group IIIA it is +3.
3. The oxidation number of hydrogen is +1, and the oxidation number of fluorine is −1.
4. The oxidation number of oxygen is −2.
5. The oxidation number of a halogen is −1.
6. The oxidation number of nonmetal in group VIA is −2.

The oxidation number rules are a hierarchy, meaning that rule 1 is the most important and rule 6 is the least important. If two rules conflict, the rule closest to the top of the list is obeyed while the one lower on the list is ignored.

Many simple compounds follow the oxidation number rules directly. Since the charge of any element is zero, the oxidation number of any element must be zero, according to rule 1. In compounds such as $CaCl_2$, calcium is +2 according to rule 2, and each chlorine is −1 by rule 5; also, the most important rule, rule 1, is obeyed since +2 and $2 \times (-1)$ add up to zero, the charge on $CaCl_2$. Also, in potassium hydroxide, KOH, potassium is +1 according to rule 2; oxygen is −2 according to rule 4; and hydrogen is +1 according to rule 3. The oxidation numbers all obey rule 1 since $+1 +1 - 2 = 0$, which is the charge on KOH.

Some compounds, however, do not obey one or more of the rules. Since all substances must obey rule 1, we may write rule 1 as an equation in which the total charge is equal to the sum of the elements' oxidation numbers, with each oxidation number multiplied by the number of times the element appears in the formula:

$$\text{Total charge} = (\text{ox. no.1})(\text{subscript 1}) + \\ + (\text{ox. no. 2})(\text{subscript 2}) + \ldots \quad (13.4)$$

For example, the oxidation numbers for the elements in perchloric acid, $HClO_4$, are +1 for hydrogen, −1 for chlorine, and −2 for each oxygen if rules 3, 4, and 5 are strictly followed. These assignments violate rule 1, however, since the oxidation numbers add up to −8 and the $HClO_4$ molecule must have a charge of zero. We, therefore, ignore rule 5 in favor of rule 1 and write the equation as

$$0 \text{ charge} = (\text{ox. no. H})(1) + (\text{ox. no. Cl})(1) + (\text{ox. no. O})(4)$$
$$0 = (+1)(1) + (\text{ox. no. Cl})(1) + (-2)(4)$$
$$= \text{ox. no. Cl} - 7$$
$$\text{ox. no. Cl} = +7$$

In perchloric acid the oxidation number of the chlorine atom is +7.

Oxidation numbers for polyatomic ions are determined using the same method, being sure that the oxidation numbers add up to the charge on the ion. For example, we might assign all the sulfur and oxygen atoms in the sulfate ion, SO_4^{2-}, oxidation numbers of -2 according to rules 4 and 6. That would disobey rule 1, however, since the sum of these oxidation numbers is $-2 - 8 = -10$, whereas the actual charge of the sulfate ion is -2. Consequently, we abandon rule 6 and work with rules 1 and 4 to write the equation

$$
\begin{aligned}
-2 \text{ charge} &= (\text{ox. no. S})(1) &+& \quad (\text{ox. no. O})(4) \\
-2 &= \text{ox. no. S} &+& \quad (-2)(4) \\
&= \text{ox. no. S} &-& \quad 8 \\
\text{ox. no. S} &= +6
\end{aligned}
$$

Finally, the rules specify oxidation numbers for only 25 of the 111 known elements. However, by using the oxidation number rules and the formulas of the polyatomic ions, chemists can determine the oxidation numbers of most of the other elements. For example, the oxidation numbers for chromium and oxygen in the dichromate ion, $Cr_2O_7^{2-}$, can be determined using rules 1 and 4:

$$
\begin{aligned}
-2 \text{ charge} &= (\text{ox. no. Cr})(2) &+& \quad (\text{ox. no. O})(7) \\
-2 &= (\text{ox. no. Cr})(2) &+& \quad (-2)(7) \\
&= (\text{ox. no. Cr})(2) &-& \quad 14 \\
(\text{ox. no. Cr})(2) &= +12 \\
\text{ox. no. Cr} &= +\frac{12}{2} = +6
\end{aligned}
$$

Some compounds may contain two elements that are not covered by the oxidation number rules. One such compound is nickel(II) carbonate, $NiCO_3$. In situations like this one we take advantage of knowing that the carbonate ion is CO_3^{2-} and the nickel must be a $+2$ ion, Ni^{2+}. For the Ni^{2+}, rule 1 applies directly, and the oxidation number is $+2$. For the carbonate ion we write

$$
\begin{aligned}
-2 \text{ charge} &= (\text{ox. no. C})(1) &+& \quad (\text{ox. no. O})(3) \\
-2 &= (\text{ox. no. C})(1) &+& \quad (-2)(3) \\
&= \text{ox. no. C} &-& \quad 6 \\
\text{ox. no. C} &= +4
\end{aligned}
$$

Using this procedure, we have determined that the oxidation numbers are as follows: $+2$ for nickel, $+4$ for carbon, and -2 for each oxygen.

Exercise 13.1   Determine the oxidation number of each element in the following formulas:

(a) H_2O_2 (c) K_3PO_4 (e) $Fe_2(C_2O_4)_3$ (g) SO_3^{2-} (i) NH_4^+
(b) $HClO_3$ (d) Na_2CrO_4 (f) MnO_4^- (h) N_2O_5 (j) $FeNH_4(SO_4)_2$

Solution

(a) $H = +1$; $O = -1$ (g) $S = +4$; $O = -2$
(b) $H = +1$; $Cl = +5$; $O = -2$ (h) $N = +5$; $O = -2$
(c) $K = +1$; $P = +5$; $O = -2$ (i) $N = -3$; $H = +1$
(d) $Na = +1$; $Cr = +6$; $O = -2$ (j) $Fe = +2$; $N = -3$; $H = +1$;
(e) $Fe = +3$; $C = +3$; $O = -2$ $S = +6$; $O = -2$
(f) $Mn = +7$; $O = -2$

Using Oxidation Numbers

Oxidation numbers are used to determine whether or not a substance has been oxidized or reduced. When the permanganate ion reacts in acid solution to form Mn^{2+}, we find that the oxidation number of the manganese is $+7$ in the permanganate ion and $+2$ in the Mn^{2+} ion. The change in oxidation number indicates that an oxidation-reduction process has taken place. In addition, the fact that the oxidation number was reduced from $+7$ to $+2$ tells us that a reduction of manganese has taken place. Also, the fact that the oxidation number changes by 5 tells us that five electrons have been gained by each manganese atom in the reduction process.

Exercise 13.2

Possible reactants and products for oxidation-reduction reactions are given below. In each case, determine the oxidation numbers to tell whether an oxidation or a reduction has occurred and, if so, how many electrons were lost or gained from the starting material.

(a) $Cr_2O_7^{2-}$ to CrO_4^{2-} (d) I^- to IO_3^- (f) Fe to Fe_2O_3
(b) $C_2O_4^{2-}$ to CO_2 (e) $BaCl_2$ to $BaSO_4$ (g) C_2H_4 to C_2H_6
(c) NO_3^- to NO_2

Solution

(a) No change occurs in any oxidation numbers; not a redox process.
(b) C changes from $+3$ to $+4$. Two electrons per $C_2O_4^{2-}$ are gained in this oxidation.
(c) N changes from $+5$ to $+4$. One electron per NO_3^- is used in this reduction.
(d) I changes from -1 to $+5$. Six electrons per I^- are used in this oxidation.
(e) Ba does not change; no redox process occurs (Cl_2 and SO_4 are ignored).
(f) Fe changes from 0 to $+3$. Three electrons per Fe are lost in this oxidation.
(g) C changes from -2 to -3. Two electrons per C_2H_4 are gained in this reduction.

In a redox equation we may now identify what is occurring. For example, Fe^{2+} is often titrated with permanganate ions. The unbalanced reaction is

$$Fe^{2+} \quad + \quad MnO_4^- \quad \rightarrow \quad Mn^{2+} \quad + \quad Fe^{3+} \qquad (13.5)$$

From this reaction we see that Fe^{2+} is oxidized to Fe^{3+}. The manganese has an oxidation number of $+7$ in the permanganate ion and of $+2$ in the product; therefore the manganese is reduced. We can also say that the permanganate ion is reduced. Because the substance oxidized causes the reduction of the other reactant, this substance is called the reducing agent. Fe^{2+} is oxidized and is also the reducing agent. Similarly, the MnO_4^- ion is reduced and is therefore the oxidizing agent.

Although the manganese in the permanganate ion is the atom actually reduced, chemists never say that the manganese atom is the reducing agent. The terms *oxidizing agent* and *reducing agent* are used with the entire formula unit, which contains the elements that are reduced or oxidized, not the elements themselves.

Exercise 13.3

In each of the following unbalanced equations, identify the element that is oxidized, the element that is reduced, and the changes in oxidation number. Also identify the oxidizing and reducing agents.

(a) O_2 + N_2H_4 → H_2O_2 + N_2
(b) XeO_3 + I^- → Xe + I_2
(c) I_2 + OCl^- → IO_3^- + Cl^-
(d) NO_3^- + Cu → NO_2 + Cu^{2+}
(e) PbO_2 + Cl^- → $PbCl_2$ + Cl_2

Solution

The table below lists the required information. The change in oxidation number is indicated after each element in the first two columns.

	Element Oxidized	Element Reduced	Oxidizing Agent	Reducing Agent
(a)	N (+2)	O (−1)	O_2	N_2H_4
(b)	I (+1)	Xe (−6)	XeO_3	I^-
(c)	I (+5)	Cl (−2)	OCl^-	I_2
(d)	Cu (+2)	N (−1)	NO_3^-	Cu
(e)	Cl (+1)	Pb (−2)	PbO_2	Cl^-

Balancing Redox Reactions

Redox reactions tend to be complex, and attemps to balance them by inspection often fail to achieve an answer within a reasonable length of time. Over the years chemists have devised several methods for balancing redox reactions. The simplest and most versatile is called the **ion-electron method**. To use the ion-electron method, six steps must be performed, in the order given, steps 1–6 for reactions that occur in acid (H^+) solution. A seventh step is added if the reaction occurs in basic (OH^-) solution, or if H^+ appears on one side of the equation and OH^- appears on the other side.

Ion-Electron Method

1. Write two half-reactions, one representing the oxidation, and the other the reduction, that occur in the reaction. It is not necessary to know which is which at this point.
2. In each half-reaction, balance all atoms except hydrogen and oxygen.
3. Balance oxygen atoms in each half-reaction by adding one H_2O molecule for each oxygen atom needed. Never use O_2, OH^-, or any other form of oxygen.

4. Balance the hydrogen atoms by adding hydrogen ions, H^+. Never use H_2, OH^-, or any other form of hydrogen.
5. Balance the charges by adding the proper number of electrons (e^-). If steps 1–4 have been done properly, electrons will be added to the left side of one half-reaction and to the right side of the other.
6. Multiply each half-reaction by the appropriate number so that the two half-reactions have the same number of electrons. Add the half-reactions, and cancel the electrons (**they must cancel**). Also cancel all common ions and molecules. Simplify the coefficients of the equation if possible.
7. Add one OH^- ion for each H^+ ion to both sides of the equation in step 6. Combine the H^+ and OH^- ions on one side of the reaction into H_2O molecules. Cancel H_2O molecules that appear on both sides of the equation, and simplify if possible.

Before using the ion-electron method, however, it is worthwhile to try to balance a reaction by inspection. For example, the unbalanced equation for the reaction of magnesium metal with acid may be written as

$$Mg \quad + \quad H^+ \quad \rightarrow \quad Mg^{2+} \quad + \quad H_2$$

By inspection we see that placing the coefficient 2 in front of H^+ will balance the hydrogen atoms and the charge in this equation:

$$Mg \quad + \quad 2H^+ \quad \rightarrow \quad Mg^{2+} \quad + \quad H_2 \qquad (13.6)$$

There is no need to use the longer ion-electron method.

In a second example, however, the ion-electron method must be used. Standard solutions of iodine are prepared by reacting iodide ions with the iodate ion in acid solution. The skeleton reaction is

$$I^- \quad + \quad IO_3^- \quad \rightarrow \quad I_2$$

The first step of the ion-electron method requires two half-reactions, which are written as

$$I^- \quad \rightarrow \quad I_2$$
$$IO_3^- \quad \rightarrow \quad I_2$$

Even though the skeleton reaction has only one product, there is no reason why both reactants cannot yield the same product, one by oxidation and the other by reduction. Usually two pairs of reactants can be identified to obtain the half-reactions. In addition, H^+, OH^-, or H_2O may be included in the skeleton reaction. These are generally ignored since they are added in later steps.

The second step requires that the iodine atoms be balanced by using the coefficient 2 in both half-reactions:

$$2I^- \quad \rightarrow \quad I_2$$
$$2IO_3^- \quad \rightarrow \quad I_2$$

The third step applies only to the second half-reaction since the first one contains no oxygen. Six water molecules are needed to balance the six oxygens in two iodate ions:

$$2I^- \quad \rightarrow \quad I_2$$

$$2IO_3^- \quad \rightarrow \quad I_2 \quad + \quad \mathbf{6H_2O}$$

The fourth step also involves only the second half-reaction, where 12 H^+ ions are required:

$$2I^- \quad \rightarrow \quad I_2$$

$$\mathbf{12H^+} \quad + \quad 2IO_3^- \quad \rightarrow \quad I_2 \quad + \quad 6H_2O$$

At this point all the atoms are balanced, and we use step 5 to balance the charges with electrons. First we must count the charge on each side of each half-reaction. The first half-reaction has a total charge of -2 on the left and 0 on the right. The second half-reaction has a total charge of $+10$ on the left and 0 on the right. Two electrons on the right side of the first half-reaction are added to equalize the charges at -2. Ten electrons are added to the left side of the second half-reaction, resulting in a total charge of 0 on both sides:

$$2I^- \quad \rightarrow \quad I_2 \quad + \quad \mathbf{2e^-}$$

$$\mathbf{10e^-} \quad + \quad 12H^+ \quad + \quad 2IO_3^- \quad \rightarrow \quad I_2 \quad + \quad 6H_2O$$

In step 6 we can equalize the electrons in the two half-reactions by multiplying the entire first half-reaction by 5:

$$10I^- \quad \rightarrow \quad 5I_2 \quad + \quad 10e^-$$

$$10e^- \quad + \quad 12H^+ \quad + \quad 2IO_3^- \quad \rightarrow \quad I_2 \quad + \quad 6H_2O$$

Adding the equations yields

$$10I^- \quad + \quad 10e^- \quad + \quad 12H^+ \quad + \quad 2IO_3^- \quad \rightarrow$$
$$5I_2 \quad + \quad 10e^- \quad + \quad I_2 \quad + \quad 6H_2O$$

We then cancel 10 electrons from each side, add the iodine molecules on the right to obtain 6 I_2, and divide all of the coefficients by 2 to obtain the final balanced equation:

$$5I^- \quad + \quad 6H^+ \quad + \quad IO_3^- \quad \rightarrow \quad 3I_2 \quad + \quad 3H_2O \quad (13.7)$$

All atoms must be balanced in the reaction. In addition, in ionic reactions the charges must also balance. In this equation we count a total charge of 0 on both sides of the arrow.

In a third example, the reaction between the permanganate ion and iodide ions occurs in neutral solutions. The unbalanced skeleton reaction is

$$MnO_4^- \quad + \quad I^- \quad \rightarrow \quad I_2 \quad + \quad MnO_2$$

The obvious pairs for the half-reactions are

$$MnO_4^- \rightarrow MnO_2$$
$$I^- \rightarrow I_2$$

In the second half-reaction the iodine atoms need to be balanced:

$$MnO_4^- \rightarrow MnO_2$$
$$2I^- \rightarrow I_2$$

The first half-reaction needs two water molecules to balance the oxygen atoms:

$$MnO_4^- \rightarrow MnO_2 + \mathbf{2H_2O}$$
$$2I^- \rightarrow I_2$$

Four hydrogen ions balance the hydrogen atoms:

$$\mathbf{4H^+} + MnO_4^- \rightarrow MnO_2 + 2H_2O$$
$$2I^- \rightarrow I_2$$

The next step is the balancing of charges. We find that the first half-reaction has a total charge of +3 on the left and 0 on the right, while the second half-reaction has a total charge of −2 on the left and 0 on the right. We add three electrons to the first half-reaction on the left and two electrons to the second half-reaction on the right:

$$\mathbf{3e^-} + 4H^+ + MnO_4^- \rightarrow MnO_2 + 2H_2O$$
$$2I^- \rightarrow I_2 + \mathbf{2e^-}$$

To equalize the electrons, we multiply the first half-reaction by 2 and the second half-reaction by 3:

$$6e^- + 8H^+ + 2MnO_4^- \rightarrow 2MnO_2 + 4H_2O$$
$$6I^- \rightarrow 3I_2 + 6e^-$$

We add the equations:

$$6e^- + 6I^- + 8H^+ + 2MnO_4^- \rightarrow$$
$$2MnO_2 + 4H_2O + 3I_2 + 6e^-$$

and cancel the 6 electrons:

$$6I^- + 8H^+ + 2MnO_4^- \rightarrow$$
$$2MnO_2 + 4H_2O + 3I_2$$

This reaction is balanced in acid solution. To convert to a basic solution, we use step 7 and add 8 OH^- to each side:

$$8OH^- + 6I^- + 8H^+ + 2MnO_4^- \rightarrow 2MnO_2 + 4H_2O + 3I_2 + 8OH^-$$

The 8 H^+ and 8 OH^- on the left are combined to make 8 H_2O:

$$8H_2O + 6I^- + 2MnO_4^- \rightarrow 2MnO_2 + 4H_2O + 3I_2 + 8OH^-$$

We then cancel 4 H_2O from each side to simplify the final equation:

$$4H_2O + 6I^- + 2MnO_4^- \rightarrow 2MnO_2 + 3I_2 + 8OH^- \qquad (13.8)$$

Exercise 13.4

Balance each of the following half-reactions in acid solution:
(a) $Fe(s) \rightarrow Fe^{3+}$
(b) $Cl_2 \rightarrow Cl^-$
(c) $Cr^{3+} \rightarrow CrO_4^{2-}$
(d) $NO_3^- \rightarrow NO_2$
(e) $S_2O_3^{2-} \rightarrow SO_4^{2-}$

Solution

(a) $Fe(s) \rightarrow Fe^{3+} + 3e^-$
(b) $2e^- + Cl_2 \rightarrow 2Cl^-$
(c) $4H_2O + Cr^{3+} \rightarrow CrO_4^{2-} + 8H^+ + 3e^-$
(d) $e^- + 2H^+ + NO_3^- \rightarrow NO_2 + H_2O$
(e) $5H_2O + S_2O_3^{2-} \rightarrow 2SO_4^{2-} + 10H^+ + 8e^-$

Exercise 13.5

Balance each of the following skeleton redox reactions in the solution indicated:
(a) $Cr_2O_7^{2-} + CH_3CH_2OH \rightarrow Cr^{3+} + CH_3COOH$ (acid solution)
(b) $Cu + NO_3^- \rightarrow NO_2 + Cu^{2+}$ (acid solution)
(c) $MnO_2 + ClO_3^- \rightarrow MnO_4^- + Cl^-$ (basic solution)
(d) $Al + H_2O \rightarrow Al(OH)_4^- + H_2$ (basic solution)

Solution

(a) The balanced half-reactions are

$$6e^- + 14H^+ + Cr_2O_7^{2-} \rightarrow 2Cr^{3+} + 7H_2O$$

$$H_2O + CH_3CH_2OH \rightarrow CH_3COOH + 4H^+ + 4e^-$$

The balanced equation is

$$16H^+ + 2Cr_2O_7^{2-} + 3CH_3CH_2OH \rightarrow 4Cr^{3+} + 3CH_3COOH + 11H_2O$$

(b) The balanced half-reactions are

$$Cu \rightarrow Cu^{2+} + 2e^-$$

$$e^- + 2H^+ + NO_3^- \rightarrow NO_2 + H_2O$$

The balanced equation is

$$Cu + 2NO_3^- + 4H^+ \rightarrow 2NO_2 + Cu^{2+}$$

(c) The balanced half-reactions are

$$6e^- + 6H^+ + ClO_3^- \rightarrow Cl^- + 3H_2O$$

$$2H_2O + MnO_2 \rightarrow MnO_4^- + 4H^+ + 3e^-$$

The balanced equation is

$$2MnO_2 + 2OH^- + ClO_3^- \rightarrow$$
$$2MnO_4^- + Cl^- + H_2O$$

(d) The balanced half-reactions are

$$4H_2O + Al \rightarrow Al(OH)_4^- + 4H^+ + 3e^-$$

$$2e^- + 2H^+ + H_2O \rightarrow H_2 + H_2O$$

The balanced equation is

$$2Al + 2OH^- + 6H_2O \rightarrow 2Al(OH)_4^- + 3H_2$$

Common Oxidation-Reduction Reactions

Single-
Replacement
(Displacement)
Reactions

In **single-replacement** reactions an element replaces an atom in a compound, producing another element and a new compound. For example, the element zinc replaces the hydrogen atom in hydrogen chloride, forming the element H_2 and the new compound zinc chloride:

$$Zn + 2HCl \rightarrow ZnCl_2 + H_2 \tag{13.9}$$

Very active metals, which have the lowest ionization energies, are Li, Na, K, Rb, Cs, Ca, Sr, and Ba. These elements all react with water in single-displacement reactions to form hydrogen. One example is

$$2Na + 2H_2O \rightarrow 2NaOH + H_2 \tag{13.10}$$

Many of these reactions also produce so much heat that the hydrogen ignites.

Active metals do not react with water, but will react with acids in a single-replacement reaction. An example is

$$Mg + 2H^+ \rightarrow Mg^{2+} + H_2 \tag{13.11}$$

The common active metals are Mg, Zn, Pb, Ni, Al, Ti, Cr, Fe, Cd, Sn, and Co.

Inactive metals do not undergo simple single-replacement reactions with either water or acids. The most common inactive metals are Ag, Pt, Au, and Cu. Copper and silver react with concentrated nitric acid in a reaction that produces nitrogen oxides but not hydrogen. Gold reacts with a mixture, called aqua regia, of three parts concentrated HCl and one part concentrated HNO_3. The reaction of very active, active, and inactive metals with water and acid are summarized in Table 13.1.

TABLE 13.1 Summary of Metal Reactions with Water and Acid

Type of Metal	Examples	Comments
Very active metal	Li, Na, K, Rb, Cs, Ca, Sr, Ba	React with H_2O to produce H_2, which may ignite
Active metal	Mg, Zn, Pb, Ni, Al, Ti, Cr, Fe, Cd, Sn, Co	React with acids to form H_2, but not with H_2O
Inactive metal	Ag, Au, Cu, Pt	Do not form H_2 with acids: may react with conc. oxidizing acids HNO_3 and H_2SO_4

In addition to replacing hydrogen, metals will displace metal ions from their compounds. For instance, copper metal will react with silver nitrate in the single-replacement reaction

$$Cu \quad + \quad 2AgNO_3 \quad \rightarrow \quad Cu(NO_3)_2 \quad + \quad 2Ag \qquad (13.12)$$

The net ionic equation is written as

$$Cu \quad + \quad 2Ag^+ \quad \rightarrow \quad Cu^{2+} \quad + \quad 2Ag \qquad (13.13)$$

In these two reactions, copper is more active than silver and the reaction does occur. The reverse reaction:

$$Cu^{2+} \quad + \quad 2Ag \quad \rightarrow \quad Cu \quad + \quad 2Ag^+ \qquad (13.14)$$

does not occur, however, since silver is less active than copper.

An **activity series** is a listing of metals in the order of their activities. We can use an activity series to determine whether a certain metal will displace another metal ion from its compounds. Later in this chapter (page 379) we will introduce the concept of standard reduction potentials. A table of standard reduction potentials contains the same information as an activity series. The metal having the lower, or more negative, standard reduction potential is the more active metal.

Only the active and inactive metals will displace each other from compounds. The very active metals listed in Table 13.1 do not displace other metals. Although these metals are certainly reactive enough to result in such displacements, their high activity causes them to react preferentially with water instead.

Nonmetals such as the halogens also participate in single-displacement reactions. The activity series for the halogens is $F_2 > Cl_2 > Br_2 > I_2$. As a result, adding chlorine to a solution of potassium bromide results in the reaction

$$Cl_2 \quad + \quad 2KBr \quad \rightarrow \quad Br_2 \quad + \quad 2KCl \qquad (13.15)$$

The net ionic reaction is

$$Cl_2 \quad + \quad 2Br^- \quad \rightarrow \quad Br_2 \quad + \quad 2Cl^- \qquad (13.16)$$

Industrially important single-replacement reactions use carbon to displace oxygen from metal oxides in the refining process. For example, Fe_2O_3 is refined into iron in the reaction

$$2Fe_2O_3 \quad + \quad 3C \quad \rightarrow \quad 4Fe \quad + \quad 3CO_2 \qquad (13.17)$$

Reactions of the Permanganate Ion

Permanganate solutions have a deep violet color, and the permanganate ion, MnO_4^-, is a very versatile oxidizing agent. It reacts differently in acidic, neutral, and basic solutions.

In acid solution the half-reaction is

$$MnO_4^- \quad + \quad 8H^+ \quad + \quad 5e^- \quad \rightarrow \quad Mn^{2+} \quad + \quad 4H_2O \quad (13.18)$$

Five electrons are used in this reduction, and the soluble Mn^{2+} ion is almost colorless. In addition, this reaction is slow and the presence of Mn^{2+} ions catalyzes the process.

In neutral or slightly acid solutions the permanganate half-reaction is

$$MnO_4^- \quad + \quad 4H^+ \quad + \quad 3e^- \quad \rightarrow \quad MnO_2 \quad + \quad 2H_2O \quad (13.19)$$

The hydrogen ions in this three-electron half-reaction come from the dissociation of water molecules. The product MnO_2 is an insoluble black precipitate.

In basic solutions the reaction involves a one-electron transfer:

$$MnO_4^- \quad + \quad e^- \quad \rightarrow \quad MnO_4^{2-} \qquad (13.20)$$

The reaction mixture changes color from the deep violet of the MnO_4^- ion to a green color for the MnO_4^{2-} ion.

Reactions of Chromium(VI)

When chromium is in the $+6$ oxidation state, it forms different compounds depending on the pH of the solution. In neutral or basic solutions the chromate ion, CrO_4^{2-}, predominates. In acid solutions the dichromate ion predominates:

$$2CrO_4^{2-} \quad + \quad 2H^+ \quad \rightleftharpoons \quad Cr_2O_7^{2-} \quad + \quad H_2O \qquad (13.21$$

In very acid solutions the dichromate ion becomes protonated to form chromic acid:

$$Cr_2O_7^{2-} \quad + \quad 2H^+ \quad + \quad H_2O \quad \rightleftharpoons \quad 2H_2CrO_4 \qquad (13.22)$$

As the acidity of a solution increases, the strength of chromium(VI) as an oxidizing agent increases. Dichromate salts are dissolved in concentrated sulfuric acid to produce chromic acid, which is a very effective cleaning agent because it oxidizes most organic material. Dichromate salts dissolved in approximately 1 molar acid solutions are used for chemical analysis. For example, the reaction of dichromate with ethyl alcohol is used to test the sobriety of drivers suspected of driving while intoxicated (DWI):

$$8H^+ \quad + \quad Cr_2O_7^{2-} \quad + \quad 3CH_3CH_2OH \quad \rightarrow$$
$$2Cr^{3+} \quad + \quad 3CH_3CHO \quad + \quad 7H_2O \qquad (13.23)$$

Since the dichromate ion is orange, and the Cr^{3+} ion is green, the change in color from orange to green is a measure of the amount of alcohol present in the breath of a DWI suspect.

Iodine, Hydrogen Peroxide, and Thiosulfate

Iodine is a weak oxidizing agent. A dilute solution of iodine in alcohol, known as tincture of iodine, is an effective antiseptic for minor wounds. Because it is a weak oxidizing agent, iodine may be used in reaction mixtures where chemists want to oxidize only the more active reducing agents that are present.

Hydrogen peroxide, H_2O_2, is another weak oxidizing agent. Its mode of action is to decompose into water and atomic oxygen (O, not O_2). Atomic oxygen normally combines to form molecular O_2. However, in the brief time that it is available, atomic oxygen acts as a very good oxidizing agent if it encounters a suitable reactant. Hydrogen peroxide is used in 3 percent solutions as a household disinfectant and hair bleach. In higher concentrations, 30 percent, it is a very powerful oxidizing agent that must be handled with care. In fact, higher concentrations of H_2O_2 have been used as rocket fuel because of the oxygen this compoud supplies.

The thiosulfate ion, $S_2O_3^{2-}$, is a reducing agent, one of the very few that is stable in air because it reacts slowly with O_2. Thiosulfate solutions are used as reducing agents in chemical analysis, often with iodine as the oxidizing agent. Active metals such as zinc and magnesium are also used as reducing agents in chemical reactions.

Stoichiometry of Redox Reactions

In Chapter 6 stoichiometric calculations that may be used for any chemical reaction are discussed. Stoichiometric calculations for redox reactions are no different from the calculations for other reactions once the balanced equation has been obtained. However, some techniques are more commonly encountered in dealing with redox stoichiometry problems than with other types.

Converting Ionic Equations into Molecular Equations

The ion-electron method for balancing a redox equation results in a net ionic equation. The chemicals on the stockroom shelf are complete compounds, not individual ions. It is necessary, therefore, to translate the ions in a net ionic equation into compounds that can be measured in the laboratory. To do this, we convert a net ionic equation into a molecular equation by adding back spectator ions. The general principles are as follows:

1. A cation is converted into molecular form by adding negatively charged spectator ions to form a soluble compound. There are many possible choices; unless otherwise specified in the problem, the most convenient spectator ion to add is the chloride ion. If the chloride compound is insoluble, the next most convenient choice is the nitrate ion.

2. An anion is converted into molecular form by adding positively charged spectator ions to form a soluble compound. Again, there are many possible choices; unless otherwise specified in the problem, the most convenient spectator ion to add is the sodium ion. Hydrogen ions are added to anions to make acids if needed.

3. Whatever spectator ions are added to convert anions and cations into molecular forms must also be added to the opposite side of the equation to maintain balance.

To illustrate the process, let us determine the molecular equation for the net ionic equation

$$Ba^{2+} \quad + \quad SO_4^{2-} \quad \rightarrow \quad BaSO_4 \tag{13.24}$$

Adding chloride ions and sodium ions yields the molecular equation. To balance the final equation, NaCl must be added:

$$BaCl_2 \quad + \quad Na_2SO_4 \quad \rightarrow \quad BaSO_4 \quad + \quad 2NaCl \tag{13.25}$$

In the reaction used to determine ethyl alcohol:

$$8H^+ \quad + \quad Cr_2O_7^{2-} \quad + \quad 3CH_3CH_2OH \quad \rightarrow$$
$$2Cr^{3+} \quad + \quad 3CH_3CHO \quad + \quad 7H_2O \tag{13.26}$$

a question may be phrased in terms of potassium dichromate: for example How many grams of potassium dichromate will react with 5.00 grams o ethyl alcohol? It is not necessary to write a complete molecular equatio to solve the problem. We simply add the necessary number of K^+ ions t form potassium dichromate on the left and an equal number of potassiun ions on the right to obtain

$$8H^+ \quad + \quad K_2Cr_2O_7 \quad + \quad 3CH_3CH_2OH \quad \rightarrow$$
$$2Cr^{3+} \quad + \quad 3CH_3CHO \quad + \quad 7H_2O \quad + \quad 2K^+ \tag{13.27}$$

This form of the equation now has the information necessary to solv the problem.

Equivalent Weight, Equivalents, and Normality

Equivalent weight, along with equivalents and normality, represents an old system of measurement that is being phased out. However, the equivalent weight system is often used in the older literature. For completeness we define the meaning of these terms in redox reactions.

The **equivalent weight** of a compound in a redox reaction is equal to the the molar (molecular) mass of the compound divided by the number of electrons per mole in the balanced half-reaction:

$$\text{Equivalent weight} = \frac{\text{Molar mass}}{\text{Number of } e^- \text{ per mole}} \qquad (13.28)$$

The **equivalent** is a quantity similar to the mole. It is determined by dividing the mass of a sample by the equivalent weight:

$$\text{Equivalent} = \frac{\text{Mass of compound}}{\text{Equivalent weight}}$$
$$= (\text{Moles of compound}) (\text{Number of } e^- \text{ per mole}) \qquad (13.29)$$

The **normality** concentration unit for a solution is similar to the molarity concentration unit. It is calculated as

$$\text{Normality (N)} = \frac{\text{Equivalents}}{\text{Liters of solution}}$$
$$= (\text{Molarity}) (\text{Number of } e^- \text{ per mole}) \qquad (13.30)$$

Electrochemistry

The electrons in a balanced half-reaction show the direct relationship between a redox reaction and electricity. A nonspontaneous redox reaction may be forced to occur by adding electric energy in an **electrolytic cell**. A spontaneous redox reaction may be used to create a flow of electrons in a **galvanic cell**.

Electrolysis

In an **electrolysis** experiment a nonspontaneous chemical reaction is forced to occur when two **electrodes** are immersed in an electrically conductive sample, and the electrical voltage applied to the two electrodes is increased until electrons flow. At the electrode supplying the electrons, reduction reactions occur. This electrode is called the **cathode**. At the other electrode, the **anode**, oxidation reactions occur.

One type of sample that may be electrolyzed is a **molten salt**. Salts are composed of ions; when the salt is a solid, the ions are immobile in the crystal lattice. Heating the salt until it melts frees the ions, and the mobility of the ions in the molten salt makes the salt electrically conductive. In the electrolysis of a molten salt that does not contain any polyatomic ions, the cation of the salt will be reduced at the cathode and the anion of the salt will be oxidized at the anode. For example, sodium chloride can be melted, and the electrolysis reactions will be

$$\text{Cathode:} \qquad Na^+ + e^- \rightarrow Na \qquad (13.31)$$

Anode: $\qquad$ $2Cl^- \rightarrow Cl_2 + 2e^-$ $\qquad$ (13.32)

Electrolysis of molten salts containing polyatomic ions is much more complex. These reactions are covered in advanced chemistry courses. A diagram of an electrolytic cell is shown is Figure 13.1.

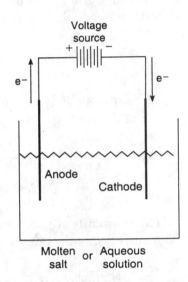

FIGURE 13.1 Setup of an electrolytic cell, described in the text.

Aqueous solutions of salts are also electrically conductive and may be electrolyzed. For solutions, two additional reactions are possible:

Cathode: $2H_2O + 2e^- \rightarrow H_2 + 2OH^-$ $\qquad$ (13.33)

Anode: $2H_2O \rightarrow O_2 + 4H^+ + 4e^-$ $\qquad$ (13.34)

There are two possible reactions at each electrode. At the cathode we will have either the reduction of water, as shown in Equation 13.33, or the reduction of a metal ion. At the anode we will have either the oxidation of water or the oxidation of the salt's anion. The following principles may be used to decide which reaction takes place at each electrode:

1. *Cathode:* If the metal ion is a very active metal, water will be reduced. If the metal ion is an inactive or an active metal, the metal ion will be reduced.

2. *Anode:* If the anion is a polyatomic ion, it generally will not be oxidized. In particular, the sulfate, nitrate, and perchlorate polyatomic anions are not oxidized in aqueous solution. Chloride, bromide, and iodide ions will be oxidized in aqueous solution. If an anion in one salt is oxidized in an aqueous electrolysis, that same anion in any other salt will also be oxidized. For example, since a solution of NaBr result in Br^- being oxidized to Br_2, we may predict that solutions of KBr, $CaBr_2$, NH_4Br, and $AlBr_3$ will all produce Br_2 at the anode.

Electrolysis is important in the industrial production of several chemical materials. Because of the need for electricity, most operations that use electrolysis are located in areas where electricity is inexpensive. Two o these are in the Pacific Northwest and in Niagara Falls close to large hydroelectric generators.

Industrial Uses for Electrolysis

The electrolysis of concentrated aqueous NaCl solutions, called brine, produces hydrogen and hydroxide ions at the cathode, as in Equation 13.33. At the anode chlorine gas is produced. If the electrodes are separated by a porous membrane, the products are H_2, NaOH, and Cl_2. In another arrangement, if the solution is stirred, the chlorine gas reacts with the sodium hydroxide to form a sodium hypochlorite (NaOCl) solution, which is better known as bleach:

$$2NaOH \; + \; Cl_2 \; \rightarrow \; NaOCl \; + \; NaCl \; + \; H_2O \qquad (13.35)$$

The electrolysis of molten NaCl produces sodium metal and chlorine gas.

Another molten-salt electrolysis is used in the production of aluminum. Although Al_2O_3 has a melting point above 2000°C, a college student, Charles Hall, discovered in 1886 that this melting point could be effectively decreased to around 1000°C when Al_2O_3 was mixed with cryolite (Na_3AlF_6). When electrolyzed, this mixture produces aluminum metal and oxygen. The more active sodium and fluorine are electrolyzed only when all of the aluminum and oxygen are used up.

Copper, the metal most used for electrical wiring, is refined by electrolysis. Copper ore is often a sulfide of copper that is refined into an impure form of copper by roasting:

$$CuS \; + \; O_2 \; \rightarrow \; Cu \; + \; SO_2 \qquad (13.36)$$

The impure copper is refined by using a bar, an ingot, of crude copper as the anode of an electrolytic cell. The cathode is a small strip of pure copper. During electrolysis the copper is oxidized to Cu^{2+} at the anode and then reduced to copper metal again at the cathode. In the process, impurities such as silver and gold drop to the bottom of the vessel as sludge. The value of the sludge comes close to paying for the electricity used in the refining.

In addition to producing industrial quantities of chemicals, electrolysis is used to electroplate thin layers of a decorative metal on a less expensive metal. Silver and gold are electroplated on iron utensils for decoration. Gold is electroplated on electrical contacts on computer circuit boards to decrease corrosion failure. Chromium is electroplated on automobile parts for decoration and resistance to corrosion.

Quantitative Electrochemistry

Every balanced half-reaction specifies the number of electrons lost or gained. Consequently, stoichiometric calculations can be used to convert between moles of electrons and moles of all other substances in the half-reaction. If the number of electrons flowing through the electrolysis cell is measured, the quantity of material reacted can be calculated. It was Michael Faraday who discovered the relationship between the mole and electric current. He started with the definition of the coulomb (C), which is the number of electrons that flow past a given point in a wire in exactly 1 second when the current is exactly 1 ampere:

$$1 \text{ coulomb} \quad = \quad 1 \text{ ampere} \quad \times \quad 1 \text{ second} \qquad (13.37)$$

Faraday found that 96,485 coulombs were equal to 1 mole of electrons:

$$1 \text{ mole } e^- \quad = \quad 96,485 \text{ coulombs} \qquad (13.38)$$

Faraday's constant, $\mathscr{F}$, is the factor label $\left(\dfrac{96,485 \text{ C}}{\text{mol } e^-}\right)$. Using Equations 13.37 and 13.38, we can determine the moles of electrons by measuring the current, I, and the time, t, that the current flows:

$$\text{moles of } e^- \quad = \quad \frac{I \times t}{96,485} \qquad (13.39)$$

The ampere (A), which is the measure of electric current, I, has units of coulombs per second (C s^{-1}), time has units of seconds (s), and Faraday's constant is 96,485 coulombs per mole of electrons.

Once the moles of electrons are calculated, the factor-label stoichiometric calculations are used to determine other quantities. For example, the half-reaction for the reduction of iodine is

$$I_2 \quad + \quad 2e^- \quad \rightarrow \quad 2I^- \qquad (13.40)$$

The moles of I$^-$ produced at an electrode with a current of 0.500 ampere for 90 minutes may be calculated by first determining the moles of electrons:

$$\text{mol } e^- \quad = \quad \frac{(0.500 \text{ C s}^{-1}) \, (90 \text{ min}) \, (60 \text{ s min}^{-1})}{96,485 \text{ C mol}^{-1}}$$

$$= \quad 0.0280 \text{ mol } e^-$$

Using the moles of electrons as the starting point, we can write the stoichiometric calculation:

$$? \text{ mol } I^- \quad = \quad 0.0280 \text{ mol } e^- \left(\frac{2 \text{ mol } I^-}{2 \text{ mol } e^-}\right) \quad = \quad 0.0280 \text{ mol } I^-$$

Chemists often bypass the stoichiometric step by incorporating the stoichiometry into Equation 13.39:

$$\text{moles of } X \quad = \quad \frac{It}{n\mathscr{F}} \qquad (13.41)$$

In this equation n is the number of electrons in the balanced half-reaction.

Exercise 13.6

A current of 2.34 A is delivered to an electrolytic cell for 85 min. How many grams of (a) Au from AuCl$_3$, (b) Ag from AgNO$_3$, and (c) Cu from CuCl$_2$ will be obtained?

Solution

(a) Au^{3+} + $3e^-$ → Au

$$mol\ Au = \frac{(2.34\ C\ s^{-1})\ (85\ min)\ (60\ s\ min^{-1})}{(3)\ (96,485\ C\ mol^{-1})}$$

$$= 4.12 \times 10^{-2}\ mol\ Au$$

$$g\ Au = 4.12 \times 10^{-2}\ mol\ Au \left(\frac{197g\ Au}{1\ mol\ Au}\right) = 8.12\ g\ Au$$

(b) Ag^- + e^- → Ag

$$mol\ Ag = \frac{(2.34\ C\ s^{-1})\ (85\ min)\ (60\ s\ min^{-1})}{(1)\ (96,485\ C\ mol^{-1})} = 0.124\ mol\ Ag$$

$$g\ Ag = 0.124\ mol\ Ag \left(\frac{108\ g\ Ag}{1\ mol\ Ag}\right) = 13.4\ g\ Ag$$

(c) Cu^{2+} + $2e^-$ → Cu

$$mol\ Cu = \frac{(2.34\ C\ s^{-1})\ (85\ min)\ (60\ s\ min^{-1})}{(2)\ (96,485\ C\ mol^{-1})}$$

$$= 6.18 \times 10^{-2}\ mol\ Cu$$

$$g\ Cu = 6.18 \times 10^{-2}\ mol\ Cu \left(\frac{63.5\ g\ Cu}{1\ mol\ Cu}\right) = 3.92\ g\ Cu$$

Galvanic Cells

Galvanic cells are used to harness the energy of spontaneous redox reactions. This is done by physically separating the chemicals in the two half-reactions so that the electrons generated by the oxidation half-reaction must flow through an electrical conductor before they can be used in the reduction half-reaction. This flow of electrons can be diverted through meters, motors, light bulbs, and other devices to perform useful work before they reach their destination.

A galvanic cell is constructed as shown in Figure 13.2. All of the reactants in the oxidation half-reaction are placed in the left beaker, and all of the reactants in the reduction half-reaction in the right beaker. If a half-reaction is written with a metal, the metal serves as the electrode for that beaker; otherwise, an inert electrode made of platinum, silver, or gold is used. Electrodes are connected to each other with a metal wire, usually copper, and a device such as a meter (voltmeter or ammeter), motor, or light bulb may be inserted in the electrical circuit. If a voltmeter is used, the positive side of the voltmeter is connected to the cathode and the negative or ground of the voltmeter is connected to the anode. To complete the circuit, a salt bridge is needed. The flow of charge is carried by electrons in the wires and by ions through the solutions and salt bridge.

In setting up a galvanic cell, we start with a balanced redox reaction. For the spontaneous reaction of permanganate with iron(II) in acid solution, the equation is

$$5Fe^{2+} + MnO_4^- + 8H^+ \rightleftharpoons 5Fe^{3+} + Mn^{2+} + 4H_2O \qquad (13.42)$$

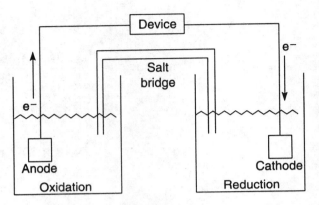

FIGURE 13.2. The galvanic cell.

To identify where the chemicals should be placed, the half-reactions are written:

$$Fe^{2+} \rightarrow Fe^{3+} + e^- \quad (13.43)$$

$$5e^- + MnO_4^- + 8H^+ \rightarrow Mn^{2+} + 4H_2O \quad (13.44)$$

Equation 13.43 is the oxidation half-reaction, and Fe^{2+} and Fe^{3+} are placed in the left beaker. Since neither Fe^{2+} nor Fe^{3+} is a metal, a platinum electrode will be used. MnO_4^-, H^+, and Mn^{2+} must be placed in the right cell since they are the components of the reduction half-reaction (Equation 13.44). Once again, a platinum electrode will be used. A voltmeter will measure the tendency of electrons to flow. The complete cell is shown in Figure 13.3.

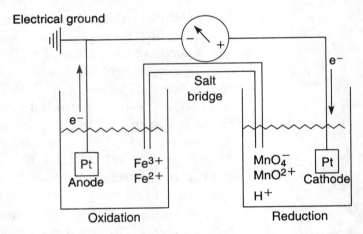

FIGURE 13.3. The galvanic cell set up to study the reaction in Equation 13.42.

To obtain consistent results from a galvanic cell, the variables of temperature, pressure, and concentration must be controlled. For this purpose electrochemists define a standard state for these experiments. Standard state for the galvanic cell is a temperature of 298 K, a pressure of 1.00 atmosphere for all gases, and concentrations of 1.00 molar for all soluble compounds. Concentrations of all solids and pure liquids are also defined as 1.00 molar.

At standard state, the galvanic cell diagram assumes that the reaction of Equation 13.42 is spontaneous and that oxidation and the anode are on the left while reduction and the cathode are on the right. Since this reaction is known to be spontaneous, the cell in Figure 13.3 is correct, and a positive voltmeter reading will be obtained. This voltmeter reading is called the **standard cell voltage**, E^0_{cell}, or the **electromotive force**, $\mathcal{EMF}$.

A nonspontaneous reaction may be converted into a spontaneous reaction by reversing the chemical equation. Then the steps outlined above are used to determine the correct setup of the galvanic cell.

In reality we often do not know whether a reaction is spontaneous or nonspontaneous. In such a situation, a chemical equation is written and the galvanic cell is constructed for that equation. When E^0_{cell} is measured, it will be either positive or negative. If E^0_{cell} is positive, the reaction is spontaneous as written. If E^0_{cell} turns out to be negative, the reaction is nonspontaneous as written and should be reversed to construct the galvanic cell.

The chemical reaction and the setup for the galvanic cell are directly related to each other. Knowing one of them allows us to determine the other. The chemicals present in the cell with the anode are written as an oxidation half-reaction; those present in the cell with the cathode, as the reduction half-reaction.

A cell diagram is a shorthand method of drawing a galvanic cell. The cell diagram "reads" the galvanic cell from left to right, starting with the anode and ending with the cathode. For the standard-state reaction of permanganate with iron(II) the cell diagram is as follows:

$$Pt \mid Fe^{2+}(1\ M),\ Fe^{3+}(1\ M) \parallel MnO_4^-(1\ M),\ Mn^{2+}(1\ M),\ H^+(1\ M) \mid Pt \quad (13.45)$$

The single vertical lines represent phase changes between the solid platinum electrodes and the solutions. The double vertical lines represent the salt bridge. Concentrations, if known, are shown in parentheses. The order in which the chemicals are written, within each cell, is not important.

Standard Reduction Potentials

The standard cell voltage is the difference between the electric potentials (voltages) of the cathode and the anode:

$$E^0_{cell} \quad = \quad E^0_{cathode} \quad - \quad E^0_{anode} \quad (13.46)$$

The $E^0_{cathode}$ is the standard reduction potential for the reaction occurring at the cathode and represents its tendency to remove electrons from the electrode surface. E^0_{anode} is the standard reduction potential for the reaction occurring at the anode and represents its tendency to remove electrons from the anode. It is impossible to independently measure the electromagnetic force values of the cathode and anode. The only measurement possible is the combined E^0_{cell}.

If it were possible to measure $E^0_{cathode}$ or E^0_{anode} for any reaction, the standard electrode potentials of all other half-reactions could be determined using Equation 13.46. As an alternative, chemists define the reduction of hydrogen, at standard state, as having a reduction potential of exactly 0.00 volt:

$$H^+(aq) \quad + \quad e^- \quad \rightarrow \quad \tfrac{1}{2}H_2(g) \quad E^0 \quad = \quad 0.00 \text{ volt} \quad (13.47)$$

This definition is used to determine the potentials of other half-reactions. For example, the reaction of

$$Zn(s) \quad + \quad 2H^+(aq) \quad \rightarrow \quad Zn^{2+}(aq) \quad + \quad H_2(g) \quad (13.48)$$

has a standard cell voltage of $E^0_{cell} = +0.76$ volt. Since the zinc oxidation occurs at the anode and the reduction of hydrogen ions occurs at the cathode, we may write

$$E^0_{cell} \quad = \quad +0.76 \text{ V} \quad = \quad E^0_{H^+} \quad - \quad E^0_{Zn}$$

The $E^0_{H^+}$ has been defined as 0.00 volt, and entering that value into the preceding equation gives

$$+0.76 \text{ V} \quad = \quad 0.00 \text{ V} \quad - \quad E^0_{Zn}$$

Rearranging this equation yields

$$E^0_{Zn} \quad = \quad -0.76 \text{ V}$$

This is the standard reduction potential for zinc.

Once the standard reduction potential for zinc is known, we may study the reaction

$$Zn(s) \quad + \quad 2Ag^+(aq) \quad \rightarrow \quad Zn^{2+}(aq) \quad + \quad 2Ag(s) \quad (13.49)$$

The standard cell voltage for this reaction is measured as $+1.56$ volts, so

$$E^0_{cell} \quad = \quad +1.56 \text{ V} \quad = \quad E^0_{Ag^+} \quad - \quad E^0_{Zn}$$

Substituting the value for the standard reduction potential of zinc into the above equation yields

$$+1.56 \text{ V} \quad = \quad E^0_{Ag^+} \quad - \quad (-0.76 \text{ V})$$

Rearranging and solving yields the standard reduction potential of silver ions:

$$E^0_{Ag^+} \quad = \quad +1.56 \text{ V} \quad - \quad 0.76 \text{ V} \quad = \quad +0.80 \text{ V}$$

In a similar manner the standard reduction potentials of all half-reactions are determined. The standard reduction potentials for most half-reactions are known, and some of these are listed in Table 13.2.

TABLE 13.2 Standard Reduction Potentials, 25°C

Half-Reaction						$E°$ (V)
$F_2(g)$ +	$2e^-$	→	$2F^-$			2.87
Co^{3+} +	e^-	→	Co^{2+}			1.82
Au^{3+} +	$3e^-$	→	Au			1.50
$Cl_2(g)$ +	$2e^-$	→	$2Cl^-$			1.36
$O_2(g)$ +	$4H^+$	+	$4e^-$	→	$2H_2O$	1.23
$Br_2(g)$ +	$2e^-$	→	2Br			1.07
$2Hg^{2+}$ +	$2e^-$	→	Hg_2^{2+}			0.92
Ag^+ +	e^-	→	Ag			0.80
Hg_2^{2+} +	$2e^-$	→	Hg			0.79
Fe^{3+} +	e^-	→	Fe^{2+}			0.77
I_2 +	$2e^-$	→	$2I^-$			0.53
Cu^+ +	e^-	→	Cu			0.52
Cu^{2+} +	$2e^-$	→	Cu			0.34
Cu^{2+} +	e^-	→	Cu^+			0.15
Sn^{4+} +	$2e^-$	→	Sn^{2+}			0.15
S +	$2H^+$	+	$2e^-$	→	H_2S	0.14
$2H^+$ +	$2e^-$	→	H_2			0.00
Pb^{2+} +	$2e^-$	→	Pb			−0.13
Sn^{2+} +	$2e^-$	→	Sn			−0.14
Ni^{2+} +	$2e^-$	→	Ni			−0.25
Co^{2+} +	$2e^-$	→	Co			−0.28
Tl^+ +	e^-	→	Tl			−0.34
Cd^{2+} +	$2e^-$	→	Cd			−0.40
Cr^{3+} +	e^-	→	Cr^{2+}			−0.41
Fe^{2+} +	$2e^-$	→	Fe			−0.44
Cr^{3+} +	$3e^-$	→	Cr			−0.74
Zn^{2+} +	$2e^-$	→	Zv			−0.76
Mn^{2+} +	$2e^-$	→	Mn			−1.18
Al^{3+} +	$3e^-$	→	Al			−1.66
Be^{2+} +	$2e^-$	→	Be			−1.70
Mg^{2+} +	$2e^-$	→	Mg			−2.37
Na^+ +	e^-	→	Na			−2.71
Ca^{2+} +	$2e^-$	→	Ca			−2.87
Sr^{2+} +	$2e^-$	→	Sr			−2.89
Ba^{2+} +	$2e^-$	→	Ba			−2.90
Rb^+ +	e^-	→	Rb			−2.92
K^+ +	e^-	→	K			−2.92
Cs^+ +	e^-	→	Cs			−2.92
Li^+ +	e^-	→	Li			−3.05

With a table of standard reduction potentials, E^0_{cell} for any redox reaction can be predicted. If E^0_{cell} is positive, the reaction is spontaneous; if it is negative, the reaction is not spontaneous.

Exercise 13.7

Write the balanced redox reaction for each of the following, determine E^0_{cell}, and state whether or not the reaction is spontaneous:
(a) the single displacement of copper(II) by zinc metal
(b) the single displacement of H^+ by iron, forming Fe^{2+}

(c) the reduction of tin(IV) to tin(II) by Fe(II) forming Fe(III)
(d) the reduction of dichromate ions to chromium(III) ions by Mn^{2+}, forming MnO_2
(e) the oxidation of AsO_3^{3-} to $H_2AsO_4^-$ by the reduction of iodine to iodide ions

Solution

(a) Cu^{2+} + Zn → Zn^{2+} + Cu

E^0_{cell} = +0.34 V − (−0.76 V) = +1.10 V

The reaction is spontaneous.

(b) Fe + $2H^+$ → Fe^{2+} + H_2

E^0_{cell} = 0.00 V − (−0.44 V) = +0.44 V

The reaction is spontaneous.

(c) Sn^{4+} + $2Fe^{2+}$ → $2Fe^{3+}$ + Sn^{2+}

E^0_{cell} = +0.15 V − (+0.77 V) = −0.62 V

The reaction is not spontaneous.

(d) $2H^+$ + $Cr_2O_7^{2-}$ + $3Mn^{2+}$ → $3MnO_2$ + $2Cr^{3+}$ + H_2O

E^0_{cell} = +1.33 V − (+1.23 V) = +0.10 V

The reaction is spontaneous.

(e) H_2O + AsO_3^{3-} + I_2 → $H_2AsO_4^-$ + $2I^-$

E^0_{cell} = +0.54 V − (+0.58 V) = −0.04 V

The reaction is not spontaneous.

Cell Voltages

In the preceding section the standard reduction potentials were used to determine the standard cell voltage expected from a galvanic cell. Standard conditions specify the temperature, pressure, and concentrations necessary to obtain these standard voltages, and the voltage measured will differ from the standard voltage if any of these variables are changed. Walter Nernst showed that

$$E = E^0 - \frac{RT}{n\mathscr{F}} \ln Q \qquad (13.50)$$

This is called the Nernst equation. E is the reduction potential under nonstandard conditions; E^0 is the standard reduction potential; $R = 0.0821$ L atm mol^{-1} K^{-1}, the universal gas law constant; T is the Kelvin temperature; n is the number of electrons in the half-reaction; $\mathscr{F} = 96,485$ C mol^{-1} is Faraday's constant; and Q is the reaction quotient for the reduction half-reaction. For 298 K the Nernst equation is often written as

$$E = E^0 - \frac{0.0591}{n} \log Q \qquad (13.51)$$

The constants R and $\mathscr{F}$ along with the temperature, 298 K, and a conversion factor from natural logarithms to base -10 logarithms are combined into the constant 0.0591.

Both Equation 13.50 and Equation 13.51 become $E = E^0$ at standard state. At standard state, all concentrations in the reaction quotient are equal to 1.00, and therefore $Q = 1.00$. The logarithm of 1.00 is zero, and the log term disappears so that $E = E^0$.

For the dichromate reduction half-reaction the Nernst equation is

$$Cr_2O_7^{2-} + 14H^+ + 6e^- \rightarrow 2Cr^{3+} + 7H_2O \qquad (13.52)$$

$$E = E^0 - \frac{0.0591}{6} \log \left(\frac{[Cr^{3+}]^2}{[Cr_2O_7^{2-}] [H^+]^{14}} \right)$$

In the Nernst equation Q is always based on the form of the equilibrium law for the reduction half-reaction.

For the complete galvanic cell, two Nernst equations are needed, one for the cathode and one for the anode. These are combined to obtain the nonstandard cell voltage, E_{cell}:

$$E_{cell} = E_{cathode} - E_{anode} \qquad (13.53)$$

The symbols E without the superscript zero indicate electrode potentials and cell voltages for systems that are not at standard state.

Exercise 13.8

One cell of a galvanic cell involves the half-reaction

$$Fe^{3+} + e^- \rightarrow Fe^{3+}$$

What is the electrode potential at 25°C if the concentration of Fe^{2+} ions is 0.0245 M and the concentration of Fe^{3+} ions is 0.187 M? ($E^0 = +0.771$ V).

Solution

The Nernst equation

$$E = E^0 - \frac{0.0591}{n} \log Q$$

is used to solve this problem, where

$$Q = \frac{[Fe^{2+}]}{[Fe^{3+}]} = \frac{0.0245}{0.187} = 0.131$$

$$E = 0.771 - \frac{0.0591}{1} \log (0.131)$$

$$= 0.771 - (0.0591)(-0.883)$$

$$= 0.771 - (0.0052)$$

$$= +0.823 \text{ V}$$

Exercise 13.9

The reduction of iron(III) with tin(II) proceeds by the reaction

$$2Fe^{3+} + Sn^{2+} \rightarrow 2Fe^{2+} + Sn^{4+}.$$

In a galvanic cell all of the product concentrations are 0.0355 M and the reactant concentrations are 0.100 M. What is the voltage of the galvanic cell at 25°C?

$$E^0(Sn) = +0.154 \text{ V} \quad \text{and} \quad E^0(Fe) = +0.771 \text{ V}$$

Solution

The Nernst equation for the entire reaction is used:

$$E_{cell} = E^0_{cell} - \frac{0.0591}{n} \log Q$$

where n = 2 and Q and E^0_{cell} are calculated as

$$Q = \frac{[Fe^{2+}]^2 [Sn^{4+}]}{[Fe^{3+}]^2 [Sn^{2+}]} = \frac{(0.0355)^2 (0.0355)}{(0.100)^2 (0.100)} = 0.0447$$

The value for Q and E^0_{cell} are substituted into the Nernst equation

$$E^0_{cell} = +0.771 - 0.154 = +0.617 \text{ V}$$

$$E = 0.617 - \frac{0.0591}{2} \log (0.0447)$$

$$= 0.617 - (-0.040)$$

$$= +0.657 \text{ V}$$

Standard Cell Voltages and Equilibrium

If the two electrodes of a galvanic cell are connected so that electrons flow freely, the reaction will proceed to equilibrium. At equilibrium $E_{cell} = 0$ and the mathematical rearrangement of the two Nernst equations in Equation 13.53 becomes

$$E^0_{cell} = E^0_{cathode} - E^0_{anode}$$

$$= \frac{RT}{n\mathscr{F}} \ln K_{eq}$$

$$\text{or} \quad = \frac{0.0591}{n} \log K_{eq} \tag{13.54}$$

where n is the total number of electrons transferred in the redox reaction, and the mathematical combination of the anode reaction quotient and the cathode reaction quotient gives the equilibrium constant, K_{eq}.

The table of standard reduction potentials also provides the information necessary to calculate the equilibrium constant for a redox reaction.

Exercise 13.10

Determine the equilibrium constant for each of the following reactions at 298 K:
(a) the single displacement of copper(II) by zinc metal
(b) the single displacement of H^+ by iron, forming Fe^{2+}
(c) the reduction of tin(iv) to tin(II) by the oxidation of Fe(II) being oxidized to Fe(III)
(d) the reduction of dichromate ions to chromium(III) ions Mn^{2+}, forming MnO_2
(e) the oxidation of AsO_3^{3-} to $H_2AsO_4^-$ by the reduction of iodine to iodide ions

Solution

In Exercise 13.7 the reactions and E^0_{cell} values were determined.

(a) Cu^{2+} + Zn → Zn^{2+} + Cu

E^0_{cell} = +0.34 V − (−0.76 V) = +1.10 V

Two electrons are transferred, and K_{eq} = 1.7 × 10³⁷.

(b) Fe + $2H^+$ → Fe^{2+} + H_2

E^0_{cell} = 0.00 V − (−0.44 V) = +0.44 V

Two electrons are transferred, and K_{eq} = 7.8 × 10¹⁴.

(c) Sn^{4+} + $2Fe^{2+}$ → $2Fe^{3+}$ + Sn^{2+}

E^0_{cell} = +0.15 V − (+0.77 V) = −0.62 V

Two electrons are transferred, and K_{eq} = 1.0 × 10⁻²¹.

(d) $2H^+$ + $Cr_2O_7^{2-}$ + $3Mn^{2+}$ →
$3MnO_2$ + $2Cr^{3+}$ + H_2O

E^0_{cell} = +1.33 V − (+1.23 V) = +0.10 V

Six electrons are transferred, and K_{eq} = 1.4 × 10¹⁰.

(e) H_2O + AsO_3^{3-} + I_2 → $H_2AsO_4^-$ + $2I^-$

E^0_{cell} = +0.54 V − (+0.58 V) = −0.04 V

Two electrons are transferred, and K_{eq} = 4.4 × 10⁻².

In these examples we see that fairly small voltages translate into very large or very small equilibrium constants, depending on the sign of E^0_{cell}.

Free-Energy Change, ΔG^0 and Standard Cell Voltages

As shown by Equation 13.54, the standard cell voltage is related to the equilibrium constant:

$$E^0_{cell} = \frac{RT}{n\mathscr{F}} \ln K_{eq}$$

The standard free-energy change, ΔG^0, is also related to the equilibrium constant:

$$\Delta G^0 = -RT \ln K_{eq}$$

The relationship between ΔG^0 and E^0_{cell} is

$$\Delta G^0 = -n\mathscr{F}E^0_{cell} \tag{13.55}$$

A major method for determining the standard free energy of a reaction is the measurement of the standard cell voltage for the reaction of interest, and then a mathematical conversion using Equation 13.55.

Exercise 13.11

Determine the standard free-energy change for each of the following reactions:

(a) the single displacement of copper(II) by zinc metal
(b) the single displacement of H^+ by iron, forming Fe^{2+}
(c) the reduction of tin(iv) to tin(II) by the oxidation of Fe(II) to Fe(III)
(d) the reduction of dichromate ions to chromium(III) ions Mn^{2+}, forming MnO_2
(e) the oxidation of AsO_3^{3-} to $H_2AsO_4^-$ by the reduction of iodine to iodide ions

Solution

In Exercise 13.7 the reactions and E^0_{cell} were determined.

(a) Cu^{2+} + Zn → Zn^{2+} + Cu
E^0_{cell} = +0.34 V − (− 0.76 V) = +1.10 V

Two electrons are transferred and $\Delta G^0 = -212$ kJ.

(b) Fe + $2H^+$ → Fe^{2+} + H_2
E^0_{cell} = 0.00 V − (−0.44 V) = +0.44 V

Two electrons are transferred, and $\Delta G^0 = -84.9$ kJ.

(c) Sn^{4+} + $2Fe^{2+}$ → $2Fe^{3+}$ + Sn^{2+}
E^0_{cell} = +0.15 V − (+0.77 V) = −0.62 V

Two electrons are transferred, and $\Delta G^0 = 120$ kJ.

(d) $2H^+$ + $Cr_2O_7^{2-}$ + $3Mn^{2+}$ →
$3MnO_2$ + $2Cr^{3+}$ + H_2O
E^0_{cell} = +1.33 V − (+1.23 V) = +0.10 V

Six electrons are transferred, and $\Delta G^0 = -57.9$ kJ.

(e) H_2O + AsO_3^{3-} + I_2 → $H_2AsO_4^-$ + $2I^-$
E^0_{cell} = +0.54 V − (+0.58 V) = −0.04 V

Two electrons are transferred, and $\Delta G^0 = 7.7$ kJ.

Using Galvanic Cells to Determine Concentrations

The Nernst equation suggests a method whereby galvanic cell measurements can be used to determine concentrations. A redox reaction that can be used for this purpose is

$$2Ag^+(aq) + Cu(s) → 2Ag(s) + Cu^{2+}(aq) \qquad (13.56)$$

The cell diagram for this reaction is

$$Cu \mid Cu^{2+} \parallel Ag^+ \mid Ag \qquad (13.57)$$

The cell voltage is represented as

$$E_{cell} = E_{cathode} - E_{anode}$$

Inserting the Nernst equations for $E_{cathode}$ and E_{anode}, we obtain

$$E_{cell} = \left(E^0_{Ag/Ag^+} - \frac{0.0591}{1} \log \frac{1}{[Ag^+]}\right) - \left(E^0_{Cu/Cu^{2+}} - \frac{0.0591}{2} \log \frac{1}{[Cu^+]}\right) \quad (13.58)$$

If $[Ag^+]$ can be kept at a constant, known value, then the value of E_{cell} determined in an experiment can be used to calculate $[Cu^{2+}]$. A saturated solution of AgCl will maintain the silver ion concentration at a constant 1.0×10^{-5} M. Since $E^0_{Ag/Ag^+} = +0.80$ volt and $E^0_{Cu/Cu^{2+}} = +0.34$ volt, Equation 13.58 becomes

$$E_{cell} = 0.164 - \frac{0.0591}{2} \log \frac{1}{[Cu^{2+}]}$$

when all three constants are entered. If $E_{cell} = +0.128$ volt for a solution that contains an unknown concentration of Cu^{2+}, we can calculate its concentration as

$$0.128 = 0.164 - \frac{0.0591}{2} \log \frac{1}{[Cu^{2+}]}$$

$$-0.036 = -\frac{0.0591}{2} \log \frac{1}{[Cu^{2+}]}$$

$$+1.218 = \log \frac{1}{[Cu^{2+}]}$$

$$16.52 = \frac{1}{[Cu^{2+}]}$$

$$[Cu^{2+}] = 0.0605 \text{ M } Cu^{2+}$$

The key to using galvanic cell measurements for determining concentrations is that all but one concentration in the Nernst equation must be known and must remain constant during the experiment. In this analysis the silver ion concentration around the cathode was held constant. This constant electrode is also known as the **reference electrode**. The anode that monitored the Cu^{2+} ion concentration is called the **indicator electrode**.

pH Measurement and pH Electrodes

The concentration of hydrogen ions can be determined by using a galvanic cell in a manner similar to that for the determination of copper(II) ions illustrated above. **pH** is defined as the negative logarithm of the hydrogen ion concentration:

$$pH = -\log [H^+] \quad (13.59)$$

As in the preceding example, one of the electrodes in the galvanic cell must be a constant reference electrode. Two common reference electrodes for pH measurement are constructed using the half-reactions

$$AgCl(s) + e^- \rightarrow Ag(s) + Cl^- \quad (13.60)$$

$$Hg_2Cl_2 + 2e^- \rightarrow 2Hg(\ell) + 2Cl^- \quad (13.61)$$

The silver-silver chloride reference electrode consists of a silver wire with a coating of insoluble silver chloride in a saturated solution of potassium chloride. The second half-reaction uses the compound calomel, Hg_2Cl_2, and the reference electrode is called a calomel electrode.

The indicator electrode for pH measurements is the **glass electrode**, which consists of a very thin glass membrane. On the inside of the glass electrode is a 1 M solution of hydrochloric acid. The outside of the glass membrane is in contact with the solution to be measured. When the glass membrane has been soaked in water for 24 hours, the glass surface becomes a hydrated gel. The hydrogen ions adsorb to this hydrated glass surface in proportion to the concentration of hydrogen ions in the solution. The 1 M HCl on the inside produces a constant positive charge to the inner membrane, while the solution to be measured produces a smaller positive charge on the outside of the membrane. The difference in charge is reflected as the electrode potential.

A galvanic cell used to measure pH follows the equations

$$E_{cell} = E_{reference} + \text{constant} + 0.0591 \log [H^+] \qquad (13.62)$$

and when the constants are combined

$$E_{cell} = C' - 0.0591 \text{ pH} \qquad (13.63)$$

The constant in Equation 13.62 arises because of the variable properties of the glass electrode. It is combined with the potential of the reference electrode (which is also constant) to yield the constant C' in Equation 13.63. In use, a pH electrode must be standardized by immersing it into a buffer solution with a known pH. Measuring E_{cell} under these conditions allows the calculation of C'. Next the electrode is rinsed with distilled water and immersed in the solution to be measured. The C' just determined and the E_{cell} value for the unknown solution allow calculation of the pH.

Glass is an excellent insulator and does not allow a large amount of electric current to pass through it. Even the very thin glass membrane of the glass electrode is a good insulator. A special instrument, the pH meter, is needed to make measurements using the glass electrode. When a pH meter is used, the calibration step is done by adjusting the meter reading to the pH of the buffer; the pH of the unknown is then read directly from the meter.

Other Uses of Galvanic Cells

Galvanic cells can also be used to convert chemical energy into electrical energy. Devices that do this are called **batteries**, and several different batteries are in common use.

The *lead-acid battery* is used to start automobiles. A battery of this type is composed of a lead anode and a lead cathode that is coated with PbO_2. The half-reactions are as follows:

$$PbO_2(s) + 4H^+(aq) + SO_4^{2-}(aq) + 2e^- \rightarrow$$
$$PbSO_4(s) + 2H_2O \text{ (cathode)} \qquad (13.64)$$

$$Pb(s) + SO_4^{2-} \rightarrow PbSO_4(s) + 2e^- \text{ (anode)} \qquad (13.65)$$

As the battery is discharged, it uses up the sulfate ions and the electrodes become coated with lead sulfate. The reactions in Equations 13.64 and 13.65 may be reversed in charging the battery. The reverse reactions regenerate the sulfate ion in solution and reduce the amount of lead sulfate contaminating the surface of the electrodes. Each pair of electrodes produces approximately 2 volts. Six pairs of electrodes are used in a 12-volt car battery.

The *alkaline battery* is the battery used most commonly in flashlights, tape recorders, and TV remote controls. The case of the battery is zinc, which is the anode. The cathode is a graphite rod inserted into a paste made of manganese dioxide, water, and potassium hydroxide. The half-reactions are as follows:

$$Zn(s) + 2OH^-(aq) \rightarrow ZnO(s) + H_2O + 2e^- \text{ (anode)} \quad (13.66)$$

$$2MnO_2(s) + H_2O + 2e^- \rightarrow Mn_2O_3(s) + 2OH^-(aq) \text{ (cathode)} \quad (13.67)$$

The total voltage is 1.54 volts. This battery is not rechargeable.

Other batteries of interest are the *nickel-cadmium* or *nicad battery*, the *mercury battery,* and the *silver oxide battery*.

Fuel cells are also used to generate electricity. In a fuel cell, hydrogen is oxidized at an anode and oxygen reduced at a cathode to form water with the production of electricity. A fuel cell is approximately twice as efficient as gas, oil, or coal-powered generators in converting chemical energy into electricity.

Important Oxidation-Reduction Reactions

Combustion Reactions

Reacting organic compounds with oxygen often results in the production of a large amount of heat along with a flame that is characteristic of the combustion process. The products of **combustion** reactions are usually carbon dioxide and water, as in the combustion of glucose:

$$C_6H_{12}O_6 + 6O_2 \rightarrow 6CO_2 + 6H_2O \quad (13.68)$$

When the amount of oxygen is limited, or there is no oxygen, the products of the reaction may include carbon monoxide or elemental carbon (soot):

$$C_6H_{12}O_6 + 3O_2 \rightarrow 6CO + 6H_2O \text{ (limited } O_2) \quad (13.69)$$

$$C_6H_{12}O_6 \rightarrow 6C + 6H_2O \text{ (no } O_2) \quad (13.70)$$

The same products, CO_2 and H_2O, are formed when glucose is metabolized in the body. However, since the process is slow and does not produce a flame, it is not called a combustion reaction. The body uses the heat and energy produced in a more efficient manner in metabolism. Even when the amount of oxygen is limited, CO and C are not produced in metabolic reactions.

Oxidation of Metals

Metallic elements have differing affinities toward oxygen. The very unreactive elements, such as platinum, gold, silver, and copper, do not react with O_2. Silver tarnishes by reacting with small amounts of hydrogen sulfide in the air. Copper reacts with water and carbon dioxide to form a carbonate compound. Some metals, particularly the alkali and alkaline earth metals, however, react readily with oxygen and are completely converted into oxides if exposed long enough.

Magnesium burns with a bright white flame in oxygen. The bright light is used in magnesium flares by the military, in flashbulbs for photography, and in fireworks. The reaction is so energetic that magnesium will continue burning even in an atmosphere of carbon dioxide:

$$2Mg + CO_2 \rightarrow 2MgO + C \qquad (13.71)$$

When finely divided into a powder, many metals burn in oxygen. Steel wool burns when placed in a flame, and powdered metals, such as aluminum, are classified as highly combustible.

Aluminum reacts very well with oxygen, as mentioned above. In large sheets or bars of the metal, however, the aluminum oxide formed produces an impervious coating so that complete oxidation does not occur. This oxide layer is only a few molecules thick and is not visible to the eye.

Iron and steel react poorly with gaseous oxygen. The formation of rust requires the presence of water for oxidation to occur; iron does not rust in pure oxygen or in water that contains no oxygen. In this complex electrochemical process, the iron actually acts as the anode of a chemical reaction when moisture is present and as the cathode when it is not. **Corrosion** and its prevention are major concerns of approximately 30 percent of working chemists and chemical engineers. Each year, damage due to corrosion of buildings, bridges, and even computer circuits costs billions of dollars to correct and repair.

Important Concepts

Oxidation and reduction
Oxidation numbers
Ion Electron method for balancing equations
Electrolytic and galvanic cells
Standard reduction potentials
Standard cell voltages
Nernst equation

Important Equations

$$E = E^0 - \frac{RT}{n\mathscr{F}} \ln K$$

$$\text{moles} = \frac{It}{n\mathscr{F}}$$

Questions on Chapter 13

1. Balance the following half-reaction in acid solution:

$$NO_3^- \rightarrow NH_4^+$$

When balanced with the smallest whole-number coefficients possible, the *sum* of all the coefficients is
(A) 13
(B) 26
(C) 15
(D) 23
(E) 21

2. For the reduction of MnO_4^- to Mn^{2+}, the correct form of the Nernst equation is

(A) $E = E^0 + \dfrac{0.0591}{3} \log \left(\dfrac{[Mn^{2+}]}{[MnO_4^-] [H^+]^8} \right)$

(B) $E = E^0 + \dfrac{0.0591}{5} \log \left(\dfrac{[Mn^{2+}]}{[MnO_4^-] [H^+]^8} \right)$

(C) $E^0 = E + \dfrac{0.0591}{5} \log \left(\dfrac{[Mn^{2+}]}{[MnO_4^-] [H^+]^8} \right)$

(D) $E = E^0 + \dfrac{0.0591}{5} \log \left(\dfrac{[MnO_4^-] [H^+]^8}{[Mn^{2+}]} \right)$

(E) $E = E^0 + \dfrac{0.0591}{5} \log \left(\dfrac{[Mn^{2+}]}{[MnO_4^-] [H^+]^8} \right)$

3. The following reactions are known to occur spontaneously:

$$Cu + 2Ag^+ \rightarrow Cu^{2+} + 2Ag$$
$$Zn + 2Ag^+ \rightarrow Zn^{2+} + 2Ag$$
$$Zn + Cu^{2+} \rightarrow Zn^{2+} + Cu$$

The activity series for the three elements as reducing agents is
(A) Cu > Ag > Zn
(B) Zn > Cu > Ag
(C) Ag > Cu > Zn
(D) Ag > Zn > Cu
(E) Zn > Ag > Cu

4. The standard reduction potential for $PbO_2 \rightarrow Pb^{2+}$ is +1.46 V, and the standard reduction potential for $Fe^{3+} \rightarrow Fe^{2+}$ is +0.77 V. What is the standard cell voltage for the reaction

$$4H^+ + PbO_2 + 2Fe^{2+} \rightarrow 2Fe^{3+} + Pb^{2+} + 2H_2O?$$

(A) −0.08 V
(B) +0.69 V
(C) +2.33 V
(D) −0.69 V
(E) −2.33 V

5. Which of the following compounds includes an element with an oxidation number of +5?
   (A) ClO_4^-
   (B) MnO_4^-
   (C) NO_2^-
   (D) SO_3^{2-}
   (E) NO_3^-

6. Which of the following metals does NOT react with water to produce hydrogen?
   (A) Zn
   (B) Li
   (C) Ca
   (D) Na
   (E) Rb

7. In the electrolysis of an aqueous solution of $CuNO_3$, which of the following is expected to occur?
   (A) formation of O_2 at the anode
   (B) formation of H_2 at the cathode
   (C) deposition of copper metal on the anode
   (D) formation of hydroxide ions at the cathode
   (E) formation of H^+ at the cathode

8. Sodium metal cannot be electrolyzed from an aqueous Na_2SO_4 solution because
   (A) the voltage needed is too high for any available instrument to achieve
   (B) water is reduced to O_2 before Na^+
   (C) Na^+ has a high over-potential that keeps it from being reduced
   (D) H^+ has a more favorable reduction potential than Na^+
   (E) Na^+ does electrolyze, but it immediately reacts with water again

9. Which of the following elements has the largest number of possible oxidation states?
   (A) Fe
   (B) Cl
   (C) Ca
   (D) Mn
   (E) Na

10. For the reaction

$$2I^- + Cl_2 \rightleftharpoons 2Cl^- + I_2$$

the standard cell voltage is $E_{cell}^0 = +0.82$ V. What is the equilibrium constant for this reaction at 45°C? ($R = 8.314$ V C mol^{-1} K^{-1}, and $\mathcal{F} = 96,485$ C mol^{-1})
   (A) 9.8×10^{25}
   (B) 1.0×10^{-26}
   (C) 1.6×10^5
   (D) 6.3×10^{-6}
   (E) 2.27

11. Which of the following E^0_{cell} values represents a nonspontaneous reaction that produces the greatest amount of product, assuming the same number of electrons is transferred in each reaction?
    (A) +2.31 V
    (B) +0.23 V
    (C) −0.12 V
    (D) −1.68 V
    (E) −1.14 V

12. A metal is electrolyzed from aqueous solution by using an electrical current of 1.23 A for 2½ h, and 3.37 g of metal is deposited. In a separate experiment the number of electrons used for the reduction of the metal is 2. What is the metal?
    (A) Al
    (B) Ni
    (C) Sn
    (D) Mg
    (E) Au

13. A galvanic cell is set up under nonstandard state conditions, and E_{cell} is measured as −0.16 V. Which of the following is true about this system?
    (A) The galvanic cell is set up incorrectly because of the negative value of E^0_{cell}.
    (B) If the contents of the two cells are mixed, the reaction will proceed in the forward direction.
    (C) The reaction is definitely nonspontaneous.
    (D) If the contents of the two cells are mixed, the reaction will proceed in the reverse direction.
    (E) The reaction is definitely spontaneous.

14. A galvanic cell is constructed; and when the temperature of the cell is increased from 20°C to 30°C, the cell voltage changes by a factor of 1.034. Which of the following conclusions may be drawn from this observation?
    (A) Neither temperature is standard state, and the observation is meaningless.
    (B) The increase is due solely to the temperature term in $\Delta G^0 = -RT \ln K$.
    (C) The information indicates that ΔS^0 for this reaction must be negative.
    (D) The reaction is spontaneous.
    (E) The voltage change must be due to the change in the equilibrium constant with temperature.

15. Which of the following is NOT commonly produced by electrolysis?
    (A) NaOCl (bleach)
    (B) Al
    (C) Fe
    (D) NaOH
    (E) H_2

16. Which of the following compounds includes an element that has the same oxidation number as the chlorine in sodium chlorate, $NaClO_3$?
    (A) $K_3Fe(CN)_6$
    (B) $KMnO_4$
    (C) $Al(NO_3)_3$
    (D) $(NH_4)_2SO_4$
    (E) $KClO_4$

17. With a current of 1.25 A, how many minutes will be required to deposit 2.00 g of copper on a platinum electrode from a copper(II) nitrate solution? (Faraday's constant $= 96,485$ C mol^{-1})
    (A) 4859
    (B) 81.0
    (C) 40.5
    (D) 1.35
    (E) 2430

18. What is the minimum number of electrons needed to balance the following half-reaction with whole number coefficients:

$$IO_3^- \quad \rightarrow \quad I_2?$$

    (A) 1
    (B) 2
    (C) 5
    (D) 10
    (E) 12

19. Which of the following pairs of constants are NOT mathematically related to each other?
    (A) equilibrium constant and Gibbs free energy
    (B) rate constant and activation energy
    (C) standard cell voltage and equilibrium constant
    (D) standard cell voltage and rate constant
    (E) Gibbs free energy and standard cell voltage

20. Which of the following statements is FALSE?
    (A) Reduction involves a gain of electrons.
    (B) Batteries are galvanic cells.
    (C) A spontaneous reaction always has a positive E^0_{cell}.
    (D) Electrolysis reactions always produce a gas at at least one electrode.
    (E) Galvanic cells can be used to determine equilibrium constants.

Answer Key   See Appendix I for explanation of answers.

1. **D**	5. **E**	9. **D**	13. **D**	17. **B**
2. **B**	6. **A**	10. **A**	14. **B**	18. **D**
3. **B**	7. **A**	11. **C**	15. **C**	19. **D**
4. **B**	8. **D**	12. **B**	16. **C**	20. **D**

CHAPTER FOURTEEN

Acids and Bases

Acids and **bases** are common in all areas of human endeavor. They range from household cleaning agents to acid rain in the environment and to concentrated industrial reagents. Acids and bases are also essential to the proper biochemical functioning of living organisms. In the form of buffer solutions they help maintain the proper pH values in cellular and body fluids. In the stomach, hydrochloric acid helps digest food. When too much hydrochloric acid is produced, bases, called antacids, are taken to relieve the indigestion or heartburn caused by the excess acid.

Acids and bases were some of the first chemicals to be manufactured and studied in detail by alchemists. Sulfuric acid, known as oil of vitriol, was obtained by distilling copper sulfate pentahydrate, which was called blue vitriol. With the modern atomic theory a much better understanding of the reactions of acids with bases has been developed. Chemists work with a combination of concepts from three separate theories to describe acids and bases.

Acid-Base Theories

Arrhenius Theory

Svante Arrhenius considered an acid to be any substance that increases the concentration of hydrogen ions, H^+, in aqueous solution. When an acid is dissolved in water, the reaction may be written in two different forms. For example, when gaseous hydrogen chloride is dissolved in water, the equation is written as

$$HCl(g) \xrightarrow{H_2O} H^+(aq) + Cl^-(aq) \qquad (14.1)$$

Modern chemistry recognizes, however, that the hydrogen ion, H^+, is unlikely to exist in aqueous solution. Instead, the hydrogen ion is hydrated or bound to one or more water molecules. H_3O^+ is used to represent the hydration of the hydrogen ion, and the reaction of HCl with water is written as

$$HCl(g) + H_2O(\ell) \rightarrow H_3O^+(aq) + Cl^-(aq) \qquad (14.2)$$

Common examples of acids are HCl, HBr, H_2SO_4, H_3PO_4, and $HC_2H_3O_2$. The **Arrhenius theory** considers bases to be substances that increase the hydroxide ion, OH^-, concentration when dissolved in water. A typical reaction is as follows:

$$KOH(s) \xrightarrow{H_2O} K^+(aq) + OH^-(aq) \qquad (14.3)$$

Common bases are NaOH, KOH, $Ca(OH)_2$, and $Al(OH)_3$.

Brönsted-Lowry Theory

For a long time it was known that ammonia, NH_3, when dissolved in water increases the hydroxide ion concentration. In fact, ammonia solutions were often called ammonium hydroxide, with the formula NH_4OH. This fit the Arrhenius theory, but not the facts since NH_4OH does not really exist. The **Brönsted-Lowry theory** solves this problem by defining acids as proton donors, as the Arrhenius theory does, but defining bases as proton acceptors. Ammonia, NH_3, is a base since it accepts protons from water molecules in the reaction

$$H_2O(\ell) + NH_3(g) \rightleftharpoons NH_4^+(aq) + OH^-(aq) \quad (14.4)$$

Ethylamine, $CH_3CH_2NH_2$, and dimethylamine, $(CH_3)_2NH$, are both bases related to ammonia. In ethylamine the ethyl group, $CH_3CH_2—$, replaces one hydrogen in ammonia. Two methyl groups, CH_3-, in dimethylamine replace two of the ammonia hydrogens.

Lewis Theory

To completely generalize acid-base theory and to account for the formation of complex ions, G. N. Lewis proposed that acids are substances that accept electron pairs from other atoms, ions, or molecules and bases are substances that donate electron pairs in forming chemical bonds. The reaction between boron trichloride, BCl_3, an electron-deficient compound, and ammonia, NH_3, which has a nonbonding pair of electrons, is an acid-base reaction according to the Lewis definitions. Ammonia is an electron-pair donor and is a base, while boron trichloride is the electron-pair acceptor and is an acid:

$$(14.5)$$

The **Lewis theory** is used mainly to explain the formation of substances called complexes; the Arrhenius and Brönsted-Lowry theories serve to explain the more traditional acid-base reactions.

Modern Concept of Acids

An acid, according to both the Arrhenius and Brönsted-Lowry theories, is any compound having one or more hydrogen atoms that are weakly bound to the rest of the molecule. When dissolved in water, hydrogen ions ionize from the rest of the molecule. Most acids are written with hydrogen as the first element in the formula. Organic acids, however, can be written with hydrogen as the first element or with the —COOH unit that is the functional group for organic acids. The following three formulas all represent acetic acid:

$$HC_2H_3O_2 \qquad CH_3COOH \qquad \begin{matrix} OH \\ | \\ CH_3C = O \end{matrix}$$

Acid-Base Nomenclature

Binary acids contain hydrogen and one other atom. The name of every binary acid starts with the prefix *hydro-* and ends with the suffix *-ic* on the root of the second atom in the formula. Table 14.1 lists several binary acid names.

TABLE 14.1 Binary Acid Names

Name	Formula
Hydrofluoric acid	HF
Hydrochloric acid	HCl
Hydrobromic acid	HBr
Hydroiodic acid	HI
Hydrosulfuric acid	H_2S

Polyatomic anions can be the anions of acids. For these acids, the ending of the polyatomic anion name is changed and the word *acid* is added. If the polyatomic anion name ends in *-ate*, it is changed to *-ic*. If the ending is *-ite*, it is changed to *-ous*. Table 14.2 illustrates this principle for several polyatomic anions.

TABLE 14.2 Names of Acids Derived from Polyatomic Anions

Polyatomic Anion	Acid Name	Acid Formula
Sulfate	Sulfuric acid	H_2SO_4
Sulfite	Sulfurous acid	H_2SO_3
Nitrate	Nitric acid	HNO_3
Nitrite	Nitrous acid	HNO_2
Hypochlorite	Hypochlorous acid	$HClO$
Chlorite	Chlorous acid	$HClO_2$
Chlorate	Chloric acid	$HClO_3$
Perchlorate	Perchloric acid	$HClO_4$

Organic acids have both common and systematic names. In the systematic name for an organic acid the suffix *-oic* and the word *acid* are added to the root name of the rest of the molecule. Some organic acids and their systematic and common names are listed in Table 14.3.

TABLE 14.3 Organic Acid Names

Systematic Name	Common Name	Formula
Methanoic acid	Formic acid	$HCOOH$
Ethanoic acid	Acetic acid	CH_3COOH
Propanoic acid	Propanoic acid	CH_3CH_2COOH
Butanoic acid	Butyric acid	$CH_3CH_2CH_2COOH$
Pentanoic acid	Valeric acid	$CH_3CH_2CH_2CH_2COOH$
Benzoic acid	Benzoic acid	C_6H_5COOH

There are two types of bases, those that have hydroxide ions in their formulas and those that contain nitrogen. The **hydroxide bases** are named by using the name of the metal, with roman numerals if necessary, and then the word *hydroxide*. For example, NaOH, Al(OH)$_3$, and Fe(OH)$_3$ are called sodium hydroxide, aluminum hydroxide, and iron(III) hydroxide, respectively.

Nitrogen bases related to ammonia are amines. Replacing a hydrogen on ammonia with a methyl, —CH$_3$, group produces methylamine. If two methyl groups replace two hydrogen atoms, the compound is called dimethylamine. If a methyl and an ethyl group, —CH$_2$CH$_3$, replace two hydrogen atoms, the compound is called either ethylmethylamine or methylethylamine.

The chloride salt of ammonia is known as ammonium chloride. The chloride salt of methylamine is called methyl ammonium chloride; an alternative name for this salt is methylamine hydrochloride. For chloride salts of nitrogen bases with common names, such as hydrazine, the hydrochloride ending, as in hydrazine hydrochloride, is ordinarily used.

Acids

Strong Acids

Strong acids are acids that dissociate completely into ions when dissolved in water. The six most important strong acids are as follows:

Hydrochloric acid	HCl	$\rightarrow$	H$^+$	+	Cl$^-$
Hydrobromic acid	HBr	$\rightarrow$	H$^+$	+	Br$^-$
Hydroiodic acid	HI	$\rightarrow$	H$^+$	+	I$^-$
Perchloric acid	HClO$_3$	$\rightarrow$	H$^+$	+	ClO$_3^-$
Nitric acid	HNO$_3$	$\rightarrow$	H$^+$	+	NO$_3^-$
Sulfuric acid	H$_2$SO$_4$	$\rightarrow$	H$^+$	+	HSO$_4^-$

For sulfuric acid, only the first hydrogen is considered strong; the second hydrogen ion dissociates only slightly. These strong acids are also called mineral acids, as opposed to organic acids.

Weak Acids

All of the remaining acids are weak, meaning that, when they are dissolved in water, only a small percentage of the molecules dissociate into ions. Most of the **weak acids** are organic acids. The most common weak mineral acids are HF, H$_2$CO$_3$, H$_3$PO$_4$, H$_3$AsO$_4$, HClO$_3$, HClO$_2$, and HClO.

Acid Strengths

The concepts of electronegativity and bonding can be used to compare the strengths of acids based on their chemical formulas. The strength of an acid is inversely proportional to the strength of the bond between the hydrogen and the remainder of the molecule. Strong acids have very weak bonds, and weak acids have stronger bonds. To determine the relative strengths of acids, an estimate of the bond strengths is needed.

As mentioned previously, a **binary acid** is composed of hydrogen and one other atom. Experimental evidence shows that acids get stronger from left to right in a period (row) of the periodic table. Thus, we find that PH$_3$ is weaker than H_2S, which is weaker than HBr. Across a period the acid strength parallels the electronegativity of the anion. This is reasonable because, as the anion attracts the electrons more strongly, the bond with hydrogen becomes weaker, while the size of the anions remains relatively constant.

Experimental evidence also shows that binary acids get stronger from the top of a group to the bottom. Thus HF is weaker than HCl, which is weaker than HBr. Electronegativity cannot explain this sequence of binary acid strengths. Instead, the size of the anion is important. An increase in anion size requires a corresponding increase in bond length. As stated in Chapter 5, longer bond lengths imply weaker bonds. In acids, a weaker bond with hydrogen means a stronger acid.

All mineral acids that are not binary acids are **oxoacids**: acids that contain hydrogen, oxygen, and another element. In all oxoacids, the oxygen atoms are bound to the central atom and the hydrogen atoms are bound to

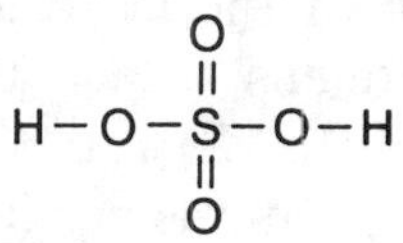

$$
\begin{array}{c}
O \\
\parallel \\
H-O-S-O-H \\
\parallel \\
O
\end{array}
$$

the oxygen atoms. A typical structure is represented by sulfuric acid:

The strength of an oxoacid always depends on the relative strength of the oxygen-hydrogen bond. In an oxoacid the strength of the O-H bond depends on (a) the number of oxygen atoms per hydrogen in the formula and (b) the electronegativity of the central atom in the formula.

Oxoacids that have the same central atom and the same number of hydrogen atoms increase in strength as the number of oxygen atoms increases:

Each extra oxygen withdraws more electron density from the O-H bond,

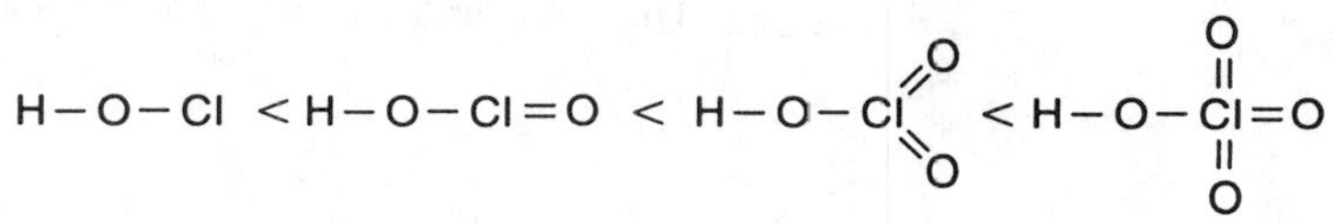

| hyporchlorous acid | chlorous acid | chloric acid | perchloric acid |

Weakest ⟵⟶ Strongest

thereby weakening it. The more oxygen atoms per hydrogen, the stronger the acid.

The strengths of oxoacids that have the same number of hydrogen and oxygen atoms but a different central atom are affected by the electronegativity of the central atom:

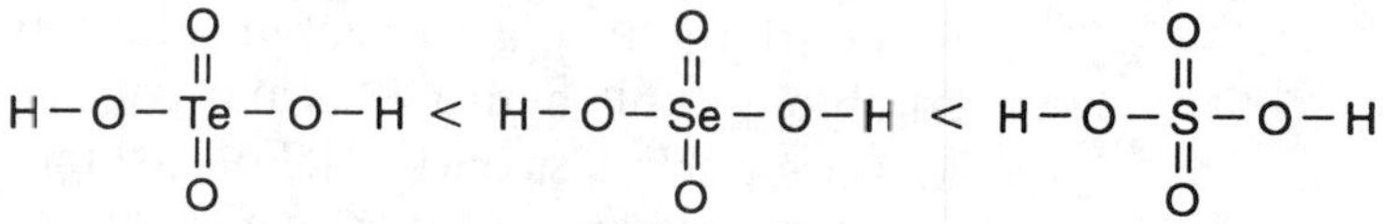

| telluric acid | selenic acid | sulfuric acid |

Weakest ⟵⟶ Strongest

The electronegativity of the central atom increases from tellurium to selenium to sulfur, weakening the O-H bond and resulting in stronger acids.

Oxoacids that have the same number of oxygen atoms but different central atoms and different numbers of hydrogens can also be compared. For instance, experiments show that

$$H_3PO_4 \quad < \quad H_2SO_4 \quad < \quad HClO_4$$

In this situation we see that the electronegativity of the central atom increases as the strength of the acid increases. In addition to the electrone-gativity of the central atom, the oxygen atoms that have no hydrogens attached to them affect the acid strength. H_3PO_4 has only one oxygen that does not have a hydrogen attached to it, and it is attracting electrons from three H-O bonds. In H_2SO_4 there are two oxygens without hydrogen attached, and their effect is concentrated on only two H-O bonds. Finally in $HClO_4$ three oxygen atoms have no hydrogen attached to them, and their effect is focused on a lone H-O bond. The effect of the electronega-tivity of the central atom and the effect of the oxygen atoms with no hydrogens attached combine to produce the observed trend in acid strengths. To repeat: when two acids are compared, the acid with more oxygen atoms per hydrogen atom will be the stronger acid.

Every **organic acid** contains the carboxyl group, which is commonly written as

$$-COOH \quad or \quad -C{\overset{\displaystyle O}{\underset{\displaystyle O-H}{}}}$$

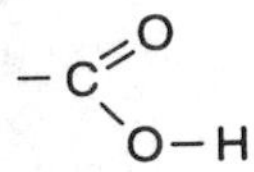

Electronegative atoms such as F, Cl, Br, I, O, and S on nearby carbon atoms will withdraw electron density from the —O—H bond and increase the strength of the acid. The addition of chloring atoms to acetic acid increases the acid strength as shown below.

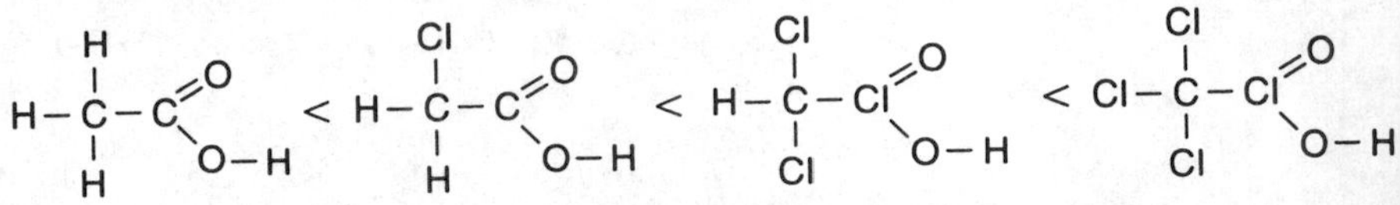

| acetic acid | chloroacetic acid | dichloroacetic acid | trichloroacetic acid |

Weakest ←—————————————————→ Strongest

Bases

Strong Bases

All metal hydroxides are **strong bases**. However, most metal hydroxides are very slightly soluble. Only the hydroxides of group IA metals, strontium and barium, have appreciable solubility; calcium hydroxide is moderately soluble. Soluble hydroxides may cause severe skin burns. Insoluble hydrox-ides are much less harmful. For instance, $Al(OH)_3$ can safely be swallowed as an antacid to neutralize excess stomach acid.

Weak Bases

All bases related to ammonia are **weak bases**. In organic compounds re-lated to ammonia, called **amines,** carbon-containing groups replace one or more of the hydrogen atoms of ammonia, NH_3. Two such bases, ethylamine and dimethylamine, were described above.

Base Strengths

The relative strengths of the weak bases may be evaluated based on the electronegativities of the organic functional groups that replace the hydrogen atoms of ammonia. Electronegative substituents such as chlorine increase the strength of organic acids. The reverse is true, however, of organic bases. For example, chloromethylamine is a weaker base than methylamine.

Anhydrides of Acids and Bases

The word *anhydride* means "without water," and the acidic and basic anhydrides are compounds that, when added to water, become common acids and bases. **Acid anhydrides** are the oxides of nonmetals, which have the following reactions with water:

$$SO_2 \quad + \quad H_2O \quad \rightarrow \quad H_2SO_3 \tag{14.6}$$

$$SO_3 \quad + \quad H_2O \quad \rightarrow \quad H_2SO_4 \tag{14.7}$$

$$CO_2 \quad + \quad H_2O \quad \rightarrow \quad H_2CO_3 \tag{14.8}$$

$$P_2O_5 \quad + \quad 3H_2O \quad \rightarrow \quad 2H_3PO_4 \tag{14.9}$$

Basic anhydrides are the oxides of metals. Some typical reactions with water are these:

$$K_2O \quad + \quad H_2O \quad \rightarrow \quad 2KOH \tag{14.10}$$

$$CaO \quad + \quad H_2O \quad \rightarrow \quad Ca(OH)_2 \tag{14.11}$$

In industrial applications CaO is called lime, and $Ca(OH)_2$ is termed slaked lime. The production of lime is a major industry that involves mining naturally occurring limestone, $CaCO_3$, and heating it to very high temperatures to drive off carbon dioxide in the reaction

$$CaCO_3 \quad \xrightarrow{\text{heat}} \quad CaO \quad + \quad CO_2 \tag{14.12}$$

Neutralization Reactions

The reactions between acids and bases are called **neutralization reactions**. They are often double-replacement reactions, and the products can be predicted by the methods described in Chapter 4. In most cases, a neutralization reaction can be described as the mixing of an acid with a base to form a salt and water:

$$\underset{\text{(acid)}}{HBr(aq)} \quad + \quad \underset{\text{(base)}}{KOH(aq)} \quad \rightarrow \quad \underset{\text{(salt)}}{KBr(aq)} \quad + \quad \underset{\text{(water)}}{H_2O(\ell)} \tag{14.13}$$

A neutralization reaction may be written as a molecular, ionic, or net ionic equation depending on the type of information the chemist is interested in communicating. For a typical neutralization reaction with soluble acids and bases the three types of reactions would be as follows:

$$HCl + NaOH \rightarrow NaCl + H_2O \quad \text{(molecular equation)} \quad (14.14)$$

$$H^+ + Cl^- + Na^+ + OH^- \rightarrow Na^+ + Cl^- + H_2O \quad \text{(ionic equation)} \quad (14.15)$$

$$H^+ + OH^- \rightarrow H_2O \quad \text{(net ionic equation)} \quad (14.16)$$

If all of the reactants are soluble strong acids and bases, the net ionic equation of a neutralization will *always* be as shown in Equation 14.16.

Acids are often used to dissolve insoluble hydroxides or oxides of metals. For instance, lanthanum ions are used to suppress interferences in atomic absorption spectroscopy. Dissolution of lanthanum oxide, La_2O_3, is achieved by reacting it with either HCl or HNO_3:

$$6HCl + La_2O_3 \rightarrow 2LaCl_3 + 3H_2O \quad (14.17)$$

$$6HNO_3 + La_2O_3 \rightarrow 2La(NO_3)_3 + 3H_2O \quad (14.18)$$

These are reactions between an acid and a basic anhydride. In both reactions the chloride and nitrate salts of lanthanum are soluble.

Acid anhydrides such as SO_3 and CO_2 will react with bases as in the following reactions:

$$2NaOH(aq) + SO_3(g) \rightarrow Na_2SO_4(aq) + H_2O(\ell) \quad (14.19)$$

$$Ca(OH)_2(aq) + CO_2(g) \rightarrow CaCO_3(s) + H_2O(\ell) \quad (14.20)$$

Acid and basic anhydrides may react with each other without any water present. For example, lime can react with sulfur trioxide in the reaction

$$SO_3(g) + CaO(s) \rightarrow CaSO_4(s) \quad (14.21)$$

Polyprotic Acids

Acids that contain more than one ionizing hydrogen are called **polyprotic acids**. Sulfuric acid, H_2SO_4, and phosphoric acid, H_3PO_4, are two examples. Although acetic acid, $HC_2H_3O_2$, has four hydrogen atoms in its formula, it is not a polyprotic acid since it has only one ionizable hydrogen.

All polyprotic acids are weak acids except sulfuric acid, which is unique in that its first proton dissociates completely but the second proton does not. One property of polyprotic acids is that the protons dissociate and react in a stepwise manner; that is, the first proton dissociates or reacts before the second proton. The stepwise dissociation of phosphoric acid is written as shown in Equations 14.22–14.24:

$$H_3PO_4 \rightleftharpoons H_2PO_4^- + H^+ \qquad (14.22)$$

$$H_3PO_4 \rightleftharpoons H_2PO_4^{2-} + H^+ \qquad (14.23)$$

$$H_3PO_4 \rightleftharpoons PO_4^{3-} + H^+ \qquad (14.24)$$

The product or products formed in the neutralization of a polyprotic acid depend on the amount of base used. When 1 mole of hydroxide ions per mole of phosphoric acid reacts, the equation is

$$H_3PO_4 + OH^- \rightarrow H_2PO_4^- + H_2O \qquad (14.25)$$

When 2 moles of hydroxide ions per mole of phosphoric acid react, the equation is

$$H_3PO_4 + 2OH^- \rightarrow H_2PO_4^{2-} + 2H_2O \qquad (14.26)$$

When 3 moles of hydroxide ions per mole of phosphoric acid react, the equation is

$$H_3PO_4 + 3OH^- \rightarrow PO_4^{3-} + 3H_2O \qquad (14.27)$$

Salts containing the $H_2PO_4^-$, $H_2PO_4^{2-}$, and PO_4^{3-} ions can be prepared by accurately adjusting the amount of base added to the phosphoric acid.

If exactly 1, 2, or 3 moles of hydroxide ions per mole of phosphoric acid are not reacted, a mixture of phosphate salts will form. For example, if 2.25 moles of OH^- are added per mole of phosphoric acid, we may deduce that the first 2 moles of OH^- convert the phosphoric acid to HPO_4^{2-}. The additional 0.25 mole of OH^- converts only some of the HPO_4^{2-} to PO_4^{3-}. Consequently, the final mixture will be a combination of HPO_4^{2-} and PO_4^{3-} salts.

rönsted-Lowry Theory; Conjugate Acid-Base Pairs:

The Brönsted-Lowry theory of acids and bases not only redefined these compounds but also gave us the concept of **conjugate acid-base pairs.** In the equilibrium reaction of acetic acid with hydroxide ions:

base 2 — acid 2: conjugate pair 2

$$HC_2H_3O_2 + OH^- \rightleftharpoons C_2H_3O_2^- + H_2O \qquad (14.28)$$

acid 1 — base 1: conjugate pair 1

$HC_2H_3O_2$ is an acid that reacts with the base OH^- in the forward reaction. The products, however, are also acids and bases. $C_2H_3O_2^-$ is a base that can accept an H^+ from the water, while water is an acid since it donate a proton in the reverse reaction. $HC_2H_3O_2$ and $C_2H_3O_2^-$ are called a conjugate acid-base pair. In a similar fashion, H_2O and OH^- are anothe conjugate acid-base pair in this equation.

Conjugate acid-base pairs always have formulas that differ by onl one H^+:

$$\text{Conjugate acid} \rightleftharpoons \text{Conjugate base} + H^+ \qquad (14.29$$

Relative Strengths of Conjugate Acids and Bases

In a conjugate acid-base pair the relative strengths of the **conjugate aci** and **conjugate base** are determined by the position of the equilibrium i Equation 14.29. If this position results in more products than reactants, th conjugate acid is stronger than the conjugate base. If there are more reac tants than products at equilibrium, the conjugate base is the stronger of th pair.

Acetic acid dissociates slightly in the reaction

$$HC_2H_3O_2 \rightleftharpoons C_2H_3O_2^- + H^+ \qquad (14.30$$

and we conclude that acetic acid is a weak acid and the acetate ion is stronger base.

The conjugate acid-base pair for ammonia may be written as

$$NH_4^+ \rightleftharpoons NH_3 + H^+ \qquad (14.3$$

Since an aqueous solution of ammonia has a much higher concentratic of ammonia than of the ammonium ion, the equilibrium lies to the right the double arrow in Equation 14.31. From this fact we conclude that th NH_4^+ ion is a stronger conjugate acid than NH_3 is a conjugate base.

Using similar logic, we can determine the relative strengths of conjuga acids and bases in a complete chemical reaction. For example, when equ numbers of moles of acetic acid and base are mixed, this reaction go virtually to completion, leaving little $HC_2H_3O_2$ and OH^-:

$$HC_2H_3O_2 + OH^- \rightarrow C_2H_3O_2^- + H_2O. \qquad (14.3$$

From the position of the equilibrium, chemists deduce that the OH^- ic is a stronger base than the acetate ion, $C_2H_3O_2^-$. At the same time, ace acid is also a stronger acid than the water molecule. Since we already knc that acetic acid is a weak acid, the water molecule must be a much weak acid. Similarly, since the acetate ion is a relatively strong base, the hydro ide ion is an even stronger base. This information tells us that in the H_2 OH^- conjugate acid-base pair water is a very weak acid and OH^- is a ve strong base.

Another reaction takes place when acetic acid is dissolved in distill water:

$$HC_2H_3O_2 + H_2O \rightleftharpoons C_2H_3O_2^- + H_3O^+ \qquad (14.$$

Again, we know that acetic acid is a weak acid, and by that definition most of it remains in molecular form. Since the reactants are favored in this equilibrium, we conclude that H_3O^+ is a stronger acid than $HC_2H_3O_2$. Also, the acetate ion is a stronger base than water. Knowing the position of equilibrium gives us another method to determine the relative strengths of conjugate acids and bases.

In aqueous solution, the strongest acid is the H_3O^+ ion (often written simply as the H^+ ion) and the strongest base is the OH^- ion. Acids that are stronger than water react with water to produce the H_3O^+ ion:

$$HCl \quad + \quad H_2O \quad \rightarrow \quad Cl^- \quad + \quad H_3O^+ \qquad (14.34)$$

Because hydrochloric acid is a very strong acid, this reaction goes all the way to completion, forming the H_3O^+ ion and leaving no HCl molecules. Bases that are stronger than water produce the OH^- ion when dissolved in water. In aqueous solutions all strong acids react completely with the weak base water. All strong bases also react completely, with water acting as a weak acid. This is known as the **leveling effect** of water.

In discussing the strengths of acids and bases, it was mentioned above that the acetate ion is a stronger base than water. This fact results in the concept that the anion of a weak acid may be considered as a base. Very strong acids such as HCl and HNO_3 have anions that are extremely weak conjugate bases. On the other hand, very weak acids have anions that are strong conjugate bases. Carbonic acid, H_2CO_3, is a very weak acid, and the carbonate ion, CO_3^{2-}, is a strong conjugate base. Carbonate salts such as sodium carbonate and calcium carbonate (limestone) are rather strong bases and are used in many industrial processes instead of more expensive hydroxide bases such as NaOH and KOH.

Later in this chapter we will see that the strengths of conjugate acids and bases can be expressed numerically as K_a and K_b values. These two values are related to the constant K_w in the equation

$$K_a K_b \quad = \quad K_w \qquad (14.35)$$

Equation 14.35 indicates that K_a is inversely proportional to K_b, meaning that strong conjugate acids have weak conjugate bases and vice versa.

Amphiprotic (Amphoteric) Substances

The words *amphiprotic* and *amphoteric* describe the same phenomenon, in which a substance may act as both a conjugate acid and a conjugate base. Amphiprotic salts are anions, and these anions must have at least one proton so that they can act as proton donors. They must also be able to accept a proton to act as bases. The anions of partially neutralized polyprotic acids are always amphiprotic. The common amphiprotic anions are the hydrogen carbonate ion, HCO_3^-; the hydrogen sulfate ion, HSO_4^-; the hydrogen sulfite ion, HSO_3^-; the dihydrogen phosphate ion, $H_2PO_4^-$; and the monohydrogen phosphate ion, HPO_4^{2-}. Each of these ions can accept a proton and act as a base. Each ion can also lose a proton and act as an acid.

Water is an amphiprotic solvent that can act as an acid and as a base as shown in the reaction

$$H_2O \quad + \quad H_2O \quad \rightleftharpoons \quad H_3O^+ \quad + \quad OH^- \qquad (14.36)$$

In this reaction one water molecule donates a proton and is an acid, while the other accepts a proton and is a base. In both cases water is an extremely weak acid and an extremely weak base.

Lewis Acids and Bases; Complexation Reactions

The primary use of the Lewis theory is to explain **complexation reactions,** which are not covered in the discussions of ionic reactions or covalent reactions. For instance, we know that silver chloride, AgCl, is an insoluble salt. It is not a hydroxide or a basic anhydride, which we know can be dissolved in acids. However, this salt does dissolve in ammonia solutions. An analysis of this process shows that the reaction is

$$AgCl(s) \quad + \quad 2NH_3 \quad \rightarrow \quad Ag(NH_3)_2^+ \quad + \quad Cl^- \quad (14.37$$

The same reaction occurs, without the Cl^- ions, when silver ions in solution react with ammonia. This reaction is a complexation reaction.

The Lewis theory explains why such ions as $Ag(NH_3)_2^+$ form. In Equation 14.37 the silver ion is a **Lewis acid,** accepting pairs of electrons, while the ammonia donates a pair of electrons to the bond, acting as a **Lewis base.** The Lewis structure shows the nonbonding pair of electrons the ammonia molecule donates:

$$H : \overset{..}{\underset{..}{N}} : H$$
$$\overset{|}{H}$$

The silver ion started as a silver atom with the electronic configuration [Kr] $5s^1$, $4d^{10}$. In forming the Ag^+ ion, it loses the $5s^1$ electron, resulting in the [Kr] $4d^{10}$ electronic configuration. Therefore it has empty $5s$ and $5p$ orbitals that may accept pairs of electrons. In actual fact, silver ions accept only two pairs of electrons from two ammonia molecules. In a similar fashion we find that all metal ions have available orbitals that may accept electron pairs. Metal ions are generally Lewis acids.

Ligands

In complexation reactions Lewis bases have many names: **ligands, complexing agents, chelates,** and **sequestering agents.** Most ligands have one pair of electrons to donate, as ammonia does. Some ligands have two pairs of electrons and some have up to six pairs. Ligands that provide more than one electron pair in forming a complex must be large, flexible molecules so that each pair of electrons can be oriented properly to form a bond. The chloride ion has four pairs of electrons but forms only one bond because the remaining six electrons cannot be aligned properly to form additional bonds.

Complexation reactions can be written generally as

$$M^{n+} \quad + \quad x\,L^{m-} \quad \rightleftharpoons \quad ML_x^{n-mx} \quad (14.3$$

where M^{n+} is a metal ion with a charge of $+n$ and L^{m-} is a liquid with a charge of $-m$.

Silver tends to accept two electron pairs, and copper accepts four. The other metal ions tend to accept six electron pairs in complexes. With the information we can accurately write most complexation reactions once the number of electron pairs that a ligand can donate has been determined.

Ligands that form only one bond are called **monodentate ligands**. Halide ions are monodentate ligands. Even though they have four available electron pairs, once one electron pair is donated, the other electron pairs are not in the proper positions to make additional bonds. Cyanide ions, CN^-; thiocyanate ions, SCN^-; and anions of weak acids are other common monodentate ligands. Ammonia is a neutral molecule that is a monodentate ligand. Water and carbon monoxide are other monodentate molecular ligands.

Ligands that can form two bonds are called **bidentate ligands**. The most common bidentate ligands are the diamines, such as ethylenediamine, $H_2NCH_2CH_2NH_2$, and the anions of diprotic organic acids, such as the oxalate ion, $^-OOCCOO^-$ or $C_2O_4^{2-}$.

One special ligand is ethylenediaminetetraacetic acid, EDTA:

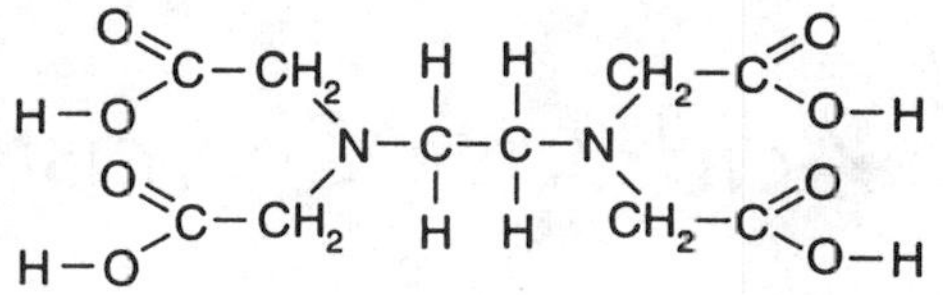

It has six pairs of electrons to donate, and the molecule is flexible enough to allow each of the six pairs to form bonds with a metal ion. One molecule of EDTA, Y^{4-}, always reacts with only one metal cation:

$$M^{n+} \quad + \quad Y^{4-} \quad \rightarrow \quad MY^{n-4}.$$

EDTA is an important molecule for chemical analysis of metal ions using simple titration methods. Also, EDTA is found in many consumer products. Cosmetics, drugs, and even foods contain EDTA, which acts as a preservative by forming complexes with metal ions. The same uncomplexed metal ions could act as catalysts to promote oxidation. Complexation reduces or eliminates the catalytic activity and increases the shelf life of consumer products.

Water was mentioned above as a monodentate ligand. In fact, when chemists write an ion with the symbol (aq) after it, they are recognizing the fact that all ions are actually complexed to water in aqueous solution. Therefore the $Na^+(aq)$ ion is actually the $Na(H_2O)_6^+$ complex ion. Complexes with other ligands simply replace the water molecules with other electron-pair donors.

The formula of a complex or a complex ion is written as any other chemical formula. For any complex ion the total charge of the ion is the sum of the charges of the ions in the complex. The complex made of Fe^{3+} and six chloride ions, $FeCl_6^{3-}$, has a charge of -3:

$$Fe^{3+} \quad + \quad 6Cl^- \quad \rightleftharpoons \quad FeCl_6^{3-}, \tag{14.39}$$

Molecular complexing agents do not affect the charge since they are neutral molecules. Thus Cu^{2+} still has a $+2$ charge when complexed with four molecules of ammonia in $Cu(NH_3)_4^{2+}$:

$$Cu^{2+} \quad + \quad 4NH_3 \quad \rightleftharpoons \quad Cu(NH_3)_4^{2+} \tag{14.40}$$

One interesting application of complexation reactions involves gold mining. Modern gold mining involves spraying dilute cyanide solutions, along with air, on gold-bearing ore. The gold, oxidized to Au^+, complexes with two CN^- ions to form the soluble complex $Au(CN)_2^-$. The liquid containing the gold complex is then treated to recover the concentrated gold.

Coordinate Covalent Bonds

The bonds formed in complexation reactions are covalent bonds. All of the properties of covalent bonds, as well as molecular structure, discussed in Chapter 5 apply also to the bonds in complexes. However, the formation of this covalent bond is unique. Instead of each atom donating one electron to the bond, one atom donates both electrons. Covalent bonds formed in this way are called **coordinate covalent bonds**. Aside from the method of formation, these bonds are true covalent bonds.

Quantitative Acid-Base Chemistry

In describing the nature of acids and bases, reference was made to their relative strengths. These strengths can be determined experimentally as the acid and base dissociation constants, K_a and K_b. The qualitative description of acid strengths given above was developed with a knowledge of the experimental values of acid strengths.

pH and pOH: Measurements of Acidity and Basicity

The acidity of a solution is expressed either as the molar hydrogen ion concentration, $[H^+]$, or the **pH** of the solution. Soren Sorensen in 1909 developed the pH system to represent acidity data in a simplified form. The pH and the hydrogen ion concentration are related by the equation

$$pH = -\log [H^+] \tag{14.41}$$

In aqueous solutions of acids and bases the pH ranges from 0 to 14. In very concentrated solutions we may have a negative pH (extremely acidic) or a pH greater than 14 (extremely basic).

In a similar fashion, the molar hydroxide ion concentration is related to the **pOH** by

$$pOH = -\log [OH^-] \tag{14.42}$$

The pH, pOH, $[H^+]$, and $[OH^-]$ are all related to each other. Water dissociates into hydrogen ions and hydroxide ions in the reaction

$$H_2O \rightleftharpoons H^+ + OH^- \tag{14.43}$$

The equilibrium law for Equation 14.43 is

$$K = [H^+][OH^-] = 1.0 \times 10^{-14} \tag{14.44}$$

The equilibrium constant in this case is designated as K_w, the **autopyrolysis constant of water**. Taking the negative logarithm of Equation 14.44 gives

$$pK_w = pH + pOH = 14.00 \qquad (14.45)$$

Equations 14.44 and 14.45 enable the chemist to determine the pH, pOH, $[H^+]$, or $[OH^-]$ and then find the other three by calculation.

Exercise 14.1

Determine $[H^+]$, $[OH^-]$, pH, and pOH, given the following data:
(a) $[H^+] = 2.3 \times 10^{-4}$ M   (c) pH = 10.67
(b) $[OH^-] = 6.3 \times 10^{-2}$ M   (d) pOH = 2.34

Solution

Starting with the given information, we use Equations 14.41–14.45 to convert:

$[H+]$	$[OH-]$	pH	pOH
(a) 2.3×10^{-4}	4.3×10^{-11}	3.64	10.36
(b) 1.6×10^{-13}	6.3×10^{-2}	12.80	1.20
(c) 2.1×10^{-11}	4.7×10^{-4}	10.67	3.33
(d) 2.2×10^{-12}	4.6×10^{-3}	11.66	2.34

When $[H^+]$ is greater than $[OH^-]$, the solution is considered to be acidic. A pH less than 7.0 also represents an acid solution. When $[H^+]$ is less than $[OH^-]$, the solution is basic and the pH is greater than 7.0. When $[H^+]$ is equal to the $[OH^-]$, the solution is neutral and the pH is 7.0.

Many of the common substances with which we come into contact are either acidic or basic. Table 14.4 lists some of these substances and their approximate pH values.

TABLE 14.4 Aproximate pH Values of Common Substances

Substance	Approximate pH
0.10 M HCl	1.00
Lemon juice	2.3
Vinegar	3.0
Wine	2.8–3.8
Pickles	3.3
Orange juice	3.5
Soft drinks	3.0–4.0
Beer	4.0–5.0
Pure rainwater	5.6
Milk	6.3–6.6
Blood	7.4
Seawater	8.3
Milk of magnesia	10.5
Ammonia	11.2
Lime water	12.4
0.1 M NaOH	13.00

[H+] and pH of Strong Acids

Except for sulfuric acid, all strong acids are monoprotic and dissociate completely when dissolved in water. Consequently, the hydrogen ion concentration of a strong acid solution is equal to the molar concentration of the acid itself:

$$[H^+] \quad = \quad M_{strong\ acid} \qquad (14.46)$$

Sulfuric acid is the only diprotic strong acid. When this acid is dissolved in water, only one hydrogen ion dissociates, and it acts as a monoprotic acid:

$$H_2SO_4 \quad \rightleftharpoons \quad H^+(aq) \quad + \quad HSO_4^-(aq) \qquad (14.47)$$

Also, for sulfuric acid the hydrogen ion concentration is equal to the molar concentration.

The pH of a strong acid solution can be written as

$$pH \quad = \quad -log\ [H^+] \quad = \quad -log\ M_{strong\ acid} \qquad (14.48)$$

[OH−], pOH, and pH of Strong Bases

Strong bases dissociate completely when dissolved in water; however, they may have more than one hydroxide ion per formula unit. The concentration of hydroxide ions is equal to the molarity of the base multiplied by the number of hydroxide ions in its chemical formula:

$$[OH^-] \quad = \quad M_{strong\ base} \times \text{number of } OH^- \text{ ions per mole} \qquad (14.49)$$

For example, a 0.200 M solution of $Ba(OH)_2$ has a hydroxide concentration of 0.400 M. Once the [OH−] is known, the pOH is calculated as

$$pOH \quad = \quad -log\ [OH^-]$$

From the pOH the pH is calculated using the relationship

$$pH \quad = \quad 14.00 - pOH$$

Exercise 14.2

Determine the pH of each of the following solutions:
(a) 0.020 M HNO_3
(b) 0.00043 M $Ba(OH)_2$
(c) 3.0 g of NaOH dissolved in 250 mL H_2O
(d) 0.00032 mol SO_3 dissolved in 3.4 L H_2O
(e) 0.00098 mol $Ca(OH)_2$ dissolved in 1.3 L H_2O

Solution

(a) $[H^+] = 0.020$ M; pH = 1.70
(b) $[OH^-] = (0.00043$ M$)$ $(2) = 0.00086$ M; pOH = 3.07 and pH = 10.9?
(c) $M_{NaOH} = 0.30$; $[OH^-] = 0.30$; pOH = 0.52 and pH = 13.48

(d) $SO_3 + H_2O \rightarrow H_2SO_4$; $M_{H_2SO_4} = 9.4 \times 10^{-5}$; $[H^+] = 9.4 \times 10^{-5}$; pH = 4.03

(e) $M_{Ca(OH)_2} = 7.5 \times 10^{-4}$; $[OH^-] = (7.5 \times 10^{-4})(2) = 1.5 \times 10^{-3}$; pOH = 2.82 and pH = 11.18

Calculations for pH can always be checked for reasonableness since acids must have pH values less than 7 and bases must have pH values greater than 7.

pH of Weak Acids and Weak Bases

Hydrofluoric acid is a weak acid that dissociates in water according to the equation

$$HF + H_2O \rightleftharpoons H_3O^+ + F^- \qquad (14.50)$$

Equation 14.50 may also be written in a shorter, more convenient form by eliminating water:

$$HF \rightleftharpoons H^+ + F^- \qquad (14.51)$$

Either Equation 14.50 or Equation 14.51 can be used to write the equilibrium law:

$$K_a = \frac{[H^+][F^-]}{[HF]} = \frac{[H_3O^+][F^-]}{[HF]} \qquad (14.52)$$

The two forms are identical, and either may be used in the calculations that follow.

The constant K_a is called the **acid dissociation constant**; values for selected weak acids are tabulated in Appendixes 4 and 5. For the example above, since we know the initial concentration of HF and the value of K_a, the hydrogen ion concentration can be calculated. The technique used is similar to the equilibrium calculations in Chapter 10.

Exercise 14.3

If 0.100 mol of HF is diluted with distilled water to a volume of 500 mL, what is the pH of the solution?

Solution

To solve this problem, we set up an equilibrium table with the reaction on the first line, and we enter the initial concentration on the INIT. CONC. line. The initial concentration of HF is calculated as

$$\frac{0.100 \text{ mol HF}}{0.500 \text{ L solution}} = 0.200 \text{ M HF}$$

REACTION	HF	⇌	H⁺	+	F⁻
INIT. CONC.	0.200 M		0.00*		0.00
CHANGE					
EQUILIBRIUM					
SOLUTION					

*The hydrogen ion concentration in distilled water is 1.0 x 10⁻⁷, but in most instances it is considered to be zero.

In the CHANGE row we enter x's to represent the stoichiometric relationships between the reactants and the products. In this table we assign a positive value to the x's under the products because they start at zero and cannot possibly decrease. As a consequence any x's under the reactant(s) must be negative.

REACTION	HF	⇌	H⁺	+	F⁻
INIT. CONC.	0.100/0.500		0.00		0.00
CHANGE	−x		+x		+x
EQUILIBRIUM					
SOLUTION					

The EQUILIBRIUM row is then the sum of the INIT. CONC. and CHANGE rows of the table:

REACTION	HF	⇌	H⁺	+	F⁻
INIT. CONC.	0.100/0.500		0.00		0.00
CHANGE	−x		+x		+x
EQUILIBRIUM	0.200 −x		+x		+x
SOLUTION					

At this point we enter the terms in the EQUILIBRIUM row into the equilibrium law, along with the value of K_a:

$$K_a = \frac{[H^+][F^-]}{[HF]}$$

$$6.6 \times 10^{-4} = \frac{(x)(x)}{0.200 - x}$$

If this equation is solved for x by ordinary means, a quadratic equation results. As before, we can try a simplifying assumption to solve the problem more quickly. The only term that can be simplified is $0.200 - x$. We use the assumption that $x \ll 0.200$ and conclude that $0.200 - x = 0.200$. (Remember that, when we finally calculate x, we must verify that the assumption is true.) Returning to the equation, we find that the assumption yields

$$6.6 \times 10^{-4} = \frac{(x)(x)}{0.200}$$
$$(6.6 \times 10^{-4})(0.200) = x^2$$
$$x = 0.0115$$

Checking the assumption, we find that 0.0115 is less than one-tenth of 0.200 and therefore qualifies as being negligible for this type of calculation. Now we substitute 0.0115 for x in the EQUILIBRIUM row and calculate the SOLUTION row:

REACTION	HF	⇌	H+	+	F−
INIT. CONC.	0.100/0.500		0.00		0.00
CHANGE	−x		+x		+x
EQUILIBRIUM	0.200 −x		+x		+x
SOLUTION	**0.189**		**0.0115**		**0.0115**

With the value for [H+] = 0.0115 M, the pH can be calculated as −log (0.0115) = 1.94.

Looking at this process a little more closely, we find that, if the assumption is valid, then

$$[H^+] = \sqrt{K_a C_a} \tag{14.53}$$

where C_a is the initial concentration of the weak acid. Evaluating the conditions under which the assumption holds, we find that it will always be valid as long as $C_a > 100 K_a$.

Weak bases such as ammonia and methylamine, CH_3NH_2, behave similarly to weak acids. The dissociation reaction for methylamine is

$$CH_3NH_2 + H_2O \rightleftharpoons CH_3NH_3^+ + OH^- \tag{14.54}$$

Although water cannot be eliminated to simplify the chemical reaction, it does not appear in the equilibrium law since it is the solvent.

$$K_b = \frac{[CH_3NH_3^+][OH^-]}{[CH_3NH_2]} \tag{14.55}$$

The constant K_b is the **base dissociation constant**. This equilibrium law is similar to the one for HF (Equation 14.52) in that it has two concentration terms in the numerator and one in the denominator. The two laws are mathematically equivalent.

Values of K_b for selected weak bases are given in Appendix 6.

Exercise 14.4

What is the pH of a 0.500 M solution of methylamine, $K_b = 4.2 \times 10^{-4}$?

Solution

First we set up the equilibrium table in the same fashion as for the weak acid example in Exercise 14.3.

REACTION	CH$_3$NH$_2$	+	H2O	⇌	CH$_3$NH$_3^+$	+	OH$^-$
INIT. CONC.	0.500		55.5		0.00		0.00
CHANGE	$-x$		$-x$		$+x$		$+x$
EQUILIBRIUM	0.500 $-x$		55.5 $-x$		$+x$		$+x$
SOLUTION							

We entered the concentration of water:

$$\frac{1000 \text{ g H}_2\text{O}}{18 \text{ g H}_2\text{O mol}^{-1}} = 55.5 \text{ M}$$

for completeness although it does not appear in the equilibrium law. The terms from the EQUILIBRIUM row are entered into the equilibrium law

$$4.2 \times 10^{-4} = \frac{(x)(x)}{0.500 - x}$$

To simplify, we assume that x is very small compared to 0.500, with the result that the 0.500 $- x$ term in the denominator becomes 0.500:

$$4.2 \times 10^{-4} = \frac{(x)(x)}{0.500}$$

Solving for x, we obtain

$$(4.2 \times 10^{-4})(0.500) = x^2$$
$$x = 0.0145$$

Once x is determined, we check the assumption and find that it is valid since 0.500 is more than ten times larger than 0.0145. The rest of the equilibrium table is completed using the calculated value of x:

REACTION	CH$_3$NH$_2$	+	H2O	⇌	CH$_3$NH$_3^+$	+	OH$^-$
INIT. CONC.	0.500		55.5		0.00		0.00
CHANGE	$-x$		$-x$		$+x$		$+x$
EQUILIBRIUM	0.500 $-x$		55.5 $-x$		$+x$		$+x$
SOLUTION	0.486		55.5		0.0145		0.0145

Using the listed [OH$^-$] we calculate pOH as 1.84, and the pH is 12.16. As with the weak acid, this entire process may be summarized in a simple equation:

$$[\text{OH}^-] = \sqrt{C_b K_b} \qquad \text{as long as } C_b > 100 \, K_b$$

In Exercises 14.3 and 14.4 there are two ways to check the accuracy of the results. First, the answers must be reasonable; a weak acid should have an acidic pH (below 7) and a weak base should have a basic pH (above 7). Second, the calculated values may be entered into the mass action expression, and the result should be close to the given K_a or K_b.

pH of Salt Solutions; Hydrolysis Reactions

When an acid is neutralized with a base, a salt is formed. If the anion of a salt is the conjugate base of a weak acid, it will react with water in a **hydrolysis reaction**. For the fluoride ion the hydrolysis reaction is as follows:

$$F^-(aq) \quad + \quad H_2O(\ell) \quad \rightleftharpoons \quad HF(aq) \quad + \quad OH^-(aq) \quad (14.56)$$

The conjugate base, F^-, of the weak acid HF will produce a basic solution, as shown by the OH^- in Equation 14.56.

If the cation of a salt is the conjugate acid of a weak base, the hydrolysis reaction will result in an acid solution, as shown by the reaction of the ammonium ion:

$$NH_4^+(aq) \quad + \quad H_2O(\ell) \quad \rightleftharpoons \quad NH_3(aq) \quad + \quad H_3O^+(aq) \quad (14.57)$$

The conjugate acid of a strong base and the conjugate base of a strong acid are extremely weak acids and bases. In fact, they are so weak that they do not hydrolyze in water. For example, Cl^- from the strong acid HCl and Na^+ from the strong base NaOH do not hydrolyze in water.

Acidity of Salt Solutions and Classification of Salts

The cation of a salt will be the conjugate acid of either a strong base or a weak base and the anion of a salt will be the conjugate base of either a strong acid or a weak acid. Table 14.5 describes the different types of salts possible.

TABLE 14.5 Classification of Salts Based on Acid and Base Used to Prepare Them

Acid Used	Base Used	Salt Type	Salt Solution Will Be
Strong	Strong	Neutral	Close to pH 7
Strong	Weak	Acidic	Acidic
Weak	Strong	Basic	Basic
Weak	Weak	Mixed	Depends on K_a and K_b

The first step in determining the pH of a salt solution is to determine the type of salt. This is done by adding H^+ to the anion and OH^- to the cation in the salt to determine the type of acid and base used to prepare the salt. For instance, ammonium chloride is composed of NH_4^+ and Cl^- ions. By adding OH⁻ to the cation and H⁺ to the anion, NH_4OH ($NH_3 + H_2O$) and HCl are obtained. From this result we conclude that ammonium chloride is an acid salt prepared from a weak base and a strong acid. We may also quickly conclude that solutions of ammonium chloride will have pH values below 7.

A mixed salt has a cation that is the conjugate acid of a weak base, and an anion that is the conjugate base of a weak acid. The acidity or alkalinity of a mixed salt will be determined by whichever of these conjugates is stronger. Considering the K_a of the weak acid and the K_b of the weak base that form the salt, we conclude that the solution will be acidic if $K_b > K_a$ and basic if $K_a > K_b$.

Exercise 14.5

Determine whether the aqueous solutions of each of the following salts will be acid, neutral, or basic:

(a) $CaCl_2$ (c) Na_2SO_3 (e) SrF_2 (g) KNO_2
(b) $NaNO_3$ (d) $KC_2H_3O_2$ (f) NH_4Br (h) Li_2CO_3

Solution

(a) Neutral   (c) Basic   (e) Basic   (g) Basic
(b) Neutral   (d) Basic   (f) Acid   (h) Basic

pH of Salt Solutions

The pH of a neutral salt is 7.00. Although we can tell whether a mixed salt solution will be acidic or basic, calculation of the pH is left for higher level courses. We concern ourselves here with calculating the pH value of acidic and basic salts only.

Ammonium chloride was determined in the preceding section to be an acid salt. Since the chloride ion does not hydrolyze, we focus on the hydrolysis of the ammonium ion discussed above to develop the equilibrium law needed to solve problems.

NH_4^+ is the conjugate acid of ammonia, and the hydrolysis reaction is written as either

$$NH_4^+ \quad + \quad H_2O \quad \rightleftharpoons \quad NH_3 \quad + \quad H_3O^+ \tag{14.58}$$

or

$$NH_4^+ \quad \rightleftharpoons \quad NH_3 \quad + \quad H^+ \tag{14.59}$$

The equilibrium law for this reaction is based on either of the two equivalent expressions:

$$K \quad = \quad \frac{[NH_3][H^+]}{[NH_4^+]} \quad = \quad \frac{[H_3O^+][NH_3]}{[NH_4^+]} \tag{14.60}$$

The equilibrium constant K is equal to K_w/K_b, where K_b is the base dissociation constant for ammonia. We can demonstrate this relationship by multiplying the equilibrium law in Equation 14.60 by $\frac{[OH^-]}{[OH^-]}$ to obtain

$$K = \left(\frac{[NH_3][H^+]}{[NH_4^+]}\right)\left(\frac{[OH^-]}{[OH^-]}\right) \tag{14.61}$$

In the numerator the product $[H^+][OH^-] = K_w$, which we substitute into Equation 14.61:

$$K = K_w\left(\frac{[NH_3]}{[NH_4^+][OH^-]}\right) \tag{14.62}$$

The term in parentheses is the reciprocal of the equilibrium law for the dissociation of ammonia, and its value is K_b. Performing the substitution yields

$$K = \frac{K_w}{K_b} \tag{14.63}$$

This value is sometimes called the hydrolysis constant for a salt, K_h, but a more accurate name is the acid dissociation constant of the Brönsted-Lowry conjugate acid, symbolized as K_a.

This derivation leads to a universally useful equation and concept. For a conjugate acid-base pair the K_a of the conjugate acid multiplied by the K_b of the conjugate base will always be equal to K_w:

$$K_w = K_a K_b \tag{14.64}$$

K_w is the ion product for the dissociation of water:

$$H_2O \rightleftharpoons H^+ + OH^-$$

and

$$K_w = [H^+][OH^-] = 1.00 \times 10^{-14} \tag{14.65}$$

From this derivation we see also that the salt of a weak base acts as a Brönsted-Lowry acid, and we expect its solutions to be acidic.

Once the equilibrium law for acid and basic salts is derived, we can start solving problems. Let us calculate the pH of a 0.100 M solution of ammonium chloride. Since the equilibrium law has already been described, the next step is to set up the equilibrium table:

REACTION	NH_4^+	$\rightleftharpoons$	NH_3	+	H^+
INIT. CONC.	0.100		0.00		0.00
CHANGE	$-x$		$+x$		$+x$
EQUILIBRIUM	$0.100-x$		$+x$		$+x$
SOLUTION					

Entering the values of K_w, K_b, and the terms from the EQUILIBRIUM line into the equilibrium law yields

$$\frac{1.0 \times 10^{-14}}{1.8 \times 10^{-5}} = \frac{(x)(x)}{0.100 - x}$$

Assuming that $0.100 \gg x$, we obtain

$$\frac{1.0 \times 10^{-14}}{1.8 \times 10^{-5}} = \frac{(x)(x)}{0.100}$$

which may be solved as

$$(5.6 \times 10^{-10})(0.100) = x^2$$
$$x = 7.4 \times 10^{-6}$$

Since x is much smaller than 0.100, the assumption was valid. We now use the value of x to calculate the values in the SOLUTION row of the table.

REACTION	NH_4^+	$\rightleftharpoons$	NH_3	+	H^+
INIT. CONC.	0.100		0.00		0.00
CHANGE	$-x$		$+x$		$+x$
EQUILIBRIUM	$0.100-x$		$+x$		$+x$
SOLUTION	**0.100**		**7.4×10^{-6}**		**7.4×10^{-6}**

The pH is then calculated to be

$$pH = -\log(7.4 \times 10^{-6}) = 5.13$$

This result is consistent with the concept that NH_4^+ is a conjugate acid of NH_3 and that the solution must be acidic.

To summarize this calculation in a simpler form, we write

$$[H^+] = \sqrt{\frac{K_w}{K_b} C_s} \quad \text{provided that } C_s > 100 \frac{K_w}{K_b} \qquad (14.66)$$

where K_b is the dissociation constant of the weak base used to produce the acidic salt and C_s is the molar concentration of the salt.

For basic salts, calculations are performed in a very similar manner. For example, NaF is a basic salt since it is formed by reacting the strong base NaOH with the weak acid HF. We may ignore Na^+ while writing the hydrolysis equation for F^- as follows:

$$F^- + H_2O \rightleftharpoons HF + OH^- \qquad (14.67)$$

The base dissociation constant is calculated by dividing K_w by the acid dissociation constant, K_a, of HF:

$$K_b = \frac{K_w}{K_a} = \frac{[HF][OH^-]}{[F^-]} \qquad (14.68)$$

Questions may then be answered by using the procedures outlined above. The general solution can be simplified to

$$[OH^-] = \sqrt{\frac{K_w}{K_a} C_s} \quad \text{provided that } C_s > 100\frac{K_w}{K_a} \qquad (14.69)$$

where C_s is the initial concentration of the salt and K_a is the acid dissociation constant of HF.

The salt KNO_3 does not change the pH of the solution since it is formed from the strong acid HNO_3 and the strong base KOH. The K^+ and NO_3^- ions are such weak Brönsted-Lowry acids and bases that they have no effect on pH.

Two simple equations suffice for calculating the pH values of weak acid, weak base, acid salt, and basic salt solutions:

weak acids and acid salts: $\quad [H^+] = \sqrt{K_a C_a} \qquad (14.70)$

weak bases and basic salts $\quad [OH^-] = \sqrt{K_b C_b} \qquad (14.71)$

For solutions of weak acids or weak bases, K_a and K_b are the acid and base dissociation constants. In salt solutions, K_a and K_b are the conjugate acid and base dissociation constants of the ions in the salt, which are calculated as K_w/K_b and K_w/K_a, respectively. Equations 17.70 and 17.71 work only when the initial concentration, C, is at least 100 times larger than the dissociation constant, K. Otherwise the problem must be solved using the quadratic equation as shown in Chapter 10.

Buffer Solutions

To this point we have considered solutions containing only pure weak acids, weak bases, or their salts dissolved in distilled water. A mixture that contains a conjugate acid-base pair is known as a **buffer solution** because the pH changes by a relatively small amount if a strong acid or base is added to it. Buffer solutions are used to control pH in many biological and chemical reactions. These solutions are governed by the same equilibrium law as are weak acids and weak bases.

For instance, a buffer can be prepared by dissolving 0.200 mole of HF and 0.100 mole of NaF in water to make 1.00 liter of solution. The dissociation reaction of HF is

$$HF(aq) \rightleftharpoons F^-(aq) + H^+(aq) \qquad (14.72)$$

and its equilibrium law is

$$K_a = \frac{[F^-][H^+]}{[HF]} = 6.8 \times 10^{-4} \qquad (14.73)$$

An equilibrium table is set up using the given information. Since we have 0.100 mole NaF, the concentration of F^- is determined as 0.100 M. The Na^+ in NaF is a spectator ion in the dissociation reaction and is not needed.

REACTION	HF	⇌	F⁻	+	H⁺
INIT. CONC.	0.200		0.100		0.00
CHANGE	$-x$		$+x$		$+x$
EQUILIBRIUM	$0.200-x$		$0.100+x$		$+x$
SOLUTION					

Substituting the information from the EQUILIBRIUM line into the equilibrium law yields

$$K_a = \frac{(0.100 + x)(x)}{0.200 - x} = 6.8 \times 10^{-4}$$

Assuming that x is small compared to both 0.100 and 0.200, we simplify the equation to

$$K_a = \frac{(0.100)(x)}{0.200} = 6.8 \times 10^{-4}$$

Solving this equation for x yields

$$x = 1.36 \times 10^{-3}$$

This value of x satisfies the assumptions made, and the last line of the equilibrium table can be completed as:

REACTION	HF	⇌	F⁻	+	H⁺
INIT. CONC.	0.200		0.100		0.00
CHANGE	$-x$		$+x$		$+x$
EQUILIBRIUM	$0.200-x$		$0.100+x$		$+x$
SOLUTION	**0.199**		**0.101**		$\mathbf{1.36 \times 10^{-3}}$

The last column in the table gives us $[H^+] = 1.36 \times 10^{-3}$ M. The pH of the buffer solution is calculated as 2.87. For almost all buffer solutions the assumptions hold true, and this type of problem is solved by simply entering the given concentrations of the conjugate acid and conjugate base directly into the equilibrium law.

Exercise 14.6

Calculate the pH of the following buffer solutions:

(a) 0.250 M acetic acid and 0.150 M sodium acetate
(b) A solution of 10.0 g each of formic acid and potassium formate dissolved in 1.00 L of H_2O

(c) 0.0345 M ethylamine and 0.0965 M ethyl ammonium chloride
(d) 0.125 M hydrazine and 0.321 M hydrazine hydrochloride

Solution

(a) $K_a = \dfrac{[C_2H_3O_2^-][H^+]}{[HC_2H_3O_2]}$. Substituting data gives

$$1.8 \times 10^{-3} = \frac{(0.150)[H^+]}{0.250}$$

$$[H^+] = 3.0 \times 10^{-3}, \text{ and pH} = 2.52$$

(b) Calculate 0.217 M formic acid and 0.417 M sodium formate.

$$K_a = \frac{[CHO_2^-][H^+]}{[HCHO_2]}. \text{ Substituting data gives}$$

$$1.8 \times 10^{-4} = \frac{(0.417)[H^+]}{0.217}$$

$$[H^+] = 9.4 \times 10^{-5}, \text{ and pH} = 4.03$$

(c) $K_b = \dfrac{[C_2H_5NH_3^+][OH^-]}{[C_2H_5NH_2]}$. Substituting data gives

$$4.3 \times 10^{-4} = \frac{(0.0965)[OH^-]}{0.0345}$$

$$[OH^-] = 1.5 \times 10^{-4}, \text{ pOH} = 3.82, \text{ and pH} = 10.18$$

(d) $K_b = \dfrac{[N_2H_5^+][OH^-]}{[N_2H_4]}$. Substituting data gives

$$9.6 \times 10^{-7} = \frac{(0.321)[OH^+]}{0.125}$$

$$[OH^-] = 3.7 \times 10^{-7}, \text{ pOH} = 6.43, \text{ and pH} = 7.57$$

Shortcuts in Buffer Calculations

The equilibrium law used for buffers involves a ratio of the concentrations of the conjugate acid and conjugate base. For a ratio, we may use the moles of conjugate acid and moles of conjugate base instead of the acid and base molarities, thereby eliminating a step or two in the calculations.

In addition, if the concentrations of the conjugate acid and conjugate base are equal, their ratio is exactly 1.00. The result is that, with equal molarities or equal numbers of moles of conjugate acid and conjugate base,

$$K_a \quad = \quad [H^+] \quad \text{and} \quad pK_a \quad = \quad pH \qquad (14.74)$$

for a buffer made from a weak acid and its conjugate base, and

$$K_b \quad = \quad [OH^-] \quad \text{and} \quad pK_b \quad = \quad pOH \qquad (14.75)$$

for a buffer made from a weak base and its conjugate base.

pH Changes in Buffers

Addition of a strong acid to a buffer will decrease the pH slightly, and addition of a strong base will increase the pH slightly. To determine the amount that the pH changes when a strong acid or base is added to a buffer, we must calculate the change in concentration of the conjugate acid and conjugate base in the buffer.

In an acetate buffer, acetic acid, $HC_2H_3O_2$, is the conjugate acid, and the acetate ion, $C_2H_3O_2^-$, is the conjugate base. Addition of a strong acid, represented as H^+, results in the reaction

$$C_2H_3O_2^- \quad + \quad H^+ \quad \rightarrow \quad HC_2H_3O_2 \qquad (14.76)$$

Addition of a strong acid increases the concentration of acetic acid and decreases the concentration of acetate ions. Addition of a strong base to this buffer increases the acetate ion concentration and decreases the acetic acid concentration as in the reaction

$$HC_2H_3O_2 \quad + \quad OH^- \quad \rightarrow \quad C_2H_3O_2^- \qquad (14.77)$$

To calculate the effect of adding a strong acid or base to a buffer the following steps are followed:

1. Determine either the molarity or the number of moles of the conjugate acid and conjugate base in the original buffer.
2. Determine the amount of strong acid or base added in the same units as the conjugate acid and base in step 1.
3a. If a strong acid is added to the buffer, add the value from step 2 to the conjugate acid and subtract it from the conjugate base.
3b. If a strong base is added to the buffer, add the value from step 2 to the conjugate base and subtract it from the conjugate acid.
4. Substitute the new values for the conjugate acid and conjugate base into the equilibrium law, and calculate the pH as shown in the previous section.

Exercise 14.7

An acetate buffer is prepared with 0.250 M acetic acid and 0.100 M $NaC_2H_3O_2$. If 0.002 mol of solid NaOH is added to 100 mL of this buffer, calculate the change in pH of the buffer due to the addition of the NaOH.

Solution

To calculate the change in pH, the pH of the original buffer is needed, along with the final pH after the base is added. First, the dissociation reaction is written for acetic acid:

$$HC_2H_3O_2 \quad \rightleftharpoons \quad H^+ \quad + \quad C_2H_3O_2^-$$

Next the equilibrium law is written:

$$K_a = \frac{[H^+][C_2H_3O_2^-]}{[HC_2H_3O_2]}$$

The value for K_a and the acetate and acetic acid concentrations are substituted into the equilibrium law:

$$1.8 \times 10^{-5} = \frac{[H^+](0.100)}{0.250}$$

The hydrogen ion concentration is calculated as $[H^+] = 4.5 \times 10^{-5}$ M, and the pH is 4.35.

To calculate the pH of the buffer after the NaOH is added we must first convert either the molarities of the conjugate acids and bases to moles or the moles of NaOH to molarity so that all of the units are the same.

$$\text{Molarity NaOH} = \frac{0.00200 \text{ mol NaOH}}{0.100 \text{ L}} = 0.0200 \text{ M}$$

Adding this value to the acetate concentration gives us 0.120 M $C_2H_3O_2^-$. Subtracting it from the acetic acid concentration yields 0.230 M $HC_2H_3O_2$. Substituting these new values into the equilibrium law, we have

$$1.8 \times 10^{-5} = \frac{[H+](0.120)}{0.230}$$
$$[H^+] = 3.45 \times 10^{-5} \text{ M}$$
$$pH = 4.46$$

There is an increase of 0.11 pH unit when the NaOH is added. This answer is reasonable since the pH is expected to rise slightly when a base is added.

Buffer Capacity

Buffer capacity is defined as the number of moles of strong acid or strong base needed to change the pH of 1 liter of buffer by 1 pH unit. Given the initial concentrations of the conjugate acid and conjugate base, buffer capacity can be calculated. A quick estimate of buffer capacity is obtained by multiplying the sum of the molarities of the conjugate acid and conjugate base by 0.4:

$$\text{Approximate buffer capacity} = \text{Total molarity} \times 0.4 \qquad (14.78)$$

Preparation of Buffers

Preparation of a buffer starts with the selection of the desired pH. Then, a table of K_a and K_b values for weak acids and bases is consulted to find an appropriate conjugate acid-base pair to use. These two steps determine the ratio of the salt to the weak acid or base. Next, the moles of acid or base that need to be buffered are estimated. The total number of moles of the conjugate acid-base pair should be at least 20 times the amount of the acid or base that needs to be buffered. The volume of buffer solution needed is determined next, and finally the method for preparing the buffer is decided upon.

Three methods are available for preparing a buffer solution. In the first method the conjugate acid and conjugate base are measured and dissolved to the desired volume. The second method involves measuring the desired amount of conjugate acid and then adding the appropriate amount of a strong base to convert some of the conjugate acid into its conjugate base. In the third method the conjugate base is measured and the necessary amount of strong acid is added to convert some of the conjugate base into its conjugate acid.

Selection of Buffer Materials

Assume that we need to prepare, at pH 5.00, 100 mL of a buffer that will be capable of buffering 6.0×10^{-5} mole of strong acid for an enzyme experiment. We need to select an appropriate weak acid or weak base to use for this buffer. Our table gives only K_a values. Instead of converting all of them to pK_a values, we realize that we need a pK_a between 4.00 and 6.00. Converting values in this range back to K_a values shows that for our buffer we require a K_a between 1.0×10^{-4} and 1.0×10^{-6}.

The possible choices are H_3AsO_4, $HCHO_2$, $HC_2H_3O_2$, HF, HNO_2, and HN_3. Since this is a biological experiment, we have to be careful that the buffer has no adverse effects on the biochemicals to be used. Therefore it is wise to avoid H_3AsO_4 because of the arsenic, HF and $HCHO_2$ because of their toxicity, HNO_2 because of its redox properties, and HN_3 because it is generally not readily available. We are left with acetic acid, $HC_2H_3O_2$, which is a very popular buffer material.

Next, we need at least 20 times the 6.0×10^{-5} mole of strong acid expected, or 1.2×10^{-3} mole of conjugate acid plus conjugate base. This will be dissolved in 100 mL of solution, so the total molarity will be 1.2×10^{-2} M. Since we already know that 100 mL of buffer is needed, the three methods of preparation can now be considered.

Method 1

As stated above, the first method involves measuring the appropriate amounts of the conjugate acid and base in the desired volume of water. The acid is acetic acid, and the conjugate base is the acetate ion. Acetate ions can be conveniently obtained from the salt sodium acetate. It was decided that the total of the conjugate acid and base should be

$$1.2 \times 10^{-2} \text{ M} = [HC_2H_3O_2] + [C_2H_3O_2^-] \quad (14.79)$$

The equilibrium law for the dissociation of acetic acid is

$$HC_2H_3O_2 = C_2H_3O_2^- + H^+ \quad (14.80)$$

$$K_a = \frac{[C_2H_3O_2^-][H^+]}{[HC_2H_3O_2]} \quad (14.81)$$

Rearranging Equation 14.81 gives

$$\frac{K_a}{[H^+]} = \frac{[C_2H_3O_2^-]}{[HC_2H_3O_2]} \quad (14.82)$$

Since the buffer pH must be 5.00, we enter 1.0×10^{-5} for $[+H]$.

$$\frac{1.8 \times 10^{-5}}{1.0 \times 10^{-5}} = \frac{[C_2H_3O_2^-]}{[HC_2H_3O_2]} \quad (14.83)$$

$$1.8 = \frac{[C_2H_3O_2^-]}{[HC_2H_3O_2]} \tag{14.84}$$

Equations 14.79 and 14.84 are used to calculate the needed concentrations of acetic acid and acetate ions:

$$1.8[HC_2H_3O_2] = [C_2H_3O_2^-] \tag{14.85}$$

Substitute $1.8[HC_2H_3O_2]$ for $[C_2H_3O]$ in Equation 14.79 to obtain

$$1.2 \times 10^{-2} = 1.8[HC_2H_3O_2] + [HC_2H_3O_2]$$
$$= 2.8[HC_2H_3O_2]$$
$$4.3 \times 10^{-3} \text{ M} = [HC_2H_3O_2]$$

Then

$$1.8(4.3 \times 10^{-3}) = [C_2H_3O_2^-]$$
$$7.7 \times 10^{-3} \text{ M} = [C_2H_3O_2^-]$$

Since the volume is 100 mL, we can calculate the number of grams of acetic acid as

$$? \text{ g HC}_2H_3O_2 = 100 \text{ mL HC}_2H_3O_2 \left(\frac{4.3 \times 10^{-3} \text{ mol HC}_2H_3O_2}{1000 \text{ mL HC}_2H_3O_2} \right) \cdot$$
$$\left(\frac{60.0 \text{ g HC}_2H_3O_2}{1 \text{ mol HC}_2H_3O_2} \right)$$
$$= 0.0258 \text{ g HC}_2H_3O_2$$

In a similar calculation the grams of sodium acetate can be determined since the molarity of sodium acetate is the same as the molarity of the acetate ion:

$$? \text{ g NaC}_2H_3O_2 = 100 \text{ mL NaC}_2H_3O_2 \left(\frac{7.7 \times 10^{-3} \text{ mol NaC}_2H_3O_2}{1000 \text{ mL NaC}_2H_3O_2} \right) \cdot$$
$$\left(\frac{82.0 \text{ g NaC}_2H_3O_2}{1 \text{ mol NaC}_2H_3O_2} \right)$$
$$= 0.0631 \text{ g NaC}_2H_3O_2$$

To prepare this buffer by Method 1 we need to weigh 0.0258 g of $HC_2H_3O_2$ and 0.0631 g of $NaC_2H_3O_2$ into a 100-mL volumetric flask, add water to the mark, and mix thoroughly.

Method 2

In the second method we have to obtain the same result by measuring only some acetic acid and neutralizing part of it with a base such as NaOH. A 0.100 M solution of NaOH can be used for this purpose. We calculate the number of grams of acetic acid needed from the 100 mL of solution and the total molarity of 1.2×10^{-2}:

$$? \text{ g HC}_2\text{H}_3\text{O}_2 \quad = \quad 100 \text{ mL HC}_2\text{H}_3\text{O}_2 \left(\frac{1.2 \times 10^{-2} \text{ mol HC}_2\text{H}_3\text{O}_2}{1000 \text{ mL HC}_2\text{H}_3\text{O}_2} \right) \cdot$$

$$\left(\frac{60.0 \text{ g HC}_2\text{H}_3\text{O}_2}{1 \text{ mol HC}_2\text{H}_3\text{O}_2} \right)$$

$$= \quad 0.0720 \text{ g HCHO}_{2\ 3\ 2}$$

The reaction of acetic acid with NaOH is

$$\text{NaOH} \quad + \quad \text{HC}_2\text{H}_3\text{O}_2 \quad \rightarrow \quad \text{NaC}_2\text{H}_3\text{O}_2 \quad + \quad \text{H}_2\text{O}$$

We can calculate the volume of NaOH needed to produce 100 mL of 7.7×10^{-3} M sodium acetate solution:

$$? \text{ mL NaOH} \quad = \quad 100 \text{ mL NaC}_2\text{H}_3\text{O}_2 \left(\frac{7.7 \times 10^{-3} \text{ mol NaC}_2\text{H}_3\text{O}_2}{1000 \text{ mL NaC}_2\text{H}_3\text{O}_2} \right) \cdot$$

$$\left(\frac{1 \text{ mol NaOH}}{1 \text{mol NaC}_2\text{H}_3\text{O}_2} \right) \left(\frac{1000 \text{ mL NaOH}}{0.100 \text{ mol NaOH}} \right)$$

$$= \quad 7.7 \text{ mL NaOH}$$

In method 2, we need to measure 7.7 mL of 0.100 M NaOH and 0.0720 of $\text{HC}_2\text{H}_3\text{O}_2$ and dissolve in enough water to make 100 mL of solution.

Method 3

In method 3, the grams of $\text{NaC}_2\text{H}_3\text{O}_2$ needed to make a 1.2×10^{-2} M solution is calculated:

$$? \text{ mL NaC}_2\text{H}_3\text{O}_2 \quad = \quad 100 \text{ mL NaC}_2\text{H}_3\text{O}_2 \left(\frac{1.2 \times 10^{-2} \text{ mol NaC}_2\text{H}_3\text{O}_2}{1000 \text{ mL NaC}_2\text{H}_3\text{O}_2} \right) \cdot$$

$$\left(\frac{82.0 \text{ g NaC}_2\text{H}_3\text{O}_2}{1 \text{ mol NaC}_2\text{H}_3\text{O}_2} \right)$$

$$= \quad 0.0984 \text{ g NaC}_2\text{H}_3\text{O}_2$$

Then the volume of 0.0500 M HCl needed to convert some of this sodium acetate into the required amount of acetic acid is determined. The reaction of sodium acetate with HCl is as follows:

$$\text{HCl} \quad + \quad \text{NaC}_2\text{H}_3\text{O}_2 \quad \rightarrow \quad \text{HC}_2\text{H}_3\text{O}_2 \quad + \quad \text{NaCl}$$

The volume of HCl needed is calculated as follows:

$$? \text{ mL HCl} \quad = \quad 100 \text{ mL HC}_2\text{H}_3\text{O}_2 \left(\frac{4.3 \times 10^{-3} \text{ mol HC}_2\text{H}_3\text{O}_2}{1000 \text{ mL HC}_2\text{H}_3\text{O}_2} \right) \cdot$$

$$\left(\frac{1 \text{ mol HCl}}{1 \text{ mol HC}_2\text{H}_3\text{O}_2} \right) \left(\frac{1000 \text{ mL HCl}}{0.0500 \text{ mol HCl}} \right)$$

$$= \quad 8.6 \text{ mL HCl}$$

In method 3 we need to weigh 0.0984 g of sodium acetate along with 8.6 mL of 0.0500 M HCl and dilute the mixture to 100 mL.

In preparing a buffer the chemist uses one of these three methods, usually the easiest one.

pH Values of Polyprotic Acids and Their Salts

Polyprotic acids dissociate in stepwise equilibria, each of which has its own dissociation constant. Each dissociation constant is smaller than the preceding one ($K_{a1} > K_{a2} > K_{a3}$). When a polyprotic acid such as H_2A dissolves in water, the possible reactions are as follows:

$$H_2A \quad \rightleftharpoons \quad HA^- \quad + \quad H^+ \qquad\qquad (14.86)$$

$$HA^- \quad \rightleftharpoons \quad A^{2-} \quad + \quad H^+ \qquad\qquad (14.87)$$

Since K_{a2} is always smaller than K_{a1}, the second dissociation must occur to a lesser extent than the first dissociation. In addition, the first dissociation produces hydrogen ions, and these hydrogen ions further suppress the second dissociation according to Le Châtelier's principle. These two considerations, along with experimental evidence, demonstrate that the first dissociation step is the only important one in determining the [H^+] and pH of a solution of a polyprotic acid.

The equation to use is

$$[H^+] \quad = \quad \sqrt{K_{a1}C_a} \qquad\qquad (14.88)$$

where C_a is the initial concentration of polyprotic acid.

Exercise 14.8

What is the pH value of each of the following solutions?

(a) 0.800 M H_3PO_4
(b) 0.0200 M H_2S
(c) 0.00400 M H_2CO_3

Solution

(a) 1.12
(b) 4.35
(c) 4.37

Similar reasoning is used for the hydrolysis of the fully deprotonated anion of a polyprotic acid, such as A^{2-} in Equation 14.87. The two hydrolysis reactions are these:

$$A^{2-} \quad + \quad H_2O \quad \rightleftharpoons \quad HA^- \quad + \quad OH^- \qquad\qquad (14.89)$$

$$HA^- \quad + \quad H_2O \quad \rightleftharpoons \quad H_2A \quad + \quad OH^- \qquad\qquad (14.90)$$

The hydrolysis reaction of Equation 14.89 has the largest equilibrium constant, and the OH^- formed in the first step suppresses the second step according to Le Châtelier's principle. The hydrolysis of a fully deprotonated anion of a polyprotic acid is calculated using the equation

$$[OH^{-1}] \quad = \quad \sqrt{\frac{K_w}{K_{a2}} C_{A^{2-}}} \qquad\qquad (14.91)$$

Exercise 14.9

What is the pH of each of the following solutions?
(a) 3.00 M Na_3PO_4
(b) 0.0500 M Na_2CO_3

Solution

(a) 13.41
(b) 11.51

Anions of polyprotic acids, such as HA^- above, are amphiprotic and can act as either conjugate acids or conjugate bases. For salts that contain these anions the hydrogen ion concentration is calculated as the square root of the product of the K_a values for that anion acting as a conjugate acid and as a conjugate base:

$$[H^+] = \sqrt{K_{a1}K_{a2}} \qquad (14.92)$$

Exercise 14.10

Calculate the pH of a solution of each of the following ions:
(a) HSO_3^-
(b) $H_2PO_4^-$
(c) HPO_4^{2-}
(d) HCO_3^-
(e) HS^-

Solution

(a) 4.55
(b) 4.67
(c) 9.77
(d) 8.34
(e) 10.00

Buffer solutions are often made using a conjugate acid and a conjugate base of a polyprotic acid. The pH of such a buffer is governed by the equilibrium law, which includes both the conjugate acid and the conjugate base present in the solution. For phosphoric acid the first dissociation step involves H_3PO_4 and $H_2PO_4^-$, and buffers in the range of pH 1.1–3.1 can be prepared from various mixtures of them. The second dissociation step involves $H_2PO_4^-$ and HPO_4^{2-}, and salts with these two ions are used to prepare buffers in the range of pH 6.2–8.2. With the HPO_4^{2-} and PO_4^{3-} anions buffers in the pH range 11.3–13.3 can be prepared.

Titration Curves

The titration technique was described in Chapter 6, along with the important calculations that apply to a wide variety of titrations. Acid-base pH calculations are often used to explain what occurs as the experiment is performed. There are four major points of interest during a titration experiment:

1. The start of the titration, where the solution contains only one acid or base.
2. The region where titrant is added up to the end point, and the solution now contains a mixture of unreacted sample and products.
3. The end point, where all of the reactant has been converted into product.
4. The region after the end point, where the solution contains product and excess titrant.

At the start of the titration the sample is a pure acid or base, and the pH is calculated as described in preceding sections. At the end point, the solution is the salt of the acid or base; again, the method of calculating the pH has been described. Between the start and the end point, however, we have a mixture of a conjugate acid and its conjugate base. If a weak acid or base is involved, this is a buffer solution. If only strong acids and bases are used, this region is unbuffered. After the end point, the pH depends on the excess titrant used.

The pH during a titration may be calculated or measured in an experiment. A plot of pH versus volume of titrant added is called a **titration curve**.

The general shapes of strong acid–strong base titration curves are shown in Figure 14.1. There are three important points about these curves. First, there is no buffer region since no weak acids or bases are present. Second, the end-point pH is always 7.0 because the products do not hydrolyze. Third, from the start the pH changes gradually until just before the end point where it changes sharply.

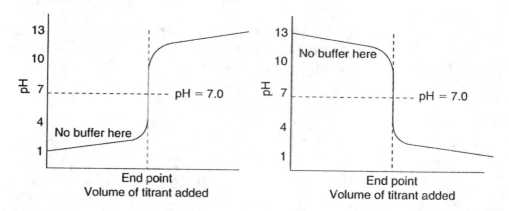

FIGURE 14.1. Titration curves for (left) a strong acid titrated with a strong base and (right) a strong base titrated with a strong acid. The region from the start to the end point is not buffered. The end-point pH is always 7.0.

Comparing Figure 14.1 with Figure 14.2, we find that weak acid and base titrations have a buffer region where a conjugate acid-base pair exists. In the middle of the buffer region, pH = pK_a. A large change in pH occurs just at the start as the buffer mixture is formed, in contrast to strong acid-base titrations. At the end point the salts of weak acids and bases hydrolyze, and the pH is not 7. Salts of weak acids hydrolyze to give basic solutions, and $pH_{ep} > 7$; the reverse is true for salts of weak bases.

Titrations of polyprotic acids produce more than one end point because of the sequence of dissociation steps. The titration of phosphoric acid with a strong base is shown in Figure 14.3. Only two end points are observed since the third occurs at a pH too high for observation. At the start, only pure H_3PO_4 is present. At each end point the acid is neutralized to pure $H_2PO_4^-$ and then HPO_4^{2-}; the pH values at the end points are calculated using Equation 14.92. Between the end points there are mixtures of a conjugate acid and its conjugate base, as shown. These are the buffer regions. At the midpoint of each buffer region the pH is equal to the pK_a that governs that particular dissociation step.

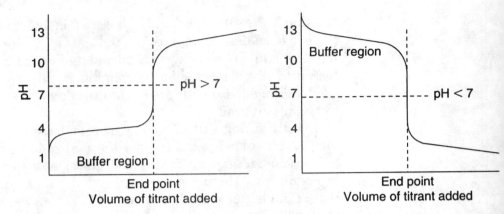

FIGURE 14.2. Titration curves for (left) a weak acid titrated with a strong base and (right) a weak base titrated with a strong acid. Between the start and the end point is a buffer region due to the presence of a conjugate acid-base mixture. Because of the hydrolysis of the products, the end point pH is not 7.0.

Figures 14.2 and 14.3 illustrate why and how a buffer can be made by partial neutralization of a weak acid. The partial neutralization results in a conjugate acid-base mixture, which is a buffer solution.

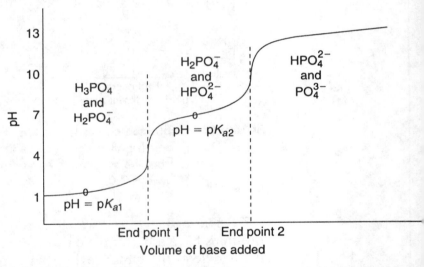

FIGURE 14.3. Titration curve for the titration of phosphoric acid with a strong base.

Henderson-Hasselbach Equation

The equilibrium law for a weak acid, HA, is written as

$$K_a = \frac{[A^-][H^+]}{[HA]} \tag{14.93}$$

Taking the logarithm of both sides of Equation 14.93 yields

$$pK_a = pH - \log\left(\frac{[A^-]}{[HA]}\right) \tag{14.94}$$

Rearrangement yields

$$pH = pK_a + \log\left(\frac{[A^-]}{[HA]}\right) = pK_a + \log\left(\frac{[\text{conjugate base}]}{[\text{conjugate acid}]}\right) \tag{14.95}$$

Equation 14.95 is known as the **Henderson-Hasselbach equation**. A similar derivation for weak bases results in

$$pOH \;=\; pK_b \;-\; \log\!\left(\frac{[\text{conjugate acid}]}{[\text{conjugate base}]}\right) \tag{14.96}$$

Equations 14.95 and 14.96 illustrate that, if the pH of a buffer is known, the ratio of the conjugate acid and conjugate base concentrations can be calculated. In addition, they show clearly that, when the concentrations of conjugate acid and conjugate base are equal, $pH = pK_a$ or $pOH = pK_b$.

pH Indicators

Indicators are weak acids and weak bases whose respective conjugate bases and conjugate acids have different colors. The reason is that the loss or gain of a proton changes the energy of the electrons within their structures. This, in turn, changes the energy of light absorbed, which is observed as a change in color.

If a conjugate acid has one color, yellow for instance, and its conjugate base has another color, blue for instance, the eye will see these colors clearly only if there is ten times more of one color than of the other. We will see yellow if the conjugate acid is ten times more concentrated than the conjugate base, and blue if the conjugate base is ten times more concentrated than the conjugate acid:

$$\frac{[\text{conjugate base}]}{[\text{conjugate acid}]} \quad < \quad 0.1 \;(\text{yellow observed}) \tag{14.97}$$

$$\frac{[\text{conjugate base}]}{[\text{conjugate acid}]} \quad > \quad 10 \;(\text{blue observed}) \tag{14.98}$$

Between these two ratios various shades of green will be observed. Since indicators are weak acids and bases, the significance of this color phenomenon is best understood with the Henderson-Hasselbach equation, Equation 14.95. Substituting 0.1 into the log term yields

$$pH \;=\; pK_a \;+\; \log\,(0.1) \;=\; pK_a \;-\; 1.0$$

so that the yellow color is observed when the pH of the solution is at least 1 pH unit below the pK_a of the indicator. For the blue color

$$pH \;=\; pK_a \;+\; \log\,(10) \;=\; pK_a + 1.0$$

and the pH of the solution must be 1 pH unit above the pK_a of the indicator.

This discussion tells us two important properties of indicators used in titrations: (1) the pH at the end point of a titration curve must change by at least 2 pH units very rapidly, and (2) the pK of the indicator must be close to the end-point pH of the titration. From the titration curves we see that the required large change in pH often occurs. Proper selection of an indicator mandates that the pH at the end point and the pK_a of the indicator be close to each other.

Important
Concepts

Arrhenius theory
Bronsted-Lowry theory
Lewis theory
Neutralization
Titration
Buffers
Strong vs weak acids and bases
Predicting relative strengths of acids
Hydrolysis

Important
Equations

$pH = -\log [H^+]$ and $pOH = -\log [OH^-]$

$$pH = pK_a + \log d\left(\frac{[\text{conjugate base}]}{[\text{conjugate acid}]}\right)$$

$$K_a = \frac{[H^+][A^-]}{[HA]}$$

$$K_w = [H^+][OH^-]$$

Questions on
Chapter 14

1. Which of the following has the highest pH?
   (A) 0.100 M HCl
   (B) 0.200 M $HC_2H_3O_2$
   (C) 0.100 M Na_2CO_3
   (D) 0.200 M NaCl
   (E) 0.500 M $NaC_2H_3O_2$

2. Which of the following CANNOT occur together in solution?
   (A) H_3PO_4 and $H_2PO_4^-$
   (B) HCO_3^- and CO_3^{2-}
   (C) Na^+ and SO_4^{2-}
   (D) $C_2O_4^{2-}$ and $H_2C_2O_4$
   (E) HPO_4^{2-} and PO_4^{3-}

3. When 0.250 mol of NaOH is added to 1.00 L of 0.100 M H_3PO_4, the
   solution will contain
   (A) HPO_4^{2-}
   (B) $H_2PO_4^-$
   (C) POD_4^{3-}
   (D) A and B
   (E) A and C

4. A buffer with a pH of 10.0 is needed. Which of the following should be
   used?
   (A) acetic acid with a K_a of 1.8×10^{-5}
   (B) ammonia with a K_b of 1.8×10^{-5}
   (C) nitrous acid with a K_a of 7.1×10^{-4}
   (D) $H_2PO_4^-$ and PO_4^{3-} with a K_a of 4.5×10^{-13}
   (E) dimethylamine with a K_b of 1.05×10^{-3}

5. pH is equal to pK_a
   (A) when [conjugate acid] = [conjugate base]
   (B) at the endpoint of a titration
   (C) in the buffer region
   (D) in the Henderson-Hasselbach equation
   (E) at equilibrium

6. The pH of a 1.23×10^{-3} M solution of $Al(OH)_3$ aqueous solution is
   (A) 2.91
   (B) 2.43
   (C) 11.09
   (D) 13.52
   (E) 11.57

7. An indicator has a K_a of 6.4×10^{-6}, the conjugate acid is red, and the conjugate base is yellow. At what pH will the solution be red?
   (A) 5.2
   (B) 5.5
   (C) 4.0
   (D) 4.7
   (E) 6.4

8. A buffer has a pH of 4.87. If the buffer is made from a weak acid (K_a = 3.30×10^{-5}), and its conjugate base, the $\dfrac{[\text{conjugate base}]}{[\text{weak acid}]}$ ratio is
   (A) 4.87
   (B) 4.48
   (C) 1.00
   (D) 2.45
   (E) 0.41

9. Which of the following statements is correct?
   (A) $HClO_2$ is a stronger acid than $HClO_3$.
   (B) HI is a weaker acid than HCl.
   (C) CH_3COOH is a stronger acid than $CH_2BrCOOH$.
   (D) HNO_3 is a stronger acid than HNO_2.
   (E) H_3PO_4 is a stronger acid than $HClO_4$.

10. What is the pH of a 0.100 M solution of K_2HPO_4? (For H_3PO_4, pK_1 = 2.15; pK_2 = 7.20; pK_3 = 12.35)
    (A) 1.00
    (B) 13.00
    (C) 9.78
    (D) 6.67
    (E) 4.10

11. Which of the following is the correct method for preparing a buffer solution?
    (A) Mix the correct amounts of a weak acid and its conjugate base.
    (B) Neutralize a weak base partially with strong acid.
    (C) Neutralize a weak acid partially with a strong base.
    (D) Add the appropriate amount of strong acid to an acid salt.
    (E) All of the above methods may be used to prepare buffers.

12. The only acid that is both a strong and a weak acid is
    (A) hydrochloric acid
    (B) perchloric acid
    (C) nitric acid
    (D) sulfuric acid
    (E) phosphoric acid

13. Which of the following is the acid anhydride of a monoprotic acid?
    (A) CaO
    (B) SO_3
    (C) FeO
    (D) CO_2
    (E) N_2O_5

14. Which of the following CANNOT be either a Lewis acid or a Lewis base?
    (A) CH_4
    (B) Cu^{2+}
    (C) CO
    (D) Fe^{3+}
    (E) NH_3

15. In the complex ion $Cu(NH_3)_4^{2+}$ the NH_3 is called
    (A) a cation
    (B) a ligand
    (C) a Lewis acid
    (D) an anion
    (E) a molecule

16. The pH of a 0.125 M solution of a weak base is 10.45. What is the pK_a of this acid?
    (A) 3.5×10^{-11}
    (B) 6.4×10^{-7}
    (C) 2.8×10^{-4}
    (D) 2.3×10^{-3}
    (E) 1.2×10^{-2}

17. A solution containing HF is titrated with KOH. At the end point of the titration the solution contains
    (A) equal amounts of HF and KOH
    (B) $H_2O, H^+, OH^-, K^+, F^-$, and HF
    (C) K^+ and F^-

(D) KF and H_2O

(E) K^+, F^-, and H_2O

18. A buffer at pH 5.32 is prepared from a weak acid with a $pK_a = 5.15$. If 100 mL of this buffer is diluted to 200 mL with distilled water, the pH of the dilute solution is
    (A) 5.62
    (B) 5.02
    (C) 5.32
    (D) The identity of the acid is needed to answer the question.
    (E) The concentrations of the acid and the salt are needed to answer the question.

19. If 50.0 mL of a 0.0134 M HCl solution is mixed with 24.0 mL of a 0.0250 M NaOH solution, what is the pH of the final mixture?
    (A) 1.87
    (B) 12.40
    (C) 5.29
    (D) 3.02
    (E) 10.98

20. If 50.0 g of formic acid ($HCHO_2, K_a = 1.8 \times 10^{-4}$) and 30.0 g of sodium formate ($NaCHO_2$) are dissolved to make 500 mL of solution, the pH of this solution is
    (A) 4.76
    (B) 3.76
    (C) 3.35
    (D) 4.12
    (E) 3.02

Answer Key

See Appendix I for explained answers.

1. **C**	5. **A**	9. **D**	13. **E**	17. **B**
2. **D**	6. **E**	10. **C**	14. **A**	18. **C**
3. **E**	7. **C**	11. **E**	15. **B**	19. **D**
4. **B**	8. **D**	12. **D**	16. **B**	20. **C**

CHAPTER FIFTEEN

Organic Chemistry and Polymers

Organic chemistry is the study of carbon-containing compounds. Before 1828 the **vital force theory**, which stated that **organic compounds** could be extracted only from living, or once living, organisms, was widely accepted. In 1828, however, the synthesis of urea, $CO(NH_2)_2$, by Friedrich Wöhler demonstrated that inorganic compounds could be converted into organic compounds, and the vital force theory was rapidly abandoned. Today, most known chemical compounds are organic compounds.

In preceding chapters we referred to many organic compounds without considering them as a separate group. This chapter describes the essential features of carbon compounds that should be appreciated.

Carbon

Carbon is the central atom in organic compounds. It exists as an element in three different forms, called **allotropes**. These allotropes are **graphite**, which is the "lead" in pencils; **diamond**, a precious stone; and **buckminsterfullerene**. Graphite consists of layers of sp^2 bonded carbon atoms in six-membered rings which form flat sheets. Each layer is weakly bonded to another with pi bonding. The loosely bound pi electrons allow electrical conduction along the plane of graphite, but graphite is a nonconductor through the planes. Diamond consists of tetrahedrally bonded carbon atoms in a covalent crystal of extraordinary hardness. Buckminsterfullerene consists of spheres of 60 carbon atoms covalently bonded together.

Carbon has a total of six electrons, four of which are valence electrons. Carbon always forms four bonds, which may be combinations of single, double, and triple bonds. This element never has a nonbonding pair of electrons. Carbon can form four single bonds with a tetrahedral, sp^3, structure. It can bond to three other atoms in a trigonal planar, sp^2, structure, which involves one double bond and two single bonds. Finally, carbon can bond with two other atoms in a linear, sp, structure. These compounds contain either two double bonds, as in CO_2, or one single and one triple bond, as in HCN.

Importance of Carbon

The most important feature of the carbon atom is that it bonds with other carbon atoms to form chains and rings of various sizes and shapes. No other atom in the periodic table can form the variety of structures that carbon can.

Isomers

Two organic compounds may have formulas with exactly the same atoms but different properties. These compounds are called **isomers**. There are three main types of isomers: structural isomers, cis-trans isomers, and stereoisomers.

Structural Isomers

Structural isomers are two or more different compounds that have the same atoms in their formulas. However, the atoms are bonded to each other in different configurations. The hydrocarbon C_5H_{12} has three different structural isomers based on the arrangement of the carbon skeleton, as shown in Figure 15.1 A compound with a single straight chain of carbon atoms is designated as **normal** with the letter *n* preceding its name, as in *n*-pentane.

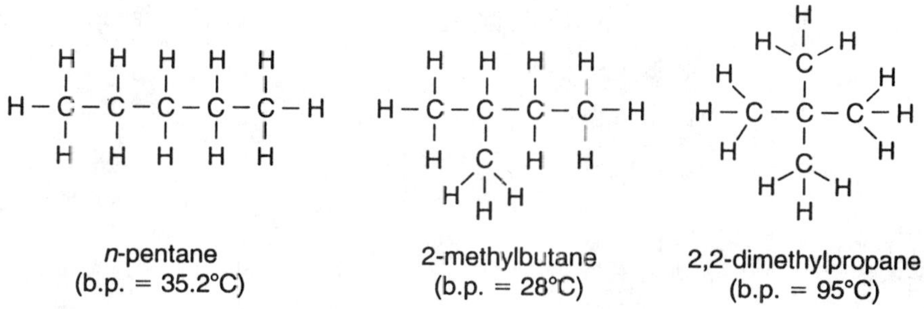

n-pentane
(b.p. = 35.2°C)

2-methylbutane
(b.p. = 28°C)

2,2-dimethylpropane
(b.p. = 95°C)

FIGURE 15.1. Structural isomers each having the formula C_5H_{12}.

Each of the three structural isomers of C_5H_{12} has different chemical and physical properties. Figure 15.1 shows the boiling points of the isomers. To explain the difference in boiling points, we see that the *n*-pentane molecules line up side by side to form many instantaneous dipoles. Because it has the largest London forces, *n*-pentane has the highest boiling point. The 2,2-dimethylpropane molecules can interact at only a few points, and this compound has the lowest boiling point because of smaller London forces.

Some of the structural isomers having the formula $C_4H_{10}O$ are shown in Figure 15.2.

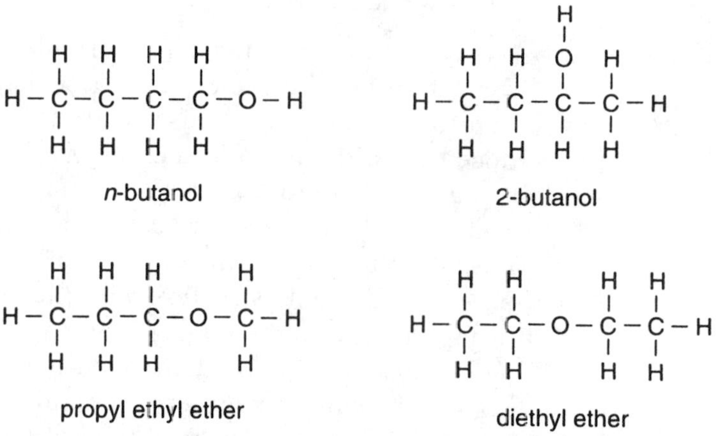

n-butanol

2-butanol

propyl ethyl ether

diethyl ether

FIGURE 15.2. Some possible isomers with the formula $C_4H_{10}O$.

Each of these compounds has distinctly different physical and chemical properties. The alcohols, with —OH groups, hydrogen-bond extensively and have high boiling points. The ethers, with C-O-C bonds, have much lower boiling points because the forces of attraction are mainly London forces.

Cis Isomers and Trans Isomers

A carbon-carbon single bond allows the carbon atoms at each end to rotate freely. A C=C double bond is a rigid structure since rotation would require the constant breaking and reforming of the pi bond. This rigidity means that the atoms bound to double-bonded carbon atoms will have fixed orientations. *Cis-* means "on the same side"; *trans-* means "on opposite sides" and refers to groups attached to double-bonded carbon atoms. Figure 15.3 illustrates the structures of *cis-* and *trans-*2-butene. In the cis form the two —CH$_3$ groups are on the same side. The trans structure has the

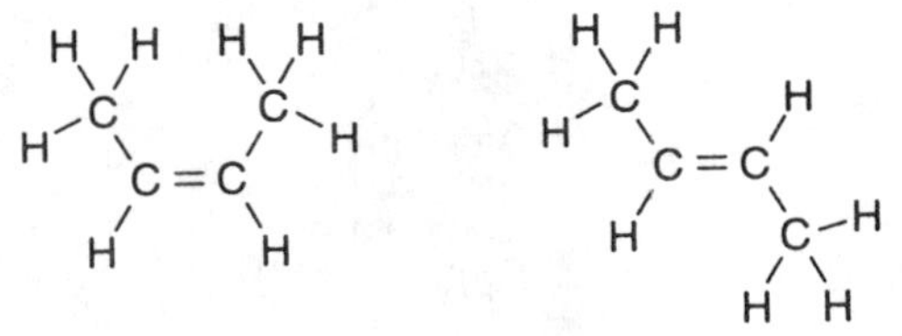

cis-2-butene   trans-2-butene

FIGURE 15.3.   Illustration of the difference between the cis and trans isomers of butene.

—CH$_3$ groups on opposing sides of the double bond.

Since the double-bonded carbon atoms cannot rotate, these two structures are distinctly different. The molecules have different chemical and physical properties as a result of their structures, as shown later in Table 15.2.

Stereoisomers

Stereoisomers have the same formulas, and every atom is bonded to the same atom. Stereoisomers are not structural isomers. The unique feature is that the arrangement of atoms around a single carbon atom can still produce two different molecules. Figure 15.4 shows a two-dimensional representation of stereoisomers. Four different groups, designated as W, X, Y, and Z, are attached to a central carbon atom. These structures are not superimposable. No matter how they are rotated, it is impossible to line up the W, X, Y, and Z of one structure with the W, X, Y, and Z of the other without lifting them from the plane of the paper.

Stereoisomers are often called **mirror images**, and the dashed line in Figure 15.4 can be considered as a mirror reflecting the two shapes. Three-dimensional molecules have the same ability to form nonsuperimposable mirror images. Your left and right hands are three-dimensional mirror

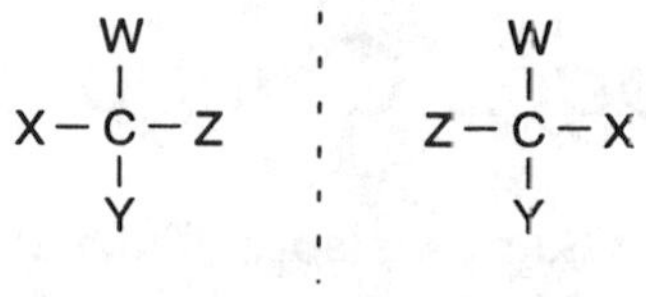

$$W \qquad\qquad W$$
$$X - C - Z \qquad Z - C - X$$
$$Y \qquad\qquad Y$$

Stereoisomers or Mirror Images

FIGURE 15.4. **Two carbon compounds that have four different groups, W, X, Y, and Z, attached to the central carbon atom. They are not superimposible by rotation. These compounds are reflections of each other, or mirror images.**

images of each other. If you hold your right hand up to a mirror, the exact image of your left hand is produced—try it and see!

Stereoisomers, unlike cis and trans isomers, have identical physical properties such as melting and boiling points. The chemical reactivity of two stereoisomers is, for the most part, identical also. However, stereoisomers often have different chemical reactivities in biological systems, where the overall shape of the molecule is important. Most amino acids have two stereoisomers.

Stereoisomers that rotate polarized light are called **optical isomers** because of this property. One isomer rotates polarized light to the right (**dextrorotatory**) and the other rotates it to the left (**levorotatory**) by an equal amount. One style of nomenclature uses D to indicate the dextrorotatory isomer and L to designate the levorotatory isomer. In all known living matter the stereoisomers are of the L type.

A substance can be a stereoisomer only if it has at least one carbon atom that has four different groups bound to it. Organic synthesis methods may be **stereospecific**, resulting in the exclusive production of one stereoisomer or the other. Other synthetic methods, however, are not stereospecific and result in a 50 : 50 mixture of D and L isomers. Such a mixture is called a **racemic mixture**. Racemic mixtures do not rotate polarized light because the rotation due to the D isomers is canceled by the equal and opposite rotation of the L isomers.

Three-Dimensional Organic Structures

Chemists and biochemists recognize that the three-dimensional shape of organic compounds is an important consideration in many reactions. Because of the complexity of these compounds, it is advantageous to build models of them rather than drawing them on paper. In all organic compounds the geometry around a carbon bound to four other atoms is tetrahedral (sp^3 hybrid). When a carbon is bound to three other atoms, the shape is trigonal planar (sp^2 hybrid); when the carbon is bound to only two other atoms, the shape is linear (sp hybrid). In addition, oxygen atoms bound to two other atoms have the bent geometry of an sp^3 hybrid. A nitrogen atom bound to three other atoms is tetrahedral, since it has a nonbonding pair of electrons. When bound to two other atoms, a nitrogen atom is trigonal planar (sp^2 hybrid).

Carbon-Hydrogen Compounds

Alkanes

Alkanes, also called **paraffins**, are compounds with the general formula C_nH_{2n+2}. These compounds contain all single, or sigma, bonds. Alkanes containing fewer than 5 carbon atoms are gases. Those containing 5–15 carbon atoms are liquids, and those with 16 or more carbon atoms are solids. As a group the alkanes are rather unreactive. Their major use is as a fuel in combustion reactions. Methane, propane, and butane are common gaseous fuels. Gasoline and kerosene are mostly liquid alkanes. Liquid alkanes are used as nonpolar solvents for chemical reactions and for cleaning. The solid alkanes, the paraffins, are often the major components of the wax used in candles.

Table 15.1 lists several alkanes and illustrates the naming system used. The first four alkanes have common names that must be remembered. From pentane on, each name has a prefix (*pent-*, *hex-*, etc.) that indicates the number of carbon atoms in the longest chain. All the names end in *-ane*.

TABLE 15.1 Names and Physical Properties of Selected Alkanes

Name	Formula: C_nH_{2n+2}	Number of Isomers	Melting Point (°C)	Boiling Point (°C)
Methane	CH_4	1	−182.5	−164.0
Ethane	C_2H_6	1	−183.3	−88.6
Propane	C_3H_8	1	−189.7	−42.1
n-Butane	C_4H_{10}	2	−138.3	−0.5
n- Pentane	C_5H_{12}	3	−129.7	36.1
n-Hexane	C_6H_{14}	5	−95.0	68.9
n-Nonane	C_9H_{20}	35	−51.0	150.8
n-Dodecane	$C_{12}H_{26}$	355	−9.6	216.3
n-Icosane	$C_{20}H_{42}$	366,319	36.8	343.0

For the normal or straight-chain alkanes the melting and boiling points increase regularly with the number of carbon atoms in the formula. Branched structural isomers have lower melting and boiling points than normal alkanes with the same numbers of carbon atoms. Increased branching decreases melting and boiling points.

Alkenes

Alkenes are compounds with the general formula C_nH_{2n}, where n must be 2 or larger. Every alkene has a double bond somewhere in its structure. A compound that contains one or more double or triple bonds is said to be **unsaturated**. A **saturated** compound has only carbon-carbon single bonds. The double bond is a reactive site in alkenes and makes them more reactive than alkanes. Alkenes such as ethylene are the major starting reactants for many chemical syntheses. When the double bond can be located in more than one position in the compound, its location is indicated by a number in front of the name. The number represents the lowest numbered carbon atom with the double bond. Compounds that have two double bonds are called dienes, and those with three double bonds are trienes.

TABLE 15.2 Names and Properties of Selected Alkenes

Name	Formula: C_nH_{2n}	Melting Point (°C)	Boiling Point (°C)
Ethylene	$CH_2{=}CH_2$	−169	−103.7
Propylene (propene)*	$CH_2{=}CHCH_3$	−185.2	−47.4
1-Butene	$CH_2{=}CHCH_2CH_3$	−185.3	−6.3
cis-2-Butene	$CH_3CH{=}CHCH_3$	−138.9	3.7
trans-2-Butene	$CH_3CH{=}CHCH_3$	−105.5	0.9
1,3-Butadiene	$CH_2{=}CHCH{=}CH_2$	−108.9	−4.4

*Propene is the systematic name, and propylene is the common name.

Table 15.2 lists, along with other alkenes, the cis and trans isomers for 2-butene discussed previously and shown in Figure 15.3. The cis isomer has —CH_3 groups on the same side of the double bond, and the trans isomer has the same groups on opposing sides of the double bond. Cis-trans isomers are not optically active; and, as stated earlier, they have different physical and chemical properties.

Exercise 15.1

Newspaper reports suggest that saturated fats (molecules with long hydrocarbon chains) and trans unsaturated fats (fats with double bonds) may be equally harmful in causing heart attacks. Suggest why this may be so.

Solution

We know that straight-chain molecules have higher melting points than branched-chain molecules, indicating that it is easier for them to be arranged in an orderly crystalline structure. Trans isomers are essentially straight molecules, while a cis isomer has a definite 120° bend. It seems reasonable that trans isomers could deposit themselves almost as easily in artery walls as straight-chain fats. Deposits of cis fats would be correspondingly more difficult to form because of their bent structure.

Alkynes

Alkynes are compounds with the general formula C_nH_{2n-2}, where n must be 2 or larger. An alkyne has a triple bond somewhere in its structures. Alkynes are very reactive. The most familiar alkyne is acetylene, which is used as a fuel in atomic spectroscopy and welding. A number in front of the name indicates the position of the triple bond.

TABLE 15.3 Names and Properties of Selected Alkynes

Name	Formula: C_nH_{2n-2}	Melting Point (°C)	Boiling Point (°C)
Acetylene (ethyne)	$CH{\equiv}CH$	−80.8	−84.0 (sublimes)
Propyne	$CH{\equiv}CCH_3$	−101.5	−23.2
1-Butyne	$CH{\equiv}CCH_2CH_3$	−125.7	8.1
2-Butyne	$CH_3C{\equiv}CCH_3$	−32.2	27

Since carbon atoms with triple bonds have only one additional bond, the alkynes do not form cis-trans isomers.

Ring Compounds

In addition to straight chains, carbon atoms can form rings. Rings of six carbon atoms are the most common since the bond angles in these rings are very close to the bond angles in sp^3 or sp^2 hybridized carbon atoms. Five-membered rings are also common, particularly in biochemical molecules.

Cyclohexane is a ring of six carbon atoms with no double bonds. It has two possible structures, shown in Figure 15.5, which can be converted from one to the other.

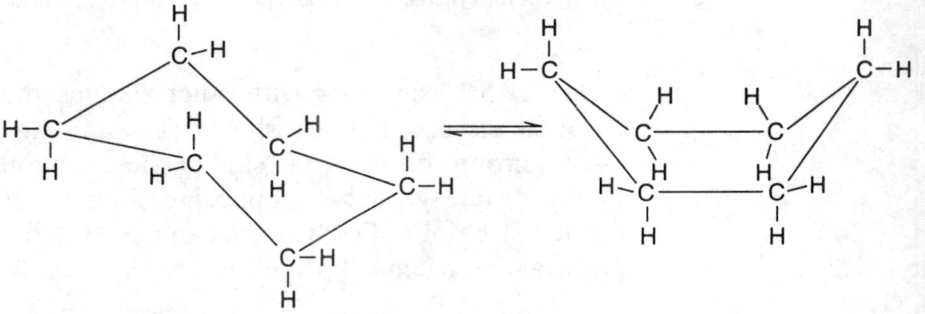

FIGURE 15.5. The chair and boat forms of cyclohexane.

The shape of the cyclohexane ring is dictated by the sp^3 hybridization of the carbon atoms, which prefer 109° bond angles. Both the chair and boat forms have these bond angles. Hydrogen atoms on the cyclohexane ring may be replaced by other functional groups to form compounds of added complexity.

Another type of ring is the **benzene** ring. In benzene the carbons have sp^2 hybridization with 120° bond angles. The benzene ring may be visualized as a ring of carbon atoms with alternating double bonds. These are actually resonance structures (as described in Chapter 5), and chemists recognize this fact by drawing a circle in the center of the ring as shown in Figure 15.6.

The benzene ring is unusually stable because the double bonds are conjugated. In a **conjugated double bond** every other bond is a double bond. The electrons in the pi orbitals are delocalized, stabilizing the struc-

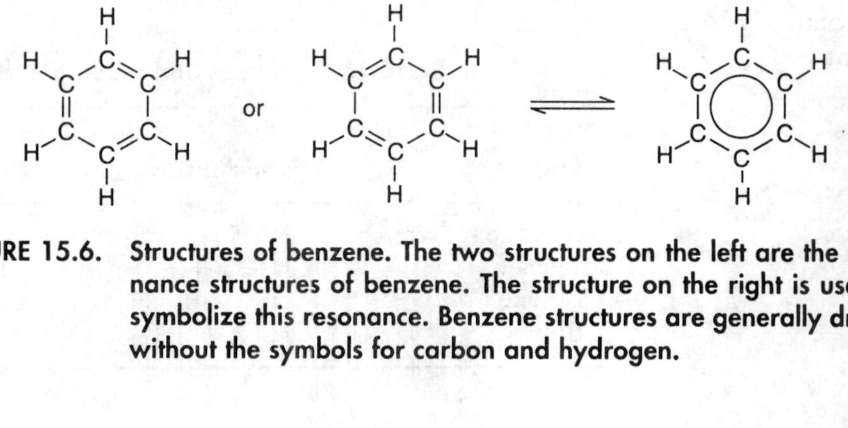

FIGURE 15.6. Structures of benzene. The two structures on the left are the resonance structures of benzene. The structure on the right is used to symbolize this resonance. Benzene structures are generally drawn without the symbols for carbon and hydrogen.

ture. This stability makes it very difficult to break the carbon-carbon bonds in benzene. The typical reactions of benzene involve replacing the hydrogen atoms with other functional groups.

Side Chains and Functional Groups

Organic molecules can be considered to be structures developed from just a few essential building blocks, called **side chains** or **functional groups**. Some of these building blocks, such as chains and rings, give the molecule its general shape. Other functional groups are responsible for the molecule's characteristic physical properties and chemical reactivity.

Alkyl Side Chains

The alkanes, without a terminal hydrogen, can be considered functional groups. Methane, CH_4, with one hydrogen removed is the methyl group, $-CH_3$. Ethane without a hydrogen is the ethyl group, $-CH_2CH_3$. In general formulas the **alkyl group** is given the symbol R. RH represents an alkane, ROH an alcohol, and R=O an aldehyde.

Aryl Side Chains

Benzene, C_6H_6, and related substances are aromatic compounds. The term *aryl* is derived from the word *aromatic*. The functional **aryl group** for benzene is $-C_6H_5$, and it is called the phenyl group.

Alcohol Functional Groups (—OH)

Every **alcohol** has the $-OH$ functional group attached to a carbon, as in ethanol, CH_3CH_2OH. Since the C-O-H bonds are rather strong, the alcohol functional group does not dissociate as the OH^- or the H^+ ion. This functional group does hydrogen-bond to other alcohols and water. A primary alcohol has the $-OH$ group bonded to a carbon that has only one other carbon bonded to it. In a secondary alcohol the $-OH$ group is attached to a carbon that is bonded to two other carbon atoms, and a tertiary alcohol has the $-OH$ bonded to a carbon that is bonded to three other carbon atoms.

Acid Functional Groups (—COOH or

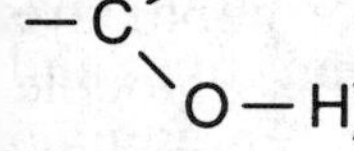

$$-C\overset{\displaystyle O}{\underset{\displaystyle O-H}{\Big\Vert}}$$

)

Organic acids have the carboxylic acid or carboxyl group. Acetic acid has the formula CH_3COOH. The electronegativity of the two oxygen atoms on the same carbon weakens the O-H bond so that hydrogen ions dissociate. Organic acids tend to be weak acids where only a few percent of all molecules dissociate. Carboxyl groups must be located on the terminal carbon of a molecule. Some organic acids have two or even three carboxyl groups.

Aldehyde Functional Groups (—C=O)

A compound with a terminal $-C=O$ group is called an **aldehyde**. Although this group is polar, only the smaller aldehydes are soluble in water. The aldehydes often have pleasant odors. They are used in perfumes and are found in many beverages such as coffee, tea, beer, and liquor. Formaldehyde, although thought to be carcinogenic, is a major component of urea-formaldehyde foam insulation. It has the structure shown in Figure 15.7.

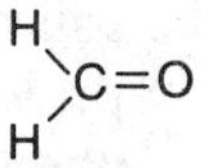

$$\underset{H}{\overset{H}{>}}C=O$$

FIGURE 15.7. Structure of formaldehyde, also called methanal.

Ketone Functional Groups

$$C-\overset{\displaystyle O}{\overset{\displaystyle \|}{C}}-C$$

Ketones are similar to aldehydes except that the double-bonded oxygen is located on a nonterminal carbon atom. Acetone, a common solvent and nail polish remover, is a ketone; its structure is shown in Figure 15.8. Ketones are found in many natural materials.

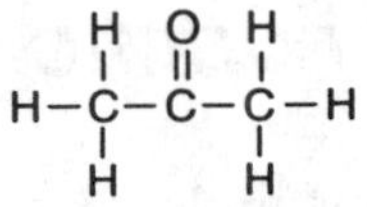

acetone
(dimethylketone)

FIGURE 15.8. Structure of acetone, a ketone commonly used as a solvent. Its systematic name is propanone.

Amine Functional Groups (—NH₂)

Amines are related to ammonia, NH_3. Replacing one or more hydrogen atoms of ammonia with a carbon chain produces an amine. Replacing one hydrogen with a carbon chain yields a primary amine such as ethylamine, $CH_3CH_2NH_2$. Replacing two hydrogen atoms results in a secondary amine, and replacing three hydrogen atoms yields a tertiary amine. Primary and secondary amines can form hydrogen bonds and are generally soluble in water. Amines are the organic version of bases.

Ether Functional Groups (—C—O—C—)

Compounds with a carbon-oxygen-carbon unit are known as ethers. Diethyl ether, $CH_3CH_2OCH_2CH_3$, was used as the first anesthetic in medical procedures. With the oxygen in the center of a carbon chain, some of its polarity is diffused in the two separate bonds it forms. As a result ethers are much less polar than ketones and aldehydes of similar size. This lesser polarity translates into lower boiling points and higher vapor pressures than those of aldehydes and ketones. There is a slight polarity, and ethers have higher boiling points than similar alkanes.

Because the oxygen is bonded to two different carbon atoms, ethers are generally less reactive than other oxygen-containing organic compounds. Because of their vapor pressures, ethers are more flammable than other organic compounds.

Halides (—X)

The halogens flourine, chlorine, bromine, and iodine are common organic functional groups. Along with hydrogen, the **halides** are terminal atoms and do not appear in the center of carbon chains. A halide is often represented by the symbol X. Thus the formula CH_3CH_2X can represent fluoroethane, chloroethane, bromoethane, or iodoethane.

Systematic Nomenclature for Organic Compounds

The original, or common, names of organic compounds were usually related to the source of the compound. For example, butyric acid was found in butter, caproic acid was isolated from goats, and vinegar was obtained from wine. When the number of known compounds caused this haphazard naming system to become unwieldy, the International Union of Pure and

Applied Chemistry, **IUPAC**, developed the systematic nomenclature system. Consequently, many organic compounds have both common and systematic IUPAC names..

The systematic name for an organic compound consists of a prefix, the parent name, and then a suffix. The parent name is based on the longest carbon chain in the molecule. Parent names for ring compounds are based on fundamental ring structures such as benzene.

Four steps are involved in constructing a name:

1. For the parent name, identify the longest continuous chain of carbon atoms in the structure. The longest chain is not always obvious, as shown in Figure 15.9. In this figure only the carbon backbone is shown. The task is more difficult when all the hydrogen atoms are added to the structure, as in Figure 15.10.

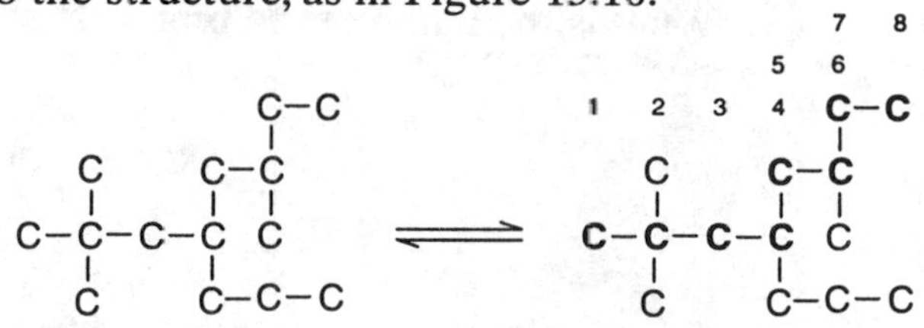

FIGURE 15.9. The longest carbon chain for the structure on the left is eight carbon

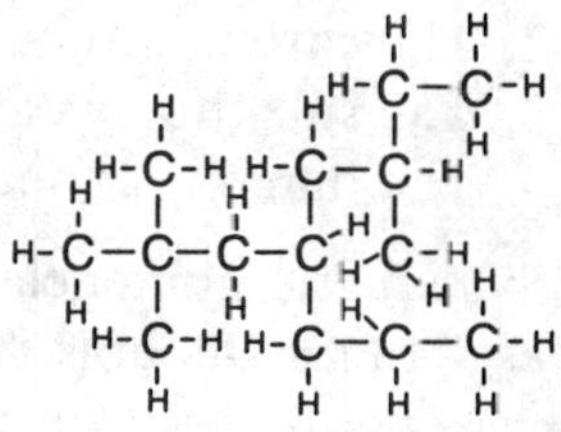

FIGURE 15.10. The compound in Figure 15.9 with all hydrogen atoms attached.

2. Number the carbon atoms in the longest chain. Start at the end closest to a side chain or functional group. In Figure 15.9 the carbon atoms are numbered from left to right.

3. Identify the substituents and the number of the carbon atom to which each is attached. For the structure in Figure 15.9 we have the following:

—CH_3 on carbon 2	2-methyl
—CH_3 on carbon 2	2-methyl
—$CH_2CH_2CH_3$ on carbon 4	4-propyl
—CH_3 on carbon 6	6-methyl

4. For the alcohol, aldehyde, ketone, and acid functional groups, use the terms obtained in step 3 as suffixes; name other functional groups, such as amines and halides, as prefixes. If identical functional groups are found, they are combined and their quantity is indicated by the prefix *di-*, *tri-*, *tetra-*, and so on.

The name of the compound in Figure 15.9 is 2,2,6-trimethyl-4-propyloctane.

Exercise 15.2

Name the following compound:

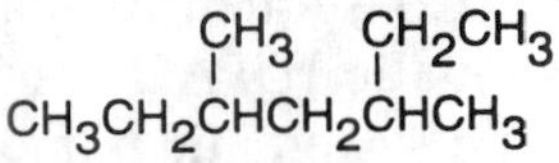

$$CH_3CH_2CHCH_2CHCH_3$$

with CH_3 and CH_2CH_3 substituents

Solution

The numbers below correspond to the four steps for constructing a name:

1. The longest carbon chain has seven carbon atoms, and the parent name is heptane.
2. The carbon atoms in this compound can be numbered from either the left or the right.
3. The compound contains a 3-methyl and a 5-methyl group.
4. Combining the methyl groups gives the name 3,5-dimethylheptane

Exercise 15.3

What is the name of the molecule shown below?

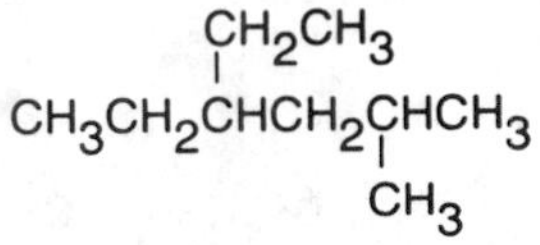

$$CH_3CH_2CHCH_2CHCH_3$$

with CH_2CH_3 and CH_3 substituents

Solution

The numbers below correspond to the four steps for constructing a name:

1. The longest chain contains six carbon atoms, and the parent name is hexane.
2. The carbon atoms are numbered from right to left.
3. The substituents are 2-methyl and 4-ethyl.
4. The name is 2-methyl-4-ethylhexane.

Systematic nomenclature for the alcohols, ketones, and acids uses suffixes: #-ol for alcohols, #-one for ketones, and #-oic acid for acids. The # sign represents the carbon number of the functional group. To illustrate this principle, Figure 15.11 shows the structure and names of three different alcohols on a pentane carbon chain.

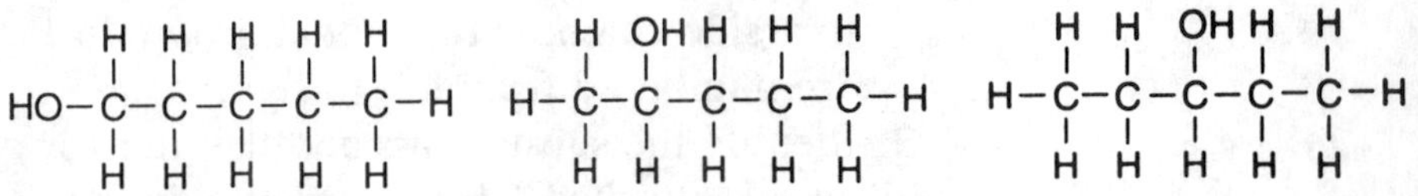

pentane-1-ol   pentane-2-ol   pentane-3-ol

FIGURE 15.11. Systematic names for the three alcohols made from *n*-pentane. Their common names are 1-pentanol, 2-pentanol, and 3-pentanol.

The simpler organic compounds are often known by their common names. Some of these are summarized in Table 15.4.

Ring Compounds

Benzene and cyclohexane are the simplest and most common parent structures for ring compounds. Because a ring is circular, the numbering of the carbon atoms follows a different procedure. If there is only one substituent, no number is necessary and the substituent is assumed to be attached to

TABLE 15.4 Common Names of Straight-Chain Organic Compounds with One to Five Carbon Atoms and the Given Functional Groups

Alkane	Acid	Alcohol	Aldehyde	Amine
Methane	Formic acid	Methanol	Formaldehyde	Methylamine
Ethane	Acetic acid	Ethanol	Acetaldehyde	Ethylamine
Propane	Propanoic acid	1-Propanol	Propionaldehyde	Propylamine
n-Butane	Butanoic acid	1-Butanol	Butyraldehyde	Butylamine
n-Pentane	Pentanoic acid	1-Pentanol	Pentanaldehyde	1-Aminopentane

the number 1 carbon atom. Chlorobenzene is a compound with a chlorine atom replacing one of the hydrogen atoms of the benzene ring. When two or more substituents are present on a ring, the carbon atoms are numbered clockwise so that one substituent is on carbon 1 and the remaining substituents are on the lowest numbered carbon atoms possible. In Figure 15.12 the correct and incorrect methods of numbering are shown for two dichlorobenzene molecules.

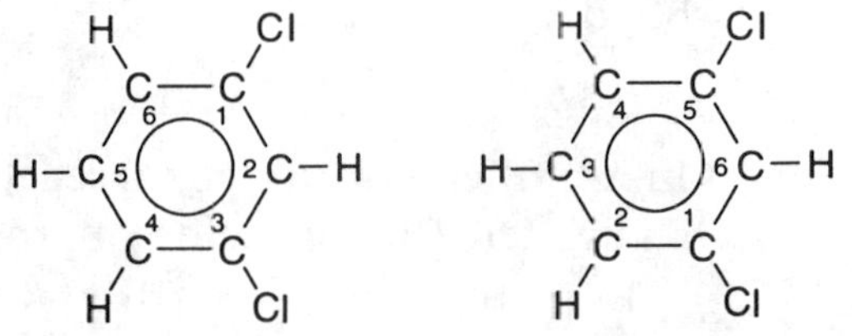

1,3-dichlorobenzene
(correctly numbered)

1,5-dichlorobenzene
(incorrectly numbered)

FIGURE 15.12. Correct and incorrect methods for numbering a ring structure.

Once the correct numbering sequence is determined, a ring compound is named in the same way as an alkane.

A frequently used system uses the prefix *ortho-*, *meta-*, or *para-* to indicate the position of a second substituent on a ring. Since the first substituent is always at carbon 1, a substituent in the ortho position is on carbon 2; the meta position is carbon 3; and the para position is carbon 4. 1,3-dichlorobenzene, shown in Figure 15.12, is also known as meta-dichlorobenzene.

Organic Reactions

There are literally thousands of different organic reaction types. Several of these are described below.

Combustion

Organic molecules may be burned in excess oxygen to produce carbon dioxide and water. Preceding chapters have shown many of these reactions.

Hydrogenation

Alkenes and alkynes have double and triple bonds. Hydrogen may be added to these bonds in a **hydrogenation** reaction, which is usually catalyzed by platinum. For example, 1-butene is hydrogenated to butane in this reaction:

$$H-C=C-C-C-H \ + \ H_2 \ \xrightarrow{\ Pt\ catalyst\ } \ H-C-C-C-C-H \tag{15.1}$$

As stated in a preceding section, compounds containing double or triple bonds are said to be unsaturated. A compound that has no double or triple bonds is termed saturated since it has the maximum number of hydrogen atoms possible.

Halogenation and
Hydrohalogenation

Halogenation is a reaction similar to the hydrogenation process. Instead of H_2, a halogen such as Cl_2 or Br_2 may be used. These reactions are generally more vigorous and do not need catalysts.

Hydrohalogenation is the corresponding reaction in which compounds such as HCl and HBr add one hydrogen and one halogen atom to a double bond.

Esterification

In **esterification** an alcohol reacts with an organic acid to produce an **ester** and water. The formation of propyl acetate is shown in Equation 15.2.

$$\underset{\text{1-propanol}}{H-C-C-C-O-H} \ + \ \underset{\text{acetic acid}}{H-C-C \overset{O}{\underset{O-H}{}}} \ \longrightarrow \ \underset{\text{propyl acetate}}{H-C-C \overset{O}{\underset{O-C-C-C-H}{}}} \ + \ H_2O \tag{15.2}$$

In the name of an ester, the name of the alcohol comes first and the name of the acid second. For example, butyl propionate is made from butyl alcohol and propionic acid. Most esters have sweet, fruity aromas. Some of them are used as substitutes for natural products. Some common esters and their aromas are listed in Table 15.5.

TABLE 15.5   Esters and Their Aromas

Name	Aroma
Octyl acetate	Orange
Ethyl formate	Rum
Methyl butyrate	Apple
Ethyl butyrate	Pineapple
Isopentyl acetate	Banana
Pentyl propionate	Apricot
Isobutyl formate	Raspberry
Benzyl acetate	Jasmine

**Peptide Bond
Synthesis**

Amino acids contain two functional groups, —NH$_2$ and —COOH. A reaction between amino acids forms a bond called the **peptide bond**:

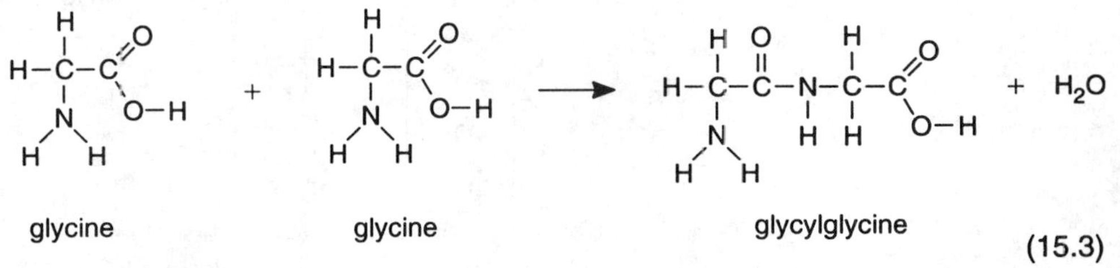

glycine   glycine   glycylglycine

(15.3)

The formation of a peptide bond is similar to the formation of an ester. Equation 15.3 shows the formation of one peptide bond, which leaves an NH$_2$ on one end and a COOH on the other end for the formation of additional peptide bonds. Long chains of amino acids joined by peptide bonds are known as proteins. Twenty-one naturally occurring amino acids produce thousands of different proteins in the body.

Polymers

Polymers are long chains of repeating structural units. One of the simplest polymers is polyethylene. Its structure is shown in Figure 15.13.

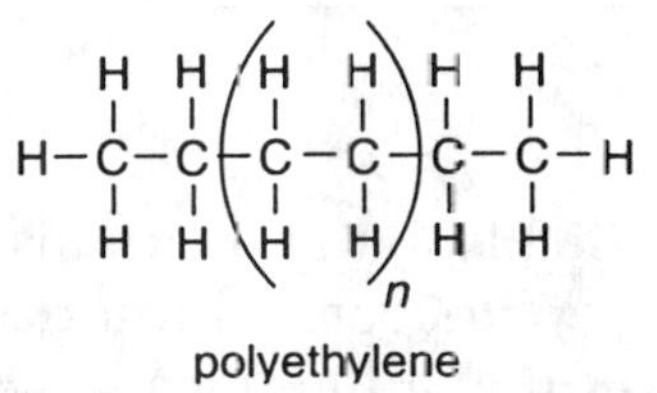

polyethylene

FIGURE 15.13. General form for drawing the structure of polymer molecules.

The number of repeating ethylene units (—CH$_2$CH$_2$—) in the complete molecule is n plus the two end groups. The value of n is usually greater than 100 and often exceeds 1000. As the name suggests, the molecule is made from ethylene, CH$_2$=CH$_2$. Ethylene is the **monomer** from which the polyethylene polymer is constructed. Polymers may be linear or branched.

Addition Polymers

A monomer that contains a double bond often reacts in a process called an **addition reaction**. Special catalysts start the reaction by forming free radicals, and the reaction proceeds to form more free radicals in a chain reaction. The net result is that the double bond opens (one bond in the double bond breaks) and reforms with two adjacent molecules. The process is illustrated in Figure 15.14.

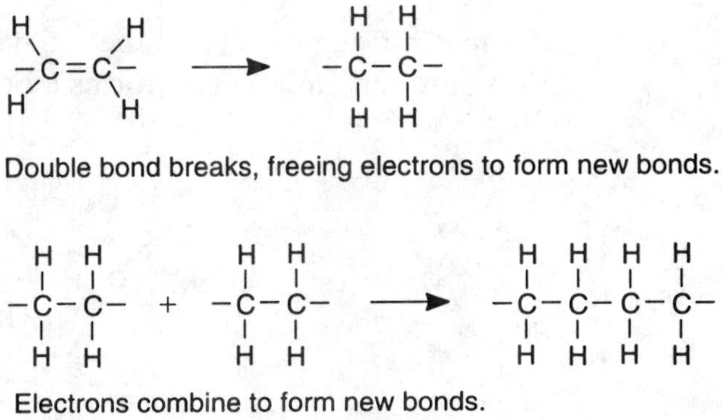

Double bond breaks, freeing electrons to form new bonds.

Electrons combine to form new bonds.

FIGURE 15.14. Elementary steps in the formation of polyethylene.

Some familiar polymers and the monomers from which they are made are listed in Table 15.6.

TABLE 15.6 Common Addition Polymers and Their Uses

Name	Monomer	Typical Uses
Polyethylene	CH_2=CH_2	Bottles, coatings
Polypropylene	CH_2=$CHCH_3$	Bottles, coatings
Polyvinyl chloride	CH_2=$CHCl$	Credit cards, pipes
Polystyrene	CH_2=CHC_6H_5	Foamed beads and blocks for packaging
Teflon	CF_2=CF_2	Nonstick surfaces

Condensation Polymers

Condensation reactions are similar to the reactions that form esters and peptide bonds. Each reactant must have two functional groups; one is an acid and the other is a base, either —OH or —NH_2. We can remember that condensation reactions produce water as a product by recalling that condensation on a cold window or a glass of ice water also produces water.

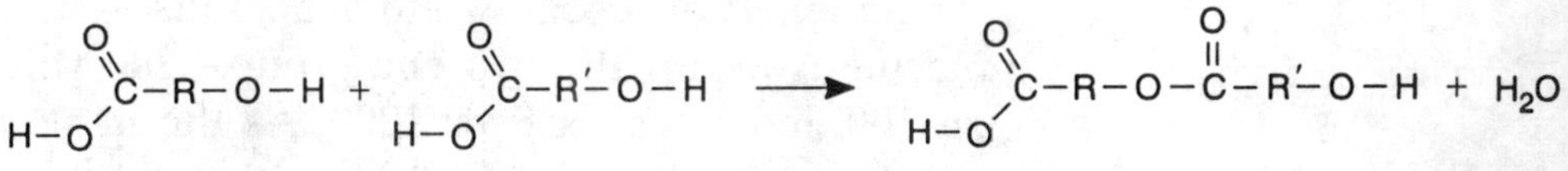

$$(15.4)$$

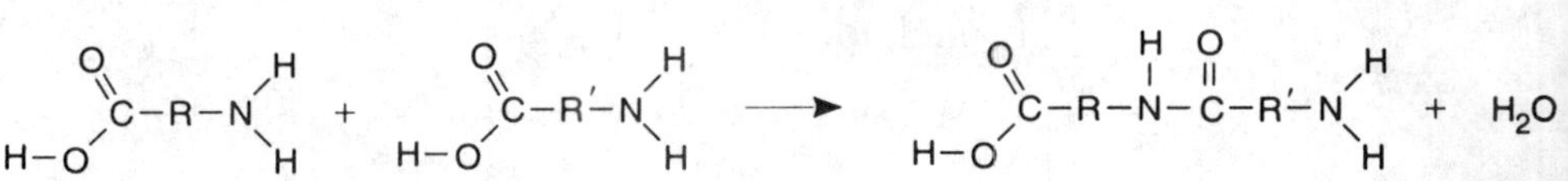

$$(15.5)$$

In the reactions in Equations 15.4 and 15.5, R and R′ represent hydrocarbon groups.

Each monomer may contain an acid and a basic functional group, as shown above, in which case there is only one reactant. Another method involves using one monomer that contains two acid groups and another that contains two basic groups. An equal molar mixture of these two monomers is used to form the polymer:

$$HOOC—R—COOH \quad + \quad H_2N—R'—NH_2$$
$$\rightarrow \quad HOOC—R—CO—NH—R'—NH_2 \quad + \quad H_2O \quad (15.6)$$

Starch and cellulose are both condensation polymers of glucose. The different physical and chemical properties of these two polymers are due to the different arrangements of their bonds. Some common condensation polymers and their uses are listed in Table 15.7.

TABLE 15.7   Common Condensation Polymers and Their Uses

Name	Monomer(s)	Typical Uses
Dacron	Terephthalic acid, ethylene glycol	Fibers, fabrics
Nylon	1,6-Hexanedicarboxylic acid, 1,6-diamino hexane	Fibers, fabrics
Proteins	Amino acids	Biological reactants, food
Disaccharides	Two sugar molecules	Biological energy source
Starch	Many glucose molecules	Food source
Cellulose	Many glucose molecules	Biological structural material
DNA	Nucleotides	Genetic code

Polymer Properties

We may deduce some of the properties of polymers from fundamental chemical principles developed in preceding chapters.

Polymers with polar, hydrogen-bonding functional groups may be soluble in water despite their tremendous size. This fact explains the solubility of proteins and polyvinyl alcohols. Most other polymers, however, are insoluble. The length of these polymers allows them to align with each other, thereby generating substantial London forces of attraction.

Although addition polymers are prepared from monomers with double bonds, the finished polymer has no double bonds. As a result, these polymers are fairly inert. The most inert is **Teflon**, in which the very strong C-F bond cannot be broken easily.

Polymers also have distinct properties related to the absorption of water and gases. Many of these properties depend on the method used to manufacture the polymer. A polymer can be manufactured or treated to increase or decrease the porosity. Branched-chain polymers have different properties than linear polymers. Polymer chemists take advantage of the specific properties of polymers in designing consumer products.

Important Concepts

Hybridization of carbon and related shapes
Isomers, structural, cis-trans and stereo
Alkanes, alkenes and alkynes
Functional groups
Nomenclature
Polymers

Questions on Chapter 15

1. The aldehyde functional group is
   (A) —C—O—H
   (B) —C=O
   (C) $—NH_2$
   (D) —COOH
   (E) $—CH_3$

2. The propyl side chain is
   (A) —COOH
   (B) $—CH_3$
   (C) $—NH_2$
   (D) $—CH_2CH_2CH_2CH_3$
   (E) $—CH_2CH_2CH_3$

3. The peptide bond is formed when an organic acid reacts with a compound containing the functional group
   (A) —C—O—H
   (B) —C=O
   (C) $—NH_2$
   (D) —COOH
   (E) $—CH_3$

4. Stereoisomers
   (A) require four different substituents attached to one carbon atom
   (B) have virtually identical physical properties
   (C) often have different biological activities
   (D) are mirror images
   (E) All of the above are true.

5. Under the appropriate reaction conditions propylene will
   (A) form an addition polymer called polypropylene
   (B) react with Br_2 to form 1,2-dibromopropane
   (C) in the presence of Pt, react with H_2 to form propane
   (D) react with HI
   (E) All of the above reactions occur.

6. The monomer used to form the polymer $[—CH_2CHCl—]_n$ is
   (A) CH_3CH_2Cl
   (B) $CH{\equiv}CCl$
   (C) CH_nCHCl_n
   (D) CHCH + HCl
   (E) $CH_2{=}CHCl$

7. The IUPAC systematic name for $CH_3CH_2CH_2OH$ is
   (A) propane-1-ol
   (B) *n*-propanol
   (C) propanol
   (D) 1-methylethane-1-ol
   (E) isopropanol

8. A protein is
   (A) a polysaccharide
   (B) desoxyribonucleic acid
   (C) a polymer of amino acids
   (D) soluble because of the —C=O groups
   (E) a polyester

9. The reaction between a compound containing one —NH_2 and a compound containing one —COOH functional group is best described as
   (A) an esterification reaction
   (B) a hydrogenation reaction
   (C) an acid-base reaction
   (D) a hydrolysis reaction
   (E) a combustion reaction

10. To have cis and trans isomers, a compound must have
   (A) *sp* bonded carbon atoms
   (B) *sp*^{3} bonded carbon atoms
   (C) *sp*^{2} bonded carbon atoms
   (D) A and B
   (E) A and C

11. For compounds with the same number of carbon atoms, the compound with the lowest boiling point is expected to be
   (A) a ketone
   (B) an amine
   (C) an acid
   (D) an alcohol
   (E) an ether

12. Which of the following organic compounds need NOT contain oxygen?
   (A) an alkyne
   (B) an alcohol
   (C) an aldehyde
   (D) a ketone
   (E) an ether

13. An organic base contains the functional group
   (A) —OH
   (B) —COOH
   (C) —NH_2
   (D) —C=O
   (E) —Cl

14. At which positions does metadibromobenzene have bromine atoms on the benzene ring?
   (A) 1 and 3
   (B) 1 and 4

(C) 1 and 2
(D) 1 and 5
(E) 1 and 6

15. Of the following molecules which is (are) totally flat?
(A) CH_4
(B) $CH_2 = CH_2$
(C) C_6H_6 (benzene)
(D) C_6H_{12} (cyclohexane)
(E) B and C

16. The bonding in the benzene molecule, C_6H_6, in any of its resonance structures, contains
(A) 6 sigma bonds and 6 pi bonds
(B) 6 sigma bonds and 12 pi bonds
(C) 12 sigma bonds and 6 pi bonds
(D) only sigma bonds
(E) 12 sigma bonds and 3 pi bonds

17. Which of the following is most likely to form hydrogen bonds?
(A) an alkyne
(B) an alcohol
(C) an aldehyde
(D) a ketone
(E) an ether

18. The following compounds have the same number of carbon atoms. Which is expected to have the lowest boiling point?
(A) an alkyne
(B) an alcohol
(C) an aldehyde
(D) a ketone
(E) an ether

19. Which of the following always have a constant percentage of carbon in all of their compounds? (Assume that there are no other functional groups on the molecule.)
(A) alkenes
(B) alcohols
(C) aldehydes
(D) ketones
(E) ethers

20. CH_2O is the empirical formula for
(A) amino acids
(B) proteins
(C) carbohydrates (sugars)
(D) aldehydes
(E) DNA and RNA

Answer Key

See Appendix I for explanations of answers.

1. **B**	5. **E**	9. **C**	13. **C**	17. **B**
2. **E**	6. **E**	10. **C**	14. **A**	18. **A**
3. **C**	7. **A**	11. **E**	15. **E**	19. **A**
4. **E**	8. **C**	12. **A**	16. **E**	20. **C**

CHAPTER SIXTEEN

Experimental Chemistry

Chemistry is an experimental science. All concepts, laws, and theories are directly supported by experimental evidence. Correctly designed and performed experiments advance knowledge about chemistry, while poor experiments confuse issues and principles and hinder the advancement of science. We need to understand the underlying concepts and techniques that are the basis of good experimental methods.

Data Gathering

Information gained in chemical experiments may be **quantitative,** that is, numerical, or it may not involve numbers, in which case the data are **qualitative** observations. If the concentration of an acid is determined to be 0.345 M, a quantitative measurement has been made. When silver nitrate is added to a solution and a white precipitate forms, the result is a qualitative observation. Both types of information are important in any experiment.

All observations and experimental details must be recorded in a **notebook.** The notebook must contain a complete description of the experiment so that any knowledgeable chemist can accurately repeat it. In particular, the description must specify the general idea of the experiment, along with the equipment and chemicals used. Diagrams are often drawn to show how an apparatus is constructed. Detailed information on the mass, volume, and source of every chemical used in the experiment is recorded. When the experiment is performed, careful observations of the reaction are noted as the experiment progresses. Finally, calculations are performed on the data gathered and conclusions are drawn. These conclusions help the chemist design the next experiment.

All information about an experiment is recorded directly in the notebook, which should be a bound, not loose-leaf or spiral, book with numbered pages. Entries are made in ink, and every entry is dated. Data should never be written on scraps of paper and then transcribed later. Erasures or removal of pages is not acceptable. Errors are crossed out in such a way that they are still readable. Although neatness is desirable, it is much more important to have a continuous record of all laboratory activity, whether a particular experiment is successful or not.

Calculations

Most calculations in chemistry invol simple algebra and two basic approaches. The first is the use of the fac-label method to convert information from one set of units into aner. The second is the use of a memorized equation or law into whichta for all variables except one are inserted. The one remaining variabl the unknown for the problem. Correct use of the second method reqs that all units be shown to ensure that they cancel properly to obtain desired units for the numerical answer.

Scientific calculators simplify math|cal operations to the touch of a few keys. Understanding the principles concepts of chemistry enables us to decide in which order to press those Understanding numbers tells us how to properly interpret the answer t|pears on the calculator screen.

Accuracy and Precision

The **accuracy** of a measurement refers closeness between the measurement obtained and the true value. cientists rarely know the true value, it is generally impossible to dete the accuracy completely. One approach to evaluating accuracy is to a measurement by two completely independent methods. If the from independent measurements agree, scientists have more co e in the accuracy of their results.

Accuracy is affected by **determinat** that is, errors due to poor technique or incorrectly calibrated ins . Careful evaluation of an experiment may eliminate determinate

Precision refers to the closeness o d measurements to each other. If the mass of an object is deter 35.43 grams, 35.41 grams, and 35.44 grams in three measuremen sults may be considered precise. There is no guarantee that the rate, however, unless the balance was properly calibrated and t methods were used in weighing the object. When proper techni ed, precise results infer, but do not guarantee, accurate results.

Precision is also a measure of **indete ors**, that is, errors that arise in estimating the last, uncertain di asurement. Indeterminate errors are random errors and canno ted. Statistical analysis deals with the theory of random errors.

Significant Figures

Every experimental measurement is ma way as to obtain the most information possible from whateve is used. As a result, measurements involve numbers in which is uncertain. Scientists characterize a measured number ba mber of **significa figures** it contains.

The number of significant figures in a n nclues all e the number from the first nonzero digit o he l d er right. For exponential numbers, the numb nt ple, mined from the digits to the left of the m If the 8.32×10^3 has three significant figures. cant.

Sometimes there are trailing zeros on the ant. number contains a decimal point, trailing

Trailing z'os that are used to complete a number, however, may or may not be sigficant. Scientists avoid writing a number such as 12,000 since it does not efinitely indicate the number of significant figures. Scientific notation used instead. Twelve thousand can be written as 1.2×10^4, 1.20×10^4, 00 $\times 10^4$, or 1.2000×10^4, indicating two, three, four, or five significa figures, respectively. It is the responsibility of the experimenter to writ mbers in such a way that there is no ambiguity. .

Exercise 16.1

Deter e the number of significant figures in each of the following meas- ured es:

(a) mL	(d) 6.02×10^{23} molecules	(g) 1.00026×10^{-3} cm
(b) 6 s	(e) 0.98 mol	(h) 2.0000
(c) 236 g	(f) 0023 m	(i) 824 mg

Solution

T bers are repeated with the significant figures in bold type:

(6 mL	(d) **6.02×10^{23}** molecules	(g) **1.00026×10^{-3}** cm
036 s	(e) **0.98** mol	(h) **2.0000** J
.236 g	(f) 00**23** m	(i) **824** mg

e numbers are **exact numbers,** which involve no uncertainty. The r of plates set on a table for dinner may be determined exactly. If ates are observed and counted, that measurement is exactly 5. In stry many defined equalities are exact. For instance, there are exactly joules in each calorie. Other exact numbers are stoichiometric coef- ts and subscripts in chemical formulas.

e reason for determining the number of significant figures in a meas- value that this number tells us how to write the answers to any lations based on that value. There are two basic rules:

The number with the fewest significant figures in a multiplication or division problem determines the number of significant figures in the answer. In these calculations an exact number is considered to have an infinite number of significant figures.

. The number with the fewest decimal places in an addition or subtrac- tion problem determines the number of decimal places in the answer. Numbers expressed in scientific notation must all be converted to the same power of 10 before determining which decimal places can be retained.

Incertainty

here are two types of uncertainty, **absolute uncertainty** and **relative un- rtainty**.

The absolute uncertainty is the uncertainty of the last digit of a measure- ent. For example, 45.47 mL is a measurement of volume, and the last digit s uncertain. The absolute uncertainty is ±0.01 mL. The measurement should be regarded as somewhere between 45.46 and 45.48 mL.

The relative uncertainty of a number is the last digit divided by the number itself. For the above example, the relative uncertainty is

$$\frac{0.01 \text{ mL}}{45.47 \text{ mL}} = 2 \times 10^{-4}.$$

The absolute uncertainty governs the principles used for addition and subtraction. The relative uncertainty governs the principles used for multiplication and division.

Rounding

Calculations, especially those done using an electronic calculator, often generate more, and sometimes fewer, significant figures or decimal places than are required by rules 1 and 2 given above. These answers must be rounded to the proper number of significant figures or decimal places. To do this, four steps are followed:

1. The number of digits to be kept in a calculation is determined using rules 1 and/or 2 above.
2. If the digit just after the kept digits is less than 5, the remaining digits are dropped. For example, rounding 6.23499 to three significant figures yields 6.23 because 4 is less than 5.
3. If the digit just after the kept digit is greater than 5, or if it is 5 with additional nonzero digits, 1 is added to the last of the kept digits. For example, rounding 5.5589 to three significant figures yields 5.56. Similarly, 6.345002 is rounded to 6.35 because the 5 has a nonzero digit after it.
4. If the digit to be rounded is just 5 or is 5 with all zeros after it, the last digit in the kept digits is rounded to the nearest even number. For example, rounding 2.335 to two decimal places yields 2.34, and rounding 6.785000 to two decimal places yields 6.78.

Exercise 16.2

Perform each of the following calculations, and report the answer with the correct number of significant figures:

(a) $23.456 + 16.0094 + 9.21$
(b) $14.98 \times 0.00234 \times 1.5$
(c) $1.46 \times 10^3 + 5.83 \times 10^4$
(d) $(8.236 \times 10^2)(5.55 \times 10^{-3})$
(e) $(23.45 - 16.12)/6.233$
(f) $(6.02 \times 10^{23})(1.00 \times 10^{-6})/(18.23)$
(g) $(44.23)/(2.33 \times 10^2 - 2.25 \times 10^2)$

Solution

(a) 48.68
(b) 0.053
(c) 5.68×10^4
(d) 4.57
(e) 1.18
(f) 3.30×10^{16}
(g) 6

Significant Figures in Atomic and Molar Masses

All of the atomic masses listed in the periodic table have four or more significant figures. These are measured values and must be included in the determination of the correct number of significant figures in any calculation that uses them. However, most calculations involve fewer than four significant figures, and the significant figures in atomic and molar masses do not affect the number of significant figures in the answers. As a result, atomic and molar masses are usually rounded to the nearest whole number. One exception is chlorine, which usually has its atomic mass rounded to 35.5.

Exercise 16.3

What percentage error is expected when the atomic mass of each of the following elements is rounded to the nearest whole number?
(a) Na
(b) Ag
(c) Pb
(d) Cl

Solution

The percentage error is calculated as

$$\text{percentage error} = \frac{\text{Measured value} - \text{True value}}{\text{True value}} \times 100$$

In this problem the measured value is the rounded atomic mass, and the true value is the atomic mass.

(a) $\dfrac{0.01}{22.99} \times 100 = +0.04\%$ (c) $\dfrac{0.2}{207.2} \times 100 = -0.1\%$

(b) $\dfrac{0.132}{107.868} \times 100 = +0.1\%$ (d) $\dfrac{0.453}{35.453} \times 100 = -1.3\%$

The error for chlorine is ten times that for the other elements. When the atomic mass is rounded to 35.5, the error for chlorine is +0.1%, which is in line with the magnitude of the rounding errors for the other elements.

Graphs

A **graph** is used to illustrate the relationship between two variables. Graphs are often a more effective method of communication than tables of data. A graph has two axes: a horizontal axis, usually called the x-axis (abscissa), and a vertical axis, called the y-axis (ordinate).

It is customary to use the x-axis for the **independent variable**, and the y-axis for the **dependent variable**, in an experiment. An independent variable is one that the experimenter selects. For instance, concentrations of standard solutions that a chemist prepares are independent variables since any concentrations may be chosen. The dependent variable is a measured property of the independent variable. For instance, the dependent variable may be the amount of light that each of the standard solutions prepared by the chemist absorbs, since the absorbed light is dependent on the concentration. Each data point is an x,y pair representing the value of the independent variable and the value of the dependent variable as determined in the experiment.

The first step in constructing a graph is to label the x- and y-axes to indicate the identity of the independent and dependent variables. Next, the axes are numbered, usually from zero to the largest value expected for each variable. Finally, each data point is plotted by drawing a horizontal line at the value of the dependent variable and a vertical line upward from the value of the independent variable. The intersection of these two lines determines where that data point belongs on the graph.

Most graphs show a linear relationship between two variables. Other graphs, such as those showing kinetic curves, have curved lines. In both cases, data points are plotted on the graph and then the best smooth line is drawn through the points. Lines are never drawn by connecting the data points with straight lines. In very accurate work a statistical analysis called the "method of least squares" is used to determine the best straight line for the data. In most cases, however, the line is drawn by eye, attempting to have all data points as close as possible to the line. The usual result is a line that has the same number of data points above and below it.

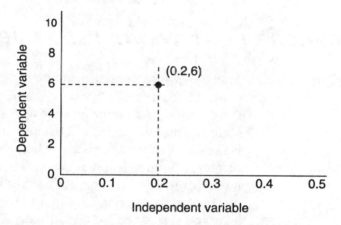

FIGURE 16.1.   The positions of the independent and dependent variables in a graph. Dashed lines show the placement of a point representing a value of 0.2 for the independent variable and of 6 for the dependent variable.

Figure 16.2 illustrates that it is incorrect to draw any line beyond the measured data points. The reason is that anything beyond the measured data is unknown. Extending the line implies information that is not verified by experimental data.

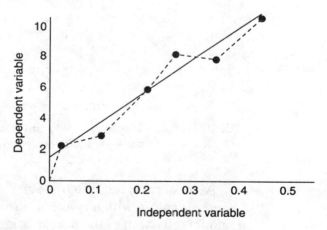

FIGURE 16.2.   The correct way to draw a line using data in a graph. The solid line is the correct line; the dashed line is incorrect.

The slope of a curve or line is often needed as an experimental result. To determine the slope of a line, two points on the line are chosen. The left-hand point has coordinates (x_1, y_1), and the right-hand point has coordinates (x_2, y_2). The values of x and y at these points are determined from the graph, and Equation 16.1 is used to determine the slope:

$$\text{Slope} = \frac{x_2 - x_1}{y_2 - y_1} \qquad (16.1)$$

In a graph with a curved line the slope is determined by drawing a tangent to the curve and then determining the slope of the tangent, as is done for a straight line.

Determination of Physical Properties

Scale Reading

Many measurements are made by comparing the level of a liquid in a container to a scale etched on the outside of the container or by observing the position of a meter pointer with reference to an adjacent scale. Such a scale is usually a series of lines in which every tenth line is numbered and is usually distinguished also by being longer than the others. The fluid level or meter pointer is never directly in contact with the scale; consequently, incorrect reading techniques can result in **parallax errors**.

The surface tension of a liquid in any container causes the liquid to have a curved surface called a **meniscus**. All glassware is calibrated on the basis that the liquid level corresponds to the bottom of the meniscus. Figure 16.3 demonstrates that, to avoid parallax errors, the eye must be at the same level as the meniscus when measuring liquids.

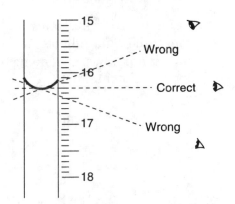

FIGURE 16.3. The correct way to read liquid levels. Parallax error results when the eye, scale, and meniscus are not lined up horizontally.

A modern meter usually has a mirror adjacent to the scale. Correct meter readings, with no parallax error, are obtained when the meter pointer and its reflection in the mirror coincide.

Determination of Mass by Weighing

The mass of a chemical substance is obtained by determining the weight of the substance. The weight of a sample is equal to the force of gravity times the mass of the sample:

$$\text{Weight} = \text{(Gravitational constant) (Mass)} \qquad (16.2)$$

If the gravitational constant is known, the mass can be calculated from the measured weight. To avoid this calculation, the mass of a sample may be directly compared to a known mass on a double-pan balance. Modern balances are single-pan balances that are calibrated with standard masses.

Proper use of a balance requires that the balance be calibrated. A sample is always weighed in an appropriate container, never directly on a balance pan. The mass of the empty container is referred to as the tare mass. A sample's mass is the difference between the tare mass and the mass of the sample and the container. A typical notebook entry for a mass determination should look like this:

$$
\begin{array}{r}
24.345 \text{ g total mass} \\
-3.862 \text{ g tare mass} \\
\hline
20.483 \text{ g sample mass}
\end{array}
$$

Liquid Volume Measurement

Graduated cylinders and graduated beakers are used to measure liquid volumes with an accuracy of ± 10 percent. More accurate liquid measurements are made with **pipets** or **burets**. Glassware of this type is usually labeled with the letters "**TD**," which stand for "to deliver" and indicate that the amount of liquid poured or delivered from the pipet or buret is the volume stated. Volumetric flasks have the label "**TC**," which stands for "to contain." Although a 100-mL volumetric flask will contain 100 mL, it will not deliver 100 mL if the liquid is poured out. The difference is the film of solution left on the inner surface of the flask itself.

Pipets come in two types, transfer and measuring. A transfer pipet has a single mark and is used for the most accurate measurements. Measuring pipets are graduated, and any volume may be delivered by stopping the flow of the liquid at the desired point. Before filling, a pipet is rinsed in the solution to be measured; then the pipet is filled above the calibration line with suction from a suction bulb. Quickly placing a finger over the top of the pipet after the suction bulb is removed allows precise control of the flow of liquid. The solution is allowed to drain to the first calibration mark, excess solution is wiped from the tip, and then the solution is allowed to drain by gravity into the receiving flask. When draining is completed, the last drop is removed by momentarily touching the tip of the pipet to the solution surface or the side of the flask. Blowing out the contents of a pipet will deliver the wrong amount of solution.

Burets are long, graduated tubes that hold between 10 and 50 mL of solution. The flow of liquid is controlled by a valve called a **stopcock**. A buret is rinsed with solution, not distilled water, before filling. When filling is completed, the stopcock is opened fully to expel any air from the tip; and, if needed, additional solution is added so that the liquid is near the top graduation mark. In use, the starting volume is recorded, solution is delivered, and, when finished, the final volume is recorded. The difference between the final and initial volumes is the volume delivered. Here is a sample notebook entry:

$$
\begin{array}{r}
23.86 \text{ mL at the end} \\
-0.23 \text{ mL at the start} \\
\hline
23.63 \text{ mL solution delivered}
\end{array}
$$

Temperature Measurement

Thermometers are used for temperature measurement. Each thermometer has a line etched near the mercury bulb. This line is the immersion depth. When the thermometer is immersed in a liquid to this etched line, the temperature reading will be the most accurate. The calibration of a thermometer is checked by immersing it in ice water, 0°C, and then in boiling water, 100°C.

Broken mercury thermometers must be disposed of carefully because of the hazards posed by elemental mercury.

Determination of Melting and Boiling Points

With sufficient liquid, the boiling point is determined by measuring the temperature as the liquid boils. Accurate determination of the normal boiling point requires that this experiment be done at 1 atmosphere of pressure.

Several instruments are available for determining melting points. For the experiment, a sample is packed into a closed-end capillary tube and inserted in the instrument, which is set to heat the sample slowly. The temperature at which the first crystals start melting is the melting point. The same result can be obtained by attaching the capillary tube to a thermometer so that the sample is next to the mercury bulb. The thermometer and attached sample are immersed in an oil with a high boiling point, and heat is applied until the sample just starts to melt.

Determination of Density

Density is an intrinsic physical property that can be used to identify unknown materials. The general equation for determining density is as follows:

$$\text{Density} \quad = \quad \frac{\text{Mass}}{\text{Volume}} \tag{16.3}$$

Equations 16.4 and 16.5 show the units used for mass and volume for substances in various phases:

$$\text{Density of solids or liquids} \quad = \quad \frac{\text{grams of material}}{\text{cubic centimeters of material}} \tag{16.4}$$

$$\text{Density of gases} \quad = \quad \frac{\text{grams of gas}}{\text{liters of gas}} \tag{16.5}$$

Since density varies somewhat with temperature, we often see the symbol d_{20}, where the subscript indicates the Celsius temperature at which the density was determined.

The density of a solid is determined by measuring first its mass and then its volume. The mass measurement was described in a preceding section. There are two methods to determine the volume of a solid. The first is to measure its dimensions and use trigonometry to calculate the volume. This method works best with a regularly shaped object such as a cylinder or a rectangular solid. The second method is to immerse the solid in a liquid and measure the volume displaced. This is commonly done by placing water in a graduated cylinder and measuring its volume. Then the solid is added and a second volume is determined. The difference in volumes is the volume of the object:

$$\text{Volume of object} = V_{final} - V_{initial} \tag{16.6}$$

Dividing the mass by the volume yields the density.

The density of a liquid is determined using a device called a **pyncnometer**, which is a small flask with a volume of approximately 5–25 mL. The exact volume is obtained by determining the mass of water needed to completely fill the pyncnometer. Since the density of water is known, the volume of the pyncnometer can be calculated. Next, the mass of unknown liquid needed to fill the pyncnometer is determined. The density is then calculated using Equation 16.4.

The density of a gas is determined by evacuating a large flask with a vacuum pump so that there is virtually no gas inside the flask. The evacuated flask is weighed, and the gas is introduced until its pressure is equal to atmospheric pressure. The flask is then weighed again to obtain the mass of the gas. The volume of the flask is determined from the amount of water it can hold or by some similar technique, and the density is determined using Equation 16.5.

Determination of Specific Heat

The specific heat of a solid, usually a metal, is determined by heating a known mass of the substance to a predetermined temperature and then submerging it in a known quantity of water in an insulated container. The final temperature of the water indicates the temperature increase of the water and the temperature decrease of the metal. The specific heat equation is as follows:

$$q = (\text{Specific heat})(\text{Mass})(\Delta T) \tag{16.7}$$

where ΔT is the temperature change.

Since the heat, q, gained by the water must be equal to the heat lost by the metal, the equality becomes

$$(\text{Specific heat})_{water}(\text{Mass})_{water}(\Delta T)_{water}$$
$$= -(\text{Specific heat})_{metal}(\text{Mass})_{metal}(\Delta T)_{metal} \tag{16.8}$$

An example of specific heat calculation is given in Chapter 12.

Sample Manipulations

Heating

Heating can be done in several ways, and the method chosen depends on the equipment on hand and safety factors. Water and aqueous solutions are usually heated with a Bunsen burner. Precautions should be taken to avoid **bumping**, which is a violent burst of boiling that may spatter hot liquid. The best way to avoid bumping is to add boiling chips to the mixture. Liquids heated in test tubes are very likely to bump, and care should be exercised that test tubes are not pointed toward other workers. Burners with open flames should be avoided when any flammable substances are in use in the laboratory.

Bumping occurs because a burner flame superheats one portion of a liquid. Hot-water baths, steam baths, sand baths, and electric heating mantles are effective heating methods that minimize bumping by spreading the applied heat. The fact that the limit for steam and hot water is approximately 100°C may be a safety feature.

Bumping also occurs when solids, particularly powders, are added to very hot liquids. For this reason solids should be added to cool liquids before heating.

Cooling

Hot solutions or objects are cooled with water or ice. A bath made of crushed ice and water is most effective. Ice by itself is not efficient since much of the flask containing the hot solution is not in contact with the ice. Only heat-resistant laboratory glassware should be used since ordinary glass will shatter with rapid temperature changes.

Lower temperatures (approx. −50°C) may be obtained using dry ice mixtures, and very low temperatures (−196°C) with liquid nitrogen. Dry ice and liquid nitrogen can cause injury, however, because of their extremely low temperatures. They also present a smaller, although real, hazard of possible suffocation.

Mixing

Preparation of solutions is the most common mixing operation in chemistry. A solid is dissolved in a solvent by adding the solid slowly, with stirring, to about half of the liquid. When dissolution is complete, the correct amount of liquid is added and mixed well. Grinding the solid to a powder and warming the mixture both speed dissolution.

Preparation of solutions with molar concentration units requires an exact total volume of solution. These solutions are prepared in **volumetric flasks**. A volumetric flask is calibrated with an etched line on its neck to hold a specified volume at a given temperature. If a solution is warmed to speed dissolution, it must be cooled to room temperature before the final volume adjustment.

When a concentrated acid is mixed with water, the acid is always added to the water. Most acids, particularly sulfuric acid, are denser than water and generate a large amount of heat when mixed with water. If water is added to sulfuric acid, it does not mix because of the density of the acid, and the high heat of mixing causes the water to boil and spatter sulfuric acid.

Drying

Drying chemical reagents before use and drying products of reactions are very common operations in the laboratory. Since the drying process involves removing water from a substance, the temperature must be above 100°C. To avoid decomposition, however, the temperature should also be as low as possible. An oven set between 105° and 110°C is recommended.

Dilution

A common practice in chemistry laboratories is to prepare a concentrated stock solution of some solute. To make other solutions, the stock solution is diluted with water in the appropriate volume ratio. The dilution law is

$$(C_{initial})(V_{initial}) = (C_{final})(V_{final}) \qquad (16.9)$$

If we have a stock solution of some concentration, $C_{initial}$, we can calculate the volume needed to prepare a given volume at any other concentration.

Exercise 16.4

Calculate the volume of a stock 6.00 M HCl solution needed to make 1.00 L of a 0.100 M HCl solution.

Solution

We can define as follows: $C_{initial}$ = 6.00 M HCl, C_{final} = 0.100 M HCl, V_{final} = 1.00 L. Entering these values in Equation 16.9 yields

$$(6.00 \text{ M HCl})(V_{initial}) \quad = \quad (0.100 \text{ M HCl}) (1.00 \text{ L})$$

$$V_{initial} \quad = \quad \frac{(0.100 \text{ M HCl}) (1.00 \text{ L})}{6.00 \text{ M HCl}}$$

$$= \quad 0.0166 \text{ L} \quad = \quad 16.6 \text{ mL}$$

To prepare the desired solution, 16.6 mL of the stock solution must be diluted to 1.00 L.

Exercise 16.5

How many milliliters of distilled water must be added to 100 mL of 0.250 M KCl to prepare a 0.100 M KCl solution?

Solution

The given values are as follows: $C_{initial}$ = 0.250 M KCl, $V_{initial}$ = 100 mL, C_{final} = 0.100 M KCl. From these data we calculate V_{final}:

$$(0.250 \text{ M KCl}) (100 \text{ mL}) \quad = \quad (0.100 \text{ M KCl})(V_{final})$$

$$V_{final} \quad = \quad 250 \text{ mL}$$

Since the final volume of solution is the sum of the initial volume and the added distilled water:

$$V_{final} \quad = \quad V_{initial} \quad + \quad V_{water}$$

$$250 \text{ mL} \quad = \quad 100 \text{ mL} \quad + \quad V_{water}$$

$$V_{water} \quad = \quad 150 \text{ mL}$$

Gas Collection

When a gas is generated in a chemical reaction, it may be collected in a **pneumatic trough**, shown in Figure 16.4. A gas-collecting bottle is filled with water, and a tube from the sealed experiment leads under water to the bottle. Any gas evolved displaces the water in the bottle. Details on how to measure the amount of gas collected are described in Chapter 4.

Gases that react with water, however, cannot be collected by displacement of water. Instead, air in a container is displaced by the gas. A gas that has a density greater than the density of air will displace air from the bottom to the top of an upright gas bottle. This process is called upward displacement. When the gas density is less than the density of air, the collecting bottle is inverted and the air is displaced downward as the gas fills the bottle from the top to the bottom. Figure 16.5 illustrates the upward and downward displacement of gas.

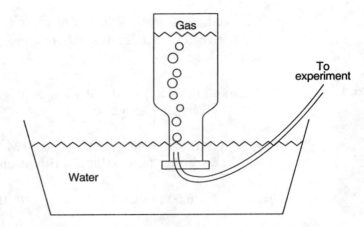

FIGURE 16.4. Diagram of a pneumatic trough.

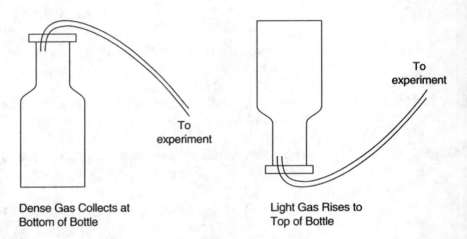

FIGURE 16.5. Experimental setups for (left) upward displacement of gas and (right) downward displacement of gas.

The density of a gas is directly proportional to its molar mass. The average molar mass of air, which is 80 percent nitrogen and 20 percent oxygen, is 29. Gases with molar masses greater than 29 are collected by upward displacement of air; gases with molar masses less than 29, by downward displacement of air.

Separation Techniques

Precipitation

Solids can be precipitated by chemical reactions such as using Ba^{2+} to **precipitate** sulfate ions as barium sulfate:

$$Ba^{2+}(aq) \quad + \quad SO_4^{2-}(aq) \quad \rightarrow \quad BaSO_4(s) \qquad (16.10)$$

To obtain a pure product the barium solution should be added slowly with rapid stirring. This procedure keeps the barium ion concentration low and the formation of barium sulfate crystals is slowed, thereby preventing the barium sulfate from entrapping impurities during rapid crystal growth. Once precipitation is complete, the mixture is heated to coagulate the small crystals into larger crystals for easy filtration.

Filtration

Filtration is used to separate solid particles from a liquid. Filter paper is folded into a cone and inserted into a funnel. A few drops of water are placed on the filter paper to hold it in place, and then the solution to be filtered is added to the funnel. As liquid flows through the paper under the force of gravity, the solid is left in the filter paper. Precipitates are washed with dilute electrolyte solutions to remove contaminants. Suction or Buchner funnels may be used to speed the filtration process.

Filter paper comes in different grades. Coarse grades allow the liquid to flow faster since the pore size is large. Coarse filter paper cannot be used for fine precipitates, which will pass through the pores. Fine precipitates require filter paper with smaller pores and consequently take longer to filter. Fine precipitates are often heated in a process called digestion in order to form larger crystals, which are more easily filtered.

Centrifugation

For very small amounts of precipitate, **centrifugation** is the preferred method of separation from the solvent. A centrifuge spins samples at high speed, forcing solids to compact at the bottom of a test tube. Each sample-containing test tube inserted in a centrifuge must be balanced by another test tube containing the same amount of liquid. This keeps the centrifuge balanced so that it does not vibrate uncontrollably and perhaps "walk" off the bench.

The clear liquid remaining after centrifugation is called the **supernatant**. When the process is finished, the supernatant is decanted (poured carefully) from the precipitate to separate the liquid from the solid.

Distillation

Distillation is a separation technique whereby a substance with a high vapor pressure (low boiling point) is separated from other substances with lower vapor pressures (higher boiling points). Distillation is performed by boiling a solution and passing the vapor formed through a condenser to recover the vaporized liquid. When a mixture of methyl alcohol (b.p. = 65°C) and ethyl alcohol (b.p. = 79°C) is heated to boiling, the vapor formed contains mostly methyl alcohol. When this vapor is condensed, the condensate is enriched in methyl alcohol while the residual in the boiling flask is enriched in ethyl alcohol. Two volatile substances may be purified but not completely separated.

A mixture of a salt in water is an example of a mixture containing a volatile and a nonvolatile substance. This type of mixture allows complete separation of the volatile substance, as in the distillation of sea water to produce pure water.

Instrumental Techniques

pH Determination

A **pH meter** or **pH paper** may be used to determine pH. A pH meter is used when a precise pH value is needed. pH paper serves to estimate the pH of a solution.

A pH meter, with a glass and reference electrode, is standardized with a standard buffer. Then the electrodes are rinsed to remove any buffer and immersed in the sample. The pH is read directly from the meter scale. More accurate pH measurements are made by standardizing the pH meter with two buffers, one with a pH slightly below that of the sample and the other with a pH slightly above that of the sample.

Litmus is a type of pH paper that tells only whether a solution is acid or basic. A clean stirring rod is dipped into the sample, and a drop is transferred to the **litmus paper**. A pink color indicates an acid solution, and a blue color a basic solution. Newer pH papers turn different colors depending on the pH. A drop of sample is placed on the pH paper with a stirring rod, and the resulting color is compared to a color chart to determine the approximate pH.

Spectroscopy

Colored solutions absorb visible light, and this absorption can be measured with a **spectrophotometer**. A spectrophotometer can be used to determine the spectrum of a compound or to determine the concentration of an unknown sample.

The **absorbance** of a sample is the quantity determined in a spectrophotometer. In the first step the wavelength of light to be used for the measurement is selected by adjusting the wavelength dial. The second step is to zero the meter with a **reagent blank**, which contains the same amounts of all reagents and solvents that were used to prepare the sample. In the last step the reagent blank is replaced with the actual sample and the meter is read. More samples can be measured as long as the wavelength is not changed. If the wavelength is changed, the instrument must be zeroed again with the reagent blank.

A spectrum is a graph of the light absorbed by a sample, that is, the absorbance, A, of the sample, versus the wavelength of light. Typically the absorbance of a sample is measured at 10-nm intervals from approximately 400 nm to 700 nm. An absorbance spectrum in the visible-wavelength region is shown in Figure 16.6.

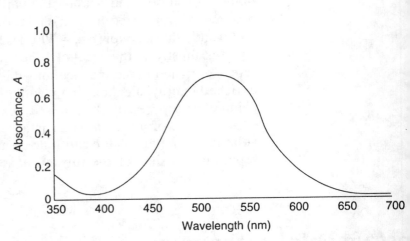

FIGURE 16.6. Absorbance spectrum for a compound that has its maximum absorbance at 515 nm. The sample has a violet color because green light is absorbed and all other wavelengths are observed by eye.

The concentration of a solute is determined at the wavelength of the largest peak in the spectrum. The absorbance of each solution of a series of concentration standards is determined, and a graph called a calibration curve is constructed. After the absorbance of the unknown sample is determined, the corresponding concentration is read from the calibration curve by drawing a horizontal line from the absorbance reading to the curve and then drawing a vertical line from the curve down to the concentration, as shown in Figure 16.7.

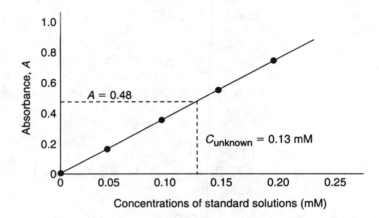

FIGURE 16.7. Calibration curve used to determine concentrations. Dots represent standard concentrations used to prepare the curve. Dashed line shows that the unknown has an absorbance of 0.48 and that the corresponding concentration is 0.13 millimolar.

The straight-line graph in Figure 16.7 is a consequence of **Beer's law**, which states that

$$\text{Absorbance } (A) \quad = \quad abc \qquad (16.11)$$

In Beer's law a is a constant called the **absorptivity**, which is characteristic of the compound and the wavelength at which the absorbance is measured. The concentration is represented by c, and the thickness of the sample, called the **optical path length**, by b. At a given wavelength, a and b are constant and there is a direct proportionality between the absorbance and the sample concentration. The slope of the line in Figure 16.7 is ab.

Experimental Reactions

The laboratory experience is a twofold process. One goal is to become familiar with the techniques and procedures used by chemists. The second is to become familiar with useful chemical reactions.

Synthesis of Gases

Some gases that are synthesized and collected are O_2, H_2, CO_2, NO, H_2S, and NH_3.

Oxygen is prepared by decomposing $KClO_3$ in the presence of MnO_2 as a catalyst:

$$2KClO_3(s) \xrightarrow[MnO_2]{heat} 2KCl(s) \quad + \quad 3O_2(g) \qquad (16.12)$$

Hydrogen is prepared by reacting an active metal, usually magnesium, with acid:

$$Mg(s) \quad + \quad 2HCl(aq) \quad \rightarrow \quad MgCl_2(aq) \quad + \quad 2H_2(g) \quad (16.13)$$

Carbon dioxide is prepared by reacting a carbonate salt with an acid. The reaction of $CaCO_3$ with HCl is one example:

$$CaCO_3(s) \quad + \quad 2HCl(aq) \quad \rightarrow$$
$$CaCl_2(aq) \quad + \quad H_2O(\ell) \quad + \quad CO_2(g) \quad (16.14)$$

Nitric oxide is produced from the reaction of copper with dilute HNO_3:

$$3Cu(s) \quad + \quad 8HNO_3(dil.\ aq) \quad \rightarrow$$
$$3Cu(NO_3)_2(aq) \quad + \quad 4H_2O \quad + \quad 2NO(g) \quad (16.15)$$

Hydrogen sulfide is produced by reacting an acid with a sulfide, for example:

$$FeS(s) \quad + \quad 2HCl(aq) \quad \rightarrow \quad FeCl_2(aq) \quad + \quad H_2S(g) \quad (16.16)$$

Ammonia is produced from the reactio of an ammonium salt with a base:

$$NH_4Cl(aq) \quad + \quad NaOH(aq) \quad \rightarrow$$
$$NaCl(aq) \quad + \quad H_2O(\ell) \quad + \quad NH_3(g) \quad (16.17)$$

As stated in a preceding section, gases that do not dissolve in, or react with, water may be collected by displacement of water in a pneumatic trough. Other gases must be collected in the absence of water. Carbon dioxide is 1.5 times as dense as air and can be collected by upward displacement of air from a collecting bottle. Ammonia, which is much lighter than air, can be collected by downward displacement of air from an inverted collecting bottle.

Synthesis of Insoluble Salts

Insoluble salts are often precipitated in double-replacement reactions or in reactions of gases with soluble substances. Some common compounds prepared by double replacement are shown in the following net ionic equations:

$$Ag^+(aq) \quad + \quad Cl^-(aq) \quad \rightarrow \quad AgCl(s) \quad (16.18)$$

$$Ba^{2+}(aq) \quad + \quad SO_4^{2-}(aq) \quad \rightarrow \quad BaSO_4(s) \quad (16.19)$$

$$Fe^{2+}(aq) \quad + \quad S^{2-}(aq) \quad \rightarrow \quad FeS(s) \quad (16.20)$$

In Equation 16.18 the chloride ion may be replaced by an iodide or a bromide ion. In Equation 16.20 Fe^{2+} can be replaced by almost any metal ion except the alkali metals.

Insoluble carbonates and sulfites are formed by bubbling $CO_2(g)$ and $SO_2(g)$ through solutions containing aqueous metal ions, for example:

$$Ca^{2+}(aq) \quad + \quad CO_2(g) \quad + \quad H_2O(\ell) \quad \rightarrow$$
$$CaCO_3(aq) \quad + \quad 2H^+(aq) \quad (16.21)$$

$$Ni^{2+}(aq) \quad + \quad SO_2(g) \quad + \quad H_2O(\ell) \quad \rightarrow$$
$$NiSO_3(s) \quad + \quad 2H^+(aq) \quad (16.22)$$

Preparation of Soluble Salts

Soluble salts are isolated from aqueous solution by removing water by evaporation with or without applying heat. To obtain a pure sample of salt, the solution must contain only the ions of that salt.

Magnesium nitrate can be prepared by reacting magnesium metal with HNO_3 until no more hydrogen is evolved. HNO_3 is the limiting reactant, and excess magnesium is removed by filtration. The filtrate can be boiled to dryness to recover $Mg(NO_3)_2(s)$:

$$Mg(s, \text{ excess}) \quad + \quad HNO_3(aq) \quad \rightarrow$$
$$Mg(NO_3)_2(aq) \quad + \quad H_2(g) \quad (16.23)$$

The preparation of calcium chloride uses the same reaction as the preparation of $CO_2(g)$ in Equation 16.14. Care is taken to avoid reacting all of the $CaCO_3(s)$ with HCl, and the reaction mixture is filtered to remove excess $CaCO_3(s)$. The solution that is left contains only $Ca^{2+}(aq)$ and $Cl^-(aq)$ ions, which can be boiled to dryness to recover the $CaCl_2(s)$.

Addition of an acid to an excess of an insoluble base anhydride such as $Fe_2O_3(s)$ can be used to produce soluble salts. Adding H_2SO_4 to an excess of $Fe_2O_3(s)$ will produce $Fe_2(SO_4)_3$:

$$Fe_2O_3(s) \quad + \quad 3H_2SO_4(aq) \quad \rightarrow \quad Fe_2(SO_4)_3(aq) \quad + \quad 3H_2O(\ell) \quad (16.24)$$

Reacting a base with an excess of an acid anhydride can also be used to prepare a soluble salt, as in the reaction

$$2NaOH(aq) \quad + \quad SO_2(g) \quad \rightarrow \quad Na_2SO_3(aq) \quad + \quad H_2O(\ell) \quad (16.25)$$

Soluble salts can be prepared by neutralization reactions as long as neither an excess of acid nor an excess of base is used in the reaction. For instance, LiBr may be prepared by reacting exactly 1 mole of LiOH for every mole of HBr in the reaction

$$LiOH(aq) \quad + \quad HBr(aq) \quad \rightarrow \quad LiBr(aq) \quad + \quad H_2O(\ell) \quad (16.26)$$

This method can be used to prepare three different sodium salts from phosphoric acid. NaH_2PO_4 is formed when 1 mole of NaOH is reacted with 1 mole of H_3PO_4. Two moles of NaOH will produce Na_2HPO_4, and 3 moles of NaOH per mole of H_3PO_4 produces Na_3PO_4.

Synthesis of Organic Compounds

The most common synthetic organic reaction is the formation of esters by the acid-catalyzed reaction of an alcohol and an organic acid. The reaction of acetic acid with 1-pentanol produces pentyl acetate, which has the odor of bananas:

$$CH_3COOH \quad + \quad CH_3CH_2CH_2CH_2CH_2OH \quad \xrightarrow{H^+}$$
$$CH_3CO_2CH_2CH_2CH_2CH_2CH_3 \quad (16.27)$$

Another common reaction is the formation of aspirin, acetyl salicylic acid, from salicylic acid and acetic acid. Although the anhydride of acetic acid is used in this reaction, the equation can be written as

$$(16.28)$$

Qualitative Analysis of Inorganic Ions

Qualitative analysis techniques are used to determine whether or not a sample contains a certain ion. In qualitative analysis an unknown and a reagent are mixed, and the result of the reaction allows us to draw a logical conclusion about the presence or absence of ions in the unknown. Many ions react in a similar manner; and although the addition of one reagent to an unknown may not identify the ion, it limits the possibilities. A sequence of reactions used to analyze a sample is called the qualitative analysis scheme—qual-scheme for short.

The qual-scheme uses selective precipitation to separate the ions in a sample into groups on the basis of their chemical characteristics listed below. When separation is by filtration, the liquid is called the **filtrate**. When the precipitate is separated by centrifugation, the liquid phase is called the **supernatant**.

Table 16.1 lists the main groups in the qual-scheme, starting with the unknown solution. The analysis starts with the sample, called the unknown, and group 1. Precipitates of the ions in each group are removed by filtration or centrifugation before the next group is precipitated.

TABLE 16.1 The Qualitative Analysis Scheme

Group Number	Solution Tested	Precipitating Agent	Precipitated Compounds
1	Unknown	0.1 M HCl	$PbCl_2$, Hg_2Cl_2, AgCl
2	Filtrate or supernatant from group 1	H_2S at pH 1	HgS, PbS, CuS, CdS, Bi_2S_3, As_2S_3, Sb_2S_3, SnS_2
3	Filtrate or supernatant from group 2	H_2S at pH 10	MnS, FeS, NiS, CoS, ZnS, $Fe(OH)_3$, $Al(OH)_3$, $Cr(OH)_3$
4	Filtrate or supernatant from group 3	CO_3^{2-} at pH 10	$MgCO_3$, $CaCO_3$, $SrCO_3$, $BaCO_3$
5	Unknown	None	Soluble ions Na^+, K^+, NH_4^+

Separation of chlorides is done first since there are only a few insoluble chlorides, which make a convenient group. The carbonates are separated last since all of the metal ions would precipitate as carbonates, and thus too many ions would precipitate, if this step were done earlier in the scheme. Groups 2 and 3 are mainly sulfides. In acid solution only sulfides with very low K_{sp} values precipitate because the concentration of S^{2-} is low in acid solution. In basic solution the sulfide concentration is much higher, and the more soluble sulfides, with relatively high K_{sp} values, precipitate along with some hydroxides.

After each group has precipitated, additional separations and confirmation tests are run to identify the individual ions. For example, in group 1 the precipitate is washed with hot water to dissolve only $PbCl_2$, which is then confirmed by another precipitation with the chromate ion, CrO_4^{2-}. If a precipitate remains after washing with hot water, ammonia is added to dissolve the silver as the complex ion $Ag(NH_3)_2^+$. Neutralization of the ammonia solution with HCl reprecipitates AgCl and confirms its presence. Any precipitate that is still left when the Ag^+ is dissolved in ammonia is most likely Hg_2Cl_2. In the presence of ammonia Hg_2Cl_2 undergoes a redox reaction to form elemental mercury, causing the precipitate to turn dark gray in the reaction

$$Hg_2Cl_2(s) \; + \; 2NH_3(aq) \; \longrightarrow$$
$$Hg(\ell) \; + \; HgNH_2Cl(s) \; + \; NH_4^+(aq) \; + \; Cl^-(aq) \qquad (16.29)$$

The reactions used and the decision-making process for qualitative analysis are often summarized in a flowchart, as shown in Figure 16.8.

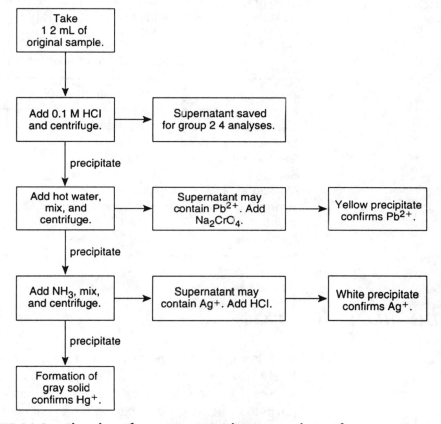

FIGURE 16.8. Flowchart for group 1 qualitative analysis of cations. Hg^+ is a dimer and is often written as Hg_2^{2+}.

Confirmation of the metal sulfides, hydroxides, and carbonates is done in a series of logical steps similar to that for the group 1 ions. A confirmation test is also performed for each metal. Some of these tests are listed in Table 16.2.

TABLE 16.2 Confirmation Spot Tests for Some Metal Ions

Cation	Test Reagent or Method	Observation
Fe^{2+}	$K_3Fe(CN)_6$	Dark blue precipitate
Fe^{3+}	$K_4Fe(CN)_6$	Dark blue precipitate
Cu^{2+}	NH_3	Dark blue solution
Ni^{2+}	Dimethylglyoxime	Red precipitate
Pb^{2+}	CrO_4^{2-}	Orange precipitate
Zn^{2+}	H_2S	White precipitate
NH_4^+	NaOH	Ammonia odor
H^+	Blue litmus paper	Paper turns red.
Na^+	Flame test	Orange flame
K^+	Flame test	Violet flame
Li^+	Flame test	Crimson red flame
Sr^{2+}	Flame test	Bright red flame

Analysis of anions is accomplished by spot tests using selected reagents. Some of these spot tests are listed in Table 16.3.

TABLE 16.3 Spot Tests for Selected Anions

Anion	Test Method	Observation
Carbonate	Add acid	Nonflammable gas evolved
Sulfide	Add acid	Rotten egg odor
Thiocyanate (SCN^-)	Add Fe^{3+}	Blood red complex
Sulfate	Add Ba^{2+}	White precipitate
Chloride	Add Ag^+	White precipitate
Bromide	Add Cl_2, water, and C_6H_{12}	Brown Br_2 in C_6H_{12} layer
Iodide	Add Cl_2, water, and C_6H_{12}	Violet I_2 in C_6H_{12} layer
Hydroxide	Red litmus paper	Paper turns blue.

Chemical Hazards

Any human endeavor has some risk associated with it. It is much more likely, however, that you will be injured in an automobile accident or, if you smoke cigarettes, that you will develop cancer than that you will come to harm in a chemistry laboratory. While chemicals can be hazardous, one aim of chemistry education is to train students in the proper handling of these substances. Elimination of all hazards in any field of endeavor is unrealistic.

The elimination of all potentially hazardous materials and techniques from the chemistry laboratory would eventually result in a society where no one understood how to handle or use chemicals properly. There are, however, certain hazards of which you should be aware so that you can take sensible precautions.

Highly Flammable Compounds

Organic compounds, particularly low-molar-mass compounds (methane, butane, etc.) and ethers, are highly flammable. They should be kept away from all sparks and flames.

Explosive Compounds

Over time, ethers react to produce explosive peroxides. Empty containers of solvents may contain explosive vapor residues. Dry picric acid is explosive. Nitrogen triiodide and nitroglycerine are shock-sensitive.

Strong Oxidizers

Concentrated perchloric acid, sulfuric acid, nitric acid, and hydrogen peroxide cause almost immediate skin injury. Perchloric acid in contact with organic material causes spontaneous combustion. White phosphorus burns spontaneously in air and emits hazardous fumes.

Compounds Incompatible with Water

The very active metals, Li, Na, K, Rb, Cs, Ca, Ba, and Sr, may react explosively with water.

Compounds with High Heats of Solution

Some substances evolve large amounts of heat when dissolved in water. If unexpected, the heat can cause spattering or can cause you to drop a hot beaker. The very active metals, their soluble oxides and hydroxides, and concentrated sulfuric and nitric acids generate heat. Calcium oxide and phosphorous pentoxide generate large amounts of heat with water. Mixing concentrated bases with concentrated acids is particularly hazardous.

Compounds with Possible Health Hazards

Benzene, chloroform, and carbon tetrachloride are suspected carcinogens and should be used only in a hood. Chlorinated organic compounds, in general, are suspected of being health hazards and should be handled carefully.

Safety Principles and Equipment

The first principle of safe experimentation in a laboratory is as follows: Never design an experiment that risks life or health. An essential part of experimental design is to assess possible safety hazards from all sources. Safety glasses are mandatory at all times; many major chemical corporations will fire a worker on the spot for failing to wear safety glasses. Protective lab clothing is worn when needed.

In experiments with hazardous materials the minimum quantities possible are used, and the work is done in a ventilated hood. When an explosion is even remotely possible, impact-resistant shields are used to protect workers. In a chemistry laboratory fire is always a possibility, and familiarity with exit routes and the location of fire extinguishers, fire blankets, and showers is essential.

Important
Concepts

Significant figures and calculations
Graphs
Meter reading
Common experimental reactions
Safety and chemical hazards

Questions on
Chapter 16

1. A 35.25-mL sample is needed. The best piece of glassware to use is
   (A) a buret
   (B) a beaker
   (C) a graduated cylinder
   (D) a volumetric flask
   (E) a pipet

2. Methane is collected by
   (A) upward displacement of air
   (B) displacement of water
   (C) downward displacement of air
   (D) displacement of mercury
   (E) filtration

3. A very fine precipitate is best isolated by
   (A) distillation
   (B) filtration
   (C) vacuum filtration
   (D) centrifugation
   (E) drying

4. The relative uncertainty in the answer to the calculation
   $\dfrac{23.00 \times 1.68}{0.1416 \times 0.1332}$ is
   (A) 10
   (B) 5×10^{-3}
   (C) 0.01
   (D) 0.0001
   (E) 5×10^{-2}

5. A 1.00 M solution of NaOH is prepared by weighing exactly 40.0 g of NaOH and adding it to exactly 1000 mL of distilled water at room temperature. Which of the following is most likely to be the largest source of error?
   (A) The wrong method is used to prepare the mixture.
   (B) The room temperature is not 25°C.
   (C) The glassware is incorrectly calibrated.
   (D) NaOH absorbs atmospheric water.
   (E) Carbon dioxide in the water neutralizes some of the NaOH.

6. The vapor pressure of a liquid is measured at several temperatures. When a graph of the data is made,
    (A) temperature is the x-axis since it is the dependent variable
    (B) pressure is the y-axis since it is the dependent variable
    (C) $1/T$ is the x-axis because of Raoult's law
    (D) mole fraction is the x-axis and is the independent variable
    (E) the temperature must be in Kelvin units

7. Safety glasses are NOT needed for which of the following?
    (A) weighing samples
    (B) boiling water
    (C) distilling alcohol
    (D) prelab writeups
    (E) titrations

8. Which of the following is LEAST useful in dissolving solids?
    (A) adding the solid slowly to the solvent
    (B) grinding the solid to small particles
    (C) drying the solid
    (D) vigorous stirring or shaking
    (E) warming the solution

9. Which of the following dissolves in both acids and bases?
    (A) CaO
    (B) CO_2
    (C) $Al(OH)_3$
    (D) $AgCl$
    (E) As_2O_3

10. A 25.0-mL sample of a monoprotic acid was titrated to the end point with 20.0 mL of 0.200 M NaOH, and the molarity of the acid was calculated as 0.160 M. After the titration was complete, it was noticed that the buret was not clean, and droplets of solution were seen on the inside of the buret. What can be deduced about the molarity of the unknown?
    (A) The calculation is wrong, and the molarity is really 0.250 M.
    (B) The recorded volume of NaOH is low, and the molarity too high.
    (C) The recorded volume of NaOH is high, and the molarity is too high.
    (D) The recorded volume of NaOH is low, and the molarity is too low.
    (E) The recorded volume of NaOH is high, and the molarity is too low.

11. A sample is brought into a laboratory and mixed with an equal volume of a preservative solution. For analysis a 5.00-mL sample is diluted to 100 mL, and the concentration of chloride ions in the diluted solution is found to be 3.0×10^{-3} M. What is the chloride concentration of the sample?
    (A) 6.0×10^{-2} M
    (B) 6.0×10^{-3} M

(C) 1.5×10^{-4} M
(D) 7.5×10^{-5} M
(E) 1.2×10^{-1} M

12. Qualitative analysis is performed on a colored solution. Addition of HCl results in a white precipitate that dissolves completely in hot water. The solution probably contained
   (A) a transition metal ion and Ag^+
   (B) Pb^{2+} and no other cations
   (C) Pb^{2+} and possibly an alkali metal ion
   (D) Hg_2^{2+} and a transition metal ion
   (E) Pb^{2+} and a transition metal ion

13. A solution is acidified, and a noticeable odor is observed. Which of the following is the most likely source of the odor?
   (A) CH_4
   (B) NH_3
   (C) CO_2
   (D) H_2S
   (E) H_2

14. Flame tests in which a small amount of solution is heated in a flame and the color of the flame is observed are routinely used to confirm the presence of which ion?
   (A) Ca
   (B) K
   (C) Na
   (D) Sr
   (E) all of these

15. The salt $CrCl_3$ may be prepared in pure form by
   (A) reacting an excess of Cr metal with HCl gas
   (B) reacting excess NaCl with Cr_2O_3
   (C) reacting 3 moles of HCl with 1 mole of $Cr(OH)_3$
   (D) reacting 1 mole of Na_2CrO_4 with 3 moles of HCl
   (E) All of the above can be used to make $CrCl_3$.

16. The most common method for determining the molarity of a solution of an acid is
   (A) gravimetric analysis (weighing a precipitate)
   (B) titration with a standard base
   (C) determination of the specific gravity of the acid
   (D) determination of the volume of gas evolved when the solution is reacted with Mg metal
   (E) determination of the pH of the acid

17. Hydrogen sulfide is used to precipitate all of the following EXCEPT
    (A) Cu^{2+}
    (B) Co^{2+}
    (C) Ca^{2+}
    (D) Fe^{3+}
    (E) Cd^{2+}

18. After a buret is filled for a titration, the bubble of air in the tip is not dislodged. What will be the effect?
    (A) No error will result if the bubble does not come out during the titration.
    (B) The volume recorded will be high if the bubble comes out.
    (C) The calculated molarity of the sample will be high if the bubble comes out.
    (D) The mass of sample will be low if the bubble comes out.
    (E) All of the above will be true.

19. If an error is made during an experiment, the appropriate action is to
    (A) stop the experiment and start over again
    (B) make a note of the error in the notebook and finish the experiment
    (C) tear the page(s) out of the notebook and start over again
    (D) adjust the results to correct for the error
    (E) continue the experiment; this is "experimental error"

20. Which of the following is appropriate when constructing a graph of experimental data?
    (A) A line is drawn connecting each data point.
    (B) The indepent variable is plotted on the y-axis.
    (C) A straight line is always drawn through the data points.
    (D) The line is extended beyond the last data point to the edge of the graph.
    (E) The axes are scaled so that the data fill the graph as completely as possible.

Answer Key

See Appendix I for explanation of answers.

1. **A**	5. **A**	9. **C**	13. **D**	17. **C**
2. **C**	6. **B**	10. **C**	14. **E**	18. **E**
3. **D**	7. **D**	11. **E**	15. **C**	19. **A**
4. **B**	8. **C**	12. **E**	16. **B**	20. **E**

Practice
Examinations

Answer Sheet: Practice Examination 1

1. Ⓐ Ⓑ Ⓒ Ⓓ Ⓔ
2. Ⓐ Ⓑ Ⓒ Ⓓ Ⓔ
3. Ⓐ Ⓑ Ⓒ Ⓓ Ⓔ
4. Ⓐ Ⓑ Ⓒ Ⓓ Ⓔ
5. Ⓐ Ⓑ Ⓒ Ⓓ Ⓔ
6. Ⓐ Ⓑ Ⓒ Ⓓ Ⓔ
7. Ⓐ Ⓑ Ⓒ Ⓓ Ⓔ
8. Ⓐ Ⓑ Ⓒ Ⓓ Ⓔ
9. Ⓐ Ⓑ Ⓒ Ⓓ Ⓔ
10. Ⓐ Ⓑ Ⓒ Ⓓ Ⓔ
11. Ⓐ Ⓑ Ⓒ Ⓓ Ⓔ
12. Ⓐ Ⓑ Ⓒ Ⓓ Ⓔ
13. Ⓐ Ⓑ Ⓒ Ⓓ Ⓔ
14. Ⓐ Ⓑ Ⓒ Ⓓ Ⓔ
15. Ⓐ Ⓑ Ⓒ Ⓓ Ⓔ
16. Ⓐ Ⓑ Ⓒ Ⓓ Ⓔ
17. Ⓐ Ⓑ Ⓒ Ⓓ Ⓔ
18. Ⓐ Ⓑ Ⓒ Ⓓ Ⓔ
19. Ⓐ Ⓑ Ⓒ Ⓓ Ⓔ
20. Ⓐ Ⓑ Ⓒ Ⓓ Ⓔ
21. Ⓐ Ⓑ Ⓒ Ⓓ Ⓔ
22. Ⓐ Ⓑ Ⓒ Ⓓ Ⓔ
23. Ⓐ Ⓑ Ⓒ Ⓓ Ⓔ
24. Ⓐ Ⓑ Ⓒ Ⓓ Ⓔ
25. Ⓐ Ⓑ Ⓒ Ⓓ Ⓔ

26. Ⓐ Ⓑ Ⓒ Ⓓ Ⓔ
27. Ⓐ Ⓑ Ⓒ Ⓓ Ⓔ
28. Ⓐ Ⓑ Ⓒ Ⓓ Ⓔ
29. Ⓐ Ⓑ Ⓒ Ⓓ Ⓔ
30. Ⓐ Ⓑ Ⓒ Ⓓ Ⓔ
31. Ⓐ Ⓑ Ⓒ Ⓓ Ⓔ
32. Ⓐ Ⓑ Ⓒ Ⓓ Ⓔ
33. Ⓐ Ⓑ Ⓒ Ⓓ Ⓔ
34. Ⓐ Ⓑ Ⓒ Ⓓ Ⓔ
35. Ⓐ Ⓑ Ⓒ Ⓓ Ⓔ
36. Ⓐ Ⓑ Ⓒ Ⓓ Ⓔ
37. Ⓐ Ⓑ Ⓒ Ⓓ Ⓔ
38. Ⓐ Ⓑ Ⓒ Ⓓ Ⓔ
39. Ⓐ Ⓑ Ⓒ Ⓓ Ⓔ
40. Ⓐ Ⓑ Ⓒ Ⓓ Ⓔ
41. Ⓐ Ⓑ Ⓒ Ⓓ Ⓔ
42. Ⓐ Ⓑ Ⓒ Ⓓ Ⓔ
43. Ⓐ Ⓑ Ⓒ Ⓓ Ⓔ
44. Ⓐ Ⓑ Ⓒ Ⓓ Ⓔ
45. Ⓐ Ⓑ Ⓒ Ⓓ Ⓔ
46. Ⓐ Ⓑ Ⓒ Ⓓ Ⓔ
47. Ⓐ Ⓑ Ⓒ Ⓓ Ⓔ
48. Ⓐ Ⓑ Ⓒ Ⓓ Ⓔ
49. Ⓐ Ⓑ Ⓒ Ⓓ Ⓔ
50. Ⓐ Ⓑ Ⓒ Ⓓ Ⓔ

51. Ⓐ Ⓑ Ⓒ Ⓓ Ⓔ
52. Ⓐ Ⓑ Ⓒ Ⓓ Ⓔ
53. Ⓐ Ⓑ Ⓒ Ⓓ Ⓔ
54. Ⓐ Ⓑ Ⓒ Ⓓ Ⓔ
55. Ⓐ Ⓑ Ⓒ Ⓓ Ⓔ
56. Ⓐ Ⓑ Ⓒ Ⓓ Ⓔ
57. Ⓐ Ⓑ Ⓒ Ⓓ Ⓔ
58. Ⓐ Ⓑ Ⓒ Ⓓ Ⓔ
59. Ⓐ Ⓑ Ⓒ Ⓓ Ⓔ
60. Ⓐ Ⓑ Ⓒ Ⓓ Ⓔ
61. Ⓐ Ⓑ Ⓒ Ⓓ Ⓔ
62. Ⓐ Ⓑ Ⓒ Ⓓ Ⓔ
63. Ⓐ Ⓑ Ⓒ Ⓓ Ⓔ
64. Ⓐ Ⓑ Ⓒ Ⓓ Ⓔ
65. Ⓐ Ⓑ Ⓒ Ⓓ Ⓔ
66. Ⓐ Ⓑ Ⓒ Ⓓ Ⓔ
67. Ⓐ Ⓑ Ⓒ Ⓓ Ⓔ
68. Ⓐ Ⓑ Ⓒ Ⓓ Ⓔ
69. Ⓐ Ⓑ Ⓒ Ⓓ Ⓔ
70. Ⓐ Ⓑ Ⓒ Ⓓ Ⓔ
71. Ⓐ Ⓑ Ⓒ Ⓓ Ⓔ
72. Ⓐ Ⓑ Ⓒ Ⓓ Ⓔ
73. Ⓐ Ⓑ Ⓒ Ⓓ Ⓔ
74. Ⓐ Ⓑ Ⓒ Ⓓ Ⓔ
75. Ⓐ Ⓑ Ⓒ Ⓓ Ⓔ

Answer Sheet: Practice Examination 2

1. Ⓐ Ⓑ Ⓒ Ⓓ Ⓔ
2. Ⓐ Ⓑ Ⓒ Ⓓ Ⓔ
3. Ⓐ Ⓑ Ⓒ Ⓓ Ⓔ
4. Ⓐ Ⓑ Ⓒ Ⓓ Ⓔ
5. Ⓐ Ⓑ Ⓒ Ⓓ Ⓔ
6. Ⓐ Ⓑ Ⓒ Ⓓ Ⓔ
7. Ⓐ Ⓑ Ⓒ Ⓓ Ⓔ
8. Ⓐ Ⓑ Ⓒ Ⓓ Ⓔ
9. Ⓐ Ⓑ Ⓒ Ⓓ Ⓔ
10. Ⓐ Ⓑ Ⓒ Ⓓ Ⓔ
11. Ⓐ Ⓑ Ⓒ Ⓓ Ⓔ
12. Ⓐ Ⓑ Ⓒ Ⓓ Ⓔ
13. Ⓐ Ⓑ Ⓒ Ⓓ Ⓔ
14. Ⓐ Ⓑ Ⓒ Ⓓ Ⓔ
15. Ⓐ Ⓑ Ⓒ Ⓓ Ⓔ
16. Ⓐ Ⓑ Ⓒ Ⓓ Ⓔ
17. Ⓐ Ⓑ Ⓒ Ⓓ Ⓔ
18. Ⓐ Ⓑ Ⓒ Ⓓ Ⓔ
19. Ⓐ Ⓑ Ⓒ Ⓓ Ⓔ
20. Ⓐ Ⓑ Ⓒ Ⓓ Ⓔ
21. Ⓐ Ⓑ Ⓒ Ⓓ Ⓔ
22. Ⓐ Ⓑ Ⓒ Ⓓ Ⓔ
23. Ⓐ Ⓑ Ⓒ Ⓓ Ⓔ
24. Ⓐ Ⓑ Ⓒ Ⓓ Ⓔ
25. Ⓐ Ⓑ Ⓒ Ⓓ Ⓔ

26. Ⓐ Ⓑ Ⓒ Ⓓ Ⓔ
27. Ⓐ Ⓑ Ⓒ Ⓓ Ⓔ
28. Ⓐ Ⓑ Ⓒ Ⓓ Ⓔ
29. Ⓐ Ⓑ Ⓒ Ⓓ Ⓔ
30. Ⓐ Ⓑ Ⓒ Ⓓ Ⓔ
31. Ⓐ Ⓑ Ⓒ Ⓓ Ⓔ
32. Ⓐ Ⓑ Ⓒ Ⓓ Ⓔ
33. Ⓐ Ⓑ Ⓒ Ⓓ Ⓔ
34. Ⓐ Ⓑ Ⓒ Ⓓ Ⓔ
35. Ⓐ Ⓑ Ⓒ Ⓓ Ⓔ
36. Ⓐ Ⓑ Ⓒ Ⓓ Ⓔ
37. Ⓐ Ⓑ Ⓒ Ⓓ Ⓔ
38. Ⓐ Ⓑ Ⓒ Ⓓ Ⓔ
39. Ⓐ Ⓑ Ⓒ Ⓓ Ⓔ
40. Ⓐ Ⓑ Ⓒ Ⓓ Ⓔ
41. Ⓐ Ⓑ Ⓒ Ⓓ Ⓔ
42. Ⓐ Ⓑ Ⓒ Ⓓ Ⓔ
43. Ⓐ Ⓑ Ⓒ Ⓓ Ⓔ
44. Ⓐ Ⓑ Ⓒ Ⓓ Ⓔ
45. Ⓐ Ⓑ Ⓒ Ⓓ Ⓔ
46. Ⓐ Ⓑ Ⓒ Ⓓ Ⓔ
47. Ⓐ Ⓑ Ⓒ Ⓓ Ⓔ
48. Ⓐ Ⓑ Ⓒ Ⓓ Ⓔ
49. Ⓐ Ⓑ Ⓒ Ⓓ Ⓔ
50. Ⓐ Ⓑ Ⓒ Ⓓ Ⓔ

51. Ⓐ Ⓑ Ⓒ Ⓓ Ⓔ
52. Ⓐ Ⓑ Ⓒ Ⓓ Ⓔ
53. Ⓐ Ⓑ Ⓒ Ⓓ Ⓔ
54. Ⓐ Ⓑ Ⓒ Ⓓ Ⓔ
55. Ⓐ Ⓑ Ⓒ Ⓓ Ⓔ
56. Ⓐ Ⓑ Ⓒ Ⓓ Ⓔ
57. Ⓐ Ⓑ Ⓒ Ⓓ Ⓔ
58. Ⓐ Ⓑ Ⓒ Ⓓ Ⓔ
59. Ⓐ Ⓑ Ⓒ Ⓓ Ⓔ
60. Ⓐ Ⓑ Ⓒ Ⓓ Ⓔ
61. Ⓐ Ⓑ Ⓒ Ⓓ Ⓔ
62. Ⓐ Ⓑ Ⓒ Ⓓ Ⓔ
63. Ⓐ Ⓑ Ⓒ Ⓓ Ⓔ
64. Ⓐ Ⓑ Ⓒ Ⓓ Ⓔ
65. Ⓐ Ⓑ Ⓒ Ⓓ Ⓔ
66. Ⓐ Ⓑ Ⓒ Ⓓ Ⓔ
67. Ⓐ Ⓑ Ⓒ Ⓓ Ⓔ
68. Ⓐ Ⓑ Ⓒ Ⓓ Ⓔ
69. Ⓐ Ⓑ Ⓒ Ⓓ Ⓔ
70. Ⓐ Ⓑ Ⓒ Ⓓ Ⓔ
71. Ⓐ Ⓑ Ⓒ Ⓓ Ⓔ
72. Ⓐ Ⓑ Ⓒ Ⓓ Ⓔ
73. Ⓐ Ⓑ Ⓒ Ⓓ Ⓔ
74. Ⓐ Ⓑ Ⓒ Ⓓ Ⓔ
75. Ⓐ Ⓑ Ⓒ Ⓓ Ⓔ

1. Ⓐ Ⓑ Ⓒ Ⓓ Ⓔ
2. Ⓐ Ⓑ Ⓒ Ⓓ Ⓔ
3. Ⓐ Ⓑ Ⓒ Ⓓ Ⓔ
4. Ⓐ Ⓑ Ⓒ Ⓓ Ⓔ
5. Ⓐ Ⓑ Ⓒ Ⓓ Ⓔ
6. Ⓐ Ⓑ Ⓒ Ⓓ Ⓔ
7. Ⓐ Ⓑ Ⓒ Ⓓ Ⓔ
8. Ⓐ Ⓑ Ⓒ Ⓓ Ⓔ
9. Ⓐ Ⓑ Ⓒ Ⓓ Ⓔ
10. Ⓐ Ⓑ Ⓒ Ⓓ Ⓔ
11. Ⓐ Ⓑ Ⓒ Ⓓ Ⓔ
12. Ⓐ Ⓑ Ⓒ Ⓓ Ⓔ
13. Ⓐ Ⓑ Ⓒ Ⓓ Ⓔ
14. Ⓐ Ⓑ Ⓒ Ⓓ Ⓔ
15. Ⓐ Ⓑ Ⓒ Ⓓ Ⓔ
16. Ⓐ Ⓑ Ⓒ Ⓓ Ⓔ
17. Ⓐ Ⓑ Ⓒ Ⓓ Ⓔ
18. Ⓐ Ⓑ Ⓒ Ⓓ Ⓔ
19. Ⓐ Ⓑ Ⓒ Ⓓ Ⓔ
20. Ⓐ Ⓑ Ⓒ Ⓓ Ⓔ
21. Ⓐ Ⓑ Ⓒ Ⓓ Ⓔ
22. Ⓐ Ⓑ Ⓒ Ⓓ Ⓔ
23. Ⓐ Ⓑ Ⓒ Ⓓ Ⓔ
24. Ⓐ Ⓑ Ⓒ Ⓓ Ⓔ
25. Ⓐ Ⓑ Ⓒ Ⓓ Ⓔ

26. Ⓐ Ⓑ Ⓒ Ⓓ Ⓔ
27. Ⓐ Ⓑ Ⓒ Ⓓ Ⓔ
28. Ⓐ Ⓑ Ⓒ Ⓓ Ⓔ
29. Ⓐ Ⓑ Ⓒ Ⓓ Ⓔ
30. Ⓐ Ⓑ Ⓒ Ⓓ Ⓔ
31. Ⓐ Ⓑ Ⓒ Ⓓ Ⓔ
32. Ⓐ Ⓑ Ⓒ Ⓓ Ⓔ
33. Ⓐ Ⓑ Ⓒ Ⓓ Ⓔ
34. Ⓐ Ⓑ Ⓒ Ⓓ Ⓔ
35. Ⓐ Ⓑ Ⓒ Ⓓ Ⓔ
36. Ⓐ Ⓑ Ⓒ Ⓓ Ⓔ
37. Ⓐ Ⓑ Ⓒ Ⓓ Ⓔ
38. Ⓐ Ⓑ Ⓒ Ⓓ Ⓔ
39. Ⓐ Ⓑ Ⓒ Ⓓ Ⓔ
40. Ⓐ Ⓑ Ⓒ Ⓓ Ⓔ
41. Ⓐ Ⓑ Ⓒ Ⓓ Ⓔ
42. Ⓐ Ⓑ Ⓒ Ⓓ Ⓔ
43. Ⓐ Ⓑ Ⓒ Ⓓ Ⓔ
44. Ⓐ Ⓑ Ⓒ Ⓓ Ⓔ
45. Ⓐ Ⓑ Ⓒ Ⓓ Ⓔ
46. Ⓐ Ⓑ Ⓒ Ⓓ Ⓔ
47. Ⓐ Ⓑ Ⓒ Ⓓ Ⓔ
48. Ⓐ Ⓑ Ⓒ Ⓓ Ⓔ
49. Ⓐ Ⓑ Ⓒ Ⓓ Ⓔ
50. Ⓐ Ⓑ Ⓒ Ⓓ Ⓔ

51. Ⓐ Ⓑ Ⓒ Ⓓ Ⓔ
52. Ⓐ Ⓑ Ⓒ Ⓓ Ⓔ
53. Ⓐ Ⓑ Ⓒ Ⓓ Ⓔ
54. Ⓐ Ⓑ Ⓒ Ⓓ Ⓔ
55. Ⓐ Ⓑ Ⓒ Ⓓ Ⓔ
56. Ⓐ Ⓑ Ⓒ Ⓓ Ⓔ
57. Ⓐ Ⓑ Ⓒ Ⓓ Ⓔ
58. Ⓐ Ⓑ Ⓒ Ⓓ Ⓔ
59. Ⓐ Ⓑ Ⓒ Ⓓ Ⓔ
60. Ⓐ Ⓑ Ⓒ Ⓓ Ⓔ
61. Ⓐ Ⓑ Ⓒ Ⓓ Ⓔ
62. Ⓐ Ⓑ Ⓒ Ⓓ Ⓔ
63. Ⓐ Ⓑ Ⓒ Ⓓ Ⓔ
64. Ⓐ Ⓑ Ⓒ Ⓓ Ⓔ
65. Ⓐ Ⓑ Ⓒ Ⓓ Ⓔ
66. Ⓐ Ⓑ Ⓒ Ⓓ Ⓔ
67. Ⓐ Ⓑ Ⓒ Ⓓ Ⓔ
68. Ⓐ Ⓑ Ⓒ Ⓓ Ⓔ
69. Ⓐ Ⓑ Ⓒ Ⓓ Ⓔ
70. Ⓐ Ⓑ Ⓒ Ⓓ Ⓔ
71. Ⓐ Ⓑ Ⓒ Ⓓ Ⓔ
72. Ⓐ Ⓑ Ⓒ Ⓓ Ⓔ
73. Ⓐ Ⓑ Ⓒ Ⓓ Ⓔ
74. Ⓐ Ⓑ Ⓒ Ⓓ Ⓔ
75. Ⓐ Ⓑ Ⓒ Ⓓ Ⓔ

Practice Examination 1

On the following pages is a complete practice examination. Try to duplicate actual test conditions. Follow the time limits, and answer all questions as directed. The periodic table found on page 36 may be used, along with the tables given with the examination, to answer the questions in Section II.

A scientific calculator is recommended for the examination. Calculators that can be programmed with chemical equations or symbols are not allowed. Calculators may not be shared between students, and calculators with communication capabilities are not allowed.

Practice Examination 1

Section I

Multiple-Choice Questions

75 questions
90 minutes
45% of total grade

Part A

Directions: The multiple-choice questions in this part consists of a list of five lettered choices to be used in responding to the three or four questions that immediately follow. Be aware that a choice may be the appropriate response to more than one question. Select the best choice for each question. Enter your choice on the answer sheet on page 484.

Questions 1–3

(A) Ca
(B) S
(C) Fe
(D) N
(E) Cs

1. Which of the above elements is the least electronegative?

2. Which of the above elements can have the greatest oxidation number?

3. Which of the above elements has the smallest atomic radius?

Questions 4–7

(A) $1s^2\ 2s^22p^6\ 3s^23p^6\ 4s^23d^5$
(B) $1s^2\ 2s^22p^6\ 3s^23p^6\ 4s^2$
(C) $1s^2\ 2s^22p^6\ 3s^23p^6\ 4s^23d^{10}4p^6\ 5s^24d^{10}5p^6$
(D) $1s^2\ 2s^22p^6\ 3s^23p^6\ 4s^23d^{10}4p^6\ 5s^24d^7$
(E) $1s^2\ 2s^22p^6\ 3s^23p^6\ 4s^23d^{10}4p^6\ 5s^16s^1$

4. The ground-state configuration for an alkaline earth metal

5. The ground-state configuration for the negative ion of a halogen

6. The ground-state configuration of a transition element in period 4

7. A possible excited-state electron configuration

Questions 8–10

(A) Calcium oxide
(B) Oxalic acid
(C) Phosphoric acid
(D) Carbon dioxide
(E) Potassium nitrite

8. Is a basic anhydride

9. Is used as an industrial cleaning agent and as a flavoring in soda pop

10. Dissolves readily in water to give a basic solution

GO ON TO THE NEXT PAGE ➤

Questions 11–14

(A) Hydrogen bonding
(B) Molecular crystals
(C) Ionic bonding
(D) Covalent bonding
(E) London forces (van der Waals forces)

11. Is used to explain the C—H bonds in organic substances

12. Is used to explain how nonpolar substances may be condensed to liquids

13. Describes the solid form of CO_2

14. Is, in general, the strongest attractive force

GO ON TO THE NEXT PAGE ➤

Part B

Directions: Each of the following questions is accompanied by five lettered choices. Select the lettered choice that best answers the question. Enter your choice on the answer sheet.

15. The mass of $CaCl_2$ (molar mass = 111.0) required to prepare 75.00 milliliters of a 2.000 molar solution of this salt is
    (A) 150 g
    (B) 16.65 g
    (C) 8.325 g
    (D) 1.65×10^4 g
    (E) 222 g

16. The pressure of 3.00 moles of neon in a flask is 2.50 atmospheres. The pressure rises to 4.60 atmospheres when 1.00 mole of hydrogen and some oxygen are added. How many moles of oxygen are added?
    (A) 1.52
    (B) 3.04
    (C) 5.52
    (D) 2.52
    (E) 4.52

17. Which of the following molecules has a Lewis structure that contains a double bond?
    (A) NH_3
    (B) NO_3^-
    (C) CH_4
    (D) Cl_2
    (E) BF_3

18. In which of the following is electromagnetic radiation listed correctly in <u>increasing</u> order of wavelength (lowest wavelength first)?
    (A) Ultraviolet < visible < infrared
    (B) Visible < infrared < microwave
    (C) X rays < infrared < ultraviolet
    (D) Microwaves < visible < infrared
    (E) Visible < ultraviolet < X rays

19. A 50.0-milliliter sample of hydrochloric acid with an unknown concentration is titrated with 0.125 molar sodium hydroxide. For this experiment, which of the following is true?
    (A) The volume of NaOH used will be less than 50.0 mL.
    (B) The end point will be at a pH greater than 7.
    (C) The color change of the indicator will be from colorless to pink.
    (D) The reaction must be standardized by adding KHP.
    (E) The equivalence point will have a pH of exactly 7.

20. Which of the following represent a pair of isotopes of element X?
    (A) $^{21}_{11}X$ and $^{24}_{12}X$
    (B) $^{19}_{9}X$ and $^{39}_{19}X$
    (C) $^{12}_{6}X$ and $^{12}_{6}X$
    (D) $^{14}_{6}X$ and $^{14}_{7}X$
    (E) $^{79}_{35}X$ and $^{81}_{35}X$

21. Which of the following ions may be detected safely by odor after an appropriate, simple chemical reaction?
    (A) CO_3^{2-} (B) Sr^{2+} (C) NO_3^-
    (D) NH_4^+ (E) MnO_4^-

GO ON TO THE NEXT PAGE ➤

22. When the skeleton equation below:

$$\_Fe_2O_3(s) + \_C_2O_4^{2-}(aq)$$
$$+ \_H^+(aq) \longrightarrow \_Fe^{2+}(aq)$$
$$+ \_CO_2(g) + \_H_2O(\ell)$$

is balanced and all coefficients are reduced to their lowest whole-number values, the coefficient for $H^+(aq)$ will be
(A) 2   (B) 3   (C) 4   (D) 6   (E) 9

23. Atoms of element Y have the ground-state electronic configuration $1s^2\ 2s^22p^6\ 3s^23p^1$. Element Y will most likely form a compound with oxygen having the formula
(A) YO   (B) YO_2 (C) Y_2O_3
(D) Y_3O_2 (E) Y_2O

24. A certain gas has a density of 1.11 grams per liter at 2.50 atmospheres of pressure and at a temperature of 165°C. What is the most probable identity of this gas? ($R = 0.0821$ liter atm mol^{-1} K^{-1})
(A) oxygen   (B) nitrogen   (C) methane
(D) carbon dioxide   (E) water

25. $$Cr_2O_7^{2-}(aq) + 3Sn^{2+}(aq) + 14H^+(aq) \rightarrow$$
$$2Cr^{3+}(aq) + 3Sn^{4+}(aq) + 7H_2O(\ell)$$

Which of the following statements about this reaction is true?
(A) Dichromate ions are oxidized by Sn(II) ions.
(B) Hydrogen ions are reduced to H_2O.
(C) Chromium is reduced from the +6 to the +3 oxidation state.
(D) The oxidation state of chromium does not change.
(E) The large coefficient for H^+ forces the reaction toward completion.

26. $$\_IO_3^-(aq) + \_H^+(aq)$$
$$\rightarrow \_I_2(aq) + \_H_2O(l)$$

When this half-reaction is balanced by entering the electrons where needed and using the smallest whole-number coefficients possible, there will be
(A) 5 electrons on the left side
(B) no electrons on either side
(C) 3 electrons on the right side
(D) 10 electrons on the left side
(E) 8 electrons on the right side

27. The reaction

$$2HgCl_2 + C_2O_4^{2-} \longrightarrow$$
$$2Cl^- + 2CO_2 + Hg_2Cl_2(s)$$

has a rate law of

$$Rate = k[HgCl_2][C_2O_4^{2-}]^2$$

The overall order of this reaction is

(A) first   (B) second   (C) zero
(D) third   (E) fourth

28. For the reaction in question 27 which of the following statements is true?
(A) The exponents in the rate law come from the coefficients in the balanced reaction.
(B) The magnitude of the rate constant indicates how far the reaction goes toward completion.
(C) Chloride ions will increase the reaction rate.
(D) The rate constant varies with the square of the $C_2O_4^{2-}$ concentration.
(E) The half-life of this reaction is $0.693/k$.

GO ON TO THE NEXT PAGE ➤

29. Which of the following represents a phase diagram?

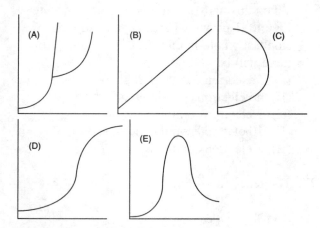

30. The critical pressure is the
    (A) end of the liquid-vapor equilibrium line on a phase diagram
    (B) the pressure above which no increase in temperature will result in vaporization of the liquid to a gas
    (C) pressure required for boiling to occur at any given temperature
    (D) pressure where solid, liquid, and gas are all at equilibrium
    (E) pressure where the compound is thermodynamically unstable

31. $2 Fe^0 + 3 Cu^{2+} \rightarrow 2 Fe^{3+} + 3 Cu^0$

    This reaction was one that was used to convince greedy nobility that the alchemists could convert the base metal iron into gold (copper freshly deposited resembles gold). If the reaction is spontaneous, which of the following is true of the standard cell voltage (potential), E^0_{cell}, and the standard free energy, ΔG^0?
    (A) E^0_{cell} and ΔG^0 are both positive.
    (B) E^0_{cell} and ΔG^0 are both negative.
    (C) E^0_{cell} is positive and ΔG^0 is negative.
    (D) E^0_{cell} is negative and ΔG^0 is positive.
    (E) E^0_{cell} and ΔG^0 are both zero.

32. Radioactive decay often results in the emission of alpha particles, beta particles, positrons, or neutrons. If in the radioactive decay of $^{210}_{83}Bi$ a single particle is observed to be emitted, which of the following is the most unlikely product?
    (A) $^{210}_{83}Bi$ (B) $^{210}_{84}Po$ (C) $^{210}_{82}Pb$
    (D) $^{206}_{81}Tl$ (E) $^{208}_{79}Au$

33. In the electrolysis of water at 26°C the total pressure inside the apparatus is 740 mm Hg. At that same temperature the vapor pressure of water is tabulated as 25 mm Hg. What is the partial pressure of the gases resulting from the electrolysis?
    (A) 740 mm Hg   (B) 1.00 atm
    (C) 715 mm Hg   (D) 25 mm Hg
    (E) 765 mg Hg

34. In which of the following chemical systems will the moles of each substance in the balanced reaction NOT change with an increase in the volume of the system but no change in the temperature?
    (A) $2H_2(g) + O_2(g) \rightarrow 2H_2O(g)$
    (B) $N_2(g) + 3H_2(g) \rightarrow 2NH_3(g)$
    (C) $4NO_2(g) + O_2(g) \rightarrow 2N_2O_5(g)$
    (D) $CH_4(g) + 2O_2(g) \rightarrow CO_2(g) + 2H_2O(g)$
    (E) $2NO_2(g) \rightarrow N_2O_4(g)$

35. Commercial nitric acid is approximately 15.4 molar. What volume of commercial nitric acid must be used to prepare 5.00 liters of 6.00 molar nitric acid?
    (A) 1.94 mL   (B) 12.8 mL   (C) 390 mL
    (D) 1950 mL   (E) 325 mL

36. How many grams of lead(II) nitrate, $Pb(NO_3)_2$ (molar mass = 331), must be weighed in order to have exactly 3.00 grams of lead atoms?
    (A) 4.80   (B) 0.626   (C) 130   (D) 3.90
    (E) 48.0

GO ON TO THE NEXT PAGE ➤

37. Which of the following does NOT provide a valid method, or enough information, to determine the molar mass of an unknown compound?
(A) The density of a gas at STP, assuming ideal gas behavior
(B) The osmotic pressure of a solute at a known temperature and a known concentration in grams per liter
(C) The freezing-point depression of a solvent with a known k_f, and the concentration of the solute in grams per kilogram of solvent
(D) The boiling-point elevation of a solvent with a known k_b, and the concentration of the solute in grams per liter of solvent
(E) The rate of effusion of the unknown gas through a pinhole, and the rate of a known gas effusing through the same pinhole under identical conditions.

38. A compound is found by qualitative analysis to be composed of carbon, hydrogen, and oxygen. Quantitative analysis reveals that the compound is 38.71 percent carbon and 9.68 percent hydrogen. What is the empirical formula of this compound?
(A) CHO   (B) CH_2O (C) CH_3O
(D) $C_2H_6O_2$ (E) CH_3

39. The physical properties of two structural isomers, cyclohexane (C_6H_{12}) and 2-hexene (C_6H_{12}), are very different, assuming ideal behavior, EXCEPT for their
(A) liquid densities at the same temperature and pressure
(B) boiling points at 1 atmosphere pressure
(C) heats of vaporization at 1 atmosphere pressure
(D) melting points at 1 atmosphere pressure
(E) gaseous densities at the same temperature and pressure

40. When the following:

$$4FeS(s) + 7O_2(g) \longrightarrow 2Fe_2O_3(s) + 4SO_2(g)$$
$$\Delta H° = -2432 \text{ kJ mol}^{-1}$$

is at equilibrium for any given pressure, P, and temperature, T, which of the following will shift the equilibrium toward the formation of products?
(A) Increasing the temperature of the system without changing the pressure
(B) Adding an inert gas to increase the pressure of the system
(C) Adding a catalyst specific for the forward reaction
(D) Removing the Fe_2O_3 as it is formed
(E) Removing the SO_2 as it is formed

41. The pH of 0.05 molar acetic acid ($K_a = 1.8 \times 10^{-5}$) is approximately
(A) 1   (B) 2   (C) 3   (D) 7   (E) 11

42. The net ionic equation for the reaction of barium carbonate with sulfuric acid is
(A) $Ba^{2+} - SO_4^{2-} \rightarrow BaSO_4$
(B) $BaCO_3 + 2H^+ \rightarrow Ba^{2+} + H_2CO_3$
(C) $BaCO_3 + 2H^+ + SO_4^{2-} \rightarrow$
$$BaSO_4 + H_2O + CO_2$$
(D) $Ba^{2+} - CO_3^{2-} + H^+ + SO_4^{2-} \rightarrow$
$$BaSO_4 + H_2O + CO_2$$
(E) $BaCO_3 + H_2SO_4 \rightarrow$
$$BaSO_4 + H_2O + CO_2$$

43. A solution of KNO_3 is known to have a 0.564 molal concentration. To calculate the concentration of this solution in terms of molarity, which of the following must be specified?
(A) The temperature of the solution
(B) The density of the solution
(C) The volume of the solution
(D) The solubility product of KNO_3
(E) The K_a of nitric acid

GO ON TO THE NEXT PAGE ➤

44. The geometry of the nitrate ion NO_3^- is best described as
    (A) a tetrahedron
    (B) a trigonal bipyramid
    (C) a linear structure
    (D) a triangular planar structure
    (E) a square pyramid

45. In which of the following are the elements listed correctly in order of <u>increasing</u> atomic radius?
    (A) $K < Ca < C < F$
    (B) $F < O < Al < Na$
    (C) $Rb < Cs < Ba < Ra$
    (D) $Si < Ge < As < Sb$
    (E) $Li < Be < B < C$

46. The substance that acts as both a Brönsted acid and a Brönsted base in an aqueous solution is
    (A) $HClO$ (B) H_2SO_4 (C) PO_4^{3-}
    (D) HSO_3^- (E) ClO_4^-

47. A 0.01 molar solution of this substance will result in a solution with the highest pH.
    (A) $HOCl$ $K_a = 3.0 \times 10^{-8}$
    (B) $HC_2H_3O_2$ $K_a = 1.8 \times 10^{-5}$
    (C) N_2H_4 $K_b = 9.6 \times 10^{-7}$
    (D) HNO_2 $K_a = 7.1 \times 10^{-4}$
    (E) CH_3NH_2 $K_b = 4.4 \times 10^{-4}$

48. To accurately measure 35.5 milliliters of 0.100 molar KOH you should use a
    (A) volumetric flask
    (B) graduated cylinder
    (C) buret
    (D) transfer pipet
    (E) Mohr pipet

49. A 0.1 molar solution of the sodium salt of this substance will give a pH closest to pH 7.
    (A) $HOCl$ $K_a = 3.0 \times 10^{-8}$
    (B) $HC_2H_3O_2$ $K_a = 1.8 \times 10^{-5}$
    (C) N_2H_4 $K_b = 9.6 \times 10^{-7}$
    (D) HNO_2 $K_a = 7.1 \times 10^{-4}$
    (E) CH_3NH_2 $K_b = 4.4 \times 10^{-4}$

50. Which of the following molecules has more than one pi bond?
    (A) CO_2 (B) SO_2 (C) NH_3
    (D) C_3H_6 (E) CH_2O

51. Which of the following is FALSE about an ideal gas?
    (A) One-half mole will occupy 11.2 L at STP.
    (B) Each atom is assumed to have no volume.
    (C) Attractive forces keep ideal gas molecules in the container.
    (D) The kinetic energy of all ideal gases is the same at STP.
    (E) The average velocity of a helium atom will be twice that of a CH_4 molecule.

52. An ideal solution of pentane and heptane is prepared, and its vapor pressure is measured as 300 mm Hg at 25°C. The vapor pressures of pentane and heptane are 480 and 40 mm Hg, respectively, at 25°C. What is the mole fraction of pentane in this mixture?
    (A) 0.625 (B) 0.591 (C) 0.133
    (D) 0.867 (E) 0.682

53.
$$Al_2(CO_3)_3 + 6HCl \rightarrow$$
$$2AlCl_3 + 3H_2O + 3CO_2$$

When 5.00 milliliters of 6.00 molar hydrochloric acid is added to 400 milligrams of aluminum carbonate (formula mass = 234) according to the above balanced reaction, what is the maximum number of moles of CO_2 gas that will be evolved?
    (A) 0.015 (B) 0.0051 (C) 0.23
    (D) 0.66   (E) 0.0017

Use the following chemical equation to answer questions 54 and 55:

$$2SO_2(g) + O_2(g) \rightleftharpoons 2SO_3(g)$$
$$\Delta H = -197 \text{ kJ}$$

54. Which of the following will NOT increase the amount of $SO_3(g)$?
    (A) Decreasing the temperature of the reaction vessel
    (B) Decreasing the volume of the reaction vessel
    (C) Adding $N_2(g)$ to increase the pressure in the reaction vessel
    (D) Adding O_2 to the reaction vessel
    (E) Adding $SO_2(g)$ to the reaction vessel

GO ON TO THE NEXT PAGE ➤

55. SO_2 and O_2 are mixed in an insulated vessel and sealed so that there is no heat exchange with the surroundings. When the reaction comes to equilibrium, which of the following best describes what has happened to the system?
(A) Total energy remains constant and the entropy increases.
(B) Total energy increases and the entropy remains constant.
(C) Total energy remains constant and the temperature increases.
(D) Total energy decreases and the temperature increases.
(E) Total energy remains constant and the temperature decreases.

56. Which of the following will give a concentration of chloride ions different from that in the other solutions? Assume that volumes are additive.

	mL of 0.250 M NaCl	mL of 0.150 M $CaCl_2$	mL of H_2O
(A)	50.0	50.0	100
(B)	80.0	80.0	80
(C)	25.0	25.0	50
(D)	90.0	0.0	74
(E)	0.0	60.0	71

57. Which of the following represents the ions formed when sodium oxalate, $Na_2C_2O_4$, is dissolved in water?
(A) $Na_2^+ + C_2O_4^{2-}$
(B) $2Na^+ + 2C^{3+} + 4O^{2-}$
(C) $2Na^+ + C_2O_4^-$
(D) $Na_2^{2+} + C_2O_4^{2-}$
(E) $2Na^+ + C_2O_4^{2-}$

58. Which of the following bonds would be expected to have the largest polarity?
(A) C—N   (B) C—F   (C) O—F
(D) N—O   (E) C—O

59. Which of the following would be expected to have the highest dipole moment?
(A) CH_4 (B) CO_2 (C) SF_6 (D) HCN
(E) Cl^-

60. The correct electron configuration for the gold(III) ion is
(A) $1s^2\ 2s^22p^6\ 3s^23p^6\ 4s^23d^{10}4p^6$ $5s^24d^{10}5p^6\ 6s^24f^{14}5d^9$
(B) $1s^2\ 2s^22p^6\ 3s^23p^6\ 4s^23d^{10}4p^6$ $5s^24d^{10}5p^6\ 6s^14f^{14}5d^{10}$
(C) $1s^2\ 2s^22p^6\ 3s^23p^6\ 4s^23d^{10}4p^6$ $5s^24d^{10}5p^6\ 6s^24f^{14}5d^6$
(D) $1s^2\ 2s^22p^6\ 3s^23p^6\ 4s^23d^{10}4p^6$ $5s^24d^{10}5p^6\ 4f^{14}5d^8$
(E) $1s^2\ 2s^22p^6\ 3s^23p^6\ 4s^23d^{10}4p^6$ $5s^24d^{10}5p^6\ 6s^24f^{14}5d^{10}6p^2$

61. A student weighed 2.145 grams of potassium acid phthalate (formula mass of KHP = 204.23), placed it in a 100-milliliter volumetric flask, and added distilled water exactly to the mark. A titration was then performed using 10.0 milliliter aliquots of the KHP and titrating with standardized 0.1036 molar sodium hydroxide solution. Phenolphthalein was used as an indicator, and each titration was stopped at the first discernible pink color that persisted for 30 seconds. In order, the results obtained were as follows:

First titration	9.74 mL
Second titration	9.86 mL
Third titration	9.98 mL
Fourth titration	10.05 mL
Fifth titration	10.18 mL
Sixth titration	10.19 mL
Seventh titration	10.17 mL

What is the most reasonable interpretation of the results obtained?
(A) All results are very close and are valid. The average is 10.02 mL.
(B) The variation in results indicates that the glassware was not dry before the experiment was started.
(C) The end point was too faint and should persist until the end of the lab period.
(D) The constant increase suggests that the KHP was not completely dissolved until the fifth titration.
(E) The increase suggests that carbon dioxide is being absorbed by the KHP.

GO ON TO THE NEXT PAGE ➤

62. Which pair of substances CANNOT be the major components of an aqueous solution?
    (A) H_2SO_4 and HSO_4^-
    (B) $H_2PO_4^-$ and HPO_4^{2-}
    (C) $HOCl$ and OCl^- (D) SO_4^{2-} and SO_3^{2-}
    (E) H_2CO_3 and CO_3^{2-}

Use the following list of ionization constants to answer questions 63 and 64.

Acid	Acid Dissociation Constant
(A) $HC_2H_3O_2$	1.8×10^{-5}
(B) HCN	6.2×10^{-10}
(C) HNO_2	7.1×10^{-4}
(D) $HCHO_2$	1.8×10^{-4}
(E) $HOBr$	2.1×10^{-9}

63. When each of these acids is titrated with a solution of KOH, which one will have the highest pH at its end point?

64. Which of these five acids and its corresponding salt can be used to make a buffer at pH 8.0?

65. Which of the following CANNOT be a reducing agent?
    (A) Ag (B) I^- (C) Fe^{3+} (D) Cr^{3+}
    (E) Cl^-

66. A 10.0-gram sample of ethane, C_2H_6, is burned in an enclosed vessel with 40.0 grams of oxygen. Which of the following best describes the mixture when the reaction is complete?
    (A) The limiting reactant is C_2H_6.
    (B) The theoretical yield of CO_2 is 29.3 g.
    (C) When the reaction is complete, 2.67 g of oxygen is left over.
    (D) When finished, the total mass of the system is 50.0 g.
    (E) All of the above are correct statements.

67. What is the molar mass of a nonelectrolyte that causes water to boil at 101.0°C when 23.2 grams are dissolved in 150 grams of distilled water? (k_b for H_2O = 0.51°C molal^{-1})
    (A) 8.6   (B) 78.9   (C) 12.6   (D) 45.1
    (E) 0.012

68. When a pure hydrocarbon is burned in air, 66 grams of CO_2 along with 27 grams of water are collected. What is the empirical formula of the hydrocarbon?
    (A) CH_2 (B) CH (C) C_2H_3
    (D) C_2H_4 (E) C_3H_4

69. Which of the following sets of quantum numbers is IMPOSSIBLE?
    (A) $4,3,1,+\frac{1}{2}$
    (B) $3,2,-2,-\frac{1}{2}$
    (C) $5,0,0,-\frac{1}{2}$
    (D) $2,2,-1,+\frac{1}{2}$
    (E) $3,2,0,+\frac{1}{2}$

70. The moles of a gas produced in an experiment are measured on a sunny day in a laboratory in New Orleans with the air conditioning in the lab working properly. Which of the following has the potential for producing the greatest error in the measurement?
    (A) The temperature was not recorded and was assumed to be 20°C.
    (B) The barometric pressure was not measured and was assumed to be 760 mm Hg.
    (C) The liquid levels were not equalized between the pneumatic trough and the flask.
    (D) The correction for the vapor pressure of water was added rather than subtracted.
    (E) The volume of gas was not marked on the flask during the experiment and was estimated from memory.

71. What ratio of the mass of Na_2HPO_4 (molar mass = 142) to the mass of NaH_2PO_4 (molar mass = 120) is needed to prepare a buffer with a pH of 7.4? (K_a for $H_2PO_4^- = 6.3 \times 10^{-8}$.)
    (A) 1.58   (B) 0.63   (C) 1.87   (D) 1.00
    (E) 0.53

72. The acid dissociation constant, K_a, for hydrofluoric acid is 6.8×10^{-4}. What percentage of HF is dissociated in a 0.0800 molar solution?
    (A) 12.3%   (B) 4.25%   (C) 9.2%
    (D) 1.12%   (E) 23.6%

GO ON TO THE NEXT PAGE ➤

73. All of the following require the use of the resonance concept to describe their geometry and physical properties EXCEPT
    (A) H_2O (B) SO_2 (C) NO_3^-
    (D) $O—C=O^-$ (E) O_3
        |
        H

74. A certain chemical reaction is described by a first-order rate law. What is the rate constant for the reaction if the half-life is determined to be 228 minutes?
    (A) 228 s^{-1} (B) $5.1 \times 10^{-5} \text{ s}^{-1}$
    (C) $3.0 \times 10^{-3} \text{ s}^{-1}$ (D) 9.52 s^{-1}
    (E) 0.42 s^{-1}

75. A student prepares ten solutions with different concentrations of $KMnO_4$ and measures the absorbance of each, using a spectrophotometer. When the results are plotted on a graph, the LEAST desirable thing to do is to
    (A) arrange the axes so that the independent variable is on the x-axis and the dependent variable is on the y-axis
    (B) plot each point by finding the coordinates corresponding to the values of the independent and dependent variable
    (C) connect the points in a dot-to-dot fashion
    (D) set the range of values on the axes to include the values found in the experiment
    (E) set the scale of the graph so that it fills the page as completely as possible

STOP

THIS IS THE END OF SECTION I.
YOU MAY USE ANY REMAINING TIME TO CHECK YOUR WORK IN THIS SECTION.

Section II
Free-Response Problems

55% of total grade
90 minutes
Suggested time for Parts A, B, and C—50 minutes
Suggested time for Part D—40 minutes

This section consists of four parts, A (25 percent), B (25 percent), C (15 percent), and D (35 percent), weighted as shown. You should spend approximately 50 minutes on parts A, B, and C and 40 minutes on part D. It is your responsibility to budget the time wisely.

RESPONSES TO THE QUESTIONS IN THIS SECTION MUST CLEARLY SHOW YOUR METHODS AND THE STEPS USED TO ARRIVE AT THE ANSWER. Partial credit is earned by demonstrating an appropriate method developed from fundamental principles while little credit is earned for an answer obtained with no method shown. Appropriate use of significant figures is recommended. Data necessary for solving problems are given with the questions, or may be found in the tables below.

Useful Information for Solving Free-Response Problems

Universal gas constant	$R = 8.314 \text{ J mol}^{-1}\text{K}^{-1}$
	$0.0821 \text{ L atm mol}^{-1}\text{K}^{-1}$
	$62.4 \text{ L mm Hg mol}^{-1}\text{K}^{-1}$
	$8.314 \text{ V C mol}^{-1}\text{K}^{-1}$
Faraday	$1 \, \mathscr{F} = 96,485 \text{ coulombs}$
	$96,485 \text{ J V}^{-1}$
Electron volt	$1 \text{ eV} = 96.5 \text{ kJ mol}^{-1}$
Speed of light	$c = 2.998 \times 10^6 \text{ m s}^{-1}$
Planck's constant	$h = 6.63 \times 10^{-34} \text{ J s}$
Boltzmann constant	$k = 1.38 \times 10^{-23} \text{ J K}^{-1}$
Avogadro's number	$N = 6.022 \times 10^{23} \text{ molecules mol}^{-1}$
At 25°C	$\dfrac{RT}{n\mathscr{F}} \ln Q = \dfrac{0.0591}{n} \log Q$

Vapor Pressure of Water as a Function of Temperature

Temperature degrees Celsius	Vapor Pressure mm Hg	Temperature degrees Celsius	Vapor Pressure mm Hg
−10	2.1	26	25.2
0.0	4.6	28	28.3
5	6.5	30	31.8
10	9.2	35	41.2
12	10.5	40	55.3
14	12.0	50	92.5
16	13.6	60	149.4
18	15.5	70	233.7
20	17.5	80	355.1
22	19.8	90	525.8
24	22.4	100	760.0

Standard Reduction Potentials, 25°C

Half-Reaction	$E°$ (V)	Half-Reaction	$E°$ (V)
$F_2(g) + 2e^- \rightarrow 2F^-$	2.87	$Co^{2+} + 2e^- \rightarrow Co$	−0.28
$Co^{3+} + e^- \rightarrow Co^{2+}$	1.82	$Tl^+ + e^- \rightarrow Tl$	−0.34
$Au^{3+} + 3e^- \rightarrow Au$	1.50	$Cd^{2+} + 2e^- \rightarrow Cd$	−0.40
$Cl_2(g) + 2e^- \rightarrow 2Cl^-$	1.36	$Cr^{3+} + e^- \rightarrow Cr^{2+}$	−0.41
$O_2(g) + 4H^+ + 4e^- \rightarrow 2H_2O$	1.23	$Fe^{2+} + 2e^- \rightarrow Fe$	−0.44
$Br_2(g) + 2e^- \rightarrow 2Br^-$	1.07	$Cr^{3+} + 3e^- \rightarrow Cr$	−0.74
$2Hg^{2+} + 2e^- \rightarrow Hg_2^{2+}$	0.92	$Zn^{2+} + 2e^- \rightarrow Zn$	−0.76
$Ag^+ + e^- \rightarrow Ag$	0.80	$Mn^{2+} + 2e^- \rightarrow Mn$	−1.18
$Hg_2^{2+} + 2e^- \rightarrow Hg$	0.79	$Al^{3+} + 3e^- \rightarrow Al$	−1.66
$Fe^{3+} + e^- \rightarrow Fe^{2+}$	0.77	$Be^{2+} + 2e^- \rightarrow Be$	−1.70
$I_2 + 2e^- \rightarrow 2I^-$	0.53	$Mg^{2+} + 2e^- \rightarrow Mg$	−2.37
$Cu^+ + e^- \rightarrow Cu$	0.52	$Na^+ + e^- \rightarrow Na$	−2.71
$Cu^{2+} + 2e^- \rightarrow Cu$	0.34	$Ca^{2+} + 2e^- \rightarrow Ca$	−2.87
$Cu^{2+} + e^- \rightarrow Cu^+$	0.15	$Sr^{2+} + 2e^- \rightarrow Sr$	−2.89
$Sn^{4+} + 2e^- \rightarrow Sn^{2+}$	0.15	$Ba^{2+} + 2e^- \rightarrow Ba$	−2.90
$S + 2H^+ + 2e^- \rightarrow H_2S$	0.14	$Rb^+ + e^- \rightarrow Rb$	−2.92
$2H^+ + 2e^- \rightarrow H_2$	0.00	$K^+ + e^- \rightarrow K$	−2.92
$Pb^{2+} + 2e^- \rightarrow Pb$	−0.13	$Cs^+ + e^- \rightarrow Cs$	−2.92
$Sn^{2+} + 2e^- \rightarrow Sn$	−0.14	$Li^+ + e^- \rightarrow Li$	−3.05
$Ni^{2+} + 2e^- \rightarrow Ni$	−0.25		

Part A

(25% of Section II grade)

Directions: Solve all parts of the following problem:

1. Hydrogen iodide decomposes according to the equation

$$2HI(g) \rightleftharpoons H_2(g) + I_2(g)$$

(a) Write the equilibrium law in terms of concentrations, K_c, and partial pressures, K_p.

(b) A 55.5-gram sample of HI (molar mass = 127.9) is transferred to an evacuated 12.0-liter flask at 95°C. (1.) What is the initial concentration, in moles per liter, of HI? (2.) What is the initial pressure, in mm Hg, of HI?

(c) When the system comes to equilibrium, 22.4 grams of I_2 is found to be in the flask. Calculate the value of K_c OR K_p. Be sure to indicate whether you are calculating K_c or K_p.

(d) An another temperature, K_c = 14.7. If 1.00 mole of HI(g), 2.00 mol H_2(g), and 0.500 mol I_2(g) are introduced into an evacuated 10.0-liter flask, determine whether the reaction proceeds in the forward or reverse direction.

GO ON TO THE NEXT PAGE ➤

Part B

(25% of Section II grade)

Directions: Completely solve EITHER problem 2 or problem 3. Only the first problem answered will be graded. Be sure to indicate which problem you are answering.

---

2. When the reaction $2A + B \rightarrow C + D$ was studied to determine its kinetic properties, the following results were obtained:

Initial Rate $(mol\ L^{-1}\ s^{-1})$	[A] $(mol\ L^{-1})$	[B] $(mol\ L^{-1})$
3.30×10^{-6}	0.200	0.100
1.32×10^{-5}	0.400	0.100
1.32×10^{-5}	0.400	0.300

(a) Determine the rate law and the value of the rate constant. Give the units for the rate constant.
(b) What is the overall order of this reaction, and what are the orders with respect to A and B?
(c) What is the initial rate of reaction when [A] = 0.500 M and [B] = 0.500 M?
(d) Which of the following is a reasonable mechanism for this reaction? Explain your conclusion.

Mechanism 1	Mechanism 2	Mechanism 3
$A + A \rightarrow K$ (slow)	$A + B \rightleftharpoons C + K$	$A + A \rightarrow L$ (slow)
$K + B \rightarrow C + L$	$A + K \rightarrow C + D$ (slow)	$B + L \rightarrow C + D$
$L + A \rightarrow D$		

3. A 50.0-milliliter solution of oxalic acid, $H_2C_2O_4$, requires 24.35 milliliters of 0.125 M NaOH to neutralize both protons. It takes 15.83 mL of $KMnO_4$ (product Mn^{2+}) to react with all of the oxalic acid in another 50.0-milliliter sample of oxalic acid (product CO_2). A 2.500-gram sample containing iron(II) chloride is dissolved in acid and titrated with 31.87 milliliters of the $KMnO_4$ solution.
(a) Write three balanced equations for the reactions in this problem.
(b) Which of the compounds above is (are) a reducing agent, and which is (are) an oxidizing agent?
(c) What is the concentration of the permanganate solution in this problem?
(d) What is the percentage of iron in the solid sample?

GO ON TO THE NEXT PAGE ➤

Part C
(15% of Section II grade)

Directions: Answer FIVE of the eight choices in this part. If more than five are answered, only the first five will be scored.

4. Give the formulas for the reactants and products in FIVE of the following word equations. In all cases a chemical reaction occurs. Unless otherwise stated, the reaction occurs in aqueous solution. Substances that exist as ions in solution should be written in ionic form. Substances that do not enter into the chemical reaction should not be listed, and the reactions do not have to be balanced.

EXAMPLE: Magnesium metal is added to a dilute solution of hydrochloric acid.

$$\text{Formula: } Mg + H^+ \longrightarrow Mg^{2+} + H_2$$

(a) Sulfur trioxide is bubbled into water.
(b) A large excess of CO_2 is bubbled into a limewater solution.
(c) Concentrated ammonia is added to solid AgCl.
(d) Solid carbon is added to hot iron(III) oxide.
(e) A concentrated solution of potassium bromide is electrolyzed.
(f) Zinc metal is added to a solution of copper(II) nitrate.
(g) Propane is ignited in excess oxygen.
(h) Concentrated hydrochloric acid is added to aqueous iron(III) nitrate.

GO ON TO THE NEXT PAGE ➤

Part D
(35% of Section II grade)

Directions: Select THREE of the following five problems. (If more than three are answered, only the first three will be graded.)

Use about 40 minutes for this part of the examination. Answers to these questions should demonstrate your ability to present logical, coherent, and convincing explanations of chemical facts and observations. Answers are judged on the accuracy of your analysis and on the appropriateness of the details and examples cited. Specific answers and examples are preferred to broad generalizations. Diagrams, illustrations, and equations may be included in your answers.

5.
$$CCl_4 \qquad CH_2CH_2 \qquad HCOOH$$

(a) Draw a Lewis electron dot structure for each of the compounds above, and describe its geometry.
(b) Using bonding principles, compare the physical properties of these molecules. Include, but do not limit yourself to, melting and boiling points, acidity, solubility in common solvents, and reactions.

6. Binary acids increase in strength from left to right across the periodic table and from top to bottom in a group of the periodic table.
(a) Explain the increase in strength across the periodic table, using bonding principles.
(b) Explain the increase in strength down a group, using bonding principles.
(c) Explain why the strong binary acids of the halides all have the same strengths in water but different strengths in glacial acetic acid.

7. Consider three unlabeled bottles that contain the white powders $NaBr$, SiO_2, and $C_6H_{12}O_2$, glucose.
(a) Describe physical tests that will distinguish the three substances.
(b) Describe chemical tests to distinguish each substance from the others.

8. Use the principles that govern the arrangement of electrons in atoms to explain each of the following facts:
(a) Some elements are paramagnetic and some are diamagnetic.
(b) Some elements form monatomic anions, some form monatomic cations, and some rarely form monatomic ions.
(c) Some metals form colored compounds while others do not.
(d) A change in size occurs when atoms lose or gain electrons and form ions.

9. Consider the dimerization reaction of NO_2:

$$2NO_2(g) \rightleftharpoons N_2O_4(g)$$

(a) Using Lewis structures, suggest why NO_2 dimerizes and CO_2 does not.
(b) What is the sign of the entropy change, ΔS^0, for this reaction in the forward direction?
(c) At 100°C the value of K_c is approximately 3.3. What is the sign for ΔH^0?
(d) Can the reverse reaction be made spontaneous? If so how?

STOP

THIS IS THE END OF SECTION II.
YOU MAY USE ANY REMAINING TIME TO CHECK YOUR WORK IN THIS SECTION.

Answer Key for Multiple-Choice Questions

1. E	16. A	31. C	46. D	61. D
2. B	17. B	32. D	47. E	62. E
3. D	18. A	33. C	48. C	63. B
4. B	19. E	34. D	49. D	64. E
5. C	20. E	35. D	50. A	65. C
6. A	21. D	36. A	51. C	66. E
7. E	22. D	37. D	52. B	67. B
8. A	23. C	38. C	53. B	68. A
9. C	24. C	39. E	54. C	69. D
10. E	25. C	40. E	55. C	70. E
11. D	26. D	41. C	56. B	71. C
12. E	27. D	42. C	57. E	72. C
13. B	28. D	43. B	58. B	73. A
14. C	29. A	44. D	59. D	74. B
15. B	30. A	45. B	60. D	75. C

Explained Answers to Multiple-Choice Questions

1. **E** Cesium is closest to the lower left corner of the periodic table, where electronegativity is lowest.
2. **B** Nitrogen has the largest number of oxidation numbers. The $+5$, $+4$, $+3$, $+2$, $+1$, and -3 are found in NO_3^-, NO_2, NO_2^-, NO, N_2O, and NH_3, respectively.
3. **D** Nitrogen is in period 2; all the other elements are in higher numbered periods with an extra shell of electrons.
4. **B** This is the configuration of calcium.
5. **C** This is the iodide ion.
6. **A** A period 4 transition element has only $3d$ electrons.
7. **E** The configuration can only occur if one $5s^2$ electron is excited to the $6s$ level as shown.
8. **A** Adding water to calcium oxide yields $Ca(OH)_2$.
9. **C** Phosphoric acid reacts with rust, which is a basic oxide, and also is one flavor in cola drinks.
10. **E** Potassium nitrite is the salt of the weak acid HNO_2. The nitrite ion hydrolyzes to give a basic solution. CaO is insoluble and the others are acids.
11. **D** Shared electrons are defined as covalent bonds. In the C—H bond C and H share electrons.
12. **E** London forces include instantaneous and induced dipoles that can form in nonpolar substances facilitating condensation.
13. **B** CO_2 crystallizes as discrete molecules in a molecular crystal.
14. **C** The attractive forces between fully charged ions are the strongest attractive forces. As evidence, ionic compounds are hard, brittle, and have high melting and boiling points.

15. **B** $\quad ? \text{ g CaCl}_2 = 0.0750 \text{ L CaCl}_2 \left(\dfrac{2.00 \text{ mol CaCl}_2}{1 \text{ L CaCl}_2} \right) \left(\dfrac{111 \text{ g CaCl}_2}{1 \text{ mol CaCl}_2} \right)$

$\qquad = 16.65 \text{ g CaCl}_2$

16. **A** Froqm the ideal gas law

$$\frac{P_i}{P_f} = \frac{n_i}{n_f}$$

after adding the hydrogen and oxygen.

$$n_f = 3.00 \text{ mol} \left(\frac{4.60 \text{ atm}}{2.50 \text{ atm}} \right) = 5.52 \text{ moles } H_2, \text{ Ne, and } O_2$$

Subtract 3.00 moles of Ne and 1.00 mole of H_2, leaving 1.52 moles of O_2.

17. **B** The Lewis structure of the nitrate ion is as follows:

18. **A** The greater the energy, the smaller the wavelength. See the chart of electromagnetic radiation in Chapter 1.

19. **E** A strong acid such as HCl, when titrated with a strong base, always has an end point at pH 7.

20. **E** The isotopes in this pair have the same atomic number but different mass numbers. Choice C represents element X with identical atomic numbers and mass numbers, not different isotopes.

21. **D** The addition of a base to a solution containing NH_4^+ forms ammonia, which has a characteristic pungent odor.

22. **D** The balanced equation is as follows:

$$Fe_2O_3(s) + C_2O_4^{2-}(aq) + 6H^+(aq) \longrightarrow 2Fe^{2+}(aq) + 2CO_2(g) + 3H_2O(\ell)$$

23. **C** The electronic configuration identifies the element as aluminum, which forms only a $+3$ ion.

24. **C** Molar mass $= \dfrac{(1.11 \text{ g/L})(0.0821 \text{ L atm mol}^{-1} \text{ K}^{-1})(438 \text{ K})}{2.50 \text{ atm}} = 16 \text{ g mol}^{-1}$

CH_4 is the only substance with this molar mass.

25. **C** Chromium is $+6$ in the dichromate ion and $+3$ in the Cr^{3+} ion

26. **D** The balanced half-reaction is as follows:

$$10e^- + 2IO_3^-(aq) + 12H^+(aq) \longrightarrow I_2(aq) + 6H_2O(\ell)$$

27. **D** The exponents of the concentrations add up to 3 and the reaction is third order.

28. **D** The exponent 2 indicates that $C_2O_4^{2-}$ is squared

29. **A** Diagram A shows the three regions for the solid, liquid, and gas phases.

30. **A** Since there is no difference between the liquid and gas phases, the liquid-gas equilibrium line ends at the critical point in the phase diagram.

31. **C** That E_{cell}^0 is positive and that ΔG^0 is negative are two of the definitions of a spontaneous reaction.

$$\Delta G^0 = -n\mathscr{F}E_{cell}^0$$

32. **D** For heavy elements (atomic number ≥ 83) an alpha particle is the most probable decay particle.

33. **C** The vapor pressure of water (25 mm Hg) is subtracted from the total pressure (740 mm Hg) to give 715 mmHg.

34. **D** This equation has the same number of moles of gas as products and reactants; $\Delta n_g = 0$. Therefore, the concentration change, due to the volume change, has no effect.

35. **D** The dilution equation $C_iV_i = C_fV_f$ is solved for V_i. Since $C_i = 15.4$ M, $C_f = 6.00$ M, and $V_f = 5.00$ L, we have

$$V_f = \frac{(6.00 \text{ M})(5.00 \text{ L})}{15.4 \text{ M}} = 1.95 \text{ L} = 1950 \text{ mL}$$

36. **A**
$$?g \text{ Pb(NO}_3)_2 = 3.00 \text{ g Pb} \left(\frac{1 \text{ mol Pb}}{207 \text{ g Pb}}\right)$$
$$\left(\frac{1 \text{ mol Pb(NO}_3)_2}{1 \text{ mol Pb}}\right)\left(\frac{331 \text{ g Pb(NO}_3)_2}{1 \text{ mol Pb(NO}_3)_2}\right)$$
$$= 4.80 \text{ g Pb(NO}_3)_2$$

37. **D** For a boiling-point elevation experiment the concentration must be given in grams per kilogram of solvent not grams per liter.

38. **C** Start by calculating the percent oxygen as $100 - 38.71 - 9.68 = 51.61$. Then convert the percent to grams and calculate the moles of each element.

$$? \text{ mol C} = 38.71 \text{ g C} \left(\frac{1 \text{ mol C}}{12 \text{ g C}}\right) = 3.226 \text{ mol C}$$

$$? \text{ mol H} = 9.68 \text{ g H} \left(\frac{1 \text{ mol H}}{1 \text{ g H}}\right) = 9.68 \text{ mol H}$$

$$? \text{ mol O} = 51.61 \text{ g O} \left(\frac{1 \text{ mol O}}{16 \text{ g O}}\right) = 3.226 \text{ mol O}$$

Dividing these three numbers by 3.226 gives 1 C, 3 H and 1 O, or CH_3O.

39. **E** Gaseous densities depend only on molar mass, which is the same for both isomers.

40. **E** The solid Fe_2O_3 has no effect on equilibrium; it does not appear in the equilibrium law; and its removal has no effect on the amount of product. Removal of SO_2 will increase the product formed.

41. **C**
$$[H^+] = \sqrt{K_aC_a} = 9.4 \times 10^{-4}$$

The negative logarithm of this is 3.02.

42. **C** Barium carbonate and sulfate are both insoluble.

43. **B** Density is required to convert mass of solvent used in molality units to volume of solution used in molarity units.

44. **D** Three atoms are bonded to the nitrogen, and there are no nonbonding pairs of electrons:

45. **B** Atoms decrease in size from left to right across the periodic table, and increase in size going down a group in the table. This relationship is true of the elements in choice B.

46. **D** The hydrogen sulfite ion can both donate H^+ and accept H^+ in aqueous solution. None of the others can.

47. **E** $CH_3 NH_2$ has the largest K_b and will have the largest pH value.

48. **C** For an odd volume such as 35.5 mL the buret is the best measuring device of those given.

49. **D** The acid with the largest K_a will have the weakest conjugate base and the pH closest to 7. Similarly the base with the largest K_b will have the weakest conjugate acid and the pH closest to 7. Calculating the pH of a 0.1 M solution of the salts of HNO_2 and CH_3NH_2 gives pH values of 8.08 and 5.82, respectively. pH 8.08 is closest to pH 7.00.

50. **A** The bonds in CO_2 are $O{=}C{=}O$; each double bond consists of one sigma and one pi bond.

51. **C** Ideal gases are assumed to have no attractive or repulsive forces.

52. **B** Use Raoult's law:

$$P_{total} = X_p \,(480 \text{ mm Hg}) + X_h \,(40 \text{ mm Hg}) = 300 \text{ mm Hg}$$

The mole fractions add up to $1.00 = X_p + X_h$. Substitute $1 - X_p = X_h$ and solve.

$$300 \text{ mm Hg} = X_p \,(480 \text{ mm Hg}) + (1 - X_p)(40 \text{ mm Hg})$$
$$= X_p \,(480 - 40) + 40 \text{ mm Hg}$$
$$260 \text{ mm Hg} = X_p \,(440 \text{ mm Hg})$$
$$\frac{260 \text{ mm Hg}}{440 \text{ mm Hg}} = X_p$$
$$0.591 = X_p$$

53. **B** Calculate:

$$? \text{ g Al}_2(CO_3)_3 = 0.005 \text{ L HCl} \times \left(\frac{6.00 \text{ mol HCl}}{1 \text{ L HCl}}\right)\left(\frac{1 \text{ mol Al}_2(CO_3)_3}{6 \text{ mol HCl}}\right)$$
$$\times \left(\frac{234 \text{ g Al}_2(CO_3)_3}{1 \text{ mol Al}_2(CO_3)_3}\right)$$
$$= 1.17 \text{ g Al}_2(CO_3)_3 = 1170 \text{ mg Al}_2(CO_3)_3$$

Since there is only 400 mg $Al_2(CO_3)_3$ given, it is the limiting reactant. Now calculate the moles of CO_2:

$$? \text{ mol CO}_2 = 0.400 \text{ g Al}_2(CO_3)_3 \left(\frac{1 \text{ mol Al}_2(CO_3)_3}{234 \text{ g Al}_2(CO_3)_3}\right)\left(\frac{3 \text{ mol CO}_2}{1 \text{ mol Al}_2(CO_3)_3}\right)$$
$$= 0.0051 \text{ mol CO}_2$$

54. **C** Adding inert N_2 does not change the partial pressures of the other gases and has no effect.

55. **C** In a closed system the total energy must remain constant. Since the reaction is exothermic, the temperature will increase.

56. **B** All the solutions give 0.1375 M Cl^- except B. The equation to use is

$$C_1V_1 + C_2V_2 + C_3V_3 = C_f(V_1 + V_2 + V_3)$$

which is an expansion of the dilution law. For B we obtain 0.183 M Cl^-.

57. **E** The subscript 2 for the sodium in the formula indicates that two is the coefficient for the Na^+ ions; the remainder is the oxalate ion.

58. **B** Carbon and fluorine are the most widely separated of the given pairs in the periodic table.

59. **D** HCN is the only unsymmetrical molecule and the only one that has any polarity. Dipole moment and polarity are similar concepts.

60. **D** Gold will lose the $6s^2$ electrons and one of its outermost d electrons.

61. **D** Regular changes in results indicate that a determinate error is involved. In this case one possibility is that the KHP solution was not thoroughly mixed. CO_2 would have the same effect but is less soluble in acidic KHP and the effect would be observed for all results.

62. **E** The major species in solution must be conjugate acid-base pairs. H_2CO_3 and CO_3^{2-} are not a conjugate and base pair. SO_4^{2-} and SO_3^{2-} are in different oxidation states and can coexist in solution.

63. **B** The weakest acid, HCN, will have the strongest conjugate base.

64. **E** To make a buffer, the pK_a of a weak acid must be within ± 1 pH unit of the desired pH. The pK_a of HOBr is 8.7.

65. **C** Fe^{3+} is the highest oxidation state for iron. A reducing agent must be oxidized, and Fe^{3+} cannot be oxidized further.

66. **E** Choice D is true from the given information.
The limiting reactant is determined as follows:

$$? \text{ g } O_2 = 10.0 \text{ g } C_2H_6 \left(\frac{1 \text{ mol } C_2H_6}{30 \text{ g } C_2H_6}\right)\left(\frac{7 \text{ mol } O_2}{2 \text{ mol } C_2H_6}\right)\left(\frac{32 \text{ g } O_2}{1 \text{ mol } O_2}\right)$$

$$= 37.3 \text{ g } O_2$$

Given 40.0 g O_2, O_2 is not the limiting reactant, so A must be correct. Since these two answers are correct, E must be correct. B and C can also be shown to be true. However, they need not be calculated since two definite correct responses require that all, a, b, c, and d, are correct.

67. **B**
$$\Delta T = 1.0°C = mk_b$$

Use the definitions of molality and the mole to obtain

$$\Delta T = \frac{\text{g/molar mass}}{\text{kg solvent}} k_b.$$

Solve for molar mass, M:

$$\text{molar mass} = \frac{gk_b}{(\Delta T)(\text{kg solvent})}$$

$$= \frac{23.2 \text{ g } (0.51°C \text{ m}^{-1})}{(1.00°C)(0.150 \text{ kg})}$$

$$= 78.9 \text{ g mol}^{-1}$$

68. **A** Calculate the moles of carbon and hydrogen as follows:

$$? \text{ mol H} = 27 \text{ g H}_2\text{O} \left(\frac{1 \text{ mol H}_2\text{O}}{18 \text{ g H}_2\text{O}} \right) \left(\frac{2 \text{ mol H}}{1 \text{ mol H}_2\text{O}} \right) = 3.0 \text{ mol H}$$

$$? \text{ mol C} = 66 \text{ g CO}_2 \left(\frac{1 \text{ mol CO}_2}{44 \text{ g CO}_2} \right) \left(\frac{1 \text{ mol C}}{1 \text{ mol CO}_2} \right) = 1.5 \text{ mol C}$$

Dividing both answers by 1.5 gives 1 mole C and 2 moles H and an empirical formula of CH_2.

69. **D** The maximum value of l is $n - 1$; therefore l and n cannot be the same.

70. **E** The error in temperature is less than $\pm 5°C$ and is $\frac{5}{293}$, about 2%.
The error in pressure is perhaps ± 20 mm Hg and is $\frac{20}{760}$, about 3%.
The error in not equalizing water levels may be as large as ± 50 mm H_2O (2 inches) or ± 4 mm Hg, about 0.5%.
The error due to adding the vapor pressure of water is about 3%.
In a typical 250-mL gas-collecting bottle a guess as to the volume is likely to be much larger than 12.5 mL, or 5%.

71. **C** Calculate the ratio of molarity from the equilibrium law:

$$\frac{K_a}{[\text{H}^+]} = \frac{[\text{Na}_2\text{HPO}_4]}{[\text{NaH}_2\text{PO}_4]} = 1.58$$

This is also the ratio of the moles of each compound in the mixture:

$$1.58 = \frac{\text{mol Na}_2\text{HPO}_4}{\text{mol NaH}_2\text{PO}_4} = \frac{\text{g Na}_2\text{HPO}_4/\text{molar mass Na}_3\text{HPO}_4}{\text{g NaH}_2\text{PO}_4/\text{molar mass NaH}_2\text{PO}_4}$$

Substituting the molar mass, M, values in this expression gives the answer:

$$\text{molar mass} = \frac{\text{gNa}_2\text{PO}_4/142}{\text{gNaH}_2\text{PO}_4/120}$$

$$\frac{\text{gNa}_2\text{PO}_4}{\text{gNaH}_2\text{PO}_4} = 1.58 \left(\frac{142}{120} \right)$$

$$= 1.87$$

72. **C** Calculate as follows:

$$[\text{H}^+] = \sqrt{K_a C_a} = 7.4 \times 10^{-3}$$

Divide this by the initial concentration, and multiply by 100 to convert to percent:

$$\% \text{ HF dissociated} = \frac{7.4 \times 10^{-3}}{0.080} \times 100 = 9.2\%$$

73. **A** Water has only one possible Lewis structure.

74. **B** The equation

$$\ln 2 = kt$$

is solved for k, but time must be converted into seconds first:

$$k = \frac{\ln 2}{(228 \text{ min})(60 \text{ s min}^{-1})}$$
$$= 5.1 \times 10^{-5}$$

75. **C** The student should draw a smooth line through the data points.

Explained Answers to Free-Response Problems

Part A

1. (a) $2HI(g) \rightleftharpoons H_2(g) + I_2(g)$

$$K_c = \frac{[H_2][I_2]}{[HI]^2}, \qquad K_p = \frac{p_{H_2} p_{I_2}}{p_{HI}^2}$$

(b) (1) ? mol HI $= 55.5 \text{ g HI} \left(\frac{1 \text{ mol HI}}{127.9 \text{ g HI}} \right) = 0.434 \text{ mol HI}$

$? \dfrac{\text{mol HI}}{\text{L HI}} = \dfrac{0.434 \text{ mol HI}}{12.0 \text{ L HI}} = 0.0362 \text{ mol HI L}^{-1}$

(2) $P = \dfrac{nRT}{V} = \dfrac{(0.434 \text{ mol HI})(0.0821 \text{ L atm mol}^{-1}\text{K}^{-1})(368 \text{ K})}{12.0 \text{ L}}$

$= 1.09 \text{ atm}$

? mm Hg $= 1.09 \text{ atm} \left(\dfrac{760 \text{ mm Hg}}{1 \text{ atm}} \right) = 828 \text{ mm Hg}$

(c) At equilibrium: ? mol $I_2 = 22.4 \text{ g } I_2 \left(\dfrac{1 \text{ mol } I_2}{253.8 \text{ g } I_2} \right) = 0.0883 \text{ mol } I_2$

$? \dfrac{\text{mol } I_2}{\text{L } I_2} = \dfrac{0.0883 \text{ mol } I_2}{12.0 \text{ L } I_2} = 7.36 \times 10^{-3} \text{ mol } I_2 \text{ L}^{-1}$

REACTION	2 HI	$\rightleftharpoons$	I_2	+	H_2
INIT. CONC.	0.0362		0.0		0.0
CHANGE	$-2x$		$+x$		$+x$
EQUILIBRIUM	$0.0362 - 2x$		x		x
SOLUTION			7.36×10^{-3}		

Since $x = 7.36 \times 10^{-3}$ (from the last two lines of the I_2 column), the table may be completed:

REACTION	2 HI	$\rightleftharpoons$	I_2	+	H_2
INIT. CONC.	0.0362		0.0		0.0
CHANGE	$-2x$		$+x$		$+x$
EQUILIBRIUM	$0.0362 - 2x$		x		x
SOLUTION	**0.0215**		7.36×10^{-3}		$\mathbf{7.36 \times 10^{-3}}$

Entering the numbers from the solution line in the equilibrium law gives

$$K_c = \frac{[H_2][I_2]}{[HI_2]} = \frac{(7.36 \times 10^{-3})(7.36 \times 10^{-3})}{(0.0215)^2} = 0.0117$$

The solution for K_p is similar. The pressure of I_2 is

$$P = \frac{nRT}{V} = \frac{(0.0883 \text{ mol } I_2)(0.0821 \text{ L atm mol}^{-1}\text{K}^{-1})(368 \text{ K})}{12.0 \text{ L}} =$$
$$0.222 \text{ atm}$$

REACTION	2 HI	⇌	I_2	+	H_2
INIT. PRESS.	1.09		0.0		0.0
CHANGE	$-2x$		$+x$		$+x$
EQUILIBRIUM	$1.09 - 2x$		x		x
SOLUTION	**0.646**		0.222		**0.222**

$$K_p = \frac{p_{H_2}p_{I_2}}{p_{HI}^2} = \frac{(0.222)(0.222)}{(0.646)^2} = 0.118$$

Rounding errors cause K_p and K_c to be slightly different, although they should be identical since $\Delta n_g = 0$.

(d)
$$Q = \frac{[H_2][I_2]}{[HI]^2} = \frac{(0.200)(0.0500)}{(0.100)^2} = 1.00$$

Since $K_c = 14.7$, the value of Q must increase to reach equilibrium. Therefore, the reaction proceeds in the forward direction.

Part B

2. (a) The rate law will be in the form

$$\text{Rate} = k[A]^x[B]^y$$

The exponent x is determined from the first two experiments in the table by writing

$$\frac{\text{Rate}_2}{\text{Rate}_1} = \frac{k[A_2]^x[B_2]^y}{k[A_1]^x[B_1]^y}$$

Entering data from the first two experiments in the table gives

$$\frac{1.32 \times 10^{-5}}{3.30 \times 10^{-6}} = \frac{k(0.400)^x(0.100)^y}{k(0.200)^x(0.100)^y}$$

Canceling the rate constants and $(0.100)^y$ terms, we have

$$\frac{1.32 \times 10^{-5}}{3.30 \times 10^{-6}} = \left(\frac{0.400}{0.200}\right)^x$$

$$4.00 = 2.00^x$$

$$x = 2$$

Taking the second and third experiments, we have

$$\frac{1.32 \times 10^{-5}}{1.32 \times 10^{-5}} = \frac{k(0.400)^x(0.300)^y}{k(0.400)^x(0.100)^y}$$

Canceling the rate constants and $(0.400)^x$ terms gives

$$\frac{1.32 \times 10^{-5}}{1.32 \times 10^{-5}} = \left(\frac{0.300}{0.100}\right)^y$$

$$1.00 = 3.00^y$$

$$y = 0$$

The rate law is as follows:

$$\text{Rate} = k[A]^2[B]^0 = k[A]^2$$

(b) This reaction is second order overall. It is second order with respect to [A] and zero order with respect to [B], as determined by the exponents in the rate law.

The rate constant is determined by substituting data from one line of the table into the rate law.

$$\text{Rate} = k[A]^2$$

$$3.30 \times 10^{-6} \text{ mol L}^{-1}\text{s}^{-1} = k(0.200 \text{ mol L}^{-1})^2$$

$$k = \frac{3.30 \times 10^{-6} \text{ mol L}^{-1}\text{s}^{-1}}{(0.200 \text{ mol L}^{-1})^2}$$

$$= 8.25 \times 10^{-5} \text{ L mol}^{-1}\text{s}^{-1}$$

(c) $\text{Initial rate} = 8.25 \times 10^{-5} \text{ L mol}^{-1}\text{s}^{-1} (0.500 \text{ mol L}^{-1})^2$
        $= 2.06 \times 10^{-5} \text{ mol L}^{-1}\text{s}^{-1}$

(d) Mechanism 3 is the most reasonable. The first step is the slow step in which two molecules of A react to form intermediate L.

Mechanism 1 is faulty since the elementary reactions do not add up to the balanced chemical equation.

Mechanism 2 is faulty since the slow step produces a rate law that is not found experimentally. Using the steady-state approximation that

$$\text{Constant} = \frac{[C][K]}{[A][B]}$$

$$[K] = \text{Constant} \left(\frac{[A][B]}{[C]}\right)$$

and the rate law for mechanism 2 is

$$\text{Rate} = k[A][K] = \frac{k'[A]^2[B]}{[C]}$$

3. (a) The reactions are as follows:

$$H_2C_2O_4 + 2\ OH^- \rightarrow C_2O_4^{2-} + 2\ H_2O$$

$$2\ MnO_4^- + 5\ C_2O_4^{2-} + 16\ H^+ \rightarrow 2\ Mn^{2+} + 10\ CO_2 + 8\ H_2O$$

$$MnO_4^- + 5\ Fe^{2+} + 8\ H^+ \rightarrow Mn^{2+} + 5\ Fe^{3+} + 4\ H_2O$$

(b) The MnO_4^- (or $KMnO_4$) is the only oxidizing agent. The reducing agents are $C_2O_4^{2-}$ (or oxalic acid) and Fe^{2+} (or $FeCl_2$).

(c) From the neutralization reaction the molarity of oxalate is calculated:

$$? \frac{\text{mol } C_2O_4^{2-}}{L\ C_2O_4^{2-}} = \frac{0.125\ \text{mol } OH^-}{1\ L\ OH^-} \left(\frac{1\ \text{mol } C_2O_4^{2-}}{2\ \text{mol } OH^-}\right)\left(\frac{24.35\ \text{mL } OH^-}{50.00\ \text{mL } C_2O_4^{2-}}\right)$$

$$= 0.0304\ M\ C_2O_4^{2-}$$

From the molarity of the oxalate, the molarity of permanganate is determined:

$$? \frac{\text{mol } MnO_4^-}{L\ MnO_4^-} = \frac{0.0304\ \text{mol } C_2O_4^{2-}}{1\ L\ C_2O_4^{2-}} \left(\frac{2\ \text{mol } MnO_4^-}{5\ \text{mol } C_2O_4^{2-}}\right)\left(\frac{50.00\ \text{mL } C_2O_4^{2-}}{15.83\ \text{mL } MnO_4^-}\right)$$

$$= 0.0385\ M\ MnO_4^-$$

(d) Use the third reaction described in the question to calculate the mass of Fe^{2+}:

$$?\ g\ Fe^{2+} = 31.87\ \text{mL } MnO_4^- \left(\frac{0.0385\ \text{mol } MnO_4^-}{1\ L\ MnO_4^-}\right)\left(\frac{5\ \text{mol } Fe^{2+}}{1\ \text{mol } MnO_4^-}\right)$$

$$\times \left(\frac{55.85\ g\ Fe^{2+}}{1\ \text{mol } Fe^{2+}}\right)$$

$$= 342.6\ \text{mg Fe}$$

The percentage of iron is as follows:

$$\%\ Fe = \frac{0.3426\ g\ Fe}{2.500\ g\ \text{sample}} \times 100 = 13.7\%\ Fe$$

Part C

4. The balanced reactions are given below. As stated in the question, reactions need not be balanced to receive credit. It is good form to include the symbols (aq) for soluble substances, (s) for insoluble substances, (ℓ) for liquids, and (g) for gases.

(a) $SO_3(g) + H_2O(\ell) \rightarrow H_2SO_4(aq)$
(extra) $H_2SO_4(aq) \rightarrow H^+(aq) + HSO_4^-(aq)$

(b) In a large excess, the solution is acidified, and the overall reaction is as follows:

$$CO_2(g) + H_2O(\ell) \longrightarrow H^+(aq) + HCO_3^-$$

A small amount of CO_2 will precipitate calcium carbonate:

$$Ca^{2+}(aq) + 2\ OH^-(aq) + CO_2(g) \longrightarrow CaCO_3(s) + H_2O(l)$$

(c) $AgCl(s) + NH_3(aq) \rightarrow Ag(NH_3)_2^+(aq) + Cl^-(aq)$
(d) $2Fe_2O_3(s) + 3C(s) \rightarrow 4Fe(s) + 3CO_2(g)$
(e) $2Br^-(aq) + 2H_2O(\ell) \rightarrow Br_2(aq) + H_2(g) + 2OH^-(aq)$
(f) $Zn(s) + Cu^{2+}(aq) \rightarrow Zn^{2+}(aq) + Cu(s)$
(g) $CH_3CH_2CH_3(g) + 5O_2(g) \rightarrow 3CO_2(g) + 4H_2O(g)$
(h) $Fe^{3+}(aq) + 6Cl^-(aq) \rightarrow Fe(Cl)_6^{3-}(aq)$

Part D

5. (a)

CCl₄   CH₂CH₂   HCOOH

CCl_4: The geometry is tetrahedral around the central carbon atom with 109° bond angles. The carbon is an sp^3 hybrid
CH_2CH_2: Both carbon atoms are trigonal planar with angles of 120°. The carbon is an sp^2 hybrid. All of the hydrogen atoms lie in the same plane as the carbon atoms. The double bond consists of a sigma bond and a pi bond.
HCOOH: The geometry around the carbon atom is trigonal planar with 120° bond angles. The H-O-C bond angle is 109° because the oxygen is an sp^3 hybrid. The C-O bond length is greater than the C=O length.

(b) Formic acid (methanoic acid), HCOOH, has the largest polarity. It can form hydrogen bonds. Carbon tetrachloride, CCl_4, and ethylene, CH_2CH_2, both are attracted by London forces only since neither is polar.
Formic acid should have the highest melting and boiling points and the lowest vapor pressure. Ethylene should have the lowest melting and boiling points and the highest vapor pressure. The chlorine atoms are more polarizable than hydrogen atoms, and the London forces are expected to be stronger in carbon tetrachloride than in ethylene.

6. (a) In binary acids, the electronegativity of the atom attached to the hydrogen governs the acid strength as long as all the acids are in the same period. The greater the electronegativity, the more the bonding electrons are drawn away from the hydrogen, weakening the bond. The weaker the bond with the hydrogen, the stronger is the acid.

(b) Binary acids in the same group of the periodic table vary in strength because of the change in bond length. As the atom attached to the hydrogen gets larger, the distance between the two nuclei must increase. The longer the bond, the weaker it is. Consequently, binary acids with longer bond lengths are stronger acids. The effect of bond length overcomes the decrease in electronegativity of atoms as you go down a group and is, therefore, a more important variable.

(c) The list HCl < HBR < HI shows the order of increasing acid strength, but not in water. These acids are all much stronger acids than water and dissociate completely in aqueous solution with the equation

$$HX + H_2O \longrightarrow H_3O^+ + X^-$$

Since they all dissociate completely, the actual acid in aqueous solution is the H_3O^+ ion. This reaction with water is called the leveling effect.

For any solvent, the strongest acid will be the protonated solvent molecule. In liquid ammonia the strongest possible acid is the ammonium ion NH_4^+. In glacial acetic acid the strongest acid is $CH_3COOH_2^+$. Since acetic acid would rather lose a proton than gain one, this acid is very strong, and HCl, HBr, and HI do not dissociate completely in acetic acid. Their relative strengths may be measured by determining their K_a values in glacial acetic acid.

7. (a) One simple test is to try to dissolve the three powders in water. SiO_2 will not dissolve, but $C_6H_{12}O_2$ and NaBr will. Another test involves the determination of the melting points. $C_6H_{12}O_2$ will char if oxygen is present while NaBr will be difficult to melt. A third possibility is to test the electrical conductivities of the solutions. NaBr will ionize into Na^+ and Br^- ions and conduct electricity; $C_6H_{12}O_2$ will not. A flame test for sodium can also be done, using the solutions or solids.

   (b) Bubbling chlorine gas through the NaBr solution will produce the brown bromine color when the bromide ion is oxidized to bromine:

   $$2\ Br^- + Cl_2 \longrightarrow Br_2 + 2\ Cl^-$$

   $C_6H_{12}O_2$ should burn readily as an organic compound. SiO_2 reacts with and dissolves in hydrofluoric acid.

8. (a) Paramagnetism is due to unpaired electrons in an element. A substance is diamagnetic if all electrons are paired. All electrons except the valence electrons must be paired. Orbital diagrams of the valence electrons indicate which atoms are paramagnetic and which are diamagnetic. Hund's rule is important. It requires that electrons be unpaired if there is room in a subshell; pairing occurs only when a subshell has no vacant orbitals.

   (b) The valence electrons of the elements represent incomplete shells of the atom. Atoms with complete shells are the noble gases, which are almost inert. Other atoms may attain an electronic configuration that is the same as that of the noble gases by gaining or losing electrons. Elements on the left side of the periodic table lose electrons and form cations; those on the right side gain electrons and form anions. The gain or loss of one electron is very common. Gaining or losing two electrons is less common, and the gain or loss of three electrons is rather rare. Elements that gain or lose four or more electrons are usually polyatomic, not monatomic, ions.
   For example, sodium loses an electron to form Na^+. The energy needed to remove another electron to make Na^{2+} is prohibitive, however, and this ion does not exist naturally. Chlorine gains an electron to form Cl^-. Adding another electron does not result in a stable Cl^{2-} ion. Chlorine will not lose seven electrons, and sodium will not gain seven electrons, to attain noble gas electron configurations. Carbon, which would have to lose or gain four electrons to achieve a noble-gas electronic configuration, does not tend to form monatomic ions but participates in covalent bonding and the formation of polyatomic ions such as CO_3^2 and $C_2O_4^{2-}$.

   (c) The transition elements form colored compounds. The reason is the small difference in energy between the d orbitals and other orbitals. As a consequence light can be absorbed to excite the electrons from one orbital to another rather easily. The low energy of light needed for this absorption is often in the visible region of the spectrum.

(d) When an atom loses electrons to form a cation, an entire shell of electrons is often removed and the size decreases drastically. When an atom gains electrons to form an anion, the added electrons are shielded from the positive charge of the nucleus and are attracted much less strongly. This result is a large expansion in size when an atom becomes an anion.

9. (a) The Lewis structures for NO_2 and CO_2 are as follows:

$$:\overset{..}{\underset{.}{O}}::\overset{.}{N}:\overset{..}{\underset{.}{O}}: \qquad :\overset{..}{O}::C::\overset{..}{O}:$$
$$\qquad NO_2 \qquad\qquad\qquad CO_2$$

The best NO_2 Lewis structure has an unpaired electron, but CO_2 has no unpaired electrons. By forming a dimer, the unpaired electrons in the two NO_2 molecules can become paired, resulting in a more stable molecule.

(b) This reaction starts with 2 moles of gas as the reactants and results in 1 mole of gas as the product. There will be a decrease in entropy in the reaction.

(c) $$\Delta G^0 = \Delta H^0 - T\Delta S^0$$

If $K_c > 1$, then ΔG^0 has a negative sign. Also, since ΔS^0 is negative, the term $-T\Delta S^0$ must be positive. It is necessary that ΔH^0 be negative, and the reaction is exothermic.

(d) The fact that both the enthalpy and the entropy are negative indicates that at some temperatures the reaction will be spontaneous and at other temperatures it will be nonspontaneous. Based on the above considerations, it will be possible to raise the temperature sufficiently to have the negative value of the enthalpy overcome by the $T\Delta S^0$ term. At high temperatures the reaction as written will not be spontaneous. That means that the reverse reaction is spontaneous. We may predict that at high tempertures N_2O_4 will decompose into NO_2 molecules.

Practice Examination 2

On the following pages is a complete practice examination. Try to duplicate actual test conditions. Follow the time limits, and answer all questions as directed. The periodic table found on page 36 of this book may be used, along with the tables given with the examination, to answer the questions in Section II.

A scientific calculator is recommended for the examination. Calculators that can be programmed with chemical equations or symbols are not allowed. Calculators may not be shared between students, and calculators with communication capabilities are not allowed.

Practice Examination 2

Section I

Multiple-Choice Questions

75 questions
90 minutes
45% of total grade

Part A

Directions: The multiple-choice questions in this part consist of a list of five lettered choices to be used in responding to the three or four questions that immediately follow. Be aware that a choice may be the appropriate response to more than one question. Select the best choice for each question. Enter your choice on the answer sheet on page 485.

Questions 1–4

(A) Sr
(B) Cu
(C) Na
(D) Fe
(E) U

1. Gives a red color in a flame test

2. Can have $+1$ and $+2$ oxidation states

3. Has the largest atomic radius

4. Has naturally radioactive isotopes

Questions 5–7

(A) Phosphates
(B) Carbonates
(C) Sulfites
(D) Oxides
(E) Sulfates

5. Which of these compounds are reducing agents?

6. Which are basic anhydrides?

7. Which are commonly used in fertilizers?

Questions 8–11

(A) Anode
(B) Cathode
(C) Salt bridge
(D) Electrode
(E) SCE

8. This is a common reference electrode.

9. Its symbol is // or |.

10. Reduction occurs here in a galvanic cell.

11. This transfers charge via ions in a galvanic cell.

Questions 12–14

(A) $KMnO_4$
(B) NH_3
(C) KHP
(D) EDTA
(E) SiO_2

12. A common oxidizing agent

13. A complexing agent that is also a base

14. The basic unit of sand

GO ON TO THE NEXT PAGE ➤

Part B

Directions: Each of the questions or incomplete statements below is followed by five suggested answers or completions. Select the one that is best in each case and fill in the corresponding oval on the answer sheet.

15. The net ionic equation for the reaction of sodium sulfite with iron(II) chloride is
    (A) $SO_4^{2-}(aq) + Fe^{2+}(aq) \rightarrow FeSO_4(s)$
    (B) $Cl^-(aq) + Si^+(aq) \rightarrow SiCl(s)$
    (C) $SO_3^{2-}(aq) + Fe^{2+}(aq) \rightarrow FeSO_3(s)$
    (D) $Na_2SO_3(s) + Fe^{2+}(aq) \rightarrow FeSO_3(s) + 2Na^+(aq)$
    (E) $SO_3^{2-}(aq) + FeCl_3(s)$
        $\rightarrow Fe_2(SO_3)_2(aq) + 3Cl^-(aq)$

16. What is the molar solubility of silver chromate? (K_{sp} for $Ag_2CrO_4 = 1.2 \times 10^{-12}$)
    (A) 1.1×10^{-6}
    (B) 1.1×10^{-4}
    (C) 6.7×10^{-5}
    (D) 5.5×10^{-7}
    (E) 8.4×10^{-5}

17. When potassium dichromate, $K_2Cr_2O_7$, dissolves in water, the ions produced are:
    (A) $2 K^+ + 2 Cr^{6+} + 7 O^{2-}$
    (B) $K_2^{2+} + Cr_2O_7^{2-}$
    (C) $2 K^+ + Cr_2^+ + O_7^{2-}$
    (D) $2 K^+ + Cr_2O_7^{2-}$
    (E) No ions are formed; $K_2Cr_2O_7$ is a nonelectrolyte.

18. Helium is placed in a tube with a pinhole, and the helium takes 36 minutes to effuse out of the tube. Then sulfur dioxide is placed in the same tube, under the same conditions. How long will the sulfur dioxide take to effuse out of the tube?
    (A) 9 min   (B) 4.5 min   (C) 2.4 h
    (D) 4.8 h   (E) 9.6 h

    Questions 19 and 20 refer to the following half-reaction for a basic solution:

    $$C_2O_4^{2-} \longrightarrow CO_3^{2-}$$

19. When the half-reaction is balanced, using the smallest possible whole-number coefficients and entering the proper number of electrons where needed,
    (A) there should be 4 electrons on the right side
    (B) there should be 3 electrons on the right side
    (C) There should be 2 electrons on the left side
    (D) there should be 2 electrons on the right side
    (E) This is not a half-reaction; no electrons are needed.

20. The hydroxide ions in the half-reaction appear as
    (A) 2 on the right side
    (B) 4 on the left side
    (C) 3 on the left side
    (D) 4 on the right side
    (E) 1 on the left side

21. The solubility product of $Fe(OH)_3$ is 1.6×10^{-39}. What is the molar solubility of iron(III) hydroxide?
    (A) 1.7×10^{-8}
    (B) 2.0×10^{-10}
    (C) 8.8×10^{-11}
    (D) 4.0×10^{-20}
    (E) 1.6×10^{-3}

22. An oxide of nitrogen is found to contain 25.9 percent nitrogen. The empirical formula for this substance is
    (A) NO (B) NO_2 (C) N_2O (D) N_2O_3
    (E) N_2O_5

23. Which of these ions has the largest radius?
    (A) K^+ (B) I^- (C) Cl^- (D) Na^+
    (E) Ba^{2+}

GO ON TO THE NEXT PAGE ➤

24. The trend for atomic radii to decrease from left to right across a period of the periodic table is ascribed to which of the following?
    (A) Electrons attract each other to compress the outer orbitals.
    (B) Increasing mass has a gravitational effect, contracting the atomic size.
    (C) Increasing nuclear charge more than offsets the repulsion of added electrons in the same shell.
    (D) Hund's rule, the Pauli exclusion principle, and the Heisenberg uncertainty principle all combine to explain this phenomenon.
    (E) The question is wrong; atomic radii increase across each period.

25. A certain gas has a volume of 2.50 liters and a pressure of 3.00 atmospheres. The pressure on the gas is reduced to 0.500 atmosphere, and the gas is allowed to expand. Determine the work involved in this process.
    (A) 31.25 L atm   (B) 6.25 L atm
    (C) 37.5 L atm   (D) − 37.5 L atm
    (E) − 6.25 L atm

26. The rate law for a reaction is found to be

    $$\text{Rate} = k[A]^2[B]$$

    Which of the following is correct?
    (A) A plot of log rate versus time will be a straight line.
    (B) The units for the rate constant are mol^2 $L^{-2}s^{-1}$.
    (C) This rate law is unlikely since it implies the simultaneous collision of two atoms of A and one of B.
    (D) It is unlikely that the first step of the mechanism is the rate-limiting step.
    (E) All third-order reactions are endothermic.

27. Which of the following describes the interaction of orbitals to form pi bonds?

    (A)   (B)   (C)

    (D)   (E)

28. Which of the following is most probably an optically active organic compound?
    (A) Acetic acid
    (B) *trans*-2-Butene
    (C) Paradichlorobenzene
    (D) 2-Bromo-2-chlorobutane
    (E) Chloroform

29. The compound with dsp^3 hybridization is
    (A) SF_6 (B) PCl_3 (C) $CHBr_3$ (D) I_3^-
    (E) BCl_3

30. Which pair has the same electronic configuration?
    (A) Ca^{2+} and Mg^{2+}
    (B) Cl^- and K^+
    (C) Fe^{2+} and Cr^{3+}
    (D) O^{2-} and S^{2-}
    (E) Ar and Ne

31. The pair with the largest difference in size is
    (A) K and Na
    (B) Cl^- and F^-
    (C) O^{2-} and F^-
    (D) Na^+ and Br^-
    (E) Cl and Br

32. The element that has a low second ionization energy and a high third ionization energy is
    (A) Fe (B) Na (C) Sr (D) Cl (E) Ar

33. One gram of an element combines with 3.9 grams of chlorine. The element also forms an oxide with the formula M_2O_3. What is the element represented by M?
    (A) Na (B) Fe (C) Al (D) B (E) Au

34. The properties of which of the following are best explained as those of a covalent network crystal?
    (A) Al_2O_3 (B) SiO_2 (C) Sn (D) Pt
    (E) $(-CF_2-)_n$

35. The most polar covalent bond is found between which two elements?
    (A) C—N (B) P—F (C) S—O
    (D) Si—C (E) O—P

GO ON TO THE NEXT PAGE ➤

36. Which of the following does NOT form hydrogen bonds?
    (A) HCN   (B) HF   (C) CH_3NH_2
    (D) CH_3COOH (E) $ClCH_2OH$

37. When 1 mole of H_3PO_4 reacts with 2 moles of KOH, one of the products is water. The other is
    (A) KH_2PO_4
    (B) K_2HPO_4
    (C) K_3PO_4
    (D) a mixture of K_2HPO_4 and K_3PO_4
    (E) a mixture of KH_2PO_4 and K_2HPO_4

38. At STP, how many liters of O_2 react with 1.50 liters of SO_2 to form SO_3?
    (A) 1.50   (B) 1.00   (C) 3.00   (D) 4.50
    (E) 0.75

39. The compound that contains 10.4 percent oxygen is
    (A) NaOH   (B) CaO   (C) Al_2O_3
    (D) BaO   (E) $Ca(OH)_2$

40. The equilibrium law for the dissociation of the weak acid HCN is
    (A) $\dfrac{[CN^-][H^+]}{[HCN]}$ (B) $\dfrac{[CN^-][H_3O^+]}{[HCN][H_2O]}$
    (C) $\dfrac{[HCN][H^+]}{[CN^-]}$ (D) $\dfrac{[HCN]}{[CN^-][H^+]}$
    (E) $\dfrac{[HCN][H_2O]}{[CN^-][H_3O^+]}$

41. The concentration of H_2 in a flask is 0.023 mole per liter, and the pressure is 346 mm Hg. If N_2 is added to bring the pressure up to 1.00 atmosphere, what is the concentration of N_2 in the flask?
    (A) 0.051 M   (B) 6.6×10^{-5} M
    (C) 0.028 M   (D) 1.19 M   (E) 414 M

42. In aqueous solution the strongest acid is
    (A) HCl   (B) H_3O^+ (C) HBr   (D) HI
    (E) All are equally strong.

43. The kinetic molecular theory is used to explain
    (A) reaction rates
    (B) bond vibrations
    (C) gas behavior
    (D) catalysts
    (E) activated complexes

44. A 35.8-milligram sample of pure iron(III) sulfate (molar mass = 400) is dissolved in 1 liter of acidified water. If a base such as solid sodium hydroxide is added, a precipitate will form. At what pH will iron(III) hydroxide begin to precipitate from this solution? (K_{sp} for $Fe(OH)_3 = 1.6 \times 10^{-39}$)
    (A) 1.6   (B) 2.3   (C) 10.4   (D) 3.6
    (E) 5.8

45. Which of the following functional groups represents an organic acid?
    (A) —COOH   (B) —OH   (C) —NH_2
    (D) —CHO   (E) —SH

46. In an experiment a student collects hydrogen by displacement of water. The water levels in the bottle and the pneumatic trough are made equal. The barometer in the laboratory reads 723.2 mm Hg, and the vapor pressure of water at room temperature of 22°C is 19.8 mm Hg. What is the pressure of the hydrogen gas collected, and what else must be done to determine the mass of hydrogen collected?
    (A) 703.4 mm Hg, the volume of H_2 must be determined
    (B) 723.2 mm Hg, the moles of H_2 must be determined
    (C) 740.0 mm Hg, the volume of H_2 must be determined
    (D) 740.0 mm Hg, the Celsius temperature must be converted to Kelvin
    (E) 703.4 mm Hg, nothing else is needed

47. Which of the following is NOT a complex ion?
    (A) $Cr_2O_7^{2-}$ (B) $Ag(NH_3)_2^+$
    (C) $FeCl_6^{3-}$ (D) $Cd(CN)_4^{2-}$ (E) HgI_4^{2-}

48. Magnesium fluoride has a $K_{sp} = 6.6 \times 10^{-9}$. What is the molar solubility of MgF_2?
    (A) 1.18×10^{-3} M   (B) 1.88×10^{-3} M
    (C) 8.12×10^{-5} M   (D) 1.65×10^{-9} M
    (E) 4.06×10^{-5} M

GO ON TO THE NEXT PAGE ➤

49. When 10.0 grams of a protein is dissolved in distilled water to prepare 500 milliliters of solution at 25 °C, the osmotic pressure is measured to be 23.2 mm Hg. What is the molar mass of the protein? ($R = 0.0821$ L atm $mol^{-1} K^{-1}$)
(A) 108 g mol^{-1} (B) 1.6×10^4 g mol^{-1}
(C) 1.5×10^3 g mol^{-1} (D) 16 g mol^{-1}
(E) 1.8×10^6 g mol^{-1}

50. Of the following, the diamagnetic element is
(A) Ca (B) Fe (C) Cr (D) Mn (E) Co

51. A hygroscopic substance
(A) reacts with atmospheric oxygen
(B) spontaneously combusts
(C) spontaneously combusts in contact with organic matter
(D) Absorbs water from the atmosphere
(E) oxidizes readily

52. Very fine precipitates are most easily separated by
(A) distillation (B) filtration (C) centrifugation (D) evaporation (E) vacuum filtration

53. Which of the following CANNOT be used to predict whether a reaction is spontaneous?
(A) ΔG^0 (B) K_c (C) E^0_{cell} (D) ΔH^0
(E) ΔS^0 and ΔH^0

54. Which of the following CANNOT be a Lewis acid?
(A) Fe^{2+} (B) Fe^{3+} (C) Cl^-
(D) BCl_3 (E) H^+

55. Which of the following is NOT a conjugate acid-base pair?
(A) H_2SO_4 and SO_4^{2-}
(B) HCl and Cl^-
(C) NH_3 and NH_2^-
(D) HPO_4^{2-} and PO_4^{3-}
(E) H_2S and HS^-

56. The shape of CH_4 is explained by
(A) the VSEPR theory
(B) Hund's rule
(C) transition-state theory
(D) quantum numbers
(E) Heisenberg's uncertainty principle

57. A reaction has the rate law

$$Rate = k[A][B]^2$$

The units for the rate constant are
(A) s^{-1} (B) mol $L^{-1}s^{-1}$ (C) L^2 $mol^{-2}s^{-1}$ (D) L $mol^{-1}s^{-1}$ (E) mol s^{-1}

58. A concentration versus time plot will be curved for all of the following EXCEPT
(A) a zero-order reaction
(B) a first-order reaction
(C) a second-order reaction
(D) a third-order reaction
(E) radioactive decay

59. A certain gas has a molar solubility in CCl_4 of 2.8×10^{-4} M when its pressure is 340 mm Hg. What is its solubility, at the same temperature, if the pressure of the gas is decreased to 200 mm Hg?
(A) 2.8×10^{-4} M (B) 1.65×10^{-4} M
(C) 1.25×10^{-4} M (D) 7.37×10^{-5} M
(E) 4.76×10^{-4} M

60. Which of the following radioactive isotopes is most likely to decay by emitting a beta particle?
(A) ^{235}U (B) ^{40}Cl (C) ^{35}Ar (D) ^{246}Cf
(E) ^{21}Na

61. Which of the following is produced commercially by electrolysis?
(A) NaOH (B) Al (C) H_2 (D) Cl_2
(E) All of these

62. Which of the following CANNOT be used to determine molar mass?
(A) Osmotic pressure
(B) Percent composition
(C) Freezing-point depression
(D) Vapor pressure
(E) Gas density

63. A compound has the formula CaX_2. X may be
(A) Br (B) O (C) P (D) N (E) Ar

GO ON TO THE NEXT PAGE ➤

64. Which of the following is correctly named?
    (A) CaF_2 calcium(II) fluoride
    (B) $Mg(C_2H_3O_2)_2$ magnesium acetate
    (C) $AlCl_3$ aluminum trichloride
    (D) FeO   iron(III) oxide
    (E) NO_2 nitric oxide

65. The reaction of sodium metal with water is classified as
    (A) a double-replacement reaction
    (B) a combustion reaction
    (C) a neutralization reaction
    (D) an oxidation reaction
    (E) a single-replacement reaction

66. Which of the following conducts electricity only slightly when dissolved in water?
    (A) $MgCl_2$ (B) $CH_3CH_2CH_2OH$
    (C) CO_2 (D) $KMnO_4$ (E) CH_2O

67. $Cu^{2+} + Sn^{2+} \longrightarrow Cu(s) + Sn^{4+}$
    $Cu^{2+} + 2e^- \longrightarrow Cu$ $E° = +0.34$ V
    $Sn^{4+} + 2e^- \longrightarrow Sn^{2+}$ $E° = +0.15$ V
    What is the standard cell voltage for the above reaction?
    (A) $+0.49$ V   (B) $+0.19$ V
    (C) -0.49 V   (D) -0.19 V
    (E) $+0.051$ V

68. Calcium chloride will react with both reactants in which of the following pairs?
    (A) Silver nitrate and sodium bromide
    (B) Silver sulfate and barium hydroxide
    (C) Iodine and potassium permanganate
    (D) Potassium nitrate and sodium phosphate
    (E) Carbon dioxide and acetic acid

69. A colorless solution is formed when which one of the following is dissolved in water?
    (A) Potassium chromate
    (B) Nickel(II) nitrate
    (C) Copper sulfate
    (D) Sodium acetate
    (E) Manganese sulfate

70. Of the following acids, the strongest is
    (A) $HClO_2$ (B) $HBrO_3$
    (C) $HClO_3$ (D) H_2SO_3 (E) H_2SeO_3

71. Which of the following molecular geometries has two different bond angles?
    (A) A tetrahedron
    (B) A linear molecule
    (C) A trigonal bipyramid
    (D) An octahedron
    (E) A trigonal planar molecule

72. The boiling point of bromine is $-7.2°C$, and its heat of vaporization is $+15$ kJ mol^{-1}. What is the entropy change when 1 mole of $Br_2(\ell)$ is converted to $Br_2(g)$ at $-7.2°C$?
    (A) -2.08 kJ K^{-1} (B) $-2,080$ J K^{-1}
    (C) 56.4 kJ K^{-1} (D) 56.4 J K^{-1}
    (E) 17.7 J K^{-1}

73. What is the mole fraction of sodium chloride in a solution that is 2.00 molal in NaCl? (Molar mass of $H_2O = 18.0$ and of NaCl = 58.5)
    (A) 0.500 (B) 0.0348 (C) 0.965
    (D) 0.117 (E) 0.883

74. A 25.0-milliliter sample of 0.100 molar silver nitrate is added to 50.00 milliliters of a 0.035 molar solution of sodium chloride. After coagulating, filtering, and drying, the precipitate weighed exactly 200 milligrams. What was the percentage yield of this experiment?
    (A) 79.6% (B) 56.0% (C) 72.5%
    (D) 32.8% (E) 100%

75. A galvanic cell is constructed to study the reaction

    $$Zn(s) + Cu^{2+}(aq) \longrightarrow Cu(s) + Zn^{2+}(aq)$$

    What is the voltage of the cell if $[Cu^{2+}] = 0.200$ M and $[Zn^{2+}] = 0.0500$ M? ($E^0_{cell} = +1.10$ V)
    (A) 1.06 V   (B) 1.10 V   (C) 1.14 V
    (D) 1.02 V   (E) 1.12 V

STOP

THIS IS THE END OF SECTION I
YOU MAY USE ANY REMAINING TIME TO CHECK YOUR WORK IN THIS SECTION.

Section II
Free-Response Problems

55% of total grade
90 minutes
Suggested time for Parts A, B, and C—50 minutes
Suggested time for Part D—40 minutes

This section consists of four parts, A (25 percent), B (25 percent), C (15 percent), and D (35 percent), weighted as shown. You should spend approximately 50 minutes on parts A, B, and C and 40 minutes on part D. It is your responsibility to budget the time wisely.

RESPONSES TO THE QUESTIONS IN THIS SECTION MUST CLEARLY SHOW YOUR METHODS AND THE STEPS USED TO ARRIVE AT THE ANSWER. Partial credit is earned by demonstrating an appropriate method developed from fundamental principles while little credit is earned for an answer obtained with no method shown. Appropriate use of significant figures is recommended. Data necessary for solving problems are given with the questions, or may be found in the tables below.

Useful Information for Solving Free-Response Problems

Universal gas constant	$R = 8.314 \text{ J mol}^{-1}\text{K}^{-1}$
	$0.0821 \text{ L atm mol}^{-1}\text{K}^{-1}$
	$62.4 \text{ L mm Hg mol}^{-1}\text{K}^{-1}$
	$8.314 \text{ V C mol}^{-1}\text{K}^{-1}$
Faraday	$1 \mathscr{F} = 96{,}485 \text{ coulombs}$
	$96{,}485 \text{ J V}^{-1}$
Electron volt	$1 \text{ eV} = 96.5 \text{ kJ mol}^{-1}$
Speed of light	$c = 2.998 \times 10^6 \text{ m s}^{-1}$
Planck's constant	$h = 6.63 \times 10^{-34} \text{ J s}$
Boltzmann constant	$k = 1.38 \times 10^{-23} \text{ J K}^{-1}$
Avogadro's number	$N = 6.022 \times 10^{23} \text{ molecules mol}^{-1}$
At 25°C	$\dfrac{RT}{n\mathscr{F}} \ln Q = \dfrac{0.0591}{n} \log Q$

Vapor Pressure of Water as a Function of Temperature

Temperature degrees Celsius	Vapor Pressure mm Hg	Temperature degrees Celsius	Vapor Pressure mm Hg
−10	2.1	26	25.2
0.0	4.6	28	28.3
5	6.5	30	31.8
10	9.2	35	41.2
12	10.5	40	55.3
14	12.0	50	92.5
16	13.6	60	149.4
18	15.5	70	233.7
20	17.5	80	355.1
22	19.8	90	525.8
24	22.4	100	760.0

Standard Reduction Potentials, 25°C

Half-Reaction	E° (V)	Half-Reaction	E° (V)
$F_2(g) + 2e^- \rightarrow 2F^-$	2.87	$Co^{2+} + 2e^- \rightarrow Co$	-0.28
$Co^{3+} + e^- \rightarrow Co^{2+}$	1.82	$Tl^+ + e^- \rightarrow Tl$	-0.34
$Au^{3+} + 3e^- \rightarrow Au$	1.50	$Cd^{2+} + 2e^- \rightarrow Cd$	-0.40
$Cl_2(g) + 2e^- \rightarrow 2Cl^-$	1.36	$Cr^{3+} + e^- \rightarrow Cr^{2+}$	-0.41
$O_2(g) + 4H^+ + 4e^- \rightarrow 2H_2O$	1.23	$Fe^{2+} + 2e^- \rightarrow Fe$	-0.44
$Br_2(g) + 2e^- \rightarrow 2Br^-$	1.07	$Cr^{3+} + 3e^- \rightarrow Cr$	-0.74
$2Hg^{2+} + 2e^- \rightarrow Hg_2^{2+}$	0.92	$Zn^{2+} + 2e^- \rightarrow Zn$	-0.76
$Ag^+ + e^- \rightarrow Ag$	0.80	$Mn^{2+} + 2e^- \rightarrow Mn$	-1.18
$Hg_2^{2+} + 2e^- \rightarrow Hg$	0.79	$Al^{3+} + 3e^- \rightarrow Al$	-1.66
$Fe^{3+} + e^- \rightarrow Fe^{2+}$	0.77	$Be^{2+} + 2e^- \rightarrow Be$	-1.70
$I_2 + 2e^- \rightarrow 2I^-$	0.53	$Mg^{2+} + 2e^- \rightarrow Mg$	-2.37
$Cu^+ + e^- \rightarrow Cu$	0.52	$Na^+ + e^- \rightarrow Na$	-2.71
$Cu^{2+} + 2e^- \rightarrow Cu$	0.34	$Ca^{2+} + 2e^- \rightarrow Ca$	-2.87
$Cu^{2+} + e^- \rightarrow Cu^+$	0.15	$Sr^{2+} + 2e^- \rightarrow Sr$	-2.89
$Sn^{4+} + 2e^- \rightarrow Sn^{2+}$	0.15	$Ba^{2+} + 2e^- \rightarrow Ba$	-2.90
$S + 2H^+ + 2e^- \rightarrow H_2S$	0.14	$Rb^- + e^- \rightarrow Rb$	-2.92
$2H^+ + 2e^- \rightarrow H_2$	0.00	$K^+ + e^- \rightarrow K$	-2.92
$Pb^{2+} + 2e^- \rightarrow Pb$	-0.13	$Cs^+ + e^- \rightarrow Cs$	-2.92
$Sn^{2+} + 2e^- \rightarrow Sn$	-0.14	$Li^+ + e^- \rightarrow Li$	-3.05
$Ni^{2+} + 2e^- \rightarrow Ni$	-0.25		

Part A
(25% of Section II grade)

Directions: Solve all parts of the following problem:

1. The molar mass and acid dissociation constant of aspirin (acetylsalicylic acid) may be determined by a titration experiment in which a 0.500-gram sample of aspirin is dissolved to make 250 milliliters of solution. Then 50.0 milliliters of this solution is titrated with 0.01225 M NaOH and the end point is determined to occur at 45.31 milliliters. The titration curve shows only one end point, at pH of 7.37.
   (a) Calculate the molar mass of the monoprotic aspirin molecule.
   (b) Calculate (1) the concentration of the sodium salt of aspirin at the end point and (2) the K_a for aspirin.
   (c) Using K_a from part (b) determine the pH range for which aspirin and its sodium salt can be used as a buffer.
   (d) Abbreviating the sodium salt of aspirin as NaAsp, write the hydrolysis reaction for the sodium salt and determine its equilibrium constant.

GO ON TO THE NEXT PAGE ➤

Part B
(25% of section II grade)

Directions: Completely solve EITHER problem 2 or problem 3. Only the first problem answered will be graded. Be sure to indicate which problem you are answering.

2. When 10.00 grams of a compound containing only carbon and hydrogen is burned in an insufficient amount of oxygen to convert all of the carbon to CO_2, 12.86 grams of water is formed along with 22.25 grams of CO_2. The only other substance left after the reaction is complete is CO.
   (a) What is the empirical formula of the hydrocarbon?
   (b) How many grams of CO are formed?
   (c) At 25°C the sample of the hydrocarbon alone had a pressure of 0.873 atmosphere in a 10.0-liter container. What is the molar mass of the hydrocarbon?
   (d) What is the molecular formula of the hydrocarbon?

3. A 250-milliliter aqueous solution of $Cu(NO_3)_2$ is electrolyzed with a current of 0.985 ampere for 1.50 hours to remove all of the copper from solution.
   (a) Write the balanced half-reactions for the anode and cathode reactions.
   (b) How many grams of copper metal are deposited on the electrode?
   (c) What was the original concentration of $Cu(NO_3)_2$?
   (d) What voltage must be applied to the electrodes to cause this reaction to occur, assuming standard state conditions and ideal behavior?

GO ON TO THE NEXT PAGE ➤

Part C
(15% of Section II grade)

Directions: Answer FIVE of the eight choices in this part. If more than five are answered, only the first five will be scored.

4. Give the formulas for the reactants and products in FIVE of the following word equations. In all cases a chemical reaction occurs. Unless otherwise stated, the reaction occurs in aqueous solution. Substances that do not enter into the chemical reaction should not be listed, and the reactions do not have to be balanced.

EXAMPLE: Magnesium metal is added to a dilute solution of hydrochloric acid

$$\text{Formula: } Mg + H^+ \longrightarrow Mg^{2+} + H_2$$

(a) Sodium acetate is added to water.
(b) To 1.50 moles of potassium hydroxide is added 1.50 moles of sulfuric acid.
(c) Potassium permanganate is decolorized by iron(II) nitrate.
(d) White phosphorus is exposed to air.
(e) Sodium cyanide is mixed with ferrous chloride.
(f) Copper metal is added to a dilute solution of nitric acid.
(g) Hydrochloric acid is added to calcium carbonate.
(h) Chlorine gas dissolved in water is added to a sodium iodide solution.

GO ON TO THE NEXT PAGE ➤

Part D
(35% of Section II grade)

Directions: Select THREE of the following five problems. (If more than three are answered, only the first three will be graded.)

Use about 40 minutes for this part of the examination. Answers to these questions should demonstrate your ability to present logical, coherent, and convincing explanations of chemical facts and observations. Answers are judged on the accuracy of your analysis and on the appropriateness of the details and examples cited. Specific answers and examples are preferred to broad generalizations. Diagrams, illustrations, and equations may be included in your answers.

5. Use chemical principles to explain each of the following;
   (a) When the cap on a bottle of soda is removed, the soda fizzes with bubbles of CO_2. More bubbles from in warm soda than in cold soda.
   (b) Before Freon was developed, many refrigerators used sulfur dioxide as a refrigerant. Why did repairmen always carry a bottle of concentrated ammonia with them?
   (c) Powdered platinum is a more effective catalyst than the same mass of platinum in a single crystal.
   (d) A mixture of solid organic compounds has a lower melting point than the pure compounds themselves.
   (e) Helium-filled party balloons deflate more quickly than air-filled balloons.

6. Use the transition-state theory and the potential energy diagram below to answer the following questions:

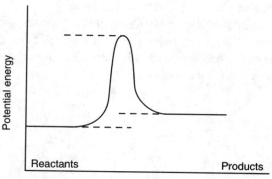

   (a) Explain why the potential energy curve has the shape shown.
   (b) Describe the transition state.
   (c) On the basis of this diagram, compare the forward and reverse rate constants.
   (d) Describe the effect of a catalyst on this reaction.
   (e) Use this diagram and the Arrhenius equation to explain why a rise in temperature must always increase the reaction rate.

GO ON TO THE NEXT PAGE ➤

7. Sulfurous acid is a diprotic acid with $K_1 = 1.2 \times 10^{-2}$ and $K_2 = 6.6 \times 10^{-8}$.
   (a) Sketch a titration curve for sulfurous acid titrated with NaOH.
   (b) Show on this curve the region where a buffer composed of $NaHSO_3$ and Na_2SO_3 would be located. From the data given, over what pH range would such a buffer be effective?
   (c) In this titration curve, show which regions are constant, and which regions will change, depending on the initial concentration of H_2SO_3.
   (d) What factor(s) must be considered in choosing an indicator to observe the end points?

8. The compound copper(II) sulfate pentahydrate is in a class of compounds called hydrates. When this compound is heated slowly from room temperature (approximately 110°C), four water molecules evaporate; at approximately 150°C the last water molecule is lost.
   (a) Sketch a heating curve for copper(II) sulfate pentahydrate as a plot of mass versus temperature.
   (b) Describe how to determine the number of water molecules of hydration that would be present if the formula were known only as $CuSO_4 \cdot nH_2O$. (Do *not* do the calculation.)
   (c) What is the difference between water of hydration and adsorbed water?
   (d) An experiment calls for the use of $CuSO_4$ but all you have is $CuSO_4 \cdot 5H_2O$. What, if any considerations are necessary before making the substitution?

9. A polymer has this general formula:

$$\left[\begin{array}{cc} H & CH_3 \\ | & | \\ -C-C- \\ | & | \\ H & H \end{array} \right]_n$$

   (a) Is this an addition or condensation polymer? Explain your reasoning.
   (b) What is the monomer used to prepare this polymer?
   (c) The subscript n is usually 100 to 10,000, and this formula indicates a linear polymer. Is this polymer soluble in water? Explain, using the intermolecular forces expected for this structure.
   (d) This polymer may also be prepared with branched side chains. Compare the properties of branched polymers with linear polymers.

STOP

THIS IS THE END OF SECTION II
YOU MAY USE ANY REMAINING TIME TO CHECK YOUR WORK IN THIS SECTION.

Answer Key for Multiple-Choice Questions

1. A	16. C	31. D	46. A	61. E
2. B	17. D	32. C	47. A	62. B
3. E	18. C	33. C	48. A	63. A
4. E	19. D	34. B	49. B	64. B
5. C	20. B	35. B	50. A	65. E
6. D	21. C	36. A	51. D	66. C
7. A	22. E	37. B	52. C	67. B
8. E	23. B	38. E	53. D	68. B
9. C	24. C	39. D	54. C	69. D
10. B	25. E	40. A	55. A	70. C
11. C	26. D	41. C	56. A	71. C
12. A	27. B	42. E	57. C	72. C
13. B	28. D	43. C	58. A	73. B
14. E	29. D	44. B	59. B	74. A
15. C	30. B	45. A	60. B	75. E

Explained Answers to Multiple-Choice Questions

1. **A** Strontium is red; copper is blue-green.
2. **B** Copper can have a $+1$ or $+2$ oxidation state.
3. **E** Uranium is in period 7; it is much larger than the others.
4. **E** The others have artificial radioactive isotopes, but none have been found in nature.
5. **C** Sulfites get oxidized to sulfates.
6. **D** Metal oxides are basic anhydrides.
7. **A** Phosphorus is an essential nutrient in fertilizers, along with nitrogen and potassium.
8. **E** The abbreviation stands for "saturated calomel electrode."
9. **C** This is the symbol for a salt bridge.
10. **B** Reduction always occurs at the cathode.
11. **C** The salt bridge completes the electrical circuit.
12. **A** Potassium permanganate is the only oxidizing agent in the list.
13. **B** Ammonia is a base; EDTA is a tetraprotic acid.
14. **E** SiO_2 is the empirical formula of sand and quartz.
15. **C** Sodium sulfite is soluble, but iron(II) sulfite is not. Iron (II) chloride is soluble.
16. **C** Solve the equation

$$K_{sp} = [Ag^+]^2[CrO_4^{2-}]$$

where $[Ag^+] = 2x$ and $[CrO_4^{2-}] = x$.

$$1.2 \times 10^{-12} = (2x)^2(x) = 4x^3$$
$$x^3 = 3.0 \times 10^{-13}$$
$$x = 6.7 \times 10^{-5}$$

17. **D** Two potassium ions and one dichromate ion are formed.
18. **C** Graham's law of effusion can be used to calculate the relative rates of effusion:

$$\sqrt{\frac{m_1}{m_2}} = \frac{V_2}{V_1} = \sqrt{\frac{64}{4}} = 4$$

Helium effuses four times faster than SO_2, so the SO_2 will take

$$(36 \text{ min})(4) = 144 \text{ min} = 2.4 \text{ hr}$$

to effuse.

19. **D** The balanced half-reaction is

$$4OH^- + C_2O_4^{2-} \longrightarrow 2CO_3^{2-} + 2H_2O + 2e^-$$

There are 2 electrons on the right side.

20. **B** See the half-reaction in the answer to question 19.

21. **C** Solve the equation

$$K_{sp} = [Fe^{2+}][OH^-]^3$$

where $[Fe^{2+}] = x$ and $[OH^-] = 3x$.

$$1.6 \times 10^{-39} = (x)(3x)^3$$
$$= 27x^4$$
$$x^4 = 5.9 \times 10^{-41}$$
$$x = 8.8 \times 10^{-11}$$

22. **E** The compound must contain $100 - 25.9 = 74.1\%$ oxygen.

$$? \text{ mol N} = 25.9 \text{ g N} \left(\frac{1 \text{ mol N}}{14 \text{ g N}} \right) = 1.85 \text{ mol N}$$

$$? \text{ mol O} = 74.1 \text{ g O} \left(\frac{1 \text{ mol O}}{16 \text{ g O}} \right) = 4.63 \text{ mol O}$$

Dividing both by 1.85 yields 1 mol N and 2.5 mol O. Therefore, the simplest ratio is N_2O_5.

23. **B** Barium and iodide ions are isoelectronic with xenon. Ba ions are much smaller than xenon because barium has more protons than electrons. I ions are larger than xenon because iodine has more electrons than protons. The other ions must be smaller since their outer electrons are in lower energy levels.

24. **C** The fact that more protons are attracting electrons from approximately the same distance causes the decrease in size.

25. **E** $$\text{Work} = -P\,\Delta V$$

where $P = 0.50$ atm. The initial volume is 2.5 L, while the final volume is 15 L as calculated from the ideal gas law.

$$\Delta V = 15 - 2.5 = 12.5 \text{ L}$$

The final pressure is always used in solving $w = -P\Delta V$
$$= -(0.5)(12.5)$$
$$= -6.25 \text{ L atm}$$

26. **D** Elementary reactions are generally bimolecular reactions. The rate law's exponents are derived from the coefficient of the rate limiting step. These two facts indicate that a rate law will rarely be more than second order if the first step is the rate limiting step.

27. **B** This diagram represents the side-to-side overlap of p orbitals to form pi bonds, which are to either side of the internuclear axis.
28. **D** 2-Bromo-2-chlorobutane has a carbon atom with four different groups bonded to it which is required of optionally active compounds.

$$CH_3CH_2\underset{\underset{Br}{|}}{\overset{\overset{Cl}{|}}{C}}CH_3$$

29. **D** I_3 has three nonbonding pairs of electrons on the central atom in addition to the two iodine atoms.
30. **B** Both Cl^- and K^+ are isoelectronic with Ar.
31. **D** Na^+ and Br^- are isoelectronic with Ne and Kr. These are two energy levels apart and must have a greater size difference than the other choices. O^{2-} and F^- are about the same size. K and Na, Cl^- and F^-, and Cl and Br differ by one energy level.
32. **C** Strontium easily loses two electrons and does not form a $+3$ ion because of the much larger third ionization energy, which corresponds to losing an electron from the next lower shell.
33. **C** The oxide indicates that element M forms a $+3$ ion and an MCl_3 chloride. The molar mass of M can be calculated as follows:

$$? \text{ g M} = 3 \text{ mol Cl} \left(\frac{35.5 \text{ g Cl}}{1 \text{ mol Cl}}\right)\left(\frac{1 \text{ g M}}{3.9 \text{ g Cl}}\right) = 27.3 \text{ g M}$$

This is the molar mass of aluminum.

34. **B** Sand and quartz, SiO_2, are tetrahedral arrays of silicon atoms connected to each other by oxygen atoms in a network crystal.
35. **B** All of the other choices are adjacent to each other in the periodic table.
36. **A** To form a hydrogen bond, hydrogen must be bonded to fluorine, oxygen, or nitrogen. Only in HCN is hydrogen not bonded to F, O, or N.
37. **B** Two hydrogen ions are replaced by two potassium ions, based on the mole ratio given.
38. **E** The reaction is

$$O_2 + 2SO_4 \longrightarrow 2SO_3$$

and the calculation is

$$? \text{ L O}_2 = 1.5 \text{ L SO}_2\left(\frac{1 \text{ mol SO}_2}{22.4 \text{ L SO}_2}\right)\left(\frac{1 \text{ mol O}_2}{2 \text{ mol SO}_2}\right)\left(\frac{22.4 \text{ L O}_2}{1 \text{ mol O}_2}\right) = 0.75 \text{ L O}_2$$

39. **D**
$$\text{Percent composition} = \frac{\text{atomic mass of element} \times n}{\text{molar mass of compound}} \times 100$$

where n is the number of atoms of the element in the compound formula. For BaO this is

$$\% \text{ O} = \tfrac{16}{153} \times 100 = 10.4\%$$

40. **A** The dissociation reaction is

$$HCN \rightleftharpoons H^+ + CN^-$$

Water is considered a pure liquid and does not appear in the equilibrium law.

41. **C** Using the ideal gas law and the variables given, we write

$$\frac{P_1 V_1}{P_2 V_2} = \frac{n_1}{n_2}$$

$P_1 = 346$ mm Hg, $n_1/V_1 = 0.023$ mol L^{-1}, $P_2 = 760$ mm $- 346 = 414$ mm Hg. Then

$$\frac{n_2}{V_2} = \frac{P_2 n_1}{P_1 V_1} = \frac{414 \text{ mm Hg}}{346 \text{ mm Hg}} \times 0.023 \text{ mol } L^{-1}$$

$$= 0.028 \text{ mol } L^{-1}$$

42. **E** In aqueous solution all strong acids are leveled to the strength of H_3O^+.

42. **C** The kinetic molecular theory explains how the motion of gases results in the observed pressure and also explains other properties, such as diffusion.

44. **B** The number of moles of $Fe_2(SO_4)_3$ dissolved in 8.95×10^{-5}, and $[Fe^{3+}] = 1.79 \times 10^{-4}$ M. The equation

$$K_{sp} = [Fe^{3+}][OH^-]^3$$

is solved for $[OH^-]$.

$$[OH]^3 = \frac{1.6 \times 10^{-39}}{1.79 \times 10^{-4}} = 8.9 \times 10^{-36}$$

$$[OH] = 2.1 \times 10^{-12}$$
$$pOH = 11.7$$
$$pH = 2.3$$

45. **A** $-COOH$ is the organic acid functional group.

46. **A** The pressure is $723.2 - 19.8 = 703.4$ mm Hg. The temperature and the universal gas law constant are known. The volume of H_2 is needed to calculate the moles of H_2 and then its mass.

47. **A** The dichromate ion is a polyatomic, not a complex, ion.

48. **A** $$K_{sp} = [Mg^{2+}][F^-]^2$$

where $[Mg^{2+}] = x$ and $[F^-] = 2x$.

$$6.6 \times 10^{-9} = (x)(2x)^2 = 4 x^3$$
$$x = 1.18 \times 10^{-3}, \text{ which is the molar solubility.}$$

49. **B** Solve

$$\Pi V = nRT$$

where n = g/molar mass. Temperature must be in Kelvin units and pressure in atmospheres

$$\text{Molar mass} = \frac{gRT}{\Pi V} = \frac{(10.0 \text{ g})(0.0821 \text{ L atm mol}^{-1}\text{K}^{-1})(298)}{(0.0305 \text{ atm})(0.500 \text{ L})}$$

$$= 1.6 \times 10^4 \text{ g mol}^{-1}$$

50. **A** All electrons are paired in calcium. All of the other choices have one or more unpaired electrons.

51. **D** All hygroscopic materials must be sealed tightly to prevent the absorption of water.

52. **C** Centrifugation is the easiest method without loss of precipitate.

53. **D** The heat of reaction, $\Delta H°$, must be combined with the entropy to determine the free-energy change. By itself $\Delta H°$ is not a definitive indication of a spontaneous reaction.

54. **C** The chloride ion cannot accept electron pairs.

55. **A** H_2SO_4 and SO_4^{2-} differ by more than one H^+ and are not a conjugate acid-base pair.

56. **A** Repulsion of electron pairs as far apart as possible dictates the shape observed for CH_4 and other molecules.

57. **C** The units moles per liter for each concentration are divided into the rate units mol $L^{-1}s^{-1}$ to obtain L^2 mol^{-2}s^{-1}.

58. **A** The rate law for a zero-order reaction is Rate = k, and the slope of the kinetic curve must be the same at all times. Consequently it is a straight line.

59. **B** Gas solubility is directly proportional to the partial pressure of the gas (Henry's law):

$$[\text{gas}] = kP_{\text{gas}}$$
$$\frac{[\text{gas}]}{2.8 \times 10^{-4}m} = \frac{k \,(200\text{mm Hg})}{k \,(340 \text{ mm Hg})}$$
$$[\text{gas}] = 2.8 \times 10^{-4} \text{ m} \left(\frac{200}{340}\right)$$
$$= 1.65 \times 10^{-4} \text{ m}$$

60. **B** Beta particles increase the atomic number when emitted. Elements with low atomic numbers emit beta particles when their masses are greater than the average mass in the periodic table. The result is to bring the proton/electron ratio closer to the stable ratio. ^{40}Cl has a mass greater than the 35.5 in the periodic table and is expected to emit a beta particle.

61. **E** The NaOH remains in solution after H_2 is produced.

62. **B** Percent composition measurements can be used to determine empirical formulas only, not molar mass.

63. **A** Only bromine forms the -1 ion required for the formula CaX_2.

64. **B** The polyatomic acetate ion must be memorized. CaF_2 is calcium fluoride, $AlCl_3$ is aluminum chloride, FeO is iron (II) oxide, and NO_2 is nitrogen dioxide.

65. **E** Sodium replaces hydrogen in water. This is also an oxidation-reduction reaction, not just an oxidation reaction.

66. **C** Carbon dioxide dissolves in water to form the weak electrolyte H_2CO_3. (a) and (d) are electrolytes while (b) and (e) are nonelectrolytes.

67. **B** $E^0_{cell} = E^0_{reduction} - E^0_{oxidation} = (+0.34) - (+0.15) V = +0.19 V$

68. **B** Chloride ions precipitate the silver ions in silver sulfate, and calcium ions precipitate with hydroxide ions from the barium hydroxide.

69. **D** All the others are colored transition metal compounds.

70. **C** In increasing order of strength, $H_2SeO_3 < H_2SO_3 < HClO_3$; also, $HClO_2 < HClO_3$, and $HBrO_3 < HClO_3$. In all comparisons $HClO_3$ is the strongest acid.

71. **C** Trigonal bipyramids have 90 degree axial and 120° equatorial angles.

72. **C** At a phase change

$$XG^0 = 0 = \Delta H^0 - T\Delta S^0$$

Therefore

$$\Delta S^0 = \frac{\Delta H^0}{T} = \frac{15,000 \text{ J}}{265.8 \text{ K}} = 56.4 \text{ J K}^{-1}$$

73. **B** A 2.00 molal solution contains 2.00 mol of solute and 1000 g H_2O = 55.5 mol H_2O.

$$X = \frac{2.00 \text{ mol NaCl}}{2.00 \text{ mol NaCl} + 55.5 \text{ mol } H_2O} = 0.0348$$

74. **A** Determine the limiting reagent:

$$? \text{ mL AgNO}_3 = 50.00 \text{ mL NaCl} \left(\frac{0.035 \text{ mol NaCl}}{\text{L NaCl}} \right) \left(\frac{1 \text{ mol AgNO}_3}{1 \text{ mol NaCl}} \right)$$

$$\times \left(\frac{1 \text{ L AgNO}_3}{0.100 \text{ mol AgNO}_3} \right)$$

$$= 17.5 \text{ mL AgNO}_3$$

Since we are given 25 mL $AgNO_3$, NaCl must be the limiting reactant.

$$? \text{ g AgCl} = 50.00 \text{ mL NaCl} \left(\frac{0.035 \text{ mol NaCl}}{\text{L NaCl}} \right) \left(\frac{1 \text{ mol AgCl}}{1 \text{ mol NaCl}} \right)$$

$$\times \left(\frac{143.3 \text{ g AgCl}}{1 \text{ mol AgCl}} \right)$$

$$= 250.8 \text{ mg AgCl (Note that the milli- units did not cancel and remain in the answer.)}$$

$$\text{Percentage yield} = \frac{\text{actual yield}}{\text{theoretical yield}} \times 100$$

$$= \frac{200 \text{ mg AgCl}}{250.8 \text{ mg AgCl}} \times 100$$

$$= 79.6\%$$

75. **E**

$$E_{cell} = E^0_{cell} - \frac{0.0591}{n} \log Q$$

$$Q = \frac{[Zn^{2+}]}{[Cu^{2+}]}$$

and $n = 2$.

$$E_{cell} = 1.10 \text{ V} - \frac{0.0591}{2} \log \left(\frac{0.0500 \text{ M}}{0.200 \text{ M}} \right) = 1.12 \text{ V}$$

Part A

Explained Answers
to Free-Response
Problems

1. (a) The reaction may be written as

$$\text{HAsp} + \text{OH}^- \longrightarrow \text{Asp}^- + \text{H}_2\text{O}$$

where HAsp is the abbreviation for the monoprotic aspirin.
Moles of aspirin titrated are

$$? \text{ mol HAsp} = 0.04531 \text{ L OH}^- \left(\frac{0.01225 \text{ mol OH}^-}{1 \text{ L OH}^-} \right) \left(\frac{1 \text{ mol HAsp}}{1 \text{ mol OH}^-} \right)$$
$$= 5.55 \times 10^{-4} \text{ mol HAsp}$$

Mass of aspirin titrated is

$$? \text{ g HAsp} = 50.0 \text{ mL HAsp} \left(\frac{0.500 \text{ g HAsp}}{250 \text{ mL HAsp}} \right) = 0.100 \text{ g HAsp}$$

Molar mass is mass calculated as

$$M = \frac{\text{mass of compound}}{\text{moles of compound}} = \frac{0.100 \text{ g HAsp}}{5.55 \times 10^{-4} \text{ mol HAsp}} = 180 \text{ g mol}^{-1}$$

(b) (1) The number of moles of aspirin in the sample titrated is

$$? \text{ mol HAsp} = 0.050 \text{ L HAsp} \left(\frac{0.500 \text{ g HAsp}}{0.250 \text{ L HAsp}} \right) \left(\frac{1 \text{ mol HAsp}}{180 \text{ g HAsp}} \right)$$
$$= 5.56 \times 10^{-4} \text{ mol HAsp}$$

The number of moles of salt at the end point is

$$? \text{ mol Asp}^- = 5.56 \times 10^{-4} \text{ mol HAsp} \left(\frac{1 \text{ mol Asp}^-}{1 \text{ mol HAsp}} \right)$$
$$= 5.56 \times 10^{-4} \text{ mol Asp}^-$$

The molarity of the salt is (the volume is the sum of the sample and titrant = 50.00 + 45.31 = 95.31 mL)

$$? \frac{\text{mol Asp}^-}{\text{L Asp}^-} = \frac{5.56 \times 10^{-4} \text{ mol Asp}^-}{0.09531 \text{ L Asp}^-} = 5.83 \times 10^{-3} \text{ M Asp}^-$$

The hydroxide ion concentration of a salt of a weak acid is

$$[\text{OH}^-] = \sqrt{\frac{K_w}{K_a} C_s}$$

The pOH at the end point is 14.00 − 7.37 = 6.63 and

$$[OH^-] = 2.34 \times 10^{-7} \text{ M OH}^-$$

(2) Rearranging the equation above gives

$$K_a = \frac{K_w C_s}{[OH^-]^2} = \frac{(1.0 \times 10^{-14})(5.83 \times 10^{-3})}{(2.34 \times 10^{-7})^2} = 1.06 \times 10^{-3}$$

(c) $$pK_a = -\log(1.06 \times 10^{-3}) = 2.97$$

A weak acid can be used to prepare buffers within ± 1 pH unit of its pK_a. The pH range of possible buffers is 1.97 to 3.97.

(d) The salt NaAsp will dissociate completely into Na^+ and Asp^- ions. The hydrolysis reaction is

$$Asp^- + H_2O \rightleftharpoons HAsp + OH^-$$

The K_a of a weak acid and the K_b of its salt (conjugate base) are related to each other by the equation

$$K_a K_b = K_w$$

For the hydrolysis reaction

$$K_b = \frac{K_w}{K_a} = \frac{1.0 \times 10^{-14}}{1.06 \times 10^{-3}} = 9.43 \times 10^{-12}$$

Part B

2. (a) Calculate the amount of hydrogen from the water, and subtract from 10.0-g sample to obtain the amount of carbon in the compound:

$$? \text{ g H} = 12.86 \text{ g } H_2O \left(\frac{1 \text{ mol } H_2O}{18 \text{ g } H_2O}\right)\left(\frac{2 \text{ mol H}}{1 \text{ mol } H_2O}\right)\left(\frac{1 \text{ g H}}{1 \text{ mol H}}\right)$$

$$= 1.429 \text{ g H}$$

$$\text{g C} = 10.000 \text{ g in sample } - 1.429 \text{ g H} = 8.571 \text{ g C}$$

Calculate the empirical formula as follows:

$$? \text{ mol H} = 1.429 \text{ g H} \left(\frac{1 \text{ mol H}}{1 \text{ g H}}\right) = 1.429 \text{ mol H}$$

$$? \text{ mol C} = 8.571 \text{ g C} \left(\frac{1 \text{ mol C}}{12 \text{ g C}}\right) = 0.714 \text{ mol C}$$

Dividing each by 0.714 gives one mole of C and 2 moles of H and the empirical formula CH_2.

(b) Calculate the grams of carbon in the CO_2, and subtract this amount from the total carbon. Use the remaining carbon to determine the grams of CO formed.

$$? \text{ g C} = 22.250 \text{ g } CO_2 \left(\frac{1 \text{ mol } CO_2}{44 \text{ g } CO_2}\right)\left(\frac{1 \text{ mol C}}{1 \text{ mol } CO_2}\right)$$

$$\left(\frac{12\ g\ C}{1\ mol\ C}\right) = 6.068\ g\ C$$

g C for CO = 8.571 g C total − 6.068 g C in CO_2 = 2.503 g C

$$?\ g\ CO = 2.503\ g\ C\left(\frac{1\ mol\ C}{12\ g\ C}\right)\left(\frac{1\ mol\ CO}{1\ mol\ C}\right)\left(\frac{28\ g\ CO}{1\ mol\ CO}\right)$$

= 5.840 g CO formed

(c) $$PV = nRT$$

Expanding the n term gives

$$PV = \frac{gRT}{molar\ mass}$$

$$molar\ mass = \frac{gRT}{PV} = \frac{(10.000\ g)(0.0821\ L\ atm\ mol^{-1}K^{-1})(298\ K)}{(0.873\ atm)(10.0\ L)}$$

$$= 28.02\ g\ mol^{-1}$$

(d) Mass of the empirical formula unit CH_2 is 14 g unit^{-1}. Then

$$\frac{28.02\ g\ mol^{-1}}{14\ g\ unit^{-1}} = 2\ formula\ units\ per\ mole$$

The molecular formula is C_2H_4.

3. (a) Cathode (reduction): $Cu^{2+}(aq) + 2e^- \longrightarrow Cu(s)$
Anode (oxidation): $2\ H_2O(\ell) \longrightarrow O_2(g) + 4\ H^+(aq) + 4\ e^-$

(b) $$mol\ Cu = \frac{It}{n\mathscr{F}} = \frac{(0.985\ A)(1.50\ h)(60\ min/h^{-1})(60\ s/min^{-1})}{(2)(96485\ C\ mol^{-1})}$$

= 0.0276 mol Cu

$$?\ g\ Cu = 0.0276\ mol\ Cu\left(\frac{63.55\ g\ Cu}{1\ mol\ Cu}\right) = 1.75\ g\ Cu$$

(c) $$?\ \frac{mol\ Cu(NO_3)_2}{L\ solution} = \frac{0.0276\ mol\ Cu}{0.250\ L\ solution}\left(\frac{1\ mol\ Cu(NO_3)_2}{1\ mol\ Cu}\right)$$

$$= 0.110\ M\ Cu(NO_3)_2$$

(d) $$E^0_{cell} = E^0_{reduction} - E^0_{oxidation} = (+0.34\ V) - (+1.23\ V) = -0.89\ V$$

A voltage of $+0.89$ V must be applied to the two electrodes to oppose the cell voltage. In actual practice a higher voltage is needed because the oxygen half-reaction has an overpotential that must be overcome before the reaction occurs.

Part C

4. The balanced equations are given below. As stated in the question, reactions need not be balanced to receive credit.
(a) $C_2H_3O_2(aq) + H_2O(\ell) \rightleftharpoons HC_2H_3O_2(aq) + OH^-(aq)$
(or) $CH_3COO^-(aq) + H_2O(\ell) \rightleftharpoons CH_3COOH(aq) + OH^-(aq)$
(b) $H_2SO_4(aq) + OH^-(aq) \longrightarrow HSO_4^-(aq) + H_2O(\ell)$
(c) $MnO_4^-(aq) + 5Fe^{2+}(aq) + 8H^+(aq) \longrightarrow$
$Mn^{2+} + 5Fe^{3+}(aq) + 4H_2O(aq)$
(d) $4P(s) + 5O_2(g) \longrightarrow 2P_2O_5(s)$

(e) $6CN^-(aq) + Fe^{3+}(aq) \longrightarrow Fe(CN)_6^{3-} (aq)$

(f) $3Cu(s) + 2NO_3^-(aq) + 8H^+(aq) \longrightarrow$
$3Cu^{2+}(aq) + 2NO(g) + 4H_2O(\ell)$

(g) $2H^+(aq) + CaCO_3(s) \longrightarrow Ca^{2+}(aq) + CO_2(g) + H_2O(\ell)$

(h) $Cl_2(aq) + 2I^-(aq) \longrightarrow 2Cl^-(aq) + I_2(aq)$ [or $I_2(s)$]

Part D

5. (a) The solubility of a gas is proportional to its partial pressure. Henry's law states that $[gas] = kP$. When the soda is uncapped the pressure rapidly decreases as does the solubility of CO_2. Also, the solubility of a gas decreases as the temperature increases; therefore more bubbles are formed in warm soda.

(b) $SO_2(g)$, a poisonous gas, might leak from the refrigeration system. The release of ammonia gas from concentrated ammonia reduces the amount of gaseous SO_2 when the reaction

$$NH_3(g) + SO_2(g) + H_2O(g) \longrightarrow NH_4SO_3(s)$$

occurs.

(c) Reactions depend on the interactions of individual molecules. Finely divided platinum has more surface area at which the molecules can react. A solid crystal of platinum has a relatively small surface area, and fewer molecules can react.

(d) The colligative properties of solutions result in increased boiling points and reduced melting points, and mixtures of solids display the same colligative behavior. Therefore a mixture of two solids generally has lower melting point than either of the pure solids. Such mixed melting points are used to confirm the identity of organic solids.

(e) All of the materials that balloons are made of have small pores. Graham's law of effusion applies to these pores. Helium, being lighter than the oxygen or nitrogen in air, will effuse faster than air. Therefore helium balloons deflate faster.

6. (a) When far apart, two molecules have a certain potential energy that is due to their structures, bonds, and interactions. The short horizontal line on the left represents this energy. As the molecules get closer, the collision begins and the molecules slow down. The kinetic energy is converted into potential energy, which is shown as the rising portion of the curve. During this rise the molecules are also deformed. At the peak, the velocities are at a minimum and the potential energy is at a maximum. When the molecules recoil from the collision, their velocities increase, converting potential energy back into kinetic energy, and the curve decreases as shown. When the molecules are once again far apart, the products have new potential energies that may be the same as, or more or less than, the potential energies of the reactants.

(b) The transition state is thought of as the geometry and energy of the molecules when they are approximately halfway between the reactants and products.

(c) The rate constant decreases as the activation energy increases. The forward reaction has a larger activation energy than the reverse reaction; consequently, the forward reaction should have a smaller rate constant than the reverse reaction.

(d) A catalyst provides an alternative pathway for the reaction that has a lower activation energy. The result is larger rate constants for both the forward and reverse reactions.

(e) The Arrhenius equation is

$$\text{Rate constant} = Ae^{-E_a/RT}$$

where E_a is the activation energy, A is a proportionality constant, R is the universal gas constant, and T is the Kelvin temperature. Increasing T in this equation decreases the numerical value of the exponential term. Since the exponential term also has a negative sign, an increase in temperature increases the rate constant.

An increase in temperature also increases the average kinetic energy of the molecules. Consequently, a greater fraction of all molecules will collide with an energy equal to or greater than the activation energy.

7. (a) The titration curve should have two equally spaced end points as shown in the titration curve below.

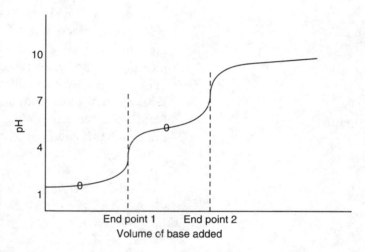

(b) The $NaHSO_3$-Na_2SO_3 buffer region would be between end point 1 and end point 2. The $pK_2 = 7.2$, and this buffer would be effective from 6.2 to 8.2.

(c) The pH just at the start of the titration (up to 10% of end point 1) and the pH of the second end point to the end will depend on the concentrations used. The rest of the curve is constant for reasonable concentrations (greater than 0.001 molar) of the reactants.

(d) The indicators chosen for the two end points should have pK_a values close to the end-point pH values. Such indicators will show distinct color changes if the pH changes rapidly by 2 pH units at the end point.

8. (a) The heating curve looks like this:

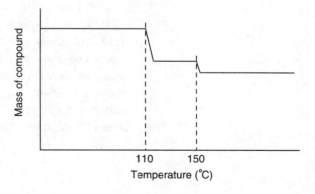

(b) To determine the number of water molecules of hydration, a weighed sample of hydrate is heated until the compound is anhydrous. The mass of the anhydrous compound is then measured, and the number of moles of anhydrous compound is determined from the mass. Moles of water are calculated from the loss in mass during the experiment. Dividing the moles of water by the moles of anhydrous compound results in a number equal to the moles of water of hydration per mole of compound.

(c) Water of hydration is an integral part of a chemical formula and of the physical structure of the crystal. A hydrate has definite physical and chemical properties that distinguish it as a true compound. Adsorbed water is a variable amount of water present in many substances; the amount depends on the vapor pressure of water in the surroundings. Adsorbed water can be removed from compounds by heating to just over 100°C. Water of hydration, however, often requires higher temperatures for its removal. Accurate experiments require that chemicals be free of adsorbed water before they are used.

(d) If the pentahydrate is used in aqueous solutions, the water in it will have no effect on the reaction itself. However, since the hydrate has a larger molar mass than the anhydrous compound, an adjustment must be made so that the correct number of moles of $CuSO_4$ are used. The ratio of the molar masses of the hydrate and the anhydrous compound is used as the factor label for this conversion. For example, if an experiment requires 10.0 g of $CuSO_4$ and the stockroom has only $CuSO_4 \cdot 5\,H_2O$, how many grams of the hydrate should be used?

$$? \text{ g } CuSO_4 \cdot 5\,H_2O = 10.0 \text{ g } CuSO_4 \left(\frac{1 \text{ mol } CuSO_4}{159.5 \text{ g } CuSO_4} \right)$$

$$\times \left(\frac{1 \text{ mol } CuSO_4 \cdot 5H_2O}{1 \text{ mol } CuSO_4} \right) \left(\frac{249.5 \text{ g } CuSO_4 \cdot 5H_2O}{1 \text{ mol } CuSO_4 \cdot 5H_2O} \right)$$

For a reaction that must have absolutely no water present, the hydrate cannot be substituted for the anhydrous compound.

9. (a) The formula shows an addition polymer. A condensation polymer would have an ester-type bond or a peptide-type bond in its structure. Also, the absence of nitrogen and oxygen means that this must be an addition polymer, although the presence of nitrogen or oxygen does not necessarily indicate a condensation polymer unless a peptide or ester bond is present.

(b) The monomer used to prepare this polymer is propylene, $CH_2{=}CHCH_3$.

(c) This polymer is not water soluble. The water-soluble polymers have polar side chains. They usually have groups that can hydrogen-bond with water. With only CH groups, this polymer has no polarity; all attractive forces are London forces. Because of the length of the polymer a large number of instantaneous dipoles can develop along the polymer chain. The sum of these forces makes this polymer a solid.

(d) Linear polymers fit together well and develop a large number of instantaneous dipoles. Branched polymers do not fit together well, and the London forces are fewer. Also, a linear polymer tends to be hard and rigid; a branched polymer is softer and more flexible. In addition, linear polymers have very high melting points and branched polymers have lower melting points.

Practice Examination 3

On the following pages is a complete practice examination. Try to duplicate actual test conditions. Follow the time limits, and answer all questions as directed. The periodic table found on page 36 may be used, along with the tables given with the examination, to answer the questions in Section II.

A scientific calculator is recommended for the examination. Calculators that can be programmed with chemical equations or symbols are not allowed. Calculators may not be shared between students, and calculators with communication capabilities are not allowed.

Practice Examination 3

Section I

Multiple Choice Questions

75 questions
90 minutes
45% of total grade

Part A

Directions: The multiple-choice questions in this part consist of a list of five lettered choices to be used in responding to the three or four questions that immediately follow. Be aware that a choice may be the appropriate response to more than one question. Select the best choice for each question. Enter your choice on the answer sheet on page 486.

Questions 1–3

(A) CH_4
(B) C_6H_6(benzene)
(C) CH_3CH_2COOH
(D) $CH_3CH_2OCH_2CH_3$
(E) $CH_2{=}CH_2$

1. Is the monomer used to make polyethylene

2. Is best described with resonance structures

3. Has the lowest boiling point of all the choices.

Questions 4–7

(A) Ideal gas law
(B) Law of conservation of matter
(C) Equilibrium law
(D) Rate law
(E) Hess's law

4. This law is fundamental to all stoichiometry calculations.

5. This law describes the order of a reaction.

6. This law may be used to determine molar masses.

7. This law can be used to predict the direction of a reaction.

Questions 8–10

(A) Na
(B) Li
(C) Si
(D) S
(E) Ar

8. Is the basis of semiconductor technology

9. Has several different allotropes

10. Has the lowest ionization energy

Questions 11–14

(A) VSEPR theory
(B) Kinetic molecular theory
(C) Transition-state theory
(D) Quantum theory
(E) Atomic theory

11. Theory used to describe reaction kinetics

12. Theory used to determine molecular goemetry

13. Theory that best explains paramagnetism

14. Theory that incorporates activation energy

GO ON TO THE NEXT PAGE ➤

Part B

15. The addition of a base to which of the following compounds will produce a gas?
    (A) $CaCO_3$
    (B) ZnS
    (C) NH_4Br
    (D) CH_3COOH
    (E) Mg

16. A gas that has a density of 3.79 grams per liter at STP may be
    (A) $CH_3CH_2CH_2CH_2CH_3$
    (B) $CH_3CH_2OCH_2CH_3$
    (C) NaCl
    (D) CH_2Cl_2
    (E) Cl_2

17. If covalent bond A is stronger than covalent bond B, then
    (A) the vibrational frequency of A is less than that of B
    (B) the length of A is generally less than that of B
    (C) the electronegativity difference in A is less than in B
    (D) A dissolves in water better than B
    (E) A absorbs light of longer wavelength than B

18. Which of the following is an integral part of collision theory?
    I. Collision frequency
    II. Collision energy
    III. Collision orientation
    (A) I only
    (B) I and II only
    (C) I and III only
    (D) II and III only
    (E) I, II, and III

19. A reaction has an equilibrium constant of 3.8×10^3. This constant will change if
    (A) a catalyst is added to the reaction
    (B) additional reactant is added
    (C) the temperature is changed
    (D) the pressure is decreased
    (E) a precipitate is formed

20. Below are K_b values for some weak bases. Which value would be suitable to prepare a buffer having a pH of 8.9?
    (A) 2.3×10^{-2}
    (B) 5.6×10^{-6}
    (C) 4.3×10^{-4}
    (D) 8.8×10^{-3}
    (E) 8.2×10^{-10}

21. Which of the following compounds is classified as an alcohol?
    (A) $CH_3CH_2CH_2COOH$
    (B) $CH_3CH=O$
    (C) $CH_3OCH_2CH_3$
    (D) $CH_3COCH_2CH_3$
    (E) $(CH_3)_2CHCH_2CH_2OH$

22. An allotrope of which nonmetallic element is electrically conductive?
    (A) sulfur
    (B) oxygen
    (C) carbon
    (D) hydrogen
    (E) chlorine

23. Water is an unusual compound in that it
    (A) forms networks of hydrogen bonds
    (B) has an unusually large difference between its melting and boiling points
    (C) dissolves a wide variety of other compounds
    (D) has a very high specific heat and heat of vaporization
    (E) has all of the above properties

GO ON TO THE NEXT PAGE ➤

24. The equilibrium law for the following reaction:

$$Na_2CO_3(s) + 2Hcl(g) \rightleftharpoons H_2O(\ell) + CO_2(g)$$

is

(A) $\dfrac{[HCl]^2}{[CO_2]}$ (B) $\dfrac{[Na_2CO_3][HCl]^2}{[H_2O][CO_2]}$

(C) $\dfrac{[CO_2]}{[H_2O]}$ (D) $\dfrac{[H_2O][CO_2]}{[Na_2CO_3][HCl]^2}$

(E) $\dfrac{[CO_2]}{[HCl]^2}$

25. The reaction

$$Cu + 2Ag^+ \rightarrow 2Ag + Cu^{2+}$$

is spontaneous. Therefore
(A) $\Delta G°$ for the reaction must be positive
(B) $E°$ for zinc must be positive
(C) $E°$ for silver must be positive
(D) $\Delta S°$ for the reaction must be positive
(E) K_{eq} must be greater than 1.00

26. When the following half-reaction:

$$C_2O_4^{2-} \longrightarrow CO_2$$

is balanced in acid solution with the smallest whole-number coefficients, it will have
(A) a coefficient of 2 for $C_2O_4^{2-}$
(B) $2e^-$ on the right side
(C) $4e^-$ on the left side
(D) $2H_2O$ on the right side
(E) $2H^+$ on the left side

27. When an element emits an alpha particle in a nuclear decay, the original element has its
(A) atomic number increased by 2 and its atomic mass increased by 4
(B) atomic number decreased by 1 and its atomic mass remains the same
(C) atomic mass decreased by 1 and its atomic number remains the same
(D) atomic mass decreased by 4 and its atomic number decreased by 2
(E) energy decreased because a gamma ray must also be emitted

28. What volume of carbon dioxide, at STP, is needed to precipitate all of the calcium ions in a 100-milliliter sample of 0.250 molar $Ca(No_3)_2$?
(A) 560 mL (B) 560 L (C) 280 mL
(D) 1.12 L (E) 280 L

29. The electromagnetic radiation with the longest wavelength is
(A) visible light
(B) ultraviolet light
(C) microwave radiation
(D) X rays
(E) infrared radiation

30. Which of the following is NOT commonly used as a catalyst?
(A) NaCl (B) Pt (C) Au (D) Enzymes (E) MnO_2

31. Given the following reactions with their equilibrium constants:

$$Cd^{2+} + 4\,CN^- \rightleftharpoons Cd(CN)_4^{2-} \quad K_f = 7.7 \times 10^{+16}$$
$$CdCO_3 \rightleftharpoons Cd^{2+} + CO_3^{2-} \quad K_{sp} = 1.8 \times 10^{-14}$$

$$\overline{CdCO_3 + 4\,CN^- \rightleftharpoons Cd(CN)_4^{2-} + CO_3^{2-}}$$

What is the equilibrium constant for the overall reaction?
(A) 1.4×10^3 (B) $9.5 \times 10^{+2}$
(C) 4.3×10^{30} (D) 2.3×10^{-31}
(E) $2.2 \times 10^{+6}$

32. Intermolecular forces are used to explain many physical properties of liquids and solids. A list of these forces in order from weakest to strongest is
(A) London forces, hydrogen bonds, dipole interactions
(B) hydrogen bonds, London forces, dipole interactions
(C) London forces, dipole interactions, hydrogen bonds
(D) dipole interactions, London forces, hydrogen bonds
(E) hydrogen bonds, dipole interactions, London forces

GO ON TO THE NEXT PAGE ➤

33. Which of the following reactions is expected to have the largest increase in entropy?
    (A) $2NO_2(g) \rightarrow N_2O_4(g)$
    (B) $KCl(aq) + AgNO_3(aq) \rightarrow$
        $AgCl(s) + KNO_3(aq)$
    (C) $MgCO_3(s) + 2HCl(aq) \rightarrow$
        $CO_2(g) + H_2O(\ell) + MgCl_2(aq)$
    (D) $C_2H_4(g) + 3O_2(g) \rightarrow$
        $2CO_2(g) + 2H_2O(g)$
    (E) $CuS(s) + O_2(g) \rightarrow Cu(s) + SO_2(g)$

34. Phosphoric acid dissociates in three steps with these equilibrium constants:

$$K_1 = 7.1 \times 10^{-3},$$

$$K_2 = 6.3 \times 10^{-8},$$

$$K_3 = 4.5 \times 10^{-13}$$

The pH of a 0.100 molar solution of K_2HPO_4 is
(A) 2.15   (B) 7.20   (C) 12.35
(D) 4.68   (E) 9.78

35. The activation energy for the reverse reaction in the following diagram is

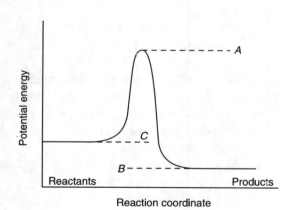

Reaction coordinate

(A) $C-A$ (B) $B-C$ (C) $C-B$
(D) A-B (E) $A-C$

36. The phase diagram below:

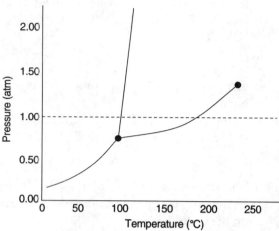

may be used to verify that
(A) An increase in temperature decreases the vapor pressure.
(B) An increase in pressure increases the boiling point.
(C) An increase in pressure has no effect on sublimation.
(D) The critical point can be determined from the ideal gas law.
(E) Raoult's law does not apply to this substance.

37. The following graph represents the disappearance of a reactant in a kinetics experiment. What is the initial rate of disappearance of this reactant?

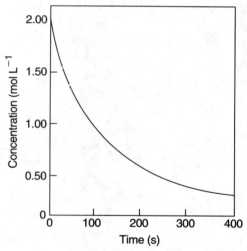

(A) 4×10^{-3} mol L^{-1} s^{-1} (B) 2.00 mol
(C) 45 mol L^{-1} s^{-1} (D) 0.022 mol L^{-1} s^{-1}
(E) 90s

GO ON TO THE NEXT PAGE ➤

38. Of the following compounds, the one expected to have the most ionic character is
   (A) Al_2O_3 (B) CCl_4 (C) N_2O
   (D) CaF_2 (E) H_2O

39. Which of the following contains nine sigma bonds and two pi bonds?
   (A) CCl_2F_2 (B) HCN   (C) HCHO
   (D) CH_3COOH (E) $CH_2CHCHCH_2$

40. The shape of a molecule with d^2sp^3 hybridization and two pairs of nonbonding electrons on the central atom is
   (A) octahedral
   (B) tetrahedral
   (C) square planar
   (D) trigonal bipyramid
   (E) trigonal planar

41. Which of the following represents an anode reaction?
   (A) $Al^{3+} + 3e^- \rightarrow Al(s)$
   (B) $Br_2 + 2e^- \rightarrow 2Br$
   (C) $2H^+ + 2e^- \rightarrow H_2(g)$
   (D) $2I^- \rightarrow I_2 + 2e^-$
   (E) $Zn^{2+} + 2e^- \rightarrow Zn(s)$

42. A cathode-ray (Crooke's) tube was used to determine
   (A) the e/m ratio of the proton
   (B) the charge of the electron
   (C) the existence of neutrons
   (D) the charge of the proton
   (E) the e/m ratio of the electron

43. A halogen, X, and an alkaline earth metal, M, will form a compound with the formula
   (A) MX   (B) MX_2 (C) MX_3
   (D) M_2X_3 (E) M_3X_2

44. The electronic configuration $1s^2\ 2s^22p^6\ 2s^23p^6$ represents all of the following EXCEPT
   (A) Ti^{4+} (B) Cr^{6+} (C) S^{2-} (D) V^{3+}
   (E) Ca^{2+}

45. The ideal gas law may be used to derive all of the following EXCEPT
   (A) Graham's law
   (B) Boyle's law
   (C) Charles's law
   (D) Avogadro's principle
   (E) Gay-Lussac's law

46. It takes 45.23 milliliters of 0.100 molar NaOH to titrate 552 milligrams of a solid monoprotic acid to the phenolphthalein end point. What is the molecular mass of the acid?
   (A) 221   (B) 122   (C) 68   (D) 1.2×10^5
   (E) 1.2×10^{-1}

47. The most polar of the following is
   (A) NH_4^+ (B) SO_4^{2-} (C) CF_4
   (D) CH_3CH_2OH (E) CH_3CH_2CHO

48. A salt that contains both ionic and covalent bonds is
   (A) KBr   (B) $HClO_4$ (C) Na_2SO_4
   (D) $AlCl_3$ (E) $CH_3CH_2CH_2CH_2Cl$

49. Which of the following has the highest pH?
   (A) The end point of a strong acid titrated with a strong base
   (B) The end point of a weak acid titrated with a strong base
   (C) The end point of a weak base titrated with a strong acid
   (D) The end point of a strong base titrated with a strong acid
   (E) The question does not provide enough information to arrive at an answer.

50. The net ionic equation for the precipitation of iron(II) nitrate with hydrogen sulfide gas is
   (A) $Fe^{2+}(aq) + S^{2-}(aq) \rightarrow FeS(s)$
   (B) $Fe(NO_3)_2(s) + H_2S(g) \rightarrow$
      $FeS(s) + 2HNO_3(aq)$
   (C) $2Fe^{3+}(aq) + 3S^{2-}(aq) \rightarrow Fe_2S_3(s)$
   (D) $H_2S(aq) + Fe^{2+}(aq) \rightarrow$
      $FeS(s) + 2H^+(aq)$
   (E) $H_2S(g) + Fe^{2+}(aq) \rightarrow$
      $FeS(s) + 2H^+(aq)$

GO ON TO THE NEXT PAGE ➤

51. Of the following, the strongest base is
    (A) NaClO   (B) NaClO$_3$ (C) NaBrO$_3$
    (D) KClO$_3$ (E) KClO$_4$

52. In aqueous solution, which of the following is
    an amphiprotic substance?
    (A) H$_2$O   (B) Cl$^-$ (C) NH$_4^+$
    (D) Cr$_2$O$_7^{2-}$ (E) CH$_3$CH$_2$COOH

53. Which of the following has three equivalent
    resonance structures?
    (A) H$_2$SO$_4$ (B) NO$_2^-$ (C) SO$_3$
    (D) HClO$_4$ (E) CO$_2$

54. A student prepares the following gases and
    collects them by displacement of water.
    Which compound will give the lowest per-
    centage yield?
    (A) H$_2$ (B) CO$_2$ (C) O$_2$ (D) NH$_3$
    (E) Cl$_2$

55. A radioactive isotope has a half-life of 4.5
    hours. What is the rate constant for this pro-
    cess?
    (A) 0.154 s^{-1} (B) 2.6 × 10^{-3} s^{-1}
    (C) 4.3 × 10^{-5} s^{-1} (D) 6.4 × 10^{-3} s^{-1}
    (E) None of these has the correct units.

56. Which of the following will NOT necessarily
    produce more product in a chemical reaction?
    (A) Increasing the temperature
    (B) Increasing the amount of reactants
    (C) Removing product as it is formed
    (D) Decreasing the volume of a reaction
        when Δn_g is negative
    (E) Increasing the volume of a reaction when
        Δn_g is positive

57. During a titration to determine the molarity of
    an unknown solution, a chemist has to look
    upward to read the initial volume of the stan-
    dard solution in the buret and look downward
    to read the final volume. The result of the ex-
    periment
    (A) will not be affected since the errors cancel
    (B) will be accurate within experimental error
    (C) will be low because the volume mea-
        sured is too high
    (D) will be low because the volume mea-
        sured is too low
    (E) will be high because the volume mea-
        sured is too low

58. All of the following are true about a boiling
    liquid EXCEPT
    (A) ΔG^0 must be zero
    (B) ΔS^0 must be positive
    (C) ΔH^0 must be positive
    (D) K_{eq} must be 1.00
    (E) ΔS^0 must equal ΔH^0

59. Which of the following will most probably
    dissolve in hexane, C$_6$H$_{12}$?
    (A) CH$_3$COOH   (B) H$_2$O
    (C) CH$_3$CH$_2$CH$_2$OH   (D) NaCl
    (E) C$_{12}$H$_{26}$

60. A 0.0250 molar solution of a weak base has a
    pH of 9.85. What is the pK_b of this weak base?
    (A) 4.15   (B) 7.1 × 10^{-5} (C) 2.0 × 10^{-7}
    (D) 6.70   (E) 7.30

61. What is the expected boiling point of a 2.50
    molal solution of Na$_2$SO$_4$? (The boiling point
    elevation constant for water is 0.52°C m^{-1}.)
    (A) 3.9°C   (B) 1.3°C   (C) 2.6°C
    (D) 103.9°C   (E) 96.1°C

62. ^{235}U has a half-life of 7.04 × 10^8 years and
    may be used to determine the length of time
    since rocks have solidified. For rocks of the
    following ages, which age can be determined
    most precisely?
    (A) Lava from Mount St. Helens, less than
        20 years old
    (B) Lava from the eruption of Mount Etna in
        700 BC.
    (C) Lava from lunar craters, 1.5 billion years
        old
    (D) Lava from Mount Vesuvius, 5 million
        years old
    (E) Lava from Mount Kenya, 20 million
        years old

63. The colored gas most closely associated with
    smog is
    (A) an oxide of sulfur
    (B) an oxide of hydrogen
    (C) a chloride of sulfur
    (D) a nitride of nitrogen
    (E) an oxide of nitrogen

GO ON TO THE NEXT PAGE ➤

64. The density of a solution must be known in order to convert between which concentration units?
    (A) Molality to mass percent
    (B) Mole fraction to molality
    (C) Molarity to mole fraction
    (D) Weight fraction to molality
    (E) Weight fraction to mole fraction

65. A compound has the empirical formula CH_2. Methane effuses through a small hole 2.65 times faster than this compound. What is the formula of the compound?
    (A) C_2H_4 (B) C_8H_8 (C) $C_{16}H_8$
    (D) C_8H_{16} (E) C_3H_6

66. Which of the following is correctly named?
    (A) CH_2CH_2 ethane
    (B) N_2O_5 nitrogen pentoxide
    (C) $FeCl_3$ iron trichloride
    (D) CH_3NH_2 methylamine
    (E) $SbCl_5$ antimony hexachloride

67. Dry ice, solid CO_2, is best described as
    (A) an ionic crystal
    (B) a molecular crystal
    (C) a covalent network crystal
    (D) a metallic crystal
    (E) a dipole crystal

68. The reaction

$$2NO_2(g) \rightleftharpoons N_2O_4(g)$$

has an equilibrium constant of 0.234 at a certain temperature. If 0.0200 mole of NO_2 and 0.0100 mole of N_2O_4 are placed in a 5.00-liter flask and allowed to come to equilibrium, the reaction that occurs
    (A) increases both the NO_2 and the N_2O_4 concentration
    (B) decreases both the NO_2 and the N_2O_4 concentration
    (C) increases the NO_2 and decreases the N_2O_4 concentrations
    (D) decreases the NO_2 and increases the N_2O_4 concentrations
    (E) changes no concentrations since the system is at equilibrium

69. The valence electron of potassium can have which of the following sets of quantum numbers?
    (A) $4, 1, 0, \frac{1}{2}$
    (B) $4, 0, 1, \frac{1}{2}$
    (C) $3, 1, 1, \frac{1}{2}$
    (D) $4, 0, 0, \frac{1}{2}$
    (E) $5, 0, 0, -\frac{1}{2}$

70. At 25°C, solvent A has a vapor pressure of 342 mm Hg and solvent B has a vapor pressure of 651 mm Hg. When mixed, A and B form an ideal solution with a vapor pressure of 445 mm Hg. The mole fraction of A in the mixture is
    (A) 0.667   (B) 0.333   (C) 0.769
    (D) 0.316   (E) 0.231

71. If 50.0 milliliters of a 0.0200 molar HCl solution is mixed with 35.0 milliliters of a 0.0180 molar NaOH solution, what is the pH of the mixture?
    (A) 2.36   (B) 0.43   (C) 2.06
    (D) 11.64   (E) 7.00

72. Barium chloride, $BaCl_2$ (molar mass = 208.2), is a hydrated salt. A 2.000-gram sample of the hydrate is heated in an oven until it does not lose additional mass. The anhydrous $BaCl_2$ has a mass of 1.708 grams. What is the formula of the hydrate?
    (A) $BaCl_2 \cdot H_2O$ (B) $BaCl_2 \cdot 2H_2O$
    (C) $BaCl_2 \cdot 3H_2O$ (D) $BaCl_2 \cdot 5H_2O$
    (E) $BaCl_2 \cdot 12H_2O$

73. The boiling points of the straight-chain aldehydes are measured, and these temperatures are plotted versus the numbers of carbon atoms in the aldehyde formulas. The graph will
    (A) have a generally negative slope equal to ΔH^0
    (B) have a generally positive slope because of increasing London forces
    (C) have a perfectly straight line if the experiments were done correctly
    (D) have a maximum at the average kinetic energy
    (E) have a straight horizontal line indicating that boiling points are constant

GO ON TO THE NEXT PAGE ➤

74. Computer disks, video tapes, and audio tapes all use the common chemical
    (A) Fe_2O_3
    (B) Teflon
    (C) SiO_2
    (D) diamond (C)
    (E) Al

75. Which of the following is not the correct formula for a complex ion?
    (A) $Fe(CN)_6^{3-}$ (B) $Cu(NH_4)_4^{2+}$
    (C) $Co(Cl)_6^{4-}$ (D) AIF_6^{3-} (E) $AgCl_2^-$

STOP

THIS IS THE END OF SECTION I
YOU MAY USE ANY REMAINING TIME TO CHECK YOUR WORK IN THIS SECTION.

Section II
Free-Response Problems

55% of total grade
90 minutes
Suggested time for Parts A, B, and C—50 minutes
Suggested time for Part D—40 minutes

This section consists of four parts, A (25 percent), B (25 percent), C (15 percent), and D (35 percent), weighted as shown. You should spend approximately 50 minutes on parts A, B, and C and 40 minutes on part D. It is your responsibility to budget the time wisely.

RESPONSES TO THE QUESTIONS IN THIS SECTION MUST CLEARLY SHOW YOUR METHODS AND THE STEPS USED TO ARRIVE AT THE ANSWER. Partial credit is earned by demonstrating an appropriate method developed from fundamental principles while little credit is earned for an answer obtained with no method shown. Appropriate use of significant figures is recommended. Data necessary for solving problems are given with the questions, or may be found in the tables below.

Useful Information for Solving Free-Response Problems

Universal gas constant	$R = 8.314$ J mol^{-1}K^{-1}
	0.0821 L atm mol^{-1}K^{-1}
	62.4 L mm Hg mol^{-1}K^{-1}
	8.314 V C mol^{-1}K^{-1}
Faraday	$1 \mathscr{F} = 96{,}485$ coulombs
	$96{,}485$ J V^{-1}
Electron volt	1 eV $= 96.5$ kJ mol^{-1}
Speed of light	$c = 2.998 \times 10^6$ m s^{-1}
Planck's constant	$h = 6.63 \times 10^{-34}$ J s
Boltzmann constant	$k = 1.38 \times 10^{-23}$ J K^{-1}
Avogadro's number	$N = 6.022 \times 10^{23}$ molecules mol^{-1}
At 25°C	$\dfrac{RT}{n\mathscr{F}} \ln Q = \dfrac{0.0591}{n} \log Q$

Vapor Pressure of Water as a Function of Temperature

Temperature degrees Celsius	Vapor Pressure mm Hg	Temperature degrees Celsius	Vapor Pressure mm Hg
− 10	2.1	26	25.2
0.0	4.6	28	28.3
5	6.5	30	31.8
10	9.2	35	41.2
12	10.5	40	55.3
14	12.0	50	92.5
16	13.6	60	149.4
18	15.5	70	233.7
20	17.5	80	355.1
22	19.8	90	525.8
24	22.4	100	760.0

GO ON TO THE NEXT PAGE ➤

Standard Reduction Potentials, 25°C

Half-Reaction	$E°$ (V)	Half-Reaction	$E°$ (V)
$F_2(g) + 2e^- \rightarrow 2F^-$	2.87	$Co^{2+} + 2e^- \rightarrow Co$	-0.28
$Co^{3+} + e^- \rightarrow Co^{2+}$	1.82	$Tl^+ + e^- \rightarrow Tl$	-0.34
$Au^{3+} + 3e^- \rightarrow Au$	1.50	$Cd^{2+} + 2e^- \rightarrow Cd$	-0.40
$Cl_2(g) + 2e^- \rightarrow 2Cl^-$	1.36	$Cr^{3+} + e^- \rightarrow Cr^{2+}$	-0.41
$O_2(g) + 4H^+ + 4e^- \rightarrow 2H_2O$	1.23	$Fe^{2+} + 2e^- \rightarrow Fe$	-0.44
$Br_2(g) + 2e^- \rightarrow 2Br^-$	1.07	$Cr^{3+} + 3e^- \rightarrow Cr$	-0.74
$2Hg^{2+} + 2e^- \rightarrow Hg_2^{2+}$	0.92	$Zn^{2+} + 2e^- \rightarrow Zn$	-0.76
$Ag^+ + e^- \rightarrow Ag$	0.80	$Mn^{2+} + 2e^- \rightarrow Mn$	-1.18
$Hg_2^{2+} + 2e^- \rightarrow Hg$	0.79	$Al^{3+} + 3e^- \rightarrow Al$	-1.66
$Fe^{3+} + e^- \rightarrow Fe^{2+}$	0.77	$Be^{2+} + 2e^- \rightarrow Be$	-1.70
$I_2 + 2e^- \rightarrow 2I^-$	0.53	$Mg^{2+} + 2e^- \rightarrow Mg$	-2.37
$Cu^+ + e^- \rightarrow Cu$	0.52	$Na^+ + e^- \rightarrow Na$	-2.71
$Cu^{2+} + 2e^- \rightarrow Cu$	0.34	$Ca^{2+} + 2e^- \rightarrow Ca$	-2.87
$Cu^{2+} + e^- \rightarrow Cu^+$	0.15	$Sr^{2+} + 2e^- \rightarrow Sr$	-2.89
$Sn^{4+} + 2e^- \rightarrow Sn^{2+}$	0.15	$Ba^{2+} + 2e^- \rightarrow Ba$	-2.90
$S + 2H^+ + 2e^- \rightarrow H_2S$	0.14	$Rb^+ + e^- \rightarrow Rb$	-2.92
$2H^+ + 2e^- \rightarrow H_2$	0.00	$K^+ + e^- \rightarrow K$	-2.92
$Pb^{2+} + 2e^- \rightarrow Pb$	-0.13	$Cs^+ + e^- \rightarrow Cs$	-2.92
$Sn^{2+} + 2e^- \rightarrow Sn$	-0.14	$Li^+ + e^- \rightarrow Li$	-3.05
$Ni^{2+} + 2e^- \rightarrow Ni$	-0.25		

Part A

90 minutes

(25% of Section II grade)

Directions: Solve all parts of the following problem:

---

1. The solubility of silver chromate, Ag_2CrO_4, is 0.0280 gram per liter at 25°C. The molar mass of silver chromate is 331.8.
   (a) Write the dissolution reaction for silver chromate and the equilibrium law for this reaction.
   (b) The equilibrium constant for the equilibrium law you wrote in part(a) is symbolized as K_{sp}. Determine the value of K_{sp}.
   (c) The K_{sp} for silver chloride, AgCl, is 1.0×10^{-10}. What is the minimum concentration of Na_2CrO_4 needed to form a precipitate of Ag_2CrO_4 in a saturated AgCl solution?

Part B
(25% of Section II grade)

Directions: Completely solve EITHER problem 2 or problem 3. Only the first problem answered will be graded. Be sure to indicate which problem you are answering.

2.

Substance	Standard Heat of Formation ΔH_f^0 (kJ mol^{-1})	Standard Entropy of Formation ΔS_f^0 (J mol^{-1} K^{-1})
$CO_2(g)$	-394	$+213.6$
$H_2O(g)$	-242	$+188.7$
$HCl(g)$	-92.5	186.7
$NaCl(s)$	-413	72.38
$Na_2CO_3(s)$	-1131	136

(a) Write a separate, balanced, formation reaction for each of the following: $Na_2CO_3(s)$, $HCl(g)$, $H_2O(g)$, $CO_2(g)$, and $NaCl(s)$.

(b) Calculate the standard enthalpy change, ΔH^0, for the reaction

$$Na_2CO_3(s) + 2HCl(g) \rightleftharpoons H_2O(g) + CO_2(g) + 2NaCl(s)$$

(c) Calculate the standard entropy change, ΔS^0, for the reaction given in part (B).

(d) Determine (1) the standard free energy change, ΔG^0, for the reaction given in part (B) and (2) the equilibrium constant at 100°C.

3. A galvanic cell is set up. Assume that an iron electrode dipping into a $Fe^{2+}(aq)$ solution is the anode and that a platinum electrode dipping into a solution containing $Co^{2+}(aq)$ and $Co^{3+}(aq)$ ions is the cathode.

(a) Write (1) the two balanced half-reactions and (2) the complete balanced chemical reaction that is being studied, using these assumptions.

(b) Show whether the complete reaction is spontaneous under standard conditions.

(c) What is the standard free-energy change, ΔG^0, for this reaction at 20°C?

(d) If the iron(II) concentration is 0.200 molar, what is the $\dfrac{[Co^{3+}]}{[Co^{2+}]}$ when the cell voltage is 2.00 volts in this galvanic cell?

Part C

(15% of Section II grade)

Directions: Answer FIVE of the eight choices in this part. If more than five are answered, only the first five will be scored.

---

4. Give the formulas for the reactants and products in FIVE of the following word equations. In all cases a chemical reaction occurs. Unless otherwise stated, the reaction occurs in aqueous solution. Substances that exist as ions in solution should be written in ionic form. Substances that do not enter into the chemical reaction should not be listed, and the reactions do not have to be balanced.

EXAMPLE: Magnesium metal is added to a dilute solution of hydrochloric acid

$$\text{Formula: } Mg + H^+ \longrightarrow Mg^{2+} + H_2$$

(a) Ethyl alcohol and acetic acid are heated with acid.
(b) Hydrochloric acid is added to iron(III) sulfide.
(c) Magnesium metal is ignited in a carbon dioxide atmosphere.
(d) Ammonia gas and hydrogen chloride gas are mixed.
(e) Dilute sulfuric acid is added to a solution of barium nitrate.
(f) Two moles of sodium hydroxide are added to 1 mole of phosphoric acid in aqueous solution.
(g) Sodium chloride is added to lead(II) nitrate.
(h) Barium hydroxide is added to ammonium chloride in aqueous solution.

Part D

(35% of Section II grade)

> *Directions:* Select THREE of the following five problems. (If more than three are answered, only the first three will be graded.)

Use about 40 minutes for this part of the examination. Answers to these questions should demonstrate your ability to present logical, coherent, and convincing explanations of chemical facts and observations. Answers are judged on the accuracy of your analysis and on the appropriateness of the details and examples cited. Specific answers and examples are preferred to broad generalizations. Diagrams, illustrations, and equations may be included in your answers.

5. Le Châtelier's principle is central to many qualitative and quantitative aspects of chemical equilibrium. Use the following equation:

$$N_2(g) + 3H_2(g) \rightleftharpoons 2NH_3(g) \qquad \Delta H^0 = -46.0 \text{ kJ mol}^{-1}$$

   to answer the questions.
   (a) Briefly but completely summarize Le Châtelier's principle.
   (b) What changes in concentration will increase the amount of NH_3 produced?
   (c) What changes in pressure will NOT increase the amount of NH_3 produced?
   (d) How should the temperature be changed to increase the amount of NH_3 produced?
   (e) Will a catalyst increase the amount of NH_3 produced?
   (f) What will happen if liquid water is present in the reaction system?

6. There exist several diagonal relationships in the periodic table.
   (a) What are they, and why do they exist?
   (b) Describe the group and period relationships in the periodic table.

7. On paper many different chemical reactions may be written. What actually happens in the laboratory depends on whether or not the reaction is spontaneous.
   (a) Define a spontaneous reaction.
   (b) A particular reaction is not spontaneous according to the correct definition for part (a). Nevertheless, some product does form. How do chemists explain this phenomenon?
   (c) Suggest several ways in which a nonspontaneous reaction may be forced to occur.

8. Use the principles of bonding and intermolecular forces to describe each of the following:
   (a) the difference between real and ideal gases
   (b) the experimental evidence for hydrogen bonding
   (c) the reaction between Cu^{2+} and NH_3
   (d) the reason why NO_2 forms dimers and CO_2 does not.
   (e) the reason why NaCl dissolves in water and AgCl does not.

9. $\qquad$ CH_4 $\qquad$ SF_6 $\qquad$ PCl_5

(a) Draw the Lewis structure of each of the three compounds above.

(b) (1) What is the octet rule, and (2) when can it be disobeyed?

(c) Determine the geometric shape of each of the structures shown above, and give bond angles if possible.

(d) Determine the hybridization, if any, of the central atom in each molecule.

(e) Why can SF_6 exist when the corresponding OF_6 does not?

STOP

THIS IS THE END OF SECTION II
YOU MAY USE ANY REMAINING TIME TO CHECK YOUR WORK IN THIS SECTION.

ANSWER KEY FOR MULTIPLE-CHOICE QUESTIONS

1. **E**	16. **D**	31. **A**	46. **B**	61. **D**
2. **B**	17. **B**	32. **C**	47. **D**	62. **C**
3. **A**	18. **E**	33. **C**	48. **C**	63. **E**
4. **B**	19. **C**	34. **E**	49. **B**	64. **C**
5. **D**	20. **B**	35. **D**	50. **E**	65. **D**
6. **A**	21. **E**	36. **B**	51. **A**	66. **D**
7. **C**	22. **C**	37. **D**	52. **A**	67. **B**
8. **C**	23. **E**	38. **D**	53. **C**	68. **C**
9. **D**	24. **E**	39. **E**	54. **D**	69. **D**
10. **A**	25. **E**	40. **C**	55. **C**	70. **A**
11. **C**	26. **B**	41. **D**	56. **A**	71. **A**
12. **A**	27. **D**	42. **E**	57. **D**	72. **B**
13. **D**	28. **A**	43. **B**	58. **E**	73. **B**
14. **C**	29. **C**	44. **D**	59. **E**	74. **A**
15. **C**	30. **A**	45. **A**	60. **D**	75. **B**

Explained Answers to Multiple-Choice Questions

1. **E** ethylene has the double bond needed for an addition reaction.
2. **B** Benzene has three conjugated double bonds and two resonance structures. Choice C, acidic acid, has a resonance structure only when ionized.
3. **A** Methane is the smallest and a totally nonpolar molecule.
4. **B** The law of conservation of matter is never violated in any calculation.
5. **D** The exponents in the rate law determine the order of reaction.
6. **A** A measured gas density can be converted into the molar mass by using the ideal gas law.
7. **C** Determining Q, the reaction quotient, and comparing that value to the equilibrium constant makes it possible to predict the reaction direction.
8. **C** Transistors and integrated circuits depend on the semiconductor properties of silicon.
9. **D** Sulfur can be easily transformed from one allotrope to another by heating.
10. **A** Sodium is closest to the lower left corner of the periodic table, where ionization energies are low.
11. **C** The transition-state theory describes energy and structural changes during collisions. Choice B describes gas behavior.
12. **A** According to the VSEPR theory, molecular shapes are defined by electron pair repulsion to keep electron pairs and atoms bonded to a central atom as far apart as possible.
13. **D** In particular Hund's rule for orbital filling requires each sublevel to fill with one unpaired electron before any electron can be paired in a sublevel. Choice E was developed before electrons were discovered.
14. **C** According to the transition-state theory, activation energy is the minimum energy needed to progress from reactants to products.
15. **C** Ammonia gas is produced when a base is added to NH_4Br.
16. **D** The molar mass is calculated:

$$? \frac{g}{mol} = \left(\frac{3.79\ g}{L} \right) \left(\frac{22.4\ L}{mol} \right) = 85\ g\ mol^{-1}$$

This is the molar mass of dichloromethane, CH_2Cl_2.
17. **B** Stronger bonds have shorter lengths.

18. **E** The frequency of effective collisions (I) is the product of the collision rate, the fraction of collisions with sufficient energy (II), and the fraction of collisions with the correct orientation (III).

19. **C** Temperature changes are the *only* changes that affect the equilibrium constant.

20. **B** The pK_b must be within ± 1 of the pOH of the desired buffer. The pOH is 5.1 and -log $(5.6 \times 10^{-6}) = 5.3$.

21. **E** $(CH_3)_2CHCH_2CH_2OH$, has the —OH functional group, which is characteristic of an alcohol.

22. **C** The electrically conductive allotrope of carbon is graphite.

23. **E** No other solvent has all of these properties.

24. **E** Solids and pure liquids do not appear in the equilibrium laws and the product appears in the numerator.

25. **E** A value of K_{eq} that is greater than 1 indicates that more product than reactant is present at equilibrium.

26. **B** The balanced half-reaction is as follows:

$$C_2O_4^{2-} \rightarrow 2CO_2 + 2e^-$$

27. **D** An alpha particle is $_2^4He$ resulting in a mass decrease of 4 and an atomic number decrease of 2.

28. **A** The chemical reaction is

$$CO_2(g) + H_2O(\ell) + Ca^{2+}(aq) \rightarrow CaCO_3(s) + 2H^+(aq)$$

The calculation is as follows:

? L CO_2 = 0.100 L $Ca(NO_3)_2$

$$\times \left(\frac{0.250 \text{ mol Ca(NO}_3)_2}{1 \text{ L Ca(NO}_3)_2} \right) \left(\frac{1 \text{ mol CO}_2}{1 \text{ mol Ca(NO}_3)_2} \right)$$

$$\times \left(\frac{22.4 \text{ L CO}_2}{1 \text{ mol CO}_2} \right)$$

$$= 0.560 \text{ L CO}_2 = 560 \text{ mL CO}_2$$

29. **C** Of the types of light given as choices, microwaves have the lowest energy and the longest wavelength.

30. **A** Platinum and gold catalyze gas-phase reactions, enzymes catalyze biological reactions, and MnO_2 catalyzes the decomposition of $KClO_3$ and H_2O_2.

31. **A** When reactions are added, their equilibrium constants are multiplied. $K_f \times K_{sp} = (7.7 \times 10^{16})(1.8 \times 10^{-14}) = 1.4 \times 10^3$

32. **C** London forces are the weakest and hydrogen bonds are the strongest.

33. **C** Reaction C has the largest increase in gas molecules, Δn_g, and the largest entropy increase.

34. **E** An amphiprotic salt has a pH that is the average of its pK_2 and pK_3. The concentration of the salt is not important.
$$pH = \frac{(-\log K_2) + (-\log K_3)}{2} = \frac{7.20 + 12.35}{2} = 9.78$$

35. **D** A−B is the height of the energy barrier when moving from right to left in the diagram.

36. **B** As pressure increases, the intersection with the gas-liquid equilibrium line moves to higher temperatures.

37. **D** A tangent drawn to the start of the reaction intersects the x-axis at approximately 90 seconds. The rate is
$$\frac{-2.00 \text{ mol L}^{-1}}{90\text{s}} = 0.022 \text{ mol L}^{-1}\text{s}^{-1}.$$
The rate is always listed as a positive number.

38. **D** The two elements, calcium and fluorine, in CaF_2 have the largest difference in electronegativity as estimated by their separation in the periodic table.

39. **E** This is 1,3-butadiene $CH_2\!\!=\!\!CHCH\!\!=\!\!CH_2$. There are six sigma C-H bonds and three sigma C-C bonds. Each double bond contains one pi bond for a total of two.

40. **C** In a square planar molecule the two nonbonding pairs of electrons are located on opposite sides of the central atom.

41. **D** Oxidation, the loss of electrons, occurs at all anodes. Half reaction (d) is the only oxidation half reaction.

42. **E** The effects of electric and magnetic fields as shown with a cathode-ray tube were used to determine the e/m ratio of the electron.

43. **B** Alkaline earth metals always form $+2$ ions, as in MX_2.

44. **D** Vanadium must be V^{5+} to have the $1s^2\,2s^22p^6\,3s^23p^6$ electronic configuration.

45. **A** Graham's law is derived from the kinetic molecular theory.

46. **B** In this calculation we start with the equivalence of the volume of NaOH and the mass of the unknown acid to write
$$? \frac{g}{mol} = \left(\frac{0.552 \text{ g acid}}{0.04523 \text{ L NaOH}}\right)\left(\frac{1 \text{ L NaOH}}{0.100 \text{ mol NaOH}}\right)\left(\frac{1 \text{ mol NaOH}}{1 \text{ mol acid}}\right)$$
$$= 122 \text{ g acid mol}^{-1}$$

47. **D** Ethyl alcohol, CH_3CH_2OH, forms hydrogen bonds because of the polarity of the —OH functional group.

48. **C** Oxygen and sulfur in the sulfate ion, Na_2SO_4, are covalently bonded in a polyatomic anion. The sodium ions and the sulfate ion form ionic bonds.

49. **B** The salt at the end point of a weak acid-strong base titration is the strongest base of the choices given because the acid is the weakest. The strongest base present at the end point will have the highest pH.

50. **E** The equation must represent the conditions given in the problem, and the only other equation that has H_2S as a gas, also has the soluble $Fe(NO_3)_2$ written as if it is insoluble.

51. **A** The strongest base will be obtained from the weakest acid. Replacing the cations with hydrogens allows us to determine the acid strength (HClO is the weakest) and correspondingly the base strength of KClO is the greatest.

52. **A** Water is the only substance that can accept and donate protons.

53. **C** SO_3 has three resonance structures, NO_2^- has two, and the others have only one.

54. **D** Ammonia is very soluble in water and very little, if any, gas will be collected resulting in a very low percentage yield.

55. **C** The equation is

$$\ln 2 = kt$$

Converting 4.5 h to 1.62×10^4 s and calculating k results in

$$k = \frac{\ln 2}{1.62 \times 10^4 \text{ s}} = 4.3 \times 10^{-5} \text{ s}^{-1}$$

56. **A** The effect of increasing temperature depends on whether the reaction is endothermic (products increase) or exothermic (products decrease).

57. **D** Looking upward results in too large a volume; looking downward results in too small a volume. The net result is a total volume smaller than was actually used and therefore a low molarity of the unknown.

58. **E** $T \Delta S^0 = \Delta H^0$, not $\Delta S^0 = \Delta H^0$ for a liquid at its boiling point.

59. **E** $C_{12}H_{26}$ is the least polar compound. NaCl is ionic (very polar) and the others contain oxygen and one polar.

60. **D** For a weak base,

$$[OH^-] = \sqrt{k_b C_b}$$

The pOH $= 14.00 - 9.85 = 4.15$. Then

$$[OH^-] = 7.1 \times 10^{-5}$$

Solving the equation yields

$$K_b = \frac{[OH^-]^2}{C_b} = \frac{5.0 \times 10^{-9}}{0.0250} = 2.0 \times 10^{-7}$$

$$pK_b = -\log(2.0 \times 10^{-7}) = 6.70$$

61. **D** Na_2SO_4 forms three ions, and the molality of all the ions is 7.50 m.

$$\Delta T = mk_b = 7.50 \text{ m}(0.52°C \text{ m}^{-1}) = 3.9°C$$

The boiling point is $100°C + 3.9°C = 103.9°C$.

62. **C** The most accurate data are obtained when the age to be dated (here, 1.5 billion years) is closest to the half-life of the isotope (here, 7.04×10^8 years).

63. **E** Nitrogen oxides, along with hydrocarbons, are a major cause of photo-chemical smog.

64. **C** Knowing the density of a solution enables the chemist to make the essential conversion from volume of solution to mass units in the denominator of these concentration units.

65. **D** Graham's law is

$$\sqrt{\frac{m_1}{m_2}} = \frac{V_2}{V_1} \quad \text{or} \quad \frac{m_1}{m_2} = \left(\frac{V_2}{V_1}\right)^2$$

The mass of the compound is

$$m_1 = m_2 \left(\frac{V_2}{V_1}\right)^2 = (16 \text{ g mol}^{-1})(2.65)^2 = 112 \text{ g mol}^{-1}$$

The number of CH_2 units in the molecule is

$$\frac{112 \text{ g/mol}}{14 \text{ g/CH}_2 \text{ unit}} = 8 \text{ CH}_2 \text{ units per mole}$$

The formula of the compound is C_8H_{16}.

66. **D** CH_3NH_2 is methylamine. Choice A is ethylene, B is dinitrogen pentoxide, C is iron(III) chloride or ferric chloride, E is antimony(V) chloride or antimony pentachloride. (Antimony is a metalloid and may be named as a metal or nonmetal.)

67. **B** Solid CO_2 is an array of molecules held together by London forces.

68. **C** The reaction quotient is

$$Q = \frac{[N_2O_4]}{[NO_2]^2} = \frac{0.002}{(0.004)^2} = 125$$

0Since $Q > K_{eq}$, the reaction proceeds in the reverse direction, increasing the NO_2 and decreasing the N_2O_4 concentrations.

69. **D** The valence electron of potassium is $4s^1$. Therefore n must be 4, ℓ for an s orbital is 0, m_ℓ then must be 0, and m_s can be either $+\frac{1}{2}$ or $-\frac{1}{2}$.

70. **A** $$P_{total} = X_A p_A + X_B p_B.$$

Substitute $(1 - X_A)$ for X_B, and solve for X_A.

$$445 = X_A(342 \text{ mm Hg}) + (1 - X_A)(651 \text{ mm Hg})$$

$$X_A = 0.667$$

71. **A** $$0.050 \text{ L HCl}) \left(\frac{0.0200 \text{ mol HCL}}{1 \text{ L HCl}}\right) = 0.00100 \text{ mol HCl}$$

$$0.035 \text{ L NaOH} \left(\frac{0.0180 \text{ mol NaOH}}{1 \text{ L NaOH}}\right) = 0.00063 \text{ mol NaOH}$$

Since 1 mol of HCl reacts with 1 mol NaOH, we conclude that the total volume of the mixture is $50 + 35 = 85$ mL or 0.085L. Then NaOH is the limiting reactant, and 0.00037 mol HCl is left over.

$$M_{HCl} = \frac{0.00037 \text{ mol HCl}}{0.085 \text{ L HCl}} = 4.35 \times 10^{-3} \text{ M}$$

The pH = 2.36.

72. **B** $$? \text{ moles BaCl}_2 = 1.708 \text{ g BaCl}_2 \left(\frac{1 \text{ mol BaCl}_2}{208.2 \text{ g BaCl}_2}\right)$$
$$= 8.20 \times 10^{-3} \text{ mol BaCl}_2$$

$$? \text{ moles H}_2\text{O} = (2.000 \text{ g} - 1.708 \text{ g}) \text{ H}_2\text{O} \left(\frac{1 \text{ mol H}_2\text{O}}{18 \text{ g H}_2\text{O}}\right)$$
$$= 1.62 \times 10^{-2} \text{ mol H}_2\text{O}$$

$$? \frac{\text{mol H}_2\text{O}}{\text{mol BaCl}_2} = \frac{1.62 \times 10^{-2} \text{ mol H}_2\text{O}}{8.20 \times 10^{-3} \text{ mol BaCl}_2}$$
$$= 2 \text{ mol H}_2\text{O/mol BaCl}_2$$

The formula of the hydrate is $BaCl_2 \cdot 2 H_2O$.

73. **B** In a homologous series, the boiling points are expected to increase as the molecule becomes larger. Response C is incorrect since a straight line may not fit the data perfectly.

74. **A** Very pure iron(III) oxide is the magnetic medium used in these recording devices.

75. **B** The formula $Cu(NH_4)_4^{2+}$ makes no sense. The charges do not add up, and the ammonium ion cannot be a ligand.

Part A

Explained Answers to Free-Response Problems

1. (a)

$$Ag_2CrO_4(s) \rightleftharpoons 2Ag^+(aq) + CrO_4^{2-}(aq)$$
$$K_{sp} = [Ag^+]^2[CrO_4^{2-}]$$

(b) $? \text{ mol } Ag_2CrO_4 = 0.0280 \text{ g } Ag_2CrO_4 \left(\dfrac{1 \text{ mol } Ag_2CrO_4}{331.8 \text{ g } Ag_2CrO_4} \right)$

$= 8.44 \times 10^{-5} \text{ mol } Ag_2CrO_4$

The molarity is 8.44×10^{-5} M Ag_2CrO_4 since the silver chromate is dissolved in 1 liter of solution.

REACTION	$Ag_2CrO_4(s)$	$\rightleftharpoons$	$2 Ag^+(aq)$	$+$	CrO_4^{2-} (aq)
INIT CONC.	Solid		O		
CHANGE	-x		+ 2x		+ x
EQUILIBRIUM	Solid		2x		x
ANSWER			1.69×10^{-4}		8.44×10^{-5}

Using the numbers on the ANSWER line we calculate the K_{sp} as

$$K_{sp} = (1.69 \times 10^{-4})^2(8.44 \times 10^{-5}) = 2.41 \times 10^{-12}$$

(c)

$$AgCl(s) \rightleftharpoons Ag^+(aq) + Cl^-(aq)$$
$$K_{sp} = [Ag^+][Cl^-] = 1.0 \times 10^{-10}$$

REACTION	AgCl(s)	$\rightleftharpoons$	$Ag^+(aq)$	$+$	$Cl^-(aq)$
INIT CONC.	Solid		OM		OM
CHANGE	$-x$	$+x$			$+x$
EQUILIBRIUM	Solid		x		x
ANSWER					

Substituting the expressions from the EQUILIBRIUM line into the equilibrium law gives

$$1.0 \times 10^{-10} = (x)(x)$$

$$x = \sqrt{1.0 \times 10^{-10}} = 1.0 \times 10^{-5} = [Ag^+] = [Cl^-]$$

The equilibrium table for silver chromate becomes as follows:

REACTION	$Ag_2CrO_4(s)$	$\rightleftharpoons$	$2\ Ag^+(aq)$	+	$CrO_4^{2-}(aq)$
INIT CONC.	Solid		1.0×10^{-5}		
CHANGE	$-x$		$+2x$		$+x$
EQUILIBRIUM	Solid		$2x + 1.0 \times 10^{-5}$		x
ANSWER					

Substituting the terms on the EQUILIBRIUM line into the equilibrium law for silver chromate gives

$$2.41 \times 10^{-12} = (2x + 1.0 \times 10^{-5})^2(x)$$

At this point assume that $2x + 1.0 \times 10^{-5} = 1.0 \times 10^{-5}$ and substitute this value into the above equation:

$$2.41 \times 10^{-12} = (1.0 \times 10^{-5})^2(x)$$
$$x = 2.41 \times 10^{-2}$$

The table shows that x is the concentration of chromate ions, so

$$? \frac{mol\ Na_2CrO_4}{L\ solution} = \frac{0.0241\ mol\ CrO_4^{2-}}{L\ solution} \left(\frac{1\ mol\ Na_2CrO_4}{1\ mol\ CrO_4^{2-}} \right)$$
$$= 0.0241\ M\ Na_2CrO_4$$

Part B   2. (a)

$$2Na(s) + C(s) + 1.5\ O_2(g) \longrightarrow Na_2CO_3(s)$$
$$0.5\ H_2(g) + 0.5\ Cl_2(g) \longrightarrow HCl(g)$$
$$H_2(g) + 0.5\ O_2(g) \longrightarrow H_2O(g)$$
$$C(s) + O_2(g) \longrightarrow CO_2(g)$$
$$Na(s) + 0.5\ Cl_2(g) \longrightarrow NaCl(s)$$

(In formation reactions fractional coefficients are allowed and only one mole of product is formed.)

(b) The standard enthalpy of this reaction is the sum of the enthalpies of the products minus the sum of the enthalpies of the reactants.

$$\Delta H^0_{reaction} = [(1 \text{ mol} \times -242 \text{ kJ mol}^{-1}) + (1 \text{ mol} \times -394 \text{ kJ mol}^{-1})$$
$$+ (2 \text{ mol} \times -413 \text{ kJ mol}^{-1})]$$
$$- [(1 \text{ mol} \times -1131 \text{ kJ mol}^{-1}) + (2 \text{ mol} \times -92.5 \text{ kJ mol}^{-1})]$$
$$= -1462 \text{ kJ} - (-1316 \text{ kJ}) = -146 \text{ kJ}$$

(c)
$$\Delta S^0_{reaction} = [(1 \text{ mol} \times 188.7 \text{ J mol}^{-1} \text{ K}^{-1})$$
$$+ (1 \text{ mol} \times 213.6 \text{ J mol}^{-1} \text{ K}^{-1})$$
$$+ (2 \text{ mol} \times 72.38 \text{ J mol}^{-1} \text{ K}^{-1})]$$
$$- [(1 \text{ mol} \times 136 \text{ J mol}^{-1} \text{ K}^{-1})$$
$$+ (2 \text{ mol} \times 186.7 \text{ J mol}^{-1} \text{ K}^{-1})]$$
$$= 547.1 \text{ J K}^{-1} - 509.4 \text{ J K}^{-1} = 37.7 \text{ J K}^{-1}$$

(d) (1)
$$\Delta G^0 = \Delta H^0 \qquad - T \Delta S^0$$
$$= -146 \text{ kJ} \quad - (373 \text{ K})(37.7 \text{ J K}^{-1})$$
$$= -146,000 \text{ J} - 14,062 \text{ J} = -160,062 \text{ J}$$
$$= -160 \text{ kJ}$$

(2)
$$\Delta G^0 = -RT \ln K_{eq.}$$

$$\ln K_{eq} = \frac{-(-160000 \text{ J})}{(8.314 \text{ J mol}^{-1} \text{K}^{-1})(373 \text{ K})} = 51.59$$

$$K_{eq} = 2.5 \times 10^{22}$$

3. (a) (1) Anode (oxidation): $Fe \rightarrow Fe^{2+} + 2 e^-$
Cathode (reduction): $Co^{3+} + e^- \rightarrow Co^{2+}$
(2) $Fe + 2 Co^{3+} \rightarrow Fe^{2+} + 2 Co^{2+}$

(b)
$$E^0_{cell} = E^0_{reduction} \quad E^0_{oxidation}$$
$$= +1.82 \text{ V} - (-0.44 \text{ V}) = +2.26 \text{ V}$$

The positive voltage indicates that this reaction is spontaneous at standard state.

(c)
$$\Delta G^0 = -n \mathscr{F} E^0_{cell}$$
$$= -2(96,485)(2.26) = -436 \text{ kJ}$$

(d)
$$E_{cell} = E^0_{cell} - \frac{0.0591}{n} \log Q$$

$$2.00 = 2.26 - \frac{0.0591}{n} \log \left(\frac{[Fe^{2+}][Co^{2+}]^2}{[Co^{3+}]^2} \right)$$

$$-0.26 = -\frac{0.0591}{2} \log \left(\frac{(0.200)[Co^{2+}]^2}{[Co^{3+}]^2} \right)$$

$$8.80 = \log \left(\frac{(0.200)[Co^{2+}]^2}{[Co^{3+}]^2} \right)$$

$$6.31 \times 10^8 = \frac{(0.200)[Co^{2+}]^2}{[Co^{3+}]^2}$$

$$3.15 \times 10^9 = \frac{[Co^{2+}]^2}{[Co^{3+}]^2}$$

$$5.62 \times 10^4 = \frac{[Co^{2+}]}{[Co^{3+}]}$$

$$1.78 \times 10^{-5} = \frac{[Co^{3+}]}{[Co^{2+}]}$$

Part C

4. The balanced reactions are given below. As stated in the question, reactions need not be balanced to receive credit.

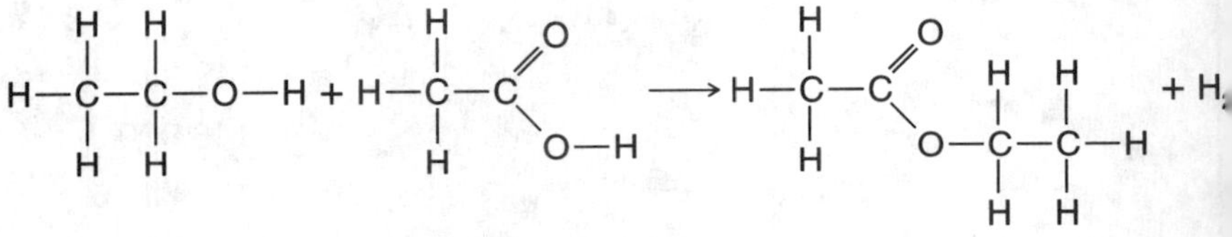

(b) $6H^+(aq) + Fe_2S_3(s) \rightarrow 2Fe^{3+}(aq) + 3H_2S(g)$
(c) $2Mg(s) + CO_2(g) \rightarrow 2MgO(s) + C(s)$
(d) $NH_3(g) + HCl(g) \rightarrow NH_4Cl(s)$
(e) $SO_4^{2-}(aq) + Ba^{2+}(aq) \rightarrow BaSO_4(s)$
(f) $2OH^-(aq) + H_3PO_4(aq) \rightarrow HPO_4^{2-}(aq) + 2H_2O(\ell)$
(g) $2Cl^-(aq) + Pb^{2+}(aq) \rightarrow PbCl_2(s)$
(h) $OH^-(aq) + NH_4^+(aq) \rightarrow NH_3(aq) + H_2O(\ell)$

or

$$\rightarrow NH_3(g) + H_2O(\ell)$$

Part D

5. (a) When a chemical system in equilibrium is disturbed in any manner, a reaction will occur in the direction and to the extent necessary to return the system to equilibrium.
   (b) Adding more H_2 or N_2 will increase the product. Removing NH_3 as it forms will also increase the amount of product.
   (c) Adding an inert gas to increase the pressure will have no effect. Increasing the volume of the system to decrease the pressure will reduce the amount of NH_3 produced.
   (d) Since the reaction is exothermic, lowering the temperature will increase the amount of product.
   (e) No, a catalyst speeds the reaction but does not affect the position of the equilibrium.
   (f) NH_3 is very soluble in water. If water is present, it will remove the NH_3 as it is formed.
6. (a) Diagonal relationships that should be discussed are as follows:
   1. Electronegativity
   2. Ionization energy
   3. Electron affinity
   4. Atomic size

(b) Group relationships involve the following:
1. Chemical properties
2. Electronic structure
3. Metallic character increases from top to bottom of a group

Period relationships involve the following:
1. Atomic radii
2. Ionic radii

7. (a) A spontaneous reaction occurs, or continues, with no outside help. Mathematically it is defined as a reaction where

$$\Delta G^0 < 0.0 \quad \text{or} \quad K_{eq} > 1.0 \quad \text{or} \quad E^0_{cell} > 0.0$$

All three of these equations are mathematically equivalent. If the value of one is known, the values of the others can be calculated.

(b) A nonspontaneous reaction may result in the formation of a small amount of product. The definition of *spontaneous* is somewhat arbitrary. An example is the dissociation of a weak acid in water. The K_a values for weak acids are less than 1.0, indicating a nonspontaneous reaction. However, the slight amount of ionization that does occur can form enough hydrogen ion (product) to make a solution significantly acidic. Therefore, a nonspontaneous reaction does procude products that have a significant effect.

(c) In an electrolytic cell, electric energy is added to force a nonspontaneous process to occur. Another method is to add an excess of one of the reactants, thereby forcing the more nearly complete conversion of the other reactant into products. Finally, the reaction may become spontaneous if the temperature is changed.

8. (a) An ideal gas molecule has no volume and no attraction toward other molecules. A real gas molecule has volume and can be attracted toward other molecules.

(b) Hydrogen bonding is used to explain why water, ammonia, and hydrogen fluoride have much higher boiling points than similar compounds in their groups. These higher values are characteristic also of the melting points and vapor pressures of other hydrogen-bonded molecules.

(c) This is a reaction between a Lewis acid, Cu^{2+}, and a Lewis base, NH_3. A Lewis acid is an electron-pair acceptor, and a Lewis base is an electron-pair donor. This reaction is also known as a complexation reaction, and the base is called a ligand.

(d) The Lewis (electron-dot) structure of NO_2 has an unpaired electron. NO_2 forms dimers to pair this electron. CO_2 does not have any unpaired electrons and does not form dimers.

(e) The dissolution process involves two steps. First, the ions must be separated by breaking the crystal lattice. The energy, called the lattic energy, needed to break the crystal lattice comes from energy released when the ions interact with the solvent. When this solvation energy is great enough to overcome the lattice energy, dissolution occurs. We may infer from the energy question that the solvation energy is large enough to overcome the lattice energy in NaCl but not in AgCl.

Entropy increase in the dissolution process is also important and results from the less ordered state of ions in solution as compared to ions in a crystal. The entropy change for NaCl and AgCl can be estimated to be similar since both are salts of monovalent ions.

9. (a) The Lewis structures are as follows:

CH₄   SF₆   PCl₅

(b) (1) The octet rule states that each atom should have an octet of electrons surrounding it in the Lewis electron-dot structure. This rule is based on the fact that the noble gases have an octet of valence electrons. For hydrogen, however, the "octet" is a single pair of electrons.

(2) Certain elements, notably boron, form compounds in which fewer than an octet of electrons surround the central atom. Also, elements except those in periods 1 and 2, can have more than an octet of electrons; such elements make use of available d orbitals for the extra electrons.

(c) The geometries for the Lewis structures in part (a) are tetrahedron, octahedron, and trigonal bipyramid, respectively. The tetrahedron has all bond angles of 109°. The octahedron has all bond angles of 90°. The trigonal bipyramid has 90° angles between the axial and equatorial atoms and 120 angles between the three equatorial atoms.

(d) The hybrids are sp^3, d^2sp^3 (also called sp^3d^2), and dsp^3, respectively.

(e) Sulfur is in period 3 and has available d orbitals for d^2sp^3 hybridization. Oxygen is in period 2 and does not have d orbitals available.

APPENDIX 1

Answer Explanations for End-of-Chapter Questions

Chapter 1

1. **E** The order of energies is as follows: microwave < infrared < visible < ultraviolet < X rays.

2. **C** Solve the equation $\lambda\nu = c$, where $c = 3.00 \times 10^8$ m s^{-1} and $\nu = 4.00 \times 10^{14}$s^{-1}.

$$\lambda = \frac{3.00 \times 10^8 \text{ m s}^{-1}}{4.00 \times 10^{14} \text{ s}^{-1}} = 7.5 \times 10^{-7} \text{ m} = 750 \text{ nm}$$

3. **E** Arsenic has a total of 15 p electrons: 6 in period 2, 6 in period 3, and 3 in period 4.

4. **B** These quantum numbers represent a d electron (the second quantum number is 2) in the third period (the first quantum number is 3). Only Fe is in the third period with an incompletely filled d sublevel.

5. **E** When $\ell = 0$ it is an s orbital; $\ell = 1$, a p orbital; $\ell = 2$, a d orbital.

6. **D** $A = 31$ and $Z = 15$. In a neutral atom the electrons and protons are each equal to Z. The difference between A and Z is the number of neutrons = 16.

7. **D** An element such as Ag that would have a d^4 or d^9 electron configuration is, according to the Aufbau principle, most likely to promote an s electron to make a d^5 or d^{10} configuration, which is more stable.

8. **C** The electronic configuration of a noble gas always ends with np^6. These gases also have an ns^2 in their structure, where n is the highest principal level.

9. **A** Energy is needed to increase the value of n, and energy is released when n decreases. The more levels by which the electron increases, the greater the energy needed.

10. **D** This is the statement of the Heisenberg uncertainty principle.

11. **C** The Millikan oil drop experiment determined the charge independent of the mass.

12. **C** The law of multiple proportions is a consequence of the atomic theory, not part of it.

13. **E** The Rydberg equation is an empirical description of experimental results.

14. **B** The l or second quantum number defines orbital shape.

15. **D** 2.36×10^{-34} is the largest common divisor of all five measurements.

16. **A** The 4 d electrons appear in the fifth period of the periodic table.

17. **B** The f orbitals in the sixth and seventh periods hold 14 electrons.

18. **C** Valence electrons are the electrons in the outermost energy level of the atom. Only the s and p electrons are in the same energy level as the period in the periodic table.

19. **D** $E = h\nu$ is the equation for determining the energy of a photon.
20. **E** Bohr's model of the atom demonstrated that the Rydberg equation could be used for all of the listed purposes.

Chapter 2

1. **A** A differentiating electron is the electron present in one atom but not in the atom just before it in the periodic table. For transition elements, these are d electrons.
2. **B** Boiling points vary regularly within groups (columns), and Ni and Pt are just above and below the Pd atom.
3. **D** Boiling points decrease for metals and increase for nonmetals from the top to the bottom of a group.
4. **A** In general, an element close to F has the higher electronegativity of any pair of atoms. Except for response A, the element closest to F is listed second.
5. **E** An element with only two valence electrons must be in the second group from the left of the table. These are the alkaline earth elements.
6. **D** Both the number of electrons and the number of protons are equal to the atomic number of Ar, 18. The number of neutrons is the difference between the atomic mass and the atomic number ($40 - 18 = 22$).
7. **C** Only H is not mentioned in the chapter as having common allotropes.
8. **A** Since Be is in the second group, it is expected to lose two electrons easily while the third ionization is very difficult. The other atoms can lose three or more electrons with relative ease and have lower-third ionization energies.
9. **D** Sr and Ba are next to each other in the second group. Although Si and C are next to each other in the fourth group, Si is a metalloid and C is not. Therefore there is a larger difference between C and Si than between Ba and Sr.
10. **D** Most elements are metals.
11. **E** We can determine the number of neutrons only if a specific isotope is selected.
12. **A** Electrons are the first parts of the atoms to encounter each other in a collision between atoms.
13. **A** Sn is the defined symbol for tin.
14. **A** In a period, the largest atom is closest to the left side of the periodic table. In a group, the atoms increase in size from top to bottom. Therefore K is a larger atom than Ca.
15. **B** Hg is the furthest from the line dividing the metals from the nonmetals and therefore is least likely to be a metalloid.

Chapter 3

1. **A** Alpha particles have the least penetrating ability, and neutrons have very great penetrating ability.
2. **A** The unknown particle needs a mass of 4 and an atomic number of 2. This is an alpha particle or a helium nucleus.
3. **C** $\ln \left(\dfrac{N_o}{N_t} \right) = kt$, and $\ln(2) = kt_{1/2}$. Given the half-life of 5730 years for ^{14}C the value of k is calculated as

$$k = \frac{\ln(2)}{5730 \text{ yr}} = 1.21 \times 10^{-4} \text{ yr}^{-1}$$

Using the first equation and setting $N_o = 100$, and since N_t is the amount that is left, we obtain

$$N_t = 100 - 70 = 30.$$

Solving the first equation for t gives

$$t = \frac{\ln(100/30)}{1.21 \times 10^{-4} \text{ yr}^{-1}} = 9950 \text{ yr}$$

4. **B** $\ln(2) = kt$. Solving for k gives

$$k = \frac{\ln(2)}{(16.3 \text{ min})(60 \text{ s/min})} = 7.1 \times 10^{-4} \text{ s}^{-1}$$

5. **D** The reaction is

$$^{1}_{0}n + ^{235}_{92}U \longrightarrow ^{139}_{56}Ba + 3^{1}_{0}n + ^{94}_{36}Kr$$

6. **B** The atomic mass of natural copper is given as 65.55 in the periodic table. Since Cu comes before Bi in the periodic table, it will probably emit either a beta particle (electron) or a positron (positive-charge electron). Emitting a beta particle will reduce the n/p ratio to a value closer to the ratio in Cu^{-65}.

7. **D** One week is 7 days $\times$ 24 hr/day = 168 hr. There are 168 hr/35.7 hr per half-life = 4.7 half-lives of ^{82}Br in 1 week. Four half-lives leaves $\frac{1}{16}$ or 144 mg of ^{82}Br. Five half-lives leaves $\frac{1}{32}$ or 72 mg of the original amount of ^{82}Br. The only answer between these two is 88.1 mg. Alternatively, k can be calculated from $\ln(2) = kt_{1/2}$, and then $\ln \frac{N_o}{N_t} = kt$ is used to calculate N_t.

8. **D** Select the isotope where the n/p ratio is closest to the ratio determined from the average atomic mass in the periodic table. The zinc isotope comes closest to this ratio.

9. **E** $\ln \left(\frac{N_o}{N_t} \right) = kt$. $N_o = 100$, $N_t = 75$, and $t = 3.24$ hr. Solve

$$\ln \left(\frac{100}{75} \right) = k(3.24 \text{ hr})$$

$$k = \frac{0.288}{3.24 \text{ hr}} \times 0.0888 \text{ hr}^{-1}$$

10. **A** $\ln(2) = kt$. Solve for k:

$$k = \frac{\ln(2)}{(32.5 \text{ days})(24 \text{ hr/day})(60 \text{ min/hr})(60 \text{s/min})} = 2.47 \times 10^{-7} \text{ s}^{-1}$$

$$\text{Rate} = kN_o = (2.47 \times 10^{-7} \text{ s}^{-1})(8.00 \times 10^7 \text{ nuclei})$$

$$= 19.8 \text{ nuclei s}^{-1} \text{ decay}$$

Chapter 4

1. **D** All potassium salts are soluble. See solubility rules.
2. **B** The sulfides are insoluble except for those that have alkali metals or ammonium ions as the cation. See solubility rules.
3. **E** MnO_4^- is defined as the permanganate ion
4. **C** Two ammonium ions and one oxalate ion are obtained. The anion does not decompose into other species, and the ammonium cation is enclosed in parentheses with a subscript of 2 indicating that two NH_4^+ ions must result.
5. **E** Iron is a transition element with more than one possible charge and requires the use of the Stock system for its name. Because it is a $+3$ ion, it is called iron (III). The NO_3 identifies the compound as a nitrate.
6. **C** The balanced reaction is

$$2C_3H_6 + 15O_2 \longrightarrow 12CO_2 + 6H_2O$$

The sum of these coefficients is 35.
7. **C** Potassium loses one electron, and the preceding noble gas in the periodic table is Ar.
8. **C** Na and F have electronic configurations of their ions that are identical to that of Ne. Each atom in the other pairs is isoelectric with different noble gases.
9. **D** Aluminum always forms a $+3$ ion and needs three Cl ions with a -1 charge each in order to form a neutral molecule.
10. **E** This is the electronic configuration of the Ar atom. Each of these ions is isoelectronic with Ar.
11. **D** The correct name for this ion is the chlorite ion.
12. **B** Calcium ions are $+2$ and oxide ions -2, so the correct formula is CaO.
13. **E** The dihydrogen phosphate ion, $H_2PO_4^-$, needs one K^+ for a correct formula. In the other formulas there is an excess of a positive or negative charge.
14. **C** The products of this reaction are hydrogen gas and aluminum bromide.
15. **D** The solubilities must be known to write correct net ionic equations; these equations do not predict solubility.

Chapter 5

1. **A** The elements Ba, Zn, C and Cl are arranged in order from the lower left (Ba) to the upper right corner of the periodic table (Cl).
2. **C** All the choices have a C atom. Of the second atom in each bond, the C atom is the most electronegative.
3. **D** In SF_2Cl_4 the two Fl atoms may be arranged opposite each other in a square planar structure for a nonpolar molecule, or next to each other for a polar molecule.
4. **C** The carbonate ion has only one double bond in each resonance structure and therefore one pi bond. Although the entire ion has a charge of -2, it is nonpolar.
5. **C** In SF_5^- there are five atoms bound to the sulfur and one nonbonding pair of electrons. This is an octahedral structure and a d^2sp^3 hybrid.

6. **D** H_2S is similar in structure to water. With two nonbonding electron pairs, the molecule has a bent structure.
7. **A** The cyanide ion, CN^-, is electronically identical to N_2.
8. **C** The octahedron is d^2sp^3, not dsp^3.
9. **C** The Lewis structure for SO_3 involves one O atom with a double bond and two O atoms with single bonds. The double bond can be placed in three positions, resulting in 3 resonance structures.
10. **B** Ammonia has a nonbonding pair of electrons.
11. **E** All of these statements are true.
12. **C** The sulfite ion is SO_3^{2-}. There are six valence electrons on each oxygen atom and on the sulfur atom, totaling 24 electrons. Two electrons are added for the -2 charge, resulting in a total of 26 electrons.
13. **B** Two nitrogen atoms give the prefix *di-* in dinitrogen and three oxygen atoms give the *tri-* in trioxide.
14. **A** A 60° angle does not occur in any hybrid structure considered in this text.
15. **A** The *sp* hybrid requires that two atoms be bound to the central atom with no nonbonding electron pairs. None of the structures named in the question fulfills these requirements. SO_2 is sp^2, SF_6 is d^2sp^3, SCl_4 is dsp^3, and SCl_2 is sp^3.

Chapter 6

1. **B** $? \text{ g KClO}_3 = 0.200 \text{ L KClO}_3 \left(\dfrac{0.150 \text{ mol KClO}_3}{1 \text{ L KClO}_3} \right) \left(\dfrac{122.5 \text{ g KClO}_3}{1 \text{ mol KClO}_3} \right)$

$= 3.68 \text{ g KClO}_3$

2. **E** The reaction is

$$\text{NaOH} + \text{HNO}_3 \longrightarrow \text{NaNO}_3 + \text{H}_2\text{O}$$

$? \text{ mL NaOH} = 35.0 \text{ mL HNO}_3 \left(\dfrac{0.345 \text{ mol HNO}_3}{1000 \text{ mL HNO}_3} \right)$

$\times \left(\dfrac{1 \text{ mol NaOH}}{1 \text{ mol HNO}_3} \right) \left(\dfrac{1000 \text{ mL NaOH}}{0.130 \text{ mol NaOH}} \right)$

$= 92.9 \text{ mL NaOH}$

3. **A** $? \text{ g CaCO}_3 = 3.00 \text{ L CO}_2 \left(\dfrac{1 \text{ mol CO}_2}{22.4 \text{ L CO}_2} \right) \left(\dfrac{1 \text{ mol CaCO}_3}{1 \text{ mol CO}_2} \right)$

$\times \left(\dfrac{100 \text{ g CaCO}_3}{1 \text{ mol CaCO}_3} \right)$

$= 13.4 \text{ g CaCO}_3$

4. **D** $? \text{ mol H} = 14.3 \text{ g H} \left(\dfrac{1 \text{ mol H}}{1.0 \text{ g H}} \right) = 14.3 \text{ mol H}$

$? \text{ mol C} = 85.7 \text{ g C} \left(\dfrac{1 \text{ mol C}}{12 \text{ g C}} \right) = 7.14 \text{ mol C}$

$\dfrac{14.3 \text{ mol H}}{7.14} = 2 \text{ mol H}$ and $\dfrac{7.14 \text{ mol C}}{7.14} = 1 \text{ mol C}$. The empirical formula is CH_2.

5. **C** One Al atom, 3 N atoms, and 9 O atoms add up to a mass of 213.

6. **D** $? \text{ mg Na}_2\text{SO}_4 = 0.100 \text{ L Na}^+ \left(\dfrac{0.00100 - \text{mol Na}^+}{1 \text{ L Na}^+} \right) \left(\dfrac{1 \text{ mol Na}_2\text{SO}_4}{2 \text{ mol Na}^+} \right)$

$$\times \left(\dfrac{142 \text{ g Na}_2\text{SO}_4}{1 \text{ mol Na}_2\text{SO}_4} \right)$$

$$= 7.1 \times 10^{-3} \text{ g Na}_2\text{SO}_4 = 7.1 \text{ mg Na}_2\text{SO}_4$$

7. **A** $? \text{ cm} = 400 \text{ nm} \left(\dfrac{10^{-9} \text{ m}}{1 \text{ nm}} \right) \left(\dfrac{1 \text{ cm}}{10^{-2} \text{ m}} \right) = 4.00 \times 10^{-5} \text{ cm}$

8. **D** $? \text{ mol Al} = 1 \text{ mol Fe} \left(\dfrac{8 \text{ mol Al}}{9 \text{ mol Fe}} \right) = \frac{8}{9} \text{ mol Al}$

9. **C** The reaction is $2 \text{ KOH} + \text{H}_2\text{SO}_4 \rightarrow \text{K}_2\text{SO}_4 + 2 \text{ H}_2\text{O}$

$$? \dfrac{\text{mol H}_2\text{SO}_4}{1 \text{ L H}_2\text{SO}_4} = \dfrac{0.125 \text{ mol KOH}}{1000 \text{ mL KOH}} \left(\dfrac{1 \text{ mol H}_2\text{SO}_4}{2 \text{ mol KOH}} \right)$$

$$\times \left(\dfrac{35.4 \text{ mL KOH}}{50.0 \text{ mL H}_2\text{SO}_4} \right)$$

$$= 0.443 \text{M H}_2\text{SO}_4$$

10. **E** The mass of the empirical formula unit is 14 g unit^{-1}.

$$\dfrac{83.5 \text{ g mol}^{-1}}{14 \text{ g unit}^{-1}} = 5.96 \text{ units mol}^{-1}$$

This rounds to 6 empirical formula units per mole and a molecular formula of C_6H_{12}.

11. **D** $? \text{ g Fe} = 1 \text{ atom Fe} \left(\dfrac{1 \text{ mol Fe}}{6.02 \times 10^{23} \text{ atoms Fe}} \right) \left(\dfrac{55.85 \text{ g Fe}}{1 \text{ mol Fe}} \right) = 9.28 \times$

10^{-23} g Fe

12. **B** $? \text{ g SO}_2 = 4.00 \text{ L SO}_2 \left(\dfrac{1 \text{ mol SO}_2}{22.4 \text{ L SO}_2} \right) \left(\dfrac{64 \text{ g SO}_2}{1 \text{ mol SO}_2} \right) = 11.4 \text{ g SO}_2$

13. **D** Molar mass of K_3PO_4 is 212. Mass of potassium is $3 \times 39 = 117$.

$$\%K = \dfrac{117 \text{ g K}}{212 \text{ g K}_3\text{PO}_4} \times 100 = 55.2\% \text{ K}$$

14. **C** $? \text{ g C} = 0.357 \text{ g CO}_2 \left(\dfrac{1 \text{ mol CO}_2}{44 \text{ g CO}_2} \right) \left(\dfrac{1 \text{ mol C}}{1 \text{ mol CO}_2} \right) \left(\dfrac{12 \text{ g C}}{1 \text{ mol C}} \right)$

$$= 0.097 \text{ g C}$$

$$\%C = \dfrac{0.097 \text{ g C}}{0.200 \text{ g sample}} \times 100 = 48.7\% \text{ C}$$

15. **B** The liter is an old metric unit of volume. The meter is the base unit of length in the S.I. system and is used to derive volume units.

16. **A** Since the question asks for the amount of product, we do the calculations using each reactant and choose the smaller answer.

$$? \text{ g AgCl} = 20.0 \text{ g AgNO}_3 \left(\dfrac{1 \text{ mol AgNO}_3}{170 \text{ g AgNO}_3} \right) \left(\dfrac{2 \text{ mol AgCl}}{2 \text{ mol AgNO}_3} \right) \left(\dfrac{143.5 \text{ g AgCl}}{1 \text{ mol AgCl}} \right)$$

$$= 16.9 \text{ g AgCl}$$

$$= 15.0 \text{ g CaCl}_2 \left(\dfrac{1 \text{ mol CaCl}_2}{111 \text{ g CaCl}_2} \right) \left(\dfrac{2 \text{ mol AgCl}}{1 \text{ mol CaCl}_2} \right) \left(\dfrac{143.5 \text{ g AgCl}}{1 \text{ mol AgCl}} \right)$$

$$= 38.8 \text{ g AgCl}$$

16.9 g AgCl is the correct answer and also defines $AgNO_3$ as the limiting reactant.

17. **C** Determine the limiting reactant (this was done in the preceding example, but another method is shown here):

$$? \text{ g AgNO}_3 = 15.0 \text{ g CaCl}_2 \left(\frac{1 \text{ mol CaCl}_2}{111 \text{ g CaCl}_2}\right)\left(\frac{2 \text{ mol AgNO}_3}{1 \text{ mol CaCL}_2}\right)\left(\frac{170 \text{ g AgNO}_3}{1 \text{ mol AgNO}_3}\right)$$

$$= 45.9 \text{ g AgNO}_3$$

This calculation shows that we need 45.9 g $AgNO_3$ to react all of the $CaCl_2$. The problem only gives us 20.0 g. Therefore $AgNO_3$ is used up first and is the limiting reactant. Now use the given amount of the limiting reactant to calculate the number of grams of CaCl, that react.

$$? \text{ g CaCl}_2 = 20.0 \text{ g AgNO}_3 \left(\frac{1 \text{ mol AgNO}_3}{170 \text{ g AgNO}_3}\right)\left(\frac{1 \text{ mol CaCl}_2}{2 \text{ mol AgNO}_3}\right)\left(\frac{111 \text{ g CaCl}_2}{1 \text{ mol CaCl}_2}\right)$$

$$= 6.53 \text{ g CaCl}_2$$

Since 6.53 g $CaCl_2$ react, $15.0 - 6.53 = 8.47$ g $CaCl_2$ must be left.

18. **B** $$? \text{ g Cl} = 5.86 \text{ g AgCl}\left(\frac{1 \text{ mol AgCl}}{143.5 \text{ g AgCl}}\right)\left(\frac{1 \text{ mol Cl}}{1 \text{ mol AgCl}}\right)\left(\frac{35.5 \text{ g Cl}}{1 \text{ mol Cl}}\right)$$

$$= 1.45 \text{ g Cl}$$

$$? \text{ \% Cl} = \frac{1.45 \text{ g Cl}}{50.0 \text{ g sample}} \times 100 = 2.90\%$$

19. **D** $$? \text{ L air} = 1 \text{ mol CH}_4\left(\frac{2 \text{ mol O}_2}{1 \text{ mol CH}_4}\right)\left(\frac{22.4 \text{ L O}_2}{1 \text{ mol O}_2}\right)\left(\frac{1 \text{ L air}}{0.2 \text{ L O}_2}\right)$$

$$= 224 \text{ L air}$$

20. **C** Assume a 100-g sample of the compound. Then 25% H = 25 g H and 75% C = 75 g C
Calculate moles of each:

$$? \text{ mol H} = 25 \text{ g H}\left(\frac{1 \text{ mol H}}{1 \text{ g H}}\right) = 25 \text{ mol H}$$

$$? \text{ mol C} = 75 \text{ g C}\left(\frac{1 \text{ mol C}}{12 \text{ g C}}\right) = 6.25 \text{ mol C}$$

$$\frac{6.25 \text{ mol C}}{6.25} = 1 \text{ mol C}$$

Also,

$$\frac{25 \text{ mol H}}{6.25} = 4 \text{ mol H}$$

The formula is CH_4.

Chapter 7

1. **A** This problem gives all of the information needed to solve the ideal gas law equation, $PV = nRT$, for volume:

$$V = \frac{nRT}{P} = \frac{(2.50 \text{ mol})(0.0821 \text{ L atm mol}^{-1}\text{K}^{-1})(318 \text{ K})}{1.50 \text{ atm}}$$

$$= 43.5 \text{ L}$$

All of the values given in the problem are used directly in this equation except that the temperature of 45 °C must be converted to 318 K. The other choices represent incorrect combinations of the given data.

2. **C** This is another calculation using the ideal gas law equation:

$$n = \frac{PV}{RT} = \frac{(800 \text{ mm Hg}/760 \text{ mm Hg atm}^{-1})(6.45 \text{ L})}{(0.0821 \text{ L atm mol}^{-1} \text{ K}^{-1})(297 \text{ K})}$$

$$= 0.278 \text{ mol}$$

In this example the pressure in millimeters of mercury had to be converted to atmospheres, and the Celsius temperature to Kelvin units. As in the preceding example, the incorrect responses involve simple errors in application of the ideal gas law equation.

3. **D** At STP 1 mol of an ideal gas occupies 22.4 L. The mass of 22.4 L of gas is the molar mass of the substance. The density is then

$$\text{density} = \frac{\text{mass}}{\text{liters}} = \frac{20.18 \text{ g mol}^{-1}}{22.4 \text{ L mol}^{-1}}$$

$$= 0.901 \text{ g L}^{-1}$$

Equation 4.12 could also be solved to obtain the density:

$$\frac{g}{V} = \frac{(\text{molar mass}) P}{RT} = \frac{(20.18 \text{ g mol}^{-1})(1.00 \text{ atm})}{(0.0821 \text{ L atm mol}^{-1} \text{ K}^{-1})(273)} = 0.901 \text{ g L}^{-1}$$

4. **D** To solve the problem, take the ratio of two ideal gas law equations as follows:

$$\frac{P_i V_i}{P_f V_f} = \frac{n_i R T_i}{n_f R T_f} = 1$$

and cancel variables that are kept constant, n, R, and T. Rearrange the remaining variables.

$$P_f = \frac{P_i V_i}{V_f}$$

$$\frac{(58 \text{ mm Hg})(155 \text{ mL})}{(1000 \text{ mL})} = 8.99 \text{ mm Hg}$$

Note that the units of volume must be the same for V_i and V_f, and so 1.00 L was converted to 1000 mL.

5. **B** The pressure is directly proportional to the number of moles of gas, and the error in the pressure will be directly reflected in the moles of hydrogen reported. By Dalton's law of partial pressures

$$P_{\text{total}} = p_{H_2} + p_{H_2O}$$

The vapor pressure of water at 30°C is given as 31.82 mm Hg. The correct pressure of hydrogen is

$$p_{H_2} = P_{total} - p_{H_2O}$$
$$= 745 \text{ mm Hg} - 31.82 \text{ mm Hg}$$
$$= 713.2 \text{ mm Hg}$$

The error is

$$\text{Error} = \frac{\text{measured} - \text{true}}{\text{true}} \times 100$$
$$= \frac{745 - 713.2}{713.2}$$
$$= +4.5\%$$

6. **B** This answer is obtained by using the ideal gas law equation $PV = nRT$ to calculate the pressure of each gas:

$$P_{CO_2} = \frac{nRT}{V} = \frac{(0.016 \text{ mol CO}_2)(0.0821 \text{ L atm mol}^{-1}\text{K}^{-1})(298 \text{ K})}{2.50 \text{ L}}$$
$$= 0.157 \text{ atm}$$

$$P_{CH_4} = \frac{nRT}{V} = \frac{(0.035 \text{ mol CH}_4)(0.0821 \text{ L atm mol}^{-1}\text{K}^{-1})(298 \text{ K})}{2.50 \text{ L}}$$
$$= 0.343 \text{ atm}$$

Dalton's law of partial pressures gives

$$P_{total} = 0.157 \text{ atm} + 0.343 \text{ atm} = 0.500 \text{ atm}$$

Conversion of 0.500 atm to mm Hg yields 380 mm Hg.

Another approach to solving this problem would be to add the moles of the two gases and then use the ideal gas law to calculate the total pressure directly.

$$P = \frac{nRT}{V} = \frac{(0.035 \text{ mol CH}_4 + 0.016 \text{ mol CO}_2)(0.0821 \text{ L atm mol}^{-1}\text{K}^{-1})(298 \text{ K})}{2.50 \text{ L}}$$
$$= 0.500 \text{ atm}$$

This yields a pressure of 380 mm Hg.

7. **B** Carbon dioxide is soluble to some extent in water. To obtain the amount dissolved in the water, the amount actually obtained is subtracted from the theoretical yield. The chemical reaction is

$$2C_2H_6 + 7O_2 \longrightarrow 4CO_2 + 6H_2O$$

The theoretical yield is

$$? \text{ g CO2} = 1.50\text{g C}_2\text{H}_6 \left(\frac{1 \text{ mol C}_2\text{H}_6}{30 \text{ g C}_2\text{H}_6}\right)\left(\frac{4 \text{ mol CO}_2}{2 \text{ mol C}_2\text{H}_6}\right)\left(\frac{44 \text{ g CO}_2}{1 \text{ mol CO}_2}\right)$$
$$= 4.40 \text{ g CO}_2$$

From the gas collection data:

$$n = \frac{PV}{RT} = \frac{(746 \text{ mmHg}/760 \text{ mmHg/atm})}{(0.0821 \text{ L atm mol}^{-1} \text{ K}^{-1})(298 \text{ K})}$$

$$= 0.0802 \text{ mol CO}_2$$

$$\text{g CO}_2 = 0.0814 \text{ mol CO}_2 \left(\frac{44 \text{ g CO}_2}{1 \text{ mol CO}_2} \right) = 3.53 \text{ g CO}_2$$

The difference between the theoretical yield and actual yield is

$$4.40 \text{ g} - 3.53 \text{ g} = 0.87 \text{ g CO}_2$$

This amount is apparently dissolved in the water of the pneumatic trough.

8. **B** Heating a gas increases the pressure, while increasing the volume decreases the pressure. From the information given, it is impossible to tell whether the temperature increase will dominate and cause an increase in pressure or whether the volume increase will dominate and cause an overall pressure decrease. All of the other options will definitely cause either an increase or a decrease in pressure of the gas.

9. **D** On the average, heavier molecules move more slowly.

10. **E** Both an increase in the force of the collisions with the container walls and an increase in the frequency of collisions lead to the increase in pressure with increased temperature.

11. **D** Ideal gases have no volume or attractive forces.

12. **D** The further a gas is from its condensation point (boiling point), the more it behaves as an ideal gas. Condensation can be achieved by cooling a gas and/or by increasing its pressure. Therefore low pressure and high temperature will cause a gas to be as far as possible from its condensation point and therefore to behave most like an ideal gas.

13. **E** Since a real gas has a volume associated with it, its volume must be greater than that of the corresponding ideal gas:

$$V_{\text{ideal}} = V_{\text{real}} - nb$$

Similarly, the pressure of a real gas is less than that of the ideal gas since attractions cause the trajectories of the molecules to be curved rather than linear. This curved trajectory decreases the frequency of collisions with the walls and therefore the pressure:

$$P_{\text{ideal}} = P_{\text{real}} + \frac{an^2}{V^2}$$

14. **D** The rate of effusion is inversely proportional to the square root of the molecular masses:

$$\sqrt{\frac{m_1}{m_2}} = \frac{\bar{v}_2}{\bar{v}_1}$$

Entering the given data we have

$$\sqrt{\frac{154 \text{ g } CCl_4 \text{ mol}^{-1}}{44 \text{ g } CO_2 \text{ mol}^{-1}}} = \frac{6.3 \times 10^{-2} \text{ mol } CO_2 \text{ s}^{-1}}{\bar{v}_1} = 1.87$$

$$\bar{v}_1 = \frac{6.3 \times 10^{-2}}{1.87} = 3.4 \times 10^{-2} \text{ mol } CCl_4 \text{ s}^{-1}$$

15. **D** At STP, 22.4 L of a gas is equivalent to 1 mol.
The mass of 22.4 L of this gas is equivalent to

$$22.4 \text{ L mol}^{-1} \times 3.48 \text{ g L}^{-1} = 78 \text{ g mol}^{-1}$$

Of the responses, only C_6H_6 and CaF_2 have molar masses of 78. However, CaF_2 is an ionic solid and highly unlikely to be in the gaseous state, therefore C_6H_6, benzene, is the most appropriate answer.

16. **A** Rearrange the ideal gas equation to read

$$n = \frac{PV}{RT} = \frac{(0.450 \text{ atm})(2.50 \text{ L})}{(0.0821 \text{ L atm mol}^{-1} \text{ K}^{-1})(300 \text{ K})} = 0.0457 \text{ mol}$$

17. **A**
$$\frac{P_1 V_1}{P_2 V_2} = \frac{n_1 R T_1}{n_2 R T_2}$$

R, T, and V are constants and cancel, so that $P_1/P_2 = n_1/n_2$. Entering the data from the experiment:

$$\frac{0.800 \text{ atm}}{1.10 \text{ atm}} = \frac{n_1}{n_1 + 0.100}$$

and solving for n_1 yields $n_1 = 0.532$ mol. Two-thirds of n_1 is O_2, and one-third is N_2.
Therefore there is 0.355 mol of O_2 in the flask.

18. **D**
$$\frac{P_1 V_1}{P_2 V_2} = \frac{n_1 R T_1}{n_2 R T_2}$$

In this problem n, R, and T cancel, and $P_1 V_1 = P_2 V_2$. Entering data from the problem yields

$$(245 \text{ mm Hg}) (1.50 \text{ L}) = (P_2)(0.350 \text{ L}).$$

Solving for P_2 gives 1050 mm Hg.

19. **D** The mass of air in the flask $= 5.00 \text{ L} \left(\frac{1.290 \text{ g}}{\text{L}} \right) = 6.45$ g. The flask must weigh $543.251 - 6.45 = 536.80$ g. The mass of the new gas is $566.11 - 536.80 = 29.31$ g. The density of the gas is

$$d = \frac{29.31 \text{ g}}{5.00 \text{ L}} = 5.86 \text{ g L}^{-1}.$$

$? \dfrac{\text{g}}{\text{mol}} = \dfrac{5.86 \text{ g}}{\text{L}} \left(\dfrac{22.4 \text{ L}}{1 \text{ mol}} \right) = 131 \text{ g mol}^{-1}$, which is the atomic mass of xenon.

20. **A** $? \text{ L H}_2 = 0.100 \text{gMg} \left(\dfrac{1 \text{ mol Mg}}{24.31 \text{ g Mg}} \right) \left(\dfrac{1 \text{ mol H}_2}{1 \text{ mol Mg}} \right) \left(\dfrac{22.4 \text{ L H}_2}{1 \text{ mol H}_2} \right)$

$= 0.0921 \text{ L}$

$= 92.1 \text{ mL}.$

Chapter 8

1. **B** London forces are the weakest and hydrogen bonds the strongest.
2. **B** Salts with ionic bonds have the highest melting points.
3. **D** Sublimation is the transformation of a solid directly to a gas.
4. **A** Iron is in period 3 and has the largest electron cloud, which is expected to be most polarizable.
5. **A** CF_4 is the only compound that does not have an N-H, O-H, or F-H bond in its structure.
6. **D** C_6H_{14} does not hydrogen-bond and has fewer London forces than C_8H_{18}.
7. **A** The larger the heat of vaporization, the larger the change in boiling point when the pressure is changed.
8. **C** Aluminum is a soft metal that will not even scratch glass.
9. **A** The face-centered cubic structure has three atoms in its unit cell. The simple cubic has one atom, the body-centered cubic has two atoms, and the edge-centered cubic has three atoms in the unit cell. A tetrahedron is not a unit cell.
10. **E** The unit cell and its dimensions can be used, with Avogadro's number, to determine the density.
11. **A** The lengths of the horizontal plateaus represent the heats of fusion and vaporization. Although not identical, they are closest to being the same.
12. **E** The slope of the curve for the solid, liquid, or gas has units of degree Celsius per joule. Therefore, $\dfrac{1}{\text{slope} \times \text{mass}}$ is the specific heat with the required units of $Jg^{-1} \, {}^{\circ}C^{-1}$.
13. **D** The lower left line is the equilibrium line between the solid and gas phases. It ends at the triple point at approximately 95°C.
14. **D** The point at which the liquid-gas equilibrium line intersects the dotted line representing 1 atm of pressure is the normal boiling point, approximately 180°C.
15. **A** The coordinates of these conditions fall in the liquid region of the phase diagram.
16. **E** Only 250°C and 2.00 atm pressure are clearly beyond the critical point.
17. **D** The triclinic structure has the properties listed in the question.
18. **A** To determine interatomic spacing in a crystal is the main use described in this chapter.

19. **A** All atoms in a diamond are covalently bonded, producing a very large structure.
20. **A** Viscosity, boiling point, and heat of vaporization are all directly related to the strength of intermolecular attractions. In a liquid substance with low intermolecular attractions the values for other properties will also be low.

Chapter 9

1. **C** $? \dfrac{\text{mol CdCl}_2}{\text{L CdCl}_2} = \dfrac{140 \text{ g CdCl}_2}{100 \text{ mL CdCl}_2} \left(\dfrac{1 \text{ mol CdCl}_2}{183 \text{ g CdCl}_2}\right)\left(\dfrac{1 \text{ mL}}{10^{-3}\text{L}}\right) = 7.65 \text{ M.}$

2. **E**
$$P = P^0 X_{\text{solvent}}$$

From this we get

$$X_{\text{solvent}} = \frac{P}{P^\circ} = \frac{456 \text{ mm Hg}}{832 \text{ mm Hg}} = 0.548$$

Mole fraction of solute is

$$X_{\text{solute}} = 1.000 - X_{\text{solvent}} = 1.000 - 0.548 = 0.452$$

3. **B** Surface tension changes depending on the type of molecule dissolved and its intermolecular attractive forces, rather than the amount of solute particles present. Surface tension is not a colligative property.
4. **C** The least polar substance, C_6H_6 will be most soluble in the nonpolar hexane.
5. **E** The osmotic pressure calculation uses molarity units; the others use molality or mole fraction units.
6. **D** Vapor pressure measurements may deviate significantly from Raoult's law, resulting in errors if the solution is not an ideal solution.
7. **A** The density of the solution must be measured. The other values are either not needed or readily available in tables.
8. **A** The sucrose will produce the largest molality of soluble particles resulting in the largest $\Delta T = k_b$ m.
9. **E** A release of heat energy when substances are mixed indicates stronger attractive forces in the solution than in the pure solvents.
10. **B** Enzymes have limited solubility and high molar masses. Consequently, the osmotic pressure method is the best choice.

11. **B** $25 \text{ ppb Pb}^{2+} = \dfrac{25 \text{ g Pb}^{2+}}{10^9 \text{ g solution}} \left(\dfrac{1 \text{ mol Pb}^{2+}}{207 \text{ g Pb}^{2+}}\right)\left(\dfrac{10^3 \text{ g solution}}{1 \text{ L solution}}\right)$
$= 1.2 \times 10^{-7} \text{ M Pb}^{2+}$

12. **C** Increasing temperature always decreases the solubility of a gas such as O_2.
13. **B** It is most reasonable that the vapor pressure and boiling point of any solution will lie between the vapor pressures and boiling points of the pure liquids. Only the pressure of 0.750 atm fulfills these conditions.

14. **B**
$$\Delta T = mk_f \quad \text{and} \quad m = \frac{k_f}{\Delta T} = \frac{-10.0°C}{-1.86°C} = 5.4 \text{ molal.}$$

Of the listed possibilities, only KCl will result in a solution that is 5.4 molal in ions (both K^+ and Cl^-).

15. **B** CH_3OH is an organic alcohol, methanol, and is a nonelectrolyte.

16. **D**
$$\frac{7.5°C}{0.52°C \ m^{-1}} = 14.4 \text{ molal}$$

$$\Delta T = (1.86°C \ m^{-1})(14.4 \ m) = 26.8°C$$

The freezing point is $0°C - 26.8°C = -26.8°C$.

17. **E** Glucose is a nonelectrolyte; the first three choices are ionic and the acid CH_3CH_2COOH ionizes slightly. Therefore glucose produces the lowest molality of particles (molecules or ions), resulting in the lowest boiling-point increase.

18. **A** The intermolecular attractions are stronger in the mixture than in the pure liquids, resulting in a warming of the solution. Also, since the mixture has stronger attractive forces, the vapor pressure of the liquid will be less than expected, resulting in a negative deviation from Raoult's law. Either B or C, or both B and C are true, but it is impossible to tell from this experiment.

19. **E** Two forces for dissolution are the energy, which is unfavorable since the solution cools, and the entropy change. The entropy change must be great enough to overcome the energy deficit.

20. **A**
$$X = \frac{mol_{ethanol}}{mol_{ethanol} + mol_{water}}$$

$$= \frac{20.0 \ g/46 \ g \ mol^{-1}}{20.0 \ g/46 \ g \ mol^{-1} + 30.0 \ g/18 \ g \ mol^{-1}}$$

$$= \frac{0.435}{0.435 + 1.667} = 0.207$$

Chapter 10

1. **C** A system in equilibrium is governed by the equilibrium law, which specifies a specific ratio of product to reactant concentrations.

2. **E** All of these are governed by equilibrium laws.

3. **C** Increasing the pressure by adding an inert gas does not change the concentrations of the reactants or products.

4. **E** The reaction has been reversed, causing the equilibrium constant to be inverted. In addition, the coefficients are doubled and the equilibrium constant is squared. The new equilibrium constant is

$$K = \frac{1}{(4.5 \times 10^{-3})^2} = 4.9 \times 10^{-8}$$

5. **A** The reaction is

$$Ag_2CrO_4(s) \rightleftharpoons 2 \ Ag^+(aq) + CrO_4^{2-} \ (aq)$$

and $K_{sp} = [Ag^+]^2[CrO_4^{2-}]$.

6. **B** $K_p = K_c$ when $\Delta n_g = 0$. Only the combustion of carbon has these properties.

7. **D** Only HCl and CO_2 should appear in the equilibrium law. Solids and pure liquids have constant concentrations and are included in the equilibrium constant. Response A does not have the correct exponent for HCl.

8. **A**
$$K_c = \frac{[H_2][I_2]}{[HI]^2} = 0.020$$

Initial concentration of HI $= \dfrac{0.200 \text{ mol } HT}{10.0 \text{ L}} = 0.0200$ M.

REACTION	2 HI	$\rightleftharpoons$	H_2	+	I_2
INITIAL CONDITIONS	**0.0200 M**		**0 M**		**0 M**
CHANGE	$-2x$		$+x$		$+x$
EQUILIBRIUM	$0.0200 - 2x$		$+x$		$+x$
ANSWER					

$$\frac{[H_2][I_2]}{[HI]^2} = 0.020 = \frac{(x)(x)}{(0.0200 - 2x)^2}$$

Take the square root of both sides to obtain

$$0.1414 = \frac{x}{0.0200 - 2x}$$

$$(0.1414)(0.0200 - 2x) = x$$

$$0.002828 - 0.2828x = x$$

$$0.002828 = x + 0.2828x$$

$$0.002828 = 1.2828x$$

$$\frac{0.002828}{1.2828} = x$$

$$x = 2.2 \times 10^{-3}$$

REACTION	2 HI	$\rightleftharpoons$	H_2	+	I_2
INITIAL CONDITIONS	**0.0200 M**		**0 M**		**0 M**
CHANGE	$-2x$		$+x$		$+x$
EQUILIBRIUM	$0.0200 - 2x$		$+x$		$+x$
ANSWER	0.01559 M		2.2×10^{-3} M		2.2×10^{-3} M

Since this is a 10.0-L flask, it will contain 2.2×10^{-2} or 0.022 mol $I_2 (g)$.

9. **B** For this reaction: $Q = \dfrac{P_{N_2O_4}}{P^2_{NO_2}}$

The reaction will go in the forward direction if Q is less than K_p. Q must be calculated from pressures in atmospheres. Only choice B results in a value of Q less than K_p.

10. **B** $PbI_2(s) \rightleftharpoons Pb^{2+}(aq) + 2I^-(aq)$ and $K_{sp} = [Pb^{2+}][I^-]^2$

REACTION	PbI_2	$\rightleftharpoons$	Pb^{2+}	+	$2I^-$
INITIAL CONDITIONS	Solid		0 M		0 M
CHANGE	$-x$		$+x$		$+2x$
EQUILIBRIUM	Solid		$+x$		$+2x$
ANSWER					

$$7.9 \times 10^{-9} = (x)(2x)^2$$
$$= 4x^3$$
$$1.98 \times 10^{-9} = x^3$$
$$1.25 \times 10^{-3} = x \text{ (This is also the molar solubility.)}$$

11. **D**   Molar solubility $= \dfrac{1.00 \times 10^{-4} \text{ g } AuCl_3/303 \text{ g } AuCl_3 \text{ mol}^{-1}}{1 \text{ L}}$

$$= 3.3 \times 10^{-7} \text{ M}$$

REACTION	$AuCl_3$	$\rightleftharpoons$	Au^{3+}	+	$3 Cl^-$
INITIAL CONDITIONS	Solid		0 M		0 M
CHANGE	$-x$		$+x$		$+3x$
EQUILIBRIUM	Solid		$+x$		$+3x$
ANSWER					

$$K_{sp} = [Au^{3+}][Cl^-]^3 = (x)(3x)^3$$

Since $x = 3.3 \times 10^{-7}$,

$$K_{sp} = (3.3 \times 10^{-7})(3 \times 3.3 \times 10^{-7})^3$$
$$= 3.2 \times 10^{-25}$$

12. **D** $$K_c = \frac{[CO_2][H_2O]^2}{[CH_4][O_2]^3} = \frac{(M)(M)^2}{(M)(M)^3} = \frac{1}{M} = M^{-1}$$

13. **B** A catalyst affects only the rate at which equilibrium is reached, not the amount of product formed.

14. **E** In an exothermic reaction the amount of product decreases with increasing temperature.

$$\text{Reactants} \rightleftharpoons \text{Products} + \text{Heat}$$

which is the general equation for an exothermic reaction, illustrates that adding heat by increasing the temperature forces the reaction toward the reactant side.

15. **A** The reaction rate has nothing to do with the size of the equilibrium constant.

16. **D** $$[Ag^+] = \frac{K_{sp}}{[Cl^-]} = \frac{1.0 \times 10^{-10}}{0.100} = 1.0 \times 10^{-9} \text{ M}$$

when AgCl starts to precipitate.

$$[I^-] = \frac{K_{sp}}{[Ag^+]} = \frac{8.3 \times 10^{-17}}{1.0 \times 10^{-9}} = 8.3 \times 10^{-8} \text{ M}$$

17. **E** $$K_{sp} = 1.1 \times 10^{-10} = [Ba^{2+}][SO_4^{2-}] = [x][x + 2.4 \times 10^3].$$

Assume $2.4 \times 10^{-3} \gg x$ so that

$$1.1 \times 10^{-10} = (x)(2.4 \times 10^{-3})$$

and

$$x = \frac{1.1 \times 10^{-10}}{2.4 \times 10^{-3}} = 4.6 \times 10^{-8} \text{ M}$$

Here x is the concentration of Ba^{2+} and the molar solubility of $BaSO_4$.

18. **D** When the initial amount of HI is known, only one: I_2, H_2, or HI needs to be measured to determine the equilibrium constant. Therefore, it is *not* important to measure all three concentrations.

19. **B**

REACTION	2 SO$_2$	+	O$_2$	$\rightleftharpoons$	2 SO$_3$
INITIAL CONCENTRA-TION	0.00300 M		0.00300 M		0.00300 M
CHANGE	2x		x		− 2x
EQUILIBRIUM	0.00300 + 2x		0.00300 + x		0.00300 − 2x
ANSWER	3.50 × 10^{-5} M				

From the last two lines

$$3.50 \times 10^{-5} = 0.00300 + 2x$$

Solve for x to get $x = -0.00148$, which yields

$$[O_2] = 0.00152 \text{ M} \quad \text{and} \quad [SO_3] = 0.00596 \text{ M}$$

on the answer line.
Then

$$K_{eq} = \frac{[SO_3]^2}{[SO_2]^2[O_2]} = \frac{(0.00596)^2}{(3.50 \times 10^{-5})^2(0.00152)} = 1.9 \times 10^7$$

20. **B** Since the two reactions are added to obtain the overall reaction

$$K_{overall} = K_{a1}K_{a2} = (2.3 \times 10^{-4})(4.5 \times 10^{-7}) = 1.0 \times 10^{-10}$$

Chapter 11

1. **B** The activated complex may be described as the structure of the colliding reactants.
2. **E** A zero-order reaction, Rate $= k$, satisfies the condition stated in the question.
3. **A** The x-axis (B) is the reaction coordinate, the y-axis (A) is the potential energy, and C represents the activation energy.
4. **D** This is an endothermic reaction, with the activation energy larger for the forward reaction than for the reverse reaction.
5. **C** Catalysts have an effect on the activation energy.
6. **D** The lower the activation energy, the faster the reaction.
7. **D** These are the units for a third-order rate constant.
8. **A** Adding an inert gas has no effect on the reaction rate.

9. **A** $\ln(2) = kt_{1/2}$

$$k = \frac{\ln(2)}{t_{1/2}} = \frac{0.693}{(36 \text{ min})(60 \text{ s min}^{-1})} = 3.2 \times 10^{-4} \text{ s}^{-1}$$

10. **D** $$\frac{\text{Rate}_1}{\text{Rate}_2} = \left(\frac{\text{Conc}_1}{\text{Conc}_2}\right)^x_v$$

where x is the exponent in the rate law. Consequently, $8 = 2^x$, based on the information in the question, and x must be 3.

11. **C** The reaction rate is an exponential function given by the Arrhenius equation. Since the activation energy is not given in this problem, we rely on the rule of thumb that the reaction rate doubles for each 10°C increase in temperature. A 20°C increase in temperature will increase the rate by a factor of approximately 4.

12. **C** Integrated rate equations for second-order reactions involve $\frac{1}{[A]}$ terms.

13. **C** $$? \frac{\text{mol O}_2}{\text{L s}} = \frac{2.2 \times 10^{-2} \text{ mol CO}_2}{\text{L s}} \left(\frac{15 \text{ mol O}_2}{12 \text{ mol CO}_2}\right)$$
$$= 2.8 \times 10^{-2} \text{ mol O}_2 \text{ L}^{-1}\text{s}^{-1}$$

14. **C** The Arrhenius plot is most useful in determining the stability or shelf-life of consumer products since it allows the chemist to predict the rate of reaction at any temperature.

15. **E** The Arrhenius equation is

$$\ln k = \frac{-E_a}{RT} + \text{const.}$$

Consequently $\ln k$ is plotted versus $\frac{1}{T}$.

16. **C** $$\frac{255 \text{ s}}{85 \text{ s half-life}^{-1}} = 3 \text{ half-lives}$$
$$\left(\frac{1}{2}\right)^3 = \frac{1}{8}$$

17. **C** the sum of the exponents of all concentrations is the order of the reaction.

18. **D** $$k[A]^2[B] = k\left[\frac{A}{2}\right]^2[4B]$$

19. **A** in the oven the rate is 2^{10} or 1024 times faster than at 25°C.

$$(2 \text{ days})(1024) = 2048 \text{ days}$$

is the shelf-life at 25°C.

20. **C** The main purpose of the catalytic converter is to reduce hydrocarbon emissions by combusting any unburned or partially burned fuel.

Chapter 12

1. **D** $q_v = -$ (heat capacity)$(\Delta T) = -$ (3245 J °C^{-1})(6.795°C) $= -$ 22.05 kJ

   The sign is negative since heat is released in the reaction.

2. **B** $$\Delta H = q_p$$

   In question 1, q_v was determined. To convert between q_v and q_p requires calculation of the work or $P \, \Delta V$. However, $CH_4 + 2\,O_2 \rightarrow CO_2 + 2\,H_2O$ and $\Delta n_g = 0$ so no volume change is expected and $q_p = q_v$.

   $$\Delta H° = \frac{q_p}{mol\ CH_4} = \frac{22.05\ kJ}{0.4\ g/16\ g\ mol^{-1}} = -822\ kJ$$

3. **A** A system where ΔG^0 is always positive will always be nonspontaneous. For this to occur, ΔH^0 must be positive and ΔS^0 must be negative.

4. **B** The condensation of water indicates that the solution becomes cold and the solution process is endothermic. Consequently, ΔH^0 must be positive; and if solution occurs, ΔG^0 must be negative, requiring that ΔS^0 be positive.

5. **C** When liquid CH_4 is burned, the greatest decrease in the moles of gas $(\Delta n_g = -2)$ is obtained.

6. **E** During a phase change $\Delta G^0 = 0$ and T $\Delta S^0 = \Delta H^0$.
   Calculate

   $$\Delta S^0 = \frac{\Delta H^0}{T} = \frac{+43900\ J}{373\ K} = +118\ J\ K^{-1}$$

7. **A** The atoms in a metal act in a similar manner, and therefore the heat absorbed depends on the number of atoms, not their mass.

8. **E** $w = -P\Delta V = -$ (1.00 atm)(10.0 L) $= -$ 10.0 L atm

9. **D** Both forms of the universal gas constant are needed. The ratio of the two forms of this constant has units of $\dfrac{L\ atm}{J}$ is used as the factor label for the conversion.

10. **B** Except for small molecules, the entropy change is a large positive value.

11. **A** Entropy can be experimentally determined. Only changes in the other thermodynamic quantities can be measured.

12. **B** The reaction is

    $$2CH_3OH(\ell) + 3O_2(g) \longrightarrow 2CO_2(g) + 4H_2O(g)$$

    $$\Delta H° = [(2\ mol)(-393.5\ kJ\ mol^{-1}) + (4\ mol)(-241.8\ kJ\ mol^{-1})]$$
    $$-\ [(2\ mol)(-238.6\ kJ\ mol^{-1})]$$
    $$= -\ 1277\ kJ$$

13. **E** The rate of a reaction cannot be determined from thermodynamic quantities.

14. **C** The ΔH^0 value for first reaction is subtracted from the value for second reaction.

    $$\Delta H^0 = \Delta H^0(\text{second react}) - \Delta H^0(\text{first react})$$
    $$= -\ 113.14\ kJ - 57.93\ kJ$$
    $$= -\ 171.07\ kJ$$

15. **D** Only changes in temperature change ΔG^0. The fact that the temperature change is measured in Celsius degrees is not significant. Thermodynamic calculations involving temperature require conversion to the Kelvin scale.

16. **A**
$$\Delta G^0 = -RT \ln K_{eq} = 0.00$$

since the natural log of 1.00 is zero.

$$\Delta G^0 = \Delta H^0 - T\Delta S^0$$

and since $\Delta G^0 = 0$, we find

$$\Delta H^0 = T\Delta S^0$$

$$T = \frac{\Delta H^0}{\Delta S^0} = \frac{15300 \text{ J mol}^{-1}}{22.6 \text{ J mol}^{-1}\text{ K}^{-1}} = 677 \text{ K}$$

$$°C = 677 \text{ K} - 273 \text{ K} = 404°C$$

17. **E**
$$\Delta H^0 = -(2 \text{ mol})(-396 \text{ kJ mol}^{-1})$$
$$= +792 \text{ kJ (heats of formation for elements} = 0)$$
$$\Delta S^0 = (3 \text{ mol O}_2)(205 \text{ J mol}^{-1}\text{K}^{-1}) + (2 \text{ mol S})(31.8 \text{ J mol}^{-1}\text{K}^{-1})$$
$$- (2 \text{ mol SO}_3)(256 \text{ J mol}^{-1}\text{K}^{-1})$$
$$= 167 \text{ J K}^{-1}$$
$$\Delta G^0 = 792 \text{ kJ} - (298\text{K})(0.167 \text{ kJ K}^{-1}) = 742 \text{ kJ}$$

18. **B** We expect the combustion of organic compounds to produce heat and be exothermic, ΔH^0 negative. Since 15 mol of reactant gas produces 12 mol of product gas, we expect a decrease in entropy, ΔS^0 negative.
19. **C** Heat must be added to evaporate a liquid, and therefore ΔH^0 is positive. Since the liquid becomes a gas, ΔS^0 is also positive.
20. **E** Combustion of organic compounds produces heat; therefore ΔH^0 is negative.

Chapter 13

1. **D** The balanced half-reaction is
$$8e^- + 10H^+ + NO_3^- \longrightarrow NH_4^+ + 3H_2O$$

2. **B** The half-reaction is
$$5e^- + 8H^+ + MnO_4^- \longrightarrow Mn^{2+} + 4H_2O$$

and B is the correct form.
3. **B** The first two reactions show that Cu and Zn metals are more effective reducing agents than Ag. The last reaction shows that Zn is a better reducing agent than Cu. Consequently, Zn is the strongest reducing agent, and Ag the weakest, of the three.

4. **B**

$$E^0_{cell} = E^0_{reduction} - E^0_{oxidation}$$

Since Fe is oxidized and Pb is reduced,

$$E^0_{cell} = +1.46 - (+0.77) = +0.69 \text{ V}$$

5. **E** The nitrogen in the nitrate ion has an oxidation number of $+5$.

6. **A** Zinc reacts with acids. The others are very active and react with water.

7. **A**

$$2H_2O \longrightarrow O_2 + 4H^+ + 4e^-$$

occurs at the anode.

$$Cu^{2+} + 2e^- \longrightarrow Cu$$

occurs at the cathode.

8. **D** H ions are reduced before Na ions.

9. **B** Chlorine can have $-1, +1, +3, +5,$ and $+7$ for its oxidation states.

10. **A**

$$\Delta G^0 = -n\mathscr{F}E^0_{cell}$$

and

$$\Delta G^0 = -RT \ln K$$

Therefore

$$-n\mathscr{F}E^0_{cell} = -RT \ln K$$

Calculate

$$\ln K = \frac{-n\mathscr{F}E^0_{cell}}{-RT} = \frac{(2)(96485 \text{ C mol}^{-1})(0.82 \text{ V})}{(8.314 \text{ V C mol}^{-1}\text{K}^{-1})(318 \text{ K})} = 59.85$$

$$K = 9.8 \times 10^{25}$$

11. **C** A nonspontaneous reaction must have a negative value for E^0_{cell}. The value closest to zero, here -0.12 V, will produce the greatest amount of product.

12. **B**

$$\text{mol} = \frac{It}{n\mathscr{F}} = \frac{(1.23 \text{ A})(2.5 \text{ h})(60 \text{ min h}^{-1})(60 \text{ s min}^{-1})}{(2)(96485 \text{ C mol}^{-1})} = 0.0574 \text{ mol}$$

$$\text{Molar mass} = \frac{\text{g compound}}{\text{mol compound}} = \frac{3.37 \text{ g}}{0.0574 \text{ mol}} = 58.7 \text{ g mol}^{-1}$$

Nickel has a molar mass of 58.7.

13. **D** Since the reaction is not at standard state, we cannot tell whether or not it would be spontaneous under standard conditions. The chemicals in the cell will react in the reverse direction when mixed.

14. **B** The ratio of Kelvin temperatures is

$$\frac{303}{293} = 1.034$$

Thus the change is due simply to the temperature change. This indicates also that for this reaction K is the same at these two temperatures and $\Delta H° = 0.0$ kJ.

15. **C** Iron is produced in high-temperature kilns by reduction with carbon; the others are produced by electrolysis.

16. **C** Chlorine has an oxidation number of $+5$. The nitrogen in the nitrate ion, NO_3^- is also $+5$.

17. **B**
$$Cu^{2+} + 2e^- \longrightarrow Cu^0$$
$$mol = \frac{g\ Cu}{molar\ mass} = \frac{It}{n\mathscr{F}}$$

Rearranging the equation yields

$$t = \frac{(gCu)n\mathscr{F}}{(molar\ mass)I} = \frac{(2.00\ g)(2)(96,485\ C\ mol^{-1})}{(63.5\ g\ mol^{-1})(1.25C\ s^{-1})} = 4862\ s = 81\ min$$

18. **D** The balanced half-reaction is

$$10e^- + 12H^+ + 2IO_3^- \longrightarrow I_2 + 6H_2O$$

19. **D** The standard cell voltage is a measure of the equilibrium constant or Gibbs free energy, not a rate constant.

20. **D** Electrolysis does not necessarily produce a gas at either the anode or the cathode.

Chapter 14

1. **C** Carbonic acid is a weaker acid than acetic acid, and its salt will be a stronger base, giving a solution with a higher pH. NaCl has no effect on the pH and A and B are acids with pH values less than 7.

2. **D** In solution only conjugate acid-base pairs exist. The oxalate ion and oxalic acid differ by more than one H^+. The ions of sodium sulfate (choice C) can exist in solution together.

3. **E** The solution contains 0.100 mol of H_3PO_4, and the addition of 0.250 mol of NaOH represents 2.5 mol base for each mole of phosphoric acid. The first 2 mol of base convert the H_3PO_4 to HPO_4^{2-}. The next 0.5 mol of base converts only half of the HPO_4^{2-} to PO_4^{3-}, and the resulting solution is a mixture of these two ions.

4. **B** We need a weak acid with a pK_a within 1 pH unit of 10.00 or a weak base with a pK_b within 1 pH unit of 4.00 (pOH). Ammonia comes closest to these requirements.

5. **A** When the concentrations of the conjugate acid and base are equal, pH = pK_a.

6. **E**
$$[OH^-] = 3 \times 1.23 \times 10^{-3} = 3.69 \times 10^{-3} M$$
$$pOH = -\log(3.69 \times 10^{-3}) = 2.43$$
$$pH = 14.00 - 2.43 = 11.57$$

7. **C** $pK_a = 5.19$. At pH values below 4.19 the indicator will be red, and at pH values above 6.19 the indicator will be yellow. From 4.19 to 6.19 it will be various shades of orange, the combination of red and yellow.

8. **D** Using the Henderson-Hasselbach equation gives

$$pH = pK_a + \log\left(\frac{[\text{conj. base}]}{[\text{conj. acid}]}\right)$$

Solving this yields

$$4.87 = 4.48 + \log\left(\frac{[\text{conj. base}]}{[\text{conj. acid}]}\right)$$

$$0.39 = \log\left(\frac{[\text{conj. base}]}{[\text{conj. acid}]}\right)$$

$$2.45 = \frac{[\text{conj. base}]}{[\text{conj. acid}]}$$

9. **D** The greater number of oxygen atoms on HNO_3 weakens the bond with hydrogen, causing it to be a strong acid. Nitrous acid, HNO_2, is a weak acid.

10. **C** The anion is amphiprotic and can act as both an acid and a base.

$$pH = \frac{pK_2 + pK_3}{2} = \frac{7.20 + 12.35}{2} = 9.78$$

11. **E** Each of these methods results in a solution containing a conjugate acid and its conjugate base in significant amounts, therefore resulting in a buffer solution.

12. **D** Sulfuric acid, H_2SO_4, dissociates its first proton completely and is a strong acid. The second proton does not dissociate completely and is weak.

13. **E** The reaction is $N_2O_5 + H_2O \rightarrow 2\,HNO_3$.

14. **A** CH_4 lacks the capacity either to accept or to donate electron pairs.

15. **B** In this ion, NH_3 is the ligand, which is another name for a Lewis base.

16. **B**
$$pOH = 14.00 - 10.45 = 3.55$$

and

$$[OH^-] = 2.82 \times 10^{-4} M$$

For a weak base

$$[OH^-] = \sqrt{K_b C_b}$$

Then

$$K_b = \frac{[OH^-]^2}{C_b} = \frac{7.95 \times 10^{-8}}{0.125} = 6.4 \times 10^{-7}$$

17. **B** An aqueous solution always contains H^+ and OH^- ions. In this solution the major solutes are K^+ and F^-, while a small amount of F^- hydrolyzes to form HF.

18. **C** Addition of distilled water to a buffer does not change the pH unless a very large amount of water is added to a small volume of buffer.

19. **D** The equation is

$$NaOH + HCl \longrightarrow NaCl + H_2O$$

$$\text{mmol HCl} = (0.0134 \text{ M})(50.0 \text{ mL}) = 0.670 \text{ mmol HCl}$$

$$\text{mmol NaOH} = (0.0250 \text{ M})(24.0 \text{ mL}) = 0.600 \text{ mmol NaOH}$$

There is an excess of 0.070 mmol HCl, and the total volume is

$$50.0 + 24.0 = 74.0 \text{ mL}$$

$$M_{acid} = \frac{0.070}{74} = 9.46 \times 10^{-4} \text{ M}$$

$$pH = -\log (9.46 \times 10^{-4}) = 3.02$$

20. **C** This is a buffer solution:

$$[HCHO_2] = \frac{50.0 \text{ g}/46 \text{ g mol}^{-1}}{0.500 \text{ L}} = 2.17$$

$$[NaCHO_2] = \frac{30.0 \text{ g}/68 \text{ g mol}^{-1}}{0.500 \text{ L}} = 0.882$$

$$[H^+] = \frac{K_a[HCHO_2]}{[NaCHO_2]} = \frac{1.8 \times 10^{-4} (2.17)}{0.882} = 4.4 \times 10^{-4}$$

$$pH = -\log (4.4 \times 10^{-4}) = 3.35$$

Chapter 15

1. **B** A terminal $-C{=}O$ is an aldehyde functional group.
2. **E** Propane contains three carbons, and propyl groups also contain three carbon atoms.
3. **C** Condensation reactions between organic acids and amines form peptide bonds.
4. **E** All of these are properties of stereo isomers.
5. **E** All of these reactions occur.
6. **E** Since $[-CH_2CHCl-]_n$ does not contain a peptide or ester bond, it must be an addition polymer formed from a monomer that contains a double bond.
7. **A** Propane-1-ol is the correct IUPAC name.

8. **C** Proteins are condensation polymers of the 21 natural amino acids.

9. **C** These are the functional groups for an organic acid and an organic base, and they participate in a neutralization or acid-base reaction. They could also form a peptide bond, but that is not one of the choices.

10. **C** Cis-trans isomers involve side groups attached to double-bonded carbon atoms only. In carbon compounds sp^2 bonding represents a double bond.

11. **E** An ether has the lowest polarity of all choices and should have the lowest boiling point.

12. **A** An alkyne contains triple bonds but does not contain oxygen.

13. **C** $-NH_2$ is the organic base functional group.

14. **A** Meta positioning represents one group on the 1 carbon and another on the 3 carbon in a benzene ring.

15. **E** Both benzene and ethylene are flat molecules because of the double bonds, which are sp^2 (trigonal planar) in geometry.

16. **E** There are 6 C—C sigma bonds, 6 C—H sigma bonds, and 3 pi bonds in the benzene ring.

17. **B** The alcohol is the only compound with an —OH group, needed for hydrogen bonding.

18. **A** An alkyne has virtually no polarity. Every other choice has an oxygen that is polar to some extent, resulting in a higher boiling point.

19. **A** The general formula for alkenes is C_nH_{2n}, and the percentage of carbon will always be 85.7%.

20. **C** The name carbohydrate is derived from the empirical formula for these compounds, CH_2O.

Chapter 16

1. **A** A buret will measure this volume most accurately.

2. **C** Methane does not dissolve in water, so displacement of water is used to collect this compound.

3. **D** Centrifugation is best. Fine precipitates clog filters. Drying and distillation are very time consuming and do not remove any soluble ions present.

4. **B** The answer to the calculation must have three significant figures and is 2.05×10^3. The relative uncertainty is

$$\frac{0.01 \times 10^3}{2.05 \times 10^3} = 0.005 \text{ or } 5 \times 10^{-3}$$

5. **A** To prepare a molar solution, the solvent is added to the solute to achieve the total volume of solution desired. By adding the solute to 1 L of water the final volume will not be 1 L.

6. **B** Pressure is the dependent variable and is the y-axis of the graph.

7. **D** Prelab writeups are done at home or in the library before entering the lab. Safety glasses are always required for any work in the lab.

8. **C** Drying the solid allows an accurate determination of the compound measured but has little effect on the dissolution process.

9. **C** $Al(OH)_3$ is amphiprotic. An acid will neutralize the hydroxide ions, and a base will form a hydroxy complex, which is soluble.

10. **C** For a monoprotic acid titrated with a monobasic base, $M_aV_a = M_bV_b$. The molarity of the acid is calculated as

$$M_a = \frac{M_b V_b}{V_a}.$$

Droplets left in the buret mean that the volume of base reported is larger than the volume that the buret actually delivered. Since the V_b reported is larger than it should be, the M_a calculated using the above equation is too high.

11. **E** $C_i V_i = C_f V_f$. When the analysis is started,

$$C_i(5.00\text{ mL}) = (3.0 \times 10^{-3}\text{ M})(100\text{ mL})$$
$$= 6.0 \times 10^{-2}\text{ M}.$$

The preservative step adds an equal volume of preservative to the sample. Choose any two volumes so that the final volume is twice the initial sample volume. Then

$$C_i(50\text{ mL}) = (6.0 \times 10^{-2}\text{ M})(100\text{ mL})$$
$$= 1.2 \times 10^{-1}\text{ M}$$

12. **E** Unlike $PbCl_2$, the other chloride precipitates, $AgCl$ and Hg_2CL_2, are not soluble in hot water. Since all the precipitate dissolves, they are not present. Also, since the unknown was colored, we may deduce that a transition metal ion is present.

13. **D** CO_2 and H_2S are the only gases produced when a solution is acidified. CO_2 has no odor, but H_2S smells like rotten eggs. NH_3 is formed when a solution is made alkaline.

14. **E** All of these ions are confirmed with flame tests.

15. **C** $CrCl_3$ is a soluble salt. Reacting precisely 3 moles of HCl with 1 mole of $Cr(OH)_3$ will produce a solution containing only Cr^{3+} and Cl^- ions, which can be dried to obtain pure $CrCl_3$. The other mixtures contain other ions in addition to Cr^{3+} and Cl^-. This results either in an impure product or reactions that will not form $CrCl_3$.

16. **B** Titration is the most common method. Choices A and D are possible, but not widely used, methods; E and C are imprecise methods.

17. **C** Calcium sulfide is relatively soluble and is not precipitated in the qual-scheme.

18. **E** This is the only choice left since A, B, C, and D are all correct.

19. **A** The correct approach is to abandon the experiment and start again.

20. **E** The data for the experiment should fill most of the graph.

Electronic Configurations of the Elements

H	$1s^1$
He	$1s^2$
Li	$1s^2\ 2s^1$
Be	$1s^2\ 2s^2$
B	$1s^2\ 2s^22p^1$
C	$1s^2\ 2s^22p^2$
N	$1s^2\ 2s^22p^3$
O	$1s^2\ 2s^22p^4$
F	$1s^2\ 2s^22p^5$
Ne	$1s^2\ 2s^22p^6$
Na	$1s^2\ 2s^22p^6\ 3s^1$
Mg	$1s^2\ 2s^22p^6\ 3s^2$
Al	$1s^2\ 2s^22p^6\ 3s^23p^1$
Si	$1s^2\ 2s^22p^6\ 3s^23p^2$
P	$1s^2\ 2s^22p^6\ 3s^23p^3$
S	$1s^2\ 2s^22p^6\ 3s^23p^4$
Cl	$1s^2\ 2s^22p^6\ 3s^23p^5$
Ar	$1s^2\ 2s^22p^6\ 3s^23p^6$
K	$1s^2\ 2s^22p^6\ 3s^23p^6\ 4s^1$
Ca	$1s^2\ 2s^22p^6\ 3s^23p^6\ 4s^2$
Sc	$1s^2\ 2s^22p^6\ 3s^23p^6\ 4s^23d^1$
Ti	$1s^2\ 2s^22p^6\ 3s^23p^6\ 4s^23d^2$
V	$1s^2\ 2s^22p^6\ 3s^23p^6\ 4s^23d^3$
Cr	$1s^2\ 2s^22p^6\ 3s^23p^6\ 4s^13d^5$
Mn	$1s^2\ 2s^22p^6\ 3s^23p^6\ 4s^23d^5$
Fe	$1s^2\ 2s^22p^6\ 3s^23p^6\ 4s^23d^6$
Co	$1s^2\ 2s^22p^6\ 3s^23p^6\ 4s^23d^7$
Ni	$1s^2\ 2s^22p^6\ 3s^23p^6\ 4s^23d^8$
Cu	$1s^2\ 2s^22p^6\ 3s^23p^6\ 4s^13d^{10}$
Zn	$1s^2\ 2s^22p^6\ 3s^23p^6\ 4s^23d^{10}$
Ga	$1s^2\ 2s^22p^6\ 3s^23p^6\ 4s^23d^{10}4p^1$
Ge	$1s^2\ 2s^22p^6\ 3s^23p^6\ 4s^23d^{10}4p^2$
As	$1s^2\ 2s^22p^6\ 3s^23p^6\ 4s^23d^{10}4p^3$
Se	$1s^2\ 2s^22p^6\ 3s^23p^6\ 4s^23d^{10}4p^4$
Br	$1s^2\ 2s^22p^6\ 3s^23p^6\ 4s^23s^{10}4p^5$
Kr	$1s^2\ 2s^22p^6\ 3s^23p^6\ 4s^23d^{10}4p^6$
Rb	$1s^2\ 2s^22p^6\ 3s^23p^6\ 4s^23d^{10}4p^6\ 5s^1$
Sr	$1s^2\ 2s^22p^6\ 3s^23p^6\ 4s^23d^{10}4p^6\ 5s^2$
Y	$1s^2\ 2s^22p^6\ 3s^23p^6\ 4s^23d^{10}4p^6\ 5s^24d^1$
Zr	$1s^2\ 2s^22p^6\ 3s^23p^6\ 4s^23d^{10}4p^6\ 5s^24d^2$

Nb	$1s^2\ 2s^22p^6\ 3s^23p^6\ 4s^23d^{10}4p^6\ 5s^14d^4$
Mo	$1s^2\ 2s^22p^6\ 3s^23p^6\ 4s^23d^{10}4p^6\ 5s^14d^5$
Tc	$1s^2\ 2s^22p^6\ 3s^23p^6\ 4s^23d^{10}4p^6\ 5s^24d^5$
Ru	$1s^2\ 2s^22p^6\ 3s^23p^6\ 4s^23d^{10}4p^6\ 5s^14d^7$
Rh	$1s^2\ 2s^22p^6\ 3s^23p^6\ 4s^23s^{10}4p^6\ 5s^14d^8$
Pd	$1s^2\ 2s^22p^6\ 3s^23p^6\ 4s^23d^{10}4p^64d^{10}$
Ag	$1s^2\ 2s^22p^6\ 3s^23p^6\ 4s^23d^{10}4p^6\ 5s^14s^{10}$
Cd	$1s^2\ 2s^22p^6\ 3s^23p^6\ 4s^23d^{10}4p^6\ 5s^24d^{10}$
In	$1s^2\ 2s^22p^6\ 3s^23p^6\ 4s^23d^{10}4p^6\ 5s^24d^{10}5p^1$
Sn	$1s^2\ 2s^22p^6\ 3s^23p^6\ 4s^23d^{10}4p^6\ 5s^24d^{10}5p^2$
Sb	$1s^2\ 2s^22p^6\ 3s^23p^6\ 4s^23d^{10}4p^6\ 5s^24d^{10}5p^3$
Te	$1s^2\ 2s^22p^6\ 3s^23p^6\ 4s^23d^{10}4p^6\ 5s^24d^{10}5p^4$
I	$1s^2\ 2s^22p^6\ 3s^23p^6\ 4s^23d^{10}4p^6\ 5s^24d^{10}5p^5$
Xe	$1s^2\ 2s^22p^6\ 3s^23p^6\ 4s^23d^{10}4p^6\ 5s^24d^{10}5p^6$
Cs	$1s^2\ 2s^22p^6\ 3s^23p^6\ 4s^23d^{10}4p^6\ 5s^24d^{10}5p^6\ 6s^1$
Ba	$1s^2\ 2s^22p^6\ 3s^23p^6\ 4s^23d^{10}4p^6\ 5s^24d^{10}5p^6\ 6s^2$
La	$1s^2\ 2s^22p^6\ 3s^23p^6\ 4s^23d^{10}4p^6\ 5s^24d^{10}5p^6\ 6s^24f^1$
Ce	$1s^2\ 2s^22p^6\ 3s^23p^6\ 4s^23d^{10}4p^6\ 5s^24d^{10}5p^6\ 6s^24f^2$
Pr	$1s^2\ 2s^22p^6\ 3s^23p^6\ 4s^23d^{10}4p^6\ 5s^24d^{10}5p^6\ 6s^24f^3$
Nd	$1s^2\ 2s^22p^6\ 3s^23p^6\ 4s^23d^{10}4p^6\ 5s^24d^{10}5p^6\ 6s^24f^4$
Pm	$1s^2\ 2s^22p^6\ 3s^23p^6\ 4s^23d^{10}4p^6\ 5s^24d^{10}5p^6\ 6s^24f^5$
Sm	$1s^2\ 2s^22p^6\ 3s^23p^6\ 4s^23d^{10}4p^6\ 5s^24d^{10}5p^6\ 6s^24f^6$
Eu	$1s^2\ 2s^22p^6\ 3s^23p^6\ 4s^23d^{10}4p^6\ 5s^24d^{10}5p^6\ 6s^24f^7$
Gd	$1s^2\ 2s^22p^6\ 3s^23p^6\ 4s^23d^{10}4p^6\ 5s^24d^{10}5p^6\ 6s^24f^75d^1$
Tb	$1s^2\ 2s^22p^6\ 3s^23p^6\ 4s^23d^{10}4p^6\ 5s^24d^{10}5p^6\ 6s^24f^9$
Dy	$1s^2\ 2s^22p^6\ 3s^23p^6\ 4s^23d^{10}4p^6\ 5s^24d^{10}5p^6\ 6s^24f^{10}$
Ho	$1s^2\ 2s^22p^6\ 3s^23p^6\ 4s^23d^{10}4p^6\ 5s^24d^{10}5p^6\ 6s^24f^{11}$
Er	$1s^2\ 2s^22p^6\ 3s^23p^6\ 4s^23d^{10}4p^6\ 5s^24d^{10}5p^6\ 6s^24f^{12}$
Tm	$1s^2\ 2s^22p^6\ 3s^23p^6\ 4s^23d^{10}4p^6\ 5s^24d^{10}5p^6\ 6s^24f^{13}$
Yb	$1s^2\ 2s^22p^6\ 3s^23p^6\ 4s^23d^{10}4p^6\ 5s^24d^{10}5p^6\ 6s^24f^{14}$
Lu	$1s^2\ 2s^22p^6\ 3s^23p^6\ 4s^23d^{10}4p^6\ 5s^24d^{10}5p^6\ 6s^24f^{14}5d^1$
Hf	$1s^2\ 2s^22p^6\ 3s^23p^6\ 4s^23d^{10}4p^6\ 5s^24d^{10}5p^6\ 6s^24f^{14}5d^2$
Ta	$1s^2\ 2s^22p^6\ 3s^23p^6\ 4s^23d^{10}4p^6\ 5s^24d^{10}5p^6\ 6s^24f^{14}5d^3$
W	$1s^2\ 2s^22p^6\ 3s^23p^6\ 4s^23d^{10}4p^6\ 5s^24d^{10}5p^6\ 6s^24f^{14}5d^4$
Re	$1s^2\ 2s^22p^6\ 3s^23p^6\ 4s^23d^{10}4p^6\ 5s^24d^{10}5p^6\ 6s^24f^{14}5d^5$
Os	$1s^2\ 2s^22p^6\ 3s^23p^6\ 4s^23d^{10}4p^6\ 5s^24d^{10}5p^6\ 6s^24f^{14}5d^6$
Ir	$1s^2\ 2s^22p^6\ 3s^23p^6\ 4s^23d^{10}4p^6\ 5s^24d^{10}5p^6\ 6s^24f^{14}5d^7$
Pt	$1s^2\ 2s^22p^6\ 3s^23p^6\ 4s^23d^{10}4p^6\ 5s^24d^{10}5p^6\ 6s^14f^{14}5d^9$
Au	$1s^2\ 2s^22p^6\ 3s^23p^6\ 4s^23d^{10}4p^6\ 5s^24d^{10}5p^6\ 6s^14f^{14}5d^{10}$
Hg	$1s^2\ 2s^22p^6\ 3s^23p^6\ 4s^23d^{10}4p^6\ 5s^24d^{10}5p^6\ 6s^24f^{14}5d^{10}$
Tl	$1s^2\ 2s^22p^6\ 3s^23p^6\ 4s^23d^{10}4p^6\ 5s^24d^{10}5p^6\ 6s^24f^{14}5d^{10}6p^1$
Pb	$1s^2\ 2s^22p^6\ 3s^23p^6\ 4s^23d^{10}4p^6\ 5s^24d^{10}5p^6\ 6s^24f^{14}5d^{10}6p^2$
Bi	$1s^2\ 2s^22p^6\ 3s^23p^6\ 4s^23d^{10}4p^6\ 5s^24d^{10}5p^6\ 6s^24f^{14}5d^{10}6p^3$
Po	$1s^2\ 2s^22p^6\ 3s^23p^6\ 4s^23d^{10}4p^6\ 5s^24d^{10}5p^6\ 6s^24f^{14}5d^{10}6p^4$
At	$1s^2\ 2s^22p^6\ 3s^23p^6\ 4s^23d^{10}4p^6\ 5s^24d^{10}5p^6\ 6s^24f^{14}5d^{10}6p^5$
Rn	$1s^2\ 2s^22p^6\ 3s^23p^6\ 4s^23d^{10}4p^6\ 5s^24d^{10}5p^6\ 6s^24f^{14}5d^{10}6p^6$
Fr	$1s^2\ 2s^22p^6\ 3s^23p^6\ 4s^23d^{10}4p^6\ 5s^24d^{10}5p^6\ 6s^24f^{14}5d^{10}6p^6\ 7s^1$
Ra	$1s^2\ 2s^22p^6\ 3s^23p^6\ 4s^23d^{10}4p^6\ 5s^24d^{10}5p^6\ 6s^24f^{14}5d^{10}6p^6\ 7s^2$
Ac	$1s^2\ 2s^22p^6\ 3s^23p^6\ 4s^23d^{10}4p^6\ 5s^24d^{10}5p^6\ 6s^24f^{14}5d^{10}6p^6\ 7s^26d^1$
Th	$1s^2\ 2s^22p^6\ 3s^23p^6\ 4s^23d^{10}4p^6\ 5s^24d^{10}5p^6\ 6s^24f^{14}5d^{10}6p^6\ 7s^26d^2$
Pa	$1s^2\ 2s^22p^6\ 3s^23p^6\ 4s^23d^{10}4p^6\ 5s^24d^{10}5p^6\ 6s^24f^{14}5d^{10}6p^6\ 7s^25f^26d^1$

U	$1s^2$	$2s^22p^6$	$3s^23p^6$	$4s^23d^{10}4p^6$	$5s^24d^{10}5p^6$	$6s^24f^{14}5d^{10}6p^6$	$7s^25f^36d^1$
Np	$1s^2$	$2s^22p^6$	$3s^23p^6$	$4s^23d^{10}4p^6$	$5s^24d^{10}5p^6$	$6s^24f^{14}5d^{10}6p^6$	$7s^25f^46d^1$
Pu	$1s^2$	$2s^22p^6$	$3s^23p^6$	$4s^23d^{10}4p^6$	$5s^24d^{10}5p^6$	$6s^24f^{14}5d^{10}6p^6$	$7s^25f^6$
Am	$1s^2$	$2s^22p^6$	$3s^23p^6$	$4s^23d^{10}4p^6$	$5s^24d^{10}5p^6$	$6s^24f^{14}5d^{10}6p^6$	$7s^25f^7$
Cm	$1s^2$	$2s^22p^6$	$3s^23p^6$	$4s^23d^{10}4p^6$	$5s^24d^{10}5p^6$	$6s^24f^{14}5d^{10}6p^6$	$7s^25f^76d^1$
Bk	$1s^2$	$2s^22p^6$	$3s^23p^6$	$4s^23d^{10}4p^6$	$5s^24d^{10}5p^6$	$6s^24f^{14}5d^{10}6p^6$	$7s^25f^9$
Cf	$1s^2$	$2s^22p^6$	$3s^23p^6$	$4s^23d^{10}4p^6$	$5s^24d^{10}5p^6$	$6s^24f^{14}5d^{10}6p^6$	$7s^25f^{10}$
Es	$1s^2$	$2s^22p^6$	$3s^23p^6$	$4s^23d^{10}4p^6$	$5s^24d^{10}5p^6$	$6s^24f^{14}5d^{10}6p^6$	$7s^25f^{11}$
Fm	$1s^2$	$2s^22p^6$	$3s^23p^6$	$4s^23d^{10}4p^6$	$5s^24d^{10}5p^6$	$6s^24f^{14}5d^{10}6p^6$	$7s^25f^{12}$
Md	$1s^2$	$2s^22p^6$	$3s^23p^6$	$4s^23d^{10}4p^6$	$5s^24d^{10}5p^6$	$6s^24f^{14}5d^{10}6p^6$	$7s^25f^{13}$
No	$1s^2$	$2s^22p^6$	$3s^23p^6$	$4s^23d^{10}4p^6$	$5s^24d^{10}5p^6$	$6s^24f^{14}5d^{10}6p^6$	$7s^25f^{14}$
Lr	$1s^2$	$2s^22p^6$	$3s^23p^6$	$4s^23d^{10}4p^6$	$5s^24d^{10}5p^6$	$6s^24f^{14}5d^{10}6p^6$	$7s^25f^{14}6d^1$

Thermodynamic Data for Selected Elements, Compounds, and Ions (25°C)

Substance	ΔH_f° (kJ/mol^{-1})	S^0 (J mol^{-1}K^{-1})	ΔG_f° (kJ/mol^{-1})
Aluminum			
Al(s)	0	28.3	0
AlCl$_3$(s)	−704	110.7	−629
Al$_2$O$_3$(s)	−1676	51.0	−1576.4
Al$_2$(SO$_4$)$_3$(s)	−3441	239	−3100
Barium			
Ba(s)	0	66.9	0
BaCO$_3$(s)	−1219	112	−1139
BaCl$_2$(s)	−860.2	125	−810.8
Ba(OH)$_2$(s)	−998.22	−8	−875.3
Ba(NO$_3$)$_2$(s)	−992	214	−795
BaSO$_4$(s)	−1465	132	−1353
Bromine			
Br$_2$(ℓ)	0	152.2	0
Br$_2$(g)	+30.9	245.4	3.11
HBr(g)	−36	198.5	53.1
Calcium			
Ca(s)	0	41.4	0
CaCO$_3$(s)	−1207	92.9	−1128.8
CaF$_2$(s)	−741	80.3	−1166
CaCl$_2$(s)	−795.8	114	−750.2
CaO(s)	−635.5	40	−604.2
Ca(OH)$_2$(s)	−986.6	76.1	896.76
CaSO$_4$(s)	−1433	107	−1320.3
Carbon			
C(s,graphite)	0	5.69	0
C(s,diamond)	+1.88	2.4	+2.9
CCl$_4$(ℓ)	−134	214.4	−65.3
CO(g)	−110	197.9	−137.3
CO$_2$(g)	−394	213.6	−394.4
CO$_2$(aq)	−413.8	117.6	−385.98
H$_2$CO$_3$(aq)	−699.65	187.4	−623.08
HCO$_3^-$(aq)	−691.99	91.2	−586.77

Substance	ΔH_f° (kJ/mol^{-1})	S^0 (J mol^{-1}K^{-1})	ΔG_f° (kJ/mol^{-1})
Carbon			
CO_3^{2-}(aq)	-677.14	-56.9	-527.81
HCN(g)	$+135.1$	201.7	$+124.7$
CN^-(aq)	$+150.6$	94.1	$+172.4$
CH_4(g)	-74.9	186.2	-50.79
C_2H_2(g)	$+227$	200.8	$+209$
C_2H_4(g)	$+51.9$	219.8	$+68.12$
C_2H_6(g)	-84.5	229.5	-32.9
C_3H_8(g)	-104	269.9	-23
C_4H_{10}(g)	-126	310.2	-17.0
$C_6H_6(\ell)$	$+49.0$	173.3	$+124.3$
$CH_3OH(\ell)$	-238	126.8	-166.2
$C_2H_5OH(\ell)$	-278	161	-174.8
$HCHO_2$(g)	-363	251	$+335$
$HC_2H_3O_2(\ell)$	-487.0	160	-392.5
$HCHO$(g)	-108.6	218.8	-102.5
CH_3CHO(g)	-167	250	-129
$(CH_3)_2CO(\ell)$	-248.1	200.4	-155.4
$C_6H_5CO_2H$(s)	-385.1	167.6	-245.3
Chlorine			
Cl_2(g)	0	223.0	0
HCl(g)	-92.5	186.7	-95.27
HCl(aq)	-167.2	56.5	-131.2
$HClO$(aq)	-131.3	106.8	-80.21
Chromium			
Cr(s)	0	23.8	0
$CrCl_2$(s)	-326	115	-282
$CrCl_3$(s)	-563.2	126	-493.7
Copper			
Cu(s)	0	33.15	0
$CuCl$(s)	-137.2	86.2	-119.87
$CuCl_2$(s)	-172	119	-131
$CuSO_4$(s)	-771.4	109	-661.8
Fluorine			
F_2(g)	0	202.7	0
F^-(aq)	-332.6	-13.8	-278.8
HF(g)	-271	173.5	-273
Hydrogen			
H_2(g)	0	130.6	0
$H_2O(\ell)$	-286	69.96	-237.2
H_2O(g)	-242	188.7	-228.6
Iron			
Fe(s)	0	27	0
Fe_2O_3(s)	-822.2	90.0	-741.0
Fe_3O_4(s)	-1118.4	146.4	-1015.4
Lead			
Pb(s)	0	64.8	0
$PbCl_2$(s)	-359.4	136	-314.1
PbS(s)	-100	91.2	-98.7
$PbSO_4$(s)	-920.1	149	-811.3

Substance	ΔH_f° (kJ/mol^{-1})	S^0 (J mol^{-1}K^{-1})	ΔG_f° (kJ/mol^{-1})
Lithium			
Li(s)	0	28.4	0
LiF(s)	-611.7	35.7	-583.3
LiCl(s)	-408	59.29	-383.7
Magnesium			
Mg(s)	0	32.5	0
MgCO$_3$(s)	-1113	65.7	-1029
MgF$_2$(s)	-1113	79.9	-1056
MgCl$_2$(s)	-641.8	89.5	-592.5
MgO(s)	-601.7	26.9	-569.4
Mg(OH)$_2$(s)	-924.7	63.1	-833.9
Manganese			
Mn(s)	0	32.0	0
MnO$_4^-$(aq)	-542.7	191	-449.4
KMnO$_4$(s)	-813.4	171.71	-713.8
MnO$_2$(s)	-520.9	53.1	-466.1
Nitrogen			
N$_2$(g)	0	191.5	0
NH$_3$(g)	-46.0	192.5	-16.7
NH$_4$Cl(s)	-314.4	94.6	-203.9
NO(g)	$+90.4$	210.6	$+86.69$
NO$_2$(g)	$+34$	240.5	$+51.84$
N$_2$O(g)	$+81.5$	220.0	$+103.6$
HNO$_3$(ℓ)	-174.1	155.6	-79.9
Oxygen			
O$_2$(g)	0	205.0	0
O$_3$(g)	$+143$	238.8	$+163$
OH$^-$(aq)	-230.0	-10.75	-157.24
Potassium			
K(s)	0	64.18	0
KF(s)	-567.3	66.6	-537.8
KCl(s)	-436.8	82.59	-408.3
KOH(s)	-424.8	78.9	-379.1
K$_2$SO$_4$(s)	-1433.7	176	-1316.4
Silver			
Ag(s)	0	42.55	0
AgCl(s)	-127.1	96.2	-109.8
AgNO$_3$(s)	-124	141	-32
Sodium			
Na(s)	0	51.0	0
NaF(s)	-571	51.5	-545
NaCl(s)	-413	72.38	-384.0
NaOH(s)	-426.8	64.18	-382
Na$_2$SO$_4$(s)	-1384.49	149.49	-1266.83
Sulfur			
S(s,rhombic)	0	31.8	0
SO$_2$(g)	-297	248	-300
SO$_3$(g)	-396	256	-370
H$_2$SO$_4$(aq)	-909.3	20.1	-744.5
SF$_6$(g)	-1209	292	-1105

Substance	ΔH_f° (kJ/mol^{-1})	S° (J mol^{-1}K^{-1})	ΔG_f° (kJ/mol^{-1})
Tin			
Sn(s,white)	0	51.6	0
SnCl$_4$(ℓ)	−511.3	258.6	−440.2
Zinc			
Zn(s)	0	41.6	0
ZnCl$_2$(s)	−415.1	111	−369.4

APPENDIX 4

Ionization Constants of Weak Acids

Monoprotic Acid	Name	K_a
HIO_3	Iodic acid	1.69×10^{-1}
HNO_2	Nitrous acid	7.1×10^{-4}
HF	Hydrofluoric acid	6.8×10^{-4}
$HCHO_2$	Formic acid	1.8×10^{-4}
$HC_3H_5O_3$	Lactic acid	1.38×10^{-4}
$HC_7H_5O_2$	Benzoic acid	6.28×10^{-5}
$HC_4H_7O_2$	Butanoic acid	1.52×10^{-5}
HN_3	Hydrazoic acid	1.8×10^{-5}
$HC_2H_3O_2$	Acetic acid	1.8×10^{-5}
$HC_3H_5O_2$	Propanoic acid	1.34×10^{-5}
$HOCl$	Hypochlorous acid	3.0×10^{-8}
HCN	Hydrocyanic acid	6.2×10^{-10}
HC_6H_5O	Phenol	1.3×10^{-10}
HOI	Hypoiodous acid	2.3×10^{-11}
H_2O_2	Hydrogen peroxide	1.8×10^{-12}

APPENDIX 5

Ionization Constants of Polyprotic Acids

Polyprotic Acid	Name	K_{a_1}	K_{a_2}	K_{a_3}
H_2SO_4	Sulfuric acid	large	1.0×10^{-2}	
H_2CrO_4	Chromic acid	5.0	1.5×10^{-6}	
$H_2C_2O_4$	Oxalic acid	5.6×10^{-2}	5.4×10^{-5}	
H_3PO_3	Phosphorous acid	3×10^{-2}	1.6×10^{-7}	
H_2SO_3	Sulfurous acid	1.2×10^{-2}	6.6×10^{-8}	
H_2SeO_3	Selenous acid	4.5×10^{-3}	1.1×10^{-8}	
$H_2C_3H_2O_4$	Malonic acid	1.4×10^{-3}	2.0×10^{-6}	
$H_2C_8H_4O_4$	Phthalic acid	1.1×10^{-3}	3.9×10^{-6}	
$H_2C_4H_4O_6$	Tartaric acid	9.2×10^{-4}	4.3×10^{-5}	
H_2CO_3	Carbonic acid	4.5×10^{-7}	4.7×10^{-11}	
H_3PO_4	Phosphoric acid	7.1×10^{-3}	6.3×10^{-8}	4.5×10^{-13}
H_3AsO_4	Arsenic acid	5.6×10^{-3}	1.7×10^{-7}	4.0×10^{-12}
$H_3C_6H_5O_7$	Citric acid	7.1×10^{-4}	1.7×10^{-5}	6.3×10^{-6}

APPENDIX 6

Ionization Constants of Weak Bases

Weak Base	Name	K_b
$(CH_3)_2NH$	Dimethylamine	9.6×10^{-4}
CH_3NH_2	Methylamine	4.4×10^{-4}
$CH_3CH_2NH_2$	Ethylamine	4.3×10^{-4}
$(CH_3)_3\,N$	Trimethylamine	7.4×10^{-5}
NH_3	Ammonia	1.8×10^{-5}
N_2H_4	Hydrazine	9.6×10^{-7}
C_5H_5N	Pyridine	1.5×10^{-9}
$C_6H_5NH_2$	Aniline	4.1×10^{-10}

APPENDIX 7

Solubility Product Constants

Salt	Dissolution Reaction	K_{sp}
Fluorides		
MgF_2	$MgF_2(s) \rightleftharpoons Mg^{2+}(aq) + 2F^-(aq)$	6.6×10^{-9}
CaF_2	$CaF_2(s) \rightleftharpoons Ca^{2+}(aq) + 2F^-(aq)$	3.9×10^{-1}
BaF_2	$BaF_2(s) \rightleftharpoons Ba^{2+}(aq) + 2F^-(aq)$	1.7×10^{-6}
PbF_2	$PbF_2(s) \rightleftharpoons Pb^{2+}(aq) + 2F^-(aq)$	3.6×10^{-8}
Chlorides		
$CuCl$	$CuCl(s) \rightleftharpoons Cu^+(aq) + Cl^-(aq)$	1.9×10^{-7}
$AgCl$	$AgCl(s) \rightleftharpoons Ag^+(aq) + Cl^-(aq)$	1.8×10^{-1}
$PbCl_2$	$PbCl_2 \rightleftharpoons Pb^{2+}(aq) + 2Cl^-(aq)$	1.7×10^{-5}
Bromides		
$CuBr$	$CuBr(s) \rightleftharpoons Cu^+(aq) + Br^-(aq)$	5×10^{-9}
$AgBr$	$AgBr(s) \rightleftharpoons Ag^+(aq) + Br^-(aq)$	5.0×10^{-1}
$PbBr_2$	$PbBr_2(s) \rightleftharpoons Pb^{2+}(aq) + 2Br^-(aq)$	2.1×10^{-6}
Iodides		
CuI	$CuI(s) \rightleftharpoons Cu^+(aq) + I^-(aq)$	1×10^{-1}
AgI	$AgI(s) \rightleftharpoons Ag^+(aq) + I^-(aq)$	8.3×10^{-1}
PbI_2	$PbI_2(s) \rightleftharpoons Pb^{2+}(aq) + 2I^-(aq)$	7.9×10^{-9}
Hydroxides		
$Mg(OH)_2$	$Mg(OH)_2(s) \rightleftharpoons Mg^{2+}(aq) + 2OH^-(aq)$	7.1×10^{-1}
$Ca(OH)_2$	$Ca(OH)_2(s) \rightleftharpoons Ca^{2+}(aq) + 2OH^-(aq)$	6.5×10^{-6}
$Mn(OH)_2$	$Mn(OH)_2(s) \rightleftharpoons Mn^{2+}(aq) + 2OH^-(aq)$	1.6×10^{-1}
$Fe(OH)_2$	$Fe(OH)_2(s) \rightleftharpoons Fe^{2+}(aq) + 2OH^-(aq)$	7.9×10^{-1}
$Fe(OH)_3$	$Fe(OH)_3(s) \rightleftharpoons Fe^{3+}(aq) + 3OH^-(aq)$	1.6×10^{-3}
$Ni(OH)_2$	$Ni(OH)_2(s) \rightleftharpoons Ni^{2+}(aq) + 2OH^-(aq)$	6×10^{-1}
$Cu(OH)_2$	$Cu(OH)_2(s) \rightleftharpoons Cu^{2+}(aq) + 2OH^-(aq)$	4.8×10^{-2}
$Cr(OH)_3$	$Cr(OH)_3(s) \rightleftharpoons Cr^{3+}(aq) + 3OH^-(aq)$	2×10^{-3}
$Zn(OH)_2$	$Zn(OH)_2(s) \rightleftharpoons Zn^{2+}(aq) + 2OH^-(aq)$	3.0×10^{-1}
$Cd(OH)_2$	$Cd(OH)_2(s) \rightleftharpoons Cd^{2+}(aq) + 2OH^-(aq)$	5.0×10^{-15}
Sulfites		
$CaSO_3$	$CaSO_3(s) \rightleftharpoons Ca^{2+}(aq) + SO_3^{2-}(aq)$	3×10^{-7}
$BaSO_3$	$BaSO_3(s) \rightleftharpoons Ba^{2+}(aq) + SO_3^{2-}(aq)$	8×10^{-7}
Sulfates		
$CaSO_4$	$CaSO_4(s) \rightleftharpoons Ca^{2+}(aq) + SO_4^{2-}(aq)$	2.4×10^{-5}
$BaSO_4$	$BaSO_4(s) \rightleftharpoons Ba^{2+}(aq) + SO_4^{2-}(aq)$	1.1×10^{-1}
Ag_2SO_4	$Ag_2SO_4(s) \rightleftharpoons 2Ag^+(aq) + SO_4^{2-}(aq)$	1.5×10^{-5}
$PbSO_4$	$PbSO_4(s) \rightleftharpoons Pb^{2+}(aq) + SO_4^{2-}(aq)$	6.3×10^{-7}
Chromates		
Ag_2CrO_4	$Ag_2CrO_4(s) \rightleftharpoons 2Ag^+(aq) + CrO_4^{2-}(aq)$	1.2×10^{-1}
Hg_2CrO_4	$Hg_2CrO_4(s) \rightleftharpoons Hg_2^{2+}(aq) + CrO_4^{2-}(aq)$	2.0×10^{-9}
$PbCrO_4$	$PbCrO_4(s) \rightleftharpoons Pb^{2-}(aq) + CrO_4^{2-}(aq)$	1.8×10^{-1}

Salt	Dissolution Reaction	K_{sp}
Carbonates		
$MgCO_3$	$MgCO_3(s) \rightleftharpoons Mg^{2+}(aq) + CO_3^{2-}(aq)$	3.5×10^{-8}
$CaCO_3$	$CaCO_3(s) \rightleftharpoons Ca^{2+}(aq) + CO_3^{2-}(aq)$	4.5×10^{-9}
$SrCO_3$	$SrCO_3(s) \rightleftharpoons Sr^{2+}(aq) + CO_3^{2-}(aq)$	9.3×10^{-10}
$BaCO_3$	$BaCO_3(s) \rightleftharpoons Ba^{2+}(aq) + CO_3^{2-}(aq)$	5.0×10^{-9}
$MnCO_3$	$MnCO_3(s) \rightleftharpoons Mn^{2+}(aq) + CO_3^{2-}(aq)$	5.0×10^{-10}
$CuCO_3$	$CuCO_3(s) \rightleftharpoons Cu^{2+}(aq) + CO_3^{2-}(aq)$	2.3×10^{-10}
Ag_2CO_3	$Ag_2CO_3(s) \rightleftharpoons 2Ag^+(aq) + CO_3^{2-}(aq)$	8.1×10^{-12}
Hg_2CO_3	$Hg_2CO_3(s) \rightleftharpoons Hg_2^{2+}(aq) + CO_3^{2-}(aq)$	8.9×10^{-17}
$ZnCO_3$	$ZnCO_3(s) \rightleftharpoons Zn^{2+}(aq) + CO_3^{2-}(aq)$	1.0×10^{-10}
$PbCO_3$	$PbCO_3(s) \rightleftharpoons Pb^{2+}(aq) + CO_3^{2-}(aq)$	7.4×10^{-14}
Sulfides		
MnS	$MnS(s) \rightleftharpoons Mn^{2+}(aq) + S^{2-}(aq)$	3.0×10^{-11}
FeS	$FeS(s) \rightleftharpoons Fe^{2+}(aq) + S^{2-}(aq)$	8.0×10^{-19}
CoS	$CoS(s) \rightleftharpoons Co^{2+}(aq) + S^{2-}(aq)$	5.0×10^{-22}
NiS	$NiS(s) \rightleftharpoons Ni^{2+}(aq) + S^{2-}(aq)$	4.0×10^{-20}
CuS	$CuS(s) \rightleftharpoons Cu^{2+}(aq) + S^{2-}(aq)$	8.0×10^{-37}
Cu_2S	$Cu_2(s) \rightleftharpoons 2Cu^+(aq) + S^{2-}(aq)$	3.0×10^{-49}
Ag_2S	$Ag_2S(s) \rightleftharpoons 2Ag^+(aq) + S^{2-}(aq)$	8.0×10^{-51}
Tl_2S	$Tl_2S(s) \rightleftharpoons 2Tl^+(aq) + S^{2-}(aq)$	6.0×10^{-22}
ZnS	$ZnS(s) \rightleftharpoons Zn^{2+}(aq) + S^{2-}(aq)$	2.0×10^{-25}
CdS	$CdS(s) \rightleftharpoons Cd^{2+}(aq) + S^{2-}(aq)$	1.0×10^{-27}
HgS	$HgS(s) \rightleftharpoons Hg^{2+}(aq) + S^{2-}(aq)$	2.0×10^{-53}
SnS	$SnS(s) \rightleftharpoons Sn^{2+}(aq) + S^{2-}(aq)$	1.3×10^{-26}
PbS	$PbS(s) \rightleftharpoons Pb^{2+}(aq) + S^{2-}(aq)$	3.0×10^{-28}
In_2S_3	$In_2S_3 \rightleftharpoons 2In^{3+}(aq) + 3S^{2-}(aq)$	4.0×10^{-70}

Glossary

Absolute uncertainty   The uncertainty of ± 1 in the last digit of a measurement. If this uncertainty is different from ± 1, it is written as part of the number; for example, 23.45 ± 0.05 indicates an uncertainty of ± 5 in the last digit.

Absolute zero   The lowest possible temperature, 0.0 K or $-273.16°C$.

Absorbance, *A*   A measure of the amount of light absorbed by a chemical.

Absorptivity, *a*   A constant the value of which depends on the sample and the wavelength at which the measurement is made in spectroscopy.

Accuracy   The degree of closeness between a measured value and the true value.

Acid   Any substance that donates protons, or as Lewis acids are electron-pair acceptors.

Acid anhydride   The oxide of a nonmetal that forms an acid when dissolved in water.

Acid dissociation constant, K_a   The value of the equilibrium law for the dissociation of a weak acid.

Activated complex   The structures of colliding molecules at the moment of collision, generally thought to be intermediate between the structures of the products and of the reactants.

Activation energy   The increase in potential energy, due to a molecular collision, necessary to convert a reactant into a product.

Activity series   A listing of elemental substances in the order of their ability to be oxidized or reduced. This listing makes it possible to predict whether an element will cause the oxidation or the reduction of an ion of another element.

Addition reaction   The reaction in which a double bond opens to form two additional single bonds.

Adhesive force   The attractive force between two dissimilar substances.

Alcohol   An organic compound with an —OH group.

Aldehyde   An organic compound with a terminal —CHO group.

Alkali metals   The extremely reactive elements in the first group (column) of the periodic table. They all have ns^1 electrons as valence electrons.

Alkaline earth metals   The very reactive elements in the second group (column) of the periodic table. They all have ns^2 electrons as valence electrons.

Alkanes   Organic compounds with the general formula C_nH_{2n+2}.

Alkenes   Organic compounds with double bonds in their structures.

Alkyl group   A functional group that is alkane in nature.

Alkynes   Organic compounds with triple bonds in their structures.

Allotrope(s)   One or more distinct forms of an element; classification as an allotrope is based on structure and physical properties. For example, diamond and graphite are two allotropes of carbon.

Alpha particle   A helium nucleus.

Amines   Compounds, related to ammonia, in which one or more of the hydrogen atoms in ammonia have been replaced by organic functional groups.

Amino acid   An organic acid that contains both an amine and an acid functional group on adjacent carbon atoms.

Amorphous   A term meaning "without structure."

Amphiprotic (amphoteric)   A term designating a substance that can act as both a conjugate acid and a conjugate base.

Amphoteric   *See* **Amphiprotic.**

Anhydride   The oxide of a metal or nonmetal that reacts with water to form an acid or a base, respectively.

Anion   An ion with a negative charge.

Aqueous   A term designating a system that involves water or a chemical mixture or solution having water as the solvent.

Arrhenius equation   The equation that relates temperature to rate constant. $K = Ae^{-Ea/RT}$.

Arrhenius theory   The theory that an acid increases hydrogen ion concentration when dissolved and that a base increases hydroxide ion concentration when dissolved.

Aryl group   A functional group that is aromatic in nature.

Atom   A fundamental particle of chemistry. At present, 109 atoms are known and are arranged in an orderly manner in the periodic table.

Atomic mass, A   The relative mass of an element as compared to the mass of the isotope C-12, which is defined as exactly 12.

Atomic number, Z   The number of an element in the periodic table; also, a number representing the number of protons in the nucleus of an atom.

Atomic orbital   The orbital structure of an element; also, an orbital within an element.

Atomic symbol   A one- or two-letter abbreviation of an element's name. Some symbols (e.g., Pb for lead) are derived from Latin names of the elements.

Autopyrolysis constant of water, K_w   The value of the equilibrium law for the dissociation of water into H^+ and OH^-.

Avogadro's number   A quantity equal to 6.02×10^{23}.

Avogadro's principle   A statement of the direct relationship between the moles of a gas and the volume of that gas.

Axial atom   A term used to describe the position of an atom in a covalent molecule of the AX_5 or AX_6 basic structure. The axial atoms are on the vertical axis of the molecule in positions similar to the Earth's North and South Poles.

Azimuthal quantum number, l   The quantum number that specifies the sublevel in which an electron is located; l may be any number from zero up to $n - 1$.

Balanced reaction   A chemical equation that has the smallest whole-number coefficients for the reactants and products so that there is the same number of atoms of each element on both sides of the arrow.

Barometer   A closed-end manometer used for measuring atmospheric pressure.

Base   Any compound that increases the hydroxide concentration of a solution or is a proton acceptor. Lewis bases are electron-pair donors.

Base anhydride   The oxide of a metal that forms a base when dissolved in water.

Base dissociation constant, K_b   The value of the equilibrium law for the dissociation of a weak base.

Basic structure   One of five basic geometries—linear, triangular planar, tetrahedral, trigonal planar, or octahedral—that a molecule may take.

Battery   A galvanic cell used to produce electricity for consumer items such as flashlights, portable radios, and heart pacemakers.

Beer's law   The statements that the absorbance of a sample is the product of the absorptivity, optical path length, and sample concentration; $A = abc$.

Beta particle, β An electron.

Bidentate ligand A Lewis base that donates two pairs of electrons.

Binary acid An acid that contains hydrogen and one other element in its formula.

Body-centered cubic (bcc) A cubic structure in which one atom is at each of the eight corners and one atom is in the center of the unit cell.

Bohr atom The model of the atom developed by Niels Bohr. This model views electrons as circling the nucleus like a miniature solar system.

Boiling point, normal The temperature at which the vapor pressure of a liquid is equal to 760 millimeters of mercury (1.00 atmospheres); also, the temperature at which a gas condenses. Also called condensation point.

Boiling-point-elevation constant, k_b The temperature increase of the boiling point per molal noun of solute particles.

Bonding electron pair A pair of electrons that participate in a covalent bond.

Bond order The average number of bonds per atom covalently bonded to a central atom.

Boyle's law The law that expresses the inverse relationship between the volume and the pressure of a gas; $PV = $ constant.

Bragg equation The equation that relates the atomic dimensions in a crystal to the angles at which monochromatic X rays will undergo constructive reinforcement.

Brönsted-Lowry theory The theory that acids are proton donors and bases are proton acceptors.

Buckminsterfullerene The allotrope of carbon that has the formula C_{60}.

Buffer capacity The moles of strong acid or strong base required to change the pH of 1 liter of buffer by 1 pH unit.

Buffer solution An aqueous solution containing a conjugate acid and its conjugate base in a molar ratio greater than 0.1 and less than 10.0.

Bumping The violent boiling that occurs when a solution becomes superheated.

Buret A tube approximately 1 centimeter in diameter that is used for measuring liquid volumes of 10–100 milliliters.

Calorimeter An instrument used to determine heat energy.

Catalyst A substance that speeds up the rate of a chemical reaction by providing an alternative reaction pathway with a lower activation energy.

Cation An ion with a positive charge.

Cell voltage, E The voltage of a galvanic cell under nonstandard state conditions.

Centrifugation The process of separating a solid from a liquid by spinning it rapidly to artificially increase the gravitational force.

Chain reaction A nuclear reaction that produces more neutrons than were needed to initiate it, therefore causing more reactions than occurred in the preceding step.

Charles's law The law that expresses the direct relationship between the temperature and volume of a gas: $P/V = $ constant.

Chelate A Lewis base that usually has more than one pair of electrons to donate.

Cis isomer An isomer with substituents on the same side of the double bond.

Clausius-Clapeyron equation The equation that relates vapor pressure to heat of vaporization.

Closed system A system in which mass cannot be lost to or gained from the surroundings.

Coefficient A number placed in front of a chemical formula to represent the number of molecules of that substance that are included in the equation. This number multiplies the number of atoms in the formula unit.

Cohesive force   The sum of all the attractive forces in a pure substance.

Colligative property   Any one of several physical properties of a solution that change depending on the amount of solute particles present in the solution.

Collision theory   The theory of kinetics, which relates reaction rates to the frequency, energy, and orientation of molecules in collisions.

Complex   *See* **Complex ion.**

Complexation reaction   A reaction between a Lewis acid and a Lewis base.

Complexing agent   *See* **Lewis base.**

Complex ion   A combination of one or more compounds or anions with a metal ion by coordinate covalent bonding. Also called a complex.

Compound   A combination of two or more elements into a distinct substance with definite physical properties.

Concentrated   A qualitative term indicating a large amount of solute in a given amount of solvent.

Concentration   An expression of the amount of solute mixed with a solvent.

Concentration versus time curve   A graph of reactant or product concentration as a function of time.

Condensation   The conversion of a gas into a liquid.

Condensation point   *See* **Boiling point.**

Condensation reaction   A polymerization reaction between an acid and either an alcohol or an amine.

Conjugate acid   Any substance that has a proton that may be donated to a base.

Conjugate acid-base pair   A pair of substances whose formulas differ by one H^+ ion.

Conjugated double bonds   A series of two or more double bonds, each separated by only a single bond in a molecule.

Cooling curve   A graph showing the changes that occur while a substance is cooling.

Coordinate covalent bond   The covalent bond between two atoms that is formed when one substance donates both electrons.

Covalent bond   The bond between two atoms that arises from the sharing of a pair of electrons.

Covalent compound   A chemical compound in which the atoms are held together with covalent bonds.

Covalent crystal   A crystal that consists of only one molecule. All atoms are joined to others with covalent bonds. Also called network crystal.

Critical mass   The minimum mass of a fissile (fissionable) material needed to sustain a nuclear chain reaction.

Critical point   The temperature and pressure above which a gas cannot be condensed to a liquid.

Crystal lattice   The arrangement of atoms, ions, or molecules in a crystal structure.

Crystallization point   *See* **Melting point.**

Cyclotron   A machine for accelerating charged particles, which are usually used to bombard targets in an effort to generate nuclear reactions.

Dalton's law of partial pressures   The law that the total pressure of a gas is the sum of the individual pressures of all the gases in the mixture; $P_{total} = p_1 + p_2 + \cdots$.

Decay   The spontaneous emission of a particle in a radioactive event.

ΔE The energy change due to a chemical reaction. It is equal to the heat and work of the reaction or to the change in potential energy of the products as compared to that of the reactants.

ΔG^0 The standard free-energy change for a reaction. The temperature is 298 K unless otherwise indicated.

ΔG_f^0 The standard free-energy change of formation corresponding to the formation of 1 mole of product from its elements at 298 K.

ΔH The enthalpy change occurring in a chemical process. Without the superscript zero it indicates an extensive property. Often called the heat of reaction.

ΔH^0 The standard enthalpy change occurring in a reaction; refers to the heat produced or absorbed when the moles of reactants specified in the chemical reaction react at standard state.

ΔH_f^0 The standard heat of formation, which is the heat produced or absorbed when 1 mole of a product is formed.

ΔS The change in entropy between the final state and the initial state in a chemical process. Without the superscript zero it indicates an extensive property.

ΔS^0 The standard entropy change of a chemical process; an intensive property based on the moles of substance in the balanced chemical reaction.

Dependent variable   The variable that an experiment measures; its value depends on the value of the independent variable.

Derived structure   A molecular structure that is derived from one of the five basic structures.

Detergent   A chemical substance that has both polar and nonpolar properties and is soluble in both polar and nonpolar solvents.

Determinate error   An error associated with faulty instruments, calibrations, or techniques.

Dextrorotatory   A term describing an optical isomer that rotates polarized light to the right.

Diagonal relationship   A term describing the fact that some properties of atoms vary regularly from the lower left corner to the upper right corner of the periodic table. Electronegativity, ionization energy, and electron affinity are some of these diagonal relationships.

Diamond   An allotrope of carbon in which all carbon atoms have sp^3 hybridization.

Diatomic   A term describing a molecule that contains only two atoms (e.g., HCl, H_2).

Differentiating electron   The electron that differentiates one element from an adjacent element in the periodic table.

Diffraction   The combination of light waves that results in either constructive or destructive reinforcement.

Diffusion   The movement of molecules from one place to another by random motion.

Dilute   A qualitative term indicating a small amount of solute in a given amount of solvent.

Dimer   A substance composed of two identical molecular or ionic units.

Dipole   A polar molecule. The term *dipole* reminds us that a polar molecule has only two poles, one positive and one negative.

Direct relationship   A relationship between two variables whereby one must increase when the other increases.

Dispersion forces   *See* **London forces.**

Dissociation   The breakup of an ionic compound into ions.

Double-replacement reaction   A chemical equation in which the cation of one substance replaces the cation of a second substance. At the same time, the cation of the second substance replaces the cation of the first substance.

dsp^3 **Hybrid orbital**   An orbital formed from one *s*, three *p*, and one *d* orbital. The electrons in these orbitals are all equal in energy. Structures are all related to the trigonal bipyramid.

d^2*sp*^{3} **Hybrid orbital**   An orbital formed from one *s*, three *p*, and two *d* orbitals. The electrons in the hybrid all have the same energy. Structures are all related to the octahedron.

Ductile   A term describing the property of being able to be drawn into wire forms.

Dynamic equilibrium   The state in which a chemical process is going in the forward direction at the same rate that it is going in the reverse direction and the concentrations of reactants and products remain constant. Equilibrium follows the kinetic period, in which reaction occurs and the concentrations of reactants and products change.

EDTA   Ethylene diamine tetraacetic acid, a very useful complexing agent.

Effusion   The movement of molecules through a small hole from one container to another.

Electrode   A metal placed in a liquid to transfer electrons in a galvanic or electrolytic cell.

Electrolysis   The process of using electric current to reduce a chemical substance at the cathode and oxidize a chemical substance at the anode.

Electrolyte   A substance that dissociates or ionizes completely into ions in solution.

Electrolytic cell   An arrangement of electrodes and a power source used to force nonspontaneous redox reactions to occur.

Electron affinity   The energy released or absorbed in adding an electron to an atom.

Electron deficient   A term describing a Lewis structure that has fewer than an octet of electrons around one or more of its atoms, except hydrogen.

Electron   1. The unit of negative charge in the atom. The diffuse electron cloud surrounds the dense nucleus. 2. One of the three particles, along with the proton and neutron, that make up an atom. An electron has a negative charge and virtually no mass in comparison to the neutron and proton. Electrons are arranged in an orderly fashion around the nucleus in a diffuse electron cloud. There are as many electrons as protons in an element.

Electronic configuration   A listing of the electrons within an atom, based on the sublevels that are filled and the relative energies of these sublevels. For example, the electronic configuration for silicon is $1s^2, 2s^2, 2p^6, 3s^2, 3p^2$.

Electronegativity   A measure of an atom's tendency to attract electrons. Fluorine has the highest, and francium the lowest, electronegativity in the periodic table.

Electroneutrality, law of   A statement of the fact that no chemical compound has a net charge. In addition, an element has no net charge.

Electrostatic potential energy   The energy of attraction of two oppositely charged particles, or the energy of repulsion of two like-charged particles.

Element   Any one of the 109 distinct particles, known as atoms, that are currently known. Each has distinct chemical and physical properties.

Elementary reaction   One reaction in a mechanism. It is usually bimolecular or unimolecular, and its coefficients are the exponents in the rate law.

Empirical formula The formula that gives only the simplest whole-number ratio of the atoms that make up a compound. *See also* **Molecular formula; Structural formula.**

Endothermic A term describing any process that absorbs heat from the surroundings. Endothermic processes cool the system.

End point The point, where neither reactant is in excess, that marks the end of a titration experiment.

Enthalpy The heat content of a chemical substance. Enthalpy is related to the internal potential energy of the substance.

Entropy A measure of the randomness of a chemical substance.

Enzyme One of many naturally occurring catalysts found in biological materials.

Enzyme-substrate complex The activated complex formed in an enzyme-catalyzed reaction.

Equatorial atom A term used to describe the position of an atom in a covalent molecule of the AX_5 or AX_6 basic structure. The equatorial atoms are around the center of the molecule in positions similar to the Earth's equator.

Equilibrium constant, K The numerical value of the equilibrium law. The only variable that has an effect on the equilibrium constant is temperature.

Equilibrium law The basic equation governing chemical equilibrium. Each balanced chemical equation has its own equilibrium law.

Equilibrium table A table of data used to summarize the numerical data and stoichiometric relationships of an equilibrium system.

Equivalent A value that is determined for a substance by dividing its mass by the equivalent weight.

Equivalent weight The mass of a compound that loses or gains 1 mole of electrons in an oxidation-reduction reaction. In acid-base reactions it is the mass that furnishes or reacts with 1 mole of H^+ ions.

Escape energy The minimum kinetic energy of a liquid molecule that is needed for transformation into a gas.

Ether An organic compound containing the $-C-O-C-$ functional group.

Eudiometer A closed-end manometer.

Evaporation The transformation of a liquid into a gas at a temperature below the boiling point.

Exact number A number that has no uncertainty. Exact numbers include stoichiometric coefficients, formula subscripts, and most defined quantities.

Excess reactant Any reactant that is not completely consumed in a chemical reaction.

Exothermic A term describing any process that gives off heat to the surroundings. Exothermic processes heat the system.

Extrinsic property A physical or chemical property that varies in proportion to the amount of matter.

Face-centered cubic (fcc) A cubic structure in which atoms are at the corners and an atom is on each cube face of the unit cell.

Factor label A ratio used to convert a number with one set of units into the equivalent number with different units.

Faraday's constant, $\mathscr{F}$ The relationship between the coulomb and moles of electrons; 96,485 C = 1 mol e^-.

Filtrate The liquid that passes through a filter.

First law of thermodynamics The law that states that in any chemical or physical process all energy is conserved.

First-order reaction   A reaction with a rate law having exponents that add up to 1. The rate law is Rate $= k[A]$.

Fissile   A term describing a nucleus that is capable of undergoing nuclear fission.

Fluorescence   A property of some atoms and molecules that allows them to absorb photons of light and reemit them very rapidly, but with a different energy. The emitted light always has a lower energy and longer wavelength than the absorbed light.

Formal charge   The charge on an atom in a covalent compound, calculated by assuming that all bonding electrons are equally shared.

Formation reaction   A chemical reaction in which the reactants are elements at standard state and the product is 1 mole of one compound.

Formula   The representation of a chemical substance using chemical symbols and appropriate subscripts for the numbers of atoms and superscripts to represent charges if the substance is an ion.

Free radical   A molecule that contains an unpaired electron in its Lewis structure.

Freezing-point-depression constant, k_f   The temperature decrease in the freezing point per molal °Cm^{-1} of solute particles.

Functional group   A group of atoms on an organic compound that represent a characteristic chemical entity.

Galvanic cell   The experimental setup used to convert chemical energy into electric energy. All batteries are galvanic cells.

Gamma ray   A high-energy photon often emitted in a nuclear reaction.

Gas   A state of matter characterized by the ability to flow and fill any container completely without regard to the amount of gas in the container.

Gay-Lussac's law   The law that expresses the direct relationship between the temperature and pressure of a gas; $P/T =$ constant.

Gibbs free energy   The maximum energy from any chemical reaction.

Graham's law of effusion   The law that relates the rate at which gases pass through a small hole to the mass of the molecule; $\sqrt{m_1/m_2} = \bar{v}_2/\bar{v}_1$.

Gram-atomic mass   *See* **Atomic mass.**

Gram-molar mass   *See* **Molar Mass.**

Graph   A pictorial method of presenting and evaluating experimental data.

Graphite   An allotrope of carbon in which carbon has sp^2 hybridization.

Gravitational potential energy   The attractive energy of any two masses toward each other.

Group   A column in the periodic table.

Half-life   The time required for half of the reactants to be consumed in a chemical reaction or a radioactive decay.

Halide   An organic compound with a halogen (e.g. $CH_3 CH_2 Cl$) in its structure.

Halogen   An element in the next to last group of the periodic table. Halogens are reactive elements with ns^2, np^5 valence electron structures.

Halogenation   The addition of a halogen to a double or triple bond.

Heat capacity   The amount of heat energy that a system needs in order for its temperature to change by 1°C.

Heating curve   A graph showing the changes that occur while a substance is heated.

Heat of combustion   The heat released when 1 mole of sample, usually an organic compound, is completely burned in oxygen to form CO_2 and H_2O.

Heat of fusion   The heat energy needed to convert a solid into a liquid. The units are either joules per gram or joules per mole.

Heat of reaction   *See ΔH.*

Heat of vaporization   The heat energy needed to convert a liquid into a gas. The units are either joules per gram or joules per mole.

Henderson-Hasselbach equation   A derivation of the equilibrium law obtained by taking the negative logarithm of the equilibrium law; $pH = pK_a + \log([\text{conjugate base}]/[\text{conjugate acid}])$.

Henry's law   The law that expresses the relationship between the solubility of a gas and its partial pressure; $c = kp$.

Hess's law   The law that states that heats of reaction are additive when chemical reactions are added.

Hund's rule   The rule that every orbital in a sublevel must fill with one electron before a second electron of opposite spin can be added to any orbital in that sublevel.

Hybrid orbital   An orbital constructed by combining electrons, usually from s and p orbitals, into a new orbital where all the electrons have the same properties. These orbitals are designated as sp, sp^2, sp^3, dsp^3, and d^2sp^3.

Hydrate   A substance that contains a fixed number of water molecules. The water molecules are written separately from the formula itself and connected to it with a dot in the center of the line between the chemical formula and the water molecules (e.g. $CuSO_4 \cdot 5\ H_2O$).

Hydrogenation   The addition of H_2 to a double or triple bond.

Hydrogen bonding   An extra-strength dipole-dipole attractive force due to a large electronegativity difference between hydrogen and nitrogen, oxygen, or fluorine.

Hydrohalogenation   The addition of a hydrogen and a halogen to a double or triple bond by using a binary acid such as HF, HCl, HBr, or HI.

Hydrolysis reaction   The reaction of a substance, usually a conjugate acid or base, with water.

Ideal gas   A gas that obeys the ideal gas law; conceptually, a gas molecule with no volume and no attractive forces with other molecules.

Ideal gas law   The law that relates temperature, pressure, volume, and moles of gas; $PV = nRT$.

Independent variable   The variable in an experiment that is under the control of the experimenter.

Indeterminate error   An error in estimating the uncertain digit in a measurement. Also called random error.

Indicator   A chemical added to a titration experiment that changes color at the end point.

Indicator electrode   An electrode placed in a sample in order to measure the concentration of an ion in the sample.

Induced dipoles   A dipole formed by the interaction of a nonpolar substance and either a polar substance or an instantaneous dipole.

Initial conditions   A quantitative description of a chemical system at the start of a reaction.

Inspection method   A method for balancing chemical equations. The inspection involves counting the number of each atom present in the equation and then balancing by adding appropriate coefficients to the reactants or products.

Instantaneous dipole   A distortion of the electron cloud around an atom or molecule that gives the atom or molecule momentary polarity.

Intermediate   A substance that appears in the elementary reactions of a mechanism but not in the overall balanced equation.

Intermolecular forces   The attractive forces—dipole-dipole attractions, London forces, and hydrogen bonding—between molecules and atoms that allows them to condense into liquids and solidify into solids.

Internuclear axis   An imaginary line connecting the nuclei of two atoms.

Intrinsic property   A physical or chemical property that does not change with the amount of matter.

Inverse relationship   A relationship between two variables whereby one must increase if the other decreases.

Ion   An element that has lost or gained one or more electrons. *See also* **Polyatomic ion.**

Ion-electron method   A method for balancing more complex oxidation-reduction equations. It involves a logical sequence of steps described in Chapter 13.

Ionic bond   The attraction of a negative anion for a positive cation.

Ionic compound   A chemical compound composed of negatively charged anions and positively charged cations. The unit is held together by the attraction of the positive charges toward the negative charges.

Ionic crystal   A crystal formed from cations and anions where the main attractive force is the attraction of positive charges toward negative charges.

Ionization   The removal or addition of an electron from an atom or molecule. Also the formation of ions when a molecular substance dissolves in water.

Ionization energy   The energy required to remove an electron completely from an atom.

Isoelectronic   A term describing any two atoms that have identical electronic configurations. These atoms may be ions or elements.

Isolated system   A system in which neither mass nor energy is transferred to or from the surroundings.

Isomers   Distinctly different compounds that have the same elemental composition.

Isotope   A form of an element with a specified number of protons, neutrons, and electrons.

IUPAC   The International Union of Pure and Applied Chemistry, which sets nomenclature standards.

K   The symbol for the equilibrium constant, often written as K_{eq}.

K_a   The acid dissociation constant, a special term denoting the equilibrium of a weak acid. A weak acid dissociation is always in the form

$$HA + H_2O \rightleftharpoons A^- + H_3O^+.$$

K_b   The base dissociation constant, a special term denoting the equilibrium of a weak base. A weak base dissociation is always in the form

$$B + H_2O \rightleftharpoons BH^+ + OH^-.$$

K_c   The equilibrium constant used when the reactants and products are specified as concentrations.

K_d The dissociation constant, a special term used mainly to describe the dissociation of complex ions.

K_{eq} See K.

K_f The formation constant, a special term used to describe the formation of complex ions.

K_p The equilibrium constant used when the reactants and products are specified in terms of partial pressures.

K_{sp} The solubility product, a special term denoting the fact that the equilibrium is between a solid and its solution products.

K_w The autopyrolysis constant of water, equal to 1.0×10^{-14} at 25°C.

Ketone   An organic compound with a nonterminal $—C\!=\!O$ group.

Kinetic curve   A graph of reactant or product concentration as a function of time.

Kinetic energy   The energy that matter possesses because of its motion; $KE = \frac{1}{2}mv^2$.

Kinetic molecular theory   The theory of the motion of molecules in the gas phase, which explains gas pressure, effusion and diffusion rates, and the effect of temperature on the behavior of gases.

Law of Dulong and Petit   The law stating that the specific heat of a metal multiplied by its molar mass is equal to a constant of approximately 25 J mol^{-1} °C^{-1}.

Leveling effect   An expression of the fact that the strongest acid in water is the H^+ (H_3O^+) ion and the strongest base is the hydroxide ion, OH^-.

Levorotatory   A term describing an optical isomer that rotates polarized light to the left.

Lewis acid   Any substance that can accept electron pairs.

Lewis base   Any substance that can donate electron pairs. Also called ligand; complexing agent; sequestering agent.

Lewis structure   A molecular structure based on the concept that all atoms try to achieve the noble gas electronic configuration by sharing electrons.

Lewis theory   The theory that acids are electron-pair acceptors and bases are electron-pair donors.

Ligand   *See* **Lewis base.**

Limiting reactant   The reactant that is completely consumed in a reaction, causing it to stop. Also called limiting reagent.

Limiting reagent   *See* **Limiting reactant.**

Linear   A term referring to atoms aligned in a straight line; a three-atom arrangement with a 180° bond angle.

Liquid   A state of matter characterized by its ability to flow in order to fill any container from the bottom up.

Litmus paper   A type of pH paper using the indicator litmus, which is pink in acid and blue in base.

Lock and key   The analogy used to depict how an enzyme recognizes reactants on the basis of physical geometry as well as chemical characteristics.

London forces   The attractive forces from instantaneous dipoles. These forces are due to the possibility that the electron clouds around atoms and molecules are not perfectly symmetrical at all times. Also called dispersion forces.

Lone pairs   Electron pairs in Lewis structures that are not used for bonding.

Magnetic quantum number, m_l   The quantum number that specifies the orbital in which an electron is located and the orientation of the orbital in space; m_l may be any number from $-l$ to $+l$, including zero.

Malleable   A term describing the property of being able to be hammered into new shapes.

Manometer   A device used for measuring gas pressures.

Mass   A quantity of matter.

Mass fraction (wt/wt)   A concentration unit defined as the mass of one solute divided by the total mass of the solution.

Mass-volume fraction (wt/vol)   A concentration unit defined as the mass of one solute in a given total volume of solution.

Melting point, normal   The temperature at which a solid melts at 1.00 atmosphere of pressure; also, the temperature at which a liquid becomes a solid. Also called crystallization point.

Meniscus   The curved surface of a liquid in a tube or container.

Metal   A substance with characteristic properties of high electrical conductivity, malleability, and a metallic silver or yellow luster.

Metallic crystal   A crystal formed from a metal in the periodic table. Metallic crystals are malleable and ductile and conduct electricity.

Metalloid   An element that has properties of both metals and nonmetals.

Metastable   A term describing a physical situation in which a material is stable unless disturbed.

Metric base unit   One of seven basic units of measurement in the metric system. More complex units are combinations of base units.

Metric prefix   A prefix (e.g., *milli-, pico-*) used with a metric base unit to represent a specific exponential value.

Michaelis-Menton equation   The rate equation that applies to enzyme-catalyzed reactions.

Mirror image   A description of stereoisomers in which the structure of one isomer is the reflection of the other in a mirror.

Molality (m)   A concentration unit defined as the number of moles of solute dissolved in 1 kilogram of solvent.

Molarity (M)   A concentration unit defined as the number of moles of solute in 1 liter of solution.

Molar mass   The sum of the gram-atomic masses of all atoms in a chemical formula. Also called molecular mass.

Molar volume   The volume of 1 mole of gas, usually at standard temperature and pressure (STP).

Mole (mol)   The quantity of any substance that contains 6.02×10^{23} units of that substance.

Mole fraction (X)   A concentration unit defined as the number of moles of solute divided by the total number of moles in a solution.

Molecular crystal   A crystal formed from a molecule. The attractive forces that hold molecular crystals together are London forces, dipole-dipole attractions, hydrogen bonding, or a combination of these.

Molecular formula   The formula for a molecular or covalent substance, showing all of the atoms that comprise the molecular unit. A molecular formula may be simplified to an empirical formula if all of the subscripts can be divided by a common number. *See also* **Empirical formula; Structural formula.**

Molecular mass   *See* **Molar mass.**

Molecular orbital   An orbital created by the pairing of electrons from different atoms. This orbital encircles the atoms that are bonded together.

Molecule   A group of atoms bound together by covalent bonds with zero total charge.

Molten salt   A solid salt that has been heated to a temperature where it becomes a liquid. Also called a fused salt.

Monochromatic   A term describing light that has a single wavelength.

Monodentate ligand   A Lewis base that donates one pair of electrons.

Monomer   One of the individual repeating units of a polymer.

Natural abundance   The percentage of an isotope of an element found in nature.

Network crystals   *See* **Covalent crystal.**

Neutralization reactions   A chemical reaction of an acid with a base.

Neutron   One of three particles, along with the electron and proton, that make up an atom. This particle has no charge, but has a mass approximately equal to the proton mass. Neutrons and protons make up the bulk of the mass of the atom.

Noble gas   An element in the last group in the periodic table. Noble gases are unusually stable elements and all have ns^2, np^6 valence electrons.

Nonbonding electron pair   A pair of electrons in a Lewis structure that is not shared with any other atoms.

Nonelectrolyte   A substance that does not dissociate at all in solution.

Nonmetal   An element that is not metallic. Nonmetals do not conduct electricity well and do not have a shiny metallic luster. They are located in the upper right portion of the periodic table.

Nonpolar   A term describing a bond or molecule that has its charge distributed evenly. Only diatomic elements form truly nonpolar bonds. Symmetrical molecules are nonpolar.

Normal   A term describing an organic compound in which all carbon atoms are arranged in one straight chain.

Normality   The number of equivalents of a substance dissolved in 1 liter of solution.

Nuclear charge   The number of positive charges in the nucleus. This is the same as the number of protons in the nucleus (Z) an is also the atomic number.

Nuclear fission   A radioactive decay process initiated by the absorption of a neutron; it results in a large nucleus dividing roughly in half.

Nuclear fusion   The combination of two nuclei to form a new atom.

Nuclear mass   The total mass of the nucleus. This is the sum of the masses of the protons and neutrons in the nucleus. Since electrons have virtually no mass, it is also the atomic mass (A) of the isotope.

Nuclear reactor   A device that uses a nuclear reaction to create heat energy for the purpose of generating electricity.

Nucleon   Either a proton or a neutron, both of which are fundamental particles of the nucleus.

Nucleus   The center of an atom, which contains the protons and neutrons. The nucleus is extremely dense and comprises a very small fraction of the atom's volume; the rest of the atom is empty space.

Octahedron   A geometric structure of six atoms covalently bound to a central atom. Each atom is 90° from any other.

Octet rule   A simple but effective rule stating that covalent molecules tend to have octets of electrons around each atom in their structures. These octets simulate the electron configurations of the noble gases.

Open system A system in which matter and energy can be exchanged with the surroundings.

Optical isomer A stereoisomer that rotates polarized light.

Optical path length, b The thickness of a sample in a spectroscopic experiment.

Orbital A region of space that may be occupied by a maximum of two electrons. The shape of an orbital is defined by the sublevel it is in. The orientation of the orbital depends on its assigned quantum number, m_l. Every orbital in a given sublevel must be filled with one electron before a second electron may fill the orbital.

Orbital diagram A diagram in which boxes represent individual valence orbitals. Electrons are represented as arrows to show the spins of the electrons in each orbital.

Order of reaction The sum of the exponents in a rate law.

Organic acid An acid containing carbon and the —COOH functional group.

Organic compound A compound composed of carbon and usually hydrogen.

Osmotic pressure The pressure needed to stop the migration of solute through a semipermeable membrane.

Oxidation The loss of electrons; also, the increase in oxidation number.

Oxidizing agent A substance that causes another to be oxidized; also, a substance that itself is reduced.

Oxoacids An acid that contains hydrogen, oxygen, and another element in its formula, excluding organic acids.

Partial pressure The pressure of a single gas in a mixture of gases.

Parts per billion (ppb) A unit of measurement similar in concept to percent, obtained by multiplying a fraction by one billion (10^9).

Parts per million (ppm) A unit of measurement similar in concept to percent, obtained by multiplying a fraction by one million (10^6).

Pauli exclusion principle The requirement that no two electrons in an atom have the same set of four quantum numbers, n, l, m_l, and m_s.

Percent (%) A unit of measurement meaning parts per hundred, obtained by multiplying a fraction by 100.

Period A row in the periodic table.

Periodic table The table in which the elements are arranged in an orderly fashion that shows the relationships of their chemical and physical characteristics.

pH The negative logarithm of the hydrogen ion concentration in a solution; $pH = -\log H^+$.

Phase diagram A graph showing the relationship between temperature and pressure and the conversion of matter among three states: solid, liquid, and gas.

pH indicator A weak acid or a weak base whose conjugate acid and conjugate base have different colors. An indicator changes color indicating the end point of a titration.

pH meter An electronic device used to measure the pH values of solutions.

pH paper Paper with a pH indicator absorbed on it so that it changes color depending on the pH of the solution; pH paper is used to estimate pH. *See also* **Litmus paper.**

Phosphorescence A property of some atoms and molecules that allows them to absorb photons of light and reemit them seconds to hours later. The emitted light always has a lower energy, longer wavelength than the absorbed light.

Pi bond   A bond made from the sideways overlap of two *p* orbitals. The electron density of a pi bond lies outside the internuclear axis.

Pipet   A narrow tube calibrated for precise measurement of small volumes of liquids.

pK_w   The negative logarithm of the autopyrolysis constant of water, equal to 14.00.

Planar triangle   A geometric structure of four atoms, three bonded to a central atom with 120° angles between the atoms, which are all in the same plane.

Planck's constant (*h*)   The constant relating the energy of a photon to its frequency.

Pneumatic trough   An experimental setup for collecting gases by the displacement of water.

pOH   The negative logarithm of the hydroxide ion concentration in a solution; $pOH = -\log OH^-$.

Polar   A term describing the property of a covalent bond or molecule of having one end more positive than the other.

Polarizability   The tendency for an atom's electron cloud to be deformed so that polarity is created.

Polyatomic ion   An ion composed of more than one atom covalently bonded together. A polyatomic ion acts as a unit in most chemical reactions.

Polymer   A long-chain organic molecule with repeating units.

Polyprotic acid   An acid with two or more ionizable hydrogen atoms in its formula.

Positron   A positive electron.

Potential energy   The energy of matter that may, under appropriate conditions, be converted into work.

Precipitate   1. (v.) To cause the formation of a solid by a chemical reaction. 2. (n.) The solid formed as a result of a chemical reaction.

Precision   The degree of closeness of a group of repeated measurements to each other.

Pressure   The force per unit area; gas molecules exert this force by collisions with the container walls.

Principal quantum number, *n*   The quantum number that specifies the energy level of the atom in which an electron is located; *n* may be any integer from 1 to infinity.

Product   The result of a chemical reaction. Products are placed on the right-hand side of a chemical equation.

Proton   One of three particles, along with the electron and neutron, that make up an atom. The proton has a positive charge, equal in magnitude (but with the opposite sign) to the charge of the electron. The number of protons is equal to the atomic number, Z, of an element. Protons and neutrons make up the bulk of the mass of an atom.

Q   *See* **Reaction quotient.**

Qualitative   A term referring to a description of a physical or chemical property without the use of numbers or equations.

Qualitative analysis   A logical sequence of experiments and observations used to determine the composition of a sample.

Quantitative   A term referring to a description of a physical or chemical property using numbers or equations.

Quantum number   One of four numbers (n, l, m_l, m_s) used in the wave-mechanical model of the atom to describe an electron in an atom.

Racemic mixture   An equal molar mixture of L and D optical isomers.

Radioactive disintegration series   A sequence of radioactive disintegrations from a heavy isotope to a lighter, stable isotope in more than one step.

Radioactivity   The property that some unstable nuclei have of decaying spontaneously with the emission of a small particle and/or energy.

Radioisotope   A radioactive isotope of an element.

Random error   *See* **Indeterminate error.**

Randomness   A qualitative description of the disorder of the molecules in any sample.

Raoult's law   The law that expresses the relationship between the vapor pressure of a solution and the mole fraction of solute in that solution.

Rate constant k   A constant in the direct relationship between the amount of reacting substance and the rate of the reaction.

Rate-determining step   The slowest reaction in a mechanism, which limits the overall rate of reaction. Also called rate-limiting step.

Rate law   The mathematical relationship between reactant concentrations and reaction rate. The general form of a rate law is Rate = $k[A]^x[B]^y[C]^z$.

Rate-limiting step   *See* **Rate-determining step.**

Reactant   One of the starting materials in a chemical reaction. The reactants are placed on the left side of a chemical equation.

Reaction mechanism   The detailed series of elementary reactions that add up to the overall reaction. *See also* **Elementary reaction.**

Reaction profile   A plot of the potential energy of molecules as they collide in a reaction, illustrating the nature of the activation energy.

Reaction quotient, Q   The value of the ratio of the equilibrium law when a chemical system is not in a state of equilibrium. The value of Q in comparison to that of K indicates the direction of the reaction.

Reaction rate   The velocity, in moles per liter per second, at which reactants are converted into products in a chemical reaction.

Reagent blank   A solution used to set the zero point of a spectrophotometer.

Real gas   A gas in which there are attractive forces between the molecules and the molecules have a finite volume.

Redox   A word coined to combine the terms *reduction* and *oxidation*. It indicates that reduction and oxidation always occur together.

Reducing agent   A substance that causes another substance to be reduced; also, a substance that is oxidized.

Reduction   The gain of electrons; also, the decrease in oxidation number.

Reference electrode   An electrode in a galvanic cell, which has a constant potential since the concentrations of all reactants are kept constant.

Relative mass   A term describing the fact that the masses of atoms in the periodic table are relative, without units, as compared to the mass of the carbon-12 isotope.

Relative uncertainty   The absolute uncertainty of a measurement divided by the value of the measurement.

Resonance structure   A Lewis structure that can be drawn in more than one equally probable way. The actual structure is a mixture of all possible resonance structures.

Reversible process   A chemical or physical process that can be changed from one state to another and then back to the original state. A reversible process takes place in infinitesimally small steps.

S^0 The standard entropy of 1 mole of a substance.

Saturated   A term describing an organic compound in which all carbon-carbon bonds are single bonds. Saturated compounds have the maximum number of hydrogen atoms; that is, they are saturated with hydrogen.

Saturated solution   A solution that has the maximum amount of solute dissolved in it.

Scientific notation   A method of writing numbers in which the significant figures are numbers from 1 to 10 and they are multiplied by 10 raised to the appropriate power to indicate the position of the decimal point.

Second law of thermodynamics   The law that states that in all physical and chemical processes the overall entropy of the universe must increase.

Second-order reaction   A reaction with a rate law having exponents that add up to 2. The rate law is Rate = $k[A][B]$ or Rate = $[A]^2$.

Semipermeable membrane   A thin, solid material through which certain molecules can diffuse while others cannot; may be visualized as a barrier with small holes that allow only molecules of a certain size to pass through.

Sequestering agent   *See* **Lewis base.**

Shell   The old term for the principal energy level of an electron; the region in space where electrons are located around the nucleus of the atom. Energy levels are numbered starting with the energy level closest to the nucleus. The number of the principal energy level is also known as the principal quantum number.

Sigma bond   A covalent bond formed by the sharing of a pair of electrons. The electron pair is located along the internuclear axis between the two atoms that share it.

Significant figures   All the digits in a measurement except preceding zeros.

Simple cubic   A term describing a cubic structure with one atom in each of the eight corners of a unit cell.

Solid   A state of matter characterized by a rigid structure that retains its shape without a container.

Solubility   A property of a solute that refers to the maximum amount of that solute that can be dissolved in a solvent. This term can be a qualitative or quantitative description of a solute.

Solute   The substance—gas, liquid, or solid—dissolved in the solvent.

Solution   A uniform mixture of chemicals. In a solution it is impossible to distinguish separate solute and solvent particles.

Solvent   Typically, the liquid phase in which a gas, another liquid, or a solid is dissolved. In a mixture of two or more liquids the solvent is the liquid present in the largest amount.

sp **Hybrid orbital**   An orbital constructed from an *s* and a *p* orbital into one where both have equal energies. The resulting structures related to this orbital are linear.

sp^2 **Hybrid orbital**   An orbital constructed from an *s* and two *p* orbitals. The resulting orbitals all have the same energy. Structures related to this orbital are triangular planar.

sp^3 **Hybrid orbital**   An orbital constructed from an *s* and three *p* orbitals. The resulting orbitals all have the same energy. Structures related to this orbital are tetrahedral.

Specific heat An intrinsic property of matter that describes the quantity of heat energy needed to raise the temperature of 1 gram of substance by 1°C.

Spectrophotometer An instrument for determining the amount of light absorbed by a sample.

Spin quantum number, m_s The quantum number that specifies the spin of an electron as either $+\frac{1}{2}$ or $-\frac{1}{2}$. Two electrons in the same orbital must have opposite spins.

Spontaneous reaction Any reaction that occurs without outside assistance; quantitatively, any reaction that has an equilibrium constant greater than 1.

Standard cell voltage, E^0_{cell} The voltage of a galvanic cell when the system is at standard state; also, the combination of two standard reduction potentials as $E^0_{cell} = E^0_{cathode} - E^0_{anode}$

Standard reduction potential E The potential (voltage) of a reduction half-reaction at standard state.

Standard state Defined temperature, pressure, and concentrations. In electrochemistry the standard state is 1.00 atmosphere pressure, 298 K or 25°C, and 1.00 molar concentrations for all soluble compounds. Solids and pure liquids are also defined as 1.00 molar.

Standard temperature and pressure A state defined as having a temperature of 0°C and 1 atmosphere of pressure.

State function A variable whose value depends only on the initial and final states of the system. State functions are ΔH, ΔS, ΔG, and ΔE.

Steady-state assumption The assumption that, in evaluating rate constants for elementary reactions, the concentrations of intermediates may be mathematically eliminated by assuming that all prior fast steps are in chemical equilibrium.

Stereoisomers Compounds that have the same formula and same bonding but differ in the geometric arrangement of the atoms.

Stereospecific A term describing a chemical reaction that produces only one stereoisomer.

Stoichiometry Mathematical relationships between chemical substances in a chemical equation.

Stopcock The valve on the end of a buret.

STP *See* **Standard temperature and pressure.**

Strong acid An acid that dissociates completely when dissolved in water.

Strong base A base that dissociates completely when dissolved in water.

Structural formula A formula that shows the actual arrangement of atoms within the molecule and the bonds between the atoms. *See also* **Empirical formula; Molecular formula.**

Structural isomers Compounds with the same formula but with the atoms bonded in different arrangements.

Sublevel A subdivision of an energy level. Electrons in each principal energy level are localized in sublevels. Each sublevel has a distinct shape associated with it. Sublevels are numbered from zero up to one less than the number of the principal energy level. These sublevel numbers are the azimuthal quantum numbers, l. Sublevels are also designated by the letters s, p, d, f.

Subscript A number placed to the right of, and slightly below, the symbol for an element to represent the number of times that atom is present in the formula unit.

Substrate(s) The reactant(s) in an enzyme-catalyzed reaction.

Supercritical fluid   A gas at a temperature and pressure above the critical point. Such a fluid has properties of both a gas and a liquid.

Supersaturated solution   A metastable solution that has more than the maximum amount of solute dissolved in it.

Supercooling   The property of some materials capable of being cooled to temperatures below their melting points without solidifying. Supercooled solutions are also supersaturated and are metastable.

Supernatant   The liquid remaining above a solid after centrifugation.

Surface tension   The added attractive force per molecule at the surface of a liquid. Surface tension causes liquids to assume shapes that minimize surface area.

Surfactant   A substance that lowers the surface tension of liquids.

Surroundings   All parts of the universe not included in the system being studied.

Symmetrical   A term describing a geometrical property whereby a structure may be rotated by some angle less than 360° and after rotation the molecule has the same configuration as before.

System   The portion of the universe that is under study.

TC ("To Contain")   A label on glassware indicating that the item is calibrated to contain the indicated volume.

TD ("To Deliver")   A label on glassware indicating that the calibration is based on the volume delivered.

Teflon   The addition polymer of CF_2=CF_2 with extraordinary nonstick properties.

Tetrahedron   A geometric structure with four atoms bound to a central atom by covalent bonds. Each bond is equidistant from any other with a bond angle of 109°.

Thermodynamics   The study of energy changes in chemical and physical processes.

Titration   An experimental procedure for reacting two solutions in order to determine the quantity or concentration of one of the solutions.

Titration curve   A plot of pH versus the volume of titrant added to a sample.

Tracer   A radioactive element used to detect the movement of materials in a complex system.

Trans isomer   An isomer with substituents on opposite sides of a double bond.

Transition element   An element having a d electron as the differentiating electron in its electronic configuration.

Transition-state theory   The reaction-rate theory that details the events and energy changes that occur as two molecules collide.

Trans-uranium element   Any of the 17 elements from atomic number 93 to 109.

Triangular bipyramid   A geometric structure with five atoms covalently bound to a central atom. Three atoms in the equatorial position are 120° from each other. Two additional atoms in the axial positions are 90° from the equatorial atoms.

Triple point   The temperature and pressure at which all three states of matter—solid, liquid, and gas—are in equilibrium.

Unit cell   The fundamental building block of crystals. An entire crystal is formed by repetitive stacking of the unit cells.

Universal gas constant, R   The constant needed to relate the temperature, pressure, volume, and moles of gas in the ideal gas law, $PV = nRT$.

Universe   The entirety of all matter and space that exist.

Unsaturated   A term describing an organic compound that contains one or more double or triple bonds in its structure.

Unsaturated solution   A solution in which the solute concentration is less than the maximum amount possible.

Vacuum distillation   The laboratory technique of vaporizing and condensing a liquid for the purpose of purification. Vacuum distillation is used to reduce the boiling points of heat-sensitive compounds.

Valence electrons   The outermost s and p electrons in an atom. The number and the arrangement of valence electrons define chemical and physical properties.

Valence shell electron-pair repulsion (VSEPR) theory   A method of evaluating molecular structure by relating the number of bonding and nonbonding electron pairs on an atom to its geometrical structure.

van der Waals forces *See* **London forces.**

Vapor pressure   The pressure developed by a liquid or solid in a closed container at a constant temperature.

Viscosity   The ability of a fluid to flow. The more easily a fluid flows, the lower is its viscosity.

Vital force theory   The theory, now discredited, that all organic molecules must be formed in living matter.

Volumetric flask   A flask calibrated to contain a precise volume of liquid.

Volume-volume fraction (vol/vol)   A concentration unit defined as the volume of one liquid solute divided by the total volumes of the liquids mixed to prepare a solution.

Weak acid   An acid that dissociates slightly when dissolved in water.

Weak electrolyte   A substance that partially dissociates into ions in solution.

Weight   The force developed by the gravitational attraction of two masses.

Weighted average   An average that depends on the abundance of the objects being averaged.

Wetting   The spreading of a liquid on a surface that occurs because the adhesive forces overcome the cohesive forces in the liquid.

X ray   The high-energy electromagnetic radiation emitted in nuclear decay events or when certain metals are bombarded with energetic electrons.

Zero-order reaction   A reaction in which the rate is independent of reactant concentration. The rate law is Rate $= k$.

Index

BARRON'S

How to Prepare for the

AP*

Chemistry

Neil D. Jespersen, Ph.D.

Total Test Preparation Includes—

- 2 Diagnostic Exams to help you pinpoint your strengths and weaknesses
- 3 Practice Exams modeled on actual AP Chemistry Examinations
- All questions answered and explained
- Review chapters that cover the structure of matter, chemical bonding, states of matter, physical chemistry, chemical reactions, more
- Test-taking tips that can help you get a high score

Barron's Educational Series, Inc.

ISBN 0-8120-1881-8

51295>

9 780812 018813

$12.95   Canada $16.95

BARRON'S – THE FIRST CHOICE IN TEST PREP MANUALS!